Fundamentals of
Media Effects

THE MCGRAW-HILL SERIES IN MASS COMMUNICATION AND JOURNALISM

Arnold
Media Writer's Handbook: A Guide to Common Writing and Editing Problems

Baskin, Aronoff, Lattimore
Public Relations: The Profession and the Practice

Black, Bryant, Thompson
Introduction to Media Communication

Brown, Quaal
Radio-Television-Cable Management

Bryant, Thompson
Fundamentals of Media Effects

Burrows, Gross, Foust, Wood
Video Production: Disciplines and Techniques

Cremer, Keirstead, Yoakam
ENG: Television News

Dominick
The Dynamics of Mass Communication: Media in the Digital Age

Dominick, Sherman, Messere
Broadcast, Cable, the Internet, and Beyond: An Introduction to Modern Electronic Media

Frazell, Tuck
Principles of Editing: A Comprehensive Guide for Students and Journalists

Gross
Telecommunications: An Introduction to Electronic Media

Harrower
The Newspaper Designer's Handbook

Holsinger, Dilts
Media Law

Itule, Anderson
News Writing and Reporting for Today's Media

Lewis
Photojournalism: Content and Technique

Lieb
Building Basic News Sites
Editing for Clear Communication

Mencher
News Reporting and Writing

Patterson, Wilkins
Media Ethics: Issues and Cases

Pember
Mass Media Law

Rich
Creating Online Media

Sherman
Telecommunications Management

Tuggle, Carr, Huffman
Broadcast News Handbook: Writing, Reporting, Producing

Wilson, Wilson
Mass Media/Mass Culture: An Introduction

Fundamentals of Media Effects

Jennings Bryant
University of Alabama

Susan Thompson
University of Alabama

Boston   Burr Ridge, IL   Dubuque, IA   Madison, WI   New York   San Francisco   St. Louis
Bangkok   Bogotá   Caracas   Kuala Lumpur   Lisbon   London   Madrid   Mexico City
Milan   Montreal   New Delhi   Santiago   Seoul   Singapore   Sydney   Taipei   Toronto

McGraw-Hill Higher Education

*A Division of The **McGraw-Hill** Companies*

FUNDAMENTALS OF MEDIA EFFECTS
Published by McGraw-Hill, an imprint of The McGraw-Hill Companies, Inc. 1221
Avenue of the Americas, New York, NY, 10020. Copyright © 2002 by The
McGraw-Hill Companies, Inc. All rights reserved. No part of this publication
may be reproduced or distributed in any form or by any means, or stored in a
database or retrieval system, without the prior written consent of The McGraw-
Hill Companies, Inc., including, but not limited to, in any network or other
electronic storage or transmission, or broadcast for distance learning.

Some ancillaries, including electronic and print components, may
not be available to customers outside the United States.

This book is printed on acid-free paper.

4 5 6 7 8 9 0 FGR/FGR 0 9 8 7 6 5 4

ISBN 0-07-243576-3

Editorial director: *Phillip A. Butcher*
Sponsoring editor: *Valerie Raymond*
Marketing manager: *Kelly M. May*
Project manager: *Natalie J. Ruffatto*
Senior production supervisor: *Lori Koetters*
Producer, Media technology: *Jessica Bodie*
Coordinator freelance design: *Artemio Ortiz Jr.*
Associate supplement producer: *Erin Sauder*
Photo research coordinator: *Judy Kausal*
Photo researcher: *Connie Gardner*
Cover design: *Artemio Ortiz Jr.*
Interior design: *Artemio Ortiz Jr.*
Typeface: *10/12 Palatino*
Compositor: *Electronic Publishing Services, Inc., TN*
Printer: *Quebecor World Fairfield Inc.*

Library of Congress Cataloging-in-Publication Data

Bryant, Jennings.
    Fundamentals of media effects / Jennings Bryant, Susan Thompson.
        p.   Cm. — (McGraw-Hill series in mass communication and journalism)
    Includes index.
    ISBN 0-07-243576-3 (alk. Paper)
        1. Mass media—United States—Psychological aspects. 2. Mass media—Social
    aspects—United States. 3. Mass media—Political aspects—United States. 4. Mass
media—United States—Influence. I. Thompson, Susan, 1957-II. Title. III. Series.
HN90.M3 B79 2002
302.23—dc21   2001042590

www.mhhe.com

About the Authors

JENNINGS BRYANT (P.h.D., Indiana University, 1974) is Professor of Communication, holder of the Reagan Senior Endowed Chair of Broadcasting, and Director of the Institute for Communication Research at the University of Alabama. He received the university's Blackmon-Moody Outstanding Professor Award for 2000 and is President-Elect of the International Communication Association.

Dr. Bryant has authored more than 70 articles in peer-reviewed journals, has written more than 80 chapters published in edited scholarly books, and has delivered more than 200 papers at conventions of national and international professional associations. Twenty-three of his articles or papers have received awards. The most recent books authored or edited by Dr. Bryant include *Media Effects: Advances in Theory and Research* (1994), *Introduction to Media Communication*, 4th ed. (1995), *Reinventing Media* (1996), *Introduction to Media Communication*, 5th ed. (1998), *Human Communication Theory*, 2nd ed. (2000), and *Television and the American Family*, 2nd ed. (2001).

In addition to his own research and writing, Dr. Bryant has been actively involved in editing and promoting the work of other scholars. He has served on the editorial boards of eleven scholarly journals, currently holds editorial board appointments on eight scholarly journals, and is founding co-editor of the journal *Media Psychology*. Dr. Bryant also serves as: Co-Editor of a series of scholarly books published by Lawrence Erlbaum Associates (LEA), Series Editor for LEA's Communication Textbook Series, and Series Editor of LEA's list of Serial Publications in Communications.

SUSAN THOMPSON (MA, University of Alabama, 1995) is a doctoral candidate in communication with a specialization in media history at the School of Communication and Information Sciences, University of Alabama. She is presently completing her dissertation, "The Antebellum Penny Press."

For several years, Thompson was the recipient of a doctoral scholarship sponsored by the Southern Progress Corporation. She has received several awards while completing her doctoral studies, including the college's Outstanding Graduate P.h.D. Research Assistant Award in 1997 and the Knox Hagood Award as outstanding graduate student for 1999. She is a member of Phi Kappa Phi and Kappa Tau Alpha Honor Societies.

Thompson has authored or co-authored several books, including *Reinventing Media* (1996) and *Introduction to Media Communication* 5th ed. (1998). She has also authored several book chapters related to media history. She has presented papers at national and international conferences.

Brief Contents

Contents

ix

SECTION THREE

Key Areas of Research

11.   Effects of Media Violence   171

12.   Media Effects from Sexual Content   194

Preface

In the third edition of *A Cognitive Psychology of Mass Communication*, Richard J. Harris noted, "the most common general perspective in studying the media is a search for the *effects* of exposure to mass communication . . . In the general public, the major concerns about the media probably center on their effects" (p. 17). Given such interest in media effects by scholars and the public, one might expect that basic textbooks on the topic would abound. But that is not the case. Although scholarly volumes analyzing media effects, including many focusing on specialized effects topics, have traditionally assumed an important place in the literature of mass communication, basic textbooks about media effects are quite scarce.

A VITAL ISSUE FOR THOSE COMING OF AGE IN AN INFORMATION SOCIETY

This paucity of textbooks in media effects is particularly problematic in our modern information age. College students are socialized into an environment in which media permeate their lives and are so omnipresent as to be essentially invisible—like water to those proverbially oblivious fish. Moreover, today's typical undergraduate students are so routinely exposed to inaccurate hype about media effects in popular culture fare, that setting the record straight about media effects has become an increasingly important part of a liberal arts education—a phenomenon often called *media literacy* or *media education*.

OUR GOAL AND CHALLENGE

Our primary goal in this volume is to represent the massive body of literature about media effects in such a way that undergraduate students can comprehend, manage, and appreciate this vitally important topic. To that end we have been ably assisted by literally thousands of our students who have eagerly raised their hands (or, less to our liking, put their heads on their desks) whenever we dared to trot out overly technical terms or ambiguous concepts. To them, and to our exceedingly fine reviewers, who willingly served as student surrogates as well as peer consultants, we are extremely grateful.

SPECIAL FEATURES

In order to assist instructors who teach courses in media effects and/or students who take these courses, we are pleased to offer several supplemental features to this textbook:

Key Terms

In each chapter, key terms that need to be understood in order for students to fully comprehend the material are identified by bold typeface and are defined on the website: www.mhhe.com/bryant

Test Bank

Instructors are provided with numerous multiple choice and true/false questions in the form of a computerized test bank, available in Windows or Macintosh formats. Roger Butner authored these questions and we hope you find them valuable. For more information, contact your McGraw-Hill sales representative.

PowerPoint Slides and Discussion Questions

Our website at www.mhhe.com/bryant offers a couple of additional features. PowerPoint slides are available for those who find them useful for class. Organized on a chapter-by-chapter basis, they include summaries of chapter concepts and key figures. Finally, to spark lively class discussions, you'll find a series of chapter questions.

ACKNOWLEDGMENTS

Over the years, numerous instructors and students who have used a volume one of us (JB) co-edited entitled *Media Effects: Advances in Theory and Research* have encouraged us to write this textbook (sometimes sounding downright urgent in their pleas), and they have offered very specific suggestions for how the book should be structured and what should be included and excluded. To them we are extremely grateful, and we are pleased to say at long last: Here 'tis!

We also would like to thank the indomitable Mary Maxwell and Dorina Miron, who helped incredibly in diverse and sundry ways large and small. Although we may forget to tell you so from time to time, we really do appreciate everything you do.

We had a team of exceptionally fine reviewers who made the book a lot better than it would have been without them. Sincere thanks to:

Oscar Patterson III, Universityof North Florida

George Comstock, Syracuse University

Daniel Riffe, Ohio University

Elizabeth Perse, University of Delaware

James Weaver, Virginia Polytechnic Institute

Mary Cassata, SUNY–Buffalo

David J. Atkin, Cleveland State University

Michael Meffert, University of Maryland

Mike Basil, University of Lethbridge

John Chapin, Pennsylvania State University

Randyll Yoder, Ohio University

Donald Singleton, Salisbury State University

Diane Furno Lumade, University of New Mexico

Susanna Priest, Texas A&M University

And our team at McGraw-Hill has been superlative. Thank you, Valerie Raymond, Natalie Ruffatto, Artemio Ortiz, and Judy Kausal.

In closing, we would like to encourage readers of this book to become a part of our editorial team also. Let us know your specific suggestions and how we may serve you better in understanding the roles and effects of media in our society.

Jennings Bryant
University of Alabama

Susan Thompson
University of Alabama

Overview
and History

CHAPTER 1

Understanding Media Effects

I think that we have created a new kind of person in a way. We have created a child who will be so exposed to the media that he will be lost to his parents by the time he is twelve.

—David Bowie, *Melody Maker* (London), January 22, 1972

In 1995 a Louisiana couple, 18-year-old Benjamin Darras and 19-year-old Sarah Edmonson, became obsessed with *Natural Born Killers,* a violent movie about a young duo who engage in a random killing spree after taking hallucinogenic drugs. Darras and Edmonson watched the video up to six times a day. They wanted to become the main characters Mickey and Mallory, who murder innocents for the sheer thrill of it, feel no remorse, and ultimately escape punishment for their evil deeds.

One day in early March, Darras and Edmonson smoked some grass, dropped some acid, loaded some guns, and went out joy riding in search of a Grateful Dead concert. Like their heroes in the film, they also went looking for victims. They never found the concert, but they did find victims, the first of them in rural Mississippi. There, Darras gunned down a cotton gin manager named Bill Savage. The next day, after traveling to Louisiana, Edmonson put a bullet in the throat of Patsy Byers, a Louisiana grocery store clerk and mother of three, and left her for dead.

Instances of monkey see–monkey do effects from mass media fare are rare, but they usually receive tremendous attention in the press because of their sensational nature. As you will learn in the chapters throughout this text, a great deal of research has revealed that people learn from mediated communication (Bandura, 1977, 1986, 1994, in press), and numerous studies have found a causal link between the viewing of media violence and an increase in aggressive behavior (Bandura, 1978, 1979, 1982, 1985; Centerwall, 1989; Liebert & Schwartzberg, 1977; Williams, 1986). Interestingly, no research findings or theoretical formulations have adequately explained why the great majority of people who watch violent movies seemingly exhibit no ill effects, whereas a few go out and imitate the actions they see on the screen, no matter how gruesome those actions. Our knowledge of the link between media violence and aggression is growing, however, and several different theories explaining why media violence may beget real world violence have been proposed and tested.

Measuring the effects of viewing screen violence represents one important facet of media effects research, but the study of media effects encompasses many other types of research as well. Social scientists are also interested in the persuasive powers of mass mediated messages (advertisements, propaganda, communication campaigns, etc.), the impact of new communication technologies, the effects of viewing sexually explicit media fare, reactions to frightening or disturbing media content, effects from political communication, and much more as you will learn.

This chapter provides a foundation for the concepts, theories, and research studies covered throughout the remainder of the text. The book is divided into three sections. In the first—in addition to this introductory chapter—we explore the importance of media effects in historical perspective. We provide historical evidence for media effects (and for societal concern about them) since the dawn of mass communication, and we offer our version of the history of media effects research. The next section includes several of the concepts and theories that serve as the basis for different types of media effects research. Social cognitive theory, priming, cultivation, diffusion of innovations, uses and gratifications, agenda setting, and various persuasion theories are covered, along with some of the relevant research in each of the areas. The final section covers key areas of media effects research, including media violence, effects of sexual content, reactions to disturbing or frightening media content, news effects, communication campaign effects, effects on health, advertising effects, political communication effects, effects of minority portrayals, entertainment effects, and new media technologies.

Following a review of communication processes, we turn in this chapter, to a discussion of different types of communication models. We then explore the means social scientists use to measure media effects—both quantitative and qualitative research methodologies. We close with a word about the importance of studying media effects in today's information society.

PROCESSES OF COMMUNICATION

> Communication can be any or all of the following: an *action on* others; an *inter-action with* others and a *reaction to* others (McQuail & Windahl, 1993, p. 5)

Communication may take several different forms. It may be interpersonal in nature, it may involve the use of a personal communication medium, or it may be described as mass communication. When two people have a conversation, they are engaging in *interpersonal communication*. When two people talk to each other on the telephone or by means of electronic mail, *media* (or *mediated*) *communication* occurs. When a news anchor talks to a camera and his or her image and voice are transmitted to a large number of viewers watching in homes scattered throughout the land, *mass communication* takes place.

The act of communicating by way of interpersonal, beyond media, or mass media channels involves a *process*. In its simplest form, communication historically has been perceived as a sender delivering a message via a channel to a receiver, *usually* producing some kind of effect. We hear a joke and we laugh. We see a sad movie and we cry. We listen to a lecture and we learn—or we become confused. These examples illustrate that communication may be thought of as a *cause* that produces some kind of *effect*.

We emphasize the word *usually* in the previous paragraph because not all communication produces effects. The effects of any communication are subject to the conditions under which the communication occurs: the receptivity of listeners, readers, or viewers as well as numerous other factors. Certain factors may keep us from attending to the messages as we should, thereby mitigating effects or preventing them entirely. Someone may whisper something to us and cause us to miss the punch line of a joke. We may be more interested in our date than in the movie, and not pay any attention whatsoever to the actions on the screen. We may sit through a lecture with our mind on an upcoming exam and walk out of the classroom without a clue as to what we just heard.

Even in its simplest form, communication between even two people is rarely simple and typically takes on an *interactional* or *transactional* dimension. In an interpersonal conversation, the listener may offer immediate feedback to the initial talker. In the course of a conversation or discussion, direct or electronically mediated senders and receivers may alternate repeatedly in their respective roles, and all of them as communicators.

In contrast, the process of mass communication involves a single source (usually a complex entity such as a television network) reaching thousands or millions of people with the same institutionalized message. The audience members are often heterogeneous, or demographically diverse, and typically are unknown to the message source. An interpersonal relationship between a network or station and any one audience member usually does not occur, although it should be noted that program websites and, especially, interactive television and other new media technologies are beginning to offer a new, interpersonal dimension to mass communication.

COMMUNICATION MODELS

To understand processes of communication and effects from communication, some scholars have developed pictorial **models** to explain their theories and illustrate abstract notions regarding communication behavior. These models make it easier for us to identify the similarities and differences among the various types of communication. Models also help demonstrate the different processes of communication, whether linear, interactional, or transactional in nature.

A simple search for the phrase "communication model" in an academic database such as ERIC results in hundreds of hits. The ubiquity of the phrase has made it something of a cliché in academia. Models of communication have been employed in everything from psychiatry to parapsychology and just about everything in between.

Even in the field of communication, the phrase "communication model" may be used in several different ways. In this chapter, we define the term *model* as a graphic means of explicating, or facilitating the understanding of, an abstract process such as communication. (In Chapter 3 "model" is used in another sense, to describe a prevailing paradigm or overall trend in scholarly thought, such as the powerful effects model, the limited effects model, and so forth.)

The successful pictorial models identified in this chapter offer three major advantages: They *organize* concepts, they *explain* processes, and they *predict* outcomes (Deutsch, 1966). These models range from the very simple to the very complex, but all attempt to make abstruse concepts readily understandable. A familiarity with these models may prove beneficial when the various instances of media effects are described throughout this book.

In this section we will examine two broad categories of pictorial models: those that describe various communication processes and those that explicate some kinds of media effects. The examples we offer represent only a few of the many different kinds of communication models that scholars have developed. For a more comprehensive catalog of communication models, you are encouraged to consult D. McQuail and S. Windahl's *Communication Models for the Study of Mass Communication* (1993).

Models to Depict Communication Processes

A number of pictorial models illustrate the various processes of communication. In this section, we discuss and reproduce graphic models that depict three different ways of viewing communication processes: linear, interactive, and transactional representations.

Linear Models

Linear models are based on the principles of stimulus-response psychology, in which a receiver is affected (response) by a message (stimulus) that emanates from a communication source. These models depict the communication process as a series of progressive, linear steps in the transmission of ideas from one person to another.

One of the first linear models of communication, known as the **Shannon-Weaver model,** described the process of telecommunication. Claude Shannon and Warren Weaver, researchers in the Bell Telephone Laboratory in the 1940s, developed a model (see Figure 1.1) that depicts a message emanating from an

FIGURE 1.1. Shannon's and Weaver's model describes communication as a linear, one-way process. *Source:* From *The Mathematical Theory of Communication.* Copyright 1949, 1977 by the Board of Trustees of the University of Illinois Press. Used with permission of the University of Illinois Press.

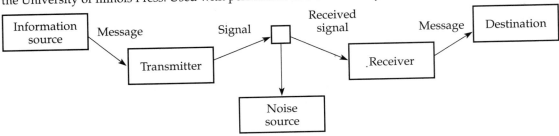

information source, which becomes a signal after passing through a transmitter. Depending upon the amount of noise or interference present, the signal passes through to a receiver, where it is decoded as a message.

In the 1950s, Bruce Westley and Malcolm M. MacLean, Jr., sought to expand upon the Shannon-Weaver model. They developed a sender-receiver model to explain types of communication other than telecommunication, such as interpersonal and mass mediated. The various versions of the **Westley-MacLean model** (see Figures 1.2a and 1.2b) differ from the Shannon-Weaver model in that they include mechanisms for *feedback,* or return flow of information from a receiver to the original source, and *gatekeeping,* a mechanism (usually a person) that has the power to control information and even prevent it from reaching a destination. The gatekeeper was thought to be an important new dimension of

FIGURE 1.2a. A selects from potential X's to communicate with B. *Source:* From Bruce Westley and Malcolm M. MacLean, Jr., "A Conceptual Model for Communication Research," *Journalism Quarterly 34,* 1957. Copyright © 1957. Used by permission of JMC Quarterly.

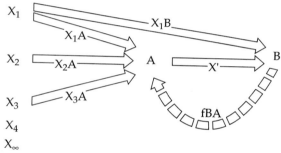

FIGURE 1.2b. Westley and MacLean's conceptual model of mass communication, in which a second type of communicator, C (channel role), is introduced. *Source:* From Bruce Westley and Malcolm M. MacLean, Jr., "A Conceptual Model for Communication Research," *Journalism Quarterly 34,* 1957. Copyright © 1957. Used by permission of JMC Quarterly.

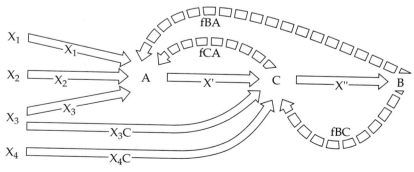

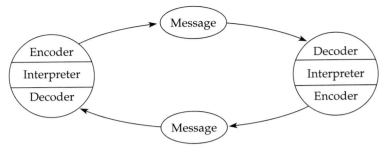

FIGURE 1.3. In Schramm's model both parties in, for example, a conversation
fulfil the same functions.
Source: From Wilbur Schramm, "How Communication Works," in *The Processes
and Effects of Mass Communication,* p.8, ed. Wilbur Schramm. Copyright © 1954.
Reprinted by permission of the Estate of Wilbur Schramm.

communication models to many in mass communication, because it serves as
an analog for editors, for example, who control and select the messages that ultimately get to readers of newspapers or viewers of news programs.

Interactive Models

One of the best definitions of communication as an *interactive* process comes
from the United States Office of Technology Assessment (OTA). A 1990 report
from the now-defunct OTA defined communication as "the process by which
messages are formulated, exchanged and interpreted" (U.S. Congress, 1990).

As with the Westley-MacLean linear model, our example of a model that
depicts communication as an interactive process also originated in the 1950s. The
Schramm interactive model emphasizes the sharing of information between
communicators, who give and receive information interactively. Developed by
communication theorist Wilbur Schramm (1954), the circular model describes
communication as interactive and interpretive, with communicators almost
simultaneously sending and receiving messages. Each person alternates in his or
her role as encoder, interpreter, and decoder of shared messages (see Figure 1.3).

Transactional Models

The same OTA report that offered the interactive definition of communication also offered two of the few models ever advanced that reveal the *transactional* nature of communication. As with a business transaction, the word
"transactional" in describing communication implies the giving and receiving
of something—in this case, information. This model takes into consideration
the character of the message and the psychological orientation of the audience
member as factors influencing the power of media effects.

The models reproduced here offer different views of communication as a
transactional process, from microanalytical and macroanalytical levels. The
OTA transactional model (see Figure 1.4) separates communication into three
distinct processes—message formulation, message interpretation, and message
exchange—and emphasizes the interdependencies of the processes. This model
offers a microanalytical view of the transactional and multidimensional nature
of communication.

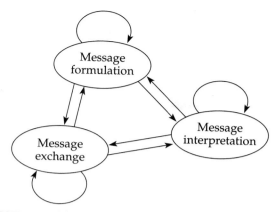

FIGURE 1.4. The Office of Technology Assessment model reveals the transactional nature of communication theories. The formation, exchange, and interpretation of messages and the interdependencies of these processes are key features of this model. *Source:* Office of Technology Assessment, U.S. Congress, Critical Connections: Communication for the Future, OTA-CIT-407 (Washington, DC: U.S. Government Printing Office, January 1990). Public Domain.

Models to Explain Media Effects

In addition to models that describe the overall processes of communication, scholars have advanced other models to depict the effects that may result whenever media communication occurs. Both micro- and macroanalytical models have been used to describe the different types and levels of media effects, from purely individual effects to influences on groups of people or even society at large.

Individual Effects

One of the most useful models to illustrate direct effects on individuals from mass mediated communication is the **Comstock psychological model** (see Figure 1.5). G. Comstock of Syracuse University and his associates (1978) developed this model to describe certain mental processes that occur while watching television. The model shows that the behavior of an individual viewer may be influenced by televised actions. A person learns some behavior by watching it presented on television, and the person may adopt the learned behavior, depending upon the salience (or psychological importance) and the personal excitement or motivation (called arousal in this model) gained by engaging in such behavior. The perceived reality of the mediated action is an important mitigating variable (i.e., the more realistic the media portrayal, the greater the psychological effect on the viewer and the greater the potential influence on the viewer's behavior).

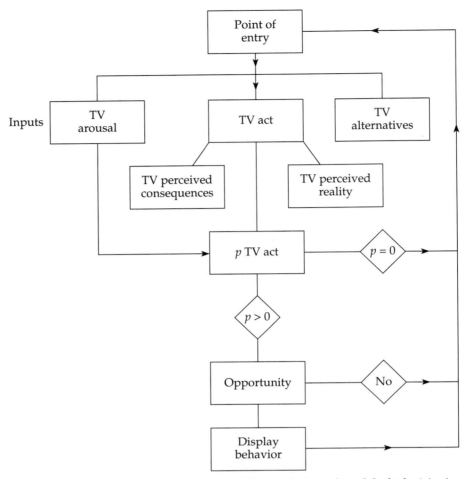

FIGURE 1.5. A simplified version of Comstock's psychological model of television's effects on individual behavior. The model is given in the form of an "itinerary" of an individual in time, starting with exposure to a given television portrayal. *Source:* From G. Comstock, S. Chaffee, N. Katzman, M. McCombs, & D. Roberts *Television and Human Behavior.* Copyright © 1978 by Columbia University.

Another good example of a model that shows individual psychological effects from media communication is the **Thorson cognitive processing model** (see Figure 1.6). Whenever cognitive (or mental) dimensions are under consideration, models are sometimes rather complex; however, such complexities are necessary to accurately depict the many factors and steps involved in the processing of mediated information. The Thorson model concentrates on the steps taken in the processing of television commercials. It takes into consideration the individual viewer's personal interest in and attention to the commercial message, the person's memory, and even language capacity, in determining the

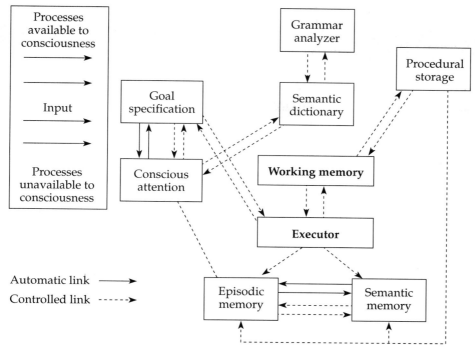

FIGURE 1.6. Thorson's cognitive processing model.
Source: B. Derwin, L. Grossberg, B. J. O'Keefe, and E. Wartells, eds., *Rethinking
Communication: Paradigm Exemplars,* vol. 2, pp. 397–410, copyright © 1989 by Sage
Publications, Inc. Reprinted by Permission of Sage Publications, Inc.

potential effects of the messages. For example, a foreign student who does not
yet have a thorough command of English would have more trouble processing
commercials than a native speaker, and would not remember the commercial
message as well.

Social Effects

As an example of a model of media effects at the societal level, we have
selected the **media system dependency model** advanced by M. L. DeFleur and
S. Ball-Rokeach (1976). This model (see Figure 1.7) focuses on the relationships
between the mass media entity (information system) and society itself (social
system). It assumes that individuals in modern society become increasingly
dependent upon mass media as a source of news and information. The level of
the dependency relationship and the strength of the media effects hinge on the
stability or instability of the society and the degree of societal importance
placed upon mass media as an information source. Relationships and interactions among media, society, and audience are demonstrated, along with media
effects. News in times of crisis serves as a good example of dependency theory
in action. Whenever a crisis occurs (e.g., the death of a leader such as President

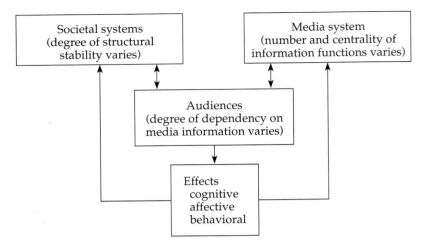

FIGURE 1.7. The dependency state.
Source: From M. L. DeFleur and S. J. Ball-Rokeach, eds., *Theories of Mass Communication.* Copyright © 1982. Reprinted/Adapted by permission of Allyn & Bacon.

Kennedy or the explosion of the space shuttle *Challenger*) people turn to the news media as a source of information and even comfort. Their dependency on the media increases during times of crisis.

These examples represent only a few of the large and growing number of pictorial models used to illustrate communication processes and effects from media communication. With this basic foundation, we now turn specifically to the topic of media effects. In these final sections, we discuss the various means of measuring or assessing media effects, and consider the social relevance of media effects research.

MEASURING MEDIA EFFECTS

The study of media effects typically assumes a basic cause-and-effect relationship. It does not, however, completely disregard the role of chance in the unfolding of events. Social scientists employ statistical tools to account for chance while accepting the notion of causality. According to D. K. Perry:

> Any discussion of media effects requires a concern with causation. Before a researcher can conclude that one concept is a cause of another, the researcher must establish three things. First, the presumed cause and the presumed effect must covary, or go together. For example, people who are heavily exposed to mediated violence should tend, on the average, to be either more or less aggressive than those who are less exposed . . . Second, the presumed cause must precede the presumed effect. Finally, a researcher must eliminate plausible rival (i.e., third variable) explanations for the observed covariation of the presumed cause and effect. (1996, pp. 25–26)

Table 1.1   Terms Used by Social Scientists

Throughout the text, we will use various terms in our discussions of concepts and theories related to media effects. The following list should provide a useful review.

Theory	Systematic explanations and predictions of phenomena. More formally, a theory is a systematic and plausible set of generalizations that explain some observable phenomena by linking constructs and variables in terms of organizing principles that are internally consistent.
Concept	A general idea derived from many specific particulars; for example, *social class* is a concept generalized from particulars like income, education, status, occupation, and esteem.
Hypothesis	A specific statement or proposal that can be tested by means of gathering empirical evidence.
Qualitative	Research methods that allow the investigator to describe a phenomenon without relying heavily on numbers. Qualitative methods allow the researcher to interpret a phenomenon more holistically using words rather than numbers.
Quantitative	Research methods that use numbers to describe the relative amount of something.
Triangulation	Use of multiple types of research methods to address questions of media effects.
Deductive reasoning	From the general to the particular; the process by which theory is tested. The researcher begins with a general idea or theory and asks a specific statement or hypothesis, then tests the hypothesis with the collection of data.
Inductive reasoning	From the particular to the general; the process by which theory is generated. The researcher begins with a simple research question and collects data that describe a particular case, then develops a theory based upon findings.
Variable	Anything to which more than one value can be assigned; for example, hair color is a variable that can have values of black, brown, blond, red, and so forth.

Throughout this text, you will read about the results of many studies that have been conducted to test for evidence of media effects. Most effects research involves the use of quantitative research methods, but studies employing more qualitative measures, or some combination of the two, have also been used. In this section we examine four research methodologies that have been used to study media effects: the laboratory experiment, survey research, field experiments, and the panel study. We also mention the importance of statistical methods in assessing the presence of media effects. Table 1.1 provides a list of terms used in the discussion of media effects.

Laboratory Experiments

By far the most popular method for measuring media effects in its most simple form, the experimental method involves having some people watch or listen to or read a certain type of media fare (violent, sexually explicit, frightening, or something else) while other people watch, read, or listen to innocuous content, then comparing any measureable changes the individuals from the two groups exhibited. The measurement tool may be either the self-reports of participants on questionnaires or automated instruments (e.g., preference analyzers), observation of participants' actions, assessments of various activities performed by the individual, or some sort of physiological measure (e.g., blood pressure, heart rate, skin temperature) or cognitive assessment (e.g., α and β brain waves) as the participant is viewing the content.

In more complex formulations, experiments often include control groups (e.g., people who did not read, hear, or see a media message). Complex research designs also are employed so that researchers can examine the effects of several variables simultaneously—for example, the impact of (*a*) frightening versus non-frightening media fare on (*b*) boys versus girls (*c*) at different ages (e.g., 3, 6, 9).

R. D. Wimmer and J. R. Dominick (1994) listed four major advantages and two disadvantages of laboratory experiments in media research. On the positive side, the experiment represents "the best social science research method for establishing causality" (p. 85). The experiment also affords the researcher much control, especially in the presentation of the variables in proper time order so that the cause is shown to precede the effect, and in the manipulation of variables. In terms of cost, experiments also involve less expense than most other research methods. Finally, the step-by-step techniques make laboratory experiments easier for others to replicate than other types of research methods. As for disadvantages, the artificial surroundings of lab experiments may affect a research participant's behavior, including the very variable that researchers are attempting to observe and measure. Another problem, experimental bias, occurs when the researcher influences the results either intentionally or unintentionally. Many researchers avoid the problem by conducting double-blind experiments, in which neither the research participants nor the researchers know which participants are part of the control group and which belong to the experimental group.

Survey Research

Another common means of measuring effects from media fare features the use of written questionnaires, telephone interviews, face-to-face interviews, or Web surveys to gauge (1) the type and extent of media exposure of an individual (e.g., number of hours the person watches violent television programs per week, or the number of pornographic magazines the person reads each week), and (2) the respondent's self-reported attitudes and tendencies toward antisocial or prosocial behaviors. For the latter measure, researchers may employ any of several scales or inventories that have been refined over time. These studies often search for specific demographic or sociographic factors that might affect the relationship between variables because surveys are commonly conducted with representative samples of the population of interest.

One caveat about using survey research to determine media effects should be added. If you recall Perry's three criteria for causation, you can readily see that the first criterion—that the presumed cause and the presumed effect must covary—can be readily accommodated through survey research. The third criterion—the elimination of rival causes—can also be addressed somewhat by survey research. Indeed, using a well-designed survey, a number of different potential contributors to a particular media effect can be evaluated in the same survey. For this reason, researchers conducting an experiment also frequently administer a survey to their research participants. In this way, they can use various statistical controls and partially account for rival causes at the same time as they determine cause-and-effect relationships by way of the tight research designs that experiments typically permit. However, the second criterion for causation presented by Perry—that the presumed cause must precede the presumed effect—is the potential trouble spot in using survey research to determine media effects. This issue of time sequence or time order cannot be determined if the questionnaire or interview assesses the presumed cause (e.g., the number of hours of violent television watched) and the presumed effect (e.g., the level of fear for personal safety) at the same time. To attempt to get around the time-course issue, researchers often administer the same survey (or similar surveys) on multiple occasions, or they administer different portions of the instrument at different times. However, because such control typically is not considered to be as certain or as effective as that exerted by tight research designs and a properly conducted experiment, the determination of causation from such procedures is frequently called into question if surveys are the only means to assess media effects. In other words, surveys are very good for determining associations or relationships between variables, but they are less compelling for determining cause and effect.

Field Experiments

Experiments conducted "in the field," or in real-world settings, have not been used to study media effects to the extent that laboratory and survey research methods have been employed, but a handful of important studies have been conducted in this manner (Williams, 1986; Parke, Berkowitz, & Leyens, 1977). Field experiments do not allow as much physical control as experiments conducted in the laboratory; however, the use of statistical controls in the field has allowed researchers to gain more control over extraneous or intervening variables. Field experiments rate high in *external validity*, or the measure of a particular study's generalizability. The attitudes or behaviors of research participants are measured in real-life settings rather than in the often sterile environment of a laboratory; therefore, the behaviors of participants are thought to be more natural. In some cases, people being studied in the field may not be aware that they are being measured and therefore may behave more naturally, although such approaches raise ethical issues. An additional advantage of the field study may be found in its expediency for studying rather complex social situations, such as the impact of television on a community receiving it for the first time.

Panel Studies

Panel studies require the researcher to either interview or send questionnaires to the same respondents at different times. This method is not employed as often in the study of media effects as other methods; however, one of the major studies in the history of media effects (Lazarsfeld, Berelson, & Gaudet, 1944) made use of a panel. Panel studies are inherently longitudinal in nature, meaning that the same respondents provide information at more than one point in time. This means that respondents must be recruited and retained over time, a situation that makes demands on the researcher's time and may involve considerable expense. However, the benefits of panel studies often outweigh these human and fiscal costs.

Triangulation

Because each of these primary research methodologies for establishing media effects has limitations, researchers often try to utilize several different methodologies to address a question or issue of media effects. For example, to determine whether watching a great deal of television drama in which the lead characters are generous and altruistic causes viewers to increase their charitable giving, it is possible to use a laboratory experiment, a field experiment, or a survey. However, it would be even better to utilize all three methodologies, that is, a so-called triangulation of methodologies. If the results of the three separate studies are similar, the cumulative findings are much more compelling than the findings from any of the independent investigations. Scholars who approach media effects questions utilizing complementary methodologies (or who use several different experiments or surveys to answer similar research questions) are often said to conduct *programmatic* research in media effects. This greatly increases the credibility of their findings not only among their peers, but also for news reporters and policy makers.

OTHER RESEARCH METHODOLOGIES OF MEDIA EFFECTS

A number of other research methodologies are also useful in understanding and predicting media effects. Two of them, content analysis and meta-analysis, are briefly profiled because of their prevalence in media effects research.

Content Analysis

Content analysis has often been used to examine the presence, absence, or quantity of certain attributes of media messages that allegedly contribute to certain types of media impact. For example, as a part of its program designed to highlight "the importance of entertainment media in shaping people's awareness of health issues" (Kaiser Family, 1999, p. 2), the Kaiser Family Foundation commissioned several content analyses of sex on television, including assessments of the prevalence of sexual messages, the types of talk about sex, the types of sexual behaviors presented or discussed, and the prevalence of messages about sexual risks or responsibilities (Kunkel et al., 1999). It should be noted that the presence or absence of such message features do not provide any direct evidence of media effects on sexual behavior; instead, such content analyses can provide a valuable profile of the type of content that might be expected to lead to prosocial or antisocial media effects. Other research methodologies must be used in conjunction with content analyses to provide evidence of effects per se.

Meta-Analysis

Throughout this textbook you will find the results from various meta-analyses of media effects. Meta-analysis is a relatively new methodology in media effects research, and it is unusual in that it does not contribute any new "primary" evidence regarding media effects. Instead, meta-analysis is a means of systematically integrating the extant findings from a large number of empirical studies on any given topic. Statistical methods are used to provide a "big picture" in terms of the magnitude as well as the direction of the effects attributable to the media in a particular area of inquiry (e.g., stereotyping, pornography). Because the procedures employed in meta-analysis are relatively objective and are designed to be quite comprehensive, a well-conducted meta-analysis can give an analytical interpretation of a body of media effects literature. This information can then be combined with traditional narrative literature reviews to provide further insight into the effects of media in society.

Statistical Methods

Most media effects studies make use of *statistics,* "the science that uses mathematical models to collect, organize, summarize, and analyze data" (Wimmer & Dominick, 1994, p. 205). Statistical methods may be *descriptive,* such as this sample hypothesis: "Readers of *six* or more mystery novels per month performed *three* times as well on problem-solving tasks as their peers who did not read mystery novels." However, probably the most common use of statistical tools in communication research involves the use of *inferential* statistics. The science of statistics assumes that random samples from populations take on the same distribution properties of the larger population; thus tests conducted upon a random sample may be generalizable to the overall population within certain well-defined limits. Statistical methods are based upon laws of probability. The methods make allowances for errors in sampling. Based upon laws of probability, statistical methods make provisions for chance. Errors due to chance, whether sampling errors (e.g., the chance selection or assignment of a sample that is not representative of a population) or something else, become part of the overall equation. Research designs allow investigators to isolate particular causes for media effects; statistical methods permit us to assign values to the strength of those causes.

IMPORTANCE OF STUDYING MEDIA EFFECTS

We live in a world in which we receive a multitude of mediated messages daily. As you will learn in the next chapter, the concern about effects from media communication, as well as evidence for effects, are as old as mass communication itself. People have always wondered how media messages are affecting them and, especially, their children. They have always been concerned for the negative effects of a particular message, or message systems, and they have been curious about the potential prosocial effects of others.

As we move further into a new millennium, the knowledge of effects from mediated communications assumes increasing importance. We have become so information oriented and information dependent that some have dubbed ours an "information society." Computers and mass media are vital cogs in our societal infrastructure. With so much of what is perceived to be wrong in today's world blamed on media communications of some sort or another, the issue of mass media effects has become one of paramount social relevance. But effects from mediated violence, pornography, advertising, or news are but the most visible surface of this fascinating and important research domain. As we hope you will discover as you read the chapters of this text, knowledge of the power of mediated communications is important for us all. It is often said that we are the "sovereign consumers" of the information age. But if our consumption is to be fruitful, we must be extremely knowledgable about the effects of media in our lives.

SUMMARY

Measuring the effects of viewing screen violence represents one important facet of media effects research, but the study of media effects encompasses many other types of research as well. Social scientists are also interested in the persuasive powers of mass mediated messages (e.g., advertisements, propaganda, communication campaigns), the impact of new communication technologies, the effects of viewing sexually explicit media fare, reactions to frightful or disturbing media content, effects from political communication, and much more.

Communication may take several different forms. It may be interpersonal in nature, it may involve the use of a personal communication medium, or it may be described as mass communication. The act of communicating via interpersonal, media, or mass media channels involves a process or series of stages. Even in its simplest form, communication between a source and a receiver may take on an interactional or transactional dimension. In the case of an interpersonal conversation, the receiver may offer immediate feedback to the source. In the course of a conversation or discussion, senders and receivers may alternate repeatedly in their respective roles. Mass communication involves one or more institutional sources (usually complex entities such as production houses in conjunction with a television network) reaching thousands or millions of people with the same transient message. The audience members are heterogeneous, or demographically diverse, and unknown to the message source.

Scholars have developed models to explain their theories and illustrate abstract ideas regarding communication processes and behavior. Models may also be used to explain media effects. Models help demonstrate the different processes of communication, whether linear, interactional, or transactional in nature. Successful pictorial models offer three major advantages: They organize concepts, they explain processes, and they predict outcomes.

The study of media effects assumes a basic cause-and-effect scenario. Social scientists employ statistical methods to account for chance as an important component of the notion of causality.

Researchers often measure media effects in laboratory settings using experimental methods. Other research methods include surveys, field experiments, and panel studies. Triangulation is the use of several research methods to address questions of media effects. Content analysis is used to examine the presence, absence, or quantity of certain attributes of media messages that allegedly contribute to certain media effects. Meta-analyses are useful for systematically integrating extant findings from a large number of empirical studies on any given topic. Most media effects studies employ statistical methods.

With so many of the problems in today's world being blamed on media communications, the issues of mass media effects has become one of paramount social relevance. Media effects is an important and fascinating research domain. A fundamental knowledge of media effects is a necessary criterion for excelling in the information age.

REFERENCES

BALL-ROKEACH, S., & DEFLEUR, M. L. (1965). A dependency model of mass media effects. *Communication Research, 3,* 3–21.

BANDURA, A. (1977). *Social learning theory.* Englewood Cliffs, NJ: Prentice Hall.

BANDURA, A. (1978). A social learning theory of aggression. *Journal of Communication, 28*(3), 12–29.

BANDURA, A. (1979). Psychological mechanisms of aggression. In M. von Cranach, K. Foppa, W. Lepenies, & D. Ploog (Eds.), *Human ethology: Claims and limits of a new discipline* (pp. 316–356). Cambridge, MA: Cambridge University Press.

BANDURA, A. (1982). Self-efficacy mechanism in human agency. *American Psychologist, 37*(2), 122–147.

BANDURA, A. (1985). *Social foundations of thought and action.* Englewood Cliffs, NJ: Prentice Hall.

BANDURA, A. (1986). *Social foundations of thought and action: A social cognitive theory.* Englewood Cliffs, NJ: Prentice Hall.

BANDURA, A. (1994). Social cognitive theory of mass communication. In J. Bryant & D. Zillmann (Eds.), *Media effects: Advances in theory and research.* Mahwah, NJ: Erlbaum.

BANDURA, A. (in press). Social cognitive theory of mass communication. In J. Bryant & D. Zillmann (Eds.), *Media effects: Advances in theory and research* (2nd ed.). Mahwah, NJ: Erlbaum.

CENTERWALL, B. S. (1989). Exposure to television as a cause of violence. *Public Communication and Behavior, 2,* 1–58.

COMSTOCK, G., CHAFFEE, S., KATZMAN, N., MCCOMBS, M., & ROBERTS, D. (1978). *Television and human behavior.* New York: Columbia University Press.

DEUTSCH, K. (1966). *The nerves of government.* New York: Free Press.

JANOWITZ, M. (1968). The study of mass communication. In D. E. Sills (Ed.), *International encyclopedia of the social sciences* (Vol. 3, p. 41). New York: Macmillan and Free Press.

KAISER FAMILY FOUNDATION (1999). *Progress on the entertainment media & public health* [Brochure]. Menlo Park, CA: Author.

KUNKEL, D., COPE, K. M., FARINOLA, W. J. M., BIELY, E., ROLLIN, E., & DONNERSTEIN, E. (1999). *Sex on tv: A biennial report to the Kaiser Family Foundation.* Menlo Park, CA: Kaiser Family Foundation.

LAZARSFELD, P., BERELSON, B., & GAUDET, H. (1944). *The people's choice.* New York: Columbia University Press.

LIEBERT, R. M., & SCHWARTZBERG, N. S. (1977). Effects of mass media. *Annual Review of Psychology, 28,* 141–183.

MCQUAIL, D., & WINDAHL, S. (1993). *Communication models for the study of mass communications* (2nd ed.). New York: Longman.

PARKE, R., BERKOWITZ, L., & LEYENS, J. (1977). Some effects of violent and nonviolent movies on the behavior of juvenile delinquents. *Advances in Experimental Social Psychology, 16,* 135–172.

PERRY, D. K. (1996). *Theory & research in mass communication: Contexts and consequences.* Mahwah, NJ: Erlbaum.

SCHRAMM, W. (1954). How communication works. In W. Schramm (Ed.), *The processes and effects of mass communication.* Urbana: University of Illinois Press.

SHANNON, C., & WEAVER, W. (1949). *The mathematical theory of communication.* Urbana: University of Illinois Press.

WESTLEY, B. H., & MACLEAN, M. (1957). A conceptual model for mass communication research. *Journalism Quarterly, 34,* 31–38.

WILLIAMS, T. M. (1986). *The impact of television.* New York: Academic.

WIMMER, R. D., & DOMINICK, J. R. (1994). *Mass media research: An introduction* (4th ed.). Belmont, CA: Wadsworth Publishing.

CHAPTER 2

Media Effects:
A Historical Perspective

Among the most alarming evils of our age and country is the injurious tendency of the publications that are daily flowing from the press.
—*U.S. Catholic Magazine*, 1847

Since the invention of the printing press in 1450, people have suggested that mass media have important effects on their audiences. Sometimes historical evidence has been utilized to chronicle pronounced changes in public opinions or behavior after widespread exposure to certain media content. At other times, media effects have been less obvious, but *concern* of the critics for media effects on others has prompted various actions against mass media. Such concerns for generalized "others" rather than self have been systematically explained as *third-person effects*, which are said to occur whenever individuals believe other audience members are more susceptible than they are to persuasive, violent, or objectable media content (Davison, 1983).

This chapter examines the concern for media effects in historical perspective and the historical evidence for actual media effects on opinions and behaviors since the invention of the printing press. The chapter also documents selected popular concern about media effects prior to and after social scientific measurement of such effects became an area of scholarly enquiry.

The existence of media effects ultimately requires a cause-and-effect perspective, with the "cause" being some kind of message conveyed by way of a communication medium. When social and behavioral scientists enter their media effects laboratories, tight control typically is undertaken to ensure that extraneous influences are minimized and that precise measurement of influences on individuals can be accomplished. They are thereby equipped to assess actual media effects on individuals in a variety of ways. In contrast, historians are usually limited to assessing cause-and-effect relationships involving media only when the effects, as indicated in recorded opinions and actions, seem obvious and powerful in retrospect.

Moreover, whereas social and behavioral scientists typically amass evidence for or against media effects by treating or examining individuals, often one at a time, historians sometimes examine aggregate data from public records and the like, thereby focusing on societal-level effects. It should be noted that the various historical examples we cite provide evidence for media effects among great numbers of people rather than individual and isolated cases of the "man bites dog" variety. We will emphasize major trends rather than idiosyncratic events of media impact that may be newsworthy because of their human interest value.

Many scholars might argue that historical examples do not provide adequate, scientific evidence of a cause-and-effect relationship. As a University of Chicago social scientist once stated:

> [T]he case method and the collection of anecdotes do not supply proof of a generalization; rather they provide illustrations, and such illustrations can be deceptive if they lead the author or others to accept them as proof. (Stouffer, 1942, p. 144)

In answer to this argument, we emphasize that historical methods are different from other research methods. The historian looks for a preponderance of evidence, usually various concurring indications of influence, that suggest cause-and-effect relationships. A book such as Harriet Beecher Stowe's *Uncle Tom's Cabin* (1852), for example, is known to have been influential because of its high sales figures and from discussions about its influence among writers and orators of the period. It should be remembered that scores of examples of null or minimal media effects may never show up on a historian's radar screen.

As will be shown, obtrusive examples of what certainly appear to be media effects on opinions and behavior are rather plentiful throughout modern history, especially when people reacted to frightful or disturbing media content and persuasive messages. Historical evidence for popular public concern about media effects also abounds and has manifested itself in different ways. The many instances of suppression of the press by authorities can be viewed as evidence of their concern for powerful media effects on the masses, as can instances of individual efforts against violent or sexually explicit material due to their suspected harmful effects on the masses, especially children.

HISTORICAL CONCERN FOR MEDIA EFFECTS

The modern-day emphasis on quantitative, experimental measures in media effects research has obscured the obvious bond that exists between the study of media history and that of media effects. Like scientific effects researchers, many media historians also search for evidence of media effects. However, the historian's laboratory is the past—the centuries since humans first used mass media to communicate with each other. Therefore, the historian's subjects can speak only through records that have survived.

Historical evidence reveals that, at first, only society's elite recognized potential societal influences from exposure to the printed word. Many leaders, due to their fear of effects from literacy and reading on the masses, sought to control publications and thereby silence opposition voices. Such fear of media influences linger today in many totalitarian societies, in which leaders suppress or control media to maintain their power.

In the 19th century, new technologies and the spread of literacy made possible the development of remarkable new forms of communication: mass communication. Since that period, concern for powerful media effects has been expressed not only by society's educated elite, but also it has been shared by individuals and groups from all strata of the population, from presidents to parents, from the intelligentsia to beginning students. These historical instances of the concern about detrimental societal affects of media messages have been strong enough and loud enough to influence lawmakers, shape public policy, and attract the interest of numerous scholars.

Western history provides many examples of attempts to control the press due to the supposed power of its messages over its audience. The control has taken various forms, such as suppression or censorship of information, use of propaganda, or physical violence against editors or reporters. The agents of control have included government officials, the clergy, and others. This section offers a brief survey of some of the more memorable instances in history when concern for media effects caused actions against the press or other media.

Suppression Due to Concern for Media Effects.

The most compelling examples of the concern for powerful media effects on the masses might be found in the many instances in which authorities have taken preemptive measures to suppress mass media messages. Soon after the appearance of the printing press, the ecclesiastical and governmental elite showed concern for the power of the printed word. They used the press for their own ends and attempted measures of censorship to prevent the publishing of opposition views. For example, in the mid-16th century, Catholics wanted Protestant material banned. In 1559, Pope Paul IV began issuing an *Index of Prohibited Books*, a listing of forbidden works. In addition to Protestant books, the list included pornography, occult books, and opposition political works. Protestant leaders such as Martin Luther defied the pope and used the printing press to spread Reformation literature to the masses. As this reform literature was disseminated to print shops throughout Europe, the repercussions against the rebels who used media without authority were extremely severe: Printers caught spreading the propaganda often were imprisoned or burned at the stake.

In early 16th-century England, King Henry VIII was so concerned about the printed word that he created the Court of the Star Chamber, which prosecuted those who published material offensive to the Crown. Henry also insisted upon a system of licensing that held the English press under strict control.

In the late 1700s in the United States, Benjamin Franklin Bache's Philadelphia *Aurora* provided a leading voice for the cause of Republicanism in the United States. His inflammatory writings galvanized public opinion and produced a number of different, notable reactions:

> On one occasion or another, Treasury Secretary Oliver Wolcott threatened to investigate the *Aurora* for treason, Federalist Speaker of the House Jonathan Dayton barred Bache from the House floor, Federalist editors and politicians subjected him to written and verbal attacks, Federalist merchants imposed an

advertising boycott on the *Aurora* and barred the paper from their establishments, the government tried Bache for sedition, and individuals and mobs physically attacked him. (Sloan, 1998, pp. 130–131)

In an effort to control opposition voices such as Bache's, the Federalists passed one of the most oppressive government measures in U.S. history, the Sedition Act of 1798. The act was passed at the time of the French Revolution in an effort to keep pro-French voices from being heard in American newspapers. "Give to any set of men the command of the press and you give them the command of public opinion, which commands everything," wrote Judge Alexander Addison in the *Columbian Centinel* on January 1, 1799 (Sloan, 1998, p. 119).

> Federalists by 1799 had come to realize a fact that had been at the essence of American public life almost since the first colonists had stepped ashore in the early 1600s. Public opinion was the basis for public policy, and the printing press was the means that provided a forum for it. (p. 119)

From the 1830s until the Civil War, many feared the powerful effects of abolitionist messages. Southerners objected vehemently to publication and circulation of such material because they believed it would encourage slave revolts. President Andrew Jackson urged Congress to pass a law to prevent incendiary material regarding the slavery debate from being circulated in the mails.

During World War I, Congress passed both the Espionage Act of 1917 and the Sedition Act of 1918. These acts made it illegal to publish information critical of the U.S. government or in support of any of the enemy powers. The government feared the effects of voices in opposition to the war effort.

Mob Violence as Media Effect

Another historical indicator of suppression due to concern for media effects might be instances of mob violence directed against mass media offices or editors in response to the publishing or showing of incendiary material. History is filled with such outbreaks of violence directed against the press (Nerone, 1994). One of the nastiest antipress mobs in history attacked producers of the Baltimore *Federal Republican,* a radical Federalist paper that opposed American participation in the War of 1812. Several people died and at least one editor was maimed for life.

Many examples of mob actions against the expression of race-related messages abound (Grimsted, 1998). During the abolitionist movement, a mob attacked and killed Elijah Lovejoy in Illinois. Frederick Douglass, the African-American editor of *The North Star*, was continually harrassed and even had his house burned by those who opposed his views. During the civil rights movement of the 1950s and 1960s, Mississippi editor Hazel Brannon Smith spoke out against racial injustices against African Americans and, as a result, faced considerable opposition from local residents and local government officials alike. A white citizens' council urged local businesses to stop advertising in her paper, subscribers canceled their subscriptions, and one white official brought a libel suit against her—all in reaction to her stand against the unfair treatment of blacks (Davies, 1998).

Not all of the mob incidents related to racial issues involved the press. At least one instance of mob action came in response to a major motion picture. In the early 20th century, release of the film *The Birth of a Nation* caused race riots and mob actions against blacks by arousing emotion and controversy. Produced by D. W. Griffith, the father of American film, *The Birth of a Nation* told the story of the Civil War, Reconstruction, and the rise of the Ku Klux Klan from a white supremacist perspective.

Public Concern for "Indecent" Material

The public concern for the ill effects of media violence and sexually explicit material is not exclusive to the 20th century. In the early 19th century, a new type of journalism emerged in England, one that would soon be copied successfully by penny dailies in the United States. In the English press, humorous reports on the activities of arrested thieves, drunks, prostitutes, and other miscreants and low-lifes of society became immensely popular among many readers, but elicited severe criticisms from social critics. In the United States, the New York *Sun*'s appearance in 1833 and its similar reports of police court activities in New York City resulted in the same mixed response: The articles made the penny sheets very popular among their devoted readers, but the emphasis on violence, sexuality, and unseemly conduct contained in the articles also caused many to criticize the sheets and express concern for the effects of such material on an innocent and expanding reading public.

The second successful penny paper, James Gordon Bennett's New York *Herald,* though immensely popular, attracted controversy almost from the start due to Bennett's habit of ridiculing his competitors in print, his language (which was not always respectable by 19th-century standards), and his extensive coverage of sensational trials that involved scandal, illicit sex, and murder. Competitors and opponents thrashed him in print and in person. On several occasions angry readers physically attacked Bennett on the streets of New York. The "moral war" on Bennett is a good 19th-century example of society's concern for printed material it considered indecent. Prominent citizens called for a boycott against the *Herald* and businesses that advertised in it. As a result, the *Herald* lost some of its mammoth circulation and Bennett soon modified the tone of his paper.

The readable style of the *Sun*, the *Herald,* and the other penny dailies, as well as their sensational and sometimes titillating news stories, made them popular and profitable. Critics continued to complain about the suspected negative effects on society, especially as other newspapers began to copy the *Herald's* techniques and a new style of journalism emerged. A commentator in 1847 complained about the sorry state of the periodical press as a purveyor of immorality. The article "Pernicious Literature" called for press reforms to avoid rather serious effects from such "contamination."

> Among the most alarming evils of our age and country is the injurious tendency of the publications that are daily flowing from the press. The licentious and anti-social works which are so profusely scattered throughout the length and breadth of the land, in the shape of annuals, brochures, and family newspapers, are sowing a seed of corruption which will bring disgrace and wretchedness upon thousands, if not lay the foundation of that sensual and selfish spirit

which will contaminate the nation at large, and threaten the downfall of its free institutions . . . In this state of things the secular press must be reformed itself . . . Until this be done, the spirit of our newspapers and the depravity of the popular appetite will exert a reciprocal influence;—one will encourage the other, and both will combine to swell and precipitate that torrent of licentiousness which is beginning to excite the profound and just apprehensions of all good men. (U.S. Catholic Magazine, 1847, pp. 46, 48)

After film became popular in the early 20th century, public concern for negative effects of violent and sexually explicit film presentations on youngsters prompted the Payne Fund Studies. These studies examined the influence of motion pictures on juvenile delinquency, attitudes, and other factors.

In the 1950s, Fredric Wertham's *Seduction of the Innocent* (1954) expressed an anticomic sentiment that resulted in the inclusion of comic book content in the meetings of the Senate Subcommittee to Investigate Juvenile Delinquency. The comic book industry began measures of self-regulation to ward off government intervention. The Comics Magazine Association of America was formed and issued the Comics Code Authority, which prohibited graphic violence and erotic depictions, among other things.

In recent years, novels such as *The Catcher in the Rye*, movies like *Natural Born Killers*, musical recordings, and even video games have been blamed for influencing audience members to commit horrible acts of violence or for causing "copycat crimes." The concern for the ill effects of viewing violence and sexual content on television and in motion pictures has led to countless studies and government-sponsored inquiries. The debate over the power of the effects of such material rages to this day.

HISTORICAL EVIDENCE FOR CHANGES IN BEHAVIOR AND OPINION DUE TO MASS MEDIA

Although actual media effects are impossible to demonstrate empirically in a historical context—owing to the difficulty of controlling for or eliminating rival causes, among other limitations—Western history is rich with more general, ancedotal examinations of media effects. Such effects include the social changes that occurred after the introduction of new communication technologies, the many instances when individuals and groups used mediated messages to achieve certain goals, and instances in which citizens took actions due to their fear of the power of media messages to sway audiences in some undesirable manner. Long before media effects were studied scientifically and measured analytically, they were assumed, felt, witnessed, and recorded.

Effects from New Media Technologies

Through the years, historians have examined new media technologies as they developed and have uncovered what they considered to be evidence for rather powerful effects at societal and cultural levels. Many studies have explored the advent of the printing press and the many societal changes it brought about (Eisenstein, 1979, 1983; Febvre & Martin, 1984). With the introduction of the printing press, paper, and movable type, more books appeared, prices fell, and literacy spread. The societal impact was considerable. Within approximately one hundred years, the audience for books exploded from a select, elite few to masses of people. By 1500 printers throughout western Europe had established more than 250 presses that produced some 35,000 editions and from 15 to 20 million copies (Febvre & Martin, 1984). Specific historical studies on the diffusion of innovations (see Chapter 7 on the diffusion of innovations) have looked at the spread of other new media technologies, such as the telegraph and the phonograph, and have also included research examining social effects from the use of the new technology (Hyde, 1994). Other historical studies have explored dynamics and changes in social processes brought about by new media technologies (Pool, 1977; Marvin, 1988).

Media Effects on Public Opinion

The influence of the abolitionist press in the years prior to the Civil War illustrates the power of the press (in this case, an alternative press) to sway public opinion. African-American newspapers such as *Freedom's Journal*, *The Colored American*, and *The North Star* advanced the cause of blacks, attacked slavery, and contributed to the growing abolitionist sentiment in the North. In the long run, the effects of such printed material served to educate, mobilize, and motivate blacks and to cultivate attitudes that were much less tolerant of human slavery and more sympathetic to the rights of African Americans among whites in the northern United States.

> Gunnar Myrdal, in *An American Dilemma*, called the black press the most important educational agency for blacks. One of the most powerful arenas in which political, economic, and cultural battles could be fought, it provided a way to tell the black experience: African-American life, concerns, achievements. It was a forum to air blacks' views and discuss issues concerning blacks. Further, coverage of blacks' achievements instilled pride and a sense of progress, identity and hope for the future. The black press also was an educator and aid to readers' intellectual development at a time when blacks were barred from formal education, and it served a vital political function. That is, it helped blacks first understand and then find their political potential. Black editors informed, inspired, unified, and mobilized readers, directing them to act on information and how. (Dicken-Garcia, 1998, p. 154)

History provides a number of other examples of media messages that seemingly proved powerful enough to influence public opinion. In the newly formed United States, a series of articles called "The Federalist Papers" appeared in the *New York Independent Journal* and were widely reprinted. This series, written by Alexander Hamilton, James Madison, and John Jay, has been credited with garnering support for adoption of the new constitutional form of government (Bent, 1969).

Another example from the antebellum period is *Uncle Tom's Cabin*, which we mentioned previously in this chapter. Historians have generally agreed that Harriet Beecher Stowe's classic novel was instrumental in fueling the fires of the abolitionist movement in the antebellum United States and helped turn public opinion against the continuance of slavery in the South.

Stowe's novel *Uncle Tom's Cabin* originally appeared in serialized form in 1852–1853 in the *National Era,* an abolitionist newspaper. It was the most widely read literature of the time. Within months of publication in book form, sales reached 300,000. The book was the single most important writing in increasing the demand that slavery be abolished. (Dicken-Garcia, 1998, p. 155)

Several other works published about this same time eventually had significant effects on thoughts and actions in the 19th and 20th centuries. These included Karl Marx and Friedrich Engels's *Communist Manifesto,* published in 1848, Charles Darwin's *Origin of Species,* and John Stuart Mill's essay "On Liberty," both published in 1859 (Cowley & Smith, 1939).

After the Civil War, William Tweed and his political machine, the Tammany Ring, took control of municipal government in New York City and eventually stole hundreds of millions of dollars from the city coffers. The stinging caricatures of Thomas Nast, an illustrator for the *New York Times,* were especially powerful in gaining public support that eventually brought down the party boss. The *New York Times'* successful crusade against the Tweed Ring and municipal corruption set the stage for the muckraking era in American journalism that soon followed (Bent, 1969).

The sensational yellow journalism of the newspapers owned by Joseph Pulitzer and William Randolph Hearst in the late 1800s resulted in great increases in circulation (over 1 million) for both newspapers—evidence of powerful media effectiveness if not effects per se. Some historians have claimed that Hearst's cries of Spanish atrocities in Cuba were responsible for turning public opinion and causing the Spanish-American War, especially after a mysterious explosion sank the U.S. battleship *Maine* near Havana.

> Hearst has been credited with inflaming public opinion and ultimately starting the war with jingoistic headlines such as "THE WHOLE COUNTRY THRILLS WITH THE WAR FEVER!" Whether or not he deserved such dubious credit, he certainly believed his newspaper was instrumental in the U.S. intervention and actually published the query "HOW DO YOU LIKE THE JOURNAL'S WAR?" in a box next to the masthead for two days. (Hoff, 1998, p. 247)

Two interesting instances of powerful media effects on public opinion in the 20th century involved a significant shift in the public perception of Standard Oil Company magnate John D. Rockefeller. One of these shifts was the result of work during the "muckraking"[1] years at the turn of the century—the Progressive era—when a group of magazine journalists wrote series after series of scathing articles to expose a number of social ills. The muckraking journalist Ida Tarbell painted Rockefeller as a ruthless capitalist who used shady methods to gain advantages over his competitors. Tarbell's articles in *McClure's Magazine* soon made the ultrarich Rockefeller one of the most hated figures in America, as evidenced in disparaging news cartoons and articles from the period. Ironically, a few years later, Rockefeller hired public relations expert Ivy Lee to improve his public image. Lee made Rockefeller's philanthropic activities more visible to the press and public and presented him as a kindly old man—grandfatherly and fun loving—and helped change public opinion favorably toward the former robber baron. The media giveth and the media taketh away!

The works of other muckraking journalists during the Progressive era have been credited with arousing public opinion and forcing social changes. The articles of Lincoln Steffens led to a focus on local corruption and a demand for better city government. Leaders in the campaign against patent medicine advertisers were the *Ladies' Home Journal,* which ran strident editorials, and *Collier's Weekly,* which published in 1905 a series of exposés under the title "The Great American Fraud." These articles contributed to a "truth in advertising" campaign that resulted in the establishment of the Federal Trade Commission and better business bureaus. Upton Sinclair's exposure of the horrible conditions of the meatpacking industry in Chicago spawned a government inquiry that led to passage of the Pure Food and Drug Act of 1907, which formed the Food and Drug Administration. The orchestrated media efforts of others precipitated improved industrial relations, child labor laws, workmen's compensation laws, and general social reform measures.

Powerful Effects: Widespread Fright Reactions to Media Content

Fright reactions in the modern sense usually involve the media presentation of monsters or supernatural beings or real-world occurrences that cause fear, especially in children. As will be shown in Chapter 13 on the effects of frightful or disturbing media content, the work of Joanne Cantor is typical of modern-day studies. Her work and that of several of her prominent students have focused on measuring the fright reactions of individual children to scary movies or television programs or to disturbing news reports. These experiments have led to much knowledge about the kind of program content that frightens children at different ages, and about ways for parents to reduce the effects of frightening program content on their children.

Media history provides numerous earlier instances of powerful effects from frightful or disturbing media content at a more societal level. *The New York Herald* on November 9, 1874, included a frightening hoax that caused audiences to react in hysteria. Reporter T. B. Connery felt that animals at the Central Park Zoo were not as secure as they should be, so he concocted a story about their escape. "The list of mutilated, trampled and injured in various ways must reach nearly two hundred persons of all ages, of which, so far as known, about sixty are very serious, and of these latter, three can hardly outlast the night," he wrote. "Twelve of the wild carnivorous beasts are still at large, their lurking places not being known for a certainty. . ." (Hoff, 1998, p. 239). The final paragraph explained that the story was "pure fabrication" and "a huge hoax," but not everyone read the entire article. A number of people took to the streets with their guns to hunt down the killer animals.

The best known historical example of fright reaction from media content is that of the *War of the Worlds* broadcast. On Halloween in 1939, Orson Welles and the Mercury Theatre on the CBS radio network presented an original adaptation of H. G. Wells's science-fiction thriller *The War of the Worlds,* in which beings from Mars invade the world and kill millions with poison gas. Many listeners were enjoying another program when the theatre presentation began, then

The first penny newspaper, the *New York Sun*, concocted a hoax in 1835 that proved so disturbing and entertaining to its audience that circulation for the paper increased to more than 19,000, the largest of any newspaper in the world at that time. Reporter Richard Adams Locke wrote that a British astronomer had discovered life on the moon while peering through his giant telescope. Readers requested reprints of the articles and other newspapers throughout the world republished the stories. Women in Bible societies talked about traveling to the moon to convert the lunar beings to Christianity. Edgar Allan Poe said the hoax "was, upon the whole, the greatest hit in the way of sensation—of merely popular sensation—ever made by any similar fiction either in America or Europe" (Poe, 1902, p. 134).

switched their radio dials to the Mercury Theatre broadcast after the original announcement had been made that the presentation was fantasy. CBS made the announcement four times during the program, but these occurred

> (1) at the beginning of the broadcast (when most people were not listening), (2) before the station break, about 8:35 (by this time, most of those who panicked were no longer listening, but fleeing), (3) right after the station break, and (4) at the end of the broadcast. Moreover, the most terrifying part of the broadcast, it should be remembered, came *before* the station break. Those listeners who failed to hear the original announcement therefore had ample opportunity to become frightened. (Lowery & DeFleur, 1995, p. 51)

Of the several million people who listened to the broadcast, about 1 million were estimated to have been frightened, and some of them actually panicked and left their homes in an effort to escape the sinister invaders (Cantril, Gaudet, & Herzog, 1940).

Evidence for Effects from Persuasive Messages

Throughout history people have been convinced of the power of particular media messages to persuade others. This singular recognition has served to shape the evolution of American media systems because advertising is predicated on the assumption of media effects. Long before the first mass-circulation newspapers appeared, advertising had gained a foothold as a major revenue producer. As the years advanced, advertising profits became the lifeblood of newspapers, magazines, and, later, of commercial radio and television (see Chapter 17 on advertising effects).

Other types of persuasive messages have proven important and effective throughout history. In Europe during the 17th century, despite tight restrictions on printing by the authorities, new ideas and renegade views found their way into print. An intellectual movement known as the Enlightenment created a revolution in thought in 18th-century Europe. Restrictions on the printed word loosened somewhat. A literate middle class emerged, and the works of Voltaire,

Widespread panic from the radio broadcast of
War of the Worlds contributed to early models of
powerful media effects.
Source: © Bettmann/CORBIS

Jean-Jacques Rousseau, and others had the persuasive power to move people
to seek more individual freedoms and rebel against tyranny.

In the 16th and early 17th centuries, noblemen and investors began to recognize the influential power of the printed word. Many books, pamphlets, and
tracts promoting colonization in America circulated at this time and throughout the colonial years. Earlier printed works such as *Divers Voyages* (Hakluyt,
1582, 1850), *A Briefe and True Report of the Newfound Land of Virginia* (Hariot,
1590, 1972), *Nova Britannia* (Johnson, 1609), *The Description of New England*
(Smith, 1616, 1957), *A Relation of Maryland* (1635, Hall & Jameson, 1910), and
Some Account of the Province of Pennsylvania (Penn, 1681; Soderlund, 1983) outlined the advantages of colonization and presented favorable accounts of life
in America. If population growth in the New World is any indication, these promotional materials and advertisements produced powerful media effects
(Thompson, 1998).

On the American frontier, editors used newspapers to promote their towns
and to attract potential settlers. Throughout the 19th century, as pioneers
moved west, newspapers appeared in the burgeoning towns and cities. Frontier editors became known as "town boosters" due to the promotional services

they performed in an effort to increase population and economic prosperity. Their efforts proved effective. One historian called the California gold rush "one of the most effective promotional campaigns in history" (quoted in Huntzicker, 1998, p. 198). During the second half of the 19th century, the number of newspapers west of the Mississippi River increased from less than 50 to more than 650.

P. T. Barnum and promotion were synonymous in mid-19th-century America. Long before the days of the public relations "fathers," Ivy Lee and Edward Bernays, Barnum mastered the art of successful publicity campaigns. Swedish singer Jenny Lind was unknown in the United States throughout most of the antebellum period, although she was famous in Europe. Barnum issued press releases, wrote letters to the editors, printed pamphlets, and even sponsored a songwriting contest, so that by the time Lind arrived in New York in 1850, more than 40,000 excited fans greeted her at the docks (Hume, 1977; Applegate, 1998). In another example, Barnum was so successful in publicizing his acquisition of Jumbo the Elephant that in the first week of Jumbo's display he earned back the $30,000 it cost him to buy and transport the animal from London to the United States (James, 1982; Applegate, 1998).

During the two world wars of the 20th century, the U.S. government took measures to spread propaganda in support of the war effort. In World War I, President Woodrow Wilson set up the Committee on Public Information (CPI), which engaged in propaganda and censorship activities. The CPI, under the direction of the muckraker George Creel, produced articles, advertisements, press releases, films, and hired speakers to promote the war effort throughout the country. Many of the scholars who served in a similar "public information" effort during World War II later became the founders of modern media effects research.

In the late 1930s, a number of newspapers began vigorous campaigns to encourage traffic safety; as a result, fatalities decreased substantially. An earlier newspaper campaign had successfully promoted a "safe-and-sane" Fourth of July. Newspaper editor James Keeley has been credited with initiating the crusade (Bent, 1969).

> On the evening of July 4, 1899, when he was beside a child gravely ill, the thunder of giant firecrackers outside disturbed her, and he telephoned his office to collect figures from thirty cities on fatalities and accidents that day. The figures showed that the celebration of a national holiday had cost more in suffering and life than the Spanish-American War. The next year the *Tribune*, demanding a "sane Fourth," presented a similar table of statistics, and thereafter other newspapers followed suit, until mortality and casualties were reduced by more than nine-tenths. (p. 220)

SUMMARY

Since the invention of the printing press in 1450, people have acknowledged the potential influence of mass media communication on audiences. The concern for powerful media effects has not been exclusive to society's elite, but has been felt by all strata of society. This concern has influenced lawmakers, shaped public policy, and attracted the interest of scholars.

History is replete with examples of media effects. These include changes that occurred due to the spread of new media technologies, instances of suppression of the press by authorities, instances of public reaction against violent or sexually explicit material, reactions against producers of inflammatory material, and reactions from frightful media content. The many successful publicity and advertising campaigns throughout history attest to the power of media communications to persuade audiences.

REFERENCES

APPLEGATE, E. (1998). *Personalities and products: A historical perspective on advertising in America.* Westport, CT: Greenwood.

BENT, S. (1969). *Newspaper crusaders: A neglected story.* Freeport, NY: Books for Libraries Press.

CANTRIL, H., GAUDET, H., & HERZOG, H. (1940). *The invasion from Mars: A study in the psychology of panic.* Princeton, NJ: Princeton University Press.

COWLEY, M., & SMITH, B. (1939). *Books that changed our minds.* New York: Doubleday, Doran & Company.

DAVIES, D. R. (1998). The contemporary newspaper/1945–present. In W. D. Sloan (Ed.), *The age of mass communication* (pp. 453–469). Northport, AL: Vision Press.

DAVISON, W. P. (1983). The third-person effect in communication. *Public Opinion Quarterly 47,* 1–15.

DICKEN-GARCIA, H. (1998). The popular press, 1833-1865. In W. D. Sloan (Ed.), *The age of mass communication* (pp. 147–170). Northport, AL: Vision Press.

EISENSTEIN, E. L. (1979). *The printing press as an agent of change: Communications and cultural transformations in early modern Europe.* Cambridge, England: Cambridge University Press.

EISENSTEIN, E. L. (1983). *The printing revolution in early modern Europe.* Cambridge, England: Cambridge University Press.

FEBVRE, L., & MARTIN, H-J. (1984). *The coming of the book: The impact of printing 1450–1800.* (D. Gerard, trans.). London: Verso Editions.

GRIMSTED, D. (1998). *American mobbing, 1828–1861: Toward Civil War.* New York: Oxford University Press.

HAKLUYT, R. (1582/1850). *Divers voyages touching the discovery of America and the islands adjacent.* New York: Burt Franklin, published by the Hakluyt Society.

HALL, C. C. (Ed.) & Jameson, J. F. (Gen. Ed.). (1910). *Original narratives of early American History: Narratives of early Maryland 1633–1684,* reproduced under the auspices of the American Historical Association. Reprint of *A relation of Maryland; together with a map of the countrey* (1635). New York: Charles Scribner's Sons.

HARIOT, T. (1590/1972). *A briefe and true report of the new found land of Virginia, by Thomas Hariot. The complete 1590 Theodor de Bry edition.* New York: Dover.

HOFF, E. E. (1998). The press and a new America, 1865–1900. In W. D. Sloan (Ed.), *The age of mass communication* (pp. 233–250). Northport, AL: Vision Press.

HUME, R. (1977, October). Selling the Swedish nightingale: Jenny Lind and P. T. Barnum. *American Heritage, 28,* 90–107.

HUNTZICKER, W. E. (1998). The pioneer press/1800–1900. In W. D. Sloan (Ed.), *The age of mass communication* (pp. 187–211). Northport, AL: Vision Press.

HYDE, J. (1994). The media and the diffusion of innovation: The phonograph and radio broadcasting. In J. D. Startt & W. D. Sloan (Eds.), *The significance of the media in American history.* Northport, AL: Vision Press.

JAMES, T., JR. (1982, May). World went mad when mighty Jumbo came to America. *Smithsonian, 13*, 134–152.

JOHNSON, R. (1609). *Nova Britannia: Offering most excellent fruites by planting in Virginia: Exciting all such as be well affected to further the same.* London: Printed for Samuel Macham.

LOWERY, S. A., & DEFLEUR, M. L. (1995). *Milestones in mass communication research: Media effects.* White Plains, NY: Longman.

MARVIN, C. (1988). *When old technologies were new: Thinking about electric communication in the late nineteenth century.* New York: Oxford University Press.

NERONE, J. (1994). *Violence against the press: Policing the public sphere in U.S. history.* New York: Oxford University Press.

O'BRIEN, F. M. (1968). *The story of The Sun.* New York: Greenwood Press.

PENN, W. (1681). *Some account of the province of Pennsylvania.* Reprinted in J. R. Soderlund (Ed.) (1938), *William Penn and the founding of Pennsylvania, 1680–1684, A documentary history* (pp. 58–66). Philadelphia: University of Pennsylvania Press.

PERNICIOUS LITERATURE. (1847, January). *United States Catholic Magazine and Monthly Review, 4*, 46–48.

POE, E. A. (1902). Richard Adams Locke. In J. A. Harrison (Ed.), *The complete works of Edgar Allan Poe* (Vol. 15, pp. 126–137). New York: Thomas Y. Crowell.

POOL, I. DE S. (Ed.). (1977). *The social impact of the telephone.* Cambridge, MA: MIT Press.

SLOAN, W. D. (1998). The partisan press/1783–1833. In W. D. Sloan (Ed.), *The age of mass communication* (pp. 119–146). Northport, AL: Vision Press.

SMITH, J. (1616). *A description of New England.* Reprinted in P. O. Barbour (Ed.) (1986). *The complete works of Captain John Smith* (Vol. 1, pp. 323–361). Chapel Hill: The University of North Carolina Press.

STOUFFER, S. A. (1942). A sociologist looks at communications research. In D. Waples (Ed.), *Print, radio, and film in a democracy: Ten papers on the administration of mass communications in the public interest—read before the Sixth Annual Institute of the Graduate Library School, The University of Chicago—August 4–9, 1941,* pp. 133–146. Chicago: The University of Chicago Press.

THOMPSON, S. (1998). Origins of advertising/1600–1833. In W. D. Sloan (Ed.), *The age of mass communication* (pp. 81–95). Northport, AL: Vision Press.

WERTHAM, F. (1954). *Seduction of the innocent.* New York: Rinehart.

ENDNOTES

1. The journalists were labeled "muckrakers" by President Theodore Roosevelt, who compared them to a character in John Bunyan's book *Pilgrim's* Progress—a man who raked muck or filth and refused to look up from his task.

CHAPTER 3

History of the Scientific Study of Media Effects

Tantalized fascination surrounds all efforts to study the effects of mass media.
—**Paul F. Lazarsfeld, 1949**

If one were to judge from the preceding chapter, effects from media communications would appear to be rather powerful. The reason for this is obvious: History is biased toward recording instances when mediated communications seem to provoke action. Major reactions that can be traced to mediated communication are much easier to locate. Except for the existence of a very detailed personal diary or some other trustworthy personal account, instances of limited media effects are difficult for the historian to identify.[1]

Several late 19th-century studies in psychology and sociology involved research on mass media and presaged the theoretical bases for more sophisticated and numerous studies in the decades to follow, but media effects research emerged categorically in the 20th century. In the past half century, graduate programs in mass communication have sprung to life at major research universities throughout the country, and the study of media effects has quickly matured and diversified. Researchers now search for evidence of media effects in a number of distinct research branches such as persuasion, media violence, sexually explicit material, fright reactions, agenda setting, new media technologies, uses and gratifications, cultivation research, and other areas.

Several communication scholars have acknowledged chinks in the armor of the established history and have offered excellent revisionary works, but their accounts either have focused more upon the history of communication studies than on media effects research and thought per se (Dennis & Wartella, 1996; Rogers, 1994) or they have concentrated on the history of communication theories (Heath & Bryant, 2000). E. Katz (1980, 1983) examined the media effects research tradition from a conceptual standpoint, offered an interesting analysis of media effects research issues, and suggested significant points of connection among the various theories of media effects. In our reexamination of the standard history of media effects research for this chapter, we employed historical research methods rather than conceptual analysis alone to note several key points of contention and identify important issues that should be addressed in the future.

The chapter first relates the "established" history of media effects research, then provides our view of the actual history, which differs somewhat from the standard version. We identify some neglected pioneers and more recent scholars of media effects who contributed significantly to our knowledge of media effects. We then point out several issues that have been obscured by the established rendition of history and offer suggestions for advancing the knowledge of media effects in the future.

THE "ESTABLISHED" HISTORY

Because of the historical bias toward chronicling powerful media effects and the concern about media's impact, it should not be surprising that in the early days of scientific effects studies, powerful effects were assumed by many. The study of media effects began during World War I in response to concerns about propaganda spread by the military and after the war by corporations (in the form of advertising and public relations efforts). At first, social scientists and the public believed that mass media produced powerful effects upon their unsuspecting audiences.

Thus begins the "established" history of media effects study in the United States. This standard history has been told and retold in countless lectures, articles, and chapters. J. W. Carey (1996) provided an eloquent summary of the established history, which we quote from time to time to enrich this discussion.

> As the "jazz age" turned into the Great Depression, the fears of propaganda and the media were confirmed by the mass movements in politics and culture typical of that period and by a series of specific and startling events of which Orson Welles' radio broadcast "The War of the Worlds" stood as an archetype. In the standard history, this random assortment of fears, alarms, jeremiads, political pronouncements, and a few pieces of empirical research were collapsed into the "hypodermic-needle model" or "bullet theory" or "model of unlimited effects" of the mass media, for they converged on a common conclusion: The media collectively, but in particularly the newer, illiterate media of radio and film, possessed extraordinary power to shape the beliefs and conduct of ordinary men and women. (p. 22)

According to the standard history, most people in the United States (including most social scientists) believed that mass media, especially electronic media such as film and radio, had incredible powers to influence their audiences. The immense power of media messages on unsuspecting audiences was described in colorful ways: Mass media supposedly fired messages like dangerous bullets, or shot messages like strong drugs pushed through hypodermic needles. These descriptions gave rise to the "bullet" or "hypodermic-needle" theory of powerful media effects.

The standard history typically attributed the rise of the bullet theory as a response to the development of a mass society of fragmented individuals receiving similar messages from the mass media of communication. Early theorists focused on the phenomenal changes in society from the late 19th to early 20th century and the resulting influences on the masses. H. Blumer (1951), noting the importance of mass behavior, wrote that due to urbanization and industrialization of the early 20th century,

> mass behaviour has emerged in increasing magnitude and importance. This is due primarily to the operation of factors which have detached people from their local cultures and local group settings. Migrations, changes of residence, newspapers, motion pictures, the radio, education—all have operated to detach individuals from customary moorings and thrust them into a wider world. In the face of this world, individuals have had to make adjustments on the basis of largely unaided selections. The convergence of their selection has made the mass a potent influence. At times its behaviour comes to approximate that of a crowd, especially under conditions of excitement. At such times it is likely to be influenced by excited appeals as these appear in the press or over the radio—appeals that play upon primitive impulses, antipathies and traditional hatreds.[2] (pp. 187–188)

A number of early books were written with an underlying acceptance of the bullet or hypodermic-needle theories;[3] that is, the immense power of mass communication messages on their audiences. These included, to name a few, Walter Lippmann's *Public Opinion* (1922), Harold Lasswell's *Propaganda Technique in the World War* (1927), and G. G. Bruntz's *Allied Propaganda and the Collapse of the German Empire in 1918* (1938). Also, the standard history relates that the bullet theory served as the basis for a series of studies sponsored by the Payne Fund in the 1920s. These studies sought to determine the influence of the motion picture on children and found that

> as an instrument of education it has unusual power to impart information, to influence specific attitudes toward objects of social value, to affect emotions either in gross or in microscopic proportions, to affect health in a minor degree through sleep disturbance, and to affect profoundly the patterns of conduct of children. (Charters, 1950, p. 406)

One media historian called journalist Walter Lippmann's *Public Opinion* "the originating book in the modern history of communication research"[4] (Carey, 1996, p. 28). Another prominent media scholar viewed it as a founding work for agenda-setting research (Rogers, 1994). In this classic work, Lippmann called upon his experiences with propaganda during World War I. The book became "a key intellectual influence in creating public apprehension about the role of propaganda in a democratic society" (Rogers, 1994, p. 236). Lippmann emphasized the role of the news media in influencing the perceptions of audiences about issues of importance.

The standard history states that the hypodermic-needle theory remained dominant until after the Depression, when empirical studies began to indicate that effects from mass media were not as powerful as originally thought. Rather than a society of fragmented individuals receiving all-powerful messages from mass media, the view shifted to one of a society of individuals who interacted within groups and thus limited the effects of media messages. Studies by Paul

Early studies such as those sponsored by the Payne Fund examined the effects of movies on children.
Source: © Sean Sexton Collection/Corbis

Lazarsfeld at Columbia University's Bureau of Applied Social Research and by other social scientists such as Carl Hovland working for the U.S. War Department, indicated that mass media had only limited effects on individuals in their audiences.

> What was also discovered, in the standard rendition, was that individuals, the members of the audience, were protected from the deleterious possibilities inherent in the mass media by a group of predispositional or mediating factors . . . Some individuals (a few) under some circumstances (rare) were directly affected by the mass media. Otherwise, media propaganda and mass culture were held at bay by an invisible shield erected by a universally resistant psyche and a universally present network of social groups. (Carey, 1996, p. 23)

The limited effects model became thoroughly established in 1960 with the publication of Joseph Klapper's *The Effects of Mass Communication.* This classic work, based on his doctoral dissertation at Columbia University, reviewed hundreds of media effects studies from the 1920s through the 1950s and attempted to make blanket generalizations on the subject of mass media effects. Klapper called for a new approach to research in the field, a "phenomenistic approach," which emphasized particular factors that limited the effects of mass media messages on individuals.

Klapper concluded that the fears of propaganda, of manipulative elites, of media-induced extremist behavior, were misplaced and hysterical . . . Given the conservative bias of the media and of social life generally, Klapper concluded that the preponderant effect was the reinforcement of the status quo . . . With the conclusion firmly established that the media had but limited effects, the research agenda was largely a mopping-up operation: the closer and more detailed specification of the specific operation of mediating and intervening factors . . . In a well-known line, interest shifted from what it was that the media did to people toward what it was people did with the media. This was then a shift in interest and attention from the source to the receiver and a relocation of the point of power in the process: The audience controlled the producers. Except for some special problems (violence and pornography are the best-known examples) and some special groups (principally children), interest in direct effects and propaganda withered away. (Carey, 1996, pp. 23–24)

In the decades following the 1960s, mass media research thrived as the field of mass communication became firmly established at research universities throughout the nation. Certain new theories and research findings did not fit neatly into the limited effects paradigm; therefore, the history was amended to include new studies that indicated moderate to powerful media effects were indeed possible (Ball-Rokeach, Rokeach, & Grube, 1984a, 1984b; Blumler & McLeod, 1974; Maccoby & Farquhar, 1975; Mendelsohn, 1973; Noelle-Neumann, 1973).

A marvelous graphic representation of the established history of media effects is included in W. J. Severin and J. W. Tankard, Jr. (1992) and reproduced here as Figure 3.1. This linear model indicates some of the major studies and research programs in mass communication—some that supposedly caused drastic shifts in scholarly thought regarding the power of media effects through the years. Table 3.1 presents a timeline that corresponds to Figure 3.1 and offers brief descriptions of the various studies that contributed to each major model.

This standard scenario of "all-powerful" effects to "limited" effects to "moderate" to "powerful" effects provided a simple and convenient history of the field of communication research. Unfortunately, as many scholars have pointed out (Carey, 1996; Wartella, 1996), the established history is not altogether satisfying. Although it contains accuracies, it also misleads due to its strict adherence to the supposed major shifts in thought about the power of media effects triggered by particular research findings. Moreover, certain research findings from these major studies (and others) that run contrary to the established picture are simply ignored. Additionally, the standard history emphasizes the importance of some scholars but neglects to mention other individuals and their studies.

In the following section, we offer a new approach for describing the history of research on mass media effects. Although the old history remains attractive because of its ease of description and topical divisions, the revised history we now relate includes additional evidence and a fresh perspective. We hope that what is lost in convenience will be gained in greater accuracy.

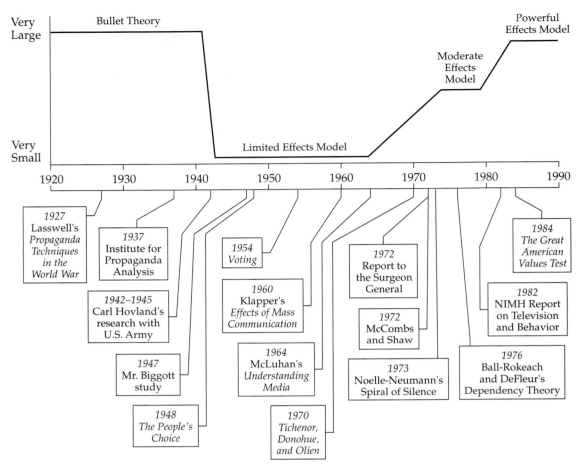

FIGURE 3.1. Size of Effect Due to Mass Communication, for Various Theories.
Source: From W. J. Severin and J. W. Tankard, Jr., *Communication Theories: Origins, Methods, and Uses in the Mass Media*, 3e. Copyright © 1992 by Allyn & Bacon. Reprinted/adapted with permission.

A REVISED HISTORY

A more accurate history of mass media effects research shares some similarities with established history but differs in important ways as well. The two versions have in common the many research studies that indicated different levels of media effects. (Moreover, the "established" history is always recounted in the improved history because that version has been accepted as gospel for so many years.) The new history differs from the standard version in these ways: the acknowledgment of early, precursory media effects studies by psychologists, sociologists, and other investigators; the reevaluation of summary findings from some of the major studies; the inclusion of particular studies through the years that did not fit neatly into the "standard" scenario; the importance attributed to particular scholars; the emphasis on the advances in effects research through the

Table 3.1 Timeline

BULLET THEORY MODEL

1927	Lasswell's *Propaganda Technique in the World War* (Lasswell, 1928). Based upon his doctoral dissertation, this qualitative work analyzed the content of propaganda messages of World War I, identifying various propaganda techniques.
1937	Institute for Propaganda Analysis. This research institute was formed in response to public fear regarding the persuasive power of propaganda via mass media. Many worried that an evil tyrant like Hitler could gain power in the United States by flooding mass communication media with propaganda messages. Studies were conducted in an effort to understand the effects of propaganda.

LIMITED EFFECTS MODEL

1942–1945	Carl Hovland's research with the U.S. Army. Hovland and his associates conducted persuasion research for the Research Branch of the U.S. Army's Information and Education division. Hovland's controlled experiments measured attitude changes among soldiers who viewed training or motivational films. They found that the films did not increase soldiers' motivations.
1947	Mr. Biggott study. This study by Cooper and Jahoda (1947) examined the effects of cartoons that poked fun at prejudice. Rather than changing any attitudes, the cartoons only strengthened or confirmed preexisting attitudes, whether prejudiced or unprejudiced.
1948	*The People's Choice.* Lazarsfeld, Berelson, and Gaudet (1948) studied voting decisions among voters in Erie County, Ohio, during the 1940 election campaign of Franklin D. Roosevelt and Wendell Wilkie. They found that interpersonal contacts were more powerful than mass media in influencing voting decisions. Mass media messages reached influential citizens called "opinion leaders," who in turn passed along information to others. This process was labeled the "two-step flow" of communication.
1954	*Voting.* Berelson, Lazarsfeld, and McPhee (1954) conducted panel surveys among voters in Elmira, New York, during the 1948 campaign that pitted Harry Truman against Thomas E. Dewey. The studies found that mass media influence played a small part in affecting voting decisions. Personal influence (interpersonal communication) was found to be the most important factor determining a person's voting decision.
1960	Klapper's *Effects of Mass Communication.* This classic work surveyed several hundred media effects studies and concluded that the effects of mass communication were limited.

MODERATE EFFECTS MODEL

1964	McLuhan's *Understanding Media.* Canadian Marshall McLuhan (1964) offered a new view toward mass media communications. He believed that media effects did not result from media content, but from the form of the medium itself. In other words, the effects occurred at a very base level, altering patterns of perception and thought.
1970	Tichenor, Donohue, and Olien. These researchers posited the "knowledge gap hypothesis," which states that "as the infusion of mass media information into a social system increases, segments of the population with higher socioeconomic status tend to acquire this information at a faster rate than the lower status segments, so that the gap in knowledge between these segments tends to increase rather than decrease" (Tichenor, Donohue, & Olien, 1970, pp. 159–160).

(continued)

Table 3.1 Timeline (concluded)

MODERATE EFFECTS MODEL (CONCLUDED)

1971   Report to the Surgeon General. This report found that a causal relationship existed between viewing televised violence and subsequent aggressive behavior, but "any such causal relation operates only on some children (who are predisposed to be aggressive)" and "operates only in some environmental contexts" (Surgeon General's Scientific Advisory Committee on Television and Social Behavior, 1972, p. 11).

1972   McCombs and Shaw (1972). These researchers conducted the first study of the agenda-setting hypothesis, which posits that news media coverage of particular issues influences their audiences' views about what issues are important.

1973   Spiral of Silence. Noelle-Neumann's (1973) theory of rather powerful media effects suggests that people become reluctant to speak an opinion that is counter to the majority opinion in society. Mass media are instrumental in shaping impressions about public opinions that are dominant or becoming dominant.

1976   Ball-Rokeach and DeFleur's Dependency Theory (1976). This theory stresses a relationship between societal systems, media systems, and audiences. It states that the degree to which audiences depend upon mass media information varies based on individual differences, the amount of disorder or conflict present in society, and the number and centrality of information functions that they serve.

POWERFUL EFFECTS MODEL

1983   NIMH Report on Television and Behavior. This report, sponsored by the National Institute of Mental Health, surveyed the research on effects of TV violence and found positive correlations between TV violence viewing and subsequent aggression among children and teens. "Not all children become aggressive, of course, but the correlations between violence and aggression are positive. In magnitude, television violence is as strongly correlated with aggressive behavior as any other behavioral variable that has been measured" (1983, p. 28).

1984   The Great American Values Test. Ball-Rokeach, Rokeach, and Grube's (1984b) elaborate study showed that when people are confronted with inconsistencies in their basic beliefs or values, they modify their values, attitudes, and behaviors accordingly. The effects of viewing a 30-minute television program on values were rather powerful.

years; and the identification of some sorely needed but missing classification rules that are fundamentally necessary for particular systematic inquiries that will advance overall knowledge and allow generalizations regarding media effects.

The history of mass media effects research does not move in pendulum swings from "all-powerful" to "limited" to "moderate" to "powerful" effects (again, except for the recounting of the established version). Instead, our history emphasizes the body of research that has, from the beginning, found overwhelming evidence for *significant* effects from mass media communications on audiences, based for the most part upon scientific methods and traditional statistical models. Additionally, the recounting of the history makes apparent an immediate need for clarifications, standardizations, and much additional research in the field of mass media effects (Thompson & Bryant, 2000).

Political Agendas in Research on Effects of Violence: Historical Perspectives

In his classic work *The Politics of TV Violence*, W. D. Rowland (1983) also offers a revised version of the history of media effects research, focusing on television violence, from the standpoint of the underlying political motives of various groups with a stake in the results (e.g., the networks, politicians, the concerned public). In the 1950s, public pressure to know more about the effects of television grew particularly intense after it became apparent that the new medium was becoming an essential part of U.S. society and culture. Through the years, elected officials have responded with major inquiries whenever public concern about the ill effects of television violence was on the rise. A number of groups have particular stakes in the results of research on media violence: politicians, the general public, industry executives, reformers, and media effects researchers.

For their part the politicians may be depicted as having found in the effects research efforts the vehicle necessary for them to project an image of concerned inquiry, while ensuring that that inquiry would force them into little, if any, legislative action. (p. 30)

Building on the prior relationships with university-based research centers and joint governmental funding, the industry continued to support and promote selected research efforts while overlooking or avoiding others . . . Throughout this process of development, the broadcasting industry alternately supported and opposed the research enterprise, carefully cultivating—and thereby shaping—certain aspects and allowing others to wither. (pp. 29–30)

The mass communication research community found the vehicle necessary for it to begin to obtain identity and ultimately to achieve legitimacy in the academy. The struggles therein for supremacy among competing social sciences carried over into the effort to interpret the new medium. A liberal, optimistic, and newly retooled American social psychology proved to be a highly attractive competitor for research funds and public recognition. (p. 27)

Source: W. D. Rowland (1983), *The politics of TV violence*, Beverly Hills: Sage, pp. 27, 29–30.

Without standard lines of demarcation, media effects researchers have often made qualitative judgment calls about the power of effects. Based upon these qualitative verdicts, what emerges is a history of research that states conclusively that, yes, various kinds of mass media effects do occur, but the levels of influence have been assumed to vary from limited to rather powerful; furthermore, researchers have recognized this—mostly they have argued this—from the beginning.

The intense debate about the power or limits of media effects still rages to this day, but knowledge in the field continues to advance. For example, as is delineated in subsequent chapters, we have discovered that media effects may be cognitive (affecting thoughts or learning), behavioral (affecting behavior), or affective (affecting attitudes and emotions). Effects may be either direct or indirect, and they may be short term, long term, or delayed. They may be self-contained or cumulative. We have learned much about individual differences, psychological factors, environmental factors, and social group characteristics that cause audience members to perceive and react to media messages in specific ways. Still, much remains to be discovered, and in the final part of this section we will take a look at some of the interesting landscapes waiting to be painted by media effects researchers in the 21st century.

Precursors

Several 19th- and early 20th-century studies in psychology, sociology, and social psychology involved the examination of particular mass media effects. Some studies were philosophical in nature and offered comments on the suspected influence of mediated communications on audiences and public opinion, rather than isolating particular social effects on mass media audiences in a controlled design or a laboratory setting. The handful of experimental studies conducted usually focused on the measure of very specific physical or psychological effects from media exposure.

We cite these studies for two reasons. Because of their emphasis on mass media and their introduction of ideas that would later become the theoretical bases of particular media effects studies, they should be considered precursors to the mass media effects studies that would arise in the 20th century. Additionally, two of these precursory studies reveal that the models for suspected powerful and limited effects from mass media communications developed almost simultaneously, contrary to the established version and its representative studies.

Two articles in the *American Journal of Sociology* in the late 19th century illustrate early differing views on the power mediated communications exerted on audiences. They introduced ideas that other social scientists would explore more fully in theoretical formations and controlled experiments during the next century. It is interesting that of these two articles, the "limited effects" view preceded the "powerful effects" view. J. W. Jenks (1895) doubted the influence of newspapers of the period on the formation of public opinion, and he proposed that the individual differences of audience members modified the influential power of communications:

> One chief reason, perhaps, of the comparatively small influence of our press is that the people know the fact that the papers are run from motives of personal profits, and that the policy of the paper is largely determined by the amount to which its opinions will affect its sales and advertising . . . [W]e all of us doubtless have our opinions formed from former prejudices, we ourselves unconsciously selecting the facts and statements that fit into these former prejudices, and thus tend to conform to our own beliefs . . . It is probably not too much to say that not 25 percent of our adult voting population have deliberately made up an opinion on a public question after anything like a reasonably full and fair study of the facts in the case. Public opinion, then, seems to be a mixture of sense and nonsense, of sentiment, of prejudice, of more or less clearly defined feelings coming from influences of various kinds that have been brought to bear upon the citizens, these influences perhaps being mostly those of sentiment rather than those acting upon the judgment. (p. 160)

V. S. Yarros took the opposite view by emphasizing the power of the newspaper as an organ of public opinion; however, he bemoaned the "mendacity, sensationalism, and recklessness" (1899, p. 374) that characterized most of the newspapers of his day. He also regretted that so many editors of the day were so incompetent yet wielded so much power over an unsuspecting public:

> The editor is glad to have the support of authority, but he is not daunted or disturbed at finding recognized authority against his position. The mature opinions

of scholars and experts he treats with a flippancy and contempt which the slightest degree of responsibility would render impossible. But the editor is irresponsible. The judicious and competent few may laugh at his ignorance and presumption, but the cheap applause of the many who mistake smartness for wit and loud assertion for knowledge affords abundant compensation. Controversy with an editor is a blunder. He always has the last word, and his space is unlimited. He is a adept at dust-throwing, question-begging, and confusing the issue. In private life he may be intellectually and morally insignificant, but his readers are imposed upon by the air of infallibility with which he treats all things, and the assurance with which he assails those who have the audacity to disagree with him. The average newspaper reader easily yields to iteration and bombast. He believes that which is said daily in print by the august and mysterious power behind the editoral "we." His sentiments and notions are formed for him by that power, and he is not even conscious of the fact. (p. 375)

The debate about the power of newspapers to either direct or reflect public opinion, which is the forerunner of the mirror/lamp metaphor of the popular culture debate of the 1950s, as well as an antecedent of the modern-day argument for and against the agenda-setting hypothesis, continues to this day. In the 20th century, articles in the *American Journal of Sociology* and elsewhere kept the debate alive before and after the publication of Lippmann's *Public Opinion* (Angell, 1941; Orton, 1927; Park, 1941; Shepard, 1909).

Several early experimental studies deserve mention as precursors to modern-day media effects, especially in the area of entertainment. These include a study of the effects of music on attention (Titchener, 1898), the effects of music on thoracic breathing (Foster & Gamble, 1906), and a study of musical enjoyment as measured by plethysmographic and pneumographic records of changes in circulation and respiration (Weld, 1912). Another early study, more theoretical than experimental, examined the nature and origin of humor as a mental process and the functions of humor (Kline, 1907).

Frances Fenton

One of the earliest (perhaps the first) studies of the effects of consumption of media violence on behavior was a doctoral dissertation by Frances Fenton. The partial and summary findings of her study appeared in two issues of the *American Journal of Sociology* in November 1910 and January 1911. Fenton pointed out that the popular notion that newspaper accounts of antisocial activities had suggestive powers on readers was well established prior to her thesis (see Fenton, 1910, pp. 345 and 350 for lists of articles). She defined *suggestion* as

the process by which ideas, images, impulsive tendencies, or any sort of stimulus, enter from without into the composition of the neural make-up or disposition and, at times more or less in the focus of consciousness, at other times not in the focus at all, are transformed into activity by the agency of a stimulus which bears an effective though unrecognized relation or similarity to the image or neural set, and in which there is in large part, or wholly, failure to anticipate the results of the suggested act. (pp. 364–365)

Fenton argued "on the basis of the psychology of suggestion" that a direct causal relationship could be assumed between reading newspaper articles on crime and on antisocial activities and subsequent criminal or antisocial acts. In her dissertation, she identified numerous cases in which individuals were known to have committed copycat-type crimes or other antisocial acts after getting ideas from a newspaper article. Due to lack of available space, the journal articles included only summary headings to describe the nature of the cases, but these headings were said to represent

> a mass of both direct and indirect evidence of the suggestive influence of the newspaper on anti-social activity gathered from a wide range of territory and from many different sources. (pp. 557–558)

She also measured the amount of such material appearing in several large-circulation newspapers of the "yellow" variety, although she emphasized that

> this was undertaken not because the actual amount of anti-social matter in a newspaper is known to bear a direct relation to the growth of crime, or because we have any evidence to show that changes in the two bear a constant relation to one another. (p. 539)

Gabriel Tarde

At about the same time that Fenton produced her study, Gabriel Tarde was undertaking his own study of crime. In *Penal Philsophy* (1912), Tarde offered a quote from A. Corre's *Crime et suicide* regarding the effects of reading about hideous crimes such as the Jack-the-Ripper murders. Corre observed that "pernicious influence" from publicity of such crimes led to "suggesto-imitative assaults," or copycat crimes. "Infectious epidemics spread with the air or the wind; epidemics of crime follow the line of the telegraph," Corre wrote (Tarde, 1912, pp. 340–341).

SOME PIONEERS IN MEDIA EFFECTS RESEARCH

In the years following World War I, innovative scholars from various disciplines at several particular institutions of learning conducted pioneering studies to examine the fledgling domain of scientific research on the effects of mass communication. These scholars, who came from disciplines outside journalism or mass communication, hailed principally from the University of Chicago, Columbia University, and Yale University. They included (among a number of others) the following: Carl Hovland, an experimental psychologist from Yale University; Paul F. Lazarsfeld, a sociologist at Columbia University; Harold Lasswell, a political scientist at the University of Chicago and, later, Yale University; Kurt Lewin, a social psychologist at the University of Iowa and, later, MIT; Samuel A. Stouffer, a sociologist from the University of Chicago; and Douglas Waples, a "professor of researches in reading" (Waples, 1942, p. xi) at the University of Chicago.[5] The importance of the first four of these scholars to the history of mass communication research has been firmly established by Wilbur Schramm prior to his death in 1987 (Rogers & Chaffee, 1997) and reiterated by Rogers (1994), and for this reason alone we greatly condense our discussion of them. We concentrate more on the final two scholars who have not received much recognition in either the standard or other revised versions of communications history, even though they made significant contributions to the media effects tradition.

Carl Hovland

Carl Hovland studied the effects of training films on the attitudes of American soldiers during World War II (Hovland, Lumsdaine, & Sheffield, 1965), and later directed experimental research that explored media effects on attitude change.[6] The tight design of the experiments conducted by Hovland became the model for much future research in media effects. Wilbur Schramm, a principle "mover and shaker" of mass communication research in the United States, said that Carl Hovland's body of research from 1945 to 1961 constituted "the largest single contribution . . . to this field any man has made" (Schramm, 1997, p. 104).

Paul Lazarsfeld

Paul F. Lazarsfeld earned a PhD in mathematics, but his diverse research interests included social psychology, sociology, and mass communication. Lazarsfeld and his research institute at Columbia University pioneered research in the effects of radio and introduced the notion that interpersonal communication was an important mediating factor in certain mass media effects. In the 1940s Lazarsfeld and his colleagues examined the influences of mass media on public opinion during a presidential campaign. They found that most people were influenced primarily through interpersonal contacts rather than by what they read in newspapers and magazines or heard on the radio, although those media were found to have some influence in and of themselves.[7] Particular individuals whom the researchers called "opinion leaders," who were often rather heavy users of mass media, were found to pass along information to others in the community who looked to them for guidance. This finding led to establishment of a two-step flow model of mass communication, in which media effects were perceived as being modified by interpersonal communication about those media messages. Subsequent research expanded the two-step flow model into one of multistep flow:

> Later studies concluded that the influence of opinion leaders was not always "downward," as in the interpretation of news events for a less informed audience. Opinion leaders were found to communicate "upward" to the media gatekeepers (i.e., newspaper editors and radio programmers) as well as share information "sideways" with other opinion leaders. Further studies of interpersonal communication showed that an individual's personal identification with an organization, religion, or other social group has a strong influence on the type of media content selected . . . Group norms apparently provide a type of "social reality" check built on similar and shared beliefs, attitudes, opinions, and concerns that tend to form barriers against mediated messages contrary to the group's point of view. Likewise, mediated messages in agreement with the group or provided by the group are usually attended to and utilized to reinforce the status quo. (Heath & Bryant, 2000, pp. 349–350)

Harold Lasswell

Harold D. Lasswell made many contributions to the study of media effects, the most notable being his five-question model—"Who says what in which channel to whom with what effects?" (Lasswell, 1948)—his studies of propaganda, and his identification of three important functions that mass communications serve in society: surveillance of the environment, correlation of society's response to events in the environment, and transmission of the cultural heritage.[8] E. M. Rogers (1994) listed five major contributions that he believed Lasswell made to communication study:

1. His five-questions model of communication led to the emphasis in communication study on determining effects. Lasswell's contemporary, Paul F. Lazarsfeld, did even more to crystallize this focus on communication effects.
2. He pioneered in content analysis methods, virtually inventing the methodology of qualitative and quantitative measurement of communication messages (propaganda messages and newspaper editorials, for example).
3. His study of political and wartime propaganda represented an important early type of communication study. The word *propaganda* later gained a negative connotation and is not used much today, although there is even more political propaganda. Propaganda analysis has been absorbed into the general body of communication research.
4. He introduced Freudian psychoanalytic theory to the social sciences in America. Lasswell integrated Freudian theory with political analysis, as in his psychoanalytic study of political leaders. He applied Freud's id-ego-superego via content analysis to political science problems. In essence, he utilized intraindividual Freudian theory at the societal level.
5. He helped create the policy sciences, an interdisciplinary movement to integrate social science knowledge with public action. The social sciences, however, generally resisted this attempt at integration and application to public policy problems. (pp. 232–233)

Kurt Lewin

Social psychologist Kurt Lewin did pioneering studies in the dynamics of group communication. While at the University of Iowa, he conducted a famous group of communication experiments to explore the differences in persuasive power on audiences in different group conditions. In the best known of these experiments, "the sweetbreads study," groups of housewives reluctant to serve glandular meats to their families learned about the benefits of beef hearts, thymus (sweetbreads), liver, and kidneys by either attending a lecture or a discussion group. The discussion group situation proved far more effective in changing the behavior of the housewives (making them more likely to serve glandular meats to their families).

According to Rogers, Lewin's "greatest academic influence was through the brilliant students whom he trained" (1994, p. 354). One of his students, Leon Festinger, directed a study to identify communication network links among married students living in a set of apartments (Festinger, Schachter, & Bach, 1950).

Later, Festinger advanced his famous theory of cognitive dissonance, which proposes that whenever an individual's attitudes and actions are in conflict, the person will adjust cognitions in an attempt to resolve the conflict.[9]

Samuel Stouffer

Paul Lazarsfeld dedicated to Stouffer his report of the Columbia University voting studies, "which profited from his skillful procedures of survey analysis" (1962, p. xxxi). He also cited Stouffer's influence on Carl Hovland's studies on attitudes and communications conducted at Yale University after World War II. Stouffer pioneered the use of empirial research, especially survey research, for social enquiries, and the use of precise statistical methods. He directed research for the Division of Information and Education of the United States Army during World War II.

After the war, Stouffer conducted several studies of communications media, but these studies deal more with the effectiveness of media and often are not labeled as effects studies.[10] His importance to the history of media effects research lies in his empirical expertise, his influence on early communication researchers such as Hovland and Lazarsfeld, and his insistence that communication research adhere to strict empirical standards. In a 1942 chapter called "A Sociologist Takes a Look at Communications Research," Stouffer applauded the careful methods of the investigation by R. C. Peterson and L. L. Thurstone (1933), one of the famous Payne Fund Studies that examined the effects of movies on children.

> A classic example of a complete experimental study in communications research was Thurstone and Peterson's study of the effects of specific motion pictures on social attitudes . . . Subsequently there have been several other studies more or less similar to Thurstone's and Peterson's, but it is surprising that there have not been more . . . This experiment demonstrated that a single movie has measurable and relatively lasting effects on children—but did anybody doubt that? Why spend a lot of money and time to demonstrate the obvious? There are two answers to this. In the first place, Thurstone showed that the direction of the effect (whether toward or against a given set of values) was not always predictable on a common-sense basis. A film glorifying a gambler had the unpredicted effect of making children feel more than ever that gambling was an evil. In the second place, Thurstone and Peterson were able to prove that effects of single films lasted over a long period of time and also that certain combinations of films had mutually reinforcing effects. It is true that they left hundreds of interesting questions unanswered. What types of children were affected most? What types of scenes within a given picture had the most effect? Were there differences in the kind of effect which would require a multidimensional rather than unidimensional attitude continuum for description? Such questions call for further research, and the Thurstone-Peterson method shows a way of answering them. (pp. 138–141)

Stouffer emphasized the importance of controlling for variables such as educational status, age, or other differences among audiences that could account for differences between the groups tested—variables that might mediate media effects. When the researcher does not control for confounding variables, he warned, "we can only hope and pray that we are controlling all the factors which would tend to differentiate" (p. 139) the control and experimental groups.

Finally, Stouffer's empirical expertise and prescience allowed him to identify problems in 1942 that continue to plague communication researchers in the 21st century—namely, the accurate measure of cumulative effects of mass media communications:

> It is a difficult matter to design an experiment which will measure the cumulative effect of, say, a year's exposure to a given medium of communication . . . The difficulty of evaluating cumulative effects of many small stimuli in the field of communications is all the more serious because there is good basis for the belief that it is in just this way that communications have their principal effect. One soft-drink ad may not invite the pause that refreshes, but hundreds, and even thousands of them, confronting the consumer in as many different social situations evidently help sell the product. (pp. 141–142)

Douglas Waples

Douglas Waples was a professor in the Graduate Library School at the University of Chicago. His significance to modern media effects research has been ignored by the standard history, but in fact it may be rather substantial. In 1940, at the same time that Lazarsfeld was conducting radio studies at Columbia University, Waples, Bernard Berelson, and F. R. Bradshaw published their work on the effects of print media, *What Reading Does to People*. The work revealed much about print media effects on attitude change.

> The studies have repeatedly shown that reading can change attitudes. They have also shown that certain reader traits and certain content elements will modify the effect of the reading. For example, the effects are modified by differences in what the readers already know about the subject. The less the reader knows about the complexities of and objections to issues discussed in the text, the greater the change in attitude will be. (pp. 108–109)

More significantly, Waples offered the earliest published version of the most famous statement about the process of communication in the history of effects research, and he added an important phrase that the later versions neglected. "Who says what in which channel to whom with what effect?" (Lasswell, 1948, p. 37) has always been credited to Lasswell in the standard—and other revised—histories of communication research. Joseph Klapper (1960) indicated the statement originated with Lasswell in 1946 (Smith, Lasswell, & Casey, 1946), but an article by Waples in the *American Journal of Sociology* in 1942 begins with the following quotation: "*Who* communicates *what* to *whom* by *what medium*, under *what conditions*, and with *what effects?*" (p. 907). Rogers (1994) credited the "who says what" statement to Lasswell, spoken during a Rockefeller Communication Seminar in 1940, a conference also attended by Waples, but the quote is not recorded in the rather detailed conference papers.[11] D. Lerner and L. M. Nelson (1977) said that Lasswell's *Propaganda Technique in the World War* "set forth the dominant paradigm" (p. 1) of the five-question line, but nothing resembling the "who says what" statement appears in that text. As for the Waples quote, whether he was quoting Lasswell, himself, or someone else is unclear; neither scholar provided a citation for the words, either in 1942 or 1948.

The identity of the speaker is less important than the substance of the Waples' quote; namely, the inclusion of the "under what conditions" phrase. This phrase, absent from any of the published Lasswell versions, adds a sophistication to the process that is essential to the sorting out of media effects at their various levels. Waples wrote the following after the quote:

> Reliable answers to this complex question at regular time intervals would greatly clarify the process of social change via communications and would simplify predictions of impending changes. (1942, p. 907)

INTEREST IN MEDIA EFFECTS CONTINUES

The number of scholars drawn to communication inquiry continued to increase throughout the 1940s and 1950s. The innovative studies and the innovators had much influence on the "founder" of the disciplinary approach to mass communication study, Wilbur Schramm (Rogers, 1994).

Wilbur Schramm

Though Schramm did not specialize exclusively in media effects (one of his principal areas of interest was in international communication and the role of mass communication in developing third-world nations), his importance must not be overlooked due to his role as consolidator and legitimizer of mass communication study—including media effects.

> Schramm was the first professor of communication so-designated; his was the first communication research institute and the first doctoral program awarding degrees in communication; and Schramm presided over the first academic unit (a "division") of communication in the world. (Rogers & Chaffee, 1997, p. 7)

Schramm initiated the first PhD program in mass communication in 1943, when he served as director of the journalism school at the University of Iowa. Three years later, he had founded the Bureau of Audience Research at Iowa, one of several communication research institutes that sprang to life during the 1940s and 1950s. These institutes were patterned somewhat after Lazarsfeld's Bureau of Applied Social Research at Columbia.

Mediating Factors

During these decades, researchers began to focus experiments on the different reactions of individuals to the same media presentations. Rather than viewing audiences as passive victims who could be manipulated by mass media messages, scholars soon realized that individual differences and environmental factors were important mediators in the process of mass media effects.

Experiments in behaviorism, motivation, persuasion, and conditioning led researchers to examine the processes of habit formation and learning. Differences among individual personality traits and psychological organization were found to be affected by the social environment in which people were raised. Moreover, studies in human perception showed that an individual's values, needs, beliefs, and attitudes were instrumental in determining how stimuli are selected from the environment and the way meaning is attributed to those stimuli within an individual's frame of reference. (Heath & Bryant, 2000, p. 347)

Studies with theoretical bases in psychology and sociology found that audience members selectively attended to media messages, depending upon their predispositions, interests, attitudes, social category, and a number of other factors. Similar variables were found to influence an individual's perception of a media message and what the person remembered about the message. These concepts were later defined as selective exposure, selective perception, selective retention, and the social categories perspective, which posits that people with similar demographic characteristics react similarly to media messages.

ATTEMPTS TO GENERALIZE ABOUT EFFECTS

Bernard Berelson

Bernard Berelson, another pioneer in media effects research, was a colleague of Waples at the University of Chicago, where Berelson served as dean of the Library School, and later a colleague of Lazarsfeld's at Columbia University and the Bureau for Applied Social Research. He coauthored with Lazarsfeld the classic voting study, *The People's Choice.*

Berelson was perhaps the first researcher to attempt to make umbrella generalizations about mass communication effects when he suggested the following formulation for research. His concern was for the influence of communication effects on public opinion, rather than media effects overall, yet his formulation could be applied to other research in media effects:

> Some kinds of *communication* on some kinds of *issues,* brought to the attention of some kinds of *people* under some kinds of *conditions,* have some kinds of *effects.* This formulation identifies five central factors (or rather groups of factors) which are involved in the process, and it is the interrelationship of these variables which represents the subject matter of theory in this field. At present, students can fill out only part of the total picture—a small part—but the development of major variables and the formulation of hypotheses and generalizations concerning them are steps in the right direction. (1948, p. 172)

Several years later Berelson noted the many complex findings that had emerged from research studies that would have to be considered in the development of any overarching theory of mass communication effects:

> The effects of communication are many and diverse. They may be short-range or long-run. They may be manifest or latent. They may be strong or weak. They may derive from any number of aspects of the communication content. They

may be considered as psychological or political or economic or sociological. They may operate upon opinions, values, information levels, skills, taste, behavior . . . Because of the variety and the complexity of the effects of communications, this topic probably represents the most neglected area in communication research. (Berelson & Janowitz, 1950, p. 395)

Joseph Klapper

Ten years later, one of Lazarsfeld's students, Joseph Klapper, produced his still valuable and classic work, *The Effects of Mass Communication* (1960). In this book, Klapper offered several overarching generalizations "in their bare bones" (p. 7) about the effects of mass media messages. Unfortunately, through the course of history, the ideas in Klapper's book have been greatly reduced to a "limited effects" notion that encouraged a "phenomenistic approach" that would identify mediating factors involved in effects, even though Klapper warned repeatedly about the grave danger in "the tendency to go overboard in blindly minimizing the effects and potentialities of mass communications" (p. 252).

Klapper's generalizations have usually been overlooked or quoted only in partial form. In most cases, only the first two generalizations have been reproduced—the two that, not surprisingly, emphasize the many studies that show limited or indirect effects of media communications. Generalizations 3, 4, and 5—those that emphasize that direct effects from media communications are indeed possible—have been ignored by the standard history. For this reason, we include all five generalizations in Figure 3.2.

FIGURE 3.2. Klapper's Generalizations

1. Mass communication *ordinarily* does not serve as a necessary and sufficient cause of audience effects, but rather functions among and through a nexus of mediating factors and influences.
2. These mediating factors are such that they typically render mass communication a contributory agent, but not the sole cause, in a process of reinforcing the existing conditions. Regardless of the condition in question—be it the vote intentions of audience members, their tendency toward or away from delinquent behavior, or their general orientation toward life and its problems—and regardless of whether the effect in question be social or individual, the media are more likely to reinforce than to change.
3. On such occasions as mass communication does function in the service of change, one of two conditions is likely to exist. Either:
   a. The mediating factors will be found to be inoperative and the effect of the media will be found to be direct; or
   b. The mediating factors, which normally favor reinforcement, will be found to be impelling toward change.
4. There are certain residual situations in which mass communication seems to produce direct effects, or directly and of itself to serve certain psychophysical functions.
5. The efficacy of mass communication, either as a contributory agent or as an agent of direct effect, is affected by various aspects of the media and communications themselves or of the communication situation, including, for example, aspects of textual organization, the nature of the source and medium, the existing climate of public opinion, and the like.

In the 1970s, the decade following the appearance of Klapper's (1960) book, psychological theories arose that had strong implications for the understanding of mass media effects. The theories of Albert Bandura (1973; 1991)—social learning theory and, later, social cognitive theory—opened up alternative lines of inquiry for communication researchers.[12] Rather than focus primarily on mass communication's effects upon attitude change, scholars in the 1970s and beyond began for the most part to examine more complex behavioral responses, changes in cognitive patterns, and media effects on learning and knowledge (Becker, McCombs, & McLeod, 1975; Chaffee, 1977; Clarke & Kline, 1974). Many of the most important of these findings are discussed throughout the remainder of this text.

Social learning theory explains how viewers learn and model behaviors they see in the mass media, based upon their environmental and cognitive predispositions. It began to serve as the basis for a bevy of research that examined the effects, especially among children, of viewing violence on film and television, the latter medium fast coming into dominance.

In the years since the 1960s, as the field of mass communication research continued to blossom and attract more scholars interested specifically in media effects, other areas of media effects research were either born or developed into maturity. These included cultivation analysis and other sociological procedures that attempt to measure the cumulative effects of mass communication, research to examine the agenda-setting hypothesis that mass media are responsible for bringing public awareness to particular issues, research to explore the reasons why audience members used particular mass media, and the many other areas of media effects.

FINAL POINTS OF CONTENTION WITH THE STANDARD HISTORY

As mentioned previously, we take issue with several aspects of the established history and, in reviewing the history, we notice the necessity for clarifications, standardizations, and additional research. In this section we identify those points of contention, and in the next section we suggest what we hope will be a productive path for media effects research in the 21st century.

Studies that indicate "limited" and "powerful" effects can be identified in every period of the history of media effects research. Although a number of studies and works during the bullet theory years did indicate that "powerful" media effects were possible (Annis & Meier, 1934; Britt & Menefee, 1939; Bruntz, 1938; Cantril, Gaudet, & Herzog, 1940; Lasswell, 1927), others found that mass media had only limited effects on their audiences. In 1926, for example, G. A. Lundberg found only a slight relationship between the opinions of Seattle residents on four public issues and on stands taken by the newspaper. He concluded that

> A modern commercial newspaper has little direct influence on the opinions of its readers on public questions. It probably seeks to discover and reflect that opinion rather than to make it. (p. 712).

The following year, an essay in the *American Journal of Sociology,* titled "The Limited Social Effect of Radio Broadcasting," questioned the powerful effects of radio on society. M. D. Beuick (1927) believed the effects of the medium would be rather limited, and that its greatest benefits would be to isolated individuals. We previously referred to the study by Waples and his associates on the effects of print media on public opinion and the "limited effects" conclusions they reached. These studies reveal that the limited effects idea was well established long before the standard history recognized its existence.

The same inconsistencies can be found during the "limited effects" years of communication research and beyond (Lazarsfeld & Stanton, 1942/1944; Lerner, 1949; Merton, 1946); furthermore, some of the major studies in the standard history contain mixed findings on the power of media communications, but these findings have been lost beneath the all-encompassing rubrics of powerful or limited effects models. For example, even though Hovland's experiments showed that the army films did not raise the motivational level of the troops, they *did* reveal significant effects in the cognitive dimension—soldiers learned a good deal of factual information by viewing the film (Hovland, Lumsdaine, & Sheffield, 1965). Also, in an even more important example previously reviewed, the findings of Klapper's *The Effects of Mass Communication* (1960) have generally been reduced to supporting only a limited- or indirect-effects scenario, yet Klapper clearly indicated that instances of direct effects were apparent from some of the research findings he reviewed, and he warned of the dangers of underestimating the power of media communications on audiences.

FUTURE OF EFFECTS RESEARCH

The challenges for media effects of the 21st century are great, but they will eventually be met if researchers continue to approach the problems with "tantalized fascination" (Lazarsfeld, 1949, p. 1). First and foremost, if we are to continue to describe media effects as either powerful, moderate, or limited, we must come up with standard, empirical lines of demarcation to separate the levels. In his influential article on "The Myth of Massive Media Impact," W. J. McGuire (1986) based his definition of small effects sizes on the percentage of variance accounted for by several dependent variables of effects; certainly statistical effect sizes would be one basis for delineating the standards. McGuire argued that powerful media effects were exaggerated, based on review of a handful of important studies in a variety of areas.

> A formidable proportion of the published studies (and presumably an even higher proportion of the unpublished studies) have failed to show overall effects sizable enough even to reach the conventionally accepted .05 level of statistical significance. Some respectable studies in several of the dozen impact areas reviewed . . . do have impacts significant at the .05 level, but even these tend to have very small effect sizes, accounting for no more than 2 or 3% of the variance in dependent variables . . . (p. 177)

Although we respect the forcefulness of McGuire's argument, we must point out that a number of studies have shown media effects significant at not only the .05 level, but at the .01 and the .001 level and beyond, and with effects sizes that account for substantial amounts of the variance (Bryant & Zillmann, 1994). Moreover, meta-analyses (statistical studies that make generalizations about effects by examining and comparing findings from many different completed research studies) of media effects reveal relatively robust effects sizes within entire genres of media effects investigations and more modest effect sizes associated with other genres (Carveth & Bryant, in press). Other studies, although recording effects in the small-to-moderate range, gain significance when one considers the vast sizes of media audiences (Andison, 1977; Wood, Wong, & Cachere, 1991). Neither these studies nor their robust effects are "mythical," but in order to classify them as "powerful" effects, a precise classification schema must first be established.

In another example, Hovland (1959) described the divergence in results from correlational studies and experimental studies on attitude change from exposure to mass communication in simple terms of *percentages of people found to be affected*. This represents another method that could be used to classify the appropriate types of studies into the various levels.

> Lazarsfeld, Berelson, and Gaudet . . . estimate that the political positions of only about 5 percent of their respondents were changed by the election campaign, and they are inclined to attribute even this small amount of change more to personal influence than to the mass media . . . Research using experimental procedures, on the other hand, indicates the possibility of considerable modifiability of attitudes through exposure to communication. In both Klapper's survey (1949) and in my chapter in the *Handbook of Social Psychology* (Hovland, 1954) a number of experimental studies are discussed in which the opinions of a third to a half or more of the audience are changed. (p. 440)

Another challenge for media effects researchers will be to identify the circumstances, conditions, or variables that account for media effects at all their various levels and forms and offer generalizations—perhaps very complex ones, even typologies of effects—that will explain the complex phenomenon of mass media effects. These are the theoretical generalizations that will advance understanding in the field of media effects. To advance such theories, communication scholars will need to use either quantitative meta-analysis techniques (when feasible) or more qualitative, intensive examination of studies in the different areas of effects research (such as that employed by Klapper), grouping the studies on the basis of their effects levels (based upon the to-be-established schema or on other theoretical criteria).

In 1960 Klapper insisted that the time for media effects generalizations had arrived. Forty years after Klapper's insistence, we can say that we know much more about the effects of media communications, but precise, blanket generalizations remain elusive, owing to the complex nature of the subject. One obvious omission in the effects literature to date is the conspicuous absence of a "no-effects model." Academic journals are severely biased toward publishing studies that show the occurrence of statistically significant media effects. Studies that find no significant effects do not normally appear—a 1944 study by Mott was a notable exception. Most studies examine a number of factors or variables, and statistically significant relationships are usually found for some but not others. No scholar has yet sifted through the thousands of effects studies to identify those particular variables or instances—reported in many studies—

when no noticable effects occurred. The statistically significant results are the ones that attract the most attention, yet the instances when media effects do not occur should be of as much interest to communication scholars as the instances when effects do occur—the no-effects scenario is, thusfar, a missing piece of the effects puzzle.[13]

In recent years, a research technique known as meta-analysis has been useful in making generalizations about the different genres of media effects. For example, Paik and Comstock (1994) conducted a major review of studies on the effects of television violence and produced a useful meta-analysis by partitioning variables (e.g., viewer attributes and types of antisocial behavior) in their research design. Meta-analysis involves finding common statistical ground among a large number of same-genre studies and then offering summary findings based on all the available evidence. Throughout this book, we include discoveries from recent meta-analyses in the various types of effects research.

Meta-analyses may be the best hope of producing blanket generalizations similar to those proposed by Klapper. If such generalizations are indeed possible, they would need to sufficiently explain the circumstances and conditions necessary for powerful or limited, direct or indirect, short-term or long-term, cumulative, cognitive, affective, or behavioral effects from mass media communications and, if possible, the factors present in a no-effects scenario. The enormity of the task stands apparent when one realizes that Klapper (1960) seems to be the only scholar in the history of media effects research who has even attempted to make such blanket generalizations on media effects across the board. Klapper offered a good starting point for those scholars of the 21st century brave enough to tackle the job of sorting through and studying the thousands of media effects studies that have been conducted through the years.

Klapper emphasized that he was "in no way committed to these particular generalizations, let alone to the exact form in which they here appear" (p. 9). He hoped that additional thought and research on the subject would "modify and perhaps annihilate the schema," and pointed out that he was "far less concerned with insuring the viability of these generalizations" than with "indicating that the time for generalization is at hand" (p. 9). "For certainly these particular generalizations do not usher in the millennium. They are imperfect and underdeveloped, they are inadequate in scope, and in some senses they are dangerous" (p. 251). It seems that, contrary to Klapper's view, his generalizations *do* usher us into the millennium. Forty years after Klapper insisted that generalizations needed to be made, the challenge remains unmet. It is our hope that this text will pique the interest of future media effects scholars who will meet the challenge of developing the long-awaited, overarching theory of media effects.

SUMMARY

The "established" history of media effects research offers a linear model of thought about the relative power of mass media messages on their audiences. In the years following World War I, scholars and the public believed that media possessed great power to influence the beliefs, attitudes, and actions of individuals in their audiences. This was called the "hypodermic-needle" theory or "bullet" theory of media influence. This model remained dominant until after the Depression when empirical studies indicated that the effects from mass media were not as powerful as originally thought. Studies by Lazarsfeld and Hovland indicated that mass media had only limited effects on individuals in their audiences. The limited effects model became firmly established in 1960 with the publication of Joseph Klapper's *The Effects of Mass Communication*. In the decades that followed, certain research findings and new theories did not fit into the limited effects model; therefore, the standard history was amended to include new studies that indicated that moderate to powerful media effects were indeed possible.

The standard scenario of "all-powerful effects to limited effects to moderate effects to powerful effects" provided a simple and convenient history of the field of media effects research. Unfortunately, the established history is neither satisfying nor accurate.

Our revised history of mass media effects research differs from the established version in the following: the acknowledgment of early, precursory media effects studies by psychologists, sociologists, and other investigators; the reevaluation of summary findings from some of the major studies; the inclusion of particular studies through the years that did not fit neatly into the "standard" scenario; the importance attributed to particular scholars; the emphasis on the advances in effects research through the years; and the identification of some sorely needed but still missing operational definitions for studies that will advance overall knowledge and allow generalizations regarding media effects.

This revised history emphasizes a body of research that has, from the beginning, found overwhelming evidence for significant effects from mass media communications on audiences, based for the most part upon scientific methods applying conventional statistical techniques. The history does not move in pendulum swings, due to the nonexistence of operational definitions to indicate the precise empirical ranges of "limited," or "moderate," or "powerful" effects. This history makes apparent the dire need for such operational definitions.

Our revised history acknowledges years of qualitative judgment calls on the part of researchers that label media effects in ranges from limited to powerful. It emphasizes that the debate about the relative power of mass media effects has been active since research on the subject began and remains an issue to this date. It also recognizes considerable advances in knowledge about media effects that have occurred through the years due to empirical investigations. Findings have indicated that media effects may be either cognitive (affecting thoughts or learning), behavioral (affecting behavior), or affective (affecting attitudes and emotions), and that the effects may be either direct, indirect, short-term, long-term, intermittent (e.g., sleeper effects), or cumulative. Findings have also revealed that individual differences, psychological factors, environmental factors, and social group characteristics cause audience members to perceive and react to media messages in specific ways.

In the future, media effects researchers will be challenged to come up with standard, empirical lines of demarcation that will classify effects as either powerful, moderate, or limited. Another challenge will be to identify the circumstances, conditions, or variables that account for media effects at their various levels and forms and make generalizations to explain the complex phenomenon of mass media effects. These generalizations should explain circumstances and conditions necessary for powerful or limited, direct or indirect, short-term or long-term, cumulative, cognitive, affective, and behavioral effects from mass media communications and, if possible, the factors present in a "no-effects" scenario. Despite these needs, we have learned a great deal about media effects through the years. Still, 40 years after Klapper's insistence that the time for media effects generalizations had arrived, we remain dependent upon his five generalizations for any overarching theory of media effects.

REFERENCES

ANDISON, F. (1977). TV violence and viewer aggression: A cumulation of study results 1956–1976. *Public Opinion Quarterly, 41*, 314–331.

ANGELL, J. R. (1941). Radio and national morale. *The American Journal of Sociology, 47*, 352–359.

ANNIS, A. D., & MEIER, N. C. (1934) The induction of opinion through suggestion by means of "planted content." *Journal of Social Psychology, 5*, 65–81.

BALL-ROKEACH, S. J., & DEFLEUR, M. L. (1976). A dependency model of mass-media effects. *Communication Research, 3*, 3–21.

BALL-ROKEACH, S. J., ROKEACH, M., & GRUBE, J. W. (1984a, November). The great American values test. *Psychology Today*, 34–41.

BALL-ROKEACH, S. J., ROKEACH, M., & GRUBE, J. W. (1984b). *The great American values test: Influencing behavior and belief through television*. New York: Free Press.

BANDURA, A. (1965). Vicarious processes: A case of no-trial learning. In L. Berkowitz (Ed.), *Advances in experimental social psychology* (Vol. 2, pp. 1–55). New York: Academic.

BANDURA, A. (1973). *Aggression: A social learning analysis*. Englewood Cliffs, NJ: Prentice Hall.

BANDURA, A. (1991). Social cognitive theory of moral thought and action. In W. M. Kurtines & J. L. Gerwitz (Eds.), *Handbook of moral behavior and development* (Vol. 1, pp. 45–103). Hillsdale, NJ: Erlbaum.

BANDURA, A., ROSS, D., & ROSS, S. A. (1963). Imitation of film-mediated aggressive models. *Journal of Abnormal and Social Psychology, 66*, 3–11.

BANDURA, A., & WALTERS, R. H. (1963). *Social learning and personality development*. New York: Holt, Rinehart and Winston.

BECKER, L. B., McCOMBS, M. E., & McLEOD, J. M. (1975). The development of political cognitions. In S. H. Chaffee (Ed.), *Political communication* (pp. 21–64). Newbury Park, CA: Sage.

BERELSON, B. (1948). Communications and public opinion. In W. Schramm (Ed.), *Communications in modern society* (pp. 168–185). Urbana, IL: University of Illinois Press.

BERELSON, B., & JANOWITZ, M. (1950). (Eds.). *Reader in public opinion and communication*. Glencoe, IL: The Free Press.

BERELSON, B. R., LAZARSFELD, P. F., & McPHEE, W. N. (1954). *Voting: A study of opinion formation in a presidential campaign*. Chicago: University of Chicago Press.

BEUICK, M. D. (1927). The limited social effect of radio broadcasting. *The American Journal of Sociology, 32*, 615–622.

BLUMER, H. (1951). The mass, the public, and public opinion. In A. M. Lee (Ed.). *New outlines of the principles of sociology* (2nd rev. ed.). New York: Barnes & Noble.

BLUMLER, J. G., & McLEOD, J. M. (1974). Communication and voter turnout in Britain. In T. Legatt (Eds.), *Sociological theory and social research* (pp. 265–312). Beverly Hills, CA: Sage.

Britt, S. H., & Menefee, S. C. (1939). Did the publicity of the Dies Committee in 1938 influence public opinion? *Public Opinion Quarterly, 3,* 449–457.

Bruntz, G. G. (1938). *Allied propaganda and the collapse of the German empire in 1918.* Stanford: Stanford University Press.

Bryant, J., & Zillmann, D. (1994). (Eds.). *Media effects: Advances in theory and research.* Mahwah, NJ: Erlbaum.

Cantor, J., Sparks, G. G., & Hoffner, C. (1988). Calming children's television fears: Mr. Rogers vs. the Incredible Hulk. *Journal of Broadcasting & Electronic Media, 32,* 271–288.

Cantor, J., & Wilson, B. J. (1984). Modifying fear responses to mass media in preschool and elementary school children. *Journal of Broadcasting, 28,* 431–443.

Cantril, H., Gaudet, H., & Herzog, H. (1940). *The invasion from Mars: A study in the psychology of panic.* Princeton, NJ: Princeton University Press.

Carey, J. W. (1996). The Chicago School and mass communication research. In E. E. Dennis & E. Wartella (Eds.), *American communication research: The remembered history* (pp. 21–38). Mahwah, N.J.: Erlbaum.

Carveth, R. A., & Bryant, J. (Eds.). (In press). *Meta-analyses of media effects.* Mahwah, NJ: Erlbaum.

Chaffee, S. H. (1977). Mass media effects. In D. Lerner & L. Nelson (Eds.), *Communication research* (pp. 210–241). Honolulu: University of Hawaii Press.

Chaffee, S. H., & Hochheimer, J. L. (1985). The beginnings of political communication research in the United States: Origins of the "limited effects" model. In E. M. Rogers & F. Balle (Eds.), *The media revolution in America and Western Europe* (pp. 60–95). Norwood, NJ: Ablex.

Charters, W. W. (1950). Motion pictures and youth. In B. Berelson & M. Janowitz (Eds.), *Reader in public opinion and communication* (pp. 397–406). Glencoe, IL: The Free Press.

Clarke, P., & Kline, F. G. (1974). Media effects reconsidered. *Communication Research, 1,* 224–240.

Cooper, E., & Jahoda, M. (1947). The evasion of propaganda: How prejudiced people respond to anti-prejudice propaganda. *Journal of Psychology, 23,* 15–25.

Dennis, E. E., & Wartella, E. (Eds.) (1996). *American communication research: The remembered history.* Mahwah, NJ: Erlbaum.

Fenton, F. (1910). The influence of newspaper presentations upon the growth of crime and other anti-social activity. *The American Journal of Sociology, 16,* 342–371.

Fenton, F. (1911). The influence of newspaper presentations upon the growth of crime and other anti-social activity. *The American Journal of Sociology, 16,* 538–564.

Festinger, L., Schachter, S., & Bach, K. (Eds.). (1950). *Social pressures in informal groups: A study of human factors in housing.* Stanford: Stanford University Press.

Foster, E., & Gamble, E. A. (1906). The effect of music on thoracic breathing. *The American Journal of Psychology, 17,* 406–414.

Heath, R. L., & Bryant, J. (2000). *Human communication theory and research: concepts, contexts, and challenges.* Mahwah, NJ: Erlbaum.

Hovland, C. I. (1954). Effects of the mass media on communication. In G. Lindzey (Ed.), *Handbook of social psychology, 2,* 1062–1103. Cambridge, MA: Addison-Wesley.

Hovland, C. I. (1959). Reconciling conflicting results derived from experimental and survey studies of attitude change. *American Psychologist, 14,* 8–17.

Hovland, C. I., Lumsdaine, A. A., & Sheffield, F. D. (1965). *Experiments on mass communication.* New York: Wiley. (Original work published 1949)

Jenks, J. W. (1895). The guidance of public opinion. *The American Journal of Sociology, 1,* 158–169.

KATZ, E. (1980). On conceptualizing media effects. In T. McCormack (Ed.), Studies in communication (Vol. 1 pp. 119–141). Greenwich, CT: JAI Press.

KATZ, E. (1983). On conceptualizing media effects. In S. Oskamp (Ed.), Television as a social issue, *Applied Social Psychology Annual, 8,* 361–374. Newbury Park, CA: Sage.

KLAPPER, J. T. (1949). *The effects of mass media, A report to the director of the public library inquiry.* New York: Columbia University Bureau of Applied Social Research.

KLAPPER, J. T. (1960). *The effects of mass communication.* New York: Free Press.

KLINE, L. W. (1907). The psychology of humor. *The American Journal of Psychology, 18,* 421–441.

LASSWELL, H. D. (1927). *Propaganda technique in the World War.* New York: Knopf.

LASSWELL, H. D. (1948). The structure and function of communication in society. In L. Bryson (Ed.), *The communication of ideas, a series of addresses* (pp. 37–51). Binghamton, NY: Vail-Ballou Press.

LAZARSFELD, P. F. (1940). *Radio and the printed page.* New York: Duell, Sloan and Pearce.

LAZARSFELD, P. F. (1949). Forward. In J. T. Klapper, *The effects of mass media, A report to the director of the public library inquiry* (pp. 1–9). New York: Columbia University Bureau of Applied Social Research.

LAZARSFELD, P. F. (1962). Introduction. In Stouffer, S. A., *Social research to test ideas, Selected writings of Samuel A. Stouffer* (pp. xv–xxxi). New York: The Free Press of Glencoe.

LAZARSFELD, P. F., BERELSON, B., & GAUDET, H. (1948). *The people's choice.* New York: Duell, Sloan, and Pearce. (Original work published 1944)

LAZARSFELD, P. F., & STANTON, F. N. (Eds.). (1942). *Radio research, 1941.* New York: Duell, Sloan, and Pearce.

LAZARSFELD, P. F., & STANTON, F. N. (Eds.). (1944). *Radio research, 1942–43.* New York: Duell, Sloan, and Pearce.

LERNER, D. (1949). *Sykewar; Psychological warfare against Germany, D-Day to VE-Day.* New York: G. W. Stewart.

LERNER, D., & NELSON, L. M. (1977). *Communication research—A half-century appraisal.* Honolulu: The University Press of Hawaii.

LIPPMANN, W. (1922). *Public opinion.* New York: Harcourt Brace.

LOWERY, S. A., & DEFLEUR, M. L. (1995). *Milestones in mass communication research, media effects* (3rd ed.). White Plains, NY: Longman.

LUNDBERG, G. A. (1926). The newspaper and public opinion. *Social Forces, 4,* 709–715.

MACCOBY, N., & FARQUHAR, J. W. (1975). Communication for health: Unselling heart disease. *Journal of Communication, 25,* 114–126.

McCOMBS, M. E., & SHAW, D. L. (1972). The agenda-setting function of mass media. *Public Opinion Quarterly, 36,* 176–187.

McGUIRE, W. J. (1986). The myth of massive media impact: Savagings and salvagings. *Public Communication and Behavior, 1,* 173–257.

McLEOD, J. M., & McDONALD, D. G. (1985). Beyond simple exposure: Media orientations and their impact on political processes. *Communication Research, 12,* 3–33.

McLUHAN, M. (1964). *Understanding media: The extensions of man.* New York: McGraw-Hill.

McQUAIL, D. (1972). *Towards a sociology of mass communications.* London: Collier-Macmillan. (Original work published 1969)

MENDELSOHN, H. (1973). Some reasons why information campaigns can succeed. *Public Opinion Quarterly, 37,* 50–61.

MERTON, R. K. (ASSISTED BY M. FISKE AND A. CURTIS). (1946). *Mass persuasion.* New York: Harper.

MOTT, F. L. (1944). Newspapers in presidential campaigns. *Public Opinion Quarterly, 8,* 348–367.

National Institute of Mental Health. (1983). Television and behavior: Ten years of scientific progress and implications for the eighties. In E. Wartella & D. C. Whitney
(Eds.), *Mass communication review yearbook*, (Vol. 4, pp. 23–35). Beverly Hills, CA: Sage.

NOELLE-NEUMANN, E. (1973). Return to the concept of powerful mass media. *Studies of
Broadcasting, 9,* 67–112.

ORTON, W. (1927). News and opinion. *The American Journal of Sociology, 33,* 80–93.

PARK, R. E. (1941). News and the power of the press. *The American Journal of Sociology,
47,* 1–11.

PETERSON, R. C., & THURSTONE, L. L. (1933). *Motion pictures and the social attitudes of children.*
New York: Macmillan.

RANNEY, A. (1983). *Channels of power.* New York: Basic Books.

ROGERS, E. M. (1994). *A history of communication study: A biographical aproach.* New York:
The Free Press.

ROGERS, E. M., & CHAFFEE, S. H. (Eds.) (1997). *The beginnings of communication study in
America, A personal memoir by Wilbur Schramm.* Thousand Oaks, CA: Sage.

SCHRAMM, W. (1997). Carl Hovland: Experiments, attitudes, and communication. In
S. H. Chaffee & E. M. Rogers (Eds.). *The beginnings of communication study in America:
A personal memoir by Wilbur Schramm* (pp. 87–105). Thousand Oaks, CA: Sage.

SEVERIN, W. J., & TANKARD, JR., J. W. (1992). *Communication theories: Origins, methods, and
uses in the mass media* (3rd ed.). New York: Longman.

SHEPARD, W. J. (1909). Public opinion. *The American Journal of Sociology, 15,* 32–60.

SMITH, B. L., LASSWELL, H. D., & CASEY, R. D. (1946). *Propaganda, communication, and public
opinion: A comprehensive reference guide.* Princeton: Princeton University Press.

STOUFFER, S. A. (1942). A sociologist looks at communications research. In D. Waples
(Ed.), *Print, radio, and film in a democracy: Ten papers on the administration of mass com-
munications in the public interest—read before the Sixth Annual Institute of the Graduate
Library School, The University of Chicago—August 4–9, 1941,* pp. 133–146. Chicago:
The University of Chicago Press.

Surgeon General's Scientific Advisory Committee on Television and Social Behavior.
(1972). *Television and growing up: The impact of televised violence.* Washington, DC: U.S.
Government Printing Office.

TARDE, G. (1912). *Penal philosophy.* Boston: Little, Brown, and Company.

THOMPSON, S., & BRYANT, J. (2000 June). *Debunking the media effects gospel: A reexamination
of media effects research history and directions for researchers of the twenty-first century.*
Paper presented at the International Communication Association 50th Annual Conference, Acapulco, Mexico.

TITCHENER, E. B. (1898). Minor studies from the psychological laboratory of Cornell
University: Distraction by musical sounds; the effect of pitch upon attention. *The
American Journal of Psychology, 99,* 332–345.

TICHENOR, P., DONOHUE, G., & OLIEN, C. (1970). Mass media flow and differential growth
in knowledge. *Public Opinion Quarterly, 34,* 159–170.

WAPLES, D. (1942a). Communications. *The American Journal of Sociology 47,* 907–917.

WAPLES, D. (Ed.). (1942b). *Print, radio, and film in a democracy.* Chicago: The University of
Chicago Press.

WAPLES, D., BERELSON, B., & BRADSHAW, F. R. (1940). *What reading does to people: A summary
of evidence on the social effects of reading and a statement of problems for research.* Chicago:
University of Chicago Press.

WARTELLA, E. (1996). The history reconsidered. In E. E. Dennis & E. Wartella (Eds.),
American communication research—The remembered history (pp. 169–180). Mahwah,
NJ: Erlbaum.

WELD, H. P. (1912). An experimental study of musical enjoyment. *The American Journal of Psychology, 23,* 245–309.

WOOD, W., WONG, F. Y., & CACHERE, G. (1991). Effects of media violence on viewers' aggression in unconstrained social interaction. *Psychological Bulletin, 109,* 371–383.

WRIGHT, C. R. (1960). Functional analysis and mass communication. *Public Opinion Quarterly, 24,* 605–620.

YARROS, V. S. (1899). The press and public opinion. *The American Journal of Sociology, 5,* 372–382.

ENDNOTES

1. Difficult but not impossible: F. L. Mott (1944) conducted a historical study and found "no correlation, positive or negative, between the support of a majority of newspapers during a campaign and success at the polls" (p. 356). Another instance of limited effects that could be argued is indicated by Isaiah Thomas's *History of Printing*, which offered state-by-state counts on the number of newspapers for and against ratification of the Constitution. In some cases, newspapers seemed to have little or no effect upon the outcome of the vote. In Delaware, for example, no newspapers favored adoption and two opposed adoption, yet Delaware was the first state to adopt the Constitution—and by unanimous vote at its convention.
2. Blumer's statement, originally written in 1939, was later called by Denis McQuail (1972/1969) "the most influential single statement of the concept of the mass, looked at from the perspective of the sociology of collective behaviour" (p. 100).
3. None used these terms, however. Many have attributed the "hypodermic needle" phrase to Lasswell, but a re-reading of Lasswell's works revealed he used no such phrase (Chaffee & Hochheimer, 1985).
4. Carey wrote: "Lippmann, in fact, redefined the problem of the media from one of morals, politics, and freedom to one of psychology and epistemology. He established the tradition of propaganda analysis and simultaneously, by framing the problem not as one of normative political theory but as one of human psychology, opened up the tradition of effects analysis that was to dominate the literature less than two decades after the publication of *Public Opinion*" (Carey, 1996, p. 30).
5. Rogers (1994) offers information about many others who made important contributions to communication study, including mass media effects research. The student is encouraged to refer to this work.
6. It should be recalled from the standard history that Hovland's U.S. Army studies reportedly showed limited media effects; however, the limits of the effects extended only to attitude change—the films proved to have much stronger effects on learning; that is, the soldiers learned a great deal from the films.
7. More recent findings (Blumler & McLeod, 1974; McLeod & McDonald, 1985; Ranney, 1983) suggest that the influence of mass media may be more powerful in the political communication process than the findings of *The People's Choice* indicated.
8. Wright (1960) added "entertainment" as another important function of mass media.
9. Rogers (1994, p. 352) offered this example of cognitive dissonance: "One effect of dissonance is for an individual to avoid exposure to conflicting messages. For example, once an individual purchases a new car, that individual tends to avoid advertisements for competing makes of cars."

10. One explored the different advantages of radio and newspaper as news sources, and identified preferences for one or the other among various classes and groups of people. Another examined the effect that radio was having on newspaper circulation. Both were included in Lazarsfeld's *Radio and the Printed Page* (1940).

11. The conference proceedings are included in the papers of Lyman Bryson at the Library of Congress (Rockefeller Foundation, "Needed Research in Communication", "Public Opinion and the Emergency", and "Memorandum on Communications Conference," U.S. Library of Congress: Papers of Lyman Bryson, Box 18, October 17, 1940, November 1, 1940, and January 18, 1941).

12. Bandura began studying children and teens and the learning of antisocial behavior by viewing models' actions on films or on television during the 1960s (e.g., Bandura, 1965; Bandura, Ross, & Ross, 1963; Bandura & Walters, 1963).

13. Some of the recent works of Cantor and her associates (Cantor, Sparks & Hoffner, 1988; Cantor & Wilson, 1984) have explored ways in which effects may be diminished, but a "no effects" model has never been advanced.

Theory and Concepts

CHAPTER 4

Social Cognitive Theory

Social cognitive theory embraces an interactional model of causation in which environmental events, personal factors, and behavior all operate as interacting determinants of each other.

—A. Bandura, 1986

For many years, psychologists, especially social psychologists, have advanced various theories about why people behave in the ways that they do. Some say behavior is based upon a person's motivations. Others propose that behavior is a response to external stimuli and subsequent reinforcements. Still others point out that people react differently in different situations, and these scholars feel that the *interaction* between a person and a situation produces a particular behavior.

It may seem strange that such issues from social and behavioral psychology would appear in a media effects textbook. Yet, as subsequent chapters will reveal, the study of effects from mediated communications often is a specialization in the social science research domains of psychology, anthropology, and sociology.

One theory in particular reappears time and again in media effects literature. It serves as the theoretical basis for many other media effects theories, including those in the critical and highly scrutinized area of media violence. For this reason, an acquaintance with this important theory, called *social cognitive theory*, is essential for a basic comprehension of media effects.

Social cognitive theory provides a framework that allows us to analyze the human cognitions (or mental functions) that produce certain behaviors. The theory describes the mental processes at work whenever a person *learns*. It is a direct offshoot of the more comprehensive and widely recognized **social learning theory.** Advanced by Albert Bandura in the 1960s, social learning theory explains behavior by examining how cognitive, behavioral, and environmental factors interact (1977, p. vii).

Social cognitive theory explains human thought and actions as a process of *triadic reciprocal causation* (Bandura, 1994). This means that thought and behavior are determined by three different factors that interact and influence each other with variable strength, at the same or at different times: (1) behavior, (2) personal characteristics such as cognitive and biological qualities (e.g., IQ, sex, height, or race), and (3) environmental factors or events.

Bandura's social cognitive theory of mass communication and the broader social learning theory serve as the foundations for volumes of research in all areas of media effects study—effects of media violence and sexually explicit material, prosocial or positive media effects, cultivation effects, persuasion, and so forth. For the student of media effects, an understanding of Bandura's theory is therefore essential because the concepts serve as a common denominator among many other media effects theories and hypotheses.

In this chapter we examine the various dimensions of social cognitive theory, including the cognitive characteristics distinct to humans, the dynamics of observational learning, the effects of modeling, and the tendency to learn from media content. The theory provides a framework to explain prosocial effects from mass media, social prompting or persuasion, and diffusion of an idea, message, or belief by way of symbolic modeling. The overall objective of the chapter is to provide an explanation of social cognitive theory, but significant studies that have drawn heavily upon the theory are also discussed.

DISTINCTLY HUMAN TRAITS

Many animals have the ability to learn, but several distinct cognitive traits set human beings apart. Social cognitive theory emphasizes the importance of these uniquely human characteristics, known as the *symbolizing, self-regulatory, self-reflective,* and *vicarious* capacities (Bandura, 1994).

Symbolizing Capacity

Human communication is based upon a system of shared meanings known as language that is constructed of various symbols. These symbols occur at more than one conceptual level—letters of the alphabet are symbols used to construct words, for example, and words serve as symbols to represent specific objects, thoughts, or ideas. The capacity to understand and use these symbols allows people to store, process, and transform observed experiences into cognitive models that guide them in future actions and decisions.

Self-Regulatory Capacity

The self-regulatory capacity includes the concepts of motivation and evaluation. People have the ability to motivate themselves to achieve certain goals. They tend to evaluate their own behavior and respond accordingly. In this way, behavior is *self-directed* and *self-regulated*.

For example, a young father and mother are motivated to achieve the goal of providing for the emotional and material needs of their toddler. If they find that they are not earning enough money to achieve their goal, they may evaluate the situation and decide to look for higher-paying jobs. They may then realize that the child's emotional needs are not being fulfilled because of their absence. In this case, one of the two may decide to start a home-based business in order to spend more time with the child. In either case, the couple evaluated, regulated, and directed their behavior in response to a common motivation or goal.

Self-Reflective Capacity

This capacity involves the process of thought verification. It is the ability of a person to perform a self-check to make sure his or her thinking is correct. Bandura identified four different self-reflective "modes" used in thought verification: the enactive, vicarious, persuasory, and logical modes (1986, 1994).

In the *enactive* mode, a person assesses the agreement between thoughts and the results of actions. For example, a young girl may think she has the potential to be an Olympic gymnast, but when she goes for her first gymnastics lesson she discovers that she is a hopeless klutz. The instructor encourages her to concentrate on her studies at school and forget about sports. In this case, her actions do not verify her thoughts and she must reassess her thinking. If, however, she shows incredible natural talent in the gym, the instructor might tell her that with hard work the Olympics might someday be possible. In this scenario, the girl's actions corroborate her thoughts and provide verification.

With the *vicarious* mode, observation of another's experiences and the outcomes of those experiences serve to confirm or refute the veracity of thoughts. The impact of television provides a good example. Suppose a woman lives in a society in which women are subservient to men and thought to be inferior in every respect. She thinks that all women live as she does. Then television comes to her village. First, she sees a woman news anchor. Then she changes the channel and watches the scantily clad Xena the Warrior Princess beat up 10 strapping male opponents. Imagine the woman's surprise! Certainly, her thoughts about female inferiority could be shocked into some kind of reassessment.

An effective advertisement serves as the best demonstration of the *persuasory* mode, especially a commercial in which a person on the street is convinced to change brands. The new product costs a little more, but it significantly outperforms the old product, so the person on the street decides to switch to the new brand. Despite the added cost, the viewer might be persuaded by the decision of the person to purchase the product advertised.

The last mode of thought verification within the self-reflective capability, the *logical* mode, involves verification by using previously acquired rules of inference. Perhaps the person who was convinced to try the new product liked it so much that he decided to try the higher-priced brands of other types of products. He would have deduced that higher cost, no matter what the product, equates to a substantial improvement in quality. Logical deduction produced this new way of thinking.

In the social cognitive view . . .

People are neither driven by inner forces nor automatically shaped and controlled by external stimuli. Rather, human functioning is explained in terms of a model of triadic reciprocality in which behavior, cognitive and other personal factors, and environmental events all operate as interacting determinants of each other. The nature of persons is defined within this perspective in terms of a number of basic capabilities.
—ALBERT BANDURA, 1986

Vicarious Capacity

This human characteristic, vicarious capacity, which is the ability to learn without direct experience, emphasizes the potential social impact of mass media—for better or worse. As an example of positive social impact, the vicarious capacity allows a person to learn all sorts of beneficial things by simply reading or watching a television program presenting these prosocial behaviors. On the negative side, people may witness and learn certain *antisocial* behaviors to which they might not otherwise have been exposed.

OBSERVATIONAL LEARNING AND MODELING

Social learning and social cognitive theories place much emphasis on the concept of *observational learning*. A person observes other people's actions and the consequences of those actions, and learns from what has been observed. The learned behavior can then be reenacted by the observer.

Modeling

The phenomenon of behavior reenactment, called **modeling,** includes four component processes: *attention, retention, motor reproduction,* and *motivation* (Bandura, 1986, 1994). These can be explained by using a simple example of observational learning, such as learning how to swing a golf club.

Attention

A person must pay attention to any behavior and perceive it accurately in order to model it successfully. The beginning golfer must watch the actions of the teacher and listen carefully to instructions—in short, pay close attention to the actions to be modeled.

Retention

Modeled behavior must be remembered or retained in order to be used again. The permanent memory stores the information by means of symbolic representations that subsequently can be converted into actions. The beginning golfer must understand the instructor's comments and remember them, along with demonstrations and corrections.

Motor reproduction

At first, motor reproduction may be difficult and even faulty, as the beginner has to "think through" all the various steps involved in making a successful swing. As the golfer practices the modeled swing, however, the cognitive process becomes less tedious. If the beginner possesses the necessary component skills, observational learning occurs at a much faster rate. In other words, the natural athletic ability or the superior motor memory of the beginner largely determines the length of time required for mastery of the modeled swing.

For various reasons, people are not always motivated to model the behaviors they learn. Using the golfer again as an example, the beginning golfer might notice that his instructor cannot drive the ball nearly as far as another instructor. The beginner may also notice that the two instructors stand differently, hold the club differently, and move different parts of the body whenever they swing the club. In this case, the beginner may choose to change instructors and learn the more successful swing of the second instructor. Or the student golfer may realize that green fees and cart fees are too expensive and thus never utilize his or her newfound knowledge. Motivation becomes a major factor in the decision to use modeled behavior.

Some instances of modeling result in actions far more consequential than the innocuous golf swing. Different learning situations dictate the importance of the four component parts. Consider, for instance, the young intern learning to perform surgery, or the fearful child learning to swim. In each case, the actual *motor reproduction* of the modeled behavior assumes paramount importance. The significance of *motivation* in the learning process may be illustrated by two people learning to speak a foreign language: an American student learning Russian for a degree requirement would not have the same motivation as a Russian immigrant suddenly learning English to survive in the United States.

Three types of situations provide the incentives that motivate a person to model learned behavior: (1) positive outcomes through direct performance of the behavior, (2) observation of another's behavior and the subsequent outcomes, and (3) evaluation based upon personal values or standards of behavior (Bandura, 1989, 1994). For instance, a child who learns an instructional song on *Barney*, then performs the song for her parents and receives much praise and encouragement, is motivated to model that learned behavior in the future. In this case, the child performed the behavior and experienced the outcome directly.

The successful Nickelodeon program *Blue's Clues* serves as a good example of the more vicarious, second type of motivational situation. In every show, the human character Steve tries to solve a mystery message from his animated puppy Blue. As they sing and play games, Steve discovers three clues, then sits in his chair to think through the problem and solve the mystery. The child sees that Steve's technique is always successful, and therefore the child is likely to model such "thinking chair" behavior whenever faced with solving his own mysterious problem.

To illustrate the third situation, consider a young boy who views and imitates the violence he sees on *Power Rangers*. Perhaps he is a sensitive child who does not wish to hurt anyone physically, and he has been told that violence is wrong, yet his ability to imitate the Red Ranger impresses the other children and makes him very popular at day care. One day he jumps, kicks his friend a little too hard, and knocks him onto the pavement, breaking the friend's arm badly. The scene is a frightful one—the bloody bone protrudes from the skin and the arm dangles. The child who kicked his friend is devastated. He cries for a week and never again imitates a Power Ranger. In this case, the child is motivated to avoid modeling the violent behavior because he has witnessed a horrible outcome. His internalized standard of conduct has become more strict.

Abstract Modeling

Rules of behavior learned in the past serve as a *guide* for new life situations (Bandura, 1994). These rules often provide an abstract framework for decision making in new situations. In other words, existing standards of behavior are not perfect or constant for each new situation. A person is merely guided by the outcomes of his or her own past experiences or the observed experiences of other people.

Abstract modeling takes learning to a higher level than mere mimicry of observed behavior. New situations generate new behaviors based upon the rules of behavior learned previously. These behaviors are themselves learned and stored in memory for future adaptation in other situations.

The use of abstract modeling offers many practical advantages (Bandura, 1986, 1994; Rosenthal & Zimmerman, 1978). One acquires personal standards for judging one's own motivations and behavior and those of others. Abstract modeling also boosts critical thinking and communication skills.

Consider, for example, the children's television program *Gullah Gullah Island*. In one episode, the children make various gifts for their father. A little girl who views this episode sees that the homemade creations please the parent. As the Christmas holiday approaches, she realizes that she has very little money to spend on gifts. She decides to make various gifts for her entire family. In this situation, the girl has gone beyond mimicry of the behavior she saw on television. She applied what she had learned in the past to a new and different situation. She performed *abstract modeling*.

EFFECTS OF MODELING

Sometimes a person observes behavior or receives information that conflicts in some way with that person's established pattern of behavior. Two major effects are associated with such situations—**inhibitory** and **disinhibitory effects** (Bandura, 1994). The inner conflict causes a person to reexamine his or her motivations to perform the established behavior.

Inhibitory Effects

Most studies on inhibitory and disinhibitory effects have examined transgressive, aggressive, or sexual behavior (Berkowitz, 1984; Liebert, Sprafkin, & Davidson, 1982; Malamuth & Donnerstein, 1984; Zillmann & Bryant, 1984). In each case, inhibitory effects occurred whenever a person refrained from reprehensible conduct for fear of the consequences, such as formal punishment by society or censure from one's own conscience.

Inhibitory effects occur whenever new information or the observation of new behavior *inhibits* or *restrains* a person from acting in a previously learned way. Disinhibitory effects *disinhibit* or lift previously learned internal restraints on certain behaviors. A smoker might decide to change his behavior if he sees his favorite uncle (who smoked all his life) suffer miserably and die of emphysema. He has experienced inhibitory behavior. On the other hand, consider a teenage girl from a strict family who counts the use of alcohol and tobacco among the ultimate of taboos. Then she goes away to college and makes friends with other students who drink and smoke. Her established mores become more relaxed. When she decides to try a beer for the first time, she has experienced disinhibitory effects.

For another example of inhibitory effects, imagine that two college freshman are taking an introductory communication course during their first semester. The two young women are friends. One watches television while studying, a habit of behavior she developed in high school. She reads during the commercials. The other student isolates herself in her room, and reads and studies without distraction. The student who works in quiet seclusion receives an "A" on the first exam, whereas the other student gets an "F." After recovering from the initial shock, the second student decides to *inhibit* her usual behavior and to model the behavior of her friend while reading and studying.

Disinhibitory Effects

A 1963 study by Bandura and his colleagues serves as an excellent example of disinhibitory effects. The researchers divided nursery school children into various control and experimental groups, then showed a film to the children in the experimental group. In the film, an adult performed physically aggressive

The famous BoBo doll study showed that children often imitate violence they see on the screen.
Source: © Albert Bandura

actions (such as pounding an air-filled, vinyl punching bag). The children who watched later imitated those aggressive acts, performing them much more frequently than did children in the control group, who saw another film. Moreover, the researchers found that the children who had watched the violent film were less inhibited about performing *other* violent acts they had learned in the past—acts that were not demonstrated on the film (Bandura, 1963). The film therefore had a *disinhibitory* effect upon the children who saw it.

Disinhibitory Devices

Many types of behavior are not socially acceptable. Murder, rape, physical violence against others, and other criminal acts serve as extreme examples of impulses that must be restrained. Other less sensational behaviors also apply.

Research has shown that people who engage in reprehensible behavior often use cognitive techniques to justify their actions to themselves. In other words, they lose their inhibitions (become disinhibited) about acting in a certain way even if those actions conflict with their internal moral standards. Researchers have identified eight such cognitive techniques or devices: moral justification, advantageous comparison, euphemistic labeling, displacement of responsibility, diffusion of responsibility, distortion of the consequences of action, dehumanization, and attribution of blame (Bandura, 1994).

The first three techniques—moral justification, advantageous comparison, and euphemistic labeling—are the most powerful of the eight in terms of cognitive and moral restructuring. This means that a person may actually change or restructure the way he or she views the undesirable behavior. Through use of disinhibitory devices, reprehensible conduct might be seen as not only *acceptable,* but actually *desirable.* As an example of such restructuring, consider the case described previously—the girl with the strict upbringing who decided to try a beer with her college friends. Certainly she may have experienced some degree of cognitive and moral restructuring that made beer drinking seem to be a desirable behavior.

Moral justification occurs whenever a person believes his or her otherwise culpable actions are serving some moral, noble, or higher purpose and are therefore justified. In such cases, inhibitive restraints on certain behaviors are released or relaxed. In the mind of the transgressor, a greater good is served. A good example of moral justification is among soldiers during wartime who legitimize aggression based on the "greater good" of protecting freedoms. A more common example would be that of a mother who spanks a misbehaving child.

Advantageous comparison involves comparing one's own deplorable actions to more serious or flagrant transgressions of others. For example, the student who watches TV while studying may justify her actions by comparing herself to her brother who does not study at *any* time, and has poor grades to show for it.

Euphemistic labeling offers not only a means of camouflaging reprehensible conduct, but may even make the conduct respectable or at least acceptable. For example, the girl who watches television while studying might euphemistically consider her viewing as an *educational* rather than a *recreational* (or mindless) experience. She convinces herself that watching television keeps her abreast of current events, and therefore it is just as important as her textbook reading assignment. The teenage girl who starts smoking cigarettes euphemistically labels the activity as "cool" or "sexy" in her mind, rather than viewing the activity as a health hazard and a nasty habit.

Two disinhibitory techniques or devices cause a transgressor to shift the responsibility for wrongdoing to another. **Displacement of responsibility** occurs when someone in authority directs a person to act in a certain reprehensible way, and the authority figure accepts responsibility for the actions. With **diffusion of responsibility,** a transgressor acts within a group and therefore does not feel personally responsible for the subsequent act. Again, soldiers at war serve as excellent examples of such devices in action.

Another device, **disregard or distortion of the consequences of action,** refers to situations in which a person performs an act without thinking about the harm that act may cause, or with the belief that the act will cause only minimal harm (Brock & Buss, 1962, 1964). The teenager who accepts the dare of his buddies and throws bricks through a store window is concerned only with the thrill of the moment—the idea of "getting away with" the wrongdoing and meeting the challenge of the dare. He gives no thought to the poor store owner who must have the window replaced.

The final devices, **dehumanization** and **attribution of blame,** focus upon the attitudes of transgressors toward their victims. Dehumanization occurs whenever a person is divested of human qualities and considered no better than a beast. Nazi soldiers dehumanized Jewish people during World War II; therefore, they were able to commit unspeakable atrocities without feelings of remorse. In the United States prior to the civil rights movement, many whites dehumanized blacks and thus prevented them from voting and enjoying advantages known by white people. Belligerent whites attacked peaceful civil rights demonstrators and justified their hostilities by attributing blame to the demonstrators or the situation rather than to themselves—they blamed the demonstrators for causing trouble and "provoking" them to hostile actions.

LEARNING FROM MEDIA CONTENT AND MODELING

Remember the death scene in the film *ET* when the alien died and the boy delivered the sad soliloquy? It was one of those "lump in the throat" scenes for audience members. Then, when ET came back to life and the child experienced such marvelous joy, it became difficult for audience members to hold back the happy tears.

When the thriller *Jaws* played in theaters in the 1970s, audiences throughout the country actually applauded after the sheriff took aim, fired, and blasted the monster shark out of the water. In the summer months that followed, newscasters reported that many people at beach resorts were afraid to set foot in the ocean because they had seen the film and feared a shark attack.

As these examples show, whenever a person sees a character on the screen expressing some strong emotion or performing some powerful action, the viewer is affected or *aroused*. The viewer remembers similar experiences and emotions, and these thoughts and images serve as cues that trigger self-arousal (Bandura, 1992; Wilson & Cantor, 1985).

Such experiences of arousal are not always fleeting in nature. Several studies have shown that audience members sometimes develop lasting emotional reactions, attitudes, and behaviors after viewing emotional content that arouses them. Vivid memories of the killer Great White shark from *Jaws* kept many people out of the ocean for years, and many who did brave the waves were cautious and uneasy. A decade earlier, the shower scene in Alfred Hitchcock's *Psycho* made many people throw back their shower curtains and opt for a much safer bath!

Examples of such fear reactions abound, but research has shown that people also learn many other reactions from media content, some of them lasting. Coping skills portrayed on the screen help people deal with their fears and phobias by lessening them and making them more tolerable (Bandura, 1982). Audience members learn to dislike whatever screen characters dislike, and they like whatever pleases or gratifies those characters (Bandura, 1986; Duncker, 1938).

Viewing Disinhibitory Devices

Media effects scholars are also interested in what happens whenever viewers see television and film characters acting in violent ways and employing the disinhibitory devices described in the previous section. How do viewers respond? How are they affected?

Research has shown that whenever viewers see television or movie characters injuring their victims and engaging in one or more of the devices, those viewers are then more likely to inflict punishment or penalty on others. Injurious conduct on the part of the viewer is linked to the sanctioned social behavior depicted on the screen (Bandura, Underwood, & Fromson, 1975).

Social Construction of Reality and Cultivation

Some studies show that the "realities" depicted on television programs do not always reflect the true state of affairs in the real world. Some scholars believe that heavy viewing of television tends to shape or cultivate viewers' perceptions and beliefs so that they are more in line with the world portrayed on television than with that of the real world. Media scholars call this media effects phenomenon the **social construction of reality.** As you will learn in Chapter 6, the research tradition associated with such effects is known as **cultivation.**

Some of the best examples of television's power to alter viewers' perceptions is revealed whenever regular television viewers are asked to estimate their chances of being aboard a plane that will crash, or their chances of being a victim of a violent crime. In the "real world" such events are extremely rare, whereas in the "world of television" they occur frequently. Most people, especially those who are heavy viewers of particular types of television programs, grossly *overestimate* their chances of being in a plane crash or becoming a victim of some criminal.

Some studies have shown that viewers tend to have misconceptions due to stereotypical portrayals on television (Buerkel-Rothfuss & Mayes, 1981; McGhee & Frueh, 1980; Tan, 1979). In 1981 N. L. Buerkel-Rothfuss and S. Mayes tested

290 college students who reportedly watched, on average, seven episodes of daytime serial dramas or "soaps" each week. Students were asked to estimate the occurrence in society of certain occupations' (e.g., doctor, lawyer, businessman, blue-collar worker, housewife), health concerns (e.g., nervous breakdown, major operation, abortion), and other life issues and crises (e.g., having an affair, being happily married, getting divorced). Students estimated how many women of every 10 and how many men of every 10 could be classified in the various categories. The researchers *controlled* for factors such as intelligence, sex, age, and self-concept; in other words, they designed their investigation in a way to make sure that any exaggerated estimates were not due to these factors rather than the viewing alone. As the researchers expected, the students who watched the most soap operas were more likely than light viewers or nonviewers to perceive the real world as similar to that of television. These students overestimated the number of doctors and lawyers, the number of extramarital affairs and divorces, the number of illegitimate births and abortions, and other events that occurred on soap operas far more frequently than in the real world.

Effects of Viewing Televised or Film Violence

Through the years, most media effects studies have examined the negative effects that result from the vicarious capacity, such as the learning of aggressive behavior by viewing televised or filmed violence. When carried to its worst extreme, the modeling of such behavior has been linked to violent and brutal "copycat" crimes such as rape and even murder. As will be discussed in Chapter 5 on priming, copycat crimes are the most disturbing examples of modeled behavior.

The sensational nature of coypcat crimes attracts the notice of print and electronic news media, and therefore examples of such crimes abound in the public's memory. It must be remembered, however, that copycat crimes are rare extremes. Millions of other viewers who watch the same film or program are *not* inspired to imitate such violent behavior. This suggests that individual factors such as a person's disposition (or predisposition to violent behavior), state of mind, emotional stability, and personal circumstances play a major role in determining whether that person will resort to violence after viewing violent fare.

Social scientists often are concerned with more subtle media effects—those that they can measure through strictly controlled experiments that do not involve harm or injury to anyone. Most studies have concentrated on identifying the effects of media violence as either *cognitive*, *affective*, or *behavioral*. Each of these will be discussed in detail in Chapter 10 on media violence.

Since the beginning of movies and television, concern about media violence has been a major force in public policy making. In her book *Violence on Television*, Cynthia A. Cooper identified three phases in the public policy debate that emerged through the years. In the first phase, the debate focused upon the rising rate of juvenile delinquency. Next, the boundaries of the debate expanded to include concern about the effects of television violence on the social behavior and well-being of society in its entirety. In the third phase, the concern of policy makers shifted from identification of detrimental effects on viewers to a proactive attempt to reduce televised violence through legislative restrictions (1996, p. vi–vii).

LEARNING GOOD THINGS FROM MASS MEDIA

In recent years, a growing body of research that examines children's television programming has yielded promising findings. These studies have shown that many children's television shows have *prosocial* or positive effects. In general, research has shown that through watching educational and nonviolent programs such as *Sesame Street* (Fisch, 2001; Fisch & Trugellio, 2001), children improve literacy, science, and mathematics skills, and learn positive social behaviors, enhance their imaginative powers, and develop problem-solving skills.

Recent studies of *Sesame Street* have supported early studies that suggested positive gains in cognitive skills and other prosocial effects for viewers compared to nonviewers, both in the United States (Wright & Huston, 1995; Wright, Huston, Scantlin, & Kotler, 2001) and abroad (UNICEF, 1996; Brederode-Santos, 1993; Ulitsa Sezam Department of Research and Content, 1998). Longitudinal studies have revealed that positive effects, in terms of academic achievement and reading skills, especially, from viewing *Sesame Street* as preschoolers continued as the children advanced to grade school (Zill, 2001; Zill, Davies, & Daly, 1994) and even high school (Anderson et al., 1998).

Studies have also found beneficial effects from programs such as *Barney & Friends* (Singer & Singer, 1998, 1995, 1994), *Gullah Gullah Island* and *Allegra's Window* (Bryant et al., 1997; Mulliken & J. A. Bryant, 1999), *Blue's Clues* (Anderson et al., 2000; Bryant et al., 1999), *Mister Rogers' Neighborhood* and *The Electric Company* (Rice, 1984; Rice & Haight, 1986; Ball & Bogatz, 1973; Ball et al., 1974), *Between the Lions* (Linebarger, 2000), *Reading Rainbow* (Leitner, 1991), *Square One TV* (Hall, Esty, & Fisch, 1990; Hall, Fisch, Esty, Debold, Miller, Bennett, & Solan, 1990), and *3-2-1 Contact* (Cambre & Fernie, 1985; Johnston, 1980; Johnston & Luker, 1983; Wagner, 1985). Positive benefits of educational programming for children are enhanced whenever parents or caregivers view programs with the children and reinforce the messages (Singer & Singer, 1983).

In a two-year assessment of Nickelodeon programs *Gullah Gullah Island* and *Allegra's Window*, children who watched regularly were able to solve problems with greater ease and exhibit more flexible thinking skills than children who did not watch the program. In addition, regular viewers learned more about appropriate social behaviors than children of similar ages who did not watch the programs (Bryant et al., 1997) and performed better on three types of problem-solving tasks (Mulliken & J. A. Bryant, 1999).

Another two-year assessment targeted viewers of *Blue's Clues*, an educational program on Nick, Jr. (Nickelodeon's network for preschoolers) and found effects for viewers were beneficial compared to effects for nonviewers (Anderson et al., 2000; Bryant et al., 1999). Nonverbal problem solving and nonhumorous riddle solving on standardized Kaufman tests were two areas that showed statistically significant differences in favor of viewers of *Blue's clues*.

Programs such as Sesame Street have prosocial or
positive effects on children.
Source: © Bettmann/CORBIS

Language development, literacy, mathematics and problem solving, science and technology, civics and social studies are other areas that have shown positive effects for viewers of educational programming (Fisch, 2001).

SOCIAL PROMPTING OR PERSUASION

Advertising campaigns and other efforts of persuasion serve as excellent examples of **social prompting,** another example of modeled behavior. Social prompting does not involve learning new behavior, and therefore it differs from observational learning and disinhibition. Social prompting implies that a person is offered an *inducement* (an incentive) to act in a particular way that has already been learned.

Most people are not inclined to try a new product unless, of course, the new product is shown to offer great benefits or inducements. Using toothpaste as an example, a viewer might be prompted to switch brands if a new, whitening toothpaste promises a beautiful smile, popularity, love, and happiness (as indicated by the actions of the models in the commercial).

Many Influences Cause Persuasion

According to social cognitive theory, many different influences of varying strengths often determine human behavior. No single pattern of influence exists to explain every instance of persuasion or modeling or adoption of a new behavior. Sometimes people are influenced by what they see on television, sometimes they are persuaded by interpersonal communication, and sometimes by a little of both. In all cases in which behavior is influenced, a combination of outside factors and personal characteristics are at work. The dynamics of those combinations differ with each person.

You will recall from Chapter 3 that the indirect influence hypothesis characterized the tradition. The limited effects hypothesis held that influential people in the community, called opinion leaders, are influenced by mass media. These opinion leaders in turn influence the majority of others through interpersonal contact.

A substantial body of evidence debunks the idea that media can *only* reinforce changes in behavior rather than initiating them. Research has shown that in some cases media influences *do* initiate change (Bandura, 1986; Liebert, Sprafkin, & Davidson, 1982) and have direct effects on viewers (Watt & van den Berg, 1978). Media influences vary in strength as do influences from other sources that ultimately determine a person's behavior (Bandura, 1994).

DIFFUSION BY WAY OF SYMBOLIC MODELING

One important area of media effects research involves the study of diffusion or spread of an innovation—a new technology, tool, behavior, farming technique— throughout a society or a large group of people. Communication scholar Everett Rogers (1963) is well known for his scholarship in this area, which is called diffusion of innovations.

Research has shown that successful diffusion of an innovation follows a similar pattern each time, an S-shaped distribution. It is the normal bell curve plotted over a period of time. The various stages of the adoption process that produce this pattern will be discussed at length in Chapter 7.

Social cognitive theory views diffusion of innovations in terms of symbolic modeling, persuasion, social prompting, and motivation. Three major events define the diffusion process:

1. When the person learns about an innovation (a new behavior, tool, product, and so on).
2. When the person adopts the innovation or performs the new behavior.
3. When the person interacts with others in a social network, either encouraging them to adopt the new behavior or confirming their own decision to adopt the behavior.

Diffusion of innovations research examines the different strengths of media and interpersonal influences in adoption of new behavior. The symbolic world of television is broadcast to masses of viewers at the same time. Satellite telecommunications have carried television programs to millions of viewers in different countries throughout the world. Social changes have occurred due to the influences of television on entire societies of viewers who model the various behaviors, styles, and ideas that they see and learn (Bandura, 1986; Singhal & Rogers, 1989; Winett et al., 1985).

RECENT RESEARCH

Social cognitive theory, as mentioned earlier in this chapter, serves as the theoretical basis for many types of media effects research covered within this text—from media violence studies and fright reactions to media content to effects from sexually explicit content and effects from persuasive media messages.

In recent years, social cognitive theory of mass communication has proved especially useful as the theoretical underpinning for communication campaigns and their design (Lapinski & Witte, 1998). Mass media campaigns intended to change health behaviors (Marcus et al., 1998; Clark & Gong, 1997; Maibach et al., 1996) have drawn heavily from social cognitive theory.

The theory has also served as the foundation for the study of media effects in a variety of other areas. These include the study of effects from news frames during the coverage of election campaigns (Rhee, 1997), the study of priming effects of media violence on aggressive constructs in memory (Bushman, 1998), the study of children's acceptance of safety rules after exposure to accidents in television dramas (Cantor & Omdahl, 1999), and even a historical content-analysis study of infant feeding messages in magazines (Potter & Sheeshka, 2000).

Research Has Shown

In the 1970s a bevy of studies examined daytime serial dramas. These content analyses of soap operas revealed that the world of daytime drama offered a distorted view of reality. Much of the content in the soaps was not consistent with the actual number of occurrences in the real world.

Katzman (1972) found that soap opera characters experience the following problems most frequently:

- Extramarital affairs/infidelity on part of spouse
- Family problems
- Difficulties at work
- Physical disabilities

Cassata, Skill, and Boadu (1979) found that the major causes of death on soap operas were:

- Homicide (number one)
- Cardiovascular disease (especially among women)

Downing (1974) and Rose (1979) found that:

- Almost 70 percent of all soap characters work as medical professionals.
- Very few characters are employed in blue-collar positions.
- Social problems are rarely portrayed.

Source: Cassata, M., T. Skill, and S. Boadu. "In Sickness and in Health." *Journal of Communication* 29(4), Autumn 1979, pp. 73–80; Downing, M. "Heroine of the Daytime Serial." *Journal of Communication* 24(2), Spring 1974, pp. 130–137; Katzman, N. "Television Soap Operas: What's Been Going on Anyway?" *Public Opinion Quarterly* 36(2), 1972, pp. 200–212; Rose, B. "Thickening the Plot." *Journal of Communication* 29(4), Autumn 1979, pp. 81–84.

Albert Bandura's social cognitive theory serves as the basis for many other theories of media effects. It provides a framework to analyze human cognitions that produce certain behaviors and describe mental processes at work whenever a person learns. Social cognitive theory is an offshoot of Bandura's more comprehensive social learning theory, which explains behavior by examining the triadic reciprocal causation process, or the interaction among cognitive, behavioral, and environmental factors.

Social cognitive theory emphasizes the importance of several distinct cognitive traits that set human beings apart. These include the symbolizing, self-regulatory, self-reflective, and vicarious capacities. The self-reflective capacity includes four different modes used in thought verification: the enactive, vicarious, persuasory, and logical modes.

Observational learning and modeling are key elements in social cognitive theory. Whenever a person observes other people's actions and the consequences of those actions, the person may learn from what has been observed. Modeling is the reenactment of learned behavior and includes four component processes: attention, retention, motor reproduction, and motivation.

New life situations require people to apply the rules of behavior learned in the past to the new and different situations. Abstract modeling takes learning to a higher level than mere mimicry of observed behavior and therefore offers many practical advantages.

Whenever a person observes behavior or receives information that conflicts with established patterns of behavior or principles of conduct, the inner conflict causes a reexamination of motivations to perform the established behavior. Inhibitory effects occur whenever a person refrains from reprehensible conduct for fear of the consequences. Disinhibitory effects lift previously learned internal restraints on certain behaviors.

People who engage in reprehensible behaviors often use cognitive techniques or devices to justify their actions. Eight such disinhibitory devices have been identified: moral justification, advantageous comparison, euphemistic labeling, displacement of responsibility, diffusion of responsibility, distortion of the consequences of action, dehumanization, and attribution of blame.

Viewers are affected or aroused by much that they see on the screen. Some experiences of arousal are not fleeting in nature. Fear reactions, coping skills, and likes and dislikes may all be learned, with lasting results, from media characters.

Social cognitive theory helps explain cultivation effects, priming effects, and prosocial effects in terms of cognitions, observational learning, and modeling. The basis for many persuasion effects or social prompting from mass media can be found in social cognitive theory, which recognizes that motivations or influences to model new behavior or adopt new ideas are dynamic and usually a combination of outside factors and personal cognitions and characteristics.

Diffusion of innovations, another important arm of media effects research, also finds a conceptual basis in social cognitive theory. Diffusion of an innovation throughout society or a large group of people is explained in terms of symbolic modeling, persuasion or social prompting, and motivation. Successful diffusion of an innovation requires three steps: learning about the innovation, adoption of the innovation, and the development of social networks after initial adoption.

REFERENCES

ANDERSON, D. N., HUSTON, A. C., WRIGHT, J. C., & COLLINS, P. A. (1998). *Sesame Street* and educational television for children. In R. G. Noll & M. E. Price (Eds.), *A communications cornucopia: Markle Foundation essays on information policy.* Washington, DC: Brookings Institution Press.

ANDERSON, D. R., BRYANT, J., WILDER, A., SANTOMERO, A., WILLIAMS, M., & CRAWLEY, A. M. (2000). Researching *Blue's Clues:* Viewing behavior and impact. *Media Psychology, 2,* 179–194.

ANDERSON, J. R., & BOWER, G. H. (1973). *Human associative memory.* Washington, DC: Winston & Sons.

BALL, S., & BOGATZ, G. A. (1973). *Reading with television: An evaluation of The Electric Company.* Princeton, NJ: Educational Testing Service.

BALL, S., BOGATZ, G. A., KARAZOW, K. M., & RUBIN, D. B. (1974). *Reading with television: A follow-up evaluation of The Electric Company.* Princeton, NJ: Educational Testing Service.

BANDURA, A. (1977). *Social learning theory.* Englewood Cliffs, NJ: Prentice-Hall.

BANDURA, A. (1982). Self-efficacy mechanism in human agency. *American Psychologist, 37,* 122–147.

BANDURA, A. (1986). *Social foundations of thought and action: A social cognitive theory.* Englewood Cliffs, NJ: Prentice-Hall.

BANDURA, A. (1989). Self-regulation of motivation and action through internal standards and goal systems. In L. A. Pervin (Ed.), *Goal concepts in personality and social psychology* (pp. 19–85). Hillsdale, NJ: Erlbaum.

BANDURA, A. (1992). Self-efficacy mechanism in psychobiological functioning. In R. Schwarzer (Ed.), *Self-efficacy: Thought control of action* (pp. 355–394). Washington, DC: Hemisphere.

BANDURA, A. (1994). Social cognitive theory of mass communication. In J. Bryant & D. Zillmann (Eds.), *Media effects: Advances in theory and research* (pp. 61–90). Hillsdale, NJ: Erlbaum.

BANDURA, A., ROSS, D., & ROSS, S. A. (1963). Imitation of film-mediated aggressive models. *Journal of Abnormal and Social Psychology, 66,* 3–11.

BANDURA, A., UNDERWOOD, B., & FROMSON, M. E. (1975). Disinhibition of aggression through diffusion of responsibility and dehumanization of victims. *Journal of Research in Personality, 9,* 253–269.

BERKOWITZ, L. (1984). Some effects of thoughts on anti- and prosocial influences of media events: A cognitive-neoassociation analysis. *Psychological Bulletin, 95,* 410–427.

BREDERODE-SANTOS, M. E. (1993). *Learning with television: The secret of Rua Sésamo.* [English translation of Portuguese, Brederode-Santos, M. E. (1991). *Com a Televiso o Segredo da Rua Sésamo.* Lison: TV Guia Editora.] Unpublished research report.

BROCK, T. C., & BUSS, A. H. (1962). Dissonance, aggression, and evaluation of pain. *Journal of Abnormal and Social Psychology, 65,* 197–202.

BROCK, T. C., & BUSS, A. H. (1964). Effects of justification for aggression and communication with the victim on postaggression dissonance. *Journal of Abnormal and Social Psychology, 68,* 404–412.

BRYANT, J., MCCOLLUM, J., RALSTON, L, RANEY, A., MCGAVIN, L., MIRON, D., MAXWELL, M., VENUGOPALAN, G., THOMPSON, S., DEWITT, D., LEWIS, K., MUNDORF, N., & SMITH, S.

(1997). Report 8: Effects of two years' viewing of *Allegra's Window* and *Gullah Gullah Island*. Report to Nick, Jr. Tuscaloosa, AL: University of Alabama, Institute for Communication Research.

BRYANT, J., MULLIKEN, L., MAXWELL, M., MUNDORF, N., MUNDORF, J., WILSON, B., SMITH, S., MCCOLLUM, J., & OWENS, J. W. (1999). *Effects of two years' viewing of Blue's Clues*. Tuscaloosa, AL: University of Alabama, Institute for Communication Research.

BUERKEL-ROTHFUSS, N. L., & MAYES, S. (1981). Soap opera viewing: The cultivation effect. *Journal of Communication, 31,* 108–115.

BUSHMAN, B. J. (1998). Priming effects of media violence on the accessibility of aggressive constructs in memory. *Personality & Social Psychology Bulletin, 24,* 537–546.

CAMBRE, M. A., & FERNIE, D. (1985). *Formative evaluation of Season IV, 3–2–1 Contact: Assessing the appeal of four weeks of educational television programs and their influence on children's science comprehension and science interest*. New York: Children's Television Workshop.

CANTOR, J., & OMDAHL, B. L. (1999). Children's acceptance of safety guidelines after exposure to televised dramas depicting accidents. *Western Journal of Communication, 63,* 58–73.

CLARK, N. M., & GONG, M. (1997). A scale for assessing health care providers' teaching and communication behavior regarding asthma. *Health Education & Behavior, 24,* 245–257.

COOPER, C. A. (1996). *Violence on television, Congressional inquiry, Public criticism and industry response, A policy analysis*. Lanham, MD: University Press of America, Inc.

DUNCKER, K. (1938). Experimental modification of children's food preferences through social suggestion. *Journal of Abnormal Social Psychology, 33,* 489–507.

FISCH, S. M. (in press). Vast wasteland or vast opportunity?: Effects of educational television on children's academic knowledge, skills, and attitudes. In J. Bryant, & D. Zillmann (Eds.) *Media effects* (2nd ed.) Mahwah, NJ: Erlbaum.

GRANOVETTER, M. (1983). The strength of weak ties: A network theory revisited. In R. Collins (Ed.), *Sociological theory 1983* (pp. 201–233). San Francisco: Jossey-Bass.

HALL, E. R., ESTY, E. T., & FISCH, S. M. (1990). Television and children's problem-solving behavior: A synopsis of an evaluation of the effects of *Square One TV*. *Journal of Mathematical Behavior, 9,* 161–174.

HALL, E. R., FISCH, S. M., ESTY, E. T., DEBOLD, E., MILLER, B. A., BENNETT, D. T., & SOLAN, S. V. (1990). *Children's problem-solving behavior and their attitudes toward mathematics: A study of the effects of Square One TV* (Vols. 1–5). New York: Children's Television Workshop.

JOHNSTON, J. (1980). *An exploratory study of the effects of viewing the first season of 3-2-1 Contact*. New York: Children's Television Workshop.

JOHNSTON, J., & LUKER, R. (1983). *The "Eriksson Study": An exploratory study of viewing two weeks of the second season of 3-2-1 Contact*. New York: Children's Television Workshop.

LANDMAN, J., & MANIS, M. (1983). Social cognition: Some historical and theoretical perspectives. In L. Berkowitz (Ed.), *Advances in experimental social psychology* (Vol. 16, pp. 49–123). New York: Academic.

LAPINSKI, M. K., & WITTE, K. (1998). Health communication campaigns. In L. D. Jackson & B. K. Duffy (Eds.), *Health communication research: A guide to developments and directions* (pp. 139–161). Westport, CT: Greenwood.

LEITNER, R. K. (1991). *Comparing the effects on reading comprehension of educational video, direct experience, and print*. Unpublished doctoral thesis, University of San Francisco, CA.

LIEBERT, R. M., SPRAFKIN, J. N., & DAVIDSON, E. S. (1982). *The early window: Effects of television on children and youth*. Elmsford, NY: Pergamon.

LINEBARGER, D. L. (2000). *Summative evaluation of Between the Lions: A final report to WGBH Educational Foundation*. Kansas City, KS: University of Kansas, Juniper Gardens Children's Project.

McGHEE, P. E., & FRUEH, T. (1980). Television viewing and the learning of sex-role stereo-types. *Sex Roles, 6*, 179–188.

MAIBACH, E. W., MAXFIELD, A., LADIN, K., & SLATER, M. (1996). Translating health psychology into effective health communication: The American Healthstyles Audience Segmentation Project. *Journal of Health Psychology, 1*, 261–277.

MALAMUTH, N. M., & DONNERSTEIN, E. (Eds.). (1984). *Pornography and sexual aggression.* New York: Academic.

MARCUS, B. H., OWEN, N., FORSYTH, L. H., CAVILL, N. A., & FRIDINGER, F. (1998). Physical activity interventions using mass media, print media, and information technology. *American Journal of Preventive Medicine, 15*, 362–378.

MULLIKEN, L., & BRYANT, J. A. (1999, May). *Effects of curriculum-based television programming on behavioral assessments of flexible thinking and structured and unstructured prosocial play behaviors.* Poster presented at the 49th annual conference of the International Communication Association, San Francisco, CA.

OSTLUND, L. E. (1974). Perceived innovation attributes as predictors of innovativeness. *Journal of Consumer Research, 1*, 23–29.

POTTER, B., & SHEESHKA, J. (2000). Content analysis of infant feeding messages in a Canadian women's magazine, 1945 to 1995. *Journal of Nutrition Education, 32*, 196–204.

RHEE, J. W. (1997). Strategy and issue frames in election campaign coverage: A social cognitive account of framing effects. *Journal of Communication, 47*, 26–48.

RICE, M. L. (1984). The words of children's television. *Journal of Broadcasting, 28*, 445–461.

RICE, M. L., & HAIGHT, P. L. (1986). "Motherese" of Mr. Rogers: A description of the dialogue of educational television programs. *Journal of Speech and Hearing Disorders, 51*, 282–287.

ROBERTSON, T. S. (1971). *Innovative behavior and communication.* New York: Holt, Rinehart & Winston.

ROGERS, E. M. (1983) *Diffusion of innovations.* New York: Free Press.

ROGERS, E. M., & SHOEMAKER, F. (1971). *Communication of innovations: A cross-cultural approach.* New York: Free Press.

ROSENTHAL, T. L., & ZIMMERMAN, B. J. (1978). *Social learning and cognition.* New York: Academic.

SINGER, J. L., & SINGER, D. G. (1994). *Barney and Friends as education and entertainment: Phase 2—Can children learn through preschool exposure to Barney and Friends?* New Haven, CT: Yale University Family Television Research and Consultation Center.

SINGER, J. L., & SINGER, D. G. (1995). *Barney and Friends as education and entertainment: Phase 3—A national study: Can children learn through preschool exposure to Barney and Friends?* New Haven, CT: Yale University Family Television Research and Consultation Center.

SINGER, J. L., & SINGER, D. G. (1998). *Barney & Friends as entertainment and education: Evaluating the quality and effectiveness of a television series for preschool children.* In J. K. Asamen, & G. L. Berry (Eds.), *Research paradigms, television, and social behavior* (pp. 305–367). Thousand Oaks, CA: Sage.

SINGER, J. L., & SINGER, D. G. (1983). Implications of childhood television viewing for cognition, imagination, and emotion. In J. Bryant & D. R. Anderson (Eds.), *Children's understanding of television: Research on attention and comprehension* (pp. 265–295). New York: Academic.

SINGHAL, A., & ROGERS, E. M. (1989). Pro-social television for development in India. In R. E. Rice & C. K. Atkin (Eds.), *Public communication campaigns* (pp. 331–350). Newbury Park, CA: Sage.

TAN, A. S. (1979). TV beauty ads and role expectations of adolescent female viewers. *Journalism Quarterly, 56*, 283–288.

TORNATZKY, L. G., & KLEIN, K. J. (1982). Innovation characteristics and innovation adoption-implementation: A meta-analysis of findings. *IEEE Transactions of Engineering and Management, EM-29*, 28–45.

Ulitsa Sezam Department of Research and Content. (1998, November). Preliminary report of summative findings. Report presented to the Children's Television Workshop, New York, NY.

UNICEF. (1996). *Executive summary: Summary assessment of Plaza Sésamo IV—Mexico.* [English translation of Spanish.] Unpublished research report. Mexico City, Mexico: Author.

WAGNER, S. (1985). *Comprehensive evaluation of the fourth season of 3-2-1 Contact.* New York: Children's Television Workshop.

WATT, J. G., JR., & VAN DEN BERG, S. A. (1978). Time series analysis of alternative media effects theories. In R. D. Ruben (Ed.), *Communication Yearbook 2* (pp. 215–224). New Brunswick, NJ: Transaction Books.

WILSON, B. J., & CANTOR, J. (1985). Developmental differences in empathy with a television protagonist's fear. *Journal of Experimental Child Psychology, 39*, 284–299.

WINETT, R. A., LECKLITER, I. N., CHINN, D. E., STAHL, B. N., & LOVE, S. Q. (1985). The effects of television modeling on residential energy conservation. *Journal of Applied Behavior Analysis, 18*, 33–44.

WRIGHT, J. C., & HUSTON, A. C. (1995). *Effects of educational TV viewing of lower income preschoolers on academic skills, school readiness, and school adjustment one to three years later: A report to the Children's Television Workshop.* Lawrence, KS: The University of Kansas, Center for Research on the Influences of Television on Children.

WRIGHT, J. C., HUSTON, A. C., SCANTLIN, R., & KOTLER, J. (2001). The Early Window project: *Sesame Street* prepares children for school. In Fisch, S. M., & Truglio, R. T., (Eds.), *"G" is for "growing": Thirty years of research on children and Sesame Street* (pp. 97–114). Mahwah, NJ: Erlbaum.

ZILL, N. (2001). Does *Sesame Street* enhance school readiness?" Evidence from a national survey of children. In S. M. Fisch, & R. T. Truglio (Eds.), *"G" is for "growing": Thirty years of research on children and Sesame Street* (pp. 115–130). Mahwah, NJ: Erlbaum.

ZILL, N., DAVIES, E., & DALY, M. (1994). *Viewing of Sesame Street by preschool children and its relationship to school readiness: Report prepared for the Children's Television Workshop.* Rockville, MD: Westat, Inc.

ZILLMANN, D., & BRYANT, J. (1984). Effects of massive exposure to pornography. In N. M. Malamuth & E. Donnerstein (Eds.), *Pornography and sexual aggression* (pp. 115–138). New York: Academic.

CHAPTER 5

Priming Effects

> *It is assumed that concepts that have some relation to each other are connected in some mental network, so that if one concept is activated, then concepts related to it are also activated.*
>
> **—Entry on "Priming"**
> **University of Alberta's *Cognitive Science Dictionary*, 1998**

In one of the lighter moments during the infamous 2000 presidential election controversy, a reporter speculated whether the great focus on chads might either prompt parents to name their newborn sons "Chad" in the near future or sour them on such a name (Constable, 2000). Other reporters talked about the ribbings that men named Chad were taking simply because they shared their name with the famous and controversial bits of paper from contested Florida ballots (Terhune, 2000; Mucha, 2000; Kornheiser, 2000). Because of the extensive media coverage, the world came to recognize "chad" as something other than a republic in Africa or a person's name. Suddenly, the term became associated with voting ballots and a hotly contested presidential election.

This example, admittedly simplistic and overly obvious, demonstrates how focused media attention can cause viewers and readers to forge mental associations related to media content. The exhaustive debate over the differences between pregnant, dimpled, and hanging chads caused viewers and readers to think twice whenever they considered the word "Chad."

When one contemplates a much more weighty and serious example—the viewing of violent media content—one can only speculate on the mental associations such content prompts in viewers. Does media violence cause viewers to make associations with angry or critical thoughts stored in their own memories? More significantly, does the viewing of mediated violence and the mental associations it arouses make viewers more likely to commit acts of violence themselves?

These types of questions lie at the heart of many social scientific investigations of media effects, as well as questions related to the psychological processes present whenever media effects do indeed occur. The cultivation hypothesis offers one framework for such investigations, but many scholars believe theories that emphasize cognitive components involved in processing information provide a more viable theoretical basis for questions such as those listed. Media effects studies that examine cognitive mechanisms often differ considerably in their assumptions and methodologies from those using the cultivation approach. Whereas cultivation research attempts to explain *long-term* media effects, cognitive research typically explores *short-term* media effects that sometimes have long-term implications. Also, whereas cultivation research has been criticized for lack of scientific controls and conceptual inadequacies, cognitive research usually employs strong experimental designs and tight controls that rarely draw criticism regarding rigor from the social scientific community.

The cognitive theoretical emphasis involves application of theories from psychology, including social psychology, to explain media effects phenomena, including social cognitive theory and priming, the subject of this chapter. **Priming** is a popular area of media effects research based upon the psychological principles of information processing by means of cognitive components. Priming theory often serves as a theoretical basis for particular studies in other areas of media effects research, including agenda setting, media violence, and political communication effects. As with the other major theories in the body of media effects research, so many studies have focused on the priming mechanism itself that an entire body of media effects literature related to priming now exists.

This chapter examines the theoretical underpinnings of priming and reviews some of the important studies that have measured priming effects resulting from mediated communication. Following a description of the priming mechanism and factors that may determine its activation, the chapter provides a glimpse into the conceptual foundations for the theory, examines a research tradition rooted in principles of cognitive psychology, and explores variables that enhance priming effects. It notes that the theoretical bases for priming theory are borrowed from the principles of cognitive psychology. Finally, the most recent research studies involving priming mechanisms and future directions in priming research receive attention.

ACTIVATION OF PRIMING

Priming occurs when exposure to mediated communication activates related thoughts that have been stored in the mind of an audience member. Media message content triggers concepts, thoughts, learning, or knowledge acquired in the past that are related to the message content. In this way, message content is connected, associated, or *reinforced* by related thoughts and concepts that it brings to mind. For a certain period of time after viewing such content, a person is more likely to have thoughts about the content, related thoughts, or memories. In some instances, the related thoughts or memories become permanently associated with the message content, or *stimulus* (Fiske & Taylor, 1991).

For example, a network newscast that features a story on the sad state of the Russian economy may cause a viewer to remember his parents' horror stories of life during the Great Depression in the United States, or recall conversations with a student from Russia whom he knew in college, or reminisce about the trip to Moscow he took while in graduate school. Any knowledge he has already acquired regarding economic depressions and the Russian economy and way of life would be associated with the new information he hears on the newscast. His interest in the news story and his reaction to it may well be affected by his existing knowledge and previous experiences. If, for example, depression stories during his childhood caused much anxiety, the story of the Russian economic hardships may cause him to recollect such feelings. In other words, his memories *primed* him to react in a particular way to the story.

The priming activation may also influence a person's behavior, causing him or her to act or react in some way, sometimes with undesirable consequences. The most sensational example of undesirable priming, in this case operating in conjunction with social learning theory, may be that of *copycat* crimes—especially murder or other violent crimes that occurred after the person was "primed" by a movie or program. While copycat crimes are rare, their occurrence in any number merits social concern and underscores the significance of media effects research. Examples of such crimes receive prominent attention as a result of the high levels of media coverage they receive. The 1971 film *A Clockwork Orange,* which depicted hoodlums who raped young girls, was blamed for a number of "copycat" rapes. Several murders in the 1980s were committed by young men said to be imitating the lead character in the Rambo movie *First Blood* (1982). In recent years, the movie *Natural Born Killers* (1994) has apparently spawned several murders.

Instances of copycat crimes are grave extremes of priming. Such cases represent a very small percentage of the population. Only a handful of people, for whatever reason, experience priming effects so completely that they actually *model* or imitate the viewed behavior. Priming effects from the viewing of media violence are normally much more subtle, but even at that level they represent cause for concern.

For most people, priming effects cause only mild reactions that usually diminish in time and may even pass unnoticed. Nevertheless, the overall evidence for priming has been substantial. The strength of the activation, the types of thoughts provoked, and the behavioral results of the activation depend upon a number of contingent factors.

CONCEPTUAL ROOTS

Priming is based upon the concept of *cognitive neoassociation.* This social psychological perspective attempts to explain a portion of the phenomenon of memory (Anderson & Bower, 1973; Landman & Manis, 1983). To understand cognitive neoassociation, one must picture the brain as a complex network of pathways that connect associative ideas, thoughts, feelings, and concepts. *Memory* can be described as the overall network. When a person watches a television program or reads a newspaper, the information being processed triggers or activates certain pathways throughout the network. Individual thoughts or feelings from past experiences are *remembered* and associated with the new information. These ideas and thoughts may stimulate other, related ideas and they may influence a person's actions.

When audiences are presented with a certain stimulus that has a specific meaning, they are "primed" to related concepts. Ideas connected to emotions trigger associated feelings and responses. For example, research has shown that thinking depressing thoughts can actually cause feelings of depression (Velten, 1968), and exposure to ideas of aggression can produce feelings of anger or even aggressive acts under some circumstances (Berkowitz & Heimer, 1989).

Audience members are likely to have thoughts with meanings similar to what they are viewing or *semantically* similar thoughts. In short, the primed ideas activate semantically related thoughts (Collins & Loftus, 1975). Watching a sad scene in a movie, for instance, causes audiences to remember similar moments in their own lives and recall emotions associated with the events. A painful separation, the death of a loved one, a tragic accident—these are events that affect everyone, and therefore everyone can relate to them whenever they see them happening to characters in the movies or on television.

Individual differences in perceptions, of course, cause priming activation strengths to vary considerably from person to person (Bargh & Chartrand, 2000). Priming effects appear to be mitigated by the recency of each individual's experiences that are called into recollection and thus their individual perceptions of the priming mechanism.

Priming and Mental Models

Scholars have begun to go beyond the network model of memory to conceptualize the priming experience as part of more expansive *mental models*. These models represent the combination of a person's knowledge of the world and memories from past experiences. They run the gamut of cognitive structuring of knowledge, from concrete, past situations or experiences, to belief structures, to more abstract thoughts or concepts. Different mental models exist for different topics, situations, or levels of abstraction. Such models are not always static, but may be expanded, refined, or altered by new information or even by primes themselves.

The effectiveness of mass media in creating mental models has been indicated by research that shows words accompanied by pictures facilitate the construction of mental models (Glenberg & Langston, 1992; Wyer & Radvansky, 1999). According to Roskos-Ewoldsen (2001):

The relevance of mental models to our understanding of the media operates at a couple of levels. First, understanding interpersonal discourse, the media, or the world in general, requires constructing a mental model to represent the event. To the extent that a person can construct such a model,

the person is said to "understand" the event . Furthermore, mental models would aid in understanding information across scenes of the program and even across episodes of a series (Zwann & Radvanski, 1998) and the type of inferences that will be drawn about the show (Graesser et al., 1994). Thus, the mental models that we construct play an integral role in how we understand the media. Second, the media clearly influence the types of mental models that we construct. For example, recently it has been found that people who watch more romantic TV programming have more idealistic expectations about marriage. We would argue that viewing this genre of TV results in the creation of mental models that reflect the idealistic images of marriage that they view on the media.

Sources: Glenberg, A. M., & Langston, W. E. (1992). Comprehension of illustrated text: Pictures help to build mental models. *Journal of Memory and Language, 31,* 129–151; Wyer, R. S., Jr., & Radvansky, G. A. (1999). The comprehension and validation of social information. *Psychological Review, 106,* 89–118; Zwann, R. A., & Radvansky, G. A. (1998). Situation models in language comprehension and memory. *Psychological Bulletin, 123,* 162–185; Graesser, A. C., Singer, M., & Trabasso, T. (1994). Constructing inferences during narrative text comprehension, 101, 371–395.

Psychologists began studying the effects of priming on social interactions several decades ago. Many of these studies have used similar procedures to examine various aspects. Researchers subtly introduce certain thoughts into the minds of the people being studied; then they test those people to determine the extent of the priming effect.

Many priming studies have focused upon the psychological phenomenon itself rather than the media effects dimension, but the findings of these studies have proven very useful for media effects scholars. R. Wyer, Jr., and T. Srull (1981) gave study participants word sets from which they were instructed to make sentences. Some participants were given words with meanings semantically related to aggression, while others received only neutral words. When evaluating a targeted person, participants who had constructed aggression-related sentences were far more critical.

Some studies have shown that priming can even occur without a person's awareness. J. Bargh and P. Pietromonaco (1982) exposed their study participants to certain words, some of which were semantically related to the idea of hostility, and then asked them to evaluate a targeted person. Those who were primed with more hostility-related words were far more negative in their evaluations of a target person than those who had not received the hostility priming.

T. Wilson and J. Capitman (1982) asked male participants to read one of two stories—a romantic "boy-meets-girl" story or a control story. Those who had read the romantic story were observed afterward to pay much closer attention to a female confederate than those who had read the control story.

A number of media effects studies have shown strong evidence for priming, especially for the priming of ideas related to aggression. One study found that children who read comic books with violent contents were more likely to have aggressive thoughts than children who read comic books with more neutral contents (Berkowitz, 1973). Another study (Berkowitz, 1970) examined the effects of listening to aggression-related humor. Young women who heard either the hostile humor of Don Rickles or a nonaggressive comedy routine by George Carlin were then asked to rate a job applicant. The women who had listened to Rickles evaluated applicants more harshly than the women who had heard Carlin.

VARIABLES THAT ENHANCE PRIMING EFFECTS

The connection between the *priming* of aggressive thoughts and the *actual display of aggression* is, generally speaking, a tenuous one, but it is substantially strengthened whenever certain variables are present. Research has shown that these **intervening variables,** or variables that strengthen the cause-effect phenomenon when they are present, include the following:

1. The perceived meaning of the communication.
2. The perceived justifiability of the witnessed aggression.

3. The extent to which audiences identify with the characters.
4. The perceived reality of the mediated communication.
5. The stimulus of prior experiences.

Perceived Meaning

L. Berkowitz and J. Alioto (1973) angered male participants and then showed them either a professional prizefight or a professional football game. The participants were given information that would enable them to interpret the events in one of two ways: either the athletes were intent on hurting each other or the athletes were simply performing their professional jobs without emotion. After watching the event, the participants had the opportunity to shock the person who had provoked them earlier. The men who had been led to believe that the athletes were intent upon hurting each other showed evidence of being "primed" with more aggressive thoughts as they administered more punishing electrical shocks.

Perceived Justifiability

Research has shown that viewers of mediated violence are also influenced in their actions by the *outcomes* of the situations they see. A number of studies have revealed that viewers believe what happens on television or in movies could also happen to them if they behave in ways similar to the characters depicted (Bandura, 1971; Comstock, 1980; Comstock et al., 1978; Huesmann, 1982). When viewers see aggressors suffering as a result of their behavior, they are less likely to imitate the aggressive behavior (Bandura, 1965, 1971). Also, when viewers are reminded of the serious and unfortunate consequences of violence, aggression is usually restrained. R. Goranson (1969) gave angry participants a chance to punish their provocateur after viewing a film in which a man received a bad beating in a prizefight. One group of participants were told the beaten man subsequently died from his injuries; the other group did not receive this information. The participants who were led to believe that the fighter died showed more restraint in punishing the provocateur than the others.

Research Has Shown

Priming effects are most enhanced when audience members:

- *Interpret* the *meaning* of a film or communication in a particular way.
- *Believe* that the violent behavior they are seeing is *justified* for some reason.
- *Identify* with the characters they see.
- *Believe* they are seeing *actual* events rather than fiction.
- See the portrayed violence and *remember* experiencing similar feelings and thoughts in the past.

Character Identification

Research has also shown that identification with a media character enhances priming effects. In one study, three groups of male participants were angered, then asked to watch a prizefight (Turner & Berkowitz, 1972). The members of one group were told to think of themselves as the winner. The men in the second group were told to think of themselves as the referee. The third group did not receive any instructions. In each group, half the participants were directed to think of the word "hit" each time the winner punched his opponent. After the movie, each participant had the opportunity to shock the person who had angered him. The most severe punishment was administered by the group of men who had pictured themselves as the winner and had thought "hit" with each punch.

Researchers have advanced various hypotheses to explain the strength of identification in causing priming effects. The "hit" word may have served as a cue for the memory to retrieve combative experiences from the past. The inducement of such memories, along with the thoughts and feelings associated with them, would only serve to intensify aggression. Eunkyung Jo and Leonard Berkowitz (1994) wrote:

> It could be that the viewers who identify with (or think of themselves as) the movie aggressor are especially apt to have aggression-related thoughts as they watch the violent events. In their minds they strike at the film victim along with the movie aggressor so that these aggression-related thoughts then prime their aggression-associated mental networks relatively strongly. (p. 54)

Perceived Reality

The perceived reality of media depictions can also intensify the strength of priming effects. Research has shown that priming effects are strongest when audiences believe they are witnessing *actual* rather than *fictional* events. In one study, angered participants saw the same war film, but only half were told it was a fictional movie (Berkowitz & Alioto, 1973). The other half were led to believe that the film depicted actual combat. When given the opportunity afterward to punish their provocateur with electrical shock, members of the latter group administered shocks that were longer in duration. Another study found similar results among three groups of fifth- and sixth-grade children (Atkin, 1983). The first group of children saw a fight being reported realistically on the news. The second group viewed the fight in the context of fantasy entertainment. The control group viewed an ordinary commercial. When tested, the first group scored significantly higher on an aggression index than the other two groups.

Memories of Prior Experiences

Another factor identified with enhancing priming effects is that of *prior learning* or *remembered experiences*. As an audience member views a violent act, he or she remembers other occasions when semantically similar thoughts or feelings cropped up. The memory reactivates a neural network and strengthens the effects of priming.

Social cognitive theory, an outgrowth of social learning theory, offers a portion of the theoretical basis for priming. The conceptual framework for social cognitive theory exists in a *triadic reciprocal model* that attempts to explain human cognitions and behavior. In this model, three components—(1) the person's behavior, (2) cognitive, biological, or other personal factors, and (3) environmental influences—interact and influence each other at different levels. This allows people to be "both products and producers of their environment" (Bandura, 1994, p. 61).

Scholars have proposed several other theoretical models to explain priming effects (Fiske & Taylor, 1991). These include the *storage bin model,* the *storage battery model,* and the *synapse view model.* Each of these models addresses the issue of *recency versus frequency* as a priming determinant; that is, are priming effects due more to information that has been stored recently or information that has been stored frequently? Even though the models differ in the relative importance they assign to the priming mechanism, empirical evidence can be found to support each model. As a result, some researchers have designed studies to illustrate the differences among the models (Higgins, 1989; Higgins, Bargh, & Lombardi, 1985).

Storage Bin Model

With this model, memory is viewed as a large storage bin in which recently primed concepts are considered strongest. Over time, new concepts are stacked atop old concepts inside the bin. Recently primed concepts are found at the top of the bin. Frequently primed concepts are found at different levels in the bin but also at the top, because it is likely that a frequently primed concept was probably primed recently as well (Wyer & Srull, 1980, 1986). Thus, recency is emphasized.

Storage Battery Model

In contrast, the storage battery model emphasizes the importance of frequently primed concepts. The frequent input serves to "charge up" the battery, so to speak, or continually reinforce certain concepts in the brain. The more frequently a concept is primed, the higher the "charge" produced and the stronger the effect.

Synapse View Model

The synapse view model demonstrates that time determines whether recently or frequently primed concepts emerge as more important. A concept that has been primed recently is stronger for a limited period of time or "in the short run," and a concept that has been primed frequently is stronger over a long period of time or "in the long run."

In recent years, media effects scholars have continued to study priming effects, especially those that result from exposure to media violence. In the *Annual Review of Sociology*, R. B. Felson (1996) reviewed much of the evidence that links mediated violence to the aggressiveness or the priming of aggressive thoughts. B. Bushman and R. Geen (1990) asked participants to watch one of three movies (highly violent, less violent, and nonviolent), then list the thoughts they had at the end of the movie. Those who watched the most violent film listed the most aggressive thoughts. Other media violence/priming studies have shown evidence for priming effects through playing video games and watching sporting events. C. Anderson and C. M. Ford (1987) measured the levels of hostility, anxiety, and depression of participants assigned to three conditions: One group played a video game containing a large amount of violence, another group played a less violent video game, and a control group did not play a game. The participants who played one of the video games showed higher levels of hostility than the control group. In terms of the anxiety measure, the group that played the highly violent video game scored significantly higher than the other two groups. In another study, football spectators reported greater feelings of hostility than spectators of a nonaggressive sporting event (Goldstein, 1986).

Other studies have also confirmed priming effects from viewing violent content. T. Langley and his associates (1992) found that male college undergraduates were more attracted to media violence after being primed. The participants wrote short stories using one of three types of word lists: aggressive words, positive or prosocial words, or neutral words. Those given the aggressive word list wrote stories that contained more aggression and violence than those given the other types of word lists. When given the chance to view film clips, participants primed with the aggressive words were more interested in clips containing violence and hostility than the group primed with neutral words. Bushman (1998) found that violent media content primed thoughts of aggression in two experiments. One required respondents to make free word associations to homonyms following the viewing of violent media content. The other experiment required participants to decide whether particular strings of letters that appeared on a computer screen were words or nonwords, with half the words having meanings associated with aggression. In both experiments, the word selections revealed a significant priming effect after viewing the mediated violence.

In recent years, priming effects have been found in areas of communication research other than media violence studies. Advertising research has focused on priming effects to examine the primed perceptions of new "extension" products introduced by well-known manufacturers (Lee, 1994). Interpretations and thoughts about media presentations have been explored after individuals were primed with either positive nonstereotypical images of blacks and women or negative stereotypes of those two groups (Power, Murphy, & Coover, 1996). A study of political communication effects determined that media focus upon moral or ethical aspects of political issues primed voters to have perceptions about candidates' integrity and perceive other political issues with ethical inter-pretations (Domke, Shah, & Wackman, 1998). Television's role in priming citizens in their evaluations of candidates and officeholders was investigated in a study that focused on the visual images of politicians that accompany TV news broadcasts (Shields, 1995). Other studies have linked presidential approval ratings to priming effects provided by media coverage of major issues such as the Gulf War or economic conditions (Pan & Kosicki, 1997; Blood, 1996). Other political communication investigators have determined that the impact of media coverage on presidential job performance evaluations has not been related to priming effects (Miller & Krosnick, 2000). Another study found that voters with a high exposure to media tended to base their voting decisions on their perceptions of the character of the candidates, as primed by mass media, even more than on party affiliation (Mendelsohn, 1996). The same study found significant interpersonal communication effects: Voters who talked about politics throughout the course of the campaign tended to base their votes upon their knowledge of issues rather than the character of the candidates. Other recent priming studies have established priming effects from music videos (Hansen & Krygowski, 1994), and the priming of racial stereotypes from local depictions of crime news (Valentino, 1999).

As the examples have shown, priming theory has become a viable theoretical basis for the explanation of many different types of media effects. The theory has found successful application in a variety of domains of media effects research, and study after study records support for the principles of the theory. In addition to violent media content, researchers now measure the extent to which other types of media content also serve to prime media audiences, such as political communications, minority portrayals, and advertisements. The number of media effects studies based upon priming theory continues to increase as more researchers seek to identify the links between media priming and the subsequent attitudes and behaviors of audience members.

SUMMARY

Priming is a popular area of media effects research that explores the cognitive components of information processing. Priming occurs when exposure to mediated communication activates related thoughts in the mind of an audience member. Media content triggers concepts, thoughts, learning, or knowledge acquired in the past and related to the message content. For a certain period of time after viewing, a person is more likely to have thoughts about the content, related thoughts, or memories. Sometimes these related thoughts become permanently associated with the message content or stimulus.

Priming may influence a person's behavior. The person may act or react in a certain way, sometimes with undesirable consequences. Instances of copycat crimes are grave extremes of priming, but only a handful of people experience priming effects so completely that they actually model or imitate the viewed behavior. For more people, priming effects cause mild reactions that diminish in time or may pass unnoticed.

Priming is based upon the concept of cognitive neoassociation which attempts to explain the phenomenon of memory. Individual thoughts or feelings from past experiences are remembered and associated with the new information. Ideas connected to emotions trigger associated feelings and responses. Audience members are likely to have thoughts with similar meanings to what they are viewing or semantically similar thoughts.

Most studies on priming use tight controls in laboratory situations. Most studies have focused upon the psychological phenomenon itself rather than the media effects dimension, but a number of media effects studies have shown strong evidence for priming.

The connection between the priming of aggressive thoughts and the actual display of aggression is not particularly strong unless certain variables are present. These include (1) the perceived meaning of the communication, (2) the perceived justifiability of the witnessed aggression, (3) the extent to which audiences identify with the characters, (4) the perceived reality of the mediated communication, and (5) the stimulus of prior experiences.

One theoretical basis for priming is social cognitive theory, an outgrowth of social learning theory. The conceptual framework for social cognitive theory exists in a triadic reciprocal model that attempts to explain human cognitions and behavior. The model includes three components: (1) the person's behavior, (2) cognitive, biological, or other personal factors, and (3) environmental influences. These components interact and influence each other at different levels.

Several theoretical models have been proposed to describe and explain priming effects. These include the storage bin model, the storage battery model, and the synapse view model. Each model addresses the issue of recency versus frequency as a priming determinant.

In recent years, a number of media violence studies have shown evidence for priming effects. Future research on priming by media effects scholars will continue to search for answers.

REFERENCES

ANDERSON, C., & FORD, C. M. (1987). Effect of the game player: Short-term effects of highly and mildly aggressive video games. *Personality and Social Psychology Bulletin, 12,* 390–402.

ANDERSON, J., & BOWER, G. (1973). *Human associative memory.* Washington, DC: Winston.

ATKIN, C. (1983). Effects of realistic TV violence vs. fictional violence on aggression. *Journalism Quarterly, 60,* 615–621.

BANDURA, A. (1965). Vicarious processes: A case of no-trial learning. In L. Berkowitz (Ed.), *Advances in experimental social psychology* (Vol. 2, pp. 1–55). New York: Academic.

BANDURA, A. (1971). *Social learning theory.* New York: General Learning Press.

BANDURA, A. (1994). Social cognitive theory of mass communication. In J. Bryant & D. Zillmann (Eds.), *Media effects: Advances in theory and research* (pp. 61–90). Hillsdale, NJ: Erlbaum.

BARGH, J., & CHARTRAND, T. (2000). The mind in the middle: A practical guide to priming and automaticity research. In H. Reis & C. Judd (Eds.), *Handbook of research methods in social and personality psychology* (pp. 253–285). Cambridge, UK: Cambridge University Press.

Bargh, J., & Pietromonaco, P. (1982). Automatic information processing and social perception: The influence of trait information presented outside of conscious awareness on impression formation. *Journal of Personality and Social Psychology, 43,* 437–449.

Berkowitz, L. (1970). Aggressive humors as a stimulus to aggressive responses. *Journal of Personality and Social Psychology, 16,* 710–717.

Berkowitz, L. (1973). Words and symbols as stimuli to aggressive responses. In J. Knutson (Ed.), *Control of aggression: Implications from basic research* (pp. 113–143). Chicago: Aldine-Atherton.

Berkowitz, L., & Alioto, J. (1973). The meaning of an observed event as a determinant of its aggressive consequences. *Journal of Personality and Social Psychology, 28,* 206–217.

Berkowitz, L., & Heimer, K. (1989). On the construction of the anger experience: Aversive events and negative priming in the formation of feelings. In L. Berkowitz (Ed.), *Advances in experimental social psychology* (Vol. 22, pp. 1–37). New York: Academic.

Blood, D. J. (1996). *Economic headline news, consumer sentiment, presidential popularity and the state of the economy: A study of their dynamic relationship, 1980–1993.* Unpublished doctoral dissertation, The University of Connecticut, Storrs.

Bushman, B. (1998). Priming effects of media violence on the accessibility of aggressive constructs in memory. *Personality & Social Psychology Bulletin, 24,* 537–545.

Bushman, B., & Geen R. (1990). Role of cognitive-emotional mediators and individual differences in the effects of media violence on aggression. *Journal of Personality and Social Psychology, 58,* 156–163.

Collins, A., & Loftus, E. (1975). A spreading-activation theory of semantic memory. *Psychological Review, 82,* 407–428.

Comstock, G. (1980). New emphasis in research on the effects of television and film violence. In E. Palmer & A. Dorr (Eds.), *Children and the faces of television* (pp. 129–148). New York: Academic.

Comstock, G., Chaffee, S., Katzman, N., McCombs, M., & Roberts, D. (1978). *Television and human behavior.* New York: Columbia University Press.

Constable, B. (2000, 28 November). Wouldn't Chadfetti be a splendid girls name? *Chicago Daily Herald,* 12.

Domke, D., Shah, D. V., & Wackman, D. B. (1998). Media priming effects: Accessibility, association, and activation. *International Journal of Public Opinion Research, 10*(1), 51–74.

Felson, R. B. (1996). Mass media effects on violent behavior. *Annual Review of Sociology, 22,* 103–128.

Fiske, S. T., & Taylor, S. E. (1991). *Social Cognition* 2nd ed. New York: McGraw-Hill.

Goldstein, J. H. (1986). *Aggression and crimes of violence.* New York: Oxford University Press.

Goranson, R. (1969). *Observed violence and aggressive behavior: The effects of negative outcomes to the observed violence.* Unpublished doctoral dissertation, University of Wisconsin–Madison.

Hansen, C. H., & Krygowski, W. (1994). Arousal-augmented priming effects. *Communication Research, 21*(1), 24–47.

Higgins, E. T. (1989). Knowledge accessibility and activation: Subjectivity and suffering from unconscious sources. In J. S. Uleman & J. A. Bargh (Eds.), *Unintended thought* (pp. 75–123). New York: Guilford.

Higgins, E. T., Bargh, J. A., & Lombardi, W. (1985). The nature of priming effects on categorization. *Journal of Experimental Psychology: Learning, Memory, and Cognition, 11,* 59–69.

Huesmann, L. (1982). Violence and aggression. In National Institute of Mental Health, *Television and Behavior: Ten years of scientific progress* (Vol. 1, pp. 36–44). Washington, DC: U.S. Government Printing Office.

Jo, E., & Berkowitz, L. (1994). A priming effect analysis of media influences: An update. In J. Bryant & D. Zillmann (Eds.), *Media effects: Advances in theory and research* (pp. 43–60). Hillsdale, NJ: Erlbaum.

Kornheiser, T. (2000, 19 November). The good, the chad and the ugly. *The Washington Post,* F01.

Landman, J., & Manis, M. (1983). Social cognition: Some historical and theoretical perspectives. In L. Berkowitz (Ed.), *Advances in experimental social psychology* (Vol. 16, pp. 49–123). New York: Academic.

Langley, T., O'Neal, E. C., Craig, K. M., & Yost, E. A. (1992) Aggression-consistent, -inconsistent, and -irrelevant priming effects on selective exposure to media violence. *Aggressive Behavior, 18,* 349–356.

Lee, J. S. (1994). *Role of brand advertising on consumer perception of a brand extension: Cognitive and affective priming effects.* Unpublished doctoral dissertation, The University of Wisconsin–Madison.

Mendelsohn, M. (1996). The media and interpersonal communications: The priming of issues, leaders, and party identification. *Journal of Politics, 58*(1), 112–125.

Miller, J. M., & Krosnick, J. A. (2000, April). News media impact on the ingredients of presidential evaluations: Politically knowledgeable citizens are guided by a trusted source. *American Journal of Political Science, 44,* 301–315.

Mucha, P. (2000, 26 November). What's in a name for Chads? Plenty of jokes, thanks to race for president. *The Houston Chronicle,* 8.

Pan, Z., & Kosicki, G. M. (1997). Priming and media impact on the evaluations of the president's performance. *Communication Research, 24*(1), 3–30.

Power, J. G., Murphy, S. T., & Coover, G. (1996). Priming prejudice: How stereotypes and counter-stereotypes influence attribution of responsibility and credibility among ingroups and outgroups. *Human Communication Research, 23*(1), 36–58.

Shields, T. G. (1995). *Network news, attributions of responsibility, and the role of visual images (television).* Unpublished doctoral dissertation, University of Kentucky.

Terhune, C. (2000, 27 November). With this name, I can say it out loud: I'm Chad and I'm proud. *Wall Street Journal,* 1.

Turner, C., & Berkowitz, L. (1972). Identification with film aggressor (covert role taking) and reactions to film violence. *Journal of Personality and Social Psychology, 21,* 256–264.

Valentino, N. A. (1999). Crime news and the priming of racial attitudes during evaluations of the president. *Public Opinion Quarterly, 63*(3), 293–320.

Velten, E. (1968). A laboratory task for the induction of mood states. *Behavior Research and Therapy, 6,* 473–482.

Wilson, T., & Capitman, J. (1982). Effects of script availability on social behavior. *Personality and Social Psychology Bulletin, 8,* 11–19.

Wyer, R., Jr., & Srull, T. (1980). The processing of social stimulus information: A conceptual integration. In R. Hastie, T. M. Ostrom, E. B. Ebbesen, R. S. Wyer, D. Hamilton, & D. E. Carlston (Eds.), *Personal memory: The cognitive basis of social perception* (pp. 227–300). Hillsdale, NJ: Erlbaum.

Wyer, R., Jr., & Srull, T. (1981). Category accessibility: Some theoretical and empirical issues concerning the processing of information. In E. Higgins, C. Herman, & M. Zanna (Eds.), *Social cognition* (Vol. 1, pp. 161–197). Hillsdale, NJ: Erlbaum.

CHAPTER 6

Cultivation

We have found that long-term exposure to television, in which frequent violence is virtually inescapable, tends to cultivate the image of a relatively mean and dangerous world.
—Gerbner, Gross, Morgan, Signorielli, & Shanahan, 2001

- 1994—Louis Harris and Associates find that 61 percent of people in the United States feel that television "contributes a lot" to violent acts in society.
- 1996—*U.S. News & World Report* pollsters find that three of every four Americans rate entertainment programs on television as having a "large impact" in contributing to violence.
- 2000—A Freedom Forum poll (Public Opinion Online, July 7, 2000) finds that 83 percent of Americans nationwide believe that television violence contributes either a great deal or somewhat to violence in real life.

Since the dawn of mass mediated entertainment, people have feared powerful and harmful media effects, especially on that segment of the population considered most vulnerable—the nation's children. As a result, the media effects tradition has been one of the most prolific, socially important, and highly scrutinized areas of mass communication research.

In the 1920s and 1930s, before television became a household fixture, feature films thrilled audiences by the millions in theaters across the country; however, those same films raised public concerns because of their violent and sometimes sexually explicit content. The Payne Fund studies brought together a group of social scientists who examined the effects of movies on the nation's youth.

Once television became entrenched in the American way of life, apprehension about negative media effects assumed a dominating presence on the public and political agenda. In the 1960s and 1970s, U.S. presidents appointed commissions and charged them with studying television violence and assessing its effects on young people.

Through the years the research findings have varied, but a number of studies have shown that the connection between viewing television violence and committing violent acts is not merely a public perception. Today, the research continues. Many answers have been determined, but many questions remain.

The **cultivation hypothesis** developed as one attempt to explain the influence of television on its viewers. The cultivation tradition grew out of a media violence research project called the Cultural Indicators Project, headed in the 1960s by George Gerbner, a University of Pennsylvania communication scholar. Since the early days of the project, cultivation research has expanded to encompass many topics in addition to media violence. Investigators now explore the relationship of long-term television viewing to the inculcation of various perceptions, values, and beliefs on the part of audiences.

Simply stated, the *cultivation hypothesis* proposes that over time, heavy viewers of television develop views of the world similar to what they see on television. Research has shown that certain characteristics among audiences tend to make cultivation effects more or less pronounced; for example, educational level has been shown to mediate cultivation effects. Among heavy viewers of television, those with higher levels of educational attainment are less likely to have their views of the world influenced by television.

The "symbolic world" of television is very different from objective reality, and this disparity has been a major point of interest for cultivation researchers. Examples of the distorted realities presented on television abound. Analyses of network television programs have revealed that most TV characters are young, energetic, and appealing. Few shows feature elderly people (age 65 or older) in starring or important roles, and when older people are used as characters they often portray sick or dying people. Needless to say, television does not accurately reflect the true proportions, conditions, or health status of the elderly population in American society today.

Violent crime serves as the most obvious example of television's distortion of reality. With all the gun battles, fist fights, karate chops, and high-speed chases that occur as standard fare on most programs, it should come as no surprise that in a given week, more than half of all the leading characters on television are involved in some kind of violent act. Actual crime statistics from the FBI tell a much different story. In a single year, less than 1 percent of the population in the United States actually falls victim to criminal acts.

The Cultural Indicators Project

- Initiated in 1967 by George Gerbner.
- First study conducted for President Johnson's National Commission on the Causes and Prevention of Violence.
- Introduced the Mean World Index, an instrument used to measure people's perceptions about violence and aggression in the world.
- Performs content analysis of televised violence each year.

- Focuses on content of network television, both prime-time dramas during the week and daytime programming on weekends.
- Investigates the "cultivation" effect on audiences due to portrayals on television on issues of gender, age-role stereotypes, the family, and so forth.

Long-term exposure to television may cause viewers to believe the world is a more violent place than it actually is.
Source: © The Everett Collection

Research has shown that among certain groups of people, heavy viewers of television tend to cultivate the same distorted pictures of reality that they see on television. Using the examples of the condition of the elderly and the frequency of criminal acts, heavy viewers tend to *underestimate* the number of elderly people in the U.S. population as well as their health status. In addition, heavy viewers consistently *overestimate* real-world crime statistics.

Cultivation analysis is one of three components in the Cultural Indicators Project. The other two research activities include institutional process analysis and message system analysis. **Institutional process analysis** examines the production, management, and distribution of media messages. **Message system analysis** involves the investigation of images in the media content, such as gender roles, portrayal of minorities, and the way certain occupations are depicted.

Since the Cultural Indicators Project began, most studies have revealed only low-level evidence of a cultivation effect, but the consistency of such findings has offered credence to the hypothesis. Gerbner and his associates insisted that cultivation has considerable implications for society, despite low-level correlations. They often made the analogy between cultivation effects upon society and global temperature changes upon climate—a variance of only a few degrees in temperature would result in another ice age, they said.

Cultivation is usually described as a *hypothesis* rather than a formal media effects *theory* due to a lack of supporting, empirical evidence to explain how the cultivation process occurs. In particular, studies have not revealed the psychological dimensions of cultivation—how television viewers learn to construct their views of social reality.

Through the years, most explanations of media effects have been firmly grounded in theories of cognitive psychology. Media effects scholars trained in this tradition have criticized the work of Gerbner and his associates for their lack of emphasis on cognitive processes (Hawkins & Pingree, 1990; Potter, 1994;

- Television as the great storyteller—wholesale distributor of images
- Mainstreaming
- Resonance
- Interaction
- Complex psychological processes

Bryant, 1986). Much of the criticism has been constructive, leading Gerbner and other cultivation researchers to make revisions and improvements in their explanation of the hypothesis. Research that explores the cognitive dimensions of cultivation continues.

In this chapter, we explore the research domain of cultivation analysis. In addition to the conceptual roots and criticisms of cultivation, we examine the theoretical bases for the hypothesis, the research tradition, and recent research, and we close with a word about the direction that cultivation research seems to be heading.

CONCEPTUAL ROOTS AND CRITICISMS

Cultivation adherents argue that television, as a "wholesale distributor of images," is different from other mass media (Morgan & Signorielli, 1990, p. 13). It serves as the *great storyteller* of our age. Programs are produced to appeal to the entire population. Even very young viewers find it easy to become enthralled by an entertaining television show.

According to these researchers, the diverse publics that make up the United States—the poor children living in a housing project in Georgia, the wealthy families living in an exclusive neighborhood in New York, the farm families in middle America, and the sorority girls on a West Coast campus—all tend to think more alike when watching television because they all receive similar messages. All television programs, from entertaining action programs to news programs, possess similar, repetitive patterns, sometimes called myths, "facts," or ideologies. These patterns are thought to influence viewers' perceptions of the world. Long-term exposure to these overall patterns of television programming is most likely to result in "the steady entrenchment of mainstream orientations for most viewers" (Gerbner et al., 1994, p. 25).

Mainstreaming is one the principal concepts that underlie cultivation analysis; another is *resonance*. The concept of **mainstreaming** assumes that dominant sets of attitudes, beliefs, values, and practices exist within cultures. Patterns also emerge across the spectrum of television programming—patterns regarding outcomes to various situations, gender roles, minority representations, and so forth. These patterns result in a "mainstream" set of attitudes, beliefs, and values that are repetitively presented on television. Heavy television viewers tend to cultivate similar mainstream views. Cultivation researchers Nancy Signorielli and Michael Morgan defined the concept in this way:

Mainstreaming means that heavy viewing may absorb or override differences in perspectives and behavior which ordinarily stem from other factors and influences. In other words, differences found in the responses of different groups of viewers, differences that usually are associated with the varied cultural, social, and political characteristics of these groups, are diminished or even absent from the responses of heavy viewers in these same groups. (1996, p. 117)

Resonance occurs when real-world events support the distorted image of reality shown on television. Whenever direct experience is in agreement with the messages from television, the messages are reinforced—they *resonate*—and the cultivation effect is amplified. For example, research has shown that the heavy television viewers who are most likely to fear crime are those who live in inner-city areas where crime rates are high (Morgan, 1983).

Cultivation researchers stress that the concept of cultivation assumes that television and its publics *interact* in a dynamic process. The extent to which a person cultivates the messages seen on television depends upon a number of factors. Some people are more susceptible to cultivation influence due to personality traits, social background, cultural mores, and even their past television viewing experiences. Gerbner and his associates explained the interaction process in this way:

Although a viewer's gender, or age, or class makes a difference in perspective, television viewing can make a similar and interacting difference. Viewing may help define what it means, for example, to be an adolescent female member of a given social class. The interaction is a continuous process (as is cultivation) beginning with infancy and going on from cradle to grave. (1994, p. 23).

Cultivation scholars define television exposure in terms of time. They assume that television messages are relatively *uniform* in nature and that viewing of television is *nonselective.* In other words, the narrative structure of various types of programs—cartoons, dramatic movies, crime shows—often resemble each other in terms of casting, action, and other factors. In this sense, scholars say, the messages are uniform. The concept of nonselective viewing is based on the idea of *ritualized viewing* or habitual viewing—watching television at certain times and being confined to whatever programs are offered for viewing at those times.

Critics say that the *conceptualizations* (precise definitions of major concepts in a theory) associated with cultivation need further explication. For example, the "uniform messages" and "underlying narratives" purportedly present in various types of television shows should be clearly articulated (Potter, 1993). Also, the validity of concepts such as resonance and mainstreaming are difficult to test using rigorous social scientific methods.

As mentioned previously, many have argued that complex psychological processes form the basis for cultivation effects, but most studies have not been directed toward identifying the cognitive components (Hawkins & Pingree, 1990; Potter, 1993). The ways in which cognitive mechanisms involved in cultivation resemble those of social learning theory need to be examined (Bryant, 1986).

The critics continue to call for more specific explication of key concepts in cultivation, and a more intense research agenda that will eventually answer questions about the cognitive processes at work in cultivation effects. The criticisms and the call for a new research agenda for the next generation of cultivation researchers (made in 1986) have not yet been answered completely.

> What I hope to see omitted is a helter-skelter, nontheoretical examination of the potential cultivation impact of consuming heavy versus light doses of specified television programming of types *a* versus *b* versus *c* on the perceptions of audiences with demographic characteristics of types *x* versus *y* versus *z*. For far too long communication scholars have conducted such investigations in other social impact domains, seemingly ad infinitum, in the false name of generalizability. (Bryant, 1986, p. 234)

THEORETICAL BASES FOR CULTIVATION

Cultivation assumes that television has become a primary source of shared meanings and messages for people in the United States and throughout the world. It has evolved into a medium with many functions for people in modern society. According to Signorielli and Morgan:

> Television has thus become our nation's (and increasingly the world's) most common and constant learning environment. It both mirrors and leads society. It serves, however, first and foremost as our storyteller; it has become the wholesale distributor of images which form the mainstream of our popular culture. The world of television shows and tells us about life—people, places, striving, power, and fate. It presents the good and bad, the happy and sad, the powerful and the weak, and lets us know who or what is successful or a failure. (1996, p. 114)

The idea of shared meanings and *symbolic interaction* through language dates back to George Herbert Mead, a philosopher at the University of Chicago at the turn of the 20th century. Some researchers feel that the concept of cultivation is more appropriately placed within the meaning paradigm, rather than within the cognitive paradigm of social psychology which has been used to support much of the media effects research tradition. In the words of Morgan and Signorielli, cultivation analysis "is designed to understand gradual, long-term shifts and transformations in the way generations are socialized (not short-term, dramatic changes in individuals' beliefs or behaviors)" (1990, p. 19).

Gerbner and his associates elaborated on the differences in theoretical bases for cultivation and other types of media effects research:

> Traditional effects research is based on evaluating specific informational, educational, political, or marketing efforts in terms of selective exposure and measurable differences between those exposed and others. Scholars steeped in those traditions find it difficult to accept the emphasis of cultivation analysis on total immersion rather than selective viewing and on the spread of stable similarities of outlook rather than on the remaining sources of cultural differentiation and change . . . Cultivation theory is based on the results of research finding a persistent and pervasive pull of the television mainstream on a great variety of conceptual currents and countercurrents. The focus on broad commonalties

of perspective among heavy viewers of otherwise varied backgrounds requires a theoretical and methodological approach different from traditional media effects research and appropriate to the distinct dynamics of television. (1994, pp. 20–21)

Other researchers insist that psychological processes underlie the cultivation process, and therefore the *cognitive paradigm* should serve as the theoretical base. R. P. Hawkins and S. Pingree (1982) have theorized that the cultivation process involves *learning* and *construction*. The viewer learns by watching television, perceiving and remembering the contents. The viewer constructs an outlook regarding the real world based upon what has been learned from television viewing.

The social cognitive theory, advanced by Albert Bandura (1986), states that the actions and behavior of a person are determined by both internal factors (intelligence and biological factors) and external factors (such as environmental events). Three components—behavior, internal factors, and external factors—interact at varying degrees and varying levels. The effects of mass communication are also influenced by the presence and interaction of the three components (Bandura, 1994).

RESEARCH TRADITION

The Cultural Indicators Project began in the late 1960s when national concern about violence prompted federal investigations and congressional funding for research. The project commenced under the auspices of President Lyndon Johnson's National Commission on the Causes and Prevention of Violence, then continued with funds from the Surgeon General's Scientific Advisory Committee on Television and Social Behavior.

Since the project began, Gerbner and his associates have periodically analyzed the content of prime-time dramatic television shows to determine the number of violent acts and criminal activities. In addition to documenting the amount of televised violence, researchers also assessed the types or nature of the violence. These reports have received a great deal of media attention through the years.

In the early 1970s, the National Institute of Mental Health offered funding support, and researchers implemented the cultivation analysis component of the project. In subsequent years, the American Medical Association, the Office of Telecommunications Policy, the Administration on Aging, the National Science Foundation, the Ad Hoc Committee on Religious Television Research, and other agencies have funded cultivation research (Morgan & Signorielli, 1990).

Since the early days of the project, researchers have explored a variety of topics in addition to television violence. For example, studies have examined the connection between television viewing and audience perceptions and actions in relation to age-role stereotypes (Gerbner et al., 1980), gender-role stereotypes (Morgan, 1982; Rothschild, 1984), and many other realms (Gerbner et al., 2001).

Cultivation research has typically involved two research methods: content analysis of television programs and survey methods to assess viewer perceptions of the world. In measuring cultivation effects related to violence, researchers developed the Mean World Index, a tool for measuring perceptions of the prevalence of violence and danger in the world (Signorielli, 1990). Among various demographic groups, heavy viewers of television score consistently higher on the Mean World Index than light viewers.

Throughout the history of cultivation research, criticisms have abounded. A number of scholars expressed concerns about statistical controls and interpretation of cultivation findings (Hirsch, 1980; Hughes, 1980; and Wober, 1978. Others questioned the causal order of effects in cultivation research and objected to certain theoretical formulations (Doob & Macdonald, 1979; Zillmann, 1980). Still other researchers argued that psychological dimensions should be incorporated into cultivation theory, that research should not merely *show* the connection between television viewing and beliefs about social reality, but *explain* it (Hawkins & Pingree, 1980, 1982; Hawkins, Pingree, & Adler, 1987; Pingree, 1983; Hawkins & Pingree, 1990). Along these lines, Hawkins and Pingree insisted that "without evidence for psychological processes, the cultivation hypothesis stands on a tenuous foundation" (1990, p. 36).

Providing empirical proof for the psychological processes to explain cultivation effects has been difficult, but research continues. A number of researchers have advanced models and tested them, but empirical support for the models remains somewhat inconsistent and incomplete (Hawkins, Pingree, & Adler, 1987; Potter, 1991a, 1991b; Rubin, Perse, & Taylor, 1988; see also Potter, 1993).

RECENT RESEARCH AND FUTURE TRENDS

Cultivation researchers continue to answer their critics and to collect evidence for cultivation effects. In recent years, researchers have expanded their domain to include countries throughout the world. Some of these studies attempt to determine "global" perceptions of social reality attributed to television viewing (Morgan, 1990), but such attempts have not addressed particular empirical problems, such as the development of simple quantitative indicators of culture that would allow researchers to apply the indicators across cultures.

Studies have examined cultivation effects in foreign countries that import considerable television programming from the United States. Findings have varied, but most indicate interactions between television viewing and cultural contexts. Most reveal a cultivation of attitudes toward violence, values, social stereotypes, and other areas of interest similar to the distorted pictures of reality shown on television. Sweden (Reimer & Rosengren, 1990), Argentina (Morgan & Shanahan, 1995), and Japan (Saito, 1991) are among the several countries that have been the focus of such cultivation analyses. In Australia, Pingree and Hawkins (1981) found that students with high levels of exposure to television programming from the United States were more likely to rate Australia as a dangerous place to live. A study in Korea found that Korean women with high levels of exposure to U.S. television programs were more likely to have liberal views regarding marriage, clothing, and music, but Korean males who were heavy viewers of U.S. programming supported traditional Korean cultural values and expressed hostility toward the United States (Kang & Morgan, 1988).

- People who watch a lot of news programs on television usually watch a lot of other television programs.
- Regular television viewers are likely to watch popular fare on their VCRs and cable—programs similar in content to those they are accustomed to seeing on television.

- The strength of cultivation or the child's resistance to it depends upon whether or not parents watch television with their child and upon the cohesiveness of the family unit.
- Children who watch a lot of television tend to eat more candy, desserts, and unhealthy foods, and they believe meals from fast-food restaurants are more nutritious than a home-cooked meal.

Other studies have updated findings from earlier investigations by collecting data from more recent television programming. For example, one recent study (Shanahan & Morgan, 1999) confirmed evidence from earlier studies that heavy viewing of television causes people to overestimate the incidence of real-world violence and hold many other inaccurate beliefs related to criminal activity and crime statistics. N. Signorielli and N. Kahlenberg (2001) found that despite significant role changes for women in the real world, television continues to depict a world with males in the majority of roles by 60 to 65 percent; this does represent an improvement from depictions in the 1970s and 1980s, when television programs contained three men to every one woman.

Researchers have also tested the cultivation effects of heavy television viewing on attitudes toward family values, the environment, and health-related topics. As for family values, one interesting study found that television depictions of the American family in the 1990s did not reflect reality, but over-represented single-parent households (Morgan, Leggett, & Shanahan, 1999). Moreover, single parents on television were usually males with live-in help, unlike real-world situations. The research found that heavy television viewers possibly romanticize single parenthood, as they tend to be more accepting of single-parent households and unwed mothers. On the issue of the environment, heavy viewers tend to cultivate a fearful withdrawal from scientific issues in general (Shanahan, Morgan, & Stenbjerre, 1997). Heavy television viewers are less likely than others to have knowledge of environmental issues. As for health-related topics, heavy television viewing affected children's views about nutrition (Signorielli & Staples, 1997).

Several recent studies have explored the cognitive processing involved in cultivation. M. Shapiro and A. Lang (1991) suggested that cultivation of beliefs that are incorrect or exaggerated stems from the tendency of heavy viewers to forget that television programming is not real. One study confirmed the hypothesis (Mares, 1996), but another interpreted the data differently (Shrum, 1999, 1997, 1995). M. L. Mares found that viewers who confused fictional programs with fact were more likely to cultivate a view of the world in line with the world shown on television. L. J. Shrum contended that viewers do not consider whether what they are watching is fact or fiction, but viewers use television

Cultivation researchers offer the following argument in answer to critics and in favor of their research approach, and as an explanation of the differences between cultivation research and standard effects research.

Traditional effects research is based on evaluating specific informational, educational, political, or marketing efforts in terms of selective exposure and measurable before/after differences between those exposed to some message and others not exposed. Scholars steeped in those traditions find it difficult to accept the emphasis of cultivation analysis on total immersion rather than selective viewing and on the spread of stable similarities of outlook rather than on the remaining sources of cultural differentiation and change.

Similarly, we are still imbued with the ideology of print culture and its ideals of freedom, diversity, and active electorate. This ideal also assumes the production and selection of information and entertainment from the point of view of a variety of competing and conflicting interests. That is why many also resist what they assume to be the emphasis of cultivation analysis on the "passive" viewer and the dissolution of authentic publics that this emphasis implies. They point to what they see as serious differences between cultivation theory and more recent excursions into reception models of mass communication. From the reception perspective, it seems logical to argue that other circumstances do intervene and can neutralize the cultivation process, that viewers construct meaning from texts is more important than how much they watch.

Source: Gerbner et al., (in press).

images whenever making cognitive judgements about social issues. Heavy television viewers answer questions more readily than others, indicating that some sort of cognitive shortcut has been forged and that answers are more readily accessible. Shrum's explanation suggests that the cultivation process strengthens a viewer's beliefs rather than changing them.

Cultivation research in the 21st century will need to consider the growing popularity of cable and satellite networks, use of videocassette recorders (VCRs), and the Internet, and the impact of these on the traditional network television audience. So far, no studies have determined great differences in viewing habits or content for heavy viewers despite the proliferation of viewer choices (Morgan, Shanahan, & Harris, 1990). Internet users watch less television than nonusers, but research has also shown that most Internet users were not among heavy television viewers to begin with (Gerbner et al., 2001).

Cultivation researchers point out that, despite the diversity of choices in media entertainment, concentrations of ownership will continue to spell similarities across media and channels. Nonetheless, cultivation research will expand its horizons to include investigations into the impact of messages from these new avenues and media technologies (Gerbner et al., 2001).

SUMMARY

The cultivation hypothesis developed as one attempt to explain the influence of television on its viewers. The tradition grew out of the Cultural Indicators Project, a media violence research project headed in the 1960s by George Gerbner.

The hypothesis proposes that over time, heavy viewers of television develop views of the world similar to what they see on television. The symbolic world of television is very different from objective reality, and this disparity is a major point of interest for cultivation researchers. Research has shown that among certain groups of people, heavy viewers of television tend to cultivate the same distorted pictures of reality that they see on television.

Cultivation analysis is one of three components in the cultural indicators project. Institutional process analysis examines the production, management, and distribution of media messages. Message system analysis involves the investigation of images in the media content, such as gender roles, portrayal of minorities, and the way certain occupations are depicted.

Cultivation is usually described as a hypothesis rather than a formal media effects theory due to a lack of supporting, empirical evidence to explain how the cultivation process occurs. In particular, studies have not revealed the psychological dimensions of cultivation or how television viewers learn to construct their views of social reality.

Media effects scholars trained in the psychological tradition have criticized the work of Gerbner and his associates for their lack of emphasis on cognitive processes. Much of the criticism has proven to be constructive, leading cultivation researchers to make revisions and improvements in their explanation of the hypothesis.

Cultivation assumes that diverse publics all become similar when watching television, because all receive similar messages. Long-term exposure to these overall patterns of television programming is likely to result in a phenomenon the researchers call mainstreaming, the assumption that dominant sets of attitudes, beliefs, values, and practices exist within cultures, and that most television programs present and perpetuate such values. Resonance, another concept associated with cultivation, occurs when real-world events support the distorted image of reality shown on television.

Cultivation research has typically involved two research methods: content analysis of television programs and survey methods to assess viewer perceptions of the world. In measuring cultivation effects related to violence, researchers developed the Mean World Index as a tool for measuring viewer perceptions of the prevalence of violence and danger in the world.

Critics say the conceptualizations (precise definitions of major concepts in a theory) associated with cultivation need further explication. According to some critics, the terms *uniform messages* and *underlying narratives* have not been clearly articulated, and the validity of concepts such as *resonance* and *mainstreaming* are difficult to test using rigorous social scientific methods.

REFERENCES

BANDURA, A. (1986). *Social foundations of thought and action: A social cognitive theory.* Englewood Cliffs, NJ: Prentice-Hall.

BANDURA, A. (1994). Social cognitive theory of mass communication. In J. Bryant & D. Zillmann (Eds.), *Media effects: Advances in theory and research* (pp. 61–90). Hillsdale, NJ: Erlbaum.

BRYANT, J. (1986). The road most traveled: Yet another cultivation critique. *Journal of Broadcasting & Electronic Media, 30,* 231–235.

DOOB, A. N., & MACDONALD, G. E. (1979). Television viewing and fear of victimization: Is the relationship causal? *Journal of Personality and Social Psychology, 37*, 170–179.

GERBNER, G., GROSS, L., MORGAN, M., & SIGNORIELLI, N. (1994). Growing up with television: The cultivation perspective. In J. Bryant & D. Zillmann (Eds.), *Media effects: Advances in theory and research* (pp. 17–41). Hillsdale, NJ: Erlbaum.

GERBNER, G., GROSS, L., MORGAN, M., SIGNORIELLI, N., & SHANAHAN, J. (In press). Growing up with television: Cultivation processes. In J. Bryant & D. Zillmann (Eds.), *Media effects: Advances in theory and research* (2nd ed.). Mahwah, NJ: Erlbaum.

GERBNER, G. GROSS, L., SIGNORIELLI, N., & MORGAN, M. (1980). Aging with television: Images on television drama and conceptions of social reality. *Journal of Communication, 30*(1), 37–47.

HAWKINS, R. P., & PINGREE, S. (1980). Some processes in the cultivation effect. *Communication Research, 7*, 193–226.

HAWKINS, R. P., & PINGREE, S. (1982). Television's influence on social reality. In D. Pearl, L. Bouthilet, & J. Lazar (Eds.), *Television and behavior: Ten years of scientific progress and implications for the eighties* (DHHS Publication No. ADM 82–1196, Vol. 2, pp. 224–247). Washington, DC: U.S. Government Printing Office.

HAWKINS, R. P., & PINGREE, S. (1990). Divergent psychological processes in constructing social reality from mass media content. In N. Signorielli & M. Morgan (Eds.), *Cultivation analysis: New directions in media effects research* (pp. 35–50). Newbury Park, CA: Sage.

HAWKINS, R. P., PINGREE, S., & ADLER, I. (1987). Searching for cognitive processes in the cultivation effect: Adult and adolescent samples in the United States and Australia. *Human Communication Research, 13*, 553–577.

HIRSCH, P. M. (1980). The "scary world" of the nonviewer and other anomalies: A reanalysis of Gerbner et al.'s findings on cultivation analysis. *Communication Research, 7*, 403–456.

HUGHES, M. (1980). The fruits of cultivation analysis: A reexamination of some effects of television watching. *Public Opinion Quarterly, 44*, 287–302.

KANG, J. G., & MORGAN, M. (1988). Culture clash: U.S. television programs in Korea. *Journalism Quarterly, 65*, 431–438.

MARES, M. (1996). The role of source confusions in television's cultivation of social reality judgements. *Human Communication Research, 23*, 278–297.

MORGAN, M. (1982). Television and adolescents' sex-role stereotypes: A longitudinal study. *Journal of Personality and Social Psychology, 43*, 947–955.

MORGAN, M. (1983). Symbolic victimization and real world fear. *Human Communication Research, 9*, 146–157.

MORGAN, M. (1990) International cultivation analysis. In N. Signorielli & M. Morgan (Eds.), *Cultivation analysis: New directions in media effects research* (pp. 225–248). Newbury Park, CA: Sage.

MORGAN, M., LEGGETT, S., & SHANAHAN, J. (1999). Television and "family values": Was Dan Quayle right? *Mass Communication and Society, 2*(1/2): 47–63.

MORGAN, M., & SHANAHAN, J. (1995). Democracy tango: Television, adolescents, and authoritarian tensions in Argentina. Cresskill, NJ: Hampton Press.

MORGAN, M., SHANAHAN, J., & HARRIS, C. (1990). VCRs and the effects of television: New diversity or more of the same? In J. Dobrow (Ed.), *Social and cultural aspects of VCR use* (pp. 107–123). Hillsdale, NJ: Erlbaum.

MORGAN, M., & SIGNORIELLI, N. (1990). Cultivation analysis: Conceptualization and methodology. In N. Signorielli & M. Morgan (Eds.), *Cultivation analysis: New directions in media effects research* (pp. 13–34). Newbury Park, CA: Sage.

PINGREE, S. (1983). Children's cognitive processes in constructing social reality. *Journalism Quarterly, 60*, 415–422.

PINGREE, S., & HAWKINS, R. P. (1981). U.S. programs on Australian television: The cultivation effect. *Journal of Communication, 31*(1), 97–105.

POTTER, W. J. (1991a). Examining cultivation from a psychological perspective: Component subprocesses. *Communication Research, 18*, 77–102.

POTTER, W. J. (1991b). The relationships between first and second order measures of cultivation. *Human Communication Research, 18*, 92–113.

POTTER, W. J. (1993). Cultivation theory and research: A conceptual critique. *Human Communication Research, 19*(4), 564–601.

POTTER, W. J. (1994). Cultivation theory and research: A methodological critique. *Journalism Monographs, 147.* Columbia, SC: Association for Education in Journalism and Mass Communication.

REIMER, B., & ROSENGREN, K. E. (1990). Cultivated viewers and readers: A life-style perspective. In N. Signorielli & M. Morgan (Eds.), *Cultivation analysis: New directions in media effects research* (pp. 181–206). Newbury Park, CA: Sage.

ROTHSCHILD, N. (1984). Small group affiliation as a mediating factor in the cultivation process. In G. Melischek, K. E. Rosengren, & J. Stappers (Eds.), *Cultural indicators: An international symposium* (pp. 377–387). Vienna: Verlag der Osterreichischen Akademie der Wissenschaften.

RUBIN, A. M., PERSE, E. M., & TAYLOR, D. S. (1988). A methodological investigation of cultivation. *Communication Research, 15*, 107–134.

SAITO, S. (1991). *Does cultivation occur in Japan?: Testing the applicability of the cultivation hypothesis on Japanese television viewers.* Unpublished master's thesis, The Annenberg School for Communication, University of Pennsylvania.

SHANAHAN, J., & MORGAN, M. (1999). *Television and its viewers: Cultivation theory and research.* Cambridge: Cambridge University Press.

SHANAHAN, J., MORGAN, M., & STENBJERRE, M. (1997). Green or brown? Television's cultivation of environmental concern. *Journal of Broadcasting & Electronic Media, 41*, 305–323.

SHAPIRO, M., & LANG, A. (1991). Making television reality: Unconscious processes in the construction of social reality. *Communication Research, 18*, 685–705.

SHRUM, L. J. (1995). Assessing the social influence of television: A social cognition perspective on cultivation effects. *Communication Research, 22*, 402–429.

SHRUM, L. J. (1997). The role of source confusion in cultivation effects may depend on processing strategy: A comment on mares (1996). *Human Communication Research, 24*, 349–358.

SHRUM, L. J. (1999). The relationship of television viewing with attitude strength and extremity: Implications for the cultivation effect. *Media Psychology, 1*, 3–25.

SIGNORIELLI, N., & KAHLENBERG, N. (2001). The world of work in the nineties. *Journal of Broadcasting & Electronic Media, 45*, 4–22.

SIGNORIELLI, N., & MORGAN, M. (1996). Cultivation analysis: Research and practice. In M. B. Salwen & D. W. Stacks (Eds.), *An integrated approach to communication theory and research* (pp. 111–126). Mahwah, NJ: Erlbaum.

SIGNORIELLI, N., & STAPLES, J. (1997). Television and children's conceptions of nutrition. *Health Communication, 9*(4), 289–301.

SIGNORIELLI, N. (1990). Television's mean and dangerous world: A continuation of the cultural indicators perspective. In N. Signorielli & M. Morgan (Eds.), *Cultivation analysis: New directions in media effects research* (pp. 85–106). Newbury Park, CA: Sage.

WOBER, J. M. (1978). Televised violence and paranoid perception: The view from Great Britain. *Public Opinion Quarterly, 42*, 315–321.

ZILLMANN, D. (1980). Anatomy of suspense. In P. H. Tannenbaum (Ed.), *The entertainment functions of television* (pp. 133–163). Hillsdale, NJ: Erlbaum.

CHAPTER 7

Diffusion of Innovations

> *One should always remember that there is nothing more difficult to take in hand, more perilous to conduct, or more uncertain in its success, than to take the lead in the introduction of a new order of things. The innovator has for enemies all those who have done well under the old conditions, and lukewarm defenders in those who may do well under the new. This coolness arises partly from fear of the opponents, who have the laws on their side, and partly from the incredulity of men, who do not readily believe in new things until they have had a long experience with them.*
>
> **—Niccolo Machiavelli, *The Prince*, 1513**

Even though it is classified as an important theory in the field of communication, diffusion of innovations theory has known practical application in many other disciplines. Literally thousands of research studies have been generated in areas such as sociology, rural sociology, anthropology, economics, and medical sociology.

Diffusion of innovations research, even though it involves message effects, normally is not included beneath the heading of media effects research because, in many cases, *interpersonal* rather than *mediated* communication characterizes certain steps in the diffusion process. In some instances, however, media communications play a fundamental role in the diffusion of an innovation, as you will learn in Chapter 15 on communication campaigns. For this reason, a basic knowledge of diffusion of innovations theory and relevant research should prove helpful.

What is meant by the phrase diffusion of innovations? **Diffusion** is "the process by which an innovation is communicated through certain channels over time among the members of a social system"; An **innovation** is "an idea, practice, or object perceived as new by an individual or other unit of adoption" (Rogers & Singhal, 1996, p. 409; Rogers, 1995).

When it comes to diffusion of innovations, communication scholar Everett Rogers wrote the book. It's appropriately called *Diffusion of Innovations* (1962, 1995). In this classic text, Rogers analyzed thousands of diffusion studies in various disciplines over the years and found certain similarities: All the studies involved (1) an innovation, (2) communication from one person to another, (3) a society or community setting, and (4) the element of time.

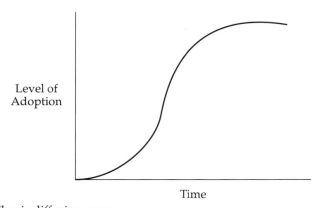

Level of
Adoption

Time

FIGURE 7.1. Classic diffusion curve.
Source: Adapted/Reprinted with the permission of the Free Press, a Division of Simon and Schuster, Inc., from Diffusion of Innovations, Fourth Edition by Everett M. Rogers, Copyright © 1962, 1971, 1983 by The Free Press.

Diffusion of innovations theory states that an innovation (i.e., an idea, new technique, new technology) diffuses or spreads throughout society in a predictable pattern. A few people will adopt an innovation as soon as they hear of it. Other people will take longer to try something new, and still others will take much longer. The pattern is that of an S-shaped curve (See Figure 7.1).

When a new media technology or other innovation is adopted rapidly by a great number of people, it is said to *explode* into being. Social scientists have borrowed a phrase from physicists to describe this adoption phenomenon, the concept of the **critical mass.** In physics, the critical mass has to do with the amount of radioactive agents needed to produce a chain reaction. In mass communication, the critical mass describes the point when adoption of an innovation takes off, when the greatest number of people begin to adopt it, and the dramatic upward line on the S-shaped curve begins its ascent (See Figure 7.2).

Rogers and other diffusion researchers have identified five separate innovation-adoption categories into which all people in a society will fall. These are termed *innovators, early adopters, early majority, late majority,* and *laggards.* Each group is discussed in the next section of this chapter.

Figure 7.3 shows the positions each of the adopter categories occupy on the S-shaped curve, revealing the different rates of adoption for each group. This S-shaped curve is actually the normal, bell-shaped curve that is distorted slightly due to the plotting of innovation adoption over time.

In this chapter we first discuss the five categories of adopters that diffusion scholars have identified. Next we examine the origins and conceptual roots of diffusion of innovations theory, and diffusion and adoption processes. We then describe some of the more important diffusion studies that researchers have conducted through the years, especially those that have advanced communication research and our particular area of focus, media effects. Finally, we explore recent diffusion research, including the popular study of news diffusion, and we plot future directions for diffusion research.

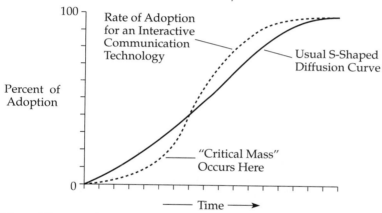

FIGURE 7.2. Adopter categorization on the basis of relative time of adoption of innovations.
Source: Adapted/Reprinted with the permission of The Free Press, a Division of Simon and Schuster, Inc., from *Diffusion of Innovations,* Fourth Edition by Everett M. Rogers. Copyright © 1995 by Everett M. Rogers. Copyright © 1962, 1971, 1983 by The Free Press.

FIGURE 7.3. The rate of adoption (1) for the usual innovation, and (2) for an interactive communication technology, showing the "critical mass."
Source: Reprinted with the permission of The Free Press, a Division of Simon & Schuster, Inc., from *Research Methods and the New Media* by Frederick Williams, Ronald E. Rice, Everett M. Rogers. Copyright © 1988 by The Free Press.

THE ADOPTER CATEGORIES

Rogers defined **adopter categories** as "the classifications of individuals within a social system on the basis of innovativeness" (1995, p. 148). In his work, first published in 1962, Rogers offered standardized titles to classify the various categories of adopters. These titles described ideal types on the continuum of innovativeness. Such standardization was needed because researchers were classifying adopter categories very differently. The five titles Rogers selected became normative in subsequent diffusion research. We now discuss each one in turn.

The Innovators

Innovators are described as venturesome and ready to try new things. Their social relationships tend to be more cosmopolitan than those of other groups. Such people tend to form cliques and communicate with one another despite geographical distances (Rogers, 1995).

The Early Adopters

Early adopters are more localite than cosmopolite. Due to their integral part in the local society, this adopter category produces the most opinion leaders of any other category. Early adopters are sought out for information about innovations, and their advice is valued. Those in this adopter category have the respect of others in the community because of their success and willingness to try innovations. The respect of others in the community is important to the early adopter, and actions are geared toward preserving that respect (Rogers, 1995).

The Early Majority

This adopter category includes people who do not wish to be the first to adopt new technologies or new ideas. Instead, the early majority prefers to deliberate, often for some period of time, before its members make a decision to adopt. These people serve the important function of *legitimizing* an innovation, or showing the rest of the community that the innovation is useful and adoption is desirable (Rogers, 1995).

The Late Majority

Members of the late majority are skeptical and cautious about the benefits of adoption. They wait until most of the community has already tried and adopted the innovation before they act. Sometimes peer pressure or social pressures serve to motivate the late majority. In other cases, economic necessity induces them to adopt the innovation (Rogers, 1995).

The Laggards

Members of this group are the last to adopt. The laggards are tied to the past, to the traditional way of doing things, and are very reluctant to try anything new. Consider, for example, a very old woman with traditional values and a rigid view of the world. This person might continue to use a 50-year-old stove rather than cook anything in the deluxe microwave oven the grandchildren gave her as a gift. She is used to the old stove. She trusts it and she trusts her knowledge of how to work it. The microwave sits in her kitchen for the remainder of her life, serving only as a stand for the African violets. Many of these people interact with others of the same mind-set. Once a laggard adopts an innovation, the rest of society may have moved so far forward that the "innovation" has become outdated (Rogers, 1995).

Diffusion of innovations is based upon the theories of a 19th-century French legal scholar and sociologist, Gabriel Tarde. In his book, *The Laws of Imitation* (1903), Tarde theorized about the S-shaped curve of innovation adoption and also about the importance of interpersonal communication. Rogers described Tarde's notion of the S-shaped curve in this way: "At first, only a few individuals adopt the new idea, then great numbers of individuals accept the innovation, and finally the rate of adoption slackens" (1995, pp. 28–29).

Tarde also introduced the notion of *opinion leadership,* an idea that was to become very important among media effects scholars several decades later. Tarde observed that certain people in the community were more interested in new ideas, new practices, and current events, and therefore were more knowledgeable about them than others. These people were valued within the community for their opinions on such matters. In many cases, the opinion leaders influenced their less knowledgeable neighbors to adopt an innovation.

CONCEPTUAL ROOTS

Imitation of others is essential to the diffusion of an innovation. If you will recall from Chapter 4, imitation is best explained by social learning theory, which also provides a solid conceptual foundation for diffusion theory. Rogers has stated outright that diffusion of innovations is firmly rooted in psychology and more specifically, social learning theory (Rogers & Singhal, 1996).

In the 1960s Albert Bandura (see Chapter 4) developed a comprehensive learning theory steeped in psychological principles. According to Bandura, diffusion of innovations is viewed in terms of symbolic modeling, persuasion, social prompting, and motivation. Three major events define the diffusion process: (1) when the person learns about the innovation, (2) when the person adopts the innovation or new behavior, and (3) when the person interacts with others in a social network, either encouraging them to adopt or confirming their own decision to adopt the innovation (Bandura, 1986). The psychological explanations for these events, in terms of social learning theory, are described below.

Step One—Learning about the Innovation

Symbolic modeling (e.g., an innovative behavior shown on television that is subsequently imitated by viewers) is the most common source of influence at the beginning of the diffusion process. Early adopters are usually those who read newspapers or watch television (Robertson, 1971). Many different cognitive factors, including those determinants of observational learning described in Chapter 4, affect the rate of adoption.

If an innovation is hard to understand and difficult to put to practical use, it will not be adopted as quickly as an innovation that is relatively simple to use (Torantzky & Klein, 1982). Some innovations must be spread through interpersonal contact and, in such situations, physical proximity affects adoption.

Step Two—Adoption of the Innovation

Whether or not a person *uses* or *adopts* the new behavior or innovation that has been learned depends upon many different factors. Research has shown that the greater the benefits, the more the incentive to adopt a particular behavior (Ostlund, 1974; Rogers & Shoemaker, 1971). For example, throughout the 1990s owners of businesses have seen the advantages of utilizing the Internet for their businesses, helping the adoption rate of the Internet to explode and critical mass to be achieved.

Adoption of innovations is also affected by **self-efficacy,** or belief in one's own abilities. Before a person decides to try something new, that person usually asks the question, "Can I do it?" If the individual perceives that he or she can indeed succeed, then it is more likely that the new behavior will be attempted and possibly adopted (Bandura, 1992). Once again using adoption of the Internet as an example, if the small business owner perceives that computers are too difficult to master, he or she would be less likely to adopt and utilize the Internet.

Status incentives are some of the most powerful motivational factors for adoption of something new. The latest hairstyles, new fashions, or use of the MP3 or e-mail by college students serve as good examples. Some people like to be the first to have and use new items or experiment with new styles. Once the majority has adopted those items or styles, their value as status symbols is gone and the early adopters must find other novel items or styles.

Adoption also depends upon a person's individual values and perceptions of self. If new behaviors or innovations conflict in some way with those values or perceptions, the person is less likely to adopt. For example, children who are brought up to view smoking and drinking as sinful and morally wrong and who have sincerely internalized these values may be more reluctant than others to experiment with such behaviors.

Research has also shown that innovations that can be tested on a limited basis before the person commits to adoption are more likely to be readily adopted. The higher the cost and the greater the effort in trying the new behavior, the less the likelihood of adopting.

Step Three—Developing Social Networks after Adoption

People are linked by various social networks. Cohesive groups such as the immediate family, close friends, clubs, co-workers, fraternities and sororities, and church members create "clusters" in the overall network of social ties. In addition to these cohesive groups, a person is also in contact with more distant groups, such as those who call a particular city or state home, that can be considered weaker links of the network.

The third step in successful diffusion of an innovation involves interpersonal communication among casual acquaintances—the weaker links of the communication network. Research has shown that cohesive, close groups or clusters of people learn of innovations through these weak social ties (Granovetter, 1983).

In the diffusion and adoption process, research has shown that public channels of communication, or communication by way of mass media, usually serve to spread the awareness of an innovation much faster than interpersonal channels. Interpersonal communications often prove essential in influencing people to adopt the idea or innovation that mass media have introduced to them.

Communication scholars have identified four key steps that effectively summarize the diffusion process (Williams, Strover, & Grant, 1994). These are knowledge, persuasion, decision, and confirmation.

Knowledge

A person or members of a community become aware of some new innovation or communication technology—high definition television (HDTV), for example, or a new software program for home computers. At this first step in the diffusion process, information is passed through some channel of communication, usually mass media or telecommunications media, but sometimes by way of interpersonal contact.

Persuasion

Step two of the diffusion process takes place mostly within the mind of the potential adopter. The individual weighs the advantages that the new technology would bring to him or her personally. Based upon these evaluations and discussions with others, the individual begins to lean toward either adoption or rejection of the innovation.

Decision

With this step, the individual makes the final decision of whether to adopt or reject. As the next step will show, however, this decision is not irreversible.

Confirmation

Once a decision is made, the individual normally seeks validation. Whether the decision was to adopt or to reject, the person continues to evaluate the consequences of the decision. If the decision was to reject, new information or economic pressures might compel the person to adopt the innovation after all.

IMPORTANT DIFFUSION STUDIES

Through the years, a number of studies of diffusion of innovations have defined the parameters, conceptualizations, and research methods that paved the way for many subsequent studies. This section provides a brief summary of several important investigations involving the diffusion of an innovation.

Wissler's Study of Diffusion of Horses among Plains Indians

One early study in the 1920s traced the diffusion of the horse from the Spanish explorers to American Indians, particularly the tribes of Plains Indians. Anthropologist Clark Wissler (1923) conducted this historical diffusion study. As with most diffusion studies in anthropology, Wissler was concerned with the effects such an innovation wrought on the society or community. He found that the introduction of horses disrupted the peaceful existence of the Plains Indians. Suddenly they began warring with neighboring tribes.

The Iowa Hybrid Corn Seed Study

The study that served as the model for subsequent diffusion of innovations research was the Iowa hybrid corn seed study conducted by Ryan and Gross (1943). In this important study, rural sociologists plotted innovation patterns of a community of farmers who had begun using a hybrid seed corn that reportedly increased corn yields by 20 percent an acre. Through hundreds of personal interviews, the researchers were able to trace the pattern of innovation adoption in the community and understand why it had taken more than a decade for the vast majority of farmers to adopt the advantageous and profitable hybrid seed corn.

The researchers uncovered several reasons why adoption of the innovation had been so slow. The farmers had to purchase the hybrid corn at a per bushel price from a certain company, and the price was relatively expensive at that time (the years of the Great Depression). Also, when farmers used hybrid seed corn they no longer needed to select beautiful ears of corn to be used as seed for the next year—a common practice among the farmers that apparently was emotionally hard to give up. Finally, agricultural innovations were rare at that time and farmers were not used to them. In subsequent years such innovations were abundant and became commonplace.

The Iowa hybrid seed corn study was one of the first diffusion studies to use statistical methods of analysis. It established the research paradigm for subsequent diffusion research projects.

Diffusion of News

A number of studies examined the diffusion of news or information, and these became of particular interest to communication scholars (Rogers, 1962; Rogers & Singhal, 1996; Williams, Strover, & Grant, 1994). P. J. Deutschmann and W. A. Danielson (1960) examined diffusion of news and found that it diffused much more rapidly than other innovations. (As Deutschmann described it to Everett Rogers, it was "damn fast diffusion.") This study was especially important because it interested many other communication researchers in the study of news diffusion at the local, national, and international levels.

In 1962 Deutschmann teamed up with Orlando Fals Borda in Colombia to conduct one of the first diffusion studies in a developing nation. Such studies

Television has diffused throughout the world,
even into very poor countries.
Source: © 2001 CORBIS

became very popular in subsequent years, especially among communication scholars interested in the diffusion of new technologies. The researchers studied the diffusion of agricultural innovations such as fertilizer and pesticides. Their results were similar to those of diffusion studies conducted in the United States among commercial farmers.

Also in the 1960s several sociologists conducted a famous study involving the diffusion of a new drug (tetracycline) among physicians. They found the familiar S-shaped curve of adoption, but were intrigued by the short (when compared to the Iowa hybrid seed corn study) 17-month period required for full adoption. The researchers discovered that interpersonal communication networks among the physicians were more influential in affecting rates of adoption than communications from mass media such as medical journals or drug company advertisements. Media channels provided the physicians with awareness of the drug and some knowledge of its properties. However, most of them tried the drug only after talking to another physician who had already used it with some success (Coleman, Katz, & Menzel, 1966).

More recently, as will be shown in the next section, communication scholars who study news diffusion have focused their attention on the emotional component that drives news diffusion, and diffusion of news through new media technologies, especially interactive media such as electronic mail or faxes. Some have concentrated their investigations on the critical mass aspect of the diffusion process (Markus, 1987). Diffusion of innovations related to health information has also been scrutinized by communication scholars.

CURRENT AND FUTURE DIFFUSION RESEARCH

One area of diffusion research that has been popular in recent years among those who study mass communication has been that of news diffusion from either broadcast or print media or both. Most studies have examined the spread of news from a mediated source that subsequently filtered through interpersonal channels. The space shuttle *Challenger* disaster in 1986 produced a bevy of studies related to news diffusion (Kubey & Peluso, 1990; Mayer et al., 1990; Riffe & Stovall, 1989; Wright et al., 1989).

Health communication has provided another prolific and highly practical realm for diffusion of innovations theory, especially AIDS-related diffusion studies and family planning promotion (Vaughan & Rogers, 2000). For instance, M. D. Basil and W. J. Brown (1994) focused on interpersonal channels of communication that developed following the media announcement by basketball great Magic Johnson that he had tested HIV positive. Diffusion theory has been applied in a study of work-site AIDS programs (Backer & Rogers, 1998) and another 1998 study identified means to enhance the effectiveness of programs that promote HIV/AIDS awareness and prevention (Svenkerud & Singhal, 1998). Diffusion theory has also been used in the identification of effective HIV/AIDS programs in Thailand (Svenkerud, Singhal, & Papa, 1998). Other scholars noticed effects from media messages that promoted family planning among Tanzanians (Vaughan & Rogers, 2000). A radio soap opera called *Twende na Wakati* (Let's Go with the Times) proved an effective way of promoting family planning by means of parasocial interaction between audience members and media characters, which included audience members' identification and involvement with the characters to the extent that they modeled their behavior after them. Interpersonal channels also affected the spread and adoption of the message.

In addition to health communication and various aspects of news diffusion (Price & Czilli, 1996; De Fleur & Cronin, 1991), other recent applications of diffusion of innovation theory have advanced knowledge in political and social sciences (Studlar, 1999; Valente & Davis, 1999; Mintrom, 1997), marketing (Dekimpe, Parker, & Sarvary, 2000), and even geography (Brown, 1999). The highly practical and applied nature of diffusion research has made it one of the most prolific of research domains. Its applicability across disciplines attests to its strength and utility as a theory.

One of the goals for communication scholarship (research and pedagogy) will be the continued use of diffusion research for solutions to practical problems. The proliferation of new media technology has become of intense interest to communication scholars, and diffusion studies in this country and throughout the world will examine the impact and spread of these innovations. More studies are needed that examine the diffusion of news from mass mediated sources. The *Challenger* disaster of 1986 allowed scholars to examine the emotional component that drives the diffusion of news in extraordinary situations, but more recent major news events that elicited emotional reactions from audiences have gone unnoticed by scholars interested in news diffusion. Studies that identify techniques that successfully communicate and diffuse health-related news and information undoubtedly will continue to be a highly important arm of research based upon diffusion theory.

Another goal will be to employ additional theories to aid in the study of diffusion, and, especially, the understanding of new media technology diffusion (Williams, Strover, & Grant, 1994; Brown, 1996; Brown & Bryant, 1989). Diffusion studies such as those conducted by S. R. Maier (2000), which examined the diffusion and use of computer-assisted reporting among reporters, should find practical application in coming years. Diffusion studies that examine spread of technologies may be conducted in combination with other approaches, such as uses and gratifications, critical mass analysis, and media system dependency theory[1] (Ball-Rokeach & DeFleur, 1976) to provide a clearer picture of the diffusion and adoption of new media technologies throughout the world. Diffusion studies tracing the spread of new media technologies have the added benefit of increasing our knowledge about social change and the role of new technologies in actually causing societal changes.

In June 2000 in Acapulco, Mexico, at the historic 50th anniversary meeting of the International Communication Association, communication scholars honored their colleague Everett Rogers for his many contributions to the field, particularly his work delineating the concept of diffusion of innovations. This extremely viable communication theory effectively crosses all disciplines in its generality, and it often spawns research that requires scholars to consider both mass media and interpersonal channels of communication. As long as innovations appear, regardless of the domain, communication studies that examine the diffusion of the innovations will continue to be generated.

SUMMARY

Diffusion of innovations is a theory of communication, but diffusion research is also conducted in other disciplines such as sociology and marketing. The theory states that an innovation diffuses throughout society in a predictable pattern: an S-shaped curve (the normal bell curve plotted over time).

Five adopter groups have been identified as occupying certain areas on the curve. These are: innovators, those who are first to adopt an innovation; early adopters, those who are next to adopt; the early majority, the great number of people who are next to adopt; the late majority, the skeptical and cautious number who wait until most of the community has already tried the innovation before they adopt for themselves; and the laggards, those who are last to adopt. Most opinion leaders belong to the early adopter group.

Diffusion of innovations is based upon the theories of Gabriel Tarde, a French scholar who wrote *The Laws of Imitation* in 1903. Tarde theorized about the S-shaped curve and introduced the notion of opinion leadership.

Diffusion of innovations is deeply rooted in psychological theory or, more particularly, social learning theory and its constituents: symbolic modeling, persuasion, social prompting, and motivation. Imitation of others is essential to the diffusion of an innovation. In terms of social learning theory, three major events define the diffusion process: (1) when the person learns about the innovation, (2) when the person adopts the innovation or new behavior, and (3) when the person interacts with others in a social network.

Four key steps summarize the diffusion process. These include knowledge or awareness of the innovation, persuasion through weighing the advantages of the innovation, decision to adopt or reject, and confirmation or validation that the decision made was the correct one.

Through the years, several diffusion studies stand out for their importance to the overall research tradition or to communication research in particular. These include Wissler's study of the diffusion of horses among the Plains Indians, the Iowa hybrid corn seed study, and several communication studies that examine the diffusion of news.

The proliferation of new media technology has become one of intense interest to communication scholars. In the future, diffusion studies in this country and throughout the world will examine the impact and spread of these innovations. Such studies will increase our knowledge of social change and the role of new media technologies in spurring such change.

REFERENCES

BACKER, T. E., & ROGERS, E. M. (1998). Diffusion of innovations theory and work-site AIDS programs. *Journal of Health Communication, 3,* 17–29.

BALL-ROKEACH, S. J., & DEFLEUR, M. L. (1976). A dependency model of mass media effects. *Communication Research, 64,* 359–372.

BANDURA, A. (1986). *Social foundations of thought and action: A social cognitive theory.* Englewood Cliffs, NJ: Prentice-Hall.

BANDURA, A. (1992). Self-efficacy mechanism in psychobiological functioning. In R. Schwarzer (Ed.), *Self-efficacy: Thought control of action* (pp. 355–394). Washington, DC: Hemisphere.

BASIL, M. D., & BROWN, W. J. (1994). Interpersonal communication in news diffusion: A study of "Magic" Johnson's announcement. *Journalism Quarterly, 71,* 305–321.

BROWN, D., & BRYANT, J. (1989). An annotated statistical abstract of communications media in the United States. In J. L. Salvaggio & J. Bryant (Eds.), *Media use in the information age: Emerging patterns of adoption and consumer use* (pp. 259–302). Hillsdale, NJ: Erlbaum.

BROWN, L. A. (1999). Change, continuity, and the pursuit of geographic understanding. *Annals of the Association of American Geographers, 89,* 1–25.

COLEMAN, J. S., KATZ, E., & MENZEL, H. (1966). *Medical innovation: Diffusion of a medical drug among doctors.* Indianapolis: Bobs-Merrill.

DE FLEUR, M. L., & CRONIN, M. M. (1991). Completeness and accuracy of recall in the diffusion of news from a newspaper vs. a television source. *Sociological Inquiry, 61,* 148–167.

DEKIMPE, M. G., PARKER, P. M., & SARVARY, M. (2000). Global diffusion of technological innovations: A coupled-hazard approach. *Journal of Marketing Research, 37,* 147–159.

DEUTSCHMANN, P. J., & DANIELSON, W. A. (1960). Diffusion of knowledge of the major news story. *Journalism Quarterly, 37,* 345–355.

GRANOVETTER, M. (1983). The strength of weak ties: A network theory revisited. In R. Collins (Ed.), *Sociological theory 1983* (pp. 201–233). San Francisco: Jossey-Bass.

KUBEY, R. W., & PELUSO, T. (1990). Emotional response as a cause of interpersonal news diffusion: The case of the space shuttle tragedy. *Journal of Broadcasting & Electronic Media, 34,* 69–76.

MAIER, S. R. (2000). Digital diffusion in newsrooms: The uneven advance of computer-assisted reporting. *Newspaper Research Journal, 21,* 95–111.

MARKUS, M. L. (1987). Toward a "critical mass" theory of intensive media: Universal access, interdependence, and diffusion. *Communication Research, 14,* 491–511.

MAYER, M. E., GUDYKUNST, W. B., PERRILL, N. K., & MERRILL, B. D. (1990). A comparison of competing models of the news diffusion process. *Western Journal of Speech Communication, 54,* 113–124.

MINTROM, M. (1997). Policy entrepreneurs and the diffusion of innovation. *American Journal of Political Science, 41,* 738–771.

OSTLUND, L. E. (1974). Perceived innovation attributes as predictor of innovativeness. *Journal of Consumer Research, 1,* 23–29.

PRICE, V., & CZILLI, E. J. (1996). Modeling patterns of news recognition and recall. *Journal of Communication, 46*(2), 55–79.

RIFFE, D., & STOVALL, J. G. (1989). Diffusion of news of shuttle disaster: What role for emotional response? *Journalism Quarterly, 66,* 551–557.

ROBERTSON, T. S. (1971). *Innovative behavior and communication.* New York: Holt, Rinehart & Winston.

ROGERS, E. M. (1995). *Diffusion of innovations.* New York: Free Press. (Original work published 1962)

ROGERS, E. M., & SHOEMAKER, F. (1971). *Communication of innovations: A cross-cultural approach.* New York: Free Press.

ROGERS, E. M., & SINGHAL, A. (1996). Diffusion of innovations. In M. B. Salwen & D. W. Stacks (Eds.), *An integrated approach to communication theory and research* (pp. 409–420). Mahwah, NJ: Erlbaum.

RYAN, B., & GROSS, N. C. (1943). The diffusion of hybrid seed corn in two Iowa communities. *Rural Sociology, 8,* 15–24.

STUDLAR, D. T. (1999). Diffusion of tobacco control in North America. *Annals of the American Academy of Political & Social Science, 566,* 68–79.

SVENKERUD, P. J., & SINGHAL, A. (1998). Enhancing the effectiveness of HIV/AIDS prevention programs targeted to unique population groups. *Journal of Health Communication, 3,* 193–217.

SVENKERUD, P. J., SINGHAL, A., & PAPA, M. J. (1998). Diffusion of innovations theory and effective targeting of HIV/AIDS programmes in Thailand. *Asian Journal of Communication, 8,* 1–30.

TARDE, G. (1903). *The laws of imitation* (E. C. Parsons, Trans.). New York: Holt.

TORANTZKY, L. G., & KLEIN, K. J. (1982). Innovation characteristics and innovation adoption-implementation: A meta-analysis of findings. *IEEE Transactions of Engineering and Management, EM-29,* 28–45.

VALENTE, T. W., & DAVIS, R. L. (1999). Accelerating the diffusion of innovations using opinion leaders. *Annals of the American Academy of Political and Social Science, 566,* 55–67.

VAUGHAN, P. W., & ROGERS, E. M. (2000). A staged model of communication effects: Evidence from an entertainment-education radio soap opera in Tanzania. *Journal of Health Communication, 5,* 203–227.

WILLIAMS, F., STROVER, S., & GRANT, A. E. (1994). Social Aspects of New Media Technologies. In J. Bryant & D. Zillmann (Eds.), *Media effects: Advances in theory and research* (pp. 463–482). Hillsdale, NJ: Erlbaum.

WISSLER, C. (1923). *Man and culture.* New York: Crowell.

WRIGHT, J. C., KUNKEL, D., PINON, M., & HUSTON, A. C. (1989). How children reacted to televised coverage of the space shuttle disaster. *Journal of Communication, 39*(2), 27–46.

ENDNOTES

1. Dependency theory predicts that relationships of dependency exist between individuals, groups, organizations, media systems, and society. Dependency relationships can be strong or weak depending upon the extent of dependency one entity places upon another for the achievement of certain fundamental goals. The theory examines these dependency relationships at various levels, thus the appeal to researchers interested in diffusion/adoption of new media technologies.

CHAPTER 8

Uses and Gratifications

Television is becoming a collage—there are so many channels that you move through them making a collage yourself. In that sense, everyone sees something a bit different.

—David Hockney, *Hockney on Photography,* **1988**

In the checkout line at the grocery store, one young woman reaches for the latest copy of *Elle* because she is interested in the new styles of bikinis that are going to be popular that season. Another woman, much older and a gardening enthusiast, picks up the current issue of *Better Homes and Gardens* to get the latest tips on spring planting arrangements. The woman's 13-year-old granddaughter begs for the latest copy of her favorite teen magazine with a fresh-faced teen idol on the cover.

In front of the television one Sunday evening, a couple and their children are arguing over which program to watch. The father wants to see the popular *60 Minutes* because it is featuring a story about a scandal that affected someone in his profession. The mother wants to watch *Martha Stewart Living* to see how to can some preserves. The young daughter is crying to watch *Lassie* on the *Disney Channel* because all her young school friends have been planning to watch it all week, and she doesn't want to be left out of the lunchroom conversation on Monday. The young son is anxious to pop *Matrix* into the VCR for an evening of fast-paced adventure.

We use these examples to demonstrate how people seek out certain kinds of media content to satisfy a variety of very personal needs. Their behavior is often goal oriented when they select media fare. Their selections are based on the information or satisfactions they anticipate they will receive by viewing a certain program or selecting a certain magazine.

The **uses and gratifications** approach assumes that individual differences among audience members cause each person to seek out different messages, use those messages differently, and respond to them differently because messages from mass media are but one of many social or psychological factors that cause audience members to select different media fare as well as to experience divergent if not idiosyncratic media effects. The approach assumes that a person's social and psychological makeup is as responsible for producing certain effects as the media messages themselves.

Rather than focus upon the direct effects from mass media on audience members, uses and gratifications research examines the *motivations and behavior of viewers,* or how and why they use the media. It always assumes that viewers actively choose programs or other media content to gratify their individual needs.

This chapter examines the uses and gratifications approach to media effects. After a brief look at the functions of mass media in society and the communication models used to explain uses and effects, we discuss several basic assumptions of the uses and gratification perspective. We then trace uses and gratifications research historically, examine recent research, and note criticisms of the approach.

SOCIETAL-LEVEL FUNCTIONS OF THE MASS MEDIA

To understand why individuals use the media, it may be helpful to examine the reasons why societies use the media. H. Lasswell (1948) identified three major functions that the media serve in society. First, the media keep viewers aware of what is going on the world around them by *surveying the environment.* Second, by providing an overview of various components of the overall environment, the media help audience members to make sense of it all, so to speak. This second function, *correlation of environmental parts,* allows audience members to form a more accurate view of the world around them. Finally, media messages serve to *transmit social norms and customs* to new generations of viewers. Transmission of the social heritage is a powerful function. For example, people in countries throughout the world who receive programs produced in the United States have complained of Western cultural imperialism, or the imposition of Western social norms and values on citizens with very different cultural norms.

Researchers have identified several other functions of mass media. C. R. Wright (1960) named another function that media serves in society, that of *entertainment.* This important function recognizes that many people use mass media for personal enjoyment. Another function, called *parasocial interaction* (Horton & Wohl, 1956), describes the phenomenon that occurs when viewers feel as though they personally know certain television and film characters and personalities simply because they see and hear them so often. *Escapism,* another function, assumes that television entertainment allows viewers to escape from real-life problems (Pearlin, 1959). Other related functions that have been identified include *anxiety reduction* (Mendelsohn, 1963) and *play* (Stephenson, 1967), two escapist functions that allow audience members to put aside the pressures and tensions of real life and experience enjoyment while being entertained with fantasy.

MODELS TO EXPLAIN USES AND EFFECTS

Communication scholars have developed several different models that attempt to explain individual-level media uses and effects, which is the principal focus of uses and gratifications research. These include the transactional model

(McLeod & Becker, 1974), the gratification seeking and audience activity model (A. Rubin & Perse, 1987), the expectancy-value model (Palmgreen & Rayburn, 1982), and the uses and dependency model (A. Rubin & Windahl, 1986).

Transactional Model

In the transactional model, two factors in combination produce an effect—the characteristics of the message and the psychological orientation of the audience member. This model combines the direct effects model and the individual differences model of years past. Exposure to a media message has powerful effects to the extent that an audience member's psychological orientation permits (McLeod & Becker, 1974). For example, a news report about severe budget cuts to a state's institutions of higher learning would be more likely to produce an effect on people involved in higher education than those with no involvement. Such a report would be very disturbing to administrators who would be forced to make reductions and professors who might not receive pay raises.

Gratification-Seeking and Audience Activity Model

In the gratification-seeking and audience activity model, many different factors and elements come to bear on the uses and effects process. Particular kinds of gratifications sought by the viewer, as well as the viewer's attitude, determine the viewer's attention to the content of those messages. Effects on the viewer's thoughts, emotions, or behavior depend on involvement with the message and behavioral intentions of the viewer (A. Rubin & Perse, 1987). For example, a person with asthma would pay more attention to a commercial for an asthma medication than a person who does not have asthma.

Expectancy-Value Model

The expectancy-value model examines the use of the media in terms of the gratifications sought and obtained in addition to the outcomes that are expected at the onset. P. Palmgreen and J. D. Rayburn (1982) proposed that the model explains a person's behavior, intentions, and attitudes as a function of two separate components: expectancy and evaluation. They defined *expectancy* as "the probability that an attitude possesses a particular attribute or that a behavior will have a particular consequence," and *evaluation* as "the degree of affect, positive or negative, toward an attitude or behavioral outcome" (pp. 562–563). For example, people might tune in a presidential debate expecting their favorite candidate to win, only to witness the opposing candidate do a much better job. They may or may not change their attitude toward their favorite candidate, but the decision would be based on their evaluation of the performances.

Uses and Dependency Model

Research has shown that dependency on a medium is the result of two major factors: viewer motives for obtaining gratifications and the availability of viewing alternatives. Each of these factors may be affected by any number of social or psychological characteristics. For example, a person with poor health and limited mobility would be more likely to be dependent upon a medium such as television for entertainment and diversion than a healthy person who enjoys many different types of activities. Furthermore, the person with limited mobility would be more likely to become dependent upon a medium such as television if he or she did not have access to other media options, such as a personal computer, a VCR, computer games, and so forth, in the home.

The **uses and dependency model** (A. Rubin & Windahl, 1986) proposes that certain elements in a media system (e.g., the system itself, the structure of society, individual differences that result in highly personal motives) cause people to use and depend upon the media. Dependency upon the media may lead to effects in itself. For example, attitude change might occur and thus affect the other elements in the model.

The greater the dependency upon a medium, the more likely that medium will have effects upon the viewer. M. M. Miller and S. D. Reese (1982) studied political effects and found that effects were more likely to occur among those who relied more upon the medium rather than those who did not rely upon the medium.

ASSUMPTIONS OF USES AND GRATIFICATIONS

Several basic assumptions lie at the heart of the uses and gratifications perspective. Scholars identified most of these assumptions in 1974. More recently, others (Palmgreen, 1984; A. Rubin, 1986; A. Rubin & Windahl, 1986) have learned more about media audiences and have expanded the list of assumptions inherent in uses and gratifications. A. Rubin (1994) provided a concise list of these assumptions.

THE ACTIVE AUDIENCE. This uses and gratifications perspective assumes that viewers are active participants in the communication process, but they are not all equally active; in other words, audience activity is variable. The communication behavior of audience members is goal directed, purposive, and motivated; they make viewing selections based on personal motivations, goals, and needs, and these same factors influence what they actually see and hear.

Additional research has attempted to explore audience involvement with the media. Studies have found that audience members differ in the level of activity (media use or involvement) and that individual members experience variability in their media activity levels and their reasons for viewing at various times. One study showed that viewers are not particularly active when they seek out programs for the motive of diversion, but they do actively seek out information when they watch news programs (Levy & Windahl, 1984).

MEDIA USE FOR GRATIFICATIONS. This perspective emphasizes that viewers use the media for a variety of reasons, sometimes to obtain information about something that interests or troubles them. It is always used or selected to gratify the needs or wants of the audience member.

Remote control devices have altered the nature of media use.
Source: © Ryan McVay/PhotoDisc

S. Finn (1992) described the motives for media use as falling under one of two headings: proactive or passive. Examples of proactive media use are watching a particular television program in order to learn more about a specific subject of interest, watching a certain movie for the express purpose of being entertained, or using the Internet to find information for a project at school or work. In other words, the media user actively seeks something from the media based upon his or her wants, needs, and motives. As the name suggests, passive motives describes the use of media in a lackadaisical (passive) sense. For example, sometimes we turn on the television simply because it is there, just to "see what's on." We are not actively seeking information, entertainment, or anything in particular. This does not mean that we will not be entertained or learn something—we very well might. It only suggests that we did not begin the viewing experience with a particular, proactive motive in mind.

Media use orientations can be described as either ritualized or instrumental (A. Rubin, 1984). Ritualized use describes habitual use of the media to pass time or divert one's attention from real-life concerns. Instrumental use characterizes active and goal-oriented use of the media. Watching news programs or a particular documentary because of a desire for news and information is an example of instrumental media use.

SOCIAL AND PSYCHOLOGICAL FACTORS. A host of social and psychological factors mediate people's communication behavior. When someone watches a newscast or dramatic program, his or her reaction to the information depends upon individual personality, social circumstances, psychological disposition, and so forth. For example, people who are not particularly mobile and those who live alone have been found to rely heavily on media use (Perse & A. Rubin, 1990; A. Rubin & R. Rubin, 1982a).

COMPETITION AND MEDIATION. Media compete with other forms of communication (i.e., functional alternatives) for selection, attention, and use to gratify our needs or wants. A viewer must pay attention to media messages in order to be influenced or affected by them. Personal choices and individual differences are strong influences that mitigate media effects. One's initiative mediates patterns and consequences of media use. Lack of sufficient individual initiative results in stronger influences from media messages.

USES AND GRATIFICATIONS RESEARCH: A BRIEF HISTORY

Most research activity in the area of uses and gratifications has examined the motives behind media use. In other words, researchers have sought to find out why people watch the television programs they watch, or why they are influenced by some commercials but not by others. Instead of focusing on what the media do to people, these studies ask the question: What do people do with the media? (Klapper, 1963; Rubin, 1994).

A series of studies in the 1940s sought to identify people's motives for listening to certain radio programs and for reading the newspaper. Some scholars conducted their studies before the phrase "uses and gratifications" was utilized (Lazarsfeld, 1940; Herzog, 1940, 1944; Berelson, 1949). While these researchers were more interested in the motives of audience members than the effects of the media content, their findings were revealing. Their studies examined radio quiz shows to determine their various appeals among audiences, daytime serials to find out what gratifications women received from listening to them, and newspaper readership to determine readers' motives. They found that listeners enjoyed the programs for various reasons, from the educational appeal of quiz shows to the opportunity for emotional release of daytime serial viewers.

By the 1970s researchers had begun to categorize the various motives for media use (Katz, Gurevitch, & Haas, 1973). Needs were found to be related to social and psychological factors. Katz and his colleagues found that viewers used the media to help them gain more understanding of themselves, the people close to them, or society at large. Also, the media were used to increase personal status and strengthen relationships.

Other researchers developed their own typology for audience gratifications (McQuail, Blumler, & Brown, 1972). They found that people use television to be diverted, to fulfill the need for personal relationships, to reinforce personal identity, and to keep abreast of happenings in the world around them.

K. E. Rosengren and S. Windahl (1972) were among the first to suggest that media uses and effects should be linked. Research should ask what effects particular gratifications may have, or what effects particular uses of the media may have. They found that people depend upon the media to fulfill certain needs, such as vicarious experience and escapism, or involvement or interaction.

Other researchers have also suggested that a synthesis of the two research realms would be logical and beneficial. These research domains are similar in that each examines the consequences of mass communication from an individual or societal level—changes in attitudes, perceptions, or behavior.

Since the mid-1970s, research has provided a greater understanding of the uses and effects of mass media. In answer to criticisms regarding lack of uniformity, uses and effects researchers have adapted similar measures for viewer motives. Based upon work by B. S. Greenberg (1974) and A. Rubin (1979), most uses and gratifications research now recognizes the following motives for media use among audience members: learning, habit, companionship, arousal, relaxation, escapism, or a way to pass time (Rubin, 1994). The studies by Greenberg and Rubin produced similar results. Both found, for example, that motives for viewing changed with a person's age. Most habitual viewers liked watching comedies rather than news. Most viewers seeking excitement tended to watch action/adventure programs.

RECENT RESEARCH

Recent research has examined uses and gratifications from a number of different perspectives. Researchers have identified links between viewing and attitudes and behaviors toward the media (Perse, 1986; A. Rubin, 1979, 1981a, 1981b, 1983, 1984, 1985; A. Rubin & Bantz, 1989), the comparison of motives for using media and viewing particular content (Cohen, Levy, & Golden, 1988; Reece, 1996; Shaw, 1997), and the identification of social and psychological characteristics that influence the use of media (Adoni, 1979; Dimmick, McCain & Bolton, 1979; Finn, 1997; Finn & Gorr, 1988; Lull, 1980; Perse & A. Rubin, 1990; A. Rubin, 1993; A. Rubin & R. Rubin, 1989; R. Rubin & A. Rubin, 1982; Windahl, Hojerback & Hedinsson, 1986).

Other research has analyzed how different backgrounds, motives, and levels of exposure have affected various outcomes, such as satisfaction or political knowledge (Alexander, 1985; Carveth & Alexander, 1985; Garramone, 1984; Perse, 1990; Perse & A. Rubin, 1988; A. Rubin, 1985; R. Rubin & McHugh, 1987). Most recently, uses and gratifications studies have identified characteristics and motives of particular media users, and used those correlations to predict various factors, such as exposure to and uses of television violence (Kremar & Greene, 1999), adoption of online services (Lin, 1999), Internet use (Papacharissi & Rubin, 2000), cellular telephone use (Leung & Wei, 2000), and home computer use (Perse & Dunn, 1998). Other studies have emphasized gratifications from overall media use (Vincent & Basil, 1997) and personality traits that predict media use (Finn, 1997). (See the box on "Uses and Gratifications Research: The VCR and Internet.)

CRITICISMS OF USES AND GRATIFICATIONS

A. Rubin (1994) reviewed the literature on uses and gratifications and identified several major criticisms of the approach. Some of the criticisms were aimed at the results of early research. Additional research has served to answer the critics on several issues.

Too Individualistic

The focus upon individual differences makes the findings of uses and gratifications research difficult to extend to other people or society as a whole (Carey & Kreiling, 1974; Elliott, 1974). In recent years, however, the consistency of findings in replicated studies (including standardization of measures in terms of viewer motives) has contributed to the generalization of results.

Uses and Gratifications Research: The VCR and Internet

Uses and gratifications research tells us much about people's *motives* or reasons for using the media or preferring particular programs or messages to others. Studies may reveal why certain types of people enjoy particular television programs, listen to certain radio stations, or read specific newspapers or magazines. A couple of recent uses and gratifications studies have produced interesting results that reveal much about people's motives for using VCRs and their reasons for preferring particular websites.

One study examined VCR use among 119 households from November 1992 to March 1993. For one week, the participants entered information about their VCR usage in a special diary. The participants were later interviewed by the researcher. The study found that most people use the VCR to record programs being broadcast while they were at work or busy with other activities, or those programs being broadcast at the same time as other interesting programs. They played back the programs in their leisure time for relaxation and entertainment. The use of VCRs did not *alter* a person's television viewing patterns; rather, their use *enhanced* previous established television viewing patterns. In other words, people still watched their favorite programs on television even though VCRs offered them the power to tape and view them at another time.

A study of websites asked the questions: "What are the benefits delivered by commercial websites, and what are the approaches that deliver the greatest benefit?" The study focused on five sites representing recognizable, brand-name products. Participants in the study browsed the sites and rated them. The researchers found that the highest; ranking websites were enjoyable, well organized, and designed with efficiency for downloading (and minimal waiting on the part of the user).

Sources: J. Eighmey (1997). Profiling user responses to commercial Web sites, *Journal of Advertising Research, 37* (3), 59. J. Eighmey & L. McCord (1995). Adding value in the information age: Uses and gratifications of the World-Wide Web. In R. R. Dholakia & D. R. Fortin (Eds.), *Proceedings of the Conference on Telecommunications and Information Markets.* Newport: University of Rhode Island. C. J. Harum Wachter (1994). Assessing the impact of VCR use on leisure attitudes and behavior (television). Unpublished doctoral dissertation, University of Illinois at Urbana-Champaign.

Lack of Synthesis of Research Findings

The various typologies that have been developed to describe audience uses and gratifications are difficult to synthesize (Anderson & Meyer, 1975; Swanson, 1979). Since the 1970s, the efforts toward consistency in typologies have produced more systematic categorizations, but differences in typologies still exist. This criticism should guide future research toward a more synthesized level.

Lack of Clarity among Key Concepts

Some researchers have argued that key concepts such as needs, motives, behavior, and so forth have not been clearly explicated (Anderson & Meyer, 1975; Blumler, 1979; Elliott, 1974). Since the 1970s these concepts have been studied and described more explicitly, but the criticism still has some validity.

Differences in the Meaning of Key Concepts

Other critics have pointed out that researchers have offered different definitions for various concepts such as motives, uses, and gratifications (Elliott,

1974; Swanson, 1977, 1979). Comparisons between studies becomes difficult when one investigator defines a key concept in one way and another defines it in another way.

The Active Audience and Use of Self-Reporting

These two related assumptions have been criticized for a perceived lack of accuracy and consistency (Elliott, 1974; Swanson, 1977, 1979). For the most part, studies have answered the criticisms by using validating scales (A. Rubin, 1979, 1981a), experimental methods (Bryant & Zillmann, 1984), and other means. Other critics have pointed out that self-reports might be affected by individual interpretations and perceptions (Babrow, 1988) and therefore caution is warranted.

SUMMARY

The uses and gratifications approach assumes that individual differences among audience members cause each person to use messages differently and react to them differently. It assumes that a person's social setting and psychological makeup are as responsible for producing certain effects as are the media messages themselves.

Uses and gratifications research examines the motivations and behavior of viewers, or how and why they use the media. It always assumes that viewers actively choose which programs or other media content they will use to gratify their individual needs.

Several basic assumptions lie at the heart of the uses and gratifications perspective. These include the active audience, media use for gratifications, viewer reactions dependent upon social and psychological factors, and other assumptions.

A series of studies in the 1940s sought to identify people's motives for listening to certain radio programs and for reading the newspaper. By the 1970s researchers had begun to type the various motives for media use. Needs were found to be related to social and psychological factors.

Many researchers believe that a synthesis of media effects research and uses research would be logical and beneficial. Such research would explore what effects particular gratifications might have, or what effects particular uses of the media might have.

Since the mid-1970s research has provided a greater understanding of the use of mass media and the effects of that use. In answer to one of the criticisms of such research in previous years, uses and effects researchers have adapted similar measures for viewer motives. Most uses and gratifications research now recognizes the following motives for media use among audience members: learning, habit, companionship, arousal, relaxation, escapism, and a way to pass time.

Communication scholars have developed several different models that attempt to explain media uses and effects. These include the transactional model, the gratification-seeking and audience-activity model, the expectancy-value model, and the uses and dependency model.

Several components and characteristics of uses and gratifications research have been criticized through the years. The more substantial criticisms include the following: findings that are too individualistic and not easily generalized, lack of synthesis among research findings, lack of clarity among key concepts, differences in the meanings of key concepts, the notion of the active audience, and the perceived lack of accuracy of self-reporting measures.

A great deal of uses and gratifications research since the 1970s has served to answer the critics on several issues. Additional research in the future should continue to offer additional strength to the overall perspective.

REFERENCES

ADONI, H. (1979). The functions of mass media in the political socialization of adolescents. *Communication Research, 6,* 84–106.

ALEXANDER, A. (1985). Adolescents' soap opera viewing and relational perceptions. *Journal of Broadcasting & Electronic Media, 29,* 295–308.

ANDERSON, J. A., & MEYER, T. P. (1975). Functionalism and the mass media. *Journal of Broadcasting, 19,* 11–22.

BABROW, A. S. (1988). Theory and method in research on audience motives. *Journal of Broadcasting & Electronic Media, 32,* 471–487.

BERELSON, B. (1949). What "missing the newspaper" means. In P. F. Lazarsfeld & F. N. Stanton (Eds.), *Communications research 1948–1949* (pp. 111–129). New York: Harper.

BLUMLER, J. G. (1979). The role of theory in uses and gratifications studies. *Communication Research, 6,* 9–36.

BRYANT, J., & ZILLMANN, D. (1984). Using television to alleviate boredom and stress: Selective exposure as a function of induced excitational states. *Journal of Broadcasting, 28,* 1–20.

CAREY, J. W., & KREILING, A. L. (1974). Popular culture and uses and gratifications: Notes toward an accommodation. In J. G. Blumler & E. Katz (Eds.). *The uses of mass communications: Current perspectives on gratifications research* (pp. 225–248). Beverly Hills, CA: Sage.

CARVETH, R., & ALEXANDER, A. (1985). Soap opera viewing motivations and the cultivation process. *Journal of Broadcasting & Electronic Media, 29,* 259–273.

COHEN, A. A., LEVY, M. R., & GOLDEN, K. (1988). Children's uses and gratifications of home VCRs: Evolution or revolution. *Communication Research, 15,* 772–780.

DIMMICK, J. W., MCCAIN, T. A., & BOLTON, W. T. (1979). Media use and the life span. *American Behavioral Scientist, 23*(1), 7–31.

ELLIOTT, P. (1974). Uses and gratifications research: A critique and a sociological alternative. In J. G. Blumler & E. Katz (Eds.), *The uses of mass communications: Current perspectives on gratifications research* (pp. 249–268). Beverly Hills, CA: Sage.

FINN, S. (1997). Origins of media exposure: Linking personality traits to TV, radio, print, and film use. *Communication Research 24,* 507–529.

FINN, S. (1992). Television addiction? An evaluation of four competing media-use models. *Journalism Quarterly, 69,* 422–435.

FINN, S., & GORR, M. B. (1988). Social isolation and social support as correlates of television viewing motivations. *Communication Research, 15,* 135–158.

GARRAMONE, G. M. (1984). Audience motivation effect: More evidence. *Communication Research, 11,* 79–96.

GREENBERG, B. S. (1974). Gratifications of television viewing and their correlates for British children. In J. G. Blumler & E. Katz (Eds.), *The uses of mass communications: Current perspectives on gratifications research* (pp. 71–92). Beverly Hills, CA: Sage.

HERZOG, H. (1940). Professor quiz: A gratification study. In P. F. Lazarsfeld (Ed.), *Radio and the printed page* (pp. 64–93). New York: Duell, Sloan, & Pearce.

HERZOG, H. (1944). What do we really know about daytime serial listeners? In P. F. Lazarsfeld & F. N. Stanton (Eds.), *Radio research 1942–1943* (pp. 3–33). New York: Duell, Sloan, & Pearce.

HORTON, D., & WOHL, R. R. (1956). Mass communication and para-social interaction. *Psychiatry, 19*, 215–229.

KATZ, E., GUREVITCH, M., & HAAS, H. (1973). On the use of the mass media for important things. *American Sociological Review, 38*, 164–181.

KLAPPER, J. T. (1963). Mass communication research: An old road resurveyed. *Public Opinion Quarterly, 27*, 515–527.

KREMAR, M., & GREENE, K. (1999). Predicting exposure to and uses of television violence. *Journal of Communication, 49*(3), 24–46.

LASSWELL, H. D. (1948). The structure and function of communication in society. In L. Bryson (Ed.), *The communication of ideas* (pp. 37–51). New York: Harper.

LAZARSFELD, P. F. (1940). *Radio and the printed page.* New York: Duell, Sloan, & Pearce.

LEUNG, L., & WEI, R. (2000). More than just talk on the move: Uses and gratifications of the cellular phone. *Journalism & Mass Communication Quarterly, 77*, 308–321.

LEVY, M. R., & WINDAHL, S. (1984). Audience activity and gratifications: A conceptual clarification and exploration. *Communication Research, 11*, 51–78.

LIN, C. A. (1999). Online-service adoption likelihood. *Journal of Advertising Research, 39*(2), 79–90.

LULL, J. (1980). The social uses of television. *Human Communication Research, 6*, 197–209.

McCOMBS, M. E., & SHAW, D. L. (1972). The agenda-setting function of mass media. *Public Opinion Quarterly, 36*, 176–187.

McLEOD, J. M., & BECKER, L. B. (1974). Testing the validity of gratification measures through political effects analysis. In J. G. Blumler & E. Katz (Eds.), *The uses of mass communications: Current perspectives on gratifications research* (pp. 137–164). Beverly Hills, CA: Sage.

McQUAIL, D., BLUMLER, J. G., & BROWN, J. R. (1972). The television audience: A revised perspective. In D. McQuail (Ed.), *Sociology of mass communications* (pp. 135–165). Middlesex, England: Penguin.

MENDELSOHN, H. (1963). Socio-psychological perspectives on the mass media and public anxiety. *Journalism Quarterly, 40*, 511–516.

MILLER, M. M., & REESE, S. D. (1982). Media dependency as interaction: Effects of exposure and reliance on political activity and efficacy. *Communication Research, 9*, 227–248.

PALMGREEN, P. (1984). Uses and gratifications: A theoretical perspective. *Communication Yearbook, 8*, 20–55.

PALMGREEN, P., & RAYBURN, J. D., II. (1982). Gratifications sought and media exposure: An expectancy value model. *Communication Research, 9*, 561–580.

PAPACHARISSI, Z., & RUBIN, A. M. (2000). Predictors of Internet use. *Journal of Broadcasting & Electronic Media, 44*, 175–197.

PEARLIN, L. I. (1959). Social and personal stress and escape television viewing. *Public Opinion Quarterly, 23*, 255–259.

PERSE, E. M. (1986). Soap opera viewing patterns of college students and cultivation. *Journal of Broadcasting & Electronic Media, 30*, 175–193.

PERSE, E. M. (1990). Involvement with local television news: Cognitive and emotional dimensions. *Human Communication Research, 16*, 556–581.

PERSE, E. M., & DUNN, D. G. (1998). The utility of home computers and media use: Implications of multimedia and connectivity. *Journal of Broadcasting & Electronic Media, 42*, 435–456.

PERSE, E. M., & RUBIN, A. M. (1988). Audience activity and satisfaction with favorite television soap opera. *Journalism Quarterly, 65*, 368–375.

PERSE, E. M., & RUBIN, A. M. (1990). Chronic loneliness and television use. *Journal of Broadcasting & Electronic Media, 34*, 37–53.

REECE, D. J. (1996). *Coming to America: The influence of cultural variables on media use among Indian sojourners (Asian Indian)*. Unpublished doctoral dissertation, University of Kentucky, Lexington.

ROSENGREN, K. E., & WINDAHL, S. (1972). Mass media consumption as a functional alternative. In D. McQuail (Ed.), *Sociology of mass communications* (pp. 166–194). Middlesex, England: Penguin.

RUBIN, A. M. (1979). Television use by children and adolescents. *Human Communication Research, 5*, 109–120.

RUBIN, A. M. (1981a). An examination of television viewing motives. *Communication Research, 8*, 141–165.

RUBIN, A. M. (1981b). A multivariate analysis of "60 Minutes" viewing motivations. *Journalism Quarterly, 58*, 529–534.

RUBIN, A. M. (1983). Television uses and gratifications: The interactions of viewing patterns and motivations. *Journal of Broadcasting, 27*, 37–51.

RUBIN, A. M. (1984). Ritualized and instrumental television viewing. *Journal of Communication, 34*(3), 67–77.

RUBIN, A. M. (1985). Uses of daytime television soap opera by college students. *Journal of Broadcasting & Electronic Media, 29*, 241–258.

RUBIN, A. M. (1986). Uses, gratifications, and media effects research. In J. Bryant & D. Zillmann (Eds.), *Perspectives on media effects* (pp. 281–301). Hillsdale, NJ: Erlbaum.

RUBIN, A. M. (1993). The effect of locus of control on communication motivation, anxiety, and satisfaction. *Communication Quarterly, 41*(2), 161–71.

RUBIN, A. M. (1994). Media effects: A uses-and-gratifications perspective. In J. Bryant & D. Zillmann (Eds.), *Media effects: Advances in theory and research* (pp. 417–436). Hillsdale, NJ: Erlbaum.

RUBIN, A. M., & BANTZ, C. R. (1989). Uses and gratifications of videocassette recorders. In J. L. Salvaggio & J. Bryant (Eds.), *Media use in the information age: Emerging patterns of adoption and consumer use* (pp. 181–195). Hillsdale, NJ: Erlbaum.

RUBIN, A. M., & PERSE, E. M. (1987). Audience activity and television news gratifications. *Communication Research, 14*, 58–84.

RUBIN, A. M., & RUBIN, R. B. (1982). Contextual age and television use. *Human Communication Research, 8*, 228–244.

RUBIN, A. M., & RUBIN, R. B. (1989). Social and psychological antecedents of VCR use. In M. R. Levy (Ed.), *The VCR age: Home video and mass communication* (pp. 92–111). Newbury Park, CA: Sage.

RUBIN, A. M., & WINDAHL, S. (1986). The uses and dependency model of mass communication. *Critical Studies in Mass Communication, 3*, 184–199.

RUBIN, R. B., & MCHUGH, M. P. (1987). Development of parasocial interaction relationships. *Journal of Broadcasting & Electronic Media, 31*, 279–292.

RUBIN, R. B., & RUBIN, A. M., (1982). Contextual age and television use: Reexamining a life-position indicator. *Communication Yearbook, 6*, 583–604.

SHAW, D. F. (1997). Gay men and computer communication: A discourse of sex and identity in cyberspace. In S. G. Jones et al. (Eds.), *Virtual culture: Identity and communication in cybersociety* (pp. 133–145). London: Sage.

STEPHENSON, W. (1967). *The play theory of mass communication.* Chicago: University of Chicago Press.

SWANSON, D. L. (1977). The uses and misuses of uses and gratifications. *Human Communication Research, 3,* 214–221.

SWANSON, D. L. (1979). Political communication research and the uses and gratifications model: A critique. *Communication Research, 6,* 37–53.

VINCENT, R. C., & BASIL, M. D. (1997). College students' news gratifications, media use and current events knowledge. *Journal of Broadcasting & Electronic Media, 41,* 380–392.

WINDAHL, S., HOJERBACK, I., & HEDINSSON, E. (1986). Adolescents without television: A study in media deprivation. *Journal of Broadcasting & Electronic Media, 30,* 47–63.

WRIGHT, C. R. (1960). Functional analysis and mass communication. *Public Opinion Quarterly, 24,* 605–620.

CHAPTER 9

Agenda Setting

> *We tell the public which way the cat is jumping. The public will take care of the cat.*
>
> **—Arthur Hays Sulzberger, *Time*, May 8, 1950**

Imagine for a moment a mayoral election without many major or salient issues, only a focus on candidate personalities. The owner of a local television station recognizes the shortage of issues and sets out to bring one into the limelight. Each morning on his way to work, a city street under construction near the television station causes infuriating traffic delays. The owner instructs his assignment editor to do a story on the unfinished construction project and get reactions from the two candidates. When the story runs on one station, the other television stations pick it up, then the local newspapers, and soon the unfinished construction on the street near the television station becomes a campaign issue. The candidates offer different proposals for raising money to finish the project. Continued coverage of the issue attracts public attention as more people learn of the problem and its proposed solution. By election day the plans to finish the construction on the street near the television station have become a significant campaign issue, all because of media coverage and, ultimately, because of the initial request of the television station owner who wanted to see the construction completed as soon as possible.

The strong link between the news stories such as the imaginary, unfinished construction project and public issue **salience,** or the importance placed upon particular issues, demonstrates a type of communication effect called **agenda setting.** B. Cohen described the concept best in his oft-quoted remark: The press, "may not be successful much of the time in telling people what to think, but it is stunningly successful in telling its readers what to think *about*" (1963, p. 13).

The agenda-setting function of the press becomes obvious when news stories bring important issues before the public; however, agenda-setting researchers often face empirical problems difficult to address. For example, how can causal directions be established? Do the media always set the agenda for the public, or does the public sometimes set the media agenda? Moreover, can the factor of media coverage be isolated and measured empirically? How can the researcher control for extraneous variables?

Agenda-setting effects are clearly indicated only when researchers are able to measure public opinion before and after media coverage of specific issues. For this reason, election campaigns have been popular among researchers because of their periodicity and other characteristics that make them suitable for agenda-setting research designs.

Initially, agenda-setting research examined the influence of news media in shaping people's perceptions of the world. Since the seminal study of public issues in the 1968 presidential campaign (McCombs & Shaw, 1972), a number of studies have confirmed the strong correspondence between news stories and the salience of issues covered to the public.

In recent years, agenda-setting research has expanded to ask the question: "Who sets the media agenda?" Each day, hundreds of news stories occur around the world, throughout the nation, in individual regions and states, and at local levels. News professionals cannot possibly pass along to the public *all* the news of the day. Space and time limitations preclude doing that. Instead, journalists and news editors must decide which stories to cover, which to run, and which to ignore. In making such decisions, news professionals invariably *set the agenda* for news consumers. They gauge the value of news on the basis of their perceptions of its importance to their readers and viewers.

Control over the flow of news information by media professionals is an important function called **gatekeeping.** Simply put, journalists, editors, and broadcasters allow a certain amount of news to pass through to the public each day, but time and space constraints force them to shut the gates and stop the flow of most information to news consumers. Scholars have been aware of this powerful gatekeeping function for many years, but only recently have they begun to examine the many factors that influence the gatekeeping process.

This chapter identifies the conceptual foundations of agenda setting and provides a brief history of the agenda-setting research tradition. It takes a look at recent trends in agenda-setting research, and considers in a concluding section the struggle of agenda setting for individual theory status, as well as the broad, paradigmatic bases upon which the hypothesis rests.

CONCEPTUAL ROOTS

Cohen was not the first to describe the notion of the press setting the public agenda. The concept can be traced to Walter Lippmann, a famous newspaper columnist and social commentator of the early 20th century. Lippmann's book, *Public Opinion* (1922), has been called the most influential, nonscholarly work in the history of the academic study of mass communication (Carey, 1996). Lippmann wrote how the news media are responsible for shaping the public's perception of the world. He emphasized that the pictures of reality created by the news media were merely *reflections* of actual reality and therefore were sometimes distorted. Lippmann said that the news-media projections of the world create a **pseudo-environment** for each news consumer. The pseudo-environment exists in addition to the *actual* environment, and people react to this pseudo-environment that media create. "For the real environment is altogether too big, too complex, and too fleeting for a direct acquaintance" (p. 16).

Agenda Building

Other scholars also described the concept of agenda setting in their writings prior to empirical assessment of the concept in the early 1970s. In 1958 Norton Long wrote: "In a sense, the newspaper is the prime mover in setting the territorial agenda. It has a great part in determining what most people will be talking about, what most people will think the facts are, and what most people will regard as the way problems are to be dealt with" (Long, 1958, p. 260). The following year, Kurt and Gladys Engel Lang wrote: "The mass media force attention to certain issues. They build up public images of political figures. They are constantly presenting objects suggesting what individuals in the mass should think about, know about, have feelings about" (1959, p. 232).

Lang and Lang's concept of **agenda building** (1991, 1981) differs from agenda setting in several ways, but primarily in its allowance for the collective influence of and reciprocity between public and media in setting the agenda. Lang and Lang summarized the role of the news media in building the agenda:

> First, the news media highlight some events, activities, groups, personalities, and so forth to make them stand out. Different kinds of issues require different amounts and kinds of coverage to gain attention. This common focus affects what people will think or talk about.
>
> Second, the object that is the focus of attention still needs to be framed. It must come to stand for something—some problem or concern. The media can play up or down the more serious aspects of a situation.
>
> The third step in the buildup links the object or event to secondary symbols, so that it becomes a part of the recognized political landscape. Something like interest aggregation is involved, since the line of division on the particular issue does not always coincide with the cleavage between the organized political parties or between other sharply defined groups. The media tend to weave discrete events into a continuing story, often a political one.
>
> Finally, spokesmen who can articulate demands must make their appearance. Their effectiveness stems in good part from their ability to command media attention. (1991, 1981, p. 286).

RESEARCH TRADITION

Phase 1: Intial Study—Chapel Hill

The first empirical test of Lippmann's ideas about agenda setting was published in 1972 by two University of North Carolina researchers, Maxwell McCombs and Donald Shaw, in what came to be known as the Chapel Hill study, for its location in North Carolina.

In 1968 the Vietnam conflict raged, African Americans struggled for civil rights, the country's youth rebelled against authority, and drug abuse became a serious problem. Robert F. Kennedy's bid for the presidency ended tragically

The 1972 Chapel Hill study tested the influence of
Presidential election campaign coverage on public
perceptions of issue importance.
Source: © CORBIS

when an assassin gunned him down in California. Hubert H. Humphrey
emerged as the Democratic nominee instead, challenging Republican Richard
M. Nixon and the independent candidate, George C. Wallace.

In this tempestuous social climate, as the nation prepared to select a new
chief executive, McCombs and Shaw designed a study to test the influence of
campaign coverage on public perceptions of the importance of issues. Prior to the
election, they asked Chapel Hill voters: "What are you most concerned about
these days? That is, regardless of what politicians say, what are the two or three
main things which you think the government should concentrate on doing something about?" (McCombs & Shaw, 1972, p. 178). The issues they identified—
foreign policy, law and order, fiscal policy, civil rights, and public welfare—were
ranked according to the percentage of respondents identifying them.

The actual content of local news media served as a measured independent
variable in the Chapel Hill study, and the dependent variable, issue salience,
was compared to topic coverage. The researchers analyzed the contents of local
newspapers, television, and radio stations for three weeks during the campaign
to identify issues that were receiving the most media attention. When McCombs
and Shaw compared these results to the public responses, they found almost
identical "agendas" on the part of the public and the news media. They named
this "transfer of salience" of issues from the media to the public "the agenda setting influence of mass communication" (McCombs & Bell, 1996, p. 96).

Phase 2: Replication

After the groundbreaking study in 1972, it might be said that agenda-setting research caught fire among communication investigators, with hundreds of studies being conducted throughout the ensuing 25 years. McCombs and Shaw (1993) reviewed the abundant research findings and identified four phases of growth in agenda-setting research: (1) publication of their original study in 1972, (2) replication and examination of contingent conditions in their second study, (3) an expansion of the original idea of agenda setting into the areas of candidate characteristics and other political aspects, and (4) a focus upon the sources of the media agenda. W. Wanta (1997) also discussed these phases and offered findings from additional research (see the box summarizing the four phases of agenda-setting research).

In 1973, G. R. Funkhouser replicated the Chapel Hill study and identified a strong correspondence between public opinion trends in the 1960s and coverage of issues in the news media during the period. Funkhouser assessed public opinion using answers to a Gallup Poll question regarding the most significant problem in the nation. He analyzed the content of issues of *Time, Newsweek,* and *U.S. News and World Report* to determine the media agenda. He then compared these findings with official statistics (e.g., the actual number of U.S. soldiers in

Agenda-Setting Research

Four Phases at a Glance

PHASE 1 *INITIAL STUDY*

Chapel Hill Study (1972), McCombs & Shaw. *Findings:* The issues considered important by the news media were also considered important by the general public.

PHASE 2 *REPLICATION*

Charlotte Voter Study (1977), Shaw & McCombs. *Findings:* Voters with greater orientation needs and those who used mass media more often than others were more likely to have agendas (issue salience) that matched the media agenda.

Laboratory Study (1982), Iyengar, Peters, & Kinder. *Findings:* Research participants who viewed stories about the weak nature of United States defense capabilities rated the issue significantly higher than those who did not see the stories.

PHASE 3 *CONTINGENT FACTORS*

1976 Candidate Study (1981), Weaver, Graber, McCombs, & Eyal. *Findings:* Dynamics of voters' perceptions of candidates and their images as portrayed by news media were examined. Contingent factors were found to affect the agenda-setting process. Voters' occupations, education levels, and their geographic locations played a part in determining whether voters' issue agendas matched the media agenda.

PHASE 4 *WHO SETS THE MEDIA AGENDA?*

Media Agenda Sources (1991), Shoemaker & Reese. *Findings:* Many influences are at work creating the media agenda each day. These include, for example, sociological factors related to the news organization and external organizations, ideological factors, individual differences among reporters and editors, and the routine of media work.

Vietnam, number of demonstrations on campus or on behalf of civil rights) to gauge congruence between *actual* reality and *perceptions* of reality on the part of the public and the media. He found a strong correlation between the amount of media coverage of an issue and the public's perceived importance of that issue; however, he also found that media coverage did not always represent the actual reality of issues and situations (Funkhouser, 1973).

The second phase of agenda-setting research (McCombs & Shaw, 1993) began with McCombs and Shaw's second study (Shaw & McCombs, 1977), in which they examined the causal directions for agenda-setting effects and contingent conditions for such effects during the 1972 presidential election campaign. Voters in Charlotte, North Carolina, were surveyed before and after the election to reveal short-term agenda-setting effects. The researchers found that voters with a greater need for orientation to their world and voters who used the mass media more frequently than others were more likely to have agendas that corresponded to the news media agenda. As for causation, the researchers claimed to find evidence to support the agenda-setting influence of the press, but the evidence was not overwhelming (1977; Westley, 1978).

In an attempt to provide stronger evidence for causal direction, the next major study of agenda setting was conducted in a laboratory setting where the researchers manipulated videotaped network television newscasts to vary the placement and emphasis given to the stories (Iyengar, Peters, & Kinder, 1982). Each day for a week, research participants viewed the altered newscasts, which were presented to them as actual and unaltered. Participants were divided into two groups. One group was shown newscasts that emphasized the weak nature of U.S. military defenses; the other group saw newscasts that did not contain these particular stories. The researchers surveyed participants before and after the weeklong experiment and found statistically significant agenda-setting effects. At the end of the week, the group that had seen the "weak defense" stories rated the issue of military defense significantly higher than the group that had not been shown the stories (Iyengar, Peters, & Kinder, 1982). Follow-up experiments provided additional empirical evidence for the agenda-setting effects of mass media (Iyengar & Kinder, 1987; Wanta, 1988).

Phase 3: Contingent Factors

Phase three of agenda-setting research began during the 1976 presidential campaign when the agenda of candidate characteristics and the alternative agenda of political interest were examined (Weaver, Graber, McCombs, & Eyal, 1981). The researchers analyzed the dynamics of how voters perceived candidate characteristics and the images of candidates portrayed in the media (McCombs, 1992). Voters in six locations—three sites in the Northeast and three in the Midwest—participated in the longitudinal study to assess contingent factors at work in the agenda-setting process. The voters' occupations, education levels, and geographic locations were found to affect the degree to which the media were responsible for setting their issue agendas at various times during the election campaign.

Phase 4: Who Sets the Media Agenda?

The fourth phase began in the 1980s when researchers began investigating sources of the media agenda. In this phase of research, the news agenda suddenly became the *dependent* rather than the independent variable (McCombs, 1992), and agenda-setting research became linked with sociology of news, gatekeeping, news diffusion, and other established lines of research. The extension of agenda-setting research into new domains has characterized this phase of the research tradition, which is also the present phase.

The early stages of agenda-setting research explored the public agenda, who was responsible for setting it, and contingent conditions present in the process. The more recent phase has zoomed in to the construction of the *media* agendas and has opened up agenda-setting research into other domains, such as exploration of sociological factors, the processes of news diffusion, and other factors possibly at work in setting the agenda.

According to G. M. Kosicki (1993), agenda-setting research evolved into its present form for several reasons. During the 1960s and 1970s, researchers rejected using the persuasion paradigm to explain agenda-setting effects, and began taking notice of the emerging cognitive paradigm.

> Agenda setting, with its apparently simple, easy-to-explain, and intuitively appealing hypothesis, seemed right for the time. On its face it is a rejection of persuasion, a "reframing" of the basic research question from "telling people what to think" to "telling them what to think about" (Cohen, 1963). This seemingly small, but clever, twist of phrase focuses attention away from persuasion and onto something new. The freshness of the model has obvious appeal. It signals not only a move away from persuasion toward other cognitive factors (Becker & Kosicki, 1991), but a move toward a particular kind of cognitive factor: an agenda of issues. (Kosicki, 1993, p. 231)

In the cognitive paradigm, three primary factors influence each other bidirectionally: a person's behavior, a person's cognitive abilities, and environmental events to which a person is exposed. "Reciprocal causation provides people with opportunities to exercise some control over events in their lives, as well as set limits of self-direction. Because of the bidirectionality of influence, people are both products and producers of their environment" (Bandura, 1994, p. 61).

The need for orientation, for example, is based upon the idea of cognitive mapping, in which people strive to orient themselves whenever they find themselves in unfamiliar settings. Agenda-setting researchers have found that voters with high needs for orientation (a high degree of interest in the election and a high degree of uncertainty about key issues) are more likely to be influenced. According to McCombs, "The concept of need for orientation provides a general psychological explanation for the agenda-setting process and subsumes a number of lower order variables and more limited explanations" (McCombs, 1994, p. 8).

Additionally, a number of influences that create the media agenda each day were identified (Shoemaker & Reese, 1991). These included sociological factors related to the news organization and external organizations, the routine of media work, ideological concerns, and individual differences between reporters and editors.

In 1993, E. M. Rogers, J. W. Dearing, and D. Bregman reviewed the literature and identified three types of studies that fall within the parameters of agenda-setting research: media agenda setting, public agenda setting, and policy agenda setting. The three types have in common an underlying concern with "the relative importance of public issues and a less obvious concern with the general functioning of public opinion in a democracy" (p. 69). The fundamental difference is that each type of study measures a different dependent variable. *The mass media news agenda* is the main dependent variable in studies of media agenda setting. Studies of public agenda setting measure the relative importance of issues to the public, while studies of policy agenda setting measure the issue agenda of a governmental body or elected official.

Investigation of news sources that may set the media agenda has continued to interest scholars in recent years (Wanta, Stephenson, Turk, & McCombs, 1989). Several of these studies have focused on the influence of a particular U.S. president on the news media agenda. In particular, these studies have identified issues covered prominently in the news media a month before and after the President's State of the Union Address to determine any influence the speech may have had.

W. Wanta and Foote (1994) examined presidential documents related to various issues, then employed a time-series statistical analysis to compare news coverage of those issues on the three national networks. The researchers identified 16 issues which they categorized into four groups: international problems, the economy, social problems, and social issues. They found significant correlations between media coverage and presidential emphasis on the issues in all categories except that of the economy, and on 7 of the 16 individual topics.

Another important finding of the Wanta and Foote study was that media coverage was most often influenced by the president. In other words, the president's issue agenda strongly influenced the media agenda. The news media appeared to influence the president on only 3 of the 16 issues examined: East-West relations, crime and drugs, and environmental concerns. See the "Research Has Shown" box.

Other recent agenda-setting research has attempted to verify the causal direction of agenda setting; that is, does the media set the public agenda or does the public agenda set the media agenda? H. B. Brosius and H. M. Kepplinger (1990) examined the importance of German television news programs in influencing issue salience among the public. They found that television coverage influenced the public agenda in several areas and, conversely, public awareness influenced news coverage in other areas. The intensity and amount of coverage given a particular issue seemed to determine the extent of television's influence in making the public aware of a problem. Public awareness was found to influence media coverage of an issue whenever public concern about the problem had increased steadily over time. See the box, "From the Public to the Media" on page 149.

The use of time-series statistical analysis (Wanta & Foote, 1994; Brosius & Kepplinger, 1992; Zhu, Watt, Snyder, Yan, & Jiang, 1993) has proven successful as a methodology in analyzing agenda-setting effects, especially in the realm of

Agenda-setting research in recent years has continued to reveal significant media effects. Wanta and Ghanem's meta-analysis of almost 100 empirical agenda-setting studies found a statistically significant positive correlation (in press). Agenda-setting effects have also been measured experimentally through online media sources. An online newspaper that brought attention to the issue of racism caused readers to rate racism as a public issue significantly higher than readers who viewed an online newspaper that did not mention racism (Wang, 2000). Experimental studies have also identified agenda-setting effects with respect to the attributes of candidates. Such studies often focus on the concept of framing or the news media's use of central themes and other referential aspects to allow audiences to readily picture topics in the news (McLeod & Detenber 1999; Miller, Andsager, & Reichert, 1998) or priming, such as the study that found significant correlations between attribute agendas and assessments of President Clinton's job performance during the Monica Lewinsky sex scandal (Wanta & Chang, 1999) and the study of the link between presidential election year news and candidate ambivalence (Kiousis, 2000).

politics. Brosius and Kepplinger found that nonlinear models often provided a better explanation of the agenda-setting process than linear models. The researchers had examined voter partisanship and identified salient issues in Germany, comparing them to issues receiving prominent news coverage.

J. Zhu and his colleagues found that media exposure alone is not the only factor affecting issue salience for the public. These researchers identified memory and social relationships as having an influence on agenda-setting effects.

The Journal of Communication (Spring, 1993) featured a symposium of articles on various aspects of agenda setting. Many of the contributors offered their views on directions for future research on the topic. A few of the questions they identified as important included:

- Why do "real-world indicators" of an issue not play an important role in the agenda-setting process?
- What are the cognitive processes involved in the agenda-setting process at the individual level?
- How can we measure the public agenda more accurately? (Rogers, Dearing, & Bregman, 1993, p. 80)

HYPOTHESIS OR THEORY?—THE DEBATE CONTINUES

Scholars are divided on whether agenda setting should be considered a theory or simply a hypothesis. McCombs and Shaw (1993) have argued in favor of agenda setting as a theory by defining a successful theory as a "fruitful" one, that is, one responsible for new questions and directions in scholarly research. They offered the following three features as indicative of the fruitfulness of agenda setting:

1. The steady historical growth of its literature.
2. Its ability to integrate a number of communication research subfields under a single theoretical umbrella as it has moved through four phases of expansion.
3. A continuing ability to generate new research problems across a variety of communication settings (pp. 58–59).

One of the most compelling arguments against agenda setting as a "theory" and the attempts of its proponents to expand its scope was provided by Kosicki, who pointed to several major problems:

- Lack of agreement between conceptual and operational definitions among researchers, causing ambiguity to cloud results.
- Ambiguity in terms of methodology, especially survey studies in which causal direction is not at all clear.
- Insufficient theory and lack of specification in terms of long-term vs. short-term agenda setting effects (pp. 106–107).

One cannot ignore the volume of research studies that have been conducted on agenda setting in assessing its value in contributing to knowledge about media effects, even if all the agenda-setting research has shown only a "subtle, highly contingent effect" (Kosicki, 1993, p. 100). Some agenda-setting critics have even argued that this domain of research embodies the heart of the media effects tradition. "The future of agenda setting is very much the future of media effects. Agenda setting is one part of that larger tapestry, and its fortunes will rise and fall along with other perspectives in the media effects tradition" (p. 118).

Whether one embraces agenda setting as a theory or a hypothesis does not reflect upon the viability of agenda-setting research. It only suggests areas that need clarification or attention in the future.

Agenda setting is often described in Cohen's quote that the press "may not be successful much of the time in telling people what to think, but it is stunningly successful in telling its readers what to think *about*." The agenda-setting function becomes obvious when major news stories bring important issues before the public.

One serious problem that agenda-setting researchers face is the control of extraneous variables. Agenda-setting effects are clearly indicated only when researchers are able to measure public opinion before and after media coverage of specific issues.

Initially, agenda-setting research examined the influence of news media in shaping people's perceptions of the world. In recent years, agenda-setting research has expanded to ask: Who sets the media agenda? Control over the flow of news information by media professionals is an important function called gatekeeping.

Walter Lippmann was the first to describe the agenda setting process in *Public Opinion* (1922). He wrote about the news media's responsibility for shaping the public's perception of the world and creating a pseudo-environment for each news consumer.

The first empirical test of Lippmann's ideas about agenda-setting was Maxwell McCombs and Donald Shaw's Chapel Hill study (1972), which tested the influence of campaign coverage on public perceptions of issue importance.

Hundreds of agenda-setting studies were conducted in the years following the Chapel Hill study. The growth in the research tradition has been divided into four phases: (1) publication of the Chapel Hill study, (2) replication and examination of contingent conditions, (3) an expansion of the original idea of agenda setting into the areas of candidate characteristics and other political aspects, and (4) a focus on the sources of the media agenda.

Agenda-setting studies have typically fallen into one of three types: media agenda setting, public agenda setting, and policy agenda setting. Each type of study measures a different dependent variable. Media agenda setting studies measure the mass media news agenda, public agenda setting studies measure the relative importance of issues to the public, and policy agenda setting studies measure the issue agenda of a governmental body or elected official.

Recent agenda-setting research has attempted to determine the causal direction of agenda setting. It attempts to answer the question: Does the media set the public agenda or does the public agenda set the media agenda?

Scholars are divided on whether agenda setting should be considered a theory or simply a hypothesis. Critics argue that agenda setting is beset with several problems: (1) a lack of agreement between conceptual and operational definitions among researchers, causing ambiguity to cloud results; (2) ambiguity in terms of methodology, especially survey studies in which causal direction is not clear; and (3) insufficient theory and lack of specification in terms of long-term compared with short-term agenda setting effects.

BANDURA, A. (1994). Social cognitive theory of mass communication. In J. Bryant & D. Zillmann, (Eds.), *Media effects: Advances in theory and research* (pp. 61–90). Hillsdale, NJ: Erlbaum.

BECKER, L. B., & KOSICKI, G. M. (1991). Einege historische und aktuelle Anmerkungen zur amerikanischen Wirkungforschung und der Versuch einer transaktionalen analyse [Some historical notes and contemporary comments on American message-producer/message-receiver transaction]. In W. Fruh (Ed.), *Medienwirkungen: Das dynamisch-transaktionale Modell: Theorie und emirische forschung* (pp. 193–213). Opladen: Westdeutscher Verlag.

BROSIUS, H .B., & KEPPLINGER, H. M. (1990). The agenda-setting function of television news. *Communication Research, 17,* 183–211.

BROSIUS, H .B., & KEPPLINGER, H. M. (1992). Beyond agenda-setting: The influence of partisanship and television. *Journalism Quarterly, 69,* 893–902.

CAREY, J. W. (1996). The Chicago school and mass communication research. In E. E. Dennis & E. Wartella (Eds.), *American communication research: The remembered history.* Mahwah, NJ: Erlbaum.

COHEN, B. C. (1963). *The press and foreign policy.* Princeton, NJ: Princeton University Press.

FUNKHOUSER, G. R. (1973). The issues of the sixties: An exploratory study in the dynamics of public opinion. *Public Opinion Quarterly, 37,* 62–75.

IYENGAR, S., & KINDER, D. R. (1987). *News that matters: Television and American opinion.* Chicago: University of Chicago Press.

IYENGAR, S., PETERS, M. D., & KINDER, D. R. (1982). Experimental demonstrations of the "not-so-minimal" consequences of television news programs. *American Political Science Review, 76,* 848–858.

KIOUSIS, S. (2000). *Beyond salience: Exploring the linkages between the agenda setting role of mass media and mass persuasion.* Unpublished doctoral dissertation, University of Texas, Austin.

KOSICKI, G. M. (1993). Problems and opportunities in agenda-setting research. *Journal of Communication, 43*(2), 100–127.

LANG, G. E., & LANG, K. (1991). Watergate: An exploration of the agenda-building process. In D. L. Protess & M. McCombs (Eds.), *Agenda setting: Readings on media, public opinion, and policymaking* (pp. 277–289). Hillsdale, NJ: Erlbaum. (Original work published 1981)

LANG, K., & LANG, G. E. (1959). The mass media and voting. In E. Burdick & A. J. Brodbeck (Eds.), *American voting behavior* (pp. 217–235). Glencoe, Ill.: Free Press.

LAZARSFELD, P., BERELSON, B., & GAUDET, H. (1948). *The people's choice.* New York: Columbia University Press.

LENNON, F. R. (1998). Argentina: 1997 elecciones. Los diarios nacionales y la campana electoral [The 1997 Argentina election. The national dailies and the electoral campaign]. Reported by The Freedom Forum and Austral University.

LIPPMANN, W. (1922). *Public opinion.* New York: Macmillan.

LONG, N. E. (1958). The local community as an ecology of games. *American Journal of Sociology, 64,* 251–261.

MCCOMBS, M. (1992). Explorers and surveyors: Expanding strategies for agenda-setting research. *Journalism Quarterly, 69,* 813–824.

MCCOMBS, M., & BELL, T. (1996). The agenda-setting role of mass communication. In M. B. Salwen & D. W. Stacks (Eds.), *An integrated approach to communication theory and research* (pp. 93–110). Mahwah, NJ: Erlbaum.

McCombs, M., & Shaw, D. (1972). The agenda-setting function of mass media. *Public Opinion Quarterly, 36,* 176–185.

McCombs, M., & Shaw, D. (1993). The evolution of agenda-setting research: Twenty-five years in the marketplace of ideas. *Journal of Communication, 43*(2), 58–67.

McLeod, D., & Detenber, B. (1999). Framing effects of television news coverage of social protest. *Journal of Communication, 49*(3), 3–23.

Miller, M., Andsager, J., & Riechert, B. (1998). Framing the candidates in presidential primaries: Issues and images in press releases and news coverage. *Journalism & Mass Communication Quarterly, 75,* 312–324.

Rogers, E. M., Dearing, J. W., & Bregman, D. (1993). The anatomy of agenda-setting research. *Journal of Communication, 43*(2), 68–84.

Shaw, D., & McCombs, M., (Eds.) (1977). *The emergence of American political issues: The agenda setting function of the press.* St. Paul, MN: West.

Shoemaker, P., & Reese, S. (1991). *Mediating the message: Theories of influence on mass media content.* New York: Longman.

Wang, T. L. (2000). Agenda-setting online: An experiment testing the effects of hyperlinks in online newspapers. *Southwestern Mass Communication Journal, 15*(2), 59–70.

Wanta, W. (1988). The effects of dominant photographs: An agenda-setting experiment. *Journalism Quarterly, 65,* 107–111.

Wanta, W. (1997). *The public and the national agenda: How people learn about important issues.* Mahwah, NJ: Erlbaum.

Wanta, W., & Chang, K. (1999, May). *Priming and the second level of agenda setting: Merging two theoretical approaches.* Paper presented to the International Communication Association, San Francisco, CA.

Wanta, W., & Foote, J. (1994). The president-news media relationship: A time series analysis of agenda-setting. *Journal of Broadcasting & Electronic Media, 38,* 437–449.

Wanta, W., & Ghanem, S. (in press). Effects of agenda-setting. In J. Bryant & R. Carveth (Eds.), *Meta-Analyses of media effects.* Mahwah, NJ: Erlbaum.

Wanta, W., Stephenson, M. A., Turk, J. V., & McCombs, M. E. (1989). How president's state of the union talk influenced news media agendas. *Journalism Quarterly, 66,* 537–541.

Weaver, D., Graber, D., McCombs, M., & Eyal, C. (1981). *Media agenda setting in a presidential election: Issues, images and interest.* New York: Praeger.

Westley, B. H. (1978). Review of *The emergence of American political issues: The agenda setting function of the press. Journalism Quarterly, 55,* 172–173.

Zhu, J., Watt, J. H., Snyder, L. B., Yan, J. (1993). Public issue priority formation: Media agenda-setting and social interaction. *Journal of Communication, 43,* 8–29.

CHAPTER 10

Persuasion

The real persuaders are our appetites, our fears and above all our vanity. The skillful propagandist stirs and coaches these internal persuaders.
—**Eric Hoffer, *The Passionate State of Mind*, 1955**

Persuasion research in mass communication examines the process of attitude formation and change in audience members and the modification of behavior based upon attitude change. Its roots are in antiquity and it remains one of the most prolific realms of modern communication scholarship.

Any individual or group that has some stake in influencing mass audiences stands to benefit from this particular arm of communication research. Advertising agents, consumer product manufacturers, politicians, and public service organizations are a few of the groups that use research findings to their practical advantage. Knowledge of persuasive influences is also important for consumers, voters, and other audience members who wish to protect themselves from being manipulated.

Persuasion research differs in an important way from most other areas of media effects research. Most persuasive messages are intentional; that is, they are designed to have an *intended effect*. Media effects in other realms of effects research (e.g., aggressive behavior after viewing violence) are usually *unintended*. The exceptions to this would be some instances of fright reactions in horror films and certain gratifications obtained from media use.

Persuasion involves certain processes of attitude change. Psychologists R. E. Petty and J. T. Cacioppo have created a popular and computerized model to explain the processes that audience members experience as they are persuaded. Their **Elaboration Likelihood Model** of persuasion identifies two separate "routes to persuasion" or one of two bridges that must be crossed before persuasion can occur (Petty & Cacioppo, 1981, 1986b; Petty & Priester, 1994, p. 98). After other theories of persuasion are presented, the Elaboration Likelihood Model will be discussed in detail in this chapter.

Following a review of the research tradition associated with studies of persuasion, we discuss the importance of attitudes, emotions, and behavior in the persuasion process. We then take a look at various models of persuasion, including models that link attitudes and actions. Finally, we examine recent directions and future trends in persuasion research. We should point out that this chapter excludes most persuasion studies related to advertising messages, health, political campaigns, and other types of communication campaigns. The research literature for each of these topics is so vast that we included a separate chapter for each.

RESEARCH TRADITION

When radio became popular in the early part of the 20th century, psychologists and sociologists began investigating the persuasive power of mass media. In the 1920s and 1930s, a respected social scientist found that propaganda messages had had *powerful* effects upon audiences during World War I (Lasswell, 1927).

In the years between the world wars, several events provided additional evidence for the power of the media to influence the masses: In 1929 news of the crash on Wall Street brought nationwide panic; in 1938 Orson Wells's *War of the Worlds* broadcast resulted in cases of hysteria that received much publicity; finally—perhaps most significantly—Adolf Hitler's rise to power in Germany underscored the frightening potential for mass persuasion by means of media communication.

During World War II, researcher Carl Hovland continued to learn about the effects of persuasive messages on attitude change through his study of soldiers who viewed military training films. Hovland found that the soldiers learned new information from the films, but the persuasive power of the films in effecting changes in attitudes and behavior was rather limited. Persuasion, Hovland found, was contingent upon any number of variables that served to moderate the effects (Hovland, Lumsdaine, & Sheffield, 1949).

After the war, Hovland continued his research on persuasion at Yale University. His research priority became the identification of the moderating variables that acted upon the persuasive process. Hovland found that successful persuasion involved a process of three important steps: (1) listeners must pay attention to a message, (2) they must comprehend the message, and (3) they must accept the message. He identified a number of variables that affected the power of a persuasive message. These included the credibility of the message source, the type of message appeal (e.g., did it arouse fear or motivate the listener), the order of the arguments presented (e.g., the different power of one-sided arguments compared with two-sided arguments), identification of the audience member with certain groups, and specific personality characteristics of audience members.

Much of the evidence for powerful and direct media effects during the early years was not based on the best research designs. For example, little effort was expended toward measuring people's attitudes *prior to* receiving the propaganda messages—a crucial factor in proving that attitude change had actually occurred due to the propaganda message.

Social scientists continued to study the effects of persuasive messages in the 1940s and 1950s, using more rigorous empirical methods. H. Hyman and P. Sheatsley (1947) found that to be successful in changing attitudes, persuasive messages had to overcome certain psychological barriers. Other social scientists

Credibility and likability of a message source affects the power of a persuasive message.
Source: © AP/Photo/Richard Drew

reported that persuasive campaign messages from the media had little effect on changing people's preferences for candidates in the 1940 presidential election (Lazarsfeld, Berelson, & Gaudet, 1948).

P. Lazarsfeld and his colleagues determined that media messages served primarily to reinforce existing attitudes rather than to change anyone's opinion. Media messages did seem to influence certain members of the community who were respected for their knowledge of current affairs. These *opinion leaders*, as the researchers called them, had the personal influence to change the attitudes of others in the community. Thus, media influence was described as a *two-step flow* or *indirect effects* situation in which media messages influenced opinion leaders who, in turn, influenced others in the community via interpersonal communication (Katz & Lazarsfeld, 1955).

Through the years, communication scholars have debated the extent to which mass mediated messages have the power to persuade audiences. Most recent research has shown that persuasion is not simply a stimulus-and-response-type situation, but a more complicated process that emphasizes the *receptivity* of the receiver, or his or her willingness to receive the message.

ATTITUDE, EMOTIONS, BEHAVIOR, AND PERSUASION

To understand the persuasion process, one must first understand the concept of *attitude*. A person's attitude can be defined as that person's "abstract evaluation of an object" (Chaiken, Wood, & Eagly, 1996, p. 702). Others have defined attitudes as "people's general predispositions to evaluate other people, objects, and issues favorably or unfavorably" (Petty & Priester, 1994, p. 94).

Whatever the definition, most contemporary research involving persuasive effects places much importance on the critical role of attitudes in the persuasion process. Attitude is viewed as the all-important mediator that stands between the acquisition of new persuasive information and subsequent behavioral change. If the new information changes a person's attitude, then behavioral change is more likely.

What actually causes a change in attitude? What internal processes come into play? Are people motivated to change their attitudes and behavior to gain rewards or avoid punishment, or do they make the change due to some other reason?

One explanation of this complex process is the **theory of cognitive dissonance** (Festinger, 1957). The best way to understand this theory is to define each of its components. We have already learned that the term "cognitive" is used to describe mental processes or thoughts. "Dissonance" in this case refers to something being *inconsistent.* Cognitive dissonance occurs when attitude and action become inconsistent with one another. For example, someone who is forced to make major dietary changes for health reasons would also have to make significant adjustments in his or her attitude, especially if the old way of eating was believed to be a "healthy" diet. According to L. Festinger's theory of cognitive dissonance, this inconsistency causes the person anxiety that must be resolved. The way it is resolved is to bring the attitude in line with the actions. The new diet is soon believed to be more healthy than the old one.

> Festinger's answer to why people come to believe what they say was thus that inconsistency between what they believe (i.e., their attitudes) and what they say (i.e., their behavior) produces a negative state of arousal that can be reduced by changing attitudes to align them with behavior. (Chaiken, Wood, & Eagly, 1996, p. 704)

Recent theorists have hypothesized that the discrepancy between behavior and attitude is not as important in producing attitude change as is the person's *perceptions about the consequences* of his or her actions (Cooper & Fazio, 1984).

> It is indeed plausible that people would be uncomfortable to think of themselves as willingly engaging in behavior with undesirable consequences. Having others think of oneself in this way should also create discomfort. However, if the role player adopts the advocated position, it would no longer seem harmful to persuade others to hold the same attitude. Attitude change thereby restores the role player's self-integrity and produces a favorable self-presentation as well. These self interpretations thus elaborate and clarify dissonance theory by providing a rationale for the generalization that taking responsibility for aversive consequences produces attitude change (Chaiken, Wood, and Eagly, 1996, p. 705).

For another example, consider the person who has been brought up to believe that homosexuality is horrible. Perhaps the person has carried strong prejudices toward homosexuals, and has even cracked jokes about homosexuals, using derisive names. Suppose such behaviors would not be tolerated in the person's workplace, where co-workers, clients, or subordinates might be gay or lesbian. The person may even come to like and respect some co-workers who have different sexual preferences, adding to the dissonance between attitude and behavior. Rather than continue with absolute intolerance, the person might ease cognitive dissonance by changing attitudes toward the homosexual community.

Many social scientists emphasize the connection between attitudes and *emotions* or affective components. Persuasive messages that contain emotional appeals can be powerful. Studies have found that emotions are very important in the formation and change of attitudes (Jorgensen, 1998).

Through the years, a number of researchers have developed various models to explain the persuasion process. Some of the major models are discussed below. Special emphasis is given to the Elaboration Likelihood Model, or ELM, which provides one of the most comprehensive explanations for persuasive processes in terms of mediated communications.

McGuire's Communication/Persuasion Matrix Model

W. J. McGuire (1985, 1989) introduced a model to explain persuasion effects by identifying *inputs* and *outputs*. Inputs, or independent variables, include the source, the message, the recipient, the channel, and the context of the presentation of the message. Inputs are variables controlled by the person or group attempting to persuade or influence audience members. Outputs, or dependent variables, are variables that fall under the control of the individual audience members. These variables include exposure to the information; attention to the information; interest, comprehension, and acquisition of new knowledge; yielding to the weight of the message and changing the attitude; remembering of the information and new attitude; retrieval of the information; the conscious decision to act according to the new attitude; action based upon that decision; reinforcement of the new behavior; and consolidation of the new attitude.

McGuire's model has several shortcomings (Petty & Priester, 1994). The first is its lack of detail regarding the process of actual *yielding* to a new attitude. Second, the model assumes that the input and output variables are *sequential*; that is, they must occur in the order listed in order to have persuasive effects. Yet more recent research has shown that the variables do not need to be sequential for persuasion to occur. The acquisition or learning and remembering of new information have been found to be independent of each other and even unnecessary steps in the persuasion process (Greenwald, 1968; McGuire, 1985; Petty

McGuire's Matrix Model:

Variables that Affect the Persuasive Power of a Communication Message

Input Variables (Controlled by Communicator)

Source	Message	Recipient	Channel	Context

Output Variables (Controlled by Receiver)

Exposure	Attention	Interest	Comprehension
Acquisition	Yielding	Memory	Retrieval
Decision	Action	Reinforcement	Consolidation

& Cacioppo, 1981). For example, a person might acquire and learn new information but refuse to change his or her attitude, or a person might conceivably misunderstand the information, learn it wrong, but still change his or her attitude in the intended way.

Cognitive Response Theory

In an attempt to explain the shortcomings of the matrix model, several researchers developed the theory of cognitive response (Greenwald, 1968; Petty, Ostrom, & Brock, 1981). According to this theory, an audience member does not yield to a new attitude after simply learning a new message. Yielding depends upon cognitive responses to the message—or what he or she *thinks* about the message. The memory of what is thought about a message is much more important than a memory of the message itself.

In some cases, however, persuasion has been shown to occur even when an audience member does not think about the content of a message. Cognitive response theory could not explain such instances (Petty, Cacioppo, & Goldman, 1981).

The Elaboration Likelihood Model

Petty and Cacioppo (1981, 1986a, 1986b) extended the theory of cognitive response and developed a theoretical model to explain the processes that occur when a person yields to a persuasive message. Their **Elaboration Likelihood Model (ELM)** explains the process of persuasion by identifying the likelihood of a person to elaborate cognitively or think very carefully about a persuasive message.

The model proposes two distinct routes that may be taken in order for persuasion to result: central and peripheral. The *central route* to persuasion requires much cognitive effort on the part of the audience member in order to judge the merit of the advocated position or persuasive message. The message recipient listens closely to what is said, then evaluates the information in light of past experiences and previous knowledge. During this process, the person forms opinions about the message—either favorable or unfavorable—and these play a major part in determining the success of the persuasive message. For example, news reports that cover debates on important national and international issues usually require a great deal of cognitive processing on the part of the viewer or reader. Whether or not a spokesperson for a particular side in an issue persuades the reader or viewer to advocate a particular position depends upon central route processing of the information.

The central route necessitates considerable cognitive effort on the part of the audience member. As a result, attitude changes resulting from the central route have shown several common characteristics, including: (1) accessibility, (2) persistency, (3) predictability of behavior, and (4) resistance to change (Petty & Priester, 1994, pp. 100–101).

The *peripheral route* to persuasion may occur in any number of ways, none of which involves considerable cognitive effort. *Simple cues* in the context of the message are more responsible for the change in attitude than a purposeful effort to process and understand information. For example, a relaxing scene by a calm, crystal blue mountain lake in a television commercial might cause the viewer to experience a nice, contented mood that becomes associated with the mountain-fresh scented detergent that is being pitched. The viewer is persuaded to try the detergent because the commercial has conditioned a certain affective response—the nice, contented mood—that is associated with the product.

The *use of experts* to pitch particular products is another example of the peripheral route to persuasion. More doctors use this aspirin. . . , more hospitals use this brand. . . , more dentists recommend this toothpaste. . . , are all examples of cues used to effectively shortcut the route to persuasion. Experts are supposed to be correct, the viewer infers; therefore, the message is judged as truthful and the viewer is persuaded to use the product (Chaiken, 1987).

Another example of the peripheral route, the *bandwagon effect*, was identified by researchers for the Institute for Propaganda Analysis in the 1930s (Lee & Lee, 1939). Audience members were made to believe that many other people already supported the position of a speaker. They inferred that with so many people in agreement, the speaker's message must be true. Such an inference served as a cue that the message of the speaker was valid, and the bandwagon effect occurred (Axsom, Yates, & Chaiken, 1987).

In contrast, persuasion by way of the central route has been shown to be more successful in long-term attitude change than persuasion through more peripheral routes. Peripheral route persuasion has been shown to be successful in the short run, but over a period of time the strength of the peripheral cues weakens. A person's mood and feelings may change, for example, or cues are no longer associated with certain messages. Petty and Cacioppo (1986a) found that in terms of resistance to attack and durability, attitude changes that occurred through the peripheral route were much weaker than those that occurred through the central route.

Predictions of the Elaboration Likelihood Model

When the likelihood for elaboration is high (e.g., when the message has personal relevance for the audience member, when there are few distractions), a person is motivated to listen to the message, mentally process, and evaluate the information. Peripheral cue variables are likely to have less impact in such a situation.

When the likelihood for elaboration is low (e.g., when the message has low personal relevance or there are many distractions), the importance of peripheral variables increases significantly. Under such circumstances, the audience member is not likely to be motivated or able to process the message with careful thought.

When the likelihood for elaboration is moderate (e.g., when the audience member has some knowledge of the issue but uncertainty about its personal relevance), the recipient may evaluate the context of the message to determine whether the message should be processed. A contextual component would be, for example, the credibility or the attractiveness of a source.

In summary, as the likelihood of mental elaboration (careful processing of a persuasive message) increases, the central route to persuasion is dominant. As the likelihood of mental elaboration decreases, the peripheral route to persuasion becomes more important in the persuasion process.

Variables that Motivate

The strength of the central route to persuasion has led researchers to examine the variables that motivate a person to think carefully about a message. One of the most important of these variables is that of *personal relevance* of the message (Brickner, Harkins, & Ostrom, 1986; Leippe & Elkin, 1987; Petty, Cacioppo, & Haugtvedt, 1992).

Two important studies illustrate the strength of the personal relevance variable. Petty and Cacioppo (1979b) told one group of undergraduates (high personal relevance group) that their university might start requiring each senior to pass a qualifying exam in his or her major subject in order to graduate. Another group of students (low personal relevance group) was told that a distant university was considering such a policy. The two groups of students then heard one of two radio editorials (either a strong argument or a weak argument) advocating the new policy. The researchers found that the high personal relevance group processed the messages more carefully than the low personal relevance group. As a message increased in personal relevance to the audience, strong arguments became more persuasive and weak arguments became less persuasive.

The other study, by R. Burnkrant and R. Unnava (1989) found that personal relevance could be increased by simply using the second person pronoun "you" rather than the third person pronouns "he" or "she." Those who received messages containing "you" were shown to listen and process the information more carefully. Like the other study, as the message increased in personal relevance to the audience, strong arguments became more persuasive and weak arguments became less persuasive.

Researchers have identified other variables that provide the necessary motivation for a receiver to think carefully about a message. One of these involves formulating a question rather than making an assertion in a message to provoke more thought processing on the part of the receiver (Howard, 1990; Petty, Cacioppo, & Heesacker, 1981; Swasy & Munch, 1985). For example, the famous soap commercial does not make the simple assertions: "Use Dial. Everyone should." Instead, it asks, "Aren't you glad you use Dial? Don't you wish everyone did?" Another variable is that of using several sources rather than a single one to present arguments (Harkins & Petty, 1981; Moore & Reardon, 1987).

"Peripheral Cue" Variables

A number of variables have been shown to affect the persuasion process by means of the peripheral route. According to R. E. Petty and J. Priester, a *peripheral cue* can be defined as "a feature of the persuasion context that allows favorable or unfavorable attitude formation even in the absence of an effortful consideration of the true merits of the object or issue" (1994, p. 106). As the likelihood of mental elaboration (careful cognitive processing of a message) decreases, peripheral cues become more potent. Petty and Priester (1994) reviewed the research findings to identify several variables that serve as simple cues. These included:

1. The likability or attractiveness of the message source.
2. The credibility of the source.
3. The number of arguments the message contained.
4. How long the arguments were.
5. How many others were perceived by the viewer to agree with the position, also known as the bandwagon effect.

The Role of Variables

For persuasion to occur, three factors must be present. A *source* must deliver a persuasive *message* to a *recipient*. Variables that affect the persuasion process may take on different roles and impact any of the three factors.

Source factor variables would include characteristics such as the attractiveness or credibility of the source. Research has shown that such variables serve as peripheral cues when the likelihood of elaboration is low, but are not as important as the quality of the argument itself when the likelihood of elaboration is high (Petty, Cacioppo, & Goldman, 1981). Research has also shown that such variables either enhanced or weakened the likelihood for persuasion, depending upon the strength of the argument (Moore, Hausknecht, & Thamodaran, 1986; Heesacker, Petty, & Cacioppo, 1983; Puckett, Petty, Cacioppo, & Fisher, 1983). An attractive or expert source made a strong argument stronger and more persuasive, but the same type of source made a weak argument weaker and even less persuasive.

Variables that could be considered message factors would include all the informational items included in a message. When the likelihood for elaboration is low, the informational items in the message serve as peripheral cues. When the likelihood for elaboration is high, the items are processed carefully and are not merely peripheral cues. Research has shown that the addition of weak arguments in support of a position for each of the low and high ELM conditions results in a different outcome. When informational items are peripheral cues, the addition of weak supporting arguments makes persuasion more likely, but when informational items are evaluated cogently as arguments themselves, weak additional arguments are less likely to affect persuasion (Alba & Marmorstein, 1987; Petty & Cacioppo, 1986a).

An example of a recipient factor would be a person's mood at the time the message is received. An experiment by Petty, Schumann, Richman, and Strathman (1993) revealed several ways in which the recipient's mood influenced the persuasion process. Participants saw a product advertisement while watching one of two television programs, either a pleasant situation comedy or a neutral documentary. In the high involvement or high elaboration likelihood condition, participants were told they could select a free gift afterward from several brands of the product in the commercial. In the low involvement or low elaboration likelihood condition, participants could select from several brands of another kind of product than that depicted in the commercial. The study revealed that viewing the pleasant program not only made people evaluate their own moods more positively, but it made them evaluate the commercial product more positively as well. This was true for both the high- and low-involvement conditions, though it must be pointed out that more positive thoughts about the product were generated when the elaboration likelihood was high rather than low. Generally speaking, mood tended to affect a person's attitude directly when involvement (elaboration likelihood) was low, but when involvement was high, the effect of mood upon attitude depended upon the number of positive thoughts generated.

Recent ELM Research

In recent years several studies and integrative chapters have increased our understanding of the elaboration likelihood model. A team of researchers found a *sleeper effect* when a communicator elaborated on ideas included in an initial communication (Priester, Wegener, Petty, & Fabrigar, 1999). The sleeper effect occurred whenever persuasive influences increased rather than decreased with the passing of time. Two other researchers provided an ELM approach to examining persuasive processes in the modification of attitudes due to aspects of identity or self-concept (Fleming & Petty, 2000). And the ELM approach has been used to argue that persuasion is influenced by matches in a person's attitudes, identity, and self-schema (Petty, Wheeler, & Bizer, 2000).

MODELS THAT LINK ATTITUDES AND ACTIONS

A large body of persuasion research has addressed the connection between a person's attitude and his or her actions or behavior. Whether or not a person changes his behavior to come into line with a change in attitude depends upon a number of factors. Most of these factors are related to particular situations or the person's disposition (Ajzen, 1988).

Scholars have developed two general purpose models that serve to explain the process that links a new or changed attitude with appropriate action or behavior. One model holds that behavior is a result of thoughtful reasoning; the other proposes that behavior is more spontaneous and is activated automatically. These two models are called, respectively, the *reasoned action and planned behavior model* and the *automatic activation model*.

Reasoned Action and Planned Behavior

M. Fishbein and I. Ajzen introduced the **reasoned action and planned behavior model** with the assumption that "people consider the implications of their actions before they decide to engage or not engage in a given behavior" (1975, p. 5). The model hypothesizes that people make the decision to behave or not to behave in a certain way based upon two criteria. The person's attitude toward the behavior itself is one important criterion. The other is the person's perceptions about how others will view the behavior. Before the person engages in a particular behavior, he or she carefully weighs the personal advantages or disadvantages of doing so. If engaging in the behavior comes at a cost, that cost is considered and carefully weighed against the perceived benefits of engaging in that behavior.

Ajzen (1991) revised the model to include the notion of planned behavior. In addition to basing intentions for action upon attitudes and the behavioral norms of others, the expanded model reveals that intentions to act are also based upon the perceived *control* the person has over the behavior.

Automatic Activation

The **automatic activation model** proposes that behavior follows automatically whenever an attitude comes to mind. The process is spontaneous and does not involve any extended reflection or reasoning on the part of the individual. R. H. Fazio (1990), the originator of the model, offered two contingent circumstances that allow attitudes to guide behavior automatically: (1) if there is spontaneous access to the attitude whenever the object of the attitude is present, and (2) if the object is perceived according to the attitude (if the attitude is favorable, it is perceived favorably; if unfavorable, it is perceived unfavorably).

RECENT RESEARCH AND FUTURE TRENDS

As we mentioned in the introduction to this chapter, the research literature related to the effects of persuasive media messages is so vast that we include separate chapters for the domains of advertising, health, political campaigns, and other communication campaigns. In this section we identify additional important research in recent years that has advanced our theoretical understanding of persuasive media effects.

W. Wood (2000) reviewed recent research on message-based persuasion and identified different types of motives that produce attitude change or resistance. Research studies on these motives have examined the functions of attitude, sometimes using cognitive dissonance theory as a basis for investigation.

Gender differences and emotions and their influence in the persuasion process have also interested researchers. M. Burgoon and R. S. Klingle (1998) reviewed research on the importance of gender differences in persuasive communications. They argued that, generally, men are more persuasive and women are more persuadable, but the sex of the communicator and the strategies of the persuasive message are important determinants. As for the connection between emotion and persuasion, P. F. Jorgensen (1998) discussed the importance of emotions in the formation and change of attitudes in the persuasion process.

The link between attitudes and persuasion has received attention in recent years. Petty and Cacioppo (1996) surveyed the different theories related to persuasion and changes in attitudes and beliefs. D. R. Roskos-Ewoldsen (1997) reviewed research on attitude accessibility as a factor in persuasion and argued that some attitudes are remembered more than others. Those that are highly accessible from memory are more likely to influence a person's reception of various messages. He also proposed a model to demonstrate the transactive relationship between persuasion and attitude accessibility.

In the future, persuasion researchers will continue to identify and study the many variables at work whenever persuasive messages reach audience members. The important influences of individual attitudes and individual emotions on the power of persuasive messages appear to be especially illuminating in our ever-increasing understanding of the persuasion process.

SUMMARY

Persuasion research in mass communication examines the process of attitude change in audience members and the modification of behavior based upon attitude change. Persuasion is an intentional process.

Research on the persuasive power of mass media began in the 1920s and 1930s when radio and films were popular. Harold Lasswell found that propaganda messages had had powerful effects upon audiences during World War I. Several events provided evidence for the influential power of the media: news of the Wall Street crash in 1929, Orson Wells's *War of the Worlds* radio broadcast in 1938, and Adolf Hitler's rise to power in Germany. During World War II, Carl Hovland found persuasion was contingent upon any number of moderating variables.

Hovland found that successful persuasion involved three steps: (1) listeners must pay attention to a message, (2) they must comprehend the message, and (3) they must accept the message. The credibility of the message source, the type of message appeal, the order of the arguments presented, identification of the audience member with certain groups, and specific personality characteristics of audience members all affected persuasive power of media messages.

In the 1940s and 1950s, persuasion was studied using more rigorous empirical methods. Hyman and Sheatsley found that attitude change required persuasive messages to pass over certain psychological barriers. Katz and Lazarsfeld described media influence as a two-step flow or indirect effects situation in which media messages influenced opinion leaders who in turn influenced others in the community through interpersonal communication. Recent research has shown that persuasion is not simply a stimulus-and-response-type situation, but a more complicated process that emphasizes the receptivity of the receiver. Most contemporary research places considerable importance on the critical role of attitudes in the persuasion process. Attitudes can be defined as "people's general predispositions to evaluate other people, objects, and issues favorably or unfavorably." Attitude is the mediator between the acquisition of persuasive information and behavioral change.

McGuire's model explained persuasion effects by identifying inputs (variables controlled by the persuasive source) and outputs (variables controlled by audience members). The model has been criticized for its lack of detail regarding the process of actual yielding to a new attitude and its assumption that the input and output variables are sequential.

The theory of cognitive response holds that yielding to persuasive messages depends upon audience members' cognitive responses to the messages. The memory of what is thought about a message is much more important than a memory of the message itself. Cognitive response theory does not explain instances when persuasion occurs even when an audience member does not think about the content of a message.

Petty and Cacioppo's Elaboration Likelihood Model (ELM) extends the theory of cognitive response and explains the processes that occur whenever a person yields to a persuasive message. It identifies the likelihood of a person to elaborate cognitively or think very carefully about a persuasive message.

The ELM proposes two distinct routes—central and peripheral. The central route requires much cognitive effort. Attitude changes resulting from the central route have shown several common characteristics: (1) accessibility, (2) persistency, (3) predictability of behavior, and (4) resistance to change. When persuasion occurs by means of the peripheral route, simple cues in the context of the message, the use of experts to pitch products, and the bandwagon effect are more responsible for attitude change than any considerable cognitive effort. As the likelihood of mental elaboration (careful processing of a persuasive message) increases, the **central route** to persuasion is dominant. As the likelihood of mental elaboration decreases, the **peripheral route** to persuasion becomes more important in the persuasion process.

REFERENCES

Ajzen, I. (1988). *Attitudes, personality, and behavior.* Homewood, IL: Dorsey.

Ajzen, I. (1991). The theory of planned behavior. *Organizational Behavior and Human Decision Processes, 50*(2), 179–211.

Alba, J. W., & Marmorstein, H. (1987). The effects of frequency knowledge on consumer decision making. *Journal of Consumer Research, 14*(1), 14–25.

Axsom, D., Yates, S., & Chaiken, S. (1987). Audience response as a heuristic cue in persuasion. *Journal of Personality and Social Psychology, 53,* 30–40.

Brickner, M. A., Harkins, S. G., & Ostrom, T. M. (1986). Effects of personal involvement: Thought provoking implications for social loafing. *Journal of Personality and Social Psychology, 51,* 763–769.

Burgoon, M., & Klingle, R. S. (1998). Gender differences in being influential and/or influenced: A challenge to prior explanations. In D. J. Canary, K. Dindia (Eds.), *Sex differences and similarities in communication: Critical essays and empirical investigations of sex and gender in interaction* (pp. 257–285). Mahwah, NJ: Erlbaum.

Burnkrant, R., & Unnava, R. (1989). Self-referencing: A strategy for increasing processing of message content. *Personality and Social Psychology Bulletin, 15,* 628–638.

Chaiken, S. (1987). The heuristic model of persuasion. In M. P. Zanna, J. Olson, & C. P. Herman (Eds.), *Social influence: The Ontario symposium, 5* (pp. 3–39). Hillsdale, NJ: Erlbaum.

Chaiken, S., & Eagly, A. H. (1976). Communication modality as a determinant of message persuasiveness and message comprehensibility. *Journal of Personality and Social Psychology, 34,* 605–614.

Chaiken, S., Wood, W., & Eagly, A. H. (1996). Principles of persuasion. E. T. Higgins & A. W. Kruglanski (Eds.), *Social psychology: Handbook of basic principles.* New York: Guilford Press.

COOPER, J., & FAZIO, R. H. (1984). A new look at dissonance theory. In L. Berkowitz (Ed.), *Advances in experimental social psychology, 17,* (pp. 229–266). San Diego, CA: Academic Press.

FAZIO, R. H. (1990). Multiple processes by which attitudes guide behavior: The MODE model as an integrative framework. *Advances in Experimental Social Psychology, 23,* 75–102.

FESTINGER, L. (1957). *A theory of cognitive dissonance.* Evanston, IL: Row, Peterson.

FISHBEIN, M., & AJZEN, I. (1976). Misconceptions about the Fishbein model: Reflections on a study by Songer-Nocks. *Journal of Experimental Social Psychology, 12,* 579–584.

FLEMING, M. A., & PETTY, R. E. (2000). Identity and persuasion: An elaboration likelihood approach. In D. J. Terry & M. A. Hogg (Eds.), *Attitudes, behavior, and social context: The role of norms and group membership. Applied social research* (pp. 171–199). Mahwah, NJ: Erlbaum.

GREENWALD, A. G. (1968). Cognitive learning, cognitive response to persuasion, and attitude change. In A. Greenwald, T. Brock, & T. Ostrom (Eds.), *Psychological foundations of attitudes* (pp. 147–170). New York: Academic Press.

HARKINS, S. G., & PETTY, R. E. (1981). The effects of source magnification cognitive effort on attitudes: An information processing view. *Journal of Personality and Social Psychology, 40,* 401–413.

HEESACKER, M., PETTY, R. E., & CACIOPPO, J. T. (1983). Field dependence and attitude change: Source credibility can alter persuasion by affecting message-relevant thinking. *Journal of Personality, 51,* 653–666.

HITCHON, J., DUCKLER, P., & THORSON, E. (1994). Effects of ambiguity and complexity on consumer response to music video commercials. *Journal of Broadcasting and Electronic Media, 38,* 289–306.

HOVLAND, C. I., LUMSDAINE, A., & SHEFFIELD, F. (1949). *Experiments on mass communication.* Princeton, NJ: Princeton University Press.

HOWARD, D. J. (1990). Rhetorical question effects on message processing and persuasion: The role of information availability and the elicitation of judgment. *Journal of Experimental Social Psychology, 26,* 217–239.

HYMAN, H., & SHEATSLEY, P. (1947). Some reasons why information campaigns fail. *Public Opinion Quarterly, 11,* 412–423.

JORGENSEN, P. F. (1998). Affect, persuasion, and communication processes. In P. A. Anderson, L. K. Guerrero (Eds.), *Handbook of communication and emotion: Research, theory, applications, and contexts* (pp. 403–422). San Diego, CA: Academic Press.

KATZ, D., & LAZARSFELD, P. R. (1955). *Personal influence.* New York: Free Press.

LASSWELL, H. W. (1927). *Propaganda techniques in the world war.* New York: Peter Smith.

LAZARSFELD, P., BERELSON, B., & GAUDET, H. (1948). *The people's choice.* New York: Columbia University Press.

LEE, A., & LEE, E. B. (1939). *The fine art of propaganda: A study of Father Coughlin's speeches.* New York: Harcourt, Brace.

LEIPPE, M. R., & ELKIN, R. A. (1987). When motives clash: Issue involvement and response involvement as determinants of persuasion. *Journal of Personality and Social Psychology, 52,* 269–278.

McGUIRE, W. J. (1985). Attitudes and attitude change. In G. Lindzey & E. Aronson (Eds.), *Handbook of social psychology* (3rd ed., Vol. 2, pp. 43–65). Newbury Park, CA: Sage.

MOORE, D. L., HAUSKNECHT, D., & THAMODARAN, K. (1986). Time compression, response opportunity, and persuasion. *Journal of Consumer Research, 13,* 85–99.

MOORE, D. L., & REARDON, R. (1987). Source magnification: The role of multiple sources in the processing of advertising appeals. *Journal of Marketing Research, 24,* 412–417.

PETTY, R. E., & CACIOPPO, J. T. (1979b). Issue-involvement can increase or decrease persuasion by enhancing message-relevant cognitive responses. *Journal of Personality and Social Psychology, 37,* 1915–1926.

PETTY, R. E., & CACIOPPO, J. T. (1981). *Attitudes and persuasion: Classic and contemporary approaches.* Dubuque, IA: W. C. Brown.

PETTY, R. E., & CACIOPPO, J. T. (1986a). *Communication and persuasion: Central and peripheral routes to attitude change.* New York: Springer/Verlag.

PETTY, R. E., & CACIOPPO, J. T. (1986b). The Elaboration Likelihood Model of persuasion. In L. Berkowitz (Ed.), *Advances in experimental social psychology, 19* (pp. 123–205). New York: Academic Press.

PETTY, R. E., & CACIOPPO, J. T. (1996). *Attitudes and Persuasion: Classic and contemporary approaches.* Boulder, CO: Westview.

PETTY, R. E., CACIOPPO, J. T., & GOLDMAN, R. (1981). Personal involvement as a determinant of argument-based persuasion. *Journal of Personality and Social Psychology, 41,* 847–855.

PETTY, R. E., CACIOPPO, J. T., & HAUGTVEDT, C. (1992). Involvement and persuasion: An appreciative look at the Sherifs' contribution to the study of self-relevance and attitude change. In D. Granberg & G. Sarup (Eds.), *Social judgment and intergroup relations: Essays in honor of Muzafer Sherif* (pp. 147–174). New York: Springer/Verlag.

PETTY, R. E., CACIOPPO, J. T., & HEESACKER, M. (1981). The use of rhetorical questions in persuasion: A cognitive response analysis. *Journal of Personality and Social Psychology, 40,* 432–440.

PETTY, R. E., OSTROM, T. M., & BROCK, T. C. (Eds.). (1981). *Cognitive responses in persuasion.* Hillsdale, NJ: Erlbaum.

PETTY, R. E., & PRIESTER, J. R. (1994). Mass media attitude change: Implications of the Elaboration Likelihood Model of Persuasion. In J. Bryant & D. Zillmann (Eds.), *Media effects: Advances in theory and research* (pp. 91–122). Hillsdale, NJ: Erlbaum.

PETTY, R. E., WELLS, G .L., & BROCK, T. C. (1976). Distraction can enhance or reduce yielding to propaganda. *Journal of Personality and Social Psychology, 34,* 874–884.

PETTY, R. E., WHEELER, S. C., & BIZER, G. Y. (2000). Attitude functions and persuasion: An elaboration likelihood approach to matched versus mismatched messages. In G. R. Maio & J. M. Olson (Eds.), *Why we evaluate: Functions of attitudes* (pp. 133–162). Mahwah, NJ: Erlbaum.

PRIESTER, J., WEGENER, D., PETTY, R., & FABRIGAR, L. (1999). Examining the psychological process underlying the sleeper effect: The Elaboration Likelihood Model explanation. *Media Psychology, 1,* 27–48.

PUCKETT, J. M., PETTY, R. E., CACIOPPO, J. T., & FISCHER, D. L. (1983). The relative impact of age and attractiveness stereotypes on persuasion. *Journal of Gerontology, 38,* 340–343.

ROSKOS-EWOLDSEN, D. R. (1997). Attitude accessibility and persuasion: Review and a transactive model. In B. R. Burleson & A. W. Kunkel (Eds.), *Communication yearbook 20* (pp. 185–225). Thousand Oaks, CA: Sage.

SMITH, S. M., & SHAFFER, D. R. (1991). Celebrity and cajolery: Rapid speech may promote or inhibit persuasion via its impact on message elaboration. *Personality and Social Psychology Bulletin, 17,* 663–669.

SWASY, J. L., & MUNCH, J. M. (1985). Examining the target of receiver elaborations: Rhetorical question effects on source processing and persuasion. *Journal of Consumer Research, 11,* 877–886.

WOOD, W. (2000). Attitude change: Persuasion and social influence. *Annual Review of Psychology, 51,* 539–570.

Key Areas of Research

CHAPTER 11

Effects of Media Violence

The currents rage deep inside us
This is the age of video violence.
—Lou Reed, "Video Violence" from album Mistrial, 1986

In 1998 a California man parked his truck on a connecting loop and proceeded to stop traffic on two busy Los Angeles freeways. As police and news helicopters gathered on the scene, the man displayed a sign that read "HMOs are in it for the money. Live free, love safe, or die." He then went back to his truck and sat inside it with his dog. He then set fire to the pickup while still inside it, but soon got out. While the dog perished inside the burning truck, the man peeled off some of his smoking clothes and walked away holding a shotgun. He stopped on the opposite side of the overpass, pressed the gun against his chin, and fired.

The grisly incident was broadcast live to viewers on at least five channels throughout Los Angeles and on one national cable channel. Several of the stations interrupted cartoons and other children's programming to show the scene live. Newscasters quickly apologized to their viewers for exposing them to the shocking scene without warning, but their apologies did nothing to abate the public criticism that followed.

One of the most important social issues of the 20th century has been the public concern for the negative effects of exposure to media violence, especially among children. Violence on newscasts is but one peripheral, albeit important, area of the media violence issue (see Chapter 14, on "News Effects"). Most concerns about violent media fare have focused on movies, television dramas, cartoons, and other fantasy shows, as well as violent video games and websites.

Through the years, many studies have revealed that viewing television violence leads to or causes aggressive behavior. Adults and children have been the research participants in these numerous experiments and studies. This chapter will review the findings of the more important studies along these lines. After a brief look at research methods used to study effects from mediated violence, including ways media violence is measured, we turn to the various types of effects from violence, such as behavioral, emotional, and so forth. A final section examines the media violence issue from a public policy standpoint.

171

When carried to perhaps its worst extreme, the modeling or imitation of screen violence has been linked to violent and brutal "copycat" crimes—rapes and even murders. As we discussed in Chapter 5 on priming, violent copycat crimes are among the most disturbing examples of imitative behavior.

The sensational nature of copycat crimes attracts the notice of print and electronic news media, and therefore examples of such crimes abound in the public's memory; in reality however, copycat crimes are extremely rare. Millions of other viewers who watch the same film or program are *not* inspired to imitate such extreme violent behavior. This suggests that other individual factors, such as a person's disposition (or predisposition to violent behavior), state of mind, emotional stability, and personal circumstances play a major role in determining whether that person will resort to violence after viewing violent fare.

Social scientists attempt to record more subtle media effects—those that they can measure through strictly controlled experiments and studies which do not involve actual harm or injury to anyone. These researchers concentrate their efforts on several major issues related to media violence. Many studies are designed to measure the amount of violence that occurs on various media. Other studies explore the *contexts* in which the violence occurs, as research has shown that such contexts are very important in determining the extent of harmful effects. (Examples of such contexts would be whether or not the violence was accidental in nature or performed with malicious intent, whether or not the perpetrator was punished, or whether or not the consequences of the violence were shown.) Most importantly, these and other studies examine viewers' exposure to such violence and attempt to answer the difficult question: What effect does media violence have on those who consume it?

Research studies on the effects of viewing violent media fare have employed a number of different methodologies. Barrie Gunter (1994) reviewed the vast body of research and identified six major research methods that have been used to study the question. These include laboratory experiments, field experiments, correlational surveys, longitudinal panel studies, natural experiments, and intervention studies. We will discuss each in turn.

Laboratory Experiments

Strictly controlled experiments in a laboratory setting have provided compelling evidence that watching media violence may cause a viewer to behave more aggressively. Such experiments are constructed to show a *causal relationship* between viewing TV violence and behaving aggressively. Critics point to the unnatural circumstances of viewing in such experiments and question whether the results have any meaning in the real world.

Field Experiments

Most of these studies have taken place among children in an institutional setting, such as a nursery school. Prior to viewing violence, the children are randomly assigned to groups (one group views violence and another sees nonviolent programming). Their levels of natural aggressiveness and attitudes are measured, then compared to measures taken *after* viewing violent fare. Field experiments avoid the problem of unnaturalness associated with laboratory experiments.

Correlational Surveys

Viewers are asked to read a list of program titles and select those programs that they watch regularly. Researchers rely on content analyses of the amount of violence in potential programs to develop a measure of the amount of violent programming exposure per viewer. Viewers are also asked about their attitudes and behavior in order to gauge some measure of aggressiveness or hostility. The two measures are then correlated to ascertain any relationship between the viewing of violence and subsequent aggressive behavior or attitudes. The major problem with such studies is that they are ultimately unable to demonstrate a causal relationship with any degree of certainty. Statistically significant correlations have been found between consumption of violent media fare and aggressive or hostile behaviors and attitudes, but most of those associations have been relatively weak.

Longitudinal Panel Studies

These studies attempt to identify relationships that may develop over a period of time between consumption of violent fare and antisocial attitudes and behaviors. According to Gunter (1994), such studies "represent perhaps the best kind of studies of TV effects. They can test causal hypotheses and they usually employ sound sampling methods" (p. 174). Researchers remain in contact with particular viewers and test them at various intervals over time to determine whether or not consumption of media violence is affecting them. Longitudinal panel studies take into account the assumption that exposure to media violence has a *cumulative* effect over time; in other words, repeated exposure to media violence has an increasing effect on aggressive behavior or attitudes as the years pass by.

Natural Experiments

With these studies, researchers make use of a natural setting where television is being introduced into the community for the first time. Through *longitudinal assessment* (similar evaluations made over a period of time), documented conduct such as criminal statistics are examined and compared before and after television becomes available in a country or community.

The results of natural experiments have varied. Through studying crime rates from 1949 to 1952, Hennigan and colleagues (1982) found that the introduction of television in certain American communities did not bring significant increases in homicides or other violent or serious crimes. Centerwall (1989) examined homicide rates from 1945 to 1975 among whites in three countries: the United States, Canada, and South Africa. He found that in the United States and Canada the murder rate among whites increased dramatically about 15 years after the rate of television set ownership in those countries increased, while homicide rates in South Africa (where TV ownership was very limited) were not so affected. A third study (Williams, 1986) provided strong evidence for the connection between viewing violent content and behaving aggressively. Of the three communities in Canada selected for study, one did not have television (notel), the second received only one channel (unitel), and the third had access to several channels (multitel). The study showed that the children in the community without television at the outset showed significant increases in aggressive behavior over a two-year period after TV was introduced. The aggressiveness of children in the other two communities did not change over the same period.

Intervention Studies

Just as vaccinations are used to inoculate people to protect them from dangerous or deadly diseases, intervention studies are designed to *intervene* and inoculate viewers against the harmful effects of viewing televised violence. With these studies, the harmful effects of viewing violence is assumed to be prevalent in the population; researchers then attempt to alleviate the negative effects in some way, that is, through some intervention strategy. Some intervention studies have indicated that increased television literacy (critical understanding of television content and production methods) may reduce the negative effects of TV violence.

MEASURING VIOLENT CONTENT

Most people agree that television programs and films contain too much violent content (Kaiser Family Foundation, 1999), but subtle differences in opinion sometimes make *media violence* an elusive term that represents something that is difficult to measure. For example, how do you define media violence? Is it harmful physical contact? Can it be verbal in nature? What about a car crash or an accidental death? What about news footage of a suicide? What about a bomb threat? Should these be considered violent?

Social scientists must address these and other highly specific questions before they can even begin to measure the amount of violence present in mass media, much less assess the effects of media violence. The research method used to determine the amount of violent content is called **content analysis.** In using this methodology, researchers must first clearly define violent content, then carefully watch various programs to code each instance of violence as it occurs. Sometimes content is classified according to program type, character type, weapon type, and the type of physical harm or damage that results.

The first content analyses of prime-time television programs were conducted in the 1950s and 1960s (Schramm, Lyle, & Parker, 1961; Smythe, 1956). These studies found that violence and criminal activities appeared frequently on the popular new medium; unfortunately, however, these early studies used different definitions and methods of measurement, making comparisons and trend studies impossible for the formative years of television.

Media violence is often difficult to define and measure.
Source: © The Everett Collection

Systematic analyses of television violence gained prowess and popularity in the 1960s programmatic study conducted by George Gerbner and his associates. Beginning in 1967 and in every year since, these cultivation researchers have analyzed and coded samples of prime-time and daytime dramas from all the major networks in the United States. Their technique of measurement, called *message system analysis*, has become one of the most widely used measures of violence on network television.

Gerbner and his colleagues defined violence as "the overt expression of physical force against self or other compelling action against one's will on pain of being hurt or killed or actually hurting or killing" (Gerbner, 1972, p. 32). Coders use the definition to generate very specific coding categories, with which they assess the number of violent acts they witness on the programs, the type of violence, the victims, the perpetrators, and the settings. The information from the coders is then synthesized to provide a **violence profile** for each program. The profile provides an objective appraisal of the amount of violence contained in each televised drama.

During the first 10 years of message system analysis, Gerbner and his associates found that the vast majority of network television programs (8 of 10) contained violent content, and a majority of characters (6 of 10) were involved in the violent acts. Children's cartoons contained more violence than all other types of shows, including action-adventure programs for adults and crime-detective programs.

In recent years, two Finnish researchers developed a coding scheme to measure the obtrusiveness of TV violence and to classify the *context*—the circumstances surrounding the violence or the message the violence conveys. The study examined violence present in fictional and nonfictional programs (Mustonen & Pulkkinen, 1997).

Other research on "reality" programming, or nonfictional television, revealed that the content of such programs was more similar to television drama than to an accurate portrayal of violence in the real world. Reality programming includes national and local newscasts, police news programs, documentaries, public affairs shows, tabloid news programs, and the like. In terms of context, the violent acts shown on such programs were rarely punished and negative consequences of violence were rarely shown (Federman, 1998; Potter et al., 1997).

It should be remembered that content analysis is simply a system of coding and describing content. The perceptions of audience members and effects of the content are entirely different questions, and researchers must employ different research strategies to answer them (Gunter, 1988; Gunter & Wober, 1988).

Measuring Viewers' Perceptions

Another method of classifying televised violence is by measuring viewers' perceptions of it. Different people react differently to television programs because each person possesses a unique set of psychological traits. Their judgments about violence do not always match those of researchers (Gunter, 1985; Van der Voort, 1986). Most people—adults and children—perceive violence in the context of a program genre and personal preferences. For example, if a program is one that parents enjoy watching, they generally perceive it as being harmless to themselves and their children. This means that programs that have been labeled as highly violent by trained content analysts may be perceived as rather harmless by actual viewers.

Despite individual differences among viewers, research has shown that people often experience similar, harmful effects after viewing certain types of violence portrayed in certain contexts. Social scientists have identified five key elements of context that make people susceptible to negative effects. Children, especially, are at high risk for learning aggressive behaviors from portrayals that feature all five of the following elements:

1. *A perpetrator who is an attractive role model.*
2. *Violence that seems justified.*
3. *Violence that goes unpunished (no remorse, criticism, or penalty).*
4. *Minimal consequences to the victims.*
5. *Violence that seems realistic to the viewer.*

(National Television Violence Study Executive Summary, 1998, p. 33)

Research has shown that in recent years many television programs include these "high-risk" contexts. In a four-year study of television programming, researchers from the University of California at Santa Barbara found that most violence on the screen is initiated by the "good guys," the screen characters that are most likely to serve as role models. Moreover, only about 15 percent of the prime-time programs from 1995 to 1998 revealed the long-term, negative

"High Risk" Contexts

DEPICTIONS THAT ENCOURAGE
AGGRESSIVE ATTITUDES AND BEHAVIORS

- Perpetrator is an attractive role model.
- Violence seems justified.
- Violence goes unpunished (no remorse, criticism, or penalty).
- Consequences to the victims are minimal.
- Violence seems realistic to the viewer.

Source: Joel Federman, (Ed.), (1998). *National television violence study,* Vol. 3, *Executive summary* (Santa Barbara: Regents of the University of California).

consequences of violent behavior. Approximately three out of four violent acts were performed without remorse or penalty, and the "bad guys" went unpunished in about 4 of 10 programs (National Television Violence Study Executive Summary, 1998).

Meta-Analyses

A number of researchers have examined the vast body of research studies and have used statistical methods to combine their findings and look for overall indications of effects as well as general trends (Andison, 1977; Carlson, Marcus-Newhall, & Miller, 1990; Hearold, 1986; Paik & Comstock, 1994; Wood, Wong, & Chachere, 1991). These **meta-analyses** have consistently found that a causal link exists between viewing violence and exhibiting aggressive behavior.

These studies have shown evidence of several major effects. The most prevalent effect is that of *imitative behavior* (Liebert & Schwartzberg, 1977). Children especially are likely to learn aggressive behaviors by watching them on television. After the behaviors are learned, they are subsequently imitated. Children are also vulnerable to another effect, *fear,* when viewing violent or disturbing subject matter (Cantor, 1994; Gunter & Furnham, 1984). *Desensitization,* a third prominent effect identified in the literature, may occur after repeated exposure to violence (Greenberg, 1975) or after only brief exposure (Drabman & Thomas, 1974; Linz, Donnerstein, & Penrod, 1988).

To better understand these effects and others, we will examine them in greater depth in the next section. The various levels of psychological effects are explained, and the different types of effects common to each are discussed in detail.

THE PSYCHOLOGICAL IMPACT OF MEDIA VIOLENCE

In terms of effects research, communication scholars have identified three different levels of psychological impact that violent media fare may have upon viewers. These levels—behavioral, affective, and cognitive—simply refer to the different types of effects that violence may have upon viewers. In this section, studies from the various methodologies described earlier will be used to illustrate each of the levels of effects.

Behavioral Effects

When a four-year-old boy watches an episode of the *Power Rangers*, then pretends he is the Red Ranger while kicking and hitting "the villain" (his two-year-old brother), that child is exhibiting a *behavioral effect* from viewing televised violence. Specifically, the child is using the mechanism of *imitation,* one of five major mechanisms through which behavioral effects may occur that we will discuss in this section. The other important mechanisms include *catharsis, arousal, disinhibition*, and *desensitization.*

Catharsis

The catharsis mechanism purportedly allows viewers to vent their aggressive impulses harmlessly through viewing televised violence or by fantasizing about violent acts. In the 1950s and 1960s, Feshbach (1955, 1961) reported the existence of a cathartic effect when participants in his experiments were able to release aggressive urges nonviolently by viewing acts of televised violence or by fantasizing about violence. In 1971, Feshbach and Singer observed teenage boys in natural settings—residential schools and homes—for six weeks. During the experimental period, the researchers controlled the boys' exposure to televised violence. They found that the boys who had watched mostly nonviolent television behaved *more aggressively* toward their peers than the boys who had watched violent programming, thus indicated some sort of catharsis effect.

It should be noted that very few of the hundreds of experimental studies have replicated Feshbach's findings or have supported the catharsis mechanism. Despite this weak body of scientific evidence, a substantial portion of the lay public believes that catharsis occurs through watching film, television, or video game violence. Media industry spokespeople happily remind the public and its elected representatives of the alleged benefits of catharsis every time a public investigation of the effects of media violence is undertaken.

Psychological Effects from Exposure to TV Violence

Cognitive
Watching TV violence influences a viewer's beliefs about the real world.

Affective (Emotional)
Watching TV violence causes an immediate or long-term emotional reaction.

Behavioral
Watching TV violence influences a person's behavior. Five major categories of behavioral effects:

  Arousal
  Catharsis
  Desensitization
  Disinhibition
  Imitation

Because of the popularity of the notion of catharsis and the lack of empirical support for cathartic or pseudocathartic effects, investigators have often tried to find some perhaps very limited conditions under which catharsis can be demonstrated. For example, Gunter (1980) has suggested that certain human cognitive skills are responsible for limited catharsis effects. One study revealed that people with strong imaginations or fantasy skills were able to relieve their anger by viewing a violent film, whereas those subjects who did not possess vivid imaginations were unable to experience such a cathartic effect (Biblow, 1973).

Arousal

The behavioral effect of this mechanism is that of excitement or, as the name says, arousal. Whenever a viewer watches a violent scene (or a particularly funny or a sexually explicit scene), he or she becomes excited or emotionally aroused, and this arousal can be measured physiologically. Viewers usually do not attribute their elevated arousal to what they are viewing. For example, if a teenage boy who is already mad about something is watching a violent program, he interprets his heightened arousal, which is in part due to excitation from the television program, as intense anger. He may therefore respond more aggressively than he would if he had not watched the violent program, particularly if an opportunity to become aggressive occurs shortly after viewing (Doob & Cline, 1972; Tannenbaum & Zillmann, 1975; Zillmann, 1988, 2000).

Disinhibition

The disinhibition mechanism operates under the assumption that as viewers grow more accustomed to seeing violence on television, especially violence that is justified by the situation or is socially sanctioned, they become less inhibited by social sanctions against committing violent acts. Research has shown that viewers do behave more aggressively after watching a program presenting sanctioned violence, especially if they were angry when they began watching (Berkowitz, 1962, 1965, 1974); however, more specialized investigations are required to indicate whether these results are due to disinhibition.

In one group of laboratory studies, a confederate angered research participants who then watched a clip from a violent film (usually a boxing match, which is a socially sanctioned form of violence). The same participants were then allowed to administer electric shocks to the person who had angered them. Other research participants were angered and shown a nonviolent film, and still other participants assigned to a control group were not angered. The researchers found that those who had seen the violent clip delivered harsher shocks than those who had not viewed violence, and that those who had been angered beforehand and viewed the sanctioned violence were the most aggressive of all. The investigators interpreted these results as providing evidence that watching sanctioned violence in the film clips served to remove some of the research participants' inhibitions, therefore permitting them to be more aggressive (Berkowitz & Alioto, 1973; Berkowitz, Corwin, & Heironimous, 1963; Berkowitz & Geen, 1966; Berkowitz & Rawlings, 1963).

Evidence for the disinhibition mechanism has also been claimed for longitudinal panel studies. In one study, researchers collected data from about 800 eight-year-olds regarding their TV viewing habits and their levels of aggressiveness. Ten years later, when the children were 18, the researchers located about half of the original group and obtained additional information. They found a strong positive correlation between viewing televised violence when young and measures of aggression as adults (Eron, Huesmann, Lefkowitz, & Walder, 1972).

Imitation

This mechanism assumes that viewers learn from what they see on television and sometimes try to mimic the actions themselves. This is especially true for young children who identify with the characters they see on television and try to imitate them. (Chapter 4 discusses the concept of *observational learning*, the essence of the imitation mechanism.)

You will recall from Chapter 4 that the laboratory experiments of Albert Bandura (1978, 1979, 1982, 1985) found that children imitate the aggressive behaviors they witness on the screen. One group of children watched a film of someone hitting and knocking about a plastic, air-filled Bobo doll. Another group watched a film that showed nonviolent behavior, and yet another group was not shown any film. The researchers then took the children to a playroom with a large number of toys—and one plastic Bobo doll. The children who had seen on film the Bobo doll being battered were not only more aggressive toward the Bobo doll than the other children, but they actually copied the violent behaviors they had witnessed in the film. Bandura attributed the copycat behavior in part to the disinhibition mechanism and in part to observational learning or the imitation mechanism.

The several intervention studies with children (described in the section on cognitive effects, see page 174) have attempted to mitigate the imitation effect. These studies have revealed that instructing children about television procedures, making them aware that viewing violence may have harmful effects on them, and teaching them critical viewing skills may reduce aggressive tendencies as they grow older (Singer & Singer, 1983; Huesmann & Eron, 1986).

Desensitization

As viewers repeatedly witness violent acts on the screen, they become less and less sensitive through the years to seeing violence and more likely to accept real-life violence. Only a few studies have examined this mechanism, but two laboratory studies in particular have provided enough evidence to give some credence to the hypothesis. In one study, children who viewed a violent program beforehand were less likely to go for adult help when they witnessed a playroom fight between two other children (Drabman & Thomas, 1974; Thomas, Horton, Lippincott, & Drabman, 1977). The other study found that children who watched 25 or more hours of television per week experienced less physiological arousal when viewing TV violence than children who watched less than four hours per week (Cline, Croft, & Courrier, 1973).

Research has shown that everyone, regardless of age, experiences an emotional reaction when viewing violent content on television and in films. Studies have examined reactions to programs that depict violence: either physical injury or threat of bodily harm. The emotional effects from watching such violence may be immediate (e.g., fright, anxiety) or long term (e.g., persistent fear of becoming a victim of crime).

The reactions of children have been of particular interest to social scientists involved in this realm of media effects research. Studies have revealed that children become very frightened when viewing certain kinds of programs. These fright reactions, which are sometimes very intense, have been observed by a number of researchers (see Blumer, 1933; Himmelweit, Oppenheim, & Vince, 1958; Preston, 1941; Schramm, Lyle, & Parker, 1961). The reactions range from loss of control over their feelings (Blumer, 1933) to horrible nightmares (Singer, 1975).

The most extensive research on children and their fright reactions has been done by Cantor and her associates (1998). Their studies have examined the correlations between viewing different types of program content and various fright responses among children (Cantor & Hoffner, 1987; Cantor & Reilly, 1982; Cantor & Sparks, 1984; Cantor, Wilson, & Hoffner, 1986; Sparks, 1986; Sparks & Cantor, 1986; Wilson, 1985). The research also explored the differences in various fright reactions of children at different ages and developmental levels. At a very young age, for example, children are more likely to be frightened by *threatening characters* and *situations.* Older children are more frightened by *threats of either realistic or abstract stimuli* rather than scary images alone.

The experiments of Cantor and associates have usually involved 3- to 11-year-olds who are randomly assigned to various groups. The children in the control group are simply shown a violent or frightening scene. The other groups of children are given certain strategies beforehand that should help them cope with the content they are about to view.

In all the studies, fright reactions are measured using one or more of four different methods. Immediately afterward, the children are asked to assess the extent of their fright by choosing one of four responses, from "not at all scared" to "very, very scared." Additionally, the researchers record and code fright reactions by evaluating the child's facial expression from a videotape made while the child is watching the program. As another supplementary measure, small sensors are attached to the child's fingers and physiological data are collected. Finally, some studies have shown behavioral measures of fear. Wilson and Cantor (1987), for example, measured fear by a child's willingness to see a live snake after watching the snake scene from *Raiders of the Lost Ark.*

Coping strategies may be cognitive or noncognitive in nature. Cognitive strategies involve changing the child's mental conceptions of the frightening content. A thorough explanation of the fantasy nature of a character or situation is one form of cognitive coping strategy. Cantor, Sparks, and Hoffner (1988) found that by showing children a behind-the-scenes video that explained and showed the makeup preparation for the actor in *The Incredible Hulk,* the children were far less fearful during the program than those children who had not seen the video. Cantor and Wilson (1984) examined the reactions of young and older children while watching the witch in the classic, *Wizard of Oz*. Some of the children were told beforehand that the witch was "just a regular person dressed up in a costume," and were reminded that the story was "make believe." Other children were not given such coping strategies. Results were different among the children. Older children were able to use the coping strategy to reduce their fears. They were significantly less frightened by the witch than other older children who had not received the explanations. The coping strategy did not work so well with the younger children. The scary witch frightened those who had received the fear-reducing strategy (the explanation) as much as those who had not. The researchers attributed the results to developmental differences in children of different ages.

An example of a noncognitive strategy is **desensitization,** which involves repeated exposure to the frightening matter in a secure and nonthreatening atmosphere; in therapy, this is called a "flooding" method. Several studies have shown that such desensitization procedures work to reduce fright reactions in children (Wilson, 1987; Wilson & Cantor, 1987).

Recent research also reveals that children experience fright reactions to television news as well as to fictional drama. In a random survey, Cantor and Nathanson (1996) found that almost 40 percent of the children of those parents surveyed had been frightened or upset by something seen on newscasts. The most fear-producing stories were those that involved violence among strangers, wars and famines abroad, and natural disasters. Younger children tended to react emotionally to upsetting images such as weapons and people dying, whereas older children were more troubled by abstract issues—fears of nuclear wars, bombing, and the reality of death (Cantor & Nathanson, 1996).

Recent research has shown that fright reactions to scary movies that occur in childhood and adolescence often linger into adulthood (See Chapter 13). Using a methodology called "recollective or retrospective reports," or "autobiographical memory," two independent teams of investigators found evidence for lingering fright reactions (Harrison & Cantor, 1999; Hoekstra, Harris, & Helmich, 1999; Cantor, 1999). Both studies involved content analyses of college students' reports of something that had frightened them in the mass media during their childhood. Remarkably, between 90 and 100 percent of the college students recalled such experiences, many poignantly. In both studies, the younger the child had been when he or she was frightened by something watched on television or film, the more intense the fright reaction was reported to be. In one investigation, more than one-quarter of the college students reported still experiencing residual anxiety from their childhood exposure to frightening media portrayals (Harrison & Cantor, 1999).

Cognitive Effects

When viewing mediated violence influences a viewer's beliefs about the real world, that viewer has experienced a *cognitive* effect. Indeed, many of the affective fright reactions just discussed may have become cognitive effects over time. The most extensive research on such cognitive effects has been performed by George Gerbner and his associates.

In the 1970s Gerbner and his colleagues analyzed data from national public opinion surveys to gauge some of the cognitive effects of television viewing. The surveys contained a large amount of useful information from each of the participants, such as how much time they spent watching television and their perceptions about the world in which they lived. The researchers found a positive correlation between the amount of time spent watching television and the prevalence of certain beliefs about the world; those who watched the most television perceived the world as a more dangerous place than light viewers (Gerbner, 1972; Gerbner & Gross, 1976; Gerbner, Gross, Eleey, Jackson-Beeck, Jeffries-Fox, & Signorielli, 1977; Gerbner, Gross, Jackson-Beeck, Jeffries-Fox, & Signorielli, 1978; Gerbner, Gross, Morgan, & Signorielli, 1980).

Through analysis of the content of network television programs, Gerbner and his associates showed the prime-time dramatic world of television to be an exceedingly violent place. They hypothesized that regular exposure to mediated violence made viewers develop an exaggerated view of real-life dangers in society.

Although widely accepted, Gerbner's methods and results have been challenged by a number of researchers (Blank, 1977a, 1977b; Coffin & Tuchman, 1973; Hughes, 1980; Hirsh, 1980; Wober & Gunter, 1988). Several of the researchers used the same database but exercised statistical controls for extraneous demographic variables and found no significant evidence for cultivation. (An extraneous demographic variable might be, for instance, the type of neighborhood in which the person lived—was it a high-crime district such as an urban ghetto or a low-crime area of affluence?)

Wober and Gunter (1982) found that a person's perception of the real world was related more to viewing certain types of programs than to the total time spent viewing. These researchers' findings indicated that people select particular types of programs that agree with, or reinforce, their personal beliefs. Such a hypothesis stands in opposition to the cultivation hypothesis.

The strength of television's influence on viewers' perceptions of the world can be mitigated by many factors. Gunter (1987) identified four leading categories of these factors which he called **levels of judgment:** program specificity, viewer perceptions or interpretations, personal judgments about crime, and situation specificity.

Program specificity means simply that television's influence on perceptions about the real world may have more to do with the types of programs watched rather than the total time spent viewing. For example, two people might watch the same amount of television each week, but one may view only violent programs while the other watches nonviolent educational shows. The perceptions of real-world crime on the part of the two viewers might be vastly different, even though both watch the same amount of TV (Weaver & Wakshlag, 1986).

The influence of television also may depend upon how viewers perceive what they are viewing, and how they interpret it (Collins, 1973; Pingree, 1983; Teevan & Hartnagel, 1976). *Viewer perceptions and interpretations* may conceivably render the most violent programs rather innocuous in their effects.

Personal judgments about crime may also modify television's influence on viewers of violent programming. Examples of such judgments would be beliefs about the prevalence of crime in society or beliefs about one's own chances of becoming a victim of crime. Tyler (1980, 1984; Tyler & Cook, 1984) found that such judgments often were not connected to viewing behavior at all, but to a person's particular, personal encounters with crime.

Situation specificity means that television's influence on personal perceptions about crime may also be moderated by the person's individual situation or setting. For example, those who live in urban areas tend to fear crime more than those who live in rural, low-crime areas (Tamborini, Zillmann, & Bryant, 1984).

MEDIA VIOLENCE RESEARCH AND PUBLIC POLICY: HISTORY AND FUTURE

Through the years, numerous studies of media effects have examined the negative effects on behavior that result from consuming media violence, whether reading, viewing, or listening to it. Since the beginning of movies and television, concern about media violence has been a major force in public policy making. The struggle for lawmakers has always been the balance that must be maintained between First Amendment rights in a free society and concern for the public welfare.

In her book *Violence on Television,* author Cynthia A. Cooper identified three phases in the public policy debate that emerged through the years. In the first phase, the debate focused upon the rising rate of juvenile delinquency. Next, the boundaries of the debate expanded to include concern about the effects of television violence on the social behavior and well-being of society in its entirety. In the third phase, the concern of policy makers shifted from identification of detrimental effects on viewers to a proactive attempt to reduce televised violence through legislative restrictions (Cooper, 1996).

Social scientists coordinated their efforts in the 1920s and 1930s to investigate the behavioral and social influences of viewing motion pictures. The Payne

National Television Violence Study

MAJOR FINDINGS:

VIOLENCE IN TV PROGRAMMING OVERALL

- Much of television violence is still glamorized (with "good guys" as perpetrators with no remorse and "bad guys" rarely being punished).
- Most violence on television continues to be sanitized (no physical harm or pain to the victim is shown).
- Much of the serious physical aggression on television is still trivialized.
- Very few programs emphasize an antiviolence theme.

- Each year of the study, about 60 percent of TV programs contained violence.
- In prime time, the number of violent programs has increased on the networks and on basic cable.
- The typical violent program contains at least six violent acts per hour.
- The average American preschooler who watches mostly cartoons is exposed to over 500 high-risk portrayals of violence each year.

Source: J. Federman, (Ed.), (1998), *National television violence study,* Vol. 3, *Executive summary* (Santa Barbara: Regents of the University of California), 29–34.

Fund Studies were a series of tests conducted on adults and children who went to movies. The studies found that the violent and sexual content of movies did not match conventional social mores, but the research evidence did not provide any wholesale support for popular public contentions of detrimental effects upon the social standards of adult movie audiences. The findings did suggest, however, that particularly "vulnerable" children who were prone to juvenile delinquency were influenced by violent and criminal behavior they watched on the screen (Blumer & Hauser, 1933; Dysinger & Ruckmick, 1933).

The next major study to gain public attention appeared in the mid-1950s. This time, the comic book industry came under intense scrutiny. A popular book, *The Seduction of the Innocent* (Wertham, 1954), contended that comic books offered children a distorted picture of reality and were responsible for problems with reading and even instances of juvenile delinquency. The author's methods and interpretations were questioned by the social scientific community, but the general public and the press challenged the findings far less severely.

In the 1950s and early 1960s, when television became a popular medium for entertainment, communication researchers in the United States and Great Britain became curious about the effects of exposure to the new medium, especially among young audiences. In their studies, researchers in the United States (Schramm, Lyle, & Parker, 1961) found a connection between viewing televised violence and aggressive behavior among youngsters, whereas a British group (Himmelweit, Oppenheim, & Vince, 1958) did not find evidence of such a causal relationship and contended that such a link would be difficult to prove.

Later, in the socially turbulent and violent 1960s, two more important reports again produced findings that conflicted with one another. First, President Lyndon Johnson's National Commission on the Causes and Prevention of Violence studied the issue and found that television could not be implicated as a primary cause for violence in society. Soon thereafter, the Surgeon General's Scientific Advisory Committee on Television and Social Behavior issued its five-volume report. According to the Surgeon General's committee, the evidence indicated that viewing violence on television *did* increase a viewer's tendencies to behave aggressively.

Throughout the 1980s, the Federal Communications Commission lifted earlier restrictions that had been placed on broadcasters to operate "in the public interest." While the loosening of restrictions signified a victory for broadcaster's First Amendment rights, the resulting changes in programming caused considerable public concern. Many children's programs disappeared, for example, and those that remained were more violent or highly commercial.

Congress reacted to the lowering of program standards with the Children's Television Act of 1990, which required broadcasters to air a certain amount of educational programming suitable for young viewers. It also placed time limits on the amount of commercials shown on children's programs.

Three years later, Congress began hearings to explore the subject of media violence and its effects on children. Due to increased public awareness and concern over the issue, the television networks decided to begin labeling programs to warn parents about violent and unsuitable content. This led to the suggestion for some device that would permit parents to control which programs could be seen on their television sets.

The Telecommunications Act of 1996 made installation of the V-chip mandatory on new models of televisions. This device allows parents to block signals and prevent certain undesirable programs containing violence, sex, or strong language from being received in their homes. The act also required the television industry to rate programs based upon suitability for certain age levels.

While many see these developments as positive steps, others point to problems inherent in such attempts to limit or prohibit children's exposure to undesirable programming (Potter & Warren, 1996). According to some, advisory warnings and blocking devices create a "forbidden fruit" effect, causing children to be extremely interested in seeing the very programs they should not see (Christenson, 1992).

At the end of the century, a three-year study on television violence conducted by researchers at several leading universities again confirmed the link between viewing violence and subsequent aggressive behavior. Released in 1998, the *National Television Violence Study* found that not only has the proportion of violent prime-time network and cable shows increased since 1994, but the *way the violence is portrayed* on these programs actually encouraged children to imitate the behavior they see. The study also found that age-based ratings did not indicate the amount of violent content in a program.

After the Columbine High School shootings in Littleton, Colorado, in April 1999, the perceived link between media violence and murderous behavior

The Media Violence and Aggression Link: More Evidence

Two recent studies provide additional evidence for the causal association of prolonged exposure to media violence and hostile behavior. Zillmann and Weaver (1999) showed research participants either innocuous films such as *Little Man Tate* and *Driving Miss Daisy* or violent films such as *Universal Soldier* and *Under Siege*. Those who viewed violent films on four consecutive days were more likely to exhibit hostile behavior whether or not they were provoked by a research assistant. According to the authors, the effects

. . . were uniform for respondent gender. Compared to men, women exhibited less hostility overall, however. The findings thus show that prolonged exposure to gratuitously violent films is capable (a) of escalating hostile behavior in provoked men and women, and (b) perhaps more importantly, of instigating such behavior in unprovoked men and women. (Zillmann & Weaver, 1999, p. 145)

The other study, conducted by the same investigators, featured prolonged exposure to four different categories of films, those containing no violence, old-style violence, gratuitous violence, and horror, along with classifications of participants' personality traits. Participants who scored high in the areas of "hostile dispositions, lack of empathy, and contempt for risks and danger" were labeled as high in psychoticism (Zillmann & Weaver, 1997; Eysenck, 1978). Men who scored high in psychoticism and viewed the gratuitously violent films were more likely to accept violence as a means of conflict resolution. The same group was more likely to endorse the death penalty for violent criminals.

Sources: Eysenck, H. J., (1978). *Sex and personality* (London: Sphere); Zillmann, D., & Weaver, J. B., III, (1999). Effects of prolonged exposure to gratuitous media violence on provoked and unprovoked hostile behavior. *Journal of Applied Social Psychology, 29,* 145–165; Zillmann, D., & Weaver, J. B., III, (1997). Psychoticism in the effect of prolonged exposure to gratuitous media violence on the acceptance of violence as a preferred means of conflict resolution. *Personality and Individual Differences, 22,* 613–627.

thrust itself squarely into the public eye once again. The reactions of horror to the senseless slayings resulted in congressional actions and a subsequent report on violence from the U.S. Surgeon General ordered by President Clinton. *Youth Violence: A Report of the Surgeon General* found a strong relationship between consumption of media violence and short-term aggression, but the aggressive behavior that typically resulted stopped far short of breaking limbs or committing murder.

Recent statistics seem to indicate that viewing violent programming does not cause as much harm as people might think. Violent crimes have been on the decline in recent years (Bureau of Justice Statistics, 1998), with 7 percent fewer crime reports in 1998 than the previous year. National statistics show a decline in youthful deaths from firearms since 1991 (Bureau of Justice Statistics, 1999), and a recent study found that the number of high school students who fight or carry weapons is smaller than in years past (Brener, Simon, Krug, & Lowry, 1999).

Still, research through the years has shown that the relationship between viewing violent programming and the demonstration of aggressive attitudes and behavior may be a strong one. Meta-analyses have revealed significant media effects for aggression, but again the aggressive behavior was not of a serious nature (Hearold, 1986; Paik & Comstock, 1994), perhaps largely because of the ethical constraints that prevent conducting the sorts of experiments that would result in pronounced harm to viewers. National reports and reviews (1993 American Psychological Association review; 1991 Centers for Disease Control report; 1993 National Academy of Science review; 1982 National Institute of Mental Health review; and 1972 Surgeon General's Report) have repeatedly documented and firmly established the link between the continuous viewing of violence and subsequent "acceptance of aggressive attitudes, as well as overt aggressive behavior" (Zillmann & Weaver, 1999, p. 145).

Some significant research in recent years has focused on reducing the negative consequences of consuming mediated violence. Nathanson (1999) found that parental involvement, whether limiting programming, talking to their children, or teaching them critical viewing skills, tends to reduce aggressive effects.

As research continues and our understanding of the effects of viewing media violence increases, changes in public policy are inevitable. Such changes occur rather slowly, however. In the meantime, the best public defense against the harmful effects of viewing violence resides in the corner of education. As more people become aware of the dangers of viewing unsuitable content and of the types of violent content that place them at highest risk for negative effects, the better they may defend themselves from those dangers. Increased public awareness should make public policy makers and industry executives more inclined to make positive changes.

SUMMARY

The public concern for the negative effects of exposure to media violence has been one of the most important social issues of the 20th century. Through the years, many studies have established a causal link between viewing media violence and subsequent aggressive behavior or attitudes.

Media effects researchers are interested in several issues related to media violence. They measure the amount of violence that occurs in various media, the context in which the violence occurs, and viewers' perceptions of the content.

Researchers have employed many different methods for studying the effects of exposure to media violence. Six of these are laboratory experiments, field experiments, correlational surveys, longitudinal panel studies, natural experiments, and intervention studies.

In measuring violent content, researchers must first define media violence. The method used to assess the amount of violence is called content analysis. Each instance of violence is coded using this technique.

Content analyses have shown that prime-time television programs contain a great deal of violent content, as do nonfictional programs. Content analyses provide a system for coding and describing content; they do not measure audience perceptions. Contextual content analyses examine the situations surrounding the portrayals of violence. Research has shown that contextual features are most important in determining what effects violence will have upon audience members.

Meta-analyses use statistical methods to combine a great number of different research studies to find overall indications of effects and general trends. Meta-analyses that examine media violence have consistently found a causal link between viewing violence and aggressive behavior. The major effects have been imitative behavior, fear, and desensitization.

Violent media fare may affect audiences at three different psychological levels: behavioral, affective (emotional), and cognitive. Behavioral effects may be exhibited through one of five different mechanisms: imitation, catharsis, arousal, disinhibition, and desensitization. Emotional effects may be immediate or extended, long-term reactions. Fright reactions of children are one example of emotional effects. Cognitive effects occur whenever viewing violent content influences a person's beliefs about the real world. The approach of cultivation analysis examines such cognitive effects.

Television's influence on viewers' perceptions can be mitigated. Four leading factors, called levels of judgment, include program specificity, viewer perceptions or interpretations, personal judgments about crime, and situation specificity.

Concern about media violence has always been a major issue for public policy makers. The debate has advanced through several stages. Most recently, the Telecommunications Act of 1996 made installation of the V-chip blocking device mandatory on new models of television sets, and required broadcasters to rate their programs based upon suitability for certain age levels.

REFERENCES

ANDISON, F. S. (1977). TV violence and viewer aggression: A cumulation of study results. *Public Opinion Quarterly, 41*, 314–331.

BANDURA, A. (1978). A social learning theory of aggression. *Journal of Communication, 28*(3), 12–29.

BANDURA, A. (1979). Psychological mechanisms of aggression. In M. von Cranach, K. Foppa, W. Lepenies, & D. Ploog (Eds.), *Human ethology: Claims and limits of a new discipline* (pp. 316–356). Cambridge: Cambridge University Press.

BANDURA, A. (1982). Self-efficacy mechanism in human agency. *American Psychologist, 37*(2), 122–147.

BANDURA, A. (1985). *Social foundations of thought and action.* Englewood Cliffs, NJ: Prentice Hall.

BANDURA, A., ROSS, D., & ROSS, S. A. (1963). Imitation of film-mediated aggressive models. *Journal of Abnormal and Social Psychology, 66,* 3–11.

BANDURA, A., UNDERWOOD, B., & FROMSON, M. E. (1975). Disinhibition of aggression through diffusion of responsibility and dehumanization of victims. *Journal of Research in Personality, 9,* 253–269.

BERKOWITZ, L. (1962). Violence in the mass media. In L. Berkowitz (Ed.), *Aggression: A social psychological analysis* (pp. 229–255). New York: McGraw-Hill.

BERKOWITZ, L. (1965). Some aspects of observed aggression. *Journal of Personality and Social Psychology, 2*(3), 359–369.

BERKOWITZ, L. (1974). Some determinants of impulsive aggression: The role of mediated associations with reinforcements for aggression. *Psychological Review, 81*(2), 165–176.

BERKOWITZ, L. (1984). Some effects of thoughts on anti- and prosocial influences of media events: A cognitive-neoassociation analysis. *Psychological Bulletin, 95,* 410–427.

BERKOWITZ, L., & ALIOTO, J. T. (1973). The meaning of an observed event as a determinant of its aggressive consequences. *Journal of Personality and Social Psychology, 28*(2), 206–217.

BERKOWITZ, L., CORWIN, R., & HEIRONIMOUS, M. (1963). Film violence and subsequent aggressive tendencies. *Public Opinion Quarterly, 27*(2), 217–229.

BERKOWITZ, L., & GEEN, R. G. (1966). Film violence and the cue properties of available targets. *Journal of Personality and Social Psychology, 3*(5), 525–530.

BERKOWITZ, L., & RAWLINGS, E. (1963). Effects of film violence on inhibitions against subsequent aggression. *Journal of Abnormal and Social Psychology, 66*(3), 405–412.

BIBLOW, F. (1973). Imaginative play and the world of aggressive behaviour. In J. L. Ian (Ed.), *The child's world of make-believe. Experimental studies of imagination play* (pp. 104–128). New York: Academic Press.

BLANK, D. M. (1977a). Final comments on the violence profile. *Journal of Broadcasting, 21,* 287–296.

BLANK, D. M. (1977b). The Gerbner violence profile. *Journal of Broadcasting, 21,* 273–279.

BLUMER, H., & HAUSER, P. M. (1933). *Movies, delinquency and crime.* New York: Macmillan.

BRENER, N. D., SIMON, T. R., KRUG, E. G., & LOWRY, R. (1999). Recent trends in violence-related behaviors among high school students in the United States. *Journal of the American Medical Association, 282,* 440–446.

BUREAU OF JUSTICE STATISTICS. (1998). Serious violent crime levels continued to decline in 1997. [Online]. Available: http://www.ojp.usdoj.gov/bjs/glace/cv2.htm

BUREAU OF JUSTICE STATISTICS. (1999). Firearm death by intent, 1991–96. [Online]. Available: http://www.ojp.usdoj.gov/bjs/glace/frmdth.txt

CANTOR, J. (1994). Fright reactions to mass media. In J. Bryant & D. Zillmann (Eds.), *Media effects: Advances in theory and research* (pp. 213–245). Hillsdale, NJ: Erlbaum.

CANTOR, J. (1998). *"Mommy, I'm scared": How TV and movies frighten children and what we can do to protect them.* San Diego, CA: Harcourt Brace.

CANTOR, J. (1999). Comments on the coincidence: Comparing the findings on retrospective reports of fear. *Media Psychology, 1,* 141–143.

CANTOR, J., & HOFFNER, C. (1987, April). *Children's fear reactions to a televised film as a function of perceived immediacy of depicted threat.* Paper presented at the Convention of the Society for Research in Child Development, Baltimore.

CANTOR, J., & NATHANSON, A. I. (1996). Children's fright reactions to television news. *Journal of Communication, 46*(4), 139–152.

CANTOR, J., & REILLY, S. (1982). Adolescents' fright reactions to television and films. *Journal of Communication, 32*(1), 87–99.

CANTOR, J., & SPARKS, G. G. (1984). Children's fear responses to mass media: Testing some Piagetian predictions. *Journal of Communication, 34*(2), 90–103.

CANTOR, J., SPARKS, G. G., & HOFFNER, C. (1988). Calming children's television fears: Mr. Rogers vs. The Incredible Hulk. *Journal of Broadcasting & Electronic Media, 32*, 271–288.

CANTOR, J., & WILSON, B. J. (1984). Modifying fear responses to mass media in preschool and elementary school children. *Journal of Broadcasting, 28*, 431–443.

CANTOR, J., WILSON, B. J., & HOFFNER, C. (1986). Emotional responses to a televised nuclear holocaust film. *Communication Research, 13*, 257–277.

CARLSON, M., MARCUS-NEWHALL, A., & MILLER, N. (1990). Effects of situational aggression cues: A quantitative review. *Journal of Personality and Social Psychology, 58*, 622–633.

CENTERWALL, B. S. (1989). Exposure to television as a cause of violence. *Public Communication and Behaviour, 2*, 1–58.

CHRISTENSON, P. (1992). The effects of parental advisory labels on adolescent music preferences. *Journal of Communication, 42*(1), 106–113.

CLINE, V. B., CROFT, R. G., & COURRIER, S. (1973). Desensitization of children to television violence. *Journal of Personality and Social Psychology, 27*(3), 360–365.

COFFIN, T. E., & TUCHMAN, S. (1973). Rating television programmes for violence: A comparison of five surveys. *Journal of Broadcasting, 17*, 3–22.

COLLINS, W. A. (1973). Effect of temporal separation between motivation, aggression and consequences: A developmental study. *Developmental Psychology, 8*, 215–221.

COOPER, C. A. (1996). *Violence on television, congressional inquiry, public criticism and industry response, A policy analysis.* Lanham, MD: University Press of America.

DOOB, A. N., & CLIMIE, R. J. (1972). Delay of . . . and effects of film violence. *Journal of Experimental Social Psychology, 8*(2), 136–142.

DRABMAN, R. S., & THOMAS, M. H. (1974). Does media violence increase children's toleration of real life aggression. *Developmental Psychology, 10*, 418–421.

DYSINGER, W. S., & RUCKMICK, C. A. (1933). *The emotional responses of children to the motion picture situation.* New York: Macmillan.

ERON, L. D., HUESMANN, L. R., LEFKOWITZ, M. M., & WALDER, L. O. (1972). Does television violence cause aggression? *American Psychologist, 27*, 253–263.

FEDERMAN, J. (Ed.). (1998). *National television violence study,* Vol. 3, *Executive summary.* Santa Barbara, CA: Center for communication and social policy, University of California, Santa Barbara.

FESHBACH, S. (1955). The drive-reducing function of fantasy behaviour. *Journal of Abnormal and Social Psychology, 50*, 3–11.

FESHBACH, S. (1961). The stimulating versus cathartic effects of vicarious aggressive activity. *Journal of Abnormal and Social Psychology, 63*, 381–385.

FESHBACH, S., & SINGER, R. D. (1971). *Television and aggression: An experimental field study.* San Francisco: Jossey-Bass.

FRIEDRICH, L. K., & STEIN, A. H. (1973). Aggressive and prosocial television programs and the natural behavior of preschool children. Chicago: University of Chicago Press.

GERBNER, G. (1972). Violence in television drama: Trends and symbolic functions. In G. A. Comstock & E. Rubinstein (Eds.), *Television and social behaviour: Vol. 1. Media content and control* (pp. 28–187). Washington, DC: U.S. Government Printing Office.

GERBNER, G., & GROSS, L. (1976). Living with television: The violence profile. *Journal of Communication, 26*, 173–199.

GERBNER, G., GROSS, L., ELEEY, M. F., JACKSON-BEECK, M., JEFFRIES-FOX, S., & SIGNORIELLI, N. (1977). Television violence profile No. 8: The highlights. *Journal of Communication, 27,* 171–180.

GERBNER, G., GROSS, L., JACKSON-BEECK, M., JEFFRIES-FOX, S., & SIGNORIELLI, N. (1978). Cultural indicators: Violence Profile No. 9. *Journal of Communication, 28,* 176–207.

GERBNER, G., GROSS, L., MORGAN, M., & SIGNORIELLI, N. (1980). The "mainstreaming" of America: Violence profile No. 11. *Journal of Communication, 30,* 10–29.

GREENBERG, B. S. (1975). British children and televised violence. *Public Opinion Quarterly, 38,* 531–547.

GUNTER, B. (1980). The cathartic potential of television drama. *Bulletin of the British Psychological Society, 33,* 448–450.

GUNTER, B. (1985). *Dimensions of television violence.* Aldershots, England: Gower.

GUNTER, B. (1987). *Television and the fear of crime.* London: John Libbey.

GUNTER, B. (1988). The perceptive audience. In J. A. Anderson (Ed.), *Communication yearbook II* (pp. 22–50). Newbury Park, CA: Sage.

GUNTER, B. (1994). The question of media violence. In J. Bryant & D. Zillmann (Eds.), *Media Effects* (pp. 163–211). Hillsdale, NJ: Erlbaum.

GUNTER, B., & FURNHAM, A. (1984). Perceptions of television violence. Effects of programme genre and type of violence on viewers' judgements of violent portrayals. *British Journal of Social Psychology, 23,* 155–164.

GUNTER, G., & WOBER, M. (1988). *Violence on television: What the viewers think.* London: John Libbey.

HARRISON, K., & CANTOR, J. (1999). Tales from the screen: Enduring fright reactions to scary media. *Media Psychology, 1,* 97–116.

HATCH, D. (2001, 22 January). Murder not a product of TV violence, report finds. *Electronic Media,* pp. 2, 89.

HEAROLD, S. (1986). A synthesis of 1043 effects of television on social behavior. In G. Comstock (Ed.), *Public communication and behavior* (Vol. 1, pp. 65–133). Orlando, FL: Academic Press.

HENNIGAN, K. M., DEL ROSARIO, M. L., HEATH, L., COOK, T. D., WHARTON, J. D., & CALDER, B. J. (1982). Impact of the introduction of television on crime in the United States: Empirical findings and theoretical implications. *Journal of Personality and Social Psychology, 42,* 461–477.

HIMMELWEIT, H., OPPENHEIM, A., & VINCE, P. (1958). *Television and the child.* London: Oxford University Press.

HIRSH, P. (1980). The "scary" world of the non-viewer and other anomalies: A reanalysis of Gerbner et al.'s findings on cultivation analysis: Part 1. *Communication Research, 7,* 403–456.

HOEKSTRA, S. J., HARRIS, R. J., & HELMICK, A. L. (1999). Autobiographical memories about the experience of seeing frightening movies in childhood. *Media Psychology, 1,* 127–140.

HUESMANN, L. R., & ERON, L. D. (Eds.). (1986). *Television and the aggressive child: A cross-national comparison.* Hillsdale, NJ: Erlbaum.

HUGHES, M. (1980). The fruits of cultivation analysis: A re-examination of television in fear of victimization, alienation and approval of violence. *Public Opinion Quarterly, 44,* 287–302.

KAISER FAMILY FOUNDATION. (1999, May). Parents and the V-chip: A Kaiser Family Foundation survey. [Online]. Available: http://www.kff.org/archive/media/entertainment/vchip/vchip_s.pdf

LIEBERT, R. M., & SCHWARTZBERG, N. S. (1977). Effects of mass media. *Annual Review of Psychology, 28,* 141–173.

LIEBERT, R. M., SPRAFKIN, J. N., & DAVIDSON, E. S. (1982). *The early window: Effects of television on children and youth* (2nd ed.). Elmsford, NY: Pergamon.

LINZ, D. G., DONNERSTEIN, E., & PENROD, S. (1988). Effects of long-term exposure to violent and sexually degrading depictions of women. *Journal of Personality and Social Psychology, 55,* 758–768.

MALAMUTH, N. M., & DONNERSTEIN, E. (Eds.). (1984). *Pornography and sexual aggression.* New York: Academic Press.

MUSTONEN, A., & PULKKINEN, L. (1997). Television violence: A development of a coding scheme. *Journal of Broadcasting & Electronic Media, 41,* 168–189.

NATHANSON, A. I. (1999). Identifying and explaining the relationship between parental mediation and children's aggression. *Communication Research, 26,* 124–143.

PAIK, H., & COMSTOCK, G. (1994). The effects of television violence on antisocial behavior: A meta-analysis. *Communication Research, 21,* 516–546.

PINGREE, S. (1983). Children's cognitive processing in constructing social reality. *Journalism Quarterly, 60,* 415–422.

POTTER, W. J., & WARREN, R. (1996). Considering policies to protect children from TV violence. *Journal of Communication, 46*(4), 116–138.

POTTER, W. J., WARREN, R., VAUGHAN, M., HOWLEY, K., LAND, A., & HAGEMEYER, J. (1997). Antisocial acts in reality programming on television. *Journal of Broadcasting & Electronic Media, 41,* 69–75.

PRESTON, M. I. (1941). Children's reactions to movie horrors and radio crime. *Journal of Pediatrics, 19,* 147–168.

SCHRAMM, W., LYLE, J., & PARKER, E. P. (1961). *Television in the lives of our children.* Stanford, CA: Stanford University Press.

SINGER, S. L. (1975). *Daydreaming and fantasy.* London: Allen & Unwin.

SINGER, J. L., & SINGER, D. G. (1983). Implications of childhood television viewing for cognition, imagination and emotion. In J. Bryant & D. R. Anderson (Eds.), *Children's understanding of television research in attention and comprehension* (pp. 331–353). New York: Academic Press.

SMYTHE, D. W. (1956). *Three years of New York television: 1951–1953.* Urbana, IL: National Association of Education Broadcasters.

SPARKS, G. G. (1986). Developmental differences in children's reports of fear induced by mass media. *Child Study Journal, 16,* 55–66.

SPARKS, G. G., & CANTOR, J. (1986). Developmental differences in fright responses to a television programme depicting a character transformation. *Journal of Broadcasting & Electronic Media, 30,* 309–323.

TAMBORINI, R., ZILLMANN, D., & BRYANT, J. (1984). Fear and victimization: Exposure to television and perceptions of crime and fear. In R. N. Bostrum (Ed.), *Communication Yearbook 8* (pp. 492–513). Beverly Hills, CA: Sage.

TANNENBAUM, P. H., & ZILLMANN, D. (1975). Emotional arousal in the facilitation of aggression through communication. In L. Berkowitz (Ed.), *Advances in experimental social psychology* (Vol. 8, pp. 149–192). New York: Academic Press.

TEEVAN, J. J., & HARTNAGEL, T. F. (1976). The effect of television violence on the perception of crime by adolescents. *Sociology and Social Research, 60,* 337–348.

THOMAS, M. H., HORTON, R. W., LIPPINCOTT, E. C., & DRABMAN, R. S. (1977). Desensitization to portrayals of real-life aggression as a function of exposure to television violence. *Journal of Personality and Social Psychology, 35*(6), 450–458.

TYLER, T. R. (1980). The impact of directly and indirectly experienced events: The origin of crime-related judgments and behaviors. *Journal of Personality and Social Psychology, 39,* 13–28.

TYLER, T. R. (1984). Assessing the risk of crime victimization and socially-transmitted information. *Journal of Social Issues, 40,* 27–38.

TYLER, T. R., & COOK, F. L. (1984). The mass media and judgements of risk: Distinguishing impact on personal and societal level judgements. *Journal of Personality and Social Psychology, 47,* 693–708.

VAN DER VOORT, T. H. A. (1986). *Television violence: A child's eye view.* Amsterdam: Elsevier Science.

WEAVER, J., & WAKSHLAG, J. (1986). Perceived vulnerability to crime, criminal victimization experience, and television viewing. *Journal of Broadcasting & Electronic Media, 30,* 141–158.

WERTHAM, F. (1954). *Seduction of the innocent.* New York; Rienhart.

WILLIAMS, T. M. (1986). *The impact of television.* New York: Academic Press.

WILSON, B. J. (1985). Developmental differences in empathy with a television protagonist's fear. *Journal of Experimental Child Psychology, 39,* 284–299.

WILSON, B. J. (1987). Reducing children's emotional reactions to mass media through rehearsed explanation and exposure to a replica of a fear object. *Human Communication Research, 14,* 3–26.

WILSON, B. J., & CANTOR, J. (1987). Reducing fear reactions to mass media: Effects of visual exposure and verbal explanation. In M. McLaughlin (Ed.), *Communication Yearbook 10* (pp. 553–573). Beverly Hills, CA: Sage.

WOBER, M., & GUNTER, B. (1982). Television and personal threat: Fact or artifact? A British survey. *British Journal of Social Psychology, 21,* 43–51.

WOBER, M., & GUNTER, B. (1988). *Television and social control.* Aldershot, England: Avebury.

WOOD, W., WONG, F. Y., & CHACHERE, J. G. (1991). Effects of media violence on viewers' aggression in unconstrained social interaction. *Psychological Bulletin, 109,* 371–383.

ZILLMANN, D. (1988). Cognition-excitation interdependencies in aggressive behavior. *Aggressive Behavior, 14,* 51–64.

ZILLMANN, D. (2000). Excitement. In A. E. Kazdin (Ed.), *Encyclopedia of psychology.* New York: American Psychological Association and Oxford University Press.

ZILLMANN, D., & BRYANT, J. (1984). Effects of massive exposure to pornography. In N. M. Malamuth & E. Donnerstein (Eds.), *Pornography and sexual aggression* (pp. 115–138). New York: Academic Press.

CHAPTER 12

Media Effects from Sexual Content

> *Sex is more exciting on the screen and between the pages than between the sheets.*
> —**Andy Warhol, *From A to B and Back Again* (1975)**

Whatever the medium—television, movies, records, magazines, music videos, advertisements, or something else—media users are inundated daily with sexually oriented messages and images. These messages range from the mildly suggestive to various levels of the *sexually explicit,* a term used to describe media depictions of individuals engaging in various kinds of sexual activities.

In Chapter 11 we explored the issue of media violence and discovered that significant links exist between the viewing of violence and subsequent acts of aggression. A recent report by the U.S. Surgeon General confirmed the causal links between viewing violent media fare and committing acts of aggression (Hatch, 2001). Sexual content in electronic and print media also has important implications because of its perceived connection with serious social concerns, such as the high incidence of teenage pregnancy and the increasing numbers of people contracting sexually transmitted diseases such as AIDS. Researchers have determined that 7 of 10 girls and 8 of 10 boys in the United States have engaged in sexual intercourse by the time they reach the age of 20, and one-fourth of all pregnant women are teenagers (Greenberg, Brown, & Buerkel-Rothfuss, 1993).

This chapter examines the media effects from sexual content. It reveals the nature and extent of sexual content in mass media. We then review results from studies that examine exposure to highly explicit sexual content, and we point out the importance of the prevailing tone of sexual content in mass media. Finally, we examine the evidence for effects from sexually violent media fare for sex offenders.

THE NATURE OF SEXUAL CONTENT

Whenever you use the word "sexual" to describe media content, you must clearly define what it means, as it occurs at many levels of intensity. In its broadest sense, it includes *all* types of media products that either show or imply

194

sexual acts or make sexual references or innuendoes, whether in humorous or dramatic context, from X-rated materials to general-audience sitcoms. In a more narrow sense, sexual content may range from rather mild sexual comments on network television to unabashedly blatant XXX videos with themes of sado-masochism, bondage, or bestiality.

The degree of sexual explicitness in media content usually depends upon how much is left to the imagination. Highly explicit materials such as X-rated[1] movies or XXX videos leave nothing to the viewer's imagination. R-rated movies contain nudity and a moderate degree of explicitness, but sexual activities are less explicit than those depicted in X-rated films. Frontal nudity does not appear on network television in the United States; therefore, the sexual explicitness on the networks is rather tame when compared to R- and X-rated movies; however, the sizzling sex scenes on daytime soap operas or prime-time serial programming or "reality fare" should leave no doubt in anyone's mind that television contains much sexual content.

Surveys and studies reveal the pervasiveness of mass media as a source of sexual information, especially for adolescents and teenagers. A recent Time/CNN poll (Stodghill, 1998) reported that almost 30 percent of teenagers in the United States said they get most of their information about sex from watching television. In contrast, 45 percent said "friends" served as their source for learning about sex, but only 7 percent identified "parents" and only 3 percent sex education as a source of information. A 1992 study in Toronto (Russell, 1998) revealed that 9 of 10 adolescent boys and 6 of 10 adolescent girls had viewed at least one pornographic movie in their lives. Another study showed that almost 30 percent of adolescent boys listed pornography as their most significant source of information on sex, and pornography rated higher than schools, parents, peers, books, and magazines (Check, 1995; Harris & Scott, 2001).

The pervasiveness of pornography is indisputable. Around 10,000 pornographic videos were released in 1999, and the porn industry takes in about $56 billion worldwide each year (Morais, 1999).

Even though programs on television leave much more to the imagination than these more explicit materials, their potential for negative effects is not necessarily diminished. The availability of television to all ages makes that medium a particularly dangerous one when considering the damaging social effects that result from the consumption of sexual content.

In any discussion of sexual content in mass media, particular terms appear from time to time and therefore need explication. Pornography and obscenity are two such terms.

Pornography

The extreme class of sexually explicit materials is commonly referred to as erotica or **pornography,** which is defined as "the graphic and explicit depictions of sexual activity" (Cline, 1994). X-rated movies or videos, certain sex magazines, sexually explicit computer and video games, and so forth belong to this class. Such materials are restricted to adult audiences only and are produced for the express purpose of pandering sexual content. They are usually considered devoid of literary merit or artistic value. Exceptions often include the magazine *Playboy*, which is also known for respectable reading content, and educational materials such as sex manuals.

In 1986 the Meese Commission classified five types of materials as pornography. These included (1) materials that depict sexual violence such as rape or other violent sex crimes, (2) nonviolent sexual materials that depict instances of degrading or humiliating activities, or scenes of domination and subordination, (3) nonviolent sexual materials without degrading activities (usually portraying a couple having consensual and nonviolent intercourse), (4) materials that depict nudity, and (5) child pornography (the sexual exploitation of children in media content) (*Final report*, 1986).

The porn industry takes in billions of dollars worldwide each year.
Source: © Bonnie Kamin/PhotoEdit

The Meese classifications are debatable, because the term "pornography" is difficult to define in a standard way. Each person's definition may be different, depending upon his or her values. For example, some people do not consider nudity to be pornographic. Others may not consider consensual and nonviolent intercourse to be pornographic.

Obscenity

Pornographic material is not always considered to be obscene. The term **obscenity** is a legal one that has been defined by the United States Supreme Court. The *Miller v. California* case in 1973 set the criteria for proclaiming material legally "obscene." Three criteria, as judged by a jury representative of the community, must be present. These include (1) the material appeals to a prurient (shameful, sick, morbid, or lustful) interest in sex; (2) the material is patently offensive or beyond the contemporary community standards regarding depictions of sexual content or activity; and (3) the material as a whole lacks "serious literary, artistic, political, or scientific value" (Cline, 1994, p. 230).

THE EXTENT OF SEXUAL CONTENT IN THE MEDIA

In recent decades, researchers have studied the extent and the explicitness of sexual content in mass media. Many of these studies have been content analyses that focus on various types of sexual media fare that children and teens are likely to see, such as R-rated movies, sex magazines, and, especially, network television programming.

Greenberg (1994) examined the sexual content trends in five types of media: music videos, X-rated videos, television, magazines, and movies. He found that the amount of sexual content and the degree of explicitness varied considerably among the media.

Music Videos

Several content analyses have measured the amount of sexual content contained in music videos. Two major studies in the 1980s examined MTV and other televised music programs during 1984. The first study (Baxter, DeRiemer, Landini, Leslie, & Singletary, 1985) found that well over half of the 62 videos analyzed contained sexual content. Sexually suggestive actions such as embraces, sexy dancing, kisses, and the wearing of sexy clothing occurred frequently. The researchers concluded that "sexually oriented suggestive behavior is portrayed frequently in music videos" (p. 336).

In another study that involved content analysis, Sherman and Dominick (1986) examined the visual aspects of 166 videos that featured a "concept," such as a story line, drama, or narrative (for at least half the video), rather than a studio performance alone. The videos were taken from MTV and the programs *Night Tracks* and *Friday Night Videos*. The researchers found that three of every four videos contained sexual content, and that the average number of sexual acts in each video was almost five. In terms of sex and violence, the study revealed that 80 percent of the videos that contained violence also contained sexual content.

X-Rated Videos

In a content analysis of sexual activities in X-rated videos, researchers found that almost 450 sexually explicit scenes appeared in the 45 videos analyzed in the study (Cowan, Lee, Levy, & Snyder, 1988). Overall, the scenes depicted one of four major themes: domination, reciprocity, exploitation, or autoeroticism. Scenes featuring satisfying and consensual sex (*reciprocity*) were the most numerous of the four types, occurring in 37 percent of the 450 scenes; however, the themes of either domination or exploitation (mostly men over women) accounted for more than 50 percent of the scenes. *Domination,* or sexual control by one person over another, occurred in 28 percent of the scenes. *Exploitation,* where one coerced another or used status to get what was wanted, was present in 26 percent of the scenes. *Autoeroticism,* which means some form of self-stimulation such as masturbation, was the least frequent theme, occurring in 9 percent of the scenes studied.

Another study compared the differences in content of X-rated videos to triple-X titles. Palys (1986) found that the XXX videos contained a much larger number of scenes depicting oral-genital sex, the touching and fondling of breasts or genitals, genital-genital sex, masturbation, and anal sex. Surprisingly, the XXX videos contained less violence and less sexual violence than the X titles.

- Domination—sexual control of one person over another.
- Reciprocity—consensual sex, satisfying to both individuals.
- Exploitation—coersion of one over another, or use of status to make another perform as desired sexually.

- Autoeroticism—self-stimulation such as masturbation.

More than half of all scenes in X-rated films feature themes of domination or exploitation, usually men over women.

Television

R-rated movies and sex magazines have been found to contain far more explicit sexual content than network television, but sexual comments and overtures are numerous and frequent on network programming (Greenberg, Stanley, Siemicki, Heeter, Soderman, & Linsangan, 1993a; Greenberg & Hofschire, 2000; Kunkel, Cope, Farinola, Biely, Rollin, & Donnerstein, 1999). Most of the sexual innuendoes on TV occur in humorous scenes. One content analysis of network and cable television programs during the 1997–1998 season revealed that 56 percent of the shows included sexual content, with 23 percent depicting sexual behaviors (Kunkel, Cope, Farinola, Biely, Rollin, & Donnerstein, 1999). References to sex between the unmarried outnumber references to sex between the married by a ratio of 6 to 1 on television programs (Greenberg & Hofschire, 2000), 24 to 1 on television soap operas (Lowry & Towles, 1989), and 32 to 1 in R-rated movies (Greenberg, Brown, & Buerkel-Rothfuss, 1993). The references to sex between the unmarried outnumber references to sex between the married by a 32 to 1 ratio.

In an analysis of network programming alone, researchers have found that daytime soap operas contain far more references to sex than programs during primetime; however, characters on the nighttime shows talk about intercourse more often and make more references to sexually deviant behavior (Greenberg, Abelman, & Nueuendorf, 1981). When soap opera characters make references to sexual encounters, most of them refer to premarital or extramarital relations rather than sex between married partners (Lowry & Towles, 1989).

From 1985 to 1994, sexual content on soap operas increased by 35 percent (Greenberg & D'Alessio, 1985; Greenberg & Busselle, 1996; Greenberg & Hofschire, 2000). Moreover, in 1994 the soaps included more portrayals of rape and other negative sexual themes.

Magazines

Sexual content in both erotic and general readership magazines has been the focus of several content analyses. Malamuth and Spinner (1980) examined the presence of sexual violence in the cartoons and photographs contained in *Playboy* and *Penthouse* over a five-year publication period in the 1970s. The number of sexually violent pictures increased in both magazines during the period. As for sexually violent cartoons, the numbers in *Penthouse* increased during the period but the numbers in *Playboy* did not. Another study of 430 different erotic magazines found that the predominant content characteristics included women, genital details of women, heterosexual activities, and particular sexual preferences such as bondage, oral sex, use of dildoes, lesbianism, sadomasochism, and so on (Winick, 1985).

Scott (1986) examined issues of several general readership magazines (*Reader's Digest, McCall's, Life, Time, Newsweek,* and the *Saturday Evening Post*) from 1950 to 1980. He found that references to sex increased 84 percent during the first decade, 16 percent during the second, and 68 percent during the third. References to extramarital intercourse, for example, increased from 18 percent in 1950 to 26 percent in 1980, while references to sexual perversions increased from 8 to 15 percent.

R-Rated Movies

Greenberg and his associates examined 16 films that had been rated R due to sexual content (1993b). The films included *Risky Business, Bachelor Party,* and *Revenge of the Nerds*—all popular among ninth- and tenth-grade audiences. The researchers found that each of the films contained an average of 17.5 sexual acts. Instances of sexual intercourse between the unmarried outnumbered scenes featuring sexual intercourse between married couples by a ratio of 32 to 1. In scenes where sex was clearly initiated by one person (16 percent of the total sex scenes), the researchers found that a man served as initiator 55 percent of the time and a woman 45 percent of the time. In the great majority of sex scenes (84 percent), either both parties initiated the sex or no one person clearly initiated the sexual activity.

EXPOSURE TO HIGHLY EXPLICIT SEXUAL CONTENT

When a person thumbs through the pages of *Hustler,* calls up a website that features child pornography, or watches an X-rated video that depicts a sexually violent crime such as rape, how does it affect that person? How is the person changed by the exposure to highly explicit sexual content? More importantly, is it possible to mitigate or lessen any negative effects of viewing such material?

Researchers have found that highly explicit sexual content may affect media users in one or more of several ways. One type of effect, of course, is sexual arousal. Other effects include changes in attitudes, values, and behaviors. Each of these areas has been studied extensively, especially the behavioral changes that result from viewing pornography.

Sexual Arousal

Several studies have demonstrated that sexually oriented media content does tend to sexually arouse the viewer or user (Abramson, Perry, Seeley, Seeley & Rothblatt, 1981, Eccles, Marshall, & Barbaree, 1988; Malamuth & Check, 1980a;

Schaefer & Colgan, 1977; Sintchak & Geer, 1975). These studies have used different types of measures. In some cases, viewers were asked to rate their level of sexual arousal after seeing sexually explicit material. In other instances, researchers used physiological measures to determine arousal, such as the measurement of penile tumescence or vaginal changes. Thermography has also been used.

Gender differences usually show up in terms of usage of sexually explicit materials and whenever arousal measures are recorded. Estimates reveal that more than 70 percent of sexually explicit videos are viewed by men rather than women (Gettleman, 1999). The industry caters to male consumers, but evidence shows that women react more positively to sexually explicit material written and directed by women, especially when themes were romantic (Mosher & Maclan, 1994; Quackenbush, Strassberg, & Turner, 1995). Regardless of content, however, evidence suggests that men are more purposive seekers of sexually explicit fare, and they tend to be more aroused by it (Malamuth, 1996), especially depictions of sexual violence or dehumanization (Murnen & Stockton, 1997).

Researchers have also studied the relationship between the explicitness of sexual content and the extent of sexual arousal. Surprisingly, these studies have shown that less explicit materials are sometimes *more* arousing than the highly explicit ones (Bancroft & Mathews, 1971). Scenes that leave much to the viewer's imagination may arouse the viewer more than those that leave no questions unanswered.

Different individuals are "turned on" by different sexual stimuli. Classic conditioning studies have shown that sexual arousal can sometimes be *learned*. This may explain the many individual differences in sexual orientation and arousal. In the 1960s researchers showed heterosexual men photos of nude women paired with boots and actually taught the men to be aroused by only the sight of women's boots (Rachman, 1966; Rachman & Hodgson, 1968).

Studies have also revealed that over time, viewers of common pornography (nonviolent sex between a man and woman) become habituated and tend to seek more uncommon porn (e.g., bondage, sadomasochism, bestiality) in order to find stimulation (Zillmann & Bryant, 1986). Also over time, heavy consumption of pornography causes viewers to report less sexual satisfaction with their intimate partners and to assign increased importance to sex without emotional involvement (Zillmann & Bryant, 1988b).

Changes in Values and Attitudes

Repeated exposure to explicit sexual materials usually results in *desensitization* of a person's attitudes and values. Desensitization is a change in values or attitudes that occurs over time as a previously taboo behavior is gradually accepted because of repeated exposure to mass media. For example, a teenage girl who sees Buffy the Vampire Slayer having a sexual relationship with her boyfriend Angel might change her mind about viewing premarital sex as a taboo. In a more extreme example, if a man watches a number of X-rated movies that depict women enjoying being raped, he may soon change his perceptions about the frequency of the occurrence of that behavior in the real world as well as his attitude about the amount of social and psychological harm rape causes, and even his beliefs about the likelihood that he would commit such a crime.

Research has revealed that exposure to sexually explicit materials produces significant changes in attitudes. For six weeks, Zillmann and Bryant (1982, 1984) showed sexually explicit films to one group and nonexplicit films to a second group. When they tested the groups, they found that the first group overestimated the popularity of the sexual activities they had viewed in the movies (e.g., fellatio, cunnilingus, anal intercourse, sadomasochism, and bestiality). The estimates of the second group were much more conservative. Later, the same researchers (Zillmann & Bryant, 1988b) used similar methods to determine if the viewing of such films caused changes in attitudes toward their sexual partners, or changes in basic values such as a desire for a marriage, monogamy, children, and so forth. They found that changes did occur. Those who saw the explicit films reported less satisfaction with their real-life partners than those in the control group. In addition to rating their partners lower in terms of physical appearance and sexual performance, the group shown explicit films were more accepting of premarital sex and extramarital sex. They reported less of a desire for marriage, monogamy, and children than the control group. The researchers explained these findings in this way:

> Only pornography shows men and women to experience the greatest sexual pleasures from coition with many partners, one after the other, or from sexual activities with several partners at the same time . . . And only this genre provides specifics such as fellatio in which women make entire male organs vanish or coition in which penises of extreme proportion cause women to scream in apparent painful ecstasy. The sexual experience of normals must pale by comparison. Partners must seem prudish, insensitive, inhibited, frigid, . . . and deficient in endowment and skill. And who, confronted with the bounty of readily attainable sexual joys that are continually presented in pornography and nowhere else, could consider his or her sexual life fulfilled? (p. 452)

Research has also provided evidence that sexual content need not be overtly explicit or pornographic to have detrimental psychological effects. For example, in three studies of 13- and 14-year-old boys and girls, Bryant and Rockwell (1994) found that under certain circumstances, massive exposure to sexual content on prime-time television (in particular, intimate sexual relations between unmarried couples) caused significant shifts in the teens' moral judgment. The studies also showed that three mitigating factors could serve to diminish or eliminate the harmful effects. In the words of the researchers:

> First, having a clear and well-defined family value system—a value system that teenagers can know and use—mediates potentially harmful media effects; the second mitigating factor we found is coming from a family in which free and open discussion of issues is encouraged and practiced . . . third, active critical viewing, or the active viewing and analysis of program content, is a most desirable trait for teenagers to have and is to be encouraged. Again, it can make a big difference in mediating the cognitive effects of mass media consumption as far as moral judgment is concerned. (p. 194)

Other studies also support the evidence for attitudinal changes related to consumption of sexually explicit material. As some have pointed out, most pornography conveys an ideological message that degrades or dehumanizes women as victims or playthings (Buchwald, Fletcher, & Roth, 1993; Russell, 1998).

Changes in Behavior

Behavioral effects from the consumption of sexually explicit media content may occur at several levels. For better or worse, people *learn* whenever they consume sexual content. The learning may be highly constructive, as in a couple undergoing sexual therapy, or it may be extremely destructive, as in copycat sexual offenses that involve violence.

Disinhibition causes changes in behavior in much the same way that desensitization causes changes in attitudes and values. After seeing an R-rated movie or an X-rated video, a person becomes less inhibited about performing the sexual behaviors witnessed—behaviors that were previously taboo. Again, when taken to an extreme, disinhibition may reduce moral judgment constraints that result in an individual committing some type of violent sex crime.

The relationship between the viewing of sexually explicit materials and the occurrence of sex crimes has received much attention through the years. Many studies have examined the numbers of rape and child molestation cases in a particular locale in relation to the amount of sexually explicit materials available there. After reviewing these studies, Court (1984) found a statistically significant correlation between the availability of explicit materials and the occurrence of violent sexual crimes.

The relationship between sexually explicit materials and the occurrence of rape in particular has been difficult to prove, however, because of several confounding variables: the variety of sexual materials, changing social norms, and the increasing number of such assaults actually being reported. Several studies have found a relationship between the crime of rape and the availability of one particular medium—sex magazines. In one study, researchers found a high correlation in all 50 states between the number of rapes and the circulation numbers for eight sex magazines (Baron & Straus, 1987). The correlations were particularly high for magazines that contained sexual violence.

Effects of Erotica on Aggression

A number of studies have shown that when individuals who had been provoked as part of the experimental protocol were exposed to sexually explicit materials, they were more likely to retaliate against or "get back at" the person who provoked them (Baron, 1979; Cantor, Zillmann, & Einsiedel, 1978; Donnerstein & Hallam, 1978; Meyer, 1972; Zillmann, 1971). In other words, viewing arousing erotic material tended to enhance aggressive tendencies in individuals. The process by which the effect occurs is known as *excitation transfer* (Zillmann, 1978, 1979, 1982). Zillmann and Bryant (1984) explained the role of excitation transfer from erotica on aggression in this way:

[E]xposure to erotica fosters increased sympathetic activity as an accompaniment to more specific genital responses . . . and that, after sexual stimulation, residues of the slowly dissipating nonspecific sympathetic activity enter into unrelated affective states and potentially intensify them. If the subsequent state is one of annoyance and anger, residual sympathetic excitation from sexual arousal thus is likely to intensify these experiences and to energize the hostile and aggressive actions incited by them. (p. 116)

When the erotic material was pleasing and nonarousing (e.g., photographs of nudes), the aggressive tendencies of provoked individuals were actually *calmed* (Baron, 1974a, 1974b; Baron & Bell, 1973; Donnerstein, Donnerstein & Evans, 1975; White, 1979). Based on these findings and others, Zillmann and Bryant (1984) developed a model called the *excitation-and-valence model* of the effects of erotica on motivated aggression. The model makes the following four predictions: (1) pleasing and nonarousing erotica reduces aggressiveness because it counteracts the provoked person's feelings of anger; (2) displeasing and nonarousing erotica increases aggressiveness because it adds to the provoked person's feelings of annoyance; (3) displeasing and nonarousing erotica increases aggressiveness because the enhanced feelings of annoyance are retained by the person and transferred to situations afterward; and (4) pleasing and arousing erotica create a situation in which calmness rather than excitation is transferred, therefore canceling out negative effects such as aggressiveness.

IMPORTANCE OF THE PREVAILING TONE

The effects of viewing sexual content in the media are also determined by context—both the context of the material and the context in which the person is exposed to it. These contextual variables, when considered as a whole, constitute what is known as a **prevailing tone.** Harris (1994) listed the following contextual variables that contribute to the prevailing tone of sexual content.

The *seriousness or triviality of the treatment* is one major aspect of the prevailing tone. Controversial topics such as rape or incest are acceptable when given serious treatment (as in a documentary) but become offensive if treated flippantly (e.g., in a comedy).

Another aspect, *artistic value and intent,* also contributes to the prevailing tone. The Bible's Song of Solomon contains many references to sexual activities, but these are a vital part of a beautiful work that carries the theme of love as shared by a married couple. The same holds true for certain works by Chaucer and Shakespeare. At the other end of the spectrum are XXX videos or films such as *Debbie Does Dallas* which are largely devoid of artistic merit.

The prevailing tone is also affected by whether or not a sex scene is *necessary to the plot,* and by the *degree of explicitness* of the sex. Scenes of explicit sex become more acceptable to a viewer if they are important in the development of the plot. For some people, sexual innuendoes are more offensive than explicit material.

Another aspect of the prevailing tone lies within the *context of viewing*. A man's reactions when thumbing through the pages of *Hustler* are likely to be very different if (1) he is alone, or he is sitting beside (2) his wife, (3) a male friend, (4) his grandmother, or (5) his preacher. The man may view the material as highly offensive or highly exciting, depending upon his context of viewing.

Cultural context also affects the prevailing tone. What may be considered inappropriate in one culture may be commonplace in another. Many men and women in primitive tribes throughout the world walk about scantily dressed or completely naked, and the behavior is entirely appropriate for that culture. In certain Islamic cultures, women must cover themselves from head to toe before appearing in public.

EXPOSURE TO SEXUALLY VIOLENT MATERIAL

In recent years much more than in years past, the media have begun to portray sex in combination with violent acts. Magazines that portray sexual violence have appeared and joined old standards like *Penthouse* and *Playboy* in depicting more images of domination and bondage (Malamuth & Spinner, 1980). Also, the horror movies of old have evolved into a new genre called *slasher films* (very popular among teenagers despite their R ratings), which depict much brute violence against women in combination with sexual acts or in a sexual context (Yang & Linz, 1990).

Should we be concerned about this tendency to mix sex with violence? Judging from the research findings, the answer is indisputably yes.

Studies using both normal populations or convicted sex offenders have shown that the mixture of sex and violence has potentially harmful effects. In one of these studies, researchers found that convicted rapists were aroused by viewing both rape and consenting sex, whereas normal participants were aroused only by depictions of consenting sex (Abel, Barlow, Blanchard, & Guild, 1977; Barbaree, Marshall, & Lanthier, 1979). A later study revealed that normal males could be aroused by depictions of rape if the victim appeared to enjoy it and experienced an orgasm (Malamuth, Heim, & Feshbach, 1980). The arousal of the males was equal to or exceeded what they experienced while viewing a film of consensual sex; however, females in the study were not aroused by the rape film.

Importance of Individual Differences

Individual differences account for great variances in the effects of sexually explicit material. A person who is more likely to use force in situations of conflict is more likely to experience the harmful effects from viewing sexually explicit material. In a study of college males, Malamuth (1981) separated force-oriented men (those who reported they would be likely to use force in their lives) from non-force-oriented men in order to determine if sexually violent media fare affected them similarly or differently. The force-oriented men were more aroused by a rape scene in which a woman was depicted as finally enjoying the assault, whereas a film of consensual sex proved to be more arousing for the non-force-oriented men.

In another study of force-oriented and non-force-oriented males by Malamuth and Check (1983), participants listened to tapes of either consenting sex, rape with the woman eventually becoming aroused (rape-arousal), or rape with the woman being disgusted during the assault rather than aroused (rape-disgust). Arousal for both groups of men, measured by self-reports and penile tumescence, was greater for the consenting sex version than for the rape-disgust version; however, the rape-arousal version proved to be a "turn on" for both groups. The non-force-oriented group became as aroused with the rape-arousal tape as with the consensual sex tape, while the force-oriented group was even more aroused by the rape-arousal tape than by the consenting sex version.

Other studies (Donnerstein, 1980; Donnerstein & Berkowitz, 1981) have involved the viewing of sexual violence and the subsequent administration of electric shock by the viewer on a confederate. These studies have concluded that a link exists between the viewing of sexual violence (especially a rape in which the woman is depicted as becoming aroused) and a propensity to inflict pain upon females.

In summary, the research findings show that harmful effects occur whenever sexually violent materials depict a woman who becomes aroused by an assault. Also, individual differences in disposition (e.g., being force-oriented or non-force-oriented) cause different people to react differently when viewing sexually violent media fare. As discussed earlier, the prevailing tone of the material is always an important consideration.

Sexual Violence in Slasher Films

The studies cited above made use of pornographic material; however, sexual violence is not limited to films exclusively for adult audiences. The highly popular, R-rated slasher movies contain a great deal of violence, usually in a sexual context (Weaver & Tamborini, 1996). According to Harris (1994):

> The main concern with such films is the juxtaposition of erotic sex and violence. For example, one scene from *Toolbox Murders* opens with a beautiful woman disrobing and getting into her bath, with the very romantic music "Pretty Baby" playing in the background. For several minutes she is shown fondling herself and masturbating in a very erotic manner. Suddenly the camera cuts to the scene of an intruder breaking into her apartment, with loud, fast-paced suspenseful music in the background. The camera and sound track cut back and forth several times between these two characters until he finally encounters the woman. He attacks her with electric tools, chasing her around the apartment, finally shooting her several times in the head with a nail gun. The scene closes after seeing her bleed profusely, finally lying on the bed to die with the sound track again playing the erotic "Pretty Baby." (pp. 261–262)

One of the main concerns regarding slasher films is their ready availability to teens. Many of these films are not rated and therefore not restricted to adult audiences; those that do receive the R rating are available to youngsters in video stores where restrictions often are not applied.

Teens take full advantage of the availability of slasher movies. A survey of 4,500 children in the United Kingdom in the 1980s found that about one in five young teenage boys (aged 13–14) had seen an illegal and sexually violent film called *I Spit on Your Grave* (Hill, Davis, Holman, & Nelson, 1984). In another study of American college students, Greenberg and his associates found that two of three watched slasher movies on a regular basis (1993b).

Researchers have also studied slasher movies for the effects of the sexual violence on young audiences. Findings suggest that men become desensitized when they repeatedly watch slasher films (Linz, Donnerstein, & Penrod, 1984), but women do not (Krafka, 1985). Over time, the men found the slasher movies to be less degrading to women, more enjoyable, less offensive, and less violent.

Reducing the Negative Effects

The negative effects of viewing sexual violence can be mitigated or lessened. In several studies, participants were trained prior to viewing in an effort to reduce desensitization effects (Intons-Peterson & Roskos-Ewoldsen, 1989; Intons-Peterson, Roskos-Ewoldsen, Thomas, Shirley, & Blut, 1989; Linz, Donnerstein, Bross, & Chapin, 1986; Linz, Fuson, & Donnerstein, 1990). Some procedures have proven more successful than others; for example, men were found to be most affected by learning that women are not responsible for sexual assaults against them.

Other researchers have given extensive debriefings to participants to make them aware of the horrors of rape and the absolute inability of a woman to be able to enjoy it (Malamuth, Heim, & Feshbach, 1980; Donnerstein & Berkowitz, 1981; Malamuth & Check, 1980b). Evaluations have revealed that these debriefings make participants less susceptible to rape myths (e.g., a woman's enjoyment of rape).

Allen and his associates (1996) conducted a meta-analysis of 10 studies that had used educational briefings to mitigate the harmful effects of sexually explicit material. Their analysis found overwhelming support for the effectiveness of debriefings in lessening harmful effects.

MORE ON BEHAVIORAL EFFECTS OF PORNOGRAPHY: THE STUDY OF SEX OFFENDERS

The link between exposure to pornography and the commission of sex crimes is a controversial one. In 1996 one researcher reviewed the many correlational studies that attempted to link sexual aggression with use of pornography and concluded that significant correlations between the two do not exist, although particular subsets of sex offenders may use pornography in significant ways (Bauserman, 1996). Other scholars and clinicians have studied the issue and found correlational links between the consumption of pornography and criminal sexual aggression (Marshall, 1989; Malamuth & Donnerstein, 1984).

In 1994 Victor B. Cline examined data from experimental laboratory studies, field studies, and clinical case histories and found four major behavioral effects that result from the consumption of pornography. As a clinical psychologist, Cline had treated hundreds of people (mostly men) who suffered from serious sexual disorders and many who had committed sex crimes such as child molestation, rape, exhibitionism, and so forth. "With only several exceptions," Cline wrote, "pornography has been a major or minor contributor or facilitator in the acquisition of their deviation or sexual addiction" (p. 233).

The Four-Factor Syndrome

The four major effects of consuming pornography are *addiction, escalation, desensitization,* and the *tendency to act out or copy* what had been viewed. Cline called these four effects the **four-factor syndrome,** because the effects occurred in the same sequence over time. Almost all his clients had experienced the four-factor syndrome.

Addiction to pornography was the first effect that Cline noticed. Once his clients began viewing pornography, they soon found themselves wanting more of it. Most of them experienced sexual stimulation followed by sexual release from masturbation.

Once addicted, an *escalation* effect occurred as time passed. As with a drug addict, the pornography addict began craving stronger (i.e., more explicit or more deviant) sexual materials to achieve the same stimulation as the initial experience. Cline found that over time, most of his clients preferred masturbating while viewing pornography to sexual intercourse and intimacy with a partner.

Desensitization was the third effect. Over time, shocking, antisocial, illegal, immoral, and deviant sexual behavior came to be viewed as acceptable and legitimate. The morals and standards of pornography addicts tended to sink lower and lower as more and more material was consumed. The addicts began to believe that deviant sexual behaviors were more commonplace than they had originally thought.

The final effect was the tendency to *act out sexually* or copy the sexual acts they had seen in pornographic materials. These activities included deviant and illegal behaviors such as sex with children, rape, sadomasochism, exhibitionism, and so forth. According to Cline, these deviant behaviors "frequently grew into a sexual addiction that they found themselves locked into and unable to change or reverse—no matter what the negative consequences in their life" (p. 234).

Four-Factor Syndrome

In a study of convicted sex offenders, consumption of pornography was found to cause four major effects, which always occurred in the same order.

- Addiction
- Escalation
- Desensitization
- Tendency to act out or copy

Correlation between Sex Crimes and Sexually Explicit Materials

More recent research has also suggested a connection between sex crimes and the use of sexually explicit materials. Zgourides, Monto, and Harris (1997) conducted a study of 176 males from the ages of 13 to 19. Of the 176, 80 were convicted sex offenders and 96 were not. The study found a significant positive correlation between the use of sexually explicit materials and the commission of sex crimes. In other words, far more sex offenders than nonoffenders reported using sexually explicit materials. Another study (Allen, D'Alessio, & Emmers-Sommer, 2000) did not find significantly different results in a comparison of pornographic consumption among sex offenders and nonoffenders, but it did find significant differences in terms of arousal and behavioral consequences. Sex offenders were more likely to become aroused and more likely to perform some sort of sexual act (whether masturbation, consensual sex, or coercive sex) after consuming sexually explicit material.

SUMMARY

Sexual content in media ranges from the mildly suggestive to various levels of the sexually explicit. Sexual content in electronic and print media has important implications due to its perceived connection with serious social concerns. The availability of television to all ages makes that medium a particularly dangerous one when considering the damaging social effects that result from the consumption of sexual content.

Pornography is the extreme class of sexually explicit materials that is available to adult audiences only. Pornography, largely devoid of literary merit or artistic value, is produced for the express purpose of pandering sexual content.

Obscenity is a legal term that describes certain pornographic material that must meet three criteria as judged by a jury representative of the community: (1) the material appeals to a prurient (shameful, sick, morbid, or lustful) interest in sex; (2) the material is patently offensive or beyond the contemporary community standards regarding depictions of sexual content or activity; (3) the material as a whole must lack serious literary, artistic, political, or scientific value.

Many studies have examined the extent and explicitness of sexual content in mass media. These studies have found that music videos, X-rated videos, television, magazines, and R-rated movies contain varying amounts and types of sexual content.

Exposure to highly explicit sexual content may affect media users in one or more of several ways. These include sexual arousal and changes in attitudes, values, and behaviors.

When provoked individuals are exposed to sexually explicit materials, they are more likely to engage in retaliatory behavior. In other words, viewing arousing erotic material tends to enhance aggressive tendencies in individuals. This effect is known as excitation transfer.

The effects of viewing sexual content in the media are altered by the context of the material and the context in which a person is exposed to it. The seriousness or triviality of the material, the artistic value and intent of the material, the degree of explicitness and the necessity of the sex scene to the development of the plot, the cultural context, and the context of viewing are contextual variables that constitute the prevailing tone.

Harmful effects occur whenever sexually violent materials depict a woman who becomes aroused by an assault. Individual differences in disposition (e.g., being force-oriented or non-force-oriented) cause people to react differently when viewing sexually violent media fare.

R-rated slasher movies, highly popular among teenagers, contain much violence, usually in a sexual context. Men become desensitized when they watch slasher films repeatedly.

The negative effects of viewing sexual violence can be mitigated. Training sessions prior to viewing or extensive debriefing sessions proved successful in lessening negative effects.

In a study of convicted sex offenders, a clinical psychologist found that use of pornography produced four major behavioral effects that occurred in the same sequence over time. These effects, known as the four-factor syndrome, included addiction, escalation, desensitization, and the tendency to act out or copy what had been viewed.

REFERENCES

ABEL, G. G., BARLOW, D. H., BLANCHARD, E. B., & GUILD, D. (1977). The components of rapists' sexual arousal. *Archives of General Psychiatry, 34,* 895–903.

ABRAMSON, P. R., PERRY, L., SEELEY, T., SEELEY, D., & ROTHBLATT, A. (1981). Thermographic measurement of sexual arousal: A discriminant validity analysis. *Archives of Sexual Behavior, 10*(2), 175–176.

ALLEN, M., D'ALESSIO, D., EMMERS, T. M., & GEBHARDT, L. (1996). The role of educational briefings in mitigating effects of experimental exposure to violent sexually explicit material: A meta-analysis. *Journal of Sex Research, 33,* 135–141.

ALLEN, M., D'ALESSIO, D., & EMMERS-SOMMER, T. M. (2000). Reactions of criminal sexual offenders to pornography: A meta-analytic summary. In M. Roloff (Ed.), *Communication Yearbook 22* (pp. 139–169). Thousand Oaks, CA: Sage.

BANCROFT, J., & MATHEWS, A. (1971). Autonomic correlates of penile erection. *Journal of Psychosomatic Research, 15,* 159–167.

BARBAREE, H. E., MARSHALL, W. L., & LANTHIER, R. D. (1979). Deviant sexual arousal in rapists. *Behavior Research and Therapy, 17,* 215–222.

BARON, R. A. (1974a). The aggression-inhibiting influence of heightened sexual arousal. *Journal of Personality and Social Psychology, 30,* 318–322.

BARON, R. A. (1974b). Sexual arousal and physical aggression: The inhibiting influence of "cheesecake" and nudes. *Bulletin of the Psychonomic Society, 3,* 337–339.

BARON, R. A. (1979). Heightened sexual arousal and physical aggression: An extension to females. *Journal of Research in Personality, 13,* 91–102.

BARON, R. A., & BELL, P. A. (1973). Effects of heightened sexual arousal on physical aggression. *Proceedings of the 81st Annual Convention of the American Psychological Association, 8,* 171–172.

BARON, L., & STRAUS, M. A. (1987). Four theories of rape: A macrosociological analysis. *Social Problems, 34,* 467–490.

BAUSERMAN, R. (1996). Sexual aggression and pornography: A review of correlational research. *Basic and Applied Social Psychology, 18*(4), 405–427.

BAXTER, R. L., DeRIEMER, C., LANDINI, A., LESLIE, L., & SINGLETARY, M. W. (1985). A content analysis of music videos. *Journal of Broadcasting & Electronic Media, 29,* 333–340.

BRYANT, J., & ROCKWELL, S. C. (1994). Effects of massive exposure to sexually oriented prime-time television programming on adolescents' moral judgment. In D. Zillmann, J. Bryant, & A. Huston (Eds.), *Media, children, and the family: Social scientific, psychodynamic, and clinical perspectives.* Hillsdale, NJ: Erlbaum.

BUCHWALD, E., FLETCHER, P., & ROTH, M. (Eds.) (1993). *Transforming a rape culture.* Minneapolis: Milkweed Eds.

CANTOR, J. R., ZILLMANN, D., & EINSIEDEL, E. F. (1978). Female responses to provocation after exposure to aggressive and erotic films. *Communication Research, 5,* 395–411.

CHECK, J. V. P. (1995). Teenage training: The effects of pornography on adolescent males. In L. Lederer & R. Delgado (Eds.), *The price we pay: The case against racist speech, hate propaganda, and pornography* (pp. 89–91). New York: Hill and Wang.

CLINE, V. B. (1994). Pornography effects: Empirical and clinical evidence. In D. Zillmann, J. Bryant, and A. Huston (Eds.), *Media, children, and the family: Social scientific, psychodynamic, and clinical perspectives.* Hillsdale, NJ: Erlbaum.

COURT, J. H. (1984). Sex and violence: A ripple effect. In N. M. Malamuth & E. Donnerstein (Eds.), *Pornography and sexual aggression* (pp. 143–172). Orlando, FL: Academic Press.

COWAN, G., LEE, C., LEVY, D., & SNYDER, D. (1988). Dominance and inequality in X-rated videocassettes. *Psychology of Women Quarterly, 12,* 299–311.

DONNERSTEIN, E. (1980). Aggressive erotica and violence against women. *Journal of Personality and Social Psychology, 39,* 269–277.

DONNERSTEIN, E., & BERKOWITZ, L. (1981). Victim reactions in aggressive erotic films as a factor in violence against women. *Journal of Personality and Social Psychology, 41,* 710–724.

DONNERSTEIN, E., DONNERSTEIN, M., & EVANS, R. (1975). Erotic stimuli and aggression: Facilitation or inhibition. *Journal of Personality and Social Psychology, 32,* 237–244.

DONNERSTEIN, E., & HALLAM, J. (1978). Facilitating effects of erotica on aggression against women. *Journal of Personality and Social Psychology, 36,* 1270–1277.

ECCLES, A., MARSHALL, W. L., & BARBAREE, H. E. (1988). The vulnerability of erectile measures to repeated assessments. *Behavior Research and Therapy, 26,* 179–183.

FINAL REPORT OF THE ATTORNEY GENERAL'S COMMISSION ON PORNOGRAPHY. (1986). Nashville, TN: Rutledge Hill Press.

GETTLEMAN, J. (1999, 28 October). XXX=$$$. *Manhattan Mercury,* p. A6.

GREENBERG, B. S. (1994). Content trends in media sex. In D. Zillmann, J. Bryant, & A. C. Huston (Eds.), *Media, children, and the family: Social scientific, psychodynamic, and clinical perspectives.* Hillsdale, NJ: Erlbaum.

GREENBERG, B. S., ABELMAN, R., & NEUENDORF, U. (1981). Sex on the soap operas: Afternoon intimacy. *Journal of Communication, 31*(3), 83–89.

GREENBERG, B. S., BROWN, J. D., & BUERKEL-ROTHFUSS, N. L. (1993). *Media, sex, and the adolescent.* Creskill, NJ: Hampton Press.

GREENBERG, B. S., & BUSSELLE (1996). Soap operas and sexual activity: A decade later. *Journal of Communication 46*(4), 153–160.

GREENBERG, B. S., & D'ALESSIO, D. (1985). Quantity and quality of sex in the soaps. *Journal of Broadcast & Electronic Media, 29,* 309–321.

GREENBERG, B. S., & HOFSCHIRE, L. (2000). Sex on entertainment television. In D. Zillmann and P. Vorderer (Eds.), *Media entertainment: The psychology of its appeal* (pp. 93–111). Mahwah, NJ: Erlbaum.

GREENBERG, B. S., STANLEY, C., SIEMICKI, M., HEETER, C., SODERMAN, A., & LINSANGAN, R. (1993a). Sex content on soaps and primetime television series most viewed by adolescents. In B.S. Greenberg, J. D. Brown, & N. L. Buerkel-Rachfuss (Eds.), *Media, sex and the adolescent*. Cresskill, NJ: Hampton Press.

GREENBERG, B. S., STANLEY, C., SIEMICKI, M., HEETER, C., SODERMAN, A., & LINSANGAN, R. (1993b). Sex content in R-rated films viewed by adolescents. In B. S. Greenberg, J. D. Brown, & N. L. Buerkel-Rachfuss (Eds.), *Media, sex and the adolescent*. Cresskill, NJ: Hampton Press.

HARRIS, R. J. (1994). The impact of sexually explicit media. In J. Bryant and D. Zillmann, *Media effects: Advances in theory and research*. Hillsdale, NJ: Erlbaum.

HARRIS, R. J., & SCOTT, C. L. (2001). Effects of sex in the media. In J. Bryant and J. A. Bryant (Eds.), *Media effects: Advances in theory and research*. Hillsdale, NJ: Erlbaum.

HILL, C., DAVIS, H., HOLMAN, R., & NELSON, G. (1984). *Video violence and children*. London: Report of an HM stationary office.

INTONS-PETERSON, M. J., & ROSKOS-EWOLDSEN, B. (1989). Mitigating the effects of violent pornography. In S. Gubar & J. Hoff-Wilson (Eds.), *For adult users only*. Bloomington: Indiana University Press.

INTONS-PETERSON, M. J., & ROSKOS-EWOLDSEN, B., THOMAS, L., SHIRLEY, M., & BLUT, D. (1989). Will educational materials reduce negative effects of exposure to sexual violence? *Journal of Social and Clinical Psychology, 8*, 256–275.

KRAFKA, C. L. (1985). *Sexually explicit, sexually violent, and violent media: Effects of multiple naturalistic exposures and debriefing on female viewers*. Unpublished doctoral dissertation, University of Wisconsin–Madison.

KUNKEL, D., COPE, K. M., FARINOLA, W. J., BIELY, E., ROLLIN, E., & DONNERSTEIN, E. (1999). *Sex on TV: Content and context*. Menlo Park, CA: Kaiser Family Foundation.

LINZ, D., DONNERSTEIN, E., BROSS, M., & CHAPIN, M. (1986). Mitigating the influence of violence on television and sexual violence in the media. In R. Blanchard (Ed.), *Advances in the study of aggression* (Vol. 2, pp. 165–194). Orlando, FL: Academic Press.

LINZ, D., DONNERSTEIN, E., & PENROD, S. (1984). The effects of multiple exposures to filmed violence against women. *Journal of Communication, 34*(3), 130–147.

LINZ, D., FUSON, I. A., & DONNERSTEIN, E. (1990). Mitigating the negative effects of sexually violent mass communications through preexposure briefings. *Communication Research, 17*, 641–674.

LOWRY, D. T., & TOWLES, D. E. (1989). Soap opera portrayals of sex, contraception, and sexually transmitted diseases. *Journal of Communication, 39*(2), 76–83.

MALAMUTH, N. M. (1981). Rape fantasies as a function of exposure to violent sexual stimuli. *Archives of Sexual Behavior, 10*, 33–47.

MALAMUTH, N. M. (1996). Sexually explicit media, gender differences, and evolutionary theory. *Journal of Communication, 46*(3), 8–31.

MALAMUTH, N. M., & CHECK, J. V. P. (1980a). Penile tumescence and perceptual responses to rape as a function of victim's perceived reactions. *Journal of Applied Social Psychology, 10*, 528–547.

MALAMUTH, N. M., & CHECK, J. V. P. (1980b). Sexual arousal to rape and consenting depictions: The importance of the woman's arousal. *Journal of Abnormal Psychology, 89*, 763–766.

MALAMUTH, N. M., & CHECK, J. V. P. (1983). Sexual arousal to rape depictions: Individual differences. *Journal of Abnormal Psychology, 92*, 55–67.

MALAMUTH, N. M., & DONNERSTEIN, E. (1984). *Pornography and Sexual Aggression*. Orlando, FL: Academic Press.

MALAMUTH, N. M., HEIM, M., & FESHBACH, S. (1980). Sexual responsiveness of college students to rape depictions: Inhibitory and disinhibitory effects. *Journal of Personality and Social Psychology, 38*, 399–408.

Malamuth, N. M., & Spinner, B. (1980). A longitudinal content analysis of sexual violence in the best-selling erotica magazines. *Journal of Sex Research, 16,* 226–237.

Marshall, W. L. (1989). Pornography and sex offenders. In D. Zillmann & J. Bryant (Eds.), *Pornography: Research advances and policy considerations.* Hillsdale, NJ: Erlbaum.

Meyer, T. P. (1972). The effects of sexually arousing and violent films on aggressive behavior. *Journal of Sex Research, 8,* 423–333.

Morais, R. C. (1999, June 14). Porn goes public. *Forbes,* p. 214.

Mosher, D. L., & Maclan, P. (1994). College men and women respond to X-rated videos intended for male or female audiences: Gender and sexual scripts. *The Journal of Sex Research, 31,* 99–113.

Murnen, S. K., & Stockton, M. (1997). Gender and self-reported sexual arousal in response to sexual stimuli: A meta-analytic review. *Sex Roles, 37,* 135–153.

Palys, T. S. (1986). Testing the common wisdom: The social content of video pornography. *Canadian Psychology, 27*(1), 22–35.

Quackenbush, D. M., Strassberg, D. S., & Turner, C. W. (1995). Gender effects of romantic themes in erotica. *Archives of Sexual Behavior, 24,* 21–35.

Rachman, S. (1966). Sexual fetishism: An experimental analogue. *Psychological Record, 16,* 293–296.

Rachman, S., & Hodgson, R. J. (1968). Experimentally-induced "sexual fetishism": Replication and development. *Psychological Record, 18,* 25–27.

Russell, D. E. H. (1998). *Dangerous relationships: Pornography, misogyny, and rape.* Thousand Oaks, CA: Sage.

Schaefer, H. H., & Colgan, A. H. (1977). The effect of pornography on penile tumescence as a function of reinforcement and novelty. *Behavior Therapy, 8,* 938–946.

Scott, J. E. (1986). An updated longitudinal content analysis of sex references in mass circulation magazines. *Journal of Sex Research, 22,* 385–392.

Sherman, B. L., & Dominick, J. R., (1986). Violence and sex in music videos: TV and rock 'n' roll. *Journal of Communication, 36*(1), 79–93.

Sintchak, G., & Geer, J. (1975). A vaginal plethysymograph system. *Psychophysiology, 12,* 113–115.

Stodghill, R. (1998, 15 June). Where'd you learn that? *Time,* pp. 52–59.

Weaver, J. B., & Tamborini, R. (Eds.) (1996). *Horror films: Current research on audience preferences and reactions.* Mahwah, NJ: Erlbaum.

White, L. A. (1979). Erotica and aggression: The influence of sexual arousal, positive effect, and negative effect on aggressive behavior. *Journal of Personality and Social Psychology, 37,* 591–601.

Winick, C. (1985). A content analysis of sexually explicit magazines sold in an adult bookstore. *Journal of Sex Research, 21,* 206–210.

Yang, N., & Linz, D. (1990). Movie ratings and the content of adult videos: The sex-violence ratio. *Journal of Communication, 40* (2), 28–42.

Zgourides, G., Monto, M., & Harris, R. (1997) Correlates of adolescent male sexual offense: Prior adult sexual contact, sexual attitudes, and use of sexually explicit materials. *International Journal of Offender Therapy and Comparative Criminology, 41*(3), 272–283.

Zillmann, D. (1971). Excitation transfer in communication-mediated aggressive behavior. *Journal of Experimental Social Psychology, 7,* 419–434.

Zillmann, D. (1978). Attribution and misattribution of excitatory reactions. In J. H. Harvey, W. J. Ickes, & R. F. Kidd (Eds.), *New directions in attribution research* (Vol. 2, pp. 335–368). Hillsdale, NJ: Erlbaum.

Zillmann, D. (1979). *Hostility and aggression.* Hillsdale, NJ: Erlbaum.

ZILLMANN, D. (1982). Transfer of excitation in emotional behavior. In J. T. Cacioppo & R. E. Petty (Eds.), *Social psychophysiology.* New York: Guilford Press.

ZILLMANN, D., & BRYANT, J. (1982). Pornography, sexual callousness, and the trivialization of rape. *Journal of Communication, 32*(4), 10–21.

ZILLMANN, D., & BRYANT, J. (1984). Effects of massive exposure to pornography. In N. M. Malamuth & E. Donnerstein (Eds.), *Pornography and sexual aggression* (pp. 115–141). Orlando, FL: Academic Press.

ZILLMANN, D., & BRYANT, J. (1986). Shifting preferences in pornography consumption. *Communication Research, 13,* 560–578.

ZILLMANN, D., & BRYANT, J. (1988a). Effects of prolonged consumption of pornography on family values. *Journal of Family Issues, 9,* 518–544.

ZILLMANN, D., & BRYANT, J. (1988b). Pornography's impact on sexual satisfaction. *Journal of Applied Social Psychology, 18,* 438–453.

ENDNOTES

1. Technically, the X-rating has not been used since 1990, when the Motion Picture Association of America began exploring less sensational NC-17 and NC-18 ratings.

Reactions to Disturbing or Frightening Media Content

No passion so effectually robs the mind of all its powers of acting and reasoning as fear.

—Edmund Burke,
The Origin of Our Ideas of the Sublime and Beautiful, 1756

In 1975 the hit movie *Jaws* appeared in theaters across the United States. That summer, the press reported that the movie had caused many people to suddenly be very afraid of swimming in the ocean. On beaches throughout the country, sunbathers avoided stepping too far into the water. They feared that ravenous Great Whites were lurking nearby, ready to clamp their razor-sharp teeth on the unsuspecting.

The emotional response that many moviegoers experienced after seeing *Jaws*, while anecdotal in nature, is a good example of a **reaction of fright or anxiety** to media content. Other anecdotal examples of fright reactions to feature films abound. In 1974, *The Exorcist*, with its disturbing scenes, caused intense responses among audiences of all ages. Other films, such as *Indiana Jones and the Temple of Doom, Invasion of the Body Snatchers,* and *Gremlins,* contained content that was especially disturbing to children.

Since the mid-1970s, Hollywood has continued to produce thrillers that contain graphic and intense content. The proliferation of cable television in millions of homes and the addition of new channels has brought many of these thrillers directly into the homes of American families. Research on exposure to disturbing content has practical benefits for society's children, especially if such research can show ways to predict when fears will be strongest or effects will be most negative. Such knowledge might allow the prevention or the reduction of fears.

In recent years, media effects researchers have learned a great deal about fright reaction to media content, including the reasons for it and ways to control it. This chapter will identify some of the more important findings from fright-reaction studies that have been conducted through the years. Children especially have been the focus of much of this research, but adults have not been ignored. Most research on children's fright reactions has involved fictional programs, while many studies on adults have examined responses to unsettling documentaries. For both age groups, most studies have explored fright as an immediate response that is rather short lived, rather than a long-term emotional response that continues for hours or days or longer, although very recent research has explored durable fright reactions. Following a brief historical look at frightening stories as entertainment and various explanations regarding the appeal of frightening content, we look at different ways in which fright is measured. Then we focus specifically on fright reactions in children and explore the dynamics of fright reactions to media content. We assess the importance of age and gender differences in gauging fear reactions, and we close with research-directed strategies for coping with fear.

215

CHAPTER 13
Reactions to
Disturbing or
Frightening
Media Content

FRIGHTENING STORIES AS ENTERTAINMENT

Throughout history, people have enjoyed hearing stories that frightened them. In the days of prerecorded history, people gathered around campfires and told horrible tales intended to frighten and entertain their audiences. These tales were passed down through the generations and have subsequently been recorded by cultural anthropologists throughout the world. Frightening myths that involve tales of witchcraft and monsters have been found in most cultures, leading researchers to believe that such themes are universal (Kluckhorn, 1960).

No one knows for certain why horror stories became so popular across cultures. Scientists speculate that such stories may have served certain purposes. Whenever people came across some phenomenon that was beyond their understanding, a myth or fable may have been used to help explain the unexplainable (Levin, 1960). Also, such stories may have allowed children to face their fears while secure in the protective embrace of their parents. The ritualistic use of such stories throughout different cultures may have helped young people learn to master their fears.

With the Age of Reason in the 1700s, audiences became much less gullible about the supernatural, but the Romantic movement in literature in the 1800s brought renewed interest in the horror genre. This time, however, audiences recognized that such tales were fictional. They read them for the enjoyment of a good fright, much like current audiences enjoy seeing a frightening film.

The works of Edgar Allan Poe in the mid-1800s brought a new threatening convention to frightening fictional stories. Instead of unbelievable monsters, Poe introduced his audiences to a different kind of villain—a terrifying lunatic who committed realistic crimes. Rather than the supernatural, Poe's readers usually feared a psychologically disturbed or psychopathic killer.

The modern horror genre developed throughout the 20th century. Classic films such as *Dracula* and *Frankenstein* appeared in 1931. The most famous incident of media-induced fright, which we mentioned previously, occurred on October 30, 1938, when thousands of people panicked during the dramatic *War of the Worlds* radio broadcast. The radio drama, set up as a series of news announcements that interrupted "regular" programming, alarmed Depression-era listeners by reporting an invasion from the planet Mars. Cantril (1940) studied

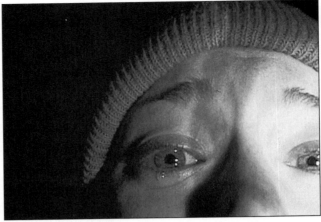

Some frightening films are considered enjoyable
entertainment.
Source: © Arisan Entertainment/Liaison

the reactions of people throughout the country and could not pinpoint a single variable that caused the fear reaction, but he found that a lack of critical ability on the part of listeners did seem to contribute. Cantril discovered that personality influences and other psychological differences tended to influence whether listeners believed what they were hearing was an actual broadcast of news.

In the 1940s and 1950s, comic books took on a more frightful aspect. Scary stories such as those from the *Tales from the Crypt* series entertained a generation of young boys in the 1950s. In the 1950s and 1960s, horror films such as Alfred Hitchcock's *Psycho* were immensely popular among audiences.

Recent years have brought more graphic depictions—more blood, gore, and realism—in books and on the screen, and audiences seem to love it. The horror writer Stephen King is one of the most successful novelists in history. King is one of today's few, elite authors whose books appear on best-seller lists prior to their release. On the big screen, box office hits such as *Friday the 13th*, *Halloween*, *Nightmare on Elm Street*, and more recently, *Scream*, have produced a number of equally popular sequels for adoring (albeit screaming) fans. Advances in the art of special effects have enhanced the graphic and realistic nature of horrible scenes in these popular films. Even on television, special effects create frightening content (especially for young viewers) on hits such as *X-Files* and *Buffy the Vampire Slayer*.

Horror has been described as stories "characterized by fear of some uncertain threat to existential nature and by disgust over its potential aftermath . . . perhaps the source of threat is supernatural in its composition" (Tamborini & Weaver, 1996). In other words, horror stories cause extreme fear. A monster or some other terrible source threatens lives, and the manner of death or the aftermath of death causes disgust.

Despite the feelings of fear and disgust, audiences are entertained—they actually seek out such experiences. This fright-as-entertainment phenomenon has piqued the interest of several communication researchers. Attempts have been made to explain the complexities that make unpleasant and horrible stories enjoyable entertainment.

217

CHAPTER 13
Reactions to
Disturbing or
Frightening
Media Content

EXPLANATIONS FOR THE APPEAL OF FRIGHT

In the previous section, we learned that myths and stories have been used throughout the ages to help people face their fears. In addition to this particular view, scientists have advanced a number of other theories to explain the appeal of frightening stories among audiences. Zillmann and Gibson (1996) provided an excellent summary of these views.

The most popular view has been that of **catharsis.** This view holds that when audience members witness graphic violence on the screen or read about it in books, they purge or rid themselves of their own violent tendencies or inclinations. Some have argued that such purgation is enjoyable (Clarens, 1967). Some have extended the notion of catharsis to include purgation of personal fears and anxieties (Douglas, 1966; Tudor, 1989). Also, the transformations that monsters undergo in many horror films supposedly provide cathartic relief for teens who are experiencing physical changes as they mature sexually (Evans, 1984).

Researchers sometimes use terms like "identification" or "vicarious experience" to explain cathartic effects from horror. Some say that viewers are able to gain sadistic pleasure by identifying with the monsters and killers (King, 1981). Viewers are able to enjoy certain taboo experiences in a vicarious manner (Wood, 1984). Deep anxieties about certain acts (especially sexual acts that frequently occur in horror) find expression and even resolution through the entertaining horror book or movie (Derry, 1987).

Another suggestion about the appeal of horror comes from Berlyne (1967, 1971), who believed that horror serves as a necessary, noxious experience that provides the viewer with feelings of gratified relief once it is finished. Of this view, Zillmann and Gibson wrote:

> It is the *termination* of this aversive state that is expected to prompt pleasurable relief. In this view, the enjoyment of horror is akin to the pleasures of the sudden end to a bad toothache—which should leave people in hopes for recurrences. (1996, p. 26)

Rosenbaum (1979) provided an explanation of the appeal of frightening content with distinctly religious overtones: People enjoy horror because it encourages a belief in a superior spiritual being capable of destroying evil forces. Ultimately, they experience feelings of "spiritual safety" (Zillmann & Gibson, 1996, p. 27).

Zillmann (1991a, 1991b) described horror as frightening because it releases empathetic responses toward victims and makes viewers apprehensive about becoming victims themselves. In other words, viewers identify with the victims and experience their terror vicariously. Horror also frightens viewers because of their apprehensions; they fear being victims themselves. Finally, horror usually features a satisfying ending that viewers enjoy.

Zillmann called his view for the enjoyment of horror a "gender-socialization approach." This explanation differed considerably from previous views. Zillmann noticed that males and females reacted very differently to horror films, and part of the enjoyment obtained from watching the film had to do with acting or reacting in those predictable ways. Zillmann and Gibson (1996) wrote:

> The precept for boys and men stipulates that exposure to horror be nondistressing. Their show of mastery of distress in the face of terror should please them and favorably impress others. Gratification is thus self-generated and of a social nature. The precept for girls and women, in contrast, stipulates that exposure to horror be distressing and duly expressed as such. Their show of appropriate sensitivity—dismay, disgust, and contempt—should give them pleasure and favorably impress others. Gratification is again self-generated and social in kind. (p. 28)

MEASURING FRIGHT

Social scientists use a variety of research methods to measure responses of fear or anxiety when a person is viewing media content. Whether studying adults or children, researchers have found that **self-reporting measures** and **measures of physiological responses** have been most useful.

With self-reporting measures, subjects are shown frightening or disturbing content, then asked to select words or phrases that best describe their reactions to the content. Adults, for example, are asked to report levels of anxiety or states of anxiety they experienced (Lazarus, Speisman, Mordkoff, & Davidson, 1962). Other descriptors such as the amount of tension or emotional arousal provide additional information. In recent years, studies have asked adults to recall media content that frightened them as children (Hoekstra, Harris, & Helmick, 1999; Harrison & Cantor, 1999). The self-reports for children must be more simply stated. Usually, researchers ask the children to express reactions in varying degrees—for instance, how scared or upset they felt after viewing the disturbing scene or content (Sparks & Cantor, 1986). Sometimes children are asked how scary they found the program to be (Osborn & Endsley, 1971) or whether or not they experienced negative sensory reactions to the content they saw (Wilson & Cantor, 1985).

Several physiological responses have been used to measure fright reactions. Among adults, the most common have been the measures of heart rate and palmar skin conductance (Falkowski & Steptoe, 1983; Koriat, Melkman, Averill, & Lazarus, 1972). When the subjects are children, experimenters have used heart rate, skin temperature (Wilson & Cantor, 1985; Zillmann, Hay, & Bryant, 1975), and facial expressions of fear (Wilson & Cantor, 1987).

FRIGHT REACTIONS IN CHILDREN

Through the years, a body of research has examined immediate and short-lived reactions of fright or anxiety among children, as well as reactions of extended duration to media content, whether movies, radio, or television. After a thorough review of the literature, scholar Joanne Cantor assessed the findings in this way:

219

CHAPTER 13
*Reactions to
Disturbing or
Frightening
Media Content*

Together, these studies suggest that transitory fright responses to dramatic mass media stimuli are quite typical, that enduring emotional disturbances occur in a substantial proportion of the audience, and that intense and debilitating reactions affect a small but appreciable minority of particularly susceptible viewers. (1994, p. 219)

In terms of other important and specific findings, the research showed that parents were usually unaware that their children experienced intense fright reactions, or they underestimated the severity or significance of their children's fright (Cantor & Reilly, 1982). Finally, through the years the research consistently showed that children actually enjoy being frightened by films or television programs, but the reasons posited by researchers for this phenomenon have been varied.

Fright reactions have been measured for many years. In the 1930s and 1940s, several studies examined reactions of fear among mass media audiences, especially children (Dysinger & Ruckmick, 1933; Eisenberg, 1936; Preston, 1941). During the period of the Payne Fund Studies, Blumer's (1933) interviews of children determined that at least 93 percent had been scared by a feature film. He described the effects of the movies upon young audiences as nothing short of "emotional possession." During this possession, normal feelings and perceptions are forgotten as viewers become lost in the vicarious viewing experience. Preston (1941) discovered that most parents were unaware of the extent of fright reactions their children experienced, and this finding has been supported by more recent research (Cantor & Reilly, 1982). Most studies in the 1950s and early 1960s followed the lead of earlier studies by focusing upon the content of motion pictures and television and their effects upon viewers (Wall & Simson, 1950; Himmelweit, Oppenheim, & Vince, 1958; Schramm, Lyle, & Parker, 1961). One famous study, however, broke with tradition and examined the harmful effects of comic books on American youth (Wertham, 1953).

Throughout the remainder of the 1960s, 1970s, and 1980s, researchers often concentrated their efforts on the *long-range effects* of mass media rather than short-term emotional effects. Enduring fright reactions, the kind that cause nightmares or long-term effects, became the focus of surveys and experiments. Hess and Goldman (1962) found that three of four parents interviewed said their children sometimes react with nightmares after viewing disturbing programs on television. Singer (1975) showed that children are in danger of having terrifying nightmares after watching disturbing media content. Years after seeing a frightening movie, children may experience such night "terrors" or, at the least, have strange or weird fantasies. Sarafino (1986) argued that frightening media content not only caused fear reactions in children, but threatened to impair psychological development (p. 56). Enduring reactions of fright were also measured by Cantor and Reilly (1982) and Palmer, Hockett, and Dean (1983).

Much research in the 1970s and 1980s underscored the prevalence of media fright reactions among children. In one study, almost 50 percent of the first graders in the study group reported having been sometimes frightened or often frightened by television programs (Lyle & Hoffman, 1972). A national survey in 1977 found that one in four of the children questioned responded that shooting and violent fighting on television had frightened them (Zill, 1977). Wilson,

Hoffner, and Cantor (1987) found even more startling results. Three of four elementary school children and preschoolers in their sample reported having been frightened by a program on television or action in a movie. Two psychiatric case studies (Buzzuto, 1975; Mathai, 1983) revealed intense and disabling states of anxiety present after watching *The Exorcist* and *Invasion of the Body Snatchers*. The viewers did not have a preexisting psychiatric problem, but the researchers found that the movie viewing occured at the same time as stressful events in the children's lives.

Since the 1990s, a number of different types of studies have offered compelling evidence for problems associated with media-induced fright among children, including lasting, detrimental effects (Cantor, 1998; Harrison & Cantor, 1999; Hoekstra, Harris, & Helmick, 1999). Singer, Slovak, Frierson, and York (1998) conducted a survey of more than 2,000 Ohio children in the third through eighth grades and found that students who watched more hours of television each day reported more symptoms of anxiety, depression, and posttraumatic stress. Another survey of parents found that the more television a child watched, the more likely the child was to have a sleep disturbance. Children with television sets in their bedroom were significantly more likely to experience sleep disturbances (Owens, Maxim, McGuinn, Nobile, Msall, & Alario, 1999).

DYNAMICS OF FEAR REACTIONS TO MEDIA CONTENT

Media effects researchers have debated the reasons for fear reactions among audiences, especially those that have the age and developmental capacity to understand that what they are witnessing never actually happened. Fright occurs despite the fact that the viewer is not in danger and understands that he or she is not in danger. Why is this? Most social scientists explain the reaction in terms of classical conditioning (Pavlov, 1927, 1960; Razran, 1949). According to classical conditioning, certain stimuli cause certain responses, and similar stimuli evoke similar, albeit less intense, responses. "This principle implies that, because of similarities between the real and the mediated stimulus, a stimulus that would evoke a fright response if experienced first hand will evoke a similar, but less intense response when encountered via the mass media" (Cantor, 1994, p. 222).

Fear-Producing Stimuli

According to Cantor (1994), three categories of stimuli that recur in media content usually result in fear responses in real life. These include (1) dangers and injuries, (2) distortions of natural forms, and (3) the experience of endangerment and fear by others (p. 222).

Dangers and Injuries

Many different kinds of events that threaten harm pop up repeatedly in scary programs. These might include natural disasters (e.g., earthquakes, tornadoes), violent confrontations between people such as interpersonal conflicts or major wars throughout the globe or even the universe, animal attacks, or major accidents (Cantor, 1994, pp. 222–223). Depictions of dangerous stimuli in mass media have produced measurable fright reactions in a number of experimental and survey research studies (Cantor, 1998; Harrison & Cantor, 1999).

221

CHAPTER 13 ·
Reactions to
Disturbing or
Frightening
Media Content

Distortions of Natural Forms

Another stimulus that tends to produce a fear response occurs when familiar sights or organisms are shown with a deformity, distortion, or mutilation. Movie monsters, for example, fall into this category. According to Cantor (1994), this set of stimuli results from "familiar organisms in unfamiliar and unnatural forms" (p. 223).

Throughout the research literature, monstrous characters are frequently mentioned as causing fear in children. Surveys and reports have revealed such fears (Blumer, 1933; Cantor & Sparks, 1984; Dorr, Doubleday, & Kovaric, 1983; Leishman, 1981; Lyle & Hoffman, 1976; Sparks, 1986), as have experiments in laboratory settings (Cantor & Wilson, 1984; Cantor, Ziemke, & Sparks, 1984; Sparks & Cantor, 1986).

Experience of Endangerment and Fear by Others

Movies and drama on television are designed to involve the audience in the situation of characters who are sometimes responding to frightful situations. The audiences are thus drawn into the plot and establish *empathy* with the characters with whom they are able to identify. Empathy is one of two primary mechanisms of this third category of responses to frightful stimuli.

This final category is the only one which involves an *indirect* response to scary content being viewed. In other words, fear is produced when audience members see characters afraid while in fearful situations.

Laboratory research studies have revealed that empathy is something that must be developed with age and is associated with the acquisition of role-play skills (Feshback, 1982; Selman & Byrne, 1978). Research has shown that preschool children are not nearly as frightened by a character's fear than by the actual frightening stimulus, while older children (ages 9 to 11) are known to experience fear simply by seeing a character's fearful expression and without witnessing the frightening stimulus itself (Wilson & Cantor, 1985).

The other mechanism that produces an indirect response of fear is that of *vicarious involvement*. This mechanism explains the fear of audiences in situations in which characters are unafraid because they are unaware that any danger is impending. Suspenseful dramas rely upon audience tensions and worries that something terrible might happen to characters with whom the audience identifies or develops an affective attachment (Zillmann, 1980; Dysinger & Ruckmick, 1933; Leishman, 1981; Tannenbaum & Gaer, 1965). The fear produced in this vicarious involvement with the characters may stem from a kind of separation anxiety—fear of being separated from the characters due to impending doom (Bowlby, 1973).

Emotional Response Factors

Cantor (1994) also identified three important factors that cause viewers to react emotionally whenever they see fearful situations on the screen: (1) realism of depiction, (2) motivations of the viewer, (3) and other factors that affect a viewer's emotionality (p. 225).

Realism of Depiction

Whenever viewers witness highly realistic, scary action on the screen, their fright responses tend to be intensely emotional. This is known as **stimulus generalization.** This notion refers to the similarity between conditioned or unconditioned stimuli from real life and what is seen on the screen. The greater the similarity between real life and screen drama, the stronger the generalization stimulus will be, and thus the fearful or emotional response to that stimulus. The stimulus generalization notion explains why people react more intensely to violent scenes that involve live action or real-life depictions, rather than, for example, violence in cartoons or between puppets (Gunter & Furnham, 1984; Osborn & Endsley, 1971; Surbeck, 1975).

Particular fears of individuals in the audience also affect the intensity of emotional responses that screen depictions evoke. Children, for instance, are more frightened by screen incidents that they can identify with—those that come within personal experiences. Experimental research has confirmed that individual fears and associated real-life experiences cause the affected individuals to react more intensely when related material is shown on the screen (Hare & Bevings, 1975; Sapolsky & Zillmann, 1978; Weiss, Katkin, & Rubin, 1968).

A process called *stimulus discrimination* has also been identified as affecting the emotional reactions of audience members. This refers to the ability of audience members at various ages to be able to (or not be able to) distinguish screen events from real-life occurrences. In young children who lack developmental maturity, for example, realizing that a TV or screen monster is not actually real or that a brutal shooting on a dramatic thriller is not indeed taking place can be very difficult and emotionally disturbing (Door, 1980). As will be shown in the next section, young children lack the developmental capacity to understand that the world of motion pictures and television is a distinctly different place from the real world. As the viewer becomes more accustomed to discriminating between productions of media technology and real-life occurrences, the intensity of the emotional response to screen depictions decreases, to a certain point.

The notion of stimulus discrimination is not entirely supported by research evidence because many adults have been shown to exhibit fear to media portrayals despite their understanding that the material is fictional (Johnson, 1980). Additional research has shown that even habitual viewing of frightening material among adults does not necessarily lessen fright responses (Feilitzen, 1975; Cantor & Reilly, 1982; Sapolsky & Zillmann, 1978).

Motivations of the Viewer

Researchers have argued that the mature adult viewer possesses a fair amount of control over responses to media content. Certain cognitive measures can be taken to enhance or to minimize fright responses (Zillmann, 1978, 1982). For example, viewers who want to be entertained and aroused by a screen drama might purposely "forget" that the events are being staged in order to enhance enjoyment. On the other hand, viewers who want to keep fright reactions to a minimum might continue to remind themselves that the actions are only mediated.

Another motivation for viewing is that of acquisition of information. Studies have shown that audience members who watch for this motivational reason tend to pay more attention to the program and thus may become more aroused by what they see. Considerable research has involved documentaries as stimulus films, as studies have shown that portrayals of violence that actually happened are significantly more arousing than programs that are known by the viewers to be purely fictional (Geen, 1975; Geen & Rakosky, 1973).

Factors Affecting Viewers' Emotional Responses

Research has shown that audience members who are previously aroused before viewing an exciting or disturbing scene retain some "arousal residue," which combines with new responses to film scenes to produce more intense emotional reactions. The theory that explains this phenomenon is called *excitation transfer* (Zillmann, 1978; Cantor, Zillmann, & Bryant, 1975; Zillmann, Mody, & Cantor, 1974). The arousing incidents may or may not be related to one another, and may or may not occur simultaneously, but excitation transfer occurs unless other factors distract the viewer or otherwise prevent the process from occurring (Girodo & Pellegrini, 1976; Schachter & Singer, 1962).

A good example of excitation transfer in action can be found in the techniques that movie producers and directors use to enhance suspense. Sound effects, for example, are very important. Different types of music can create different moods and different degrees of arousal, thus affecting the emotional impact of a film (Thayer & Levenson, 1983). Another important device to enhance the effects of a movie is that of foreshadowing or forewarning of impending threats. Studies showed that adults become more upset when a distressing event occurs if the movie forewarned them of it (Cantor, Ziemke, & Sparks, 1984; Nomikos, Opton, Averill, & Lazarus, 1968), and children experienced more fear in anticipation of the forewarned scene (Hoffner & Cantor, 1990).

AGE AND GENDER DIFFERENCES

Two of the most important factors that affect a viewer's reactions to frightening media fare are chronological age and gender. A recent meta-analysis of studies that examined media-induced fear conducted between 1987 and 1996, underscored the importance of gender and age differences, as females were found to exhibit more fear than men, and the extent of the effect increased with age (Peck, 1999). As noted previously, gender differences may have resulted from social pressures to conform to gender-specific behavior (e.g., girls who scream at horror shows, boys who demonstrate self-controlled mastery of the disturbing content).

223

CHAPTER 13
Reactions to
Disturbing or
Frightening
Media Content

The significance of gender differences among adults in differing responses to frightful media content has already been discussed in the section on explanations for the appeal of fright, so we focus this section on the importance of age and gender differences among children. The most important determining factor of fright reactions in children is that of age, due to the great developmental differences that occur during childhood, especially as children learn to distinguish fantasy from reality. Gender differences among children have been less pronounced, despite the stereotypical images of girls being more easily frightened than boys (Birnbaum & Croll, 1984) and more emotional (Fabes & Martin, 1991; Grossman & Wood, 1993).

Cantor and her associates have identified various types of stimuli that frighten children at different ages, as well as strategies that help reduce fear responses in children. Monsters, ghosts, supernatural creatures, the dark, animals, strange-looking creatures, and fast-moving creatures tend to scare young children from ages three to eight years. Slightly older children (9 to 12 years) are more frightened by threats of injury or destruction to themselves or their loved ones. Children older than 12 also are afraid of personal injury, but in addition they face social and peer pressures and accompanying fears, as well as global concerns such as politics, the economy, or the environment (Cantor, 1994, p. 231; Cantor, Wilson, & Hoffner, 1986).

The difference between the fears of very young children and those of older children can be stated plainly. Younger children fear the stimulus itself, no matter how unreal or fantastic it is. Older children are more afraid of what might occur to them, rather than simply the danger itself. Even older children fear more abstract concepts and issues that threaten *psychological* harm in addition to or instead of *physical* harm. See the box "What Frightens Children" for a summary of fear reactions at different ages.

What Frightens Children?

At different ages, children experience different types of fear reactions to what they see on the screen. The reason for this has to do with their different levels of cognitive development. Younger children tend to fear stimuli themselves, no matter how unrealistic or fanciful they may be. Older children are more afraid of what might occur to them, rather than simply the danger itself. Still older children fear more abstract issues that threaten psychological harm in addition to or instead of physical harm.

Age: 3 to 8 Years
Frightening images on the screen such as monsters, ghosts, supernatural creatures, the dark, animals, strange-looking creatures, and fast-moving creatures tend to scare young children.

Age: 9 to 12 Years
Threats of injury or destruction to the self or loved ones most frighten children in this age group.

Age: Older than 12
Personal injury is also a fear for adolescents, but they also face social and peer pressures and accompanying fears, and global concerns such as politics, the economy, or the environment.

Source: Cantor, J (1994). Fright reactions to mass media. In J. Bryant & D. Zillmann (Eds.), *Media effects: Advances in theory and research.* Hillsdale, NJ: Erlbaum, p. 231. Cantor, J., Wilson, B. J. & Hoffner, C. (1986). Emotional responses to a televised nuclear holocaust film. *Communication Research, 13,* 257–277.

225

Chapter 13
Reactions to
Disturbing or
Frightening
Media Content

The reason for these differences has to do with cognitive development of the children. Until about age seven, children remember and sort items in terms of salient attributes they perceive. After age seven, this type of organization is replaced by one based upon *concepts or functions* of the items involved rather than physical characteristics alone (Birch & Bortner, 1966; Melkman, Tversky, & Baratz, 1981). Thus, as a child grows older, he or she responds more intensely to media depictions that are based more on reality than fantasy or the unrealistic (Flavell, 1963; Kelly, 1981; Morison & Gardner, 1978; Cantor & Sparks, 1984).

A good example of the differences in cognitive development and the fear responses they produce can be shown through a study that involved *The Incredible Hulk* television program. Sparks and Cantor (1986) found that preschoolers became intensely frightened whenever the normal-looking hero turned into the monster Hulk. Older children did not fear the transformation because they understood that the creature used his powers for the forces of good.

Another excellent example is that of a study conducted after a showing of the televised movie *The Day After* in the 1980s. The movie showed a community in Kansas under nuclear attack and the devastating aftermath, though depictions of injuries were rather mild in comparison to other television programs. Cantor, Wilson, and Hoffner (1986) surveyed viewers by telephone the night after the movie played. They found that young children were least affected by the film, while children older than 12 (due to cognitive development) were highly disturbed, as were their parents. Cantor and her associates concluded that "the findings are due to the fact that the emotional impact of the film comes from the contemplation of the potential annihilation of the earth as we know it—a concept that is beyond the grasp of the young child" (1994, p. 234).

STRATEGIES FOR COPING WITH FEAR

As would be expected, the same developmental and gender differences that cause children of different ages to fear different media portrayals also affect the different types of coping strategies, though gender differences play a much smaller role in determining effective coping mechanisms (Cantor, 2001). At various ages, coping strategies have been shown to be effective in reducing or even preventing fears that are induced by mass media content.

Coping strategies fall into one of two categories: noncognitive and cognitive (Cantor, 1994). **Noncognitive strategies,** those that do not require the viewer to process verbal information, have been shown to work well among preschoolers. **Cognitive strategies,** those that require the activation of cognitive processes (e.g., talking about the fear), tend to work well with children of elementary school age and older, though noncognitive strategies have also been shown to be useful. Research has shown that adolescent girls report using more noncognitive coping strategies than boys, but gender differences could not be measured in the use of cognitive coping strategies (Hoffner, 1995; Valkenburg, Cantor, & Peeters, 2000).

Types of Noncognitive Strategies

Several types of noncognitive strategies have been used to help young children cope with media-induced fear. *Visual desensitization* allows children to be gradually exposed to disturbing content. In one study, the children were shown a rubber tarantula in order to prepare them for a scene that featured the large spiders (Wilson, 1987). The backstage view of the application of makeup to the actor in *The Incredible Hulk* served as a visual desensitization.

Physical activity serves as another type of noncognitive coping strategy. Clinging to an object of attachment is an example of this strategy. Eating or drinking while viewing a scene has been shown to reduce fears, but some researchers argued that this takes place only because the child has been distracted from the program (Manis, Keating, & Morison, 1980). Covering the eyes is another example (Wilson, 1989), but research showed that only younger children used this as a means of reducing fear; older children actually became more frightened by doing it.

Types of Cognitive Strategies

As mentioned previously, cognitive strategies are typically more appropriate for older children because of their level of development. When children are told to remember that a program is not real, they are less likely to be frightened by it. When the media presentations depict highly realistic threats, one of the most effective cognitive coping strategies is that of offering reassuring information about the minimal danger of the depicted threat.

Studies have revealed that cognitive strategies can be modified for younger children to improve their effectiveness in helping the children cope with media-induced fears. Information can be provided verbally and visually (Cantor, Sparks, & Hoffner, 1988), and simple reassuring words can be repeated to calm the children (Wilson, 1987).

SUMMARY

Fright reactions to media content among adults and especially among children have been the focus of one branch of media effects research. Self-reporting measures and measures of physiological responses have been most useful in these studies.

Research has revealed several important findings. Most fright reactions are usually transitory, but some may endure for an extended period of time. Fright reactions are debilitating in only a few cases. Parents are usually unaware of the intensity of their children's fright reactions. Finally, research has shown that, to an extent, children enjoy being frightened by films or television programs.

In the 1930s and 1940s, the Payne Fund Studies and the *War of the Worlds* study examined fright reactions among movie and radio audiences. In the 1950s and 1960s, studies focused upon the content of motion pictures and television and their long-term effects upon viewers. Research in the 1970s and 1980s iden-

227

CHAPTER 13
*Reactions to
Disturbing or
Frightening
Media Content*

tified the prevalence of media fright reactions among children. Recent research has attempted to determine ways of reducing or eliminating fright reactions among young audiences.

Viewers' attraction to disturbing content can be explained by the mechanism of excitation transfer. This is a process of physiological arousal transference that allows greater enjoyment of media presentations.

Fright occurs despite viewers' understanding that they are not in danger. According to classical conditioning, certain stimuli cause certain responses, and similar stimuli evoke similar, albeit less intense, responses.

Three categories of stimuli that recur in media content usually result in fear responses in real life: (1) dangers and injuries, (2) distortions of natural forms, and (3) the experience of endangerment and fear by others.

The type of fright reaction experienced depends heavily upon the chronological age of the viewer. This is due to differences in the cognitive development of children at various ages. These differences affect a child's ability to distinguish fantasy from reality. Very young children (ages 3 to 8) fear the stimulus itself, no matter how unreal or fantastic it may be. Older children (ages 9 to 12) are more afraid of what might occur to them, rather than simply the danger itself. Children older than 12 fear more abstract concepts and issues that threaten psychological harm in addition to or instead of physical harm.

A number of different fright stimuli have been identified for children at different ages. Monsters, ghosts, supernatural creatures, the dark, animals, strange-looking creatures, and fast-moving creatures tend to scare young children from the ages of 3 to 8; children 9 to 12 years old are more frightened by threats of injury or destruction to themselves or their loved ones. Adolescents also fear personal injury, but in addition they face social and peer pressures and accompanying fears, as well as global concerns such as politics, the economy, or the environment.

Three factors cause viewers to react emotionally whenever they see fearful situations on the screen: (1) realism of the depiction, (2) motivations of the viewer, and (3) other factors that affect a viewer's emotionality.

Strategies for coping with media-induced fears include cognitive and noncognitive techniques. Cognitive strategies require the activation of cognitive processes such as talking about the fear. These strategies tend to work well with children in elementary school or beyond, though noncongnitive strategies have also been shown to be useful. Visual desensitization and physical activity are types of noncognitive strategies. These usually work well with younger children.

REFERENCES

BERLYNE, D. E. (1967). Arousal and reinforcement. In D. Levine (Ed.), *Nebraska Symposium on Motivation* (Vol. 15, pp. 1–110). Lincoln: University of Nebraska Press.

BERLYNE, D. E. (1971). *Aesthetics and psychobiology.* Englewood Cliffs, NJ: Prentice Hall.

BIRCH, H. B., & BORTNER, M. (1966). Stimulus competition and category usage in normal children. *Journal of Genetic Psychology, 109,* 195–204.

BLUMER, H. (1933). *Movies and conduct.* New York: Macmillan.

BOWLBY, J. (1973). *Separation: Anxiety and anger.* New York: Basic Books.

BUZZUTO, J. C. (1975). Cinematic neurosis following *The Exorcist*. *Journal of Nervous and Mental Disease, 161,* 43–48.

CANTOR, J. (1994). Fright reactions to mass media. In J. Bryant & D. Zillmann (Eds.), *Media effects: Advances in theory and research* (pp. 213–245). Hillsdale, NJ: Erlbaum.

CANTOR, J. (1998). *"Mommy, I'm scared": How TV and movies frighten children and what we can do to protect them.* San Diego, CA: Harvest/Harcourt.

CANTOR, J. (in press). Fright reactions to mass media. In J. Bryant & D. Zillmann (Eds.), *Media effects: Advances in theory and research.* Mahwah, NJ: Erlbaum.

CANTOR, J., & REILLY, S. (1982). Adolescents' fright reactions to television and films. *Journal of Communication, 32*(1), 87–99.

CANTOR, J., & SPARKS, G. G. (1984). Children's fear responses to mass media: Testing some Piagetian predictions. *Journal of Communication, 34* (2), 90–103.

CANTOR, J., SPARKS, G. G., & HOFFNER, C. (1988). Calming children's television fears: *Mr. Rogers* vs. the *Incredible Hulk. Journal of Broadcasting & Electronic Media, 32,* 271–288.

CANTOR, J., & WILSON, B. J. (1984). Modifying fear responses to mass media in preschool and elementary school children. *Journal of Broadcasting, 28,* 431–443.

CANTOR, J., WILSON, B. J., & HOFFNER, C. (1986). Emotional responses to a televised nuclear holocaust film. *Communication Research, 13,* 257–277.

CANTOR, J., ZIEMKE, D., & SPARKS, G. G. (1984). Effect of forewarning on emotional responses to a horror film. *Journal of Broadcasting, 28,* 21–31.

CANTOR, J., ZILLMANN, D., & BRYANT, J. (1975). Enhancement of experienced sexual arousal in response to erotic stimuli through misattribution of unrelated residual excitation. *Journal of Personality and Social Psychology, 32,* 69–75.

CANTRIL, H. (1940). *The invasion from Mars: A study in the psychology of panic.* Princeton, NJ: Princeton University Press.

CLARENS, C. (1967). *An illustrated history of the horror film.* New York: Putnam.

DERRY, C. (1987). More dark dreams: Some notes on the recent horror film. In G.A. Waller (Ed.), *American horrors: Essays on the modern American horror film* (pp. 162–174). Urbana: University of Illinois Press.

DOOR, A. (1980). When I was a child I thought as a child. In S. B. Withey & R. P. Abeles (Eds.), *Television and social behavior: Beyond violence and children* (pp. 191–230). Hillsdale, NJ: Erlbaum.

DOOR, A., DOUBLEDAY, C., & KOVARIC, P. (1983). Emotions depicted on and stimulated by television programs. In M. Meyer (Ed.), *Children and the formal features of television* (pp. 97–143). New York: K. G. Saur.

DOUGLAS, D. (1966). *Horror!* New York: Macmillan.

DYSINGER, W. S., & RUCKMICK, C. A. (1933). *The emotional responses of children to the motion picture situation.* New York: Macmillan.

EISENBERG, A. L. (1936). *Children and radio programs.* New York: Columbia University Press.

EVANS, W. (1984). Monster movies: A sexual theory. In B. K. Grant (Ed.), *Planks of reason: Essays on the horror film* (pp. 53–64). Metuchen, NJ: Scarecrow Press.

FABES, R. A., & MARTIN, C. L. (1991). Gender and age stereotypes of emotionality. *Personality and Social Psychology Bulletin, 17,* 532–540.

FALKOWSKI, J., & STEPTOE, A. (1983). Biofeedback-assisted relaxation in the control of reactions to a challenging task and anxiety-provoking film. *Behavior Research and Therapy, 21,* 161–167.

FEILITZEN, C., VON. (1975). Findings of Scandinavian research on child and television in the process of socialization. *Fernsehen und Bildung, 9,* 54–84.

229

CHAPTER 13
*Reactions to
Disturbing or
Frightening
Media Content*

FESHBACH, N. D. (1982). Sex differences in empathy and social behavior in children. In N. Eisenberg (Ed.), *The development of prosocial behavior* (pp. 315–338). New York: Academic Press.

FLAVELL, J. (1963). *The developmental psychology of Jean Piaget.* New York: Van Nostrand.

GEEN, R. G. (1975). The meaning of observed violence: Real vs. fictional violence and consequent effects on aggression and emotional arousal. *Journal of Research in Personality, 9,* 270–281.

GEEN, R. G., & RAKOSKY, J. J. (1973). Inteptretations of observed violence and their effects on GSR. *Journal of Experimental Research in Personality, 6,* 289–292.

GIRODO, M., & PELLEGRINI, W. (1976). Exercise-produced arousal, film-induced arousal and attribution of internal state. *Perceptual and Motor Skills, 42,* 931–935.

GROSSMAN, M., & WOOD, W. (1993). Sex differences in the intensity of emotional experience: A social role interpretation. *Journal of Personality and Social Psychology, 65,* 1010–1022.

GUNTER, B., & FURNHAM, A. (1984). Perceptions of television violence: Effects of programme genre and type of violence on viewers' judgements of violent portrayals. *British Journal of Social Psychology, 23,* 155–164.

HARE, R. D., & BLEVINGS, G. (1975). Defensive responses to phobic stimuli. *Biological Psychology, 3,* 1–13.

HARRISON, K., & CANTOR, J. (1999). Tales from the screen: Enduring fright reactions to scary media. *Media Psychology, 1*(2), 97–116.

HESS, R. D., & GOLDMAN, H. (1962). Parents' views of the effects of television on their children. *Child Development, 33,* 411–426.

HIMMELWEIT, H. T., OPPENHEIM, A. N., & VINCE, P. (1958). *Television and the child.* London: Oxford University Press.

HOEKSTRA, S. J., HARRIS, R. J., & HELMICK, A. L. (1999). Autobiographical memories about the experience of seeing frightening movies in childhood. *Media Psychology, 1*(2), 117–140.

HOFFNER, C., & CANTOR, J. (1990). Forewarning of a threat and prior knowledge of outcome: Effects on children's emotional responses to a film sequence. *Human Communication Research, 16,* 323–354.

JOHNSON, B. R. (1980). General occurrence of stressful reactions to commercial motion pictures and elements in films subjectively identified as stressors. *Psychological Reports, 47,* 775–786.

KELLY, H. (1981). Reasoning about realities: Children's evaluations of television and books. In H. Kelly & H. Gardner (Eds.), *Viewing children through television* (pp. 59–71). San Francisco: Jossey-Bass.

KING, S. (1981). *Danse macabre.* New York: Everest.

KLUCKHORN, C. (1960). Recurrent themes in myths and myth making. In H. A. Murray (Eds.), *Myth and myth making* (pp. 46–59). New York: George Braziller.

KORIAT, A., MELKMAN, R., AVERILL, J. R., & LAZARUS, R. S. (1972). The self-control of emotional reactions to a stressful film. *Journal of Personality, 40,* 601–619.

LAZARUS, R. S., SPEISMAN, J. C., MORDKOFF, A. M., & DAVIDSON, L. A. (1962). A laboratory study of psychological stress produced by a motion picture film. *Psychological Monographs: General and Applied, 76* (34), 553.

LEISHMAN, K. (1981, 10 January). When is television too scary for children? *TV Guide,* pp. 4–5, 8.

LEVIN, H. (1960). Some meanings of myth. In H. A. Murray (Ed.), *Myth and myth making* (pp. 103–114). New York: George Braziller.

LYLE, J., & HOFFMAN, H. R. (1972). Children's use of television and other media. In E. A. Rubinstein, G. A. Comstock, & J. P. Murray (Eds.), *Television and social behavior* (Vol. 4, pp. 129–256). Washington, DC: U.S. Government Printing Office.

LYLE, J., & HOFFMAN, H. R. (1976). Explorations in patterns of television viewing by preschool-age children. In R. Brown (Ed.), *Children and television* (pp. 45–61). Beverly Hills, CA: Sage.

MANIS, F. R., KEATING, D. P., & MORISON, F. J. (1980). Developmental differences in the allocation of processing capacity. *Journal of Experimental Child Psychology, 29,* 156–169.

MATHAI, J. (1983). An acute anxiety state in an adolescent precipitated by viewing a horror movie. *Journal of Adolescence, 6,* 197–200.

MELKMAN, R., TVERSKY, B., & BARATZ, D. (1981). Developmental trends in the use of perpetual and conceptual attributes in grouping, clustering and retrieval. *Journal of Experimental Child Psychology, 31,* 470–486.

MORISON, P., & GARDNER, H. (1978). Dragons and dinosaurs: The child's capacity to differentiate fantasy from reality. *Child Development, 49,* 642–648.

NOMIKOS, M., OPTON, E., AVERILL, J., & LAZARUS, R. (1968). Surprise versus suspense in the production of stress reaction. *Journal of Personality and Social Psychology, 8,* 204–208.

OSBORN, D. K., & ENDSLEY, R. C. (1971). Emotional reactions of young children to TV violence. *Child Development, 42,* 321–331.

OWENS, J., MAXIM, R., McGUINN, M., NOBILE, C., MSALL, M., & ALARIO, A. (1999). Television viewing habits and sleep disturbance in school children. Pediatrics, 104(3), 552 (Abstract). [Online]. Available: http://www.pediatrics.org/cgi/content/full/104/3/c27.

PALMER, E. L., HOCKETT, A. B., & DEAN, W. W. (1983). The television family and children's fright reactions. *Journal of Family Issues, 4,* 279–292.

PAVLOV, I. P. ([1927} 1960). *Conditioned reflexes* (G.V. Anrep, Trans.). London: Oxford University Press.

PECK, E. Y. (1999). *Gender differences in film-induced fear as a function of type of emotion measure and stimulus content: A meta-analysis and a laboratory study.* Unpublished doctoral dissertation, University of Wisconsin–Madison.

PRESTON, M. I. (1941). Children's reactions to movie horrors and radio crime. *Journal of Pediatrics, 19,* 147–168.

RAZRAN, G. (1949). Stimulus generalization of conditioned responses. *Psychological Bulletin, 46,* 337–365.

ROSENBAUM, R. (1979, September). Gooseflesh. *Harpers,* pp. 86–92.

SAPOLSKY, B. S., & ZILLMANN, D. (1978). Experience and empathy: Affective reactions to witnessing childbirth. *Journal of Social Psychology, 105,* 131–144.

SARAFINO, E. P. (1986). *The fears of childhood: A guide to recognizing and reducing fearful states in children.* New York: Human Sciences Press.

SCHACHTER, S., & SINGER, J. (1962). Cognitive, social, and physiological determinants of emotional state. *Psychological Review, 69,* 379–399.

SCHRAMM, W., LYLE, J., & PARKER, E. P. (1961). *Television in the lives of our children.* Stanford, CA: Stanford University Press.

SELMAN, R. L., & BYRNE, D. (1978). A structural analysis of levels of role-taking in middle childhood. *Child Development, 45,* 803–807.

SINGER, J. L. (1975). *Daydreaming and fantasy.* London: Allen & Unwin.

SINGER, M. I., SLOVAK, K., FRIERSON, T., & YORK, P. (1998). Viewing preferences, symptoms of psychological trauma, and violent behaviors among children who watch television. *Journal of the American Academy of Child and Adolescent Psychiatry, 37*(10), 1041–1048.

231

CHAPTER 13
Reactions to
Disturbing or
Frightening
Media Content

SPARKS, G. G. (1986). Developmental differences in children's reports of fear induced by the mass media. *Child Study Journal, 16,* 55–66.

SPARKS, G. G., & CANTOR, J. (1986). Developmental differences in fright responses to a television program depicting a character transformation. *Journal of Broadcasting and Electronic Media, 30,* 309–323.

SURBECK, E. (1975). Young children's emotional reactions to T.V. violence: The effects of children's perceptions of reality. University of Georgia. *Dissertation Abstracts International, 35,* 5139–A.

TAMBORINI, R., & WEAVER, J. B., III (1996). Frightening entertainment: A historical perspective of fictional horror. In J. B. Weaver, III, & R. Tamborini (Eds.), *Horror films, current research on audience preferences and reactions* (pp. 1–13). Mahwah, NJ: Erlbaum.

TANNENBAUM, P. H., & GAER, E. P. (1965). Mood change as a function of stress of protagonist and degree of identification in a film-viewing situation. *Journal of Personality and Social Psychology, 2,* 612–616.

THAYER, J. F., & LEVENSON, R. W. (1983). Effects of music on psychophysiological responses to a stressful film. *Psychomusicology, 3,* 44–52.

TUDOR, A. (1989). *Monsters and mad scientists: A cultural history of the horror movie.* Oxford, England: Blackwell.

VALKENBURG, P. M., CANTOR, J., & PEETERS, A. L. (2000). Fright reactions to television: A child survey. *Communication Research, 27*(1), 82–97.

WALL, W. D., & SIMSON, W. A. (1950). The emotional responses of adolescent groups to certain films. *British Journal of Educational Psychology, 20,* 153–163.

WEISS, B. W., KATKIN, E. S., & RUBIN, B. M. (1968). Relationship between a factor analytically derived measure of a specific fear and performance after related fear induction. *Journal of Abnormal Psychology, 73,* 461–463.

WERTHAM, F. (1953). *Seduction of the innocent.* New York: Rinehart.

WILSON, B. J. (1987). Reducing children's emotional reactions to mass media through rehearsed explanation and exposure to a replica of a fear object. *Human Communication Research, 14,* 3–26.

WILSON, B. J. (1989). The effects of two control strategies on children's emotional reactions to a frightening movie scene. *Journal of Broadcasting & Electronic Media, 33,* 397–418.

WILSON, B. J., & CANTOR, J. (1985). Developmental differences in empathy with a television protagonist's fear. *Journal of Experimental Child Psychology, 39,* 284–299.

WILSON, B. J., & CANTOR, J. (1987). Reducing children's fear reactions to mass media: Effects of visual exposure and verbal explanation. In M. McLaughlin, (Ed.), *Communication Yearbook 10* (pp. 553–573). Beverly Hills, CA: Sage.

WILSON, B. J., HOFFNER, C., & CANTOR, J. (1987). Children's perceptions of the effectiveness of techniques to reduce fear from mass media. *Journal of Applied Developmental Psychology, 8,* 39–52.

WOOD, R. (1984). An introduction to the American horror film. In B. K. Grant (Eds.), *Planks of reason: Essays on the horror film* (pp. 164–200). Metuchen, NJ: Scarecrow Press.

ZILL, N. (1977). *National survey of children: Summary of preliminary results.* New York: Foundation for Child Development.

ZILLMANN, D. (1978). Attribution and misattribution of excitatory reactions. In J. H. Harvey, W. Ickes, & R. F. Kidd (Eds.), *New directions in attribution research* (Vol. 2, pp. 335–368). Hillsdale, NJ: Erlbaum.

ZILLMANN, D. (1980). Anatomy of suspense. In P. Tannenbaum, (Ed.), *The entertainment functions of television* (pp. 133–163). Hillsdale, NJ: Erlbaum.

ZILLMANN, D. (1982). Television viewing and arousal. In D. Pearl, L. Bouthilet, & J. Lazar (Eds.), *Television and behavior: Ten years of scientific progress and implications for the eighties* (Vol. 2, pp. 53–67). Washington, DC: U.S. Government Printing Office.

ZILLMANN, D. (1991a). Empathy: Effect from bearing witness to the emotions of others. In J. Bryant & D. Zillmann (Eds.), *Responding to the screen: Reception and reaction processes* (pp. 135–167). Hillsdale, NJ: Erlbaum.

ZILLMANN, D. (1991b). The logic of suspense and mystery. In J. Bryant & D. Zillmann (Eds.), *Responding to the screen: Reception and reaction processes* (pp. 281–303). Hillsdale, NJ: Erlbaum.

ZILLMANN, D., & GIBSON, R. (1996). Evolution of the horror genre. J. B. Weaver III & R. Tamborini (Eds.), *Horror films, current research on audience preferences and reactions* (pp. 15–31). Mahwah, NJ: Erlbaum.

ZILLMANN, D., HAY, T. A., & BRYANT, J. (1975). The effect of suspense and its resolution on the appreciation of dramatic presentations. *Journal of Research in Personality, 9,* 307–323.

ZILLMANN, D., MODY, B., & CANTOR, J. (1974). Empathetic perception of emotional displays in films as a function of hedonic and excitatory state prior to exposure. *Journal of Research in Personality, 8,* 335–349.

News Effects

During the final decade of the 20th century and as the new millenium dawned, several major news stories captured the attention and imagination of the world. In 1995 former Heisman trophy winner and football great O. J. Simpson was tried for and acquitted of the double murder of his wife and her friend. Two years later, in August 1997, the people of the world were shocked and saddened by the tragic death of Diana, Princess of Wales, in a car crash in Paris. Television networks around the globe broadcast her funeral live from London. In 1998, news of President Bill Clinton's torrid affair with White House intern Monica Lewinsky, and his subsequent public denial and later public admission of a sexual liaison with Lewinsky, significantly marred his credibility and the respectability of his presidency. In the closing months of 2000, a voting fiasco in Florida kept the nation and the world wondering long after election day who would be the 43rd president of the United States—Republican George W. Bush or Democrat Al Gore.

At first glance, the examples cited have several aspects in common. All were sensational, all involved celebrities or famous people, and all caused strong reactions of one sort or another among audiences. But these are not all the traits they shared as major news stories.

Everyone recognizes major news stories when they arise, but what specific characteristics define those news stories? When a major story breaks, by what means and how quickly does word spread among audiences? Moreover, what psychological effects do news stories have on audiences? Can the news affect a person's decisions or behavior? Do people always understand the news they see and hear on television? Do they remember news once they've seen it? At the societal level, does the news sometimes have the power to influence foreign or domestic policy? This chapter will examine the research on news effects and attempt to answer these questions.

What is news? How can it be described and defined? One good overall description of news was provided by Hachten (2001).

> News is not usually a discrete, singular event, although television news often gives that impression. News is a process with a recent past, present, and future; hence, the importance of giving background and context to a story as well as providing follow-up stories. It has also been said that news is a liquid, not a solid . . . News, as useful public knowledge, is a lot of things as distinct from rumor, titillation, diversion, gossip and, particularly, scandal, although any of these elements may contain kernels of news and unfortunately often become involved in news stories. News has a long and fascinating history; one man's news is another man's titillation, entertainment, propaganda, or diversion. (p. xviii)

Hachten went on to point out that in recent years, in the ever present quest for higher ratings, sales, and titillation, serious news has become increasingly tainted by so-called trash or tabloid journalism. At respected news organizations such as the major television networks, cable news networks, and major newspapers, Hachten noted that the "fire wall" that used to protect serious news from the encroachment of sensationalism has all but disappeared (2001, p. xxii). The JonBenet Ramsey case serves as a prime example of the disappearing fire wall. At the height of the media frenzy following the brutal murder of the child beauty queen in Colorado, assignment editors at respected news organizations suddenly found themselves looking to the *National Enquirer* and other sensational tabloids for leads.

Hachten's observations on news provide us with good descriptions that help us understand the role of the news in today's media environment, but a more precise definition would be useful for our discussion of news. In coming up with a more precise definition, one must distinguish between the several different types of news stories. These include hard news, crisis news, and soft news.

Hard News

Hard news has been defined as "the report of an event that happened or was disclosed within the previous twenty-four hours and treats an issue of ongoing concern" (Jamieson & Campbell, 1988, p. 20). According to Jamieson and Campbell, a newsworthy event has five primary characteristics. It is:

> (1) personalized—it happened to real people; (2) dramatic, conflict-filled, controversial, violent; (3) actual and concrete, not theoretical or abstract; (4) novel or deviant; and (5) linked to issues of ongoing concern to the news media. (p. 21)

If a flood has devastated an area, news reporters often focus on a particular family that is representative of many flood victims. This type of *personalization* occurs with many different types of news stories. Reporters believe that zeroing in on an individual as a vehicle to tell a major story makes the news more interesting for an audience. The second group of characteristics that define a newsworthy event, "dramatic, conflict-filled, controversial, violent," emphasizes the

News reporters often use examples whenever they present their stories. They may focus upon specific cases or situations or people representative of some population, or upon those somewhat atypical from the norm. For example, whenever a hurricane devastates an area, reporters sometimes find a particular individual or family whose great losses or whose sad story might be representative of a great number of individuals or families who experienced tragedy due to the storm. Or, a reporter may decide to focus upon a family whose losses were far greater than most in the community.

Whether exemplars are typical or atypical of larger populations, their use in news reports (and in human communication in general) has been theorized to produce important effects. In his outline of the basic tenets of exemplification theory, Zillmann (1999) noted that:

The world of exemplars appears to influence our perception and judgment of essentially all phenomena and issues of the so-called real world. (p. 73)

Some research has supported the importance of exemplification in news reporting. For example, the presentation of emotionally stirring images leaves lasting impressions and sometimes influences our perceptions and beliefs (Zillmann, 1999; Aust & Zillmann, 1996; Zillmann & Gan, 1996).

Sources: C. F. Aust & D. Zillmann (1996). Effects of victim exemplification in television news on viewer perception of social issues, *Journalism & Mass Communication Quarterly, 73,* 787–803; D. Zillmann (1999), Exemplification theory: Judging the whole by some of its parts, *Media Psychology, 1,* 69–94; D. Zillmann & S. Gan (1996). Effects of threatening images in news programs on the perception of risk to others and self, *Medienpsychologie: Zeitschrift für Individual- und Massenkommunikation, 8,* 288–305, 317–318; for more on exemplification, see D. Zillmann & H. B. Brosius (2000), *Exemplification in communication: The influence of case reports on the perception of issues,* Mahwah, NJ: Erlbaum.

dramatic element in news stories. Crime stories serve as excellent examples of news stories that abound in drama and violence. Reporters look for conflicts to create drama and make the news interesting. As the examples first cited reveal, news is also an actual, concrete event. It is something out of the ordinary—a disruption of normal routines. News reports often focus on ongoing issues or themes, such as the ritual of a presidential election every four years.

In addition to the five primary characteristics, several secondary characteristics also define hard news stories. According to Harris (1999), news stories are also usually (1) inoffensive, (2) perceived as credible, (3) packageable, and (4) oriented toward a local angle. Blatant offensiveness is usually avoided. Harris used the example of the media's reluctance to report on the AIDS epidemic in the 1980s because it meant revealing that anal intercourse was the most common means of infection (Harris, 1999; Meyer, 1990). The perception of credibility means that supermarket tabloid stories of human-animal hybrids and other strange oddities are generally avoided by mainstream media. Packageability or condensed presentation has been much more a characteristic of broadcast news than print news (Barnhurst & Multz, 1997). Finally, the use of a local angle heightens local interest in a story of national or international importance.

The primary and secondary characteristics are important in attracting the attention of media coverage. According to Harris:

The surest way to obtain coverage of one's activities is to imbue them with these primary and secondary newsworthy characteristics. The more of these an event has, the more likely the media will be to show interest. Possessing these characteristics does not necessarily ensure that the event is important or unimportant, but it does ensure that the perceived reality will be a newsworthy event. (p. 147)

Crisis News

One important branch of hard news coverage is that of *crisis news*. According to Graber (1989), crises may be defined as "natural or man-made events that pose an immediate and serious threat to the lives and property or to the peace of mind of many" (p. 305). Perse (2001) said crises "affect large numbers of people and are marked by sudden onset, uncertainty, and lack of control, emotional reactions, and threats to lives and property" (pp. 53–54). Good examples of crisis news would be coverage of the assassination of President Kennedy in 1963 and the continuing coverage of his funeral, the space shuttle *Challenger* disaster in 1986, the bombing of the Oklahoma City federal building in 1995, and Princess Diana's funeral in 1997. Natural disasters such as hurricanes or earthquakes usually spawn crisis news reporting, as do sudden military actions on the part of president or wars such as the Persian Gulf War in 1991.

In times of crisis, mass media become more important in their service to society. People in record numbers tune in to news broadcasts on television and radio for extended periods of time because of heightened interest and the need of audiences for information in a time of uncertainty or shock (Riffe & Stovall, 1989). When a crisis is discovered, mass media hurry to the scene and begin contacting various experts and officials who can fully explain what is going on. Gatekeeping relaxes somewhat during a crisis, and rumors and inaccuracies are often communicated along with factual information and must eventually be ferreted *out of* the information flow.

You will recall from Chapter 3 the functions of mass media in society—surveillance of the environment, correlation of society's response to events in the environment, socialization or transmission of social norms and customs (Lasswell, 1948), and entertainment (Wright, 1986). Perse (2001) reviewed this list and added two functions to explain the most important duties of the news media in times of crisis, namely those that bring people together and help relieve stress.

> Surveillance and correlation are the most apparent functions of the mass media during crises, but the mass media also serve solidarity-building and tension-reduction functions. (p. 60)

An example of the solidarity-building use of mass media occurred in the aftermath of Princess Diana's death, when the world found a bit of comfort in the sharing of grief by means of televised reports of her funeral. The same phenomenon had occurred in the aftermath of the *Challenger* explosion a decade earlier, when many viewers received comfort from the news coverage of mourners throughout the country (Kaye, 1989).

In times of crisis, surveillance may also become a dysfunction. Too much information sometimes causes people to become too stressful and fearful, but the

The 1986 space shuttle *Challenger* disaster was an example of crisis news.
Source: © AP, Photo/Bruce Weaver, File

correlation function may remedy the surveillance dysfunction (Perse, 2001). Correlation of the great amount of information available during crises helps audiences to digest the information and realize how exactly they will be affected.

Soft News

In addition to crisis news and other types of hard news, reporters also cover stories sometimes referred to as *soft news*. Human interest stories and news stories that are not considered fast breaking or immediate in nature may be defined as soft news. These are the kinds of stories that add special interest to newscasts and newspapers. They are usually interesting and entertaining, and sometimes heartwarming.

Research has shown that in recent years, print and broadcast news sources have opted for more soft news in an effort to compete with cable television and the Internet. Following a two-year study of news that involved national surveys, analysis of thousands of randomly selected news stories, and content analyses, Patterson (2000) assessed the news landscape in the United States and presented several arguments based upon the study's findings. He suggested that cable television and the Internet continued to attract more people in search of news while traditional news sources, such as newspapers, newsmagazines, network television, and local television stations, have noticed declines in their audiences in recent years. To keep present audiences and attract new ones, more soft news and critical journalism has been employed.

> Soft news is sometimes used in a way that implies it is all the news that is not "hard news." Hard news refers to coverage of breaking events involving top leaders, major issues, or significant disruptions in the routines of daily life, such as an earthquake or airline disaster. Information about these events is presumably important to citizens' ability to understand and respond to the world of public affairs. News that is not of this type is, by definition, "soft." (p. 3)

CRISIS EFFECTS

In times of crisis, several different kinds of effects have been identified and studied by researchers. News diffusion research focuses on the announcement and spread of news among audiences who learn of news through print or broadcast media or through interpersonal channels. Other studies of news crises examine effects on the news organizations themselves—their peculiar service to the public and their activities in response to the crises. Another type of crisis effect is that of the rally effect, which occurs when in times of crisis people rally behind a leader such as the president.

News Diffusion

One important area of research related to news effects is that of *news diffusion* (recall the news diffusion studies from Chapter 7). This realm of effects research usually focuses on crisis news. Studies examine the ways that people hear about news items and the rapidity with which news, especially crisis news, spreads.

Since news diffusion research began in the 1940s, researchers have discovered several general characteristics associated with the diffusion of news (Perse, 2001). First, when the news is an *important or high impact event*, it diffuses very rapidly. For example, when President Kennedy was assassinated in 1963, 42 percent of the people in the country had heard the news that Kennedy had been shot within 15 minutes of the assassination, and this percentage rose to 90 within one hour after the assassination (Greenberg, 1965). Second, the *timing of the release* of the news affects diffusion. In their study of news diffusion following the *Challenger* disaster, Mayer, Gudykunst, Perrill, and Merrill (1990) found that "*where* one is affects *how* one discovers the occurrence of a major news event . . . *how* one discovers the event then affects *how quickly* one hears of the event" (p. 121). If a breaking news item occurs during the evening newscast, most people will first hear of the news on television. If the breaking item occurs during the early morning hours when people are driving to work, radio may be the initial channel of news diffusion. According to Perse (2001):

How people find out about an event is due mainly to where people are when the news is released—at work or at home. For those at home, radio or television are usually the first source of news; for those at work, where media are less likely to be readily available, interpersonal communication is usually the first source. (p. 66)

Finally, *audience demographics* has been shown to have an effect on the diffusion of news, but the more important the news item, the less the effect of audience differences. For example, if an event occurs on a weekend night, young people out on the town may be more likely to hear about it before their older counterparts. In the case of a shocking news item such as the death of a world leader or world-renowned celebrity, younger people might be more likely to call and awaken their friends and relatives to share the high impact news with them.

Effects of Crisis on Media Function and Activity

In addition to news diffusion among audiences, news researchers are also interested in studying the ways the media react and conduct themselves during times of crisis. Scholars have identified the various functions the media serve in society at these critical times.

When a major crisis occurs, the media provide extended coverage of the event whether or not they have any important, new information to relate. Sometimes coverage is intended to comfort audiences who are grieving or otherwise upset.

In order to reduce tension in society, media devote a good deal of coverage to media content intended to comfort their audience. Solidarity building is functional for society in times of crisis. Media highlight the wisdom of leaders and the bravery of rescue workers or soldiers to reassure society that "we are all in this together" and that everything possible is being done for survival. So, although the media may be unable to fulfill surveillance and correlation needs, they are able to offer assurance and tension reduction. (Perse, 2001, pp. 73–74)

Rally effects

In times of national crisis when the president must take action, people in the country usually rally behind him and his approval rating subsequently goes up. The phenomenon is known as *rally effects*. Such effects were evident during the Cuban Missile Crisis in 1962 when President Kennedy ordered the naval blockade, and during the 1991 Persian Gulf War when President Bush ordered the bombing of Baghdad. Coser (1956) observed that rally effects occur whenever an external threat is present. People tend to ignore their differences and come together and mobilize against the threat.

Mass media contribute to rally effects in two ways. First, the media serve as the vehicle through which information reaches the public. Second, during times of crisis the media are often less critical of government leaders and policies in their effort toward solidarity building.

Studies of the effects of news coverage have sought to identify how much people learn from the news they see, hear, and read, what factors facilitate or impede learning, and what effects result from comprehension or miscomprehension. Other types of studies have examined news effects at the national and international level and the impact of the news on foreign policy or foreign relations.

Remembering the News

Through the years, findings have been varied, but a vast body of early studies showed that people do not learn very much from news reports and what they do learn is sometimes garbled (Gunter, 1991). Subsequent research has revealed that many different factors have an effect on how much audiences learn from news reports. Gender, age, educational level, social class—all have a marked influence on the amount of information retained by audience members. Personal interest has also been shown to determine retention of news information. People usually learn from stories that have a special interest to them individually.

Through the years, research has revealed that better-educated people usually hold jobs of higher status than less-educated people, and they tend to be better informed about current events knowledge related through the news media, whether print or broadcast. This phenomenon is called the *knowledge gap hypothesis* (Tichenor, Donohue, & Olien, 1970), which posits basically that the information rich keep getting richer and the information poor never catch up. A number of studies have shown that people with higher levels of education and higher-status jobs learn more and remember more from news reports (Gunter, 1985; Robinson & Sahin, 1984; Stauffer, Frost, & Rybolt, 1983; Renckstorff, 1980), but a few have found other factors at work as well in a rather complex mix. For example, Findahl and Hoijer (1975) found that a background knowledge of news events was related to successful learning, and many people with lower educational attainment learned as much as their more educated counterparts when background knowledge was strong.

Other variables may also play a role in determining whether audiences learn and retain what they hear on newscasts. Research in the 1970s and 1980s examined the recall factor in a variety of types of news stories based upon a typology of story types such as a short and dramatic event, a feature of elite people, a highly unexpected nature, and so forth (Galtung & Ruge, 1965). Katz, Adoni, and Parness (1977) found that the rate of recall correlated positively with the number of Galtung-Ruge criteria a story contained. Story structure has also been shown to affect recall of news items (Berry & Clifford, 1987; Findahl & Hoijer, 1984; Larson, 1981), as has the presence of visual material that accompanies TV news broadcasts and print news stories (Gunter, 1979, 1980a), but other studies have found either no correlation or impairing effects on learning due to visual accompaniments (Baggaley, 1980; Gunter, 1980b; Berry, 1983). Still other studies have uncovered complex relationships between visual accompaniments to newscaster presentations that may have a bearing on the effects of visuals and audience retention of news items (Brosius, 1989; Reese, 1984).

Studies that have examined the impact on memory from disturbing or intense visual images (e.g., blood and gore) have produced interesting findings. It seems that information related just prior to showing the image becomes inhibited in memory, but memory is enhanced for information given during the showing of the image and just afterward (Christianson & Loftus, 1987; Loftus & Burns, 1982; Newhagen & Reeves, 1992).

> Apparently, what happens cognitively is that the intense emotional image disrupts the rehearsal in working memory of the immediately preceding information, much as a moderate head injury can produce retroactive amnesia for events just preceding the impact. However, the intense picture is itself highly memorable and may enhance memory for following related information by serving as an organizational schema for construction of a memory presentation. (Harris, 1999, p. 158)

A comparison of two related studies found that photographs in newsmagazines had an effect on issue perceptions. Zillmann, Gibson, and Sargent (1999) found that the one-sided use of photographs influenced perceptions. Participants in one experiment read stories about the growing gap between rich and poor farmers, and those in another study read about amusement park safety. Issue perception was measured immediately and again 10 days after exposure to the stories. Delayed assessments were especially influenced in the direction suggested by the photographs. In the amusement park safety experiment, participant perceptions of park safety were especially influenced by photographs that projected danger.

News Effects on Knowledge and Decisions

Other studies have explored news comprehension beyond memory. For example, Gibson and Zillmann (1994) found that particular aspects of news stories impact comprehension. Study participants who read a magazine article about the problem of carjacking rated the problem more serious and occurring more frequently when the story contained an extreme example, such as a person being killed during the crime, rather than a less extreme example, such as the person being injured or escaping unharmed.

Other studies have examined media pretrial coverage and its impact on juries. Studies have consistently found that exposure to case information does affect verdicts (Carroll et al., 1986), especially in the case of sensational information about a rape or murder. Another type of effect, the influence on jury members of reading about similar crimes prior to a trial, has been shown to occur experimentally (Greene & Wade, 1987).

News Effects on Foreign Policy

Due to the transcontinental nature of news by means of the wire services and television, the news media have been known to affect foreign policy and foreign relations (Larson, 1986). Harris (1999) identified several areas in which the news has an effect on foreign affairs, including the area of diplomatic negotiations, the media's focus on particular images, and the reliance of the news media on government sources for information. Harris pointed out that diplomatic negotiations between countries are rarely secret, due to the news media, and usually highly public affairs. "Although such public scrutiny has probably placed some highly desirable curbs on corruption and extralegal chicanery, it has also made legitimate secret negotiations in the public interest much harder to keep secret" (p. 160).

Another area in which the news may have an effect on foreign affairs is in relation of the choice of stories covered to accompanying video images. Photogenic issues, or stories that can be depicted visually, are usually overcovered while less-photogenic issues are often ignored. The individual who stood in front of the line of tanks during the Tiananmen Square uprising in Beijing in 1989 provides an excellent example of a compelling visual image that affected the reaction to news story coverage. Such powerful images become associated with particular stories and become ingrained in the minds of people throughout the world.

Finally, the reliance of the news media on particular government sources also has an effect on coverage of foreign affairs. Rather than provide background information and discuss particular trends, reporters often focus their attention on particular individuals such as government leaders, spokespeople, or those who make policy. According to Harris (1999):

> Media sometimes even participate in foreign policy by serving as a direct channel of communications between government officials or policy elites in different nations . . . In some crisis situations, media may actually know more than governments and may thus reverse the usual government-to-media flow of news. During the 1991 Persian Gulf War, both U.S. President Bush and Iraqi leader Saddam Hussein regularly watched CNN to learn what was happening in the war. Furthermore, they both used the network to send messages to the other side, because that was the fastest and most reliable means of communication. (p. 161)

RECENT RESEARCH AND FUTURE TRENDS

Recent research on news effects has explored several different areas. These have included children's fright reactions to news reports, knowledge gap research, additional research on memory for news items and perceptions of issues reported in the news. Future research will probably continue along these lines.

Smith and Wilson (2000) found differences in cognitive processing of news reports by children of different ages. Older children (10 to 11 years) were more frightened than younger children (6 to 7 years) by the proximity of crime, local rather than nonlocal. Video footage had the effect of reducing fear responses of children from both age groups.

Grabe, Lang, Zhou, and Bolls (2000) provided support for the knowledge gap hypothesis in an experiment that tested physiological arousal from news processing and recognition memory. The study found that participants from different socioeconomic backgrounds and educational levels differed in their memory of facts from broadcast news stories they were shown. The participants with higher educational levels showed more physiological arousal in the processing of news stories.

News memory studies have examined differences in recall for children and adults for news stories in children's and adult news formats (Walma van der Molen & van der Voort, 2000a), and recall for children in particular (Walma van der Molen & van der Voort, 2000b). Television versions of news stories, as opposed to print versions with photographs and audio versions, were better retained by children. In a study of memory for news in young (<30) and old (>55) adults, both groups were more likely to remember stories presented in a televised format rather than an audio-only format (Frieske & Park, 1999).

As for perceptions, a study that examined the effects of news frames on the thoughts and recollections of readers found that frames determined how readers presented information about reported issues (Valkenburg, Semetko, & de Vreese, 1999). Another study of news frames found that the framing of an anarchist protest influenced viewer perceptions of the news report (McLeod & Detenber, 1999). The higher the level of status quo support contained in the frame, the less likely the viewers were to identify with the anarchist protesters or criticize the police.

SUMMARY

Hard news is the report of an event that took place or was made known within the previous 24 hours and deals with a matter or matters of continuing concern. A newsworthy event has five primary characteristics: personalized, dramatic and conflict filled, actual and concrete, novel or deviant, and linked to issues of ongoing concern to the news media. Several secondary characteristics also define hard news stories. They are usually (1) inoffensive, (2) perceived as credible, (3) packageable, and (4) oriented toward a local angle.

One important branch of hard news coverage is that of crisis news, which is natural or man-made events that might threaten the lives, property, or peace of mind of many people. These crises affect a great number of people and are characterized by their "sudden onset, uncertainty, and lack of control, emotional reactions, and threats to lives and property" (Perse, 2001, pp. 53–54). In times of crisis, mass media become more important in their service to society. Researchers have identified and studied several different kinds of crisis effects. News diffusion research focuses on the announcement and spread of news among audiences who learn of news through print and broadcast media or interpersonal channels. Other studies of news crises examine effects on the news organizations themselves—their peculiar service to the public and their activities in response to the crises. Another type of crisis effect is that of the rally effect, when in times of crisis people rally behind a leader such as the president.

Soft news includes human interest feature stories and news stories that are not considered fast breaking or immediate in nature. In recent years, print and broadcast news sources have opted for more soft news in an effort to compete with cable television and the Internet.

Studies of the effects of news coverage have sought to identify how much people learn from the news they see, hear, and read, what factors facilitate or impede learning, and what effects result from comprehension or miscomprehension. Other types of studies have examined news effects at the national and international level and the impact of the news on foreign policy or foreign relations.

Recent research on news effects has explored several different areas. These have included children's fright reactions to news reports, knowledge gap research, additional research on memory for news items and perceptions of issues reported in the news. Future research should continue along these lines.

REFERENCES

BAGGALEY, J. P. (1980). *The psychology of the TV image.* Aldershot, England: Saxon House.

BARNHURST, K. G., & MULTZ, D. (1997). American journalism and the decline in event-centered reporting. *Journal of Communication, 47*(4), 27–53.

BERRY, C. (1983). A dual effect of pictorial enhancement in learning from television news: Gunter's data revised. *Journal of Educational Television, 9,* 171–174.

BERRY, C., & CLIFFORD, B. (1987). *Learning from television news: Effects of perceptions factors and knowledge on comprehension and memory.* London: North East London Polytechnic and Independent Broadcasting Authority.

BROSIUS, H. B. (1989). Influence of presentation features and news content on learning from television news. *Journal of Broadcasting & Electronic Media, 33,* 1–14.

CARROLL, J. S., KERR, N. L., ALFINI, J. J., WEAVER, F. M., MACCOUNT, R. J., & FELDMAN, V. (1986). Free press and fair trial: The role of behavioral research. *Law and Human Behavior, 10,* 187–202.

CHRISTIANSON, S., & LOFTUS, E. F. (1987). Memory for traumatic events. *Applied Cognitive Psychology, 1,* 225–239.

COSER, L. A. (1956). *The functions of social conflict.* New York: Free Press.

FINDAHL, O., & HOIJER, B. (1975). *Man as a receiver of information: On knowledge, social privilege, and the news.* Stockholm: Swedish Broadcasting Corporation, Audience and Programme Research Department.

FINDAHL, O., & HOIJER, B. (1984). *Comprehension analysis: A review of the research and an application to radio and television news.* Lund, Sweden: Studentlitteratur.

FRIESKE, D. A., & PARK, D. C. (1999). Memory for news in young and old adults. *Psychology and Aging, 14,* 90–98.

GALTUNG, J., & RUGE, M. H. (1965). The structure of foreign news: The presentation of the Congo, Cuba and Cyprus crises in four foreign newspapers. *Journal of Peace Research, 2,* 64–91.

GIBSON, R., & ZILLMANN, D. (1994). Exaggerated versus representative exemplification in news reports: Perception of issues and personal consequences. *Communication Research, 21,* 603–624.

GRABE, M. E., LANG, A., ZHOU, S., BOLLS, P. D. (2000). Cognitive access to negatively arousing news: An experimental investigation of the knowledge gap. *Communication Research, 27,* 3–26.

GRABER, D. A. (1989). *Mass media and American politics* (3rd ed.). Washington, DC: Congressional Quarterly Press.

GREENBERG, B. S. (1965). Diffusion of news about the Kennedy assassination. In B. S. Greenberg & E. B. Parker (Eds.), *The Kennedy assassination and the American public: Social communication in crisis* (pp. 89–98). Stanford, CA: Stanford University Press.

GREENE, E., & WADE, R. (1987). Of private talk and public print: General pre-trial publicity and juror decision-making. *Applied Cognitive Psychology, 1,* 1–13.

GUNTER, B. (1979). Recall of television news items: Effects of presentation mode, picture content and serial position. *Journal of Education Television, 5,* 57–61.

GUNTER, B. (1980a). Remembering television news. Effects of picture content. *Journal of General Psychology, 102,* 127–133.

GUNTER, B. (1980b). Remembering televised news: Effects of visual format in information gain. *Journal of Educational Television, 6,* 8–11.

GUNTER, B. (1985). News sources and news awareness: A British survey. *Journal of Broadcasting, 29,* 397–406.

GUNTER, B. (1991). Responding to news and public affairs. In J. Bryant & D. Zillmann (Eds.), Responding to the screen: Reception and reaction processes (p. 229–260). Hillsdale, NJ: Erlbaum.

HACHTEN, W. A. (2001). *The troubles of journalism: A critical look at what's right and wrong with the press* (2nd ed.). Mahwah, NJ: Erlbaum.

HARRIS, R. J. (1999). *A cognitive psychology of mass communication* (3rd ed.). Mahwah, NJ: Erlbaum.

JAMIESON, K. H., & CAMPELL, K. K. (1988). *The interplay of influence: Mass media and their publics in news, advertising, politics* (2nd ed.). Belmont, CA: Wadsworth.

KATZ, E., ADONI, H., & PARNESS, P. (1977). Remembering the news: What the picture adds to recall. *Journalism Quarterly, 54,* 231–235.

KAYE, E. (1989, September). Peter Jennings. *Esquire,* pp. 158–176.

LARSEN, S. F. (1981). *Knowledge updating: Three papers on news memory, background knowledge and text processing.* Aarhus, Denmark: University of Aarhus, Institute of Psychology.

LARSON, J. F. (1986). Television and U.S. foreign policy: The case of the Iran hostage crisis. *Journal of Communication, 36*(4), 108–130.

LASSWELL, H. D. (1948). The structure and function of communication in society. In L. Bryson (Ed.), *The communication of ideas* (pp. 37–51). New York: Harper.

LOFTUS, E. F., & BURNS, T. E. (1982). Mental shock can produce retrograde amnesia. *Memory & Cognition, 10,* 318–323.

MAYER, M. E., GUDYKUNST, W. B., PERRILL, N. K., & MERRILL, B. D. (1990). A comparison of competing models of the news diffusion process. *Western Journal of Speech Communication, 54,* 113–123.

MCLEOD, D. M., & DETENBER, B. H. (1999). Framing effects of television news coverage of social protest. *Journal of Communication, 49*(3), 3–23.

MEYER, P. (1990). News media responsiveness to public health. In C. Atkin & L. Wallack (Eds.), *Mass communication and public health: Complexities and conflicts* (pp. 52–57). Newbury Park, CA: Sage.

NEWHAGEN, J. E., & REEVES, B. (1992). The evening's bad news: Effects of compelling negative television news images on memory. *Journal of Communication, 42*(2), 25–41.

PATTERSON, T. E. (2000). *Doing well and doing good: How soft news and critical journalism are shrinking the news audience and weakening democracy—and what news outlets can do about it.* Cambridge: Joan Shorenstein Center on the Press, Politics and Public Policy, Harvard University.

PERSE, E. M. (2001). *Media effects and society.* Mahwah, NJ: Erlbaum.

REESE, S. D. (1984). Visual-verbal redundancy effects on television news learning. *Journal of Broadcasting, 28,* 79–87.

RENCKSTORFF, K. (1980). *Nachrichtensendungen im Fernsehen (1): Zur Wirkung von Darstellungsforme in Fernsehnachrichten.* Berlin: Volker Spiess Verlag.

RIFFE, D., & STOVALL, J. G. (1989). Diffusion of news of shuttle disaster: What role for emotional response? *Journalism Quarterly, 66,* 551–556.

ROBINSON, J. P., & SAHIN, H. (1984). *Audience comprehension of television news: Results from some exploratory research.* London: Broadcasting Research Department, British Broadcasting Corporation.

SMITH, S. L., & WILSON, B. J. (2000). Children's reactions to a television news story: The impact of video footage and proximity of the crime. *Communication Research, 27,* 641–673.

STAUFFER, J., FROST, R., & RYBOLT, W. (1983). The attention factor in recalling network television news. *Journal of Communication, 33,* 29–37.

TICHENOR, P. J., DONOHUE, G. A., & OLIEN, C. N. (1970). Mass media flow and differential growth of knowledge. *Public Opinion Quarterly, 34,* 159–170.

VALKENBURG, P. M., SEMETKO, H. A., & DE VREESE, C. H. (1999). The effects of news frames on readers' thoughts and recall. *Communication Research, 26,* 550–569.

WALMA VAN DER MOLEN, J. H., & VAN DER VOORT, T. H. A. (2000a). Children's and adults' recall of television and print news in children's and adult news formats. *Communication Research, 27,* 132–160.

WALMA VAN DER MOLEN, J. H., & VAN DER VOORT, T. H. A. (2000b). The impact of television, print, and audio on children's recall of the news: A study of three alternative explanations for the dual-coding hypothesis. *Human Communication Research, 26,* 3–26.

WRIGHT, C. R. (1986). *Mass communication: A sociological perspective* (3rd ed.). New York: Random House.

ZILLMANN, D., GIBSON, R., & SARGENT, S. L. (1999). Effects of photographs in news magazine reports on issue perception. *Media Psychology, 1,* 207–228.

CHAPTER 15

Communication Campaign Effects

Buckle Up America
—**National Highway Traffic Safety Administration, campaign slogan**

Throughout the history of the United States, voluntary organizations and the federal government have repeatedly relied upon mass media to get messages across to the public—messages intended to offer the public certain knowledge intended to produce attitude or behavior changes. These **public communication campaigns** have been defined by Rice and Atkin (in press) as:

> (1) purposive attempts (2) to inform, persuade, or motivate behavior changes (3) in a relatively well-defined and large audience, (4) generally for noncommercial benefits to the individuals and/or society at large, (5) typically within a given time period, (6) by means or organized communication activities involving mass media, and (7) often complemented by interpersonal support. (Adapted and expanded from Rogers & Storey, 1987, p. 821)

Perhaps a simpler way of defining public communication campaigns is to offer a few well-known examples. As will be shown, communication campaigns take a variety of forms in our society, and each has specific goals. Each election year we note the success of one candidate over another, usually attributable to the success of his or her political campaign. Every single day we notice advertisements that are part of overall campaigns to sell particular products or services. On television and radio, we see and hear public service announcements that remind us to "buckle up, America"; tell us only we can prevent forest fires; urge us to help "take a bite out of crime"; or encourage us to avoid drinking and driving by introducing us to appealing individuals who have lost their lives to drunk drivers. All of these represent some rather notable public communication campaigns designed to change attitudes or behaviors.

This chapter will focus primarily on the theory, strategies, and research that support successful communication campaigns. We will discuss the concepts of communication campaigns, offer an overview of theoretical foundations that underlie campaign strategies, examine some reasons why campaigns fail, and then identify 10 principles that improve a campaign's chances for success (Rice & Atkin, in press; Atkin, 2001; McGuire, 2001). The principles for success are

247

based upon theoretical knowledge and years of careful study and research on successful and unsuccessful campaigns. Finally, we will take a look at recent research on the effectiveness of communication campaigns.

CONCEPTS OF COMMUNICATION CAMPAIGNS

When it comes to the effects of communication campaigns, much of what we know has been summarized by Rice and Atkin, based upon their collection of the theoretical and research literature, in *Public Communication Campaigns*, 3rd edition (2001). One of the works in that collection stressed the importance of some key, related concepts that are central to the understanding of communication campaigns (Paisley, 1989, 2001). The concepts include:

1. The objectives of the campaign or the media methods employed.
2. The strategy used to facilitate change.
3. The potential benefits resulting from proposed change.
4. Public perceptions about the campaign stakeholder.
5. The stakeholders themselves.

Campaign Objectives and Methods

In studying communication campaigns, it is important to understand two defining characteristics: their *objectives* and their *methods*. Objectives refer to the essence of communication appeals; that is, one group's attempts to influence the attitudes or behavior of another. Methods pertain to the genre of communication (e.g., as educational or innovative and nonconventional types), the type of communications media, and the strategies that the campaign employs.

> Thus the definition of public communication campaigns can be approached via *objectives*—are they *strategies of social control* insofar as one group intends to affect the beliefs or behavior of another group?—or via *methods*—are they a *genre of communication* that might be called noncommercial advertising? (Paisley, 1989, p. 16)

Strategy to Facilitate Change

The three basic strategies of social control that have been identified as causing changes in levels of knowledge, attitudes, or behaviors are also important in understanding campaigns. The **"three E's"** of *education, engineering,* and *enforcement* were first discerned by researchers at the U.S. Forest Service who were interested in promoting the prevention of forest fires (Paisley, 2001, p. 6).

The effectiveness of the three E's depends on several factors, including the audience's cultural heritage, form of government, and level of technological development. In a country with authoritarian leadership, enforcement is usually chosen as the appropriate strategy for communication campaigns; however, audiences are normally motivated to change because they fear the repercussions from noncompliance, rather than because the campaign messages have

The Smokey the Bear campaign shows that the measure of communication campaign successfulness is often relative.
Source: © Joseph Sohm; Chromosom Inc./CORBIS

persuaded them to adopt new behaviors. The most effective strategy for a society of people with common values is usually education. Engineering used to be an important strategy in the United States. Paisley offered the following examples of the engineering strategy:

> The early 1960s were marked by an eager faith in engineering solutions. Buoyed by successes in medicine that were linked metaphorically to social ills, John Kennedy's and Lyndon Johnson's social engineers drafted programs to combat poverty, illiteracy, inequality, and so on. Some of the programs benefited some people, but it was obvious by 1970 that social engineering was quite different from medical engineering. (pp. 6–7)

Potential Benefits from Proposed Change

Another essential concept is the *benefits* that individuals or society will gain by complying with the objectives of the campaign. For example, antismoking or other health-related campaigns stress the healthy benefits that individuals will achieve by changing their behaviors. On the flip side, campaigns may also highlight the negative aspects of particular behaviors in an attempt to motivate audiences to change. Again using antismoking campaigns as an example, individuals are bombarded with messages that stress the *costs* of failing to change their behavior. They learn that the consequences of smoking are dire: emphysema, heart disease, various types of cancer, and even death.

Campaign Stakeholders

Since the development of mass communications media such as books, newspapers, magazines, motion pictures, radio, and television, communicators have used these media to try to influence audiences in some way. Whether the goal has been to promote certain health practices, migrations, political ideals and candidates, or to raise social consciousness and promote social change, mass media have been used for various communication campaigns since their beginnings.

Throughout the history of the United States, communication campaigns have been directed by different types of **stakeholders** (Paisley, 2001). These are the individuals, groups, associations, or organizations that initiate the campaign stemming from their interest in promoting reform. Stakeholders have included (1) individuals and associations, (2) media, (3) government, and (4) social scientists. Individuals and voluntary associations were the major stakeholders in public communication campaigns during the 18th and 19th centuries. A more recent example would be the leadership of Martin Luther King, Jr., of the civil rights movement of the 1950s and 1960s, though organizations of students and other interested parties also could be considered stakeholders in the movement. The prohibition and antislavery movements of the mid-19th century, and the Mothers Against Drunk Drivers campaign and the self-exam/early detection promotions of the American Cancer Society demonstrate successful campaigns of associations in the 20th century. The muckraking articles in mass circulation newspapers and magazines at the close of the 19th century and early 20th century represent reform efforts on the part of mass media. As for the U.S. government, it has used communication campaigns to accomplish goals since its inception; consider the widespread newspaper campaign to promote ratification of the Constitution and the propaganda campaigns to sway public opinion during the two world wars.

Social scientists have also been listed among stakeholders (Paisley, 2001), even though the interest of social scientists and communicators has been in studying the dynamics of successful campaigns, developing theoretical models, and measuring effects rather than advancing a particular goal or movement toward social reform. Through the years, social scientists have offered differing views regarding the effects of communication campaigns by means of the mass media. Researchers first began to study public communication campaigns in the early 20th century, during a period of heightened concern about the success of World War I propaganda techniques. Some studies seemed to indicate that mass media had great powers to influence attitudes, but others gave rise to a model of limited and indirect effects on audiences. Effects were believed to work in an indirect manner: Certain individuals called *opinion leaders* received information from mass media and then passed it on interpersonally to others in the community. Subsequent research on the persuasion process and the documentation of several successful communication campaigns after the 1960s indicated more powerful effects. Communication campaigns were found to be effective if they followed a particular design, adhered to specific principles, and targeted appropriate audiences.

Another concept important to the success of campaigns has to do with the public's view of the stakeholder. The source of the campaign messages must be seen as an individual or group who is *entitled* to or has the right to offer the messages, place them on the public's *issues agenda,* and attempt to change the behaviors of audiences. This concept of stakeholders and the personal relevance of an issue to them is known as **entitlement.**

Paisley (1989) identified two classes of public issues: *obligations* and *opportunities.* Some issues are high on the public agenda because people feel obligated to respond due to some sense of altruism or unselfishness. Other issues rank high because people are self-interested and focus on self-improvement opportunities.

These two types of issues are also the two key motivational components in communications campaigns, which call for action motivated by altruistic leanings, by personal benefits, or both. For example, campaigns that promote a healthier environment may appeal to a person's unselfish desire to keep the earth a safe and beautiful place for future generations. A campaign to prevent illegal drug use might appeal to another person's self-interested desire to keep his teenager off drugs.

Paisley (1989, 2001) also identified two classes of stakeholders: those with *first-party entitlement* and those with *second-party entitlement.* **First-party entitlement** refers to a situation in which an aggrieved group of stakeholders is seen by the public to be directly affected by an issue. A good example would be the campaign of African Americans for civil rights in the 1960s and beyond. **Second-party entitlement** pertains to circumstances in which a group is not directly impacted by a particular issue. Again using the civil rights movement as an example, campaigns that promoted the rights of minorities with whites as the stakeholders would be considered second-party entitlement. These individuals increased their entitlement by their public sacrifice—they put themselves on the line during the civil rights movement and faced negative and even violent repercussions for their altruistic actions. According to Paisley:

> Some issues have no first-party group to claim entitlement. Whales, seal pups, and future generations of Americans are the first parties of campaigns, but they are not their own advocates. In such cases, second-party groups step forward to serve as advocates, sometimes putting themselves at risk as surrogate first parties. (2001, p. 9)

THEORETICAL BASES FOR CAMPAIGNS

The theoretical bases for campaigns are those that have been discussed in previous chapters. We will focus in this section on a review of the major persuasion models, including McGuire's model for communication and persuasion (1989), Petty and Cacioppo's elaboration likelihood model (1986), Fishbein and Ajzen's reasoned action and planned behavior model (1975), and Fazzio's automatic activation model (1990). Additionally, we will review briefly Bandura's ideas of social cognitive theory, social learning, and self-efficacy. These are some of the theoretical formulations that have been most important in explaining communication campaigns.

McGuire's Model

You will recall from Chapter 10 that McGuire's communication/persuasion matrix model emphasizes a number of steps in the persuasive process, each one building upon the other to create a hierarchy of effects. Inputs (independent variables controlled by the stakeholder) include the source, message, recipient, channel, and context of the message. Outputs (dependent variables controlled by the individual audience members) include exposure to the information, attention to the information, interest, comprehension, acquisition of new knowledge, yielding to the weight of the message and changing the attitude, remembering the information and new attitude, retrieving the information, making a conscious decision to act according to the new attitude, acting based upon the decision, reinforcing the new behavior, and consolidating the new attitude.

Elaboration Likelihood Model (ELM)

The elaboration likelihood model, you will remember, stresses central or peripheral routes to persuasion (Petty & Cacioppo, 1986). The persuasion process is influenced by the likelihood of the audience member to think carefully or *elaborate cognitively* about a persuasive appeal. The central route requires considerable cognitive effort on the part of the audience member, including evaluation in view of previous experiences and knowledge, to determine if the advocated position has merit. The peripheral route generally results from simple cues within the context of the message. Cognitive elaboration is not stressed in the peripheral route. Examples of persuasion through the peripheral route include affective (emotional) responses to messages, belief in experts who pitch the messages, and the bandwagon effect. Recall our dictum for remembering the dynamics of these two routes: As the likelihood of mental elaboration (careful processing of a persuasive message) increases, the central route to persuasion is dominant. As the likelihood of mental elaboration decreases, the peripheral route to persuasion becomes more important in the persuasion process.

Reasoned Action and Planned Behavior

This model assumes that people decide whether or not to change their behavior based upon three criteria (Fishbein & Ajzen, 1975; Ajzen, 1991):

1. Their attitudes about the behavior.
2. Their perceptions of how others will view the behavior.
3. Their perceptions of how much control they have over the behavior.

Automatic Activation Model

According to this model, when a specific attitude comes to mind, a specific behavior follows spontaneously and without serious reflection or carefully reasoned action (Fazio, 1990). This occurs whenever two contingent conditions are met: (1) the attitude may be accessed spontaneously whenever the object of the attitude presents itself, and (2) the object is perceived according to the attitude.

Social Cognitive and Social Learning Theories

The framework of social cognitive theory enables the analysis of human cognitions or mental functions that produce various behaviors. The theory explains human thought and actions as a process of triadic reciprocal causation (Bandura, 1994). Thought and behavior are determined by three different factors that interact and influence each other with variable strength, at the same or different times. The three factors are behavior, personal characteristics (cognitive and biological qualities such as IQ, sex, height, or race), and environmental factors or events.

Bandura (1977b) explained attitude and behavior change in terms of modeling principles. When audience members see credible role models performing particular behaviors, they tend to model their own behaviors after them. (This is especially true if they receive reinforcement of some nature, either positive or negative.) A number of campaigns are based upon this theoretical construct. Consider, for example, the milk mustache campaign, which features famous and successful people who obviously drink milk. Also, there have been countless advertisements in which famous actors or sports stars are featured eating a particular cereal, working out on a particular exercise machine, driving a particular car, or drinking a particular soft drink. According to social cognitive theory, the way the individual audience member thinks about and acts upon the information depends in large part on the process of triadic reciprocal causation.

Self-Efficacy

Another theoretical concept from Bandura (1977a) is that of self-efficacy, or the belief that one can indeed accomplish the behavioral change. Part of the goal of campaign stakeholders is to increase the audience's self-efficacy. For example, in any antismoking campaign (or advertisement), it is very important to make the desired audience of smokers believe that they can quit (McAlister, Ramirez, Galavotti, & Gallion, 1989).

Researchers have identified a number of ways to increase self-efficacy. These include the use of role models (Reardon, 1989), counterattitudinal advocacy (which occurs when people can see themselves engaging in behavior that is counter to the attitudes originally held), providing reasons to offer whenever others encourage the old behavior, presenting mild fear appeals (e.g., telling a smoker that his teeth will become very yellow from tobacco stains), and encouraging "deeply held but possibly unrealistic illusions" that will promote the desired behavior (Reardon, 1989; Rice & Atkin, 1994, p. 371).

Despite our preoccupation with famous examples, there are other examples of communication campaigns that flopped miserably. Indeed, one could probably select examples from various successful or unsuccessful communication campaigns through the years to make a case for powerful or limited media effects. Examples of successful campaigns include the safe-and-sane Fourth of July campaign, the early years of the Smokey the Bear campaign to prevent forest fires, and the antilitter campaigns of the 1960s. A good example of a failed campaign is the effort in Cincinnati during the 1940s to gain support for the United Nations. Another example of a failure of sorts would be Smokey the Bear of recent years; while recognizable to a new generation, many do not associate Smokey with a campaign to prevent forest fires. See the box on the Smokey the Bear campaign.

One of the early, classic communication campaign studies examined some of the reasons why campaigns fail (Hyman & Sheatsley, 1947). The study identified a number of barriers related to audiences' perceptions of messages that blocked the way for campaign success. Audience members were found to attend to messages selectively, based upon their predispositions and existing attitudes.

Measuring Campaign Success: Smokey the Bear

Smokey the Bear, symbol of one of the most famous communication campaigns in the 20th century, was "born" in 1942 when the Wartime Advertising Council needed a symbol for a forest fire prevention campaign. The Smokey campaign messages and Smokey's image have changed somewhat through the years. The first campaign message, "Careless Matches Aid the Axis—Prevent Forest Fires," was designed to appeal to the patriotic spirit of Americans during World War II. Two years later Walt Disney produced the poster that depicted Smokey in his now-famous image—in overalls and a ranger's hat. Smokey was shown putting out a campfire with water, and the slogan read "Smokey Says—Care Will Prevent 9 out of 10 Forest Fires." The most famous slogan, "Remember, Only You Can Prevent Forest Fires," was conceived by an advertising agency in 1947.

The campaign increased in magnitude during the 1950s when a live Smokey Bear was procured for exhibition and a huge Smokey Bear Junior Forest Ranger Program began. In 1950 a badly burned bear cub was rescued from a forest fire, nursed back to health, and housed at the National Zoo. This bear served as a living symbol of the Smokey the Bear campaign until it died in 1977. After it was initiated in 1953, the Junior Forest Ranger Program sent fire prevention kits and badges to millions of children who wrote to the Smokey Bear headquarters.

The Smokey the Bear campaign to prevent forest fires serves as a good example of the relativity of the measure of communication campaign successfulness. Many factors indicate that the campaign has been enormously successful through the years, including Smokey's almost universal recognizability, the dramatic drop in acreage lost to wildfires since the campaign began, and the resulting cost-benefits. A study in the 1970s, however, showed that while Smokey the Bear was recognized by 98 percent of Americans, only 7 percent associated Smokey with fire prevention.

The very longevity of Smokey Bear may also work against its effectiveness: The current theme of "Only You Can Prevent Forest Fires" assumes the campaign is well known enough that specific knowledge and behaviors will be activated by these words. Yet every year brings new children into our schools and new visitors into forest areas who have never been exposed to specific information or behavioral models about fire prevention. (Rice, 1989, p. 217)

In recent years, the subject of campaign failure has been much discussed. Backer, Rogers, and Sopory (1992) conducted interviews with leading campaign designers and scholars who are experts on the subject of communication campaigns. One of the questions the interviewees addressed was the issue of campaign failures.

According to Rice (1992), a campaign may fail for any number of reasons. Neglecting to clearly define criteria for success may limit a campaign's effectiveness, as may a lack of sophistication in audience-targeting techniques. Additionally, if the wrong medium is selected, the targeted audience may not be reached. Clearly defined goals for success are essential in order to measure success or failure, as success or failure is often relative to one's point of view. In the case of Smokey the Bear, for example, the campaign should be considered successful in the sense that acreage lost from fires diminished sixfold following the campaign; however, millions of acres continue to be lost to wildfires each year and, in that sense, the campaign failed.

Rogers (1992) listed some additional reasons why campaigns fail to achieve their goals. If unrealistic goals are set in the first place, he said, the campaign has little chance for success.

> Goals of 40% or 50% changes in human behavior are impossible. More reasonable objectives might be 3–5% change in a reasonable time frame of several years. We must set feasible objectives to ensure that the hoped-for results of a campaign are achieved. (p. 150)

Additionally, to facilitate success, Rogers suggested that multimedia messages should be used on many channels, rather than a single message on a single channel, and the messages should be shown repeatedly. Finally, message content is very important:

> Campaign planners and implementers know a lot about media, but they are often naïve about choosing strategies based on the behavioral sciences. They may rely on simple messages. An integrated team is required. Experts are needed on content, on how to make messages, and on behavior change. (p. 150)

Flora (1992) emphasized the importance of two kinds of issues in determining the success or failure of a campaign: (1) either empirical or theoretical considerations, and (2) practical issues in the execution of the campaign. She wrote:

> Most media campaigns are not theory driven. Campaign activities are not well specified or ordered sequentially. The campaign is not targeted to specific audiences or based on an understanding of the audience. High-risk youth audiences are targeted by campaigns in schools, where few truly high-risk youth are present. So we do not reach the intended youth audience with the intended message. Sometimes we reach them with messages that are not of any interest to them, and so no impact occurs. (p. 85)

SUCCESSFUL CAMPAIGN PRINCIPLES

Researchers have identified 10 underlying principles that, if adhered to by those who implement campaigns, may increase a campaign's chances for success. These principles, discussed by Rice and Atkin (in press) and based upon the framework in Atkin (2001) and McGuire (2001), "are naturally based on considerable and diverse theoretical developments, research efforts, and practical experience" (Rice & Atkin, 1994, p. 365). The principles include:

> understanding historical dimensions and key concepts; application of relevant theory; understanding the implications of theory and the interactions of campaign components; planning the campaign and matching objectives to individual costs and benefits; applying formative evaluation, analyzing and understanding the audience; analyzing and understanding the media choices; mixing multimedia and interpersonal channels when cost-effective; understanding the uses and contradictions of mass media and identifying reasonable criteria for campaign success; and using summary evaluations to assess both theory and program success. (pp. 365–384)

Rice and Atkin (in press) emphasized that the one campaign principle that underlies all others is evaluation. According to Valente, "Evaluation is the systematic application of research procedures to understand the conceptualization, design, implementation, and utility of interventions" (2001, p. 106). Comprehensive evaluation requires campaign developers to assess their needs; conduct formative research to help them develop effective messages; design methods, treatments, and instruments needed for research; conduct process research and summative research; and share results with other researchers. Valente (2001) defined formative, process, and summative research in the following ways:

> *Formative research* consists of those activities that define the scope of the problem, gather data on possible intervention strategies, learn about the intended audience, and investigate possible factors that might limit program implementation . . . *Process research* (also known as monitoring) consists of those activities conducted to measure the degree of program implementation to determine whether the program was delivered as it was intended . . . *Summative research* consists of those activities conducted to measure the program's impact, to determine the lessons learned from the study, and to disseminate research findings. (pp. 107–109)

1. Understand Historical and Conceptual Dimensions

The concepts listed previously by Paisley (1989), such as objectives, methods, strategies of change, individual or collective benefits, first-party and second-party entitlement, and stakeholders, are the keys to understanding communication campaign components. Historical dimensions are also important in that modern-day campaign coordinators can learn much by studying the successful campaigns of the past. A few of these campaigns (and their stakeholders) have included the fight to extend the vote to women (associations), the muckraking efforts of the 19th century (media), the New Deal (government), and the study of the power of propaganda campaigns (social scientists).

2. Apply and Extend Relevant Theory

Theoretical principles help campaign developers understand the underlying dynamics of persuasion and communication, and therefore design the most effective campaigns possible. McGuire's communication/persuasion model, the elaboration likelihood model, social learning theory, and the other theoretical bases discussed previously provide the essential foundations upon which successful, practical campaigns can be built.

Other theoretical models used recently to provide application of relevant theory to important campaigns have included the extended parallel process model (Stephenson & Witte, 2001), diffusion and influence through social networks (Piotrow & Kincaid, 2001), and the transtheoretical model (Buller, Woodall, Hall, Borland, Ax, Brown, & Hines, 2001). The **extended parallel process model** recognizes two separate responses to fear appeals, either cognitive or emotional, and encourages a balance between the two. Fear messages may invoke the cognitive process and generate thoughts about ways to avert danger, or fear appeals may cause a more emotional response. The fear appeal must be strong enough to make the threat significant in the minds of audience members, but not so strong that they feel paralyzed with fear and unable to respond with appropriate preventive action. The **diffusion model** emphasizes the spread of ideas or practices via interpersonal networks. The **transtheoretical model** identifies five stages in the process of behavior change on the part of audiences: precontemplation, contemplation, preparation, action, and maintenance. The messages should be tailored to audiences at particular stages in the behavioral change process.

3. Understand Theoretical Implications and Interactions of Campaign Components

Briefly stated, the theoretical models dictate the following: (*a*) campaign goals should not be set too high; (*b*) careful decisions should be made regarding the measure for the campaign's success (e.g., will it be considered successful if audiences like the message, or if it leads to behavioral or attitudinal changes, either short term or long term?); (*c*) the power of particular components may undermine the campaign's overall message (e.g., audiences may recognize Smokey the Bear but may not know what he stands for); (*d*) different components (sometimes negative) may affect each other in a positive way (e.g., people may trust a source less when they realize that it is trying to persuade them to do something; however, this also means that they may be more aware of the message being conveyed).

4. Plan the Campaign: Match Objectives to Individual Cost-Benefits

In planning the campaign, several factors must be carefully deliberated. First, *realistic goals* must be set (e.g., attitude or behavior changes that will be measured either in the short term or long term). Next, *media objectives* should be clearly defined (e.g., ratings could be used to project reach to the desired target audiences). *Timing* of the campaign's media messages is also essential (e.g., presidential election campaign messages are shown during the months prior to the election, and become more numerous as the election day approaches). *Choice of media* is important because different media offer different advantages (e.g., broadcast communications would be more useful than print media in a country where literacy rates are rather low).

Social campaigns based on product marketing principles (called *social mar-keting perspective*) have additional components that must be considered in the campaign plan. Solomon (1984, 1989) applied the **"Four P's" of marketing**—product, price, place, and promotion—to social campaigns, along with a fifth "P," positioning.

> A *product* is defined as the focus of the transaction between the marketer and the target market. A product can have a physical component or consist only of ideas, practices, or services . . . The *price* of a product or service consists of far more than just the monetary cost. Other factors to be considered are time costs (how much time it takes to obtain a product or service) and opportunity costs (which benefits or other opportunities will be missed because of taking part in obtaining a given product or service) . . . *Place* refers to the distribution chan-nels used to make the product, service, or idea available to the target group . . . *Promotion* is an extremely broad area that includes the publicity about a campaign, the mass media campaign message design and dissemination, and the campaign monitoring and modification. (Solomon, 1989, pp. 91–94)

The "fifth P," **positioning,** represents the position or location (in the minds of the audience) of the product or service in relation to others in the market. If a campaign is promoting "heart-smart" foods, then one step in the planning process is to determine the position of such foods in relation to other foods in the minds of the audience.

5. Apply Formative Evaluation

Campaigns must be monitored for a variety of reasons, the most important being the measure of their effectiveness over time. Evaluations are essential to planning, making, and implementing improvements, administering and sched-uling various components, and other aspects of the campaign. *Preproduction research* involves obtaining relevant information about the sociocultural climate that may have an impact on the campaign (Rice & Atkin, in press, 1994). For example, literacy rates, standard of living, religious beliefs of the people, and many other factors must be considered in creating campaign messages that are not only appropriate but ultimately persuasive. Production testing (pretesting) is used to revise and refine the messages that will ultimately be used in the campaign.

Atkin and Freimuth (1989, 2001) identified four stages in preproduction research:

1. *Identify audience-related factors* such as which target group is most at risk, which people are most likely to receive the messages, which ones are most likely to be persuaded and which ones are the least likely.
2. *Specify behavior-related factors* such as targeted behaviors and skills that must be taught in order to maintain behavioral changes.
3. *Identify the intermediate steps* that occur after exposure to a campaign mes-sage and before behavioral change takes place (these may include changes in attitudes, values, knowledge, skills, etc., that must take place).
4. *Identify media use factors* such as which communications media is used most by the target audience during what hours.

After preproduction test results have been evaluated, pretesting allows campaign designers to revise their messages accordingly. Pretesting is especially beneficial in clarifying key concepts, identifying the best message sources (e.g., using either a scientist, the surgeon general, or a supermodel who gave up smoking to deliver an antismoking message), and learning the proper vocabulary to use in messages that will appeal to specific audiences. Pretest results will also reveal whether audiences will comprehend the message, whether they will consider it relevant, or whether it will be inclined to cause controversy.

6. Analyze and Understand the Audience

One important way to understand audiences is in identifying subaudiences and recognizing the three major types of audiences—focal segments, interpersonal influencers, and societal policy makers (Atkin & Rice, in press). Atkin and Rice defined focal segments as "audiences grouped by levels of risk or illness, readiness, income and education, and other factors such as sensation seeking." Interpersonal influences "are opinion leaders, media advocates, and peer and role models who can mediate the campaign (positively or negatively) and help set the public agenda." Societal policy makers include those who "affect the legal, political and resource infrastructure, through, for example, regulations on media messages, environmental conditions, or safety standards, and social action such as community-based campaigns, federal allocations (e.g., the gasoline or tobacco tax), and insurance and health care programs" (Atkin & Rice, in press).

To determine which messages will be appropriate and most persuasive, the campaign planner must understand the audience and its various segments. Dervin and Frenette (2001) suggested a *sense-making* approach that goes beyond the simple transmission of messages traditionally employed in campaigns. This approach tries to "ensure as far as possible that dialogue is encouraged in every aspect of communication campaign research, design, and implementation" (Dervin & Frenette, 2001, p. 72). The method requires determination of situational factors about the audience and then identification of available informational resources for the audience that relate specifically to campaign goals. It requires that campaign organizers provide a lot of useful information in their messages. They must "conceptualize their efforts as entering into a dialogue with individuals, instead of as transmitting content" (Rice & Atkin, 1994, p. 376).

7. Analyze and Understand Media Choices

In a communication campaign, media choices refer not only to various communications media such as television, radio, newspapers, and so forth, but also to different *strategies* of media use. For example, use of public relations skills and public affairs activities may help the public visibility of the campaign and possibly shape the course of legislative actions related to the campaign issues. Press releases may result in media coverage of a campaign-related event or issue. The use of *public service announcements* (PSAs) serves as another type of media strategy. However, only the broadcaster determines the time slot in which the PSA will run, so the target audience may or may not receive it. Campaign planners also make use of *broadcast rating services* like Nielsen or Arbitron to determine which channels are most watched by their target audiences and *media books* that offer CPM[1] rates or similar data for different media such as radio, magazines, billboards, and so forth. Such data allow planners to calculate the number of people in the audience at a particular time (called the *reach*) and the number of exposures a person may receive (the *frequency*).

8. Mix Multiple Media and Interpersonal Channels when Cost-Effective

Research has shown that people are more likely to make attitudinal or behavioral changes (even long-term ones) when the media campaign is supplemented by *interpersonal* supports. For example, the use of training instructors to help those who are trying to quit smoking, or those at risk for heart disease are examples of interpersonal campaign supports, as are personal appearances by political candidates during their election campaigns. This principle stresses that interpersonal communications should be used as support for the overall media campaign. On their own, interpersonal activities may have strong persuasive effects, but mass media campaign messages continue to be more effective in terms of the number of people reached and the costs involved (Hornik, 1989).

9. Understand Uses and Contradictions of Mass Media

It is also important for the campaign planner to be aware of the broad spectrum of mass media content, some of which may be in direct contradiction to the campaign messages. Wallack (1989) identified several characteristics of media and types of media content that might deliver messages of their own that conflict with particular campaign objectives. Commercials, television programs, and motion pictures often depict individuals engaging in unhealthy activities such as smoking or abusing drugs. Portrayals sometimes glamorize these activities and others such as intense violence or promiscuous sex. Additionally, media portrayals reinforce public perceptions—sometimes inaccurate ones—concerning medical treatments, the "proper" roles of men and women, mental illness and its treatment, and many other circumstances.

10. Identify Reasonable Criteria for Campaign Success, and Use Summative Evaluation to Assess both Theory and Program Success

The watchword in the first part of this principle is the word "reasonable." It would not be reasonable to expect a communication campaign to prevent any forest fire from ever occurring again, or to stop all people from ever driving while under the influence of alcohol. Rather, a campaign that raises public awareness and results in a significant reduction in forest fires or traffic fatalities involving drunk drivers should be considered a success.

As for the second part of this final principle, summative evaluation refers to the identification and measurement of several aspects of the campaign, including the audience, the implementation of the campaign components, the effects of the campaign on individuals and society, the cost effectiveness of the project, and identification of the steps in the causal process that explain why effects did or did not occur (Flay & Cook, 1989).

Flay and Cook (1989) identified three types of evaluative models that may be used to assess the campaign's success: the advertising model, the impact-monitoring model, and the experimental model. Rice and Atkin (1994) provided a summary of the positive aspects of each model:

Ten Principles of Successful Campaigns

1. Understand historical and conceptual dimensions.
2. Apply and extend relevant theory.
3. Understand theoretical implications and inter-actions of campaign components.
4. Plan the campaign: match objectives to indi-vidual cost-benefits.
5. Apply formative evaluation.
6. Analyze and understand the audience.
7. Analyze and understand media choices.
8. Mix multiple media and interpersonal channels when cost effective.
9. Understand uses and contradictions of mass media.
10. Identify reasonable criteria for campaign suc-cess, and use summative evaluation to assess both theory and program success.

Source: Rice & Atkin (1994).

The *advertising* model focuses on the early stages of the communication hier-archy of effects: exposure, recall, liking, self-reported behavioral intentions, and message characteristics.

The *impact-monitoring* model focuses on the more distal stages and social impacts in the hierarchy of effects, through tracking of archival data such as pop-ulation trends, consumption behaviors, epidemiological information, and so on.

The *experimental* model focuses on testing hypothesized causal chains through controlled manipulation of treatments, often requiring lengthy and complex campaigns. (pp. 382–383)

Another method of campaign evaluation is the *systems-theoretical* approach (Rice & Foote, 1989, 2001). This approach has been effective in evaluating com-munication campaigns related to health in less developed countries. The approach includes seven stages, also summarized by Rice and Atkin (1994):

1. Specifying the goals and underlying assumptions of the project.
2. Specifying the process model at the project level.
3. Specifying prior states, system phases, and system constraints.
4. Specifying immediate as well as long-term intended poststates.
5. Specifying the process model at the individual level.
6. Choosing among research approaches appropriate to the system.
7. Assessing implications for design. (p. 383)

RECENT RESEARCH AND FUTURE TRENDS

Recent research on communication campaigns has examined a variety of dif-ferent types of campaigns. Public health campaigns and those that encourage personal health and safety, political campaigns, and other types of communi-cation campaigns have produced measurable effects.

In recent years, scholars have made an effort to use various theories to guide communication campaigns (Slater, 1999), especially health communica-tion campaigns (Lapinski & Witte, 1998), and this trend will likely continue. Micro-level theories such as social cognitive theory, and those at the macro level, such as diffusion of innovations, have proven useful for researchers, as well as other theories less known to communication scholars. For example, Brinson and Brown (1997) used narrative theory to predict reasons why particular public service announcements would succeed in some ways and be less than successful in other ways. The PSAs were part of the Centers for Disease Control and Prevention's overall campaign, "America Responds to AIDS."

Other health-related campaign studies have included Mi-Kim and Marangwanda's (1997) evaluation of the effectiveness of a motivational campaign among males in Zimbabwe to encourage use of contraceptives and participation in family planning, Kerr and McKenna's (2000) promotion of a walking campaign among nonactive people, and Rimal, Flora, and Schooler's (1999) examination of the effects of exposure to a campaign to improve cardiovascular health.

Recent research and analyses have shown that political communication campaigns produce significant effects (Iyengar & Simon, 2000). A variety of studies have documented campaign effects in recent presidential elections (Kaid & Bystrom, 1999).

Other types of campaigns that have come under the scrutiny of researchers in recent years include those, to name a few, that attempt to reduce racial prejudices (Vrij & Smith, 1999), stress drug abuse prevention (Stephenson, Palmgreen, Hoyle, Donohew, Lorch, & Colon, 1999; Harrington & Donohew, 1997) and encourage the use of bicycle helmets (Ressler & Toledo, 1997, 1998).

SUMMARY

Public communication campaigns may be defined as purposive attempts to inform, persuade, or motivate behavioral changes in a relatively well-defined and large audience, generally for noncommercial benefits to the individuals and/or society at large, typically within a given time period, by means or organized communication activities involving mass media, and often complemented by interpersonal support. Communication campaigns take a variety of forms in our society: advertising campaigns to sell products, public service campaigns to promote better health or societal improvements, election campaigns, and many more.

Several key concepts are central to the understanding of campaigns. These include the objectives of the campaign or the media methods employed, the strategy used to facilitate change, the potential benefits resulting from proposed change, public perceptions about the campaign stakeholder, and the stakeholders themselves. Stakeholders are the individuals, groups, associations, or organizations that initiate the campaign because of their interest in promoting reform. They have included (1) individuals and associations, (2) the media, (3) government, and (4) social scientists.

The theoretical bases for campaigns have been discussed in previous chapters. They include, primarily, the models for persuasion, social cognitive theory, and social learning theory. McGuire's communication/persuasion matrix model emphasizes a number of steps in the persuasive process, each one building upon the other to create a hierarchy of effects. The elaboration likelihood model of Petty and Cacioppo stresses central or peripheral routes to persuasion. The persuasion process is influenced by the likelihood of the audience member to think carefully or elaborate cognitively about a persuasive appeal. Fishbein and Ajzen's model of reasoned action and planned behavior posits that people decide to change their behavior depending upon their attitudes toward the behavior, their perceptions of how others will view the behavior, and their perceptions of how much control they have over the behavior. The automatic activation model assumes that specific behaviors follow when specific attitudes come to mind without serious reflection or carefully reasoned action. Social cognitive and social learning theories explain attitude and behavior changes in terms of triadic reciprocal causation and modeling principles.

Communication campaigns sometimes fail for any number of reasons. These reasons may be related to audience perception barriers that blocked the persuasive power of the messages or audience selectivity based upon predispositions and existing attitudes. Other possible reasons for failure include neglecting to clearly define the criteria for success, insufficient audience targeting techniques, the selection of the wrong medium, or the setting of unreasonable goals.

Researchers have identified 10 underlying principles that, if adhered to by those who implement campaigns, may increase a campaign's chances for success. These principles include (1) understanding historical dimensions and key concepts, (2) application of relevant theory, (3) understanding the implications of theory and the interactions of campaign components, (4) planning the campaign and matching objectives to individual costs and benefits, (5) applying formative evaluation, (6) analyzing and understanding the audience, (7) analyzing and understanding the media choices, (8) mixing multimedia and interpersonal channels when cost effective, (9) understanding the uses and contradictions of mass media, and (10) identifying reasonable criteria for campaign success, and using summative evaluations to assess both theory and program success.

Recent research has been guided by various theories at the micro and macro levels. Future research on campaigns will follow this trend.

REFERENCES

AJZEN, I. (1991). The theory of planned behavior. *Organizational Behavior and Human Decision Processes, 50,* 179–210.

ATKIN, C. K. (2001). Theory and principles of media health campaigns. In R. E. Rice & C. K. Atkin (Eds.), *Public communication campaigns* (3rd ed., pp. 49–68). Thousand Oaks, CA: Sage.

ATKIN, C., & FREIMUTH, V. (1989). Formative evaluation research in campaign design. In R. E. Rice & C. K. Atkin (Eds.), *Public communication campaigns* (2nd ed., pp. 131–150). Newbury Park, CA: Sage.

ATKIN, C. K., & FREIMUTH, V. (2001). Formative evaluation research in campaign design. In R. E. Rice & C. K. Atkin (Eds.), *Public communication campaigns* (3rd ed., pp. 125–145). Thousand Oaks, CA: Sage.

BACKER, T. E., ROGERS, E. M., &. SOPORY, P. (1992). *Designing health communication campaigns: What works?* Newbury Park, CA: Sage.

BANDURA, A. (1977a). Self-efficacy: Toward a unifying theory of behavioral change. *Psychological Review, 84,* 191–215.

BANDURA, A. (1977b). *Social learning theory.* Englewood Cliffs. NJ: Prentice Hall.

BANDURA, A. (1994). Social cognitive theory of mass communication. In J. Bryant & D. Zillmann (Eds.), *Media effects: Advances in theory and research* (pp. 61–90). Hillsdale, NJ: Erlbaum.

BRINSON, S. L., & BROWN, M. H. (1997). The AIDS risk narrative in the 1994 CDC campaign. *Journal of Health Communication, 2,* 101–112.

BULLER, D., WOODALL, W. G., HALL, J., BORLAND, R., AX, B., BROWN, M., & HINES, J. M. (2001). A web-based smoking cessation and prevention program for children aged 12–15. In R. E. Rice & C. K. Atkin (Eds.), *Public communication campaigns* (3rd ed., pp. 357–372). Thousand Oaks, CA: Sage.

DERVIN, B. (1989). Audience as listener and learner, teacher and confidante: The sense-making approach. In R. E. Rice & C. Atkin (Eds.), *Public communication campaigns* (2nd ed., pp. 43–66). Newbury Park, CA: Sage.

DERVIN, B., & FRENETTE, M. (2001). Applying sense-making methodology: Communicating communicatively with audiences as listeners, learners, teachers, confidantes. In R. E. Rice & C. K. Atkin (Eds.), *Public communication campaigns* (3rd ed., pp. 69–87). Thousand Oaks, CA: Sage.

FAZIO, R. H. (1990). Multiple processes by which attitudes guide behavior: The MODE model as an integrative framework. In M. Zanna (Ed.), *Advances in experimental social psychology* (Vol. 23, pp. 75–109). New York: Academic Press.

FISHBEIN, M., & AJZEN, I. (1975). *Belief, attitude, intention and behavior.* Reading, MA: Addison-Wesley.

FLAY, B., & COOK, T. (1989). Three models for summative evaluation of prevention campaigns with a mass media component. In R. E. Rice & C. K. Atkins (Eds.), *Public communication campaigns* (2nd ed., pp. 174–196). Newbury Park, CA: Sage.

FLORA, J. (1992). Interview. In T. E. Backer, E. M. Rogers, & P. Sopory. *Designing health communication campaigns: What works?* (pp. 84–89). Newbury Park, CA: Sage.

HARRINGTON, N. G., & DONOHEW, L. (1997). Jump Start: A targeted substance abuse prevention program. *Health Education and Behavior, 24,* 568–586.

HORNIK, R. (1989). Channel effectiveness in development communication programs. In R. E. Rice & C. K. Atkin (Eds.), *Public communication campaigns* (2nd ed., pp. 309–330). Newbury Park, CA: Sage.

HYMAN, H., & SHEATSLEY, P. (1947). Some reasons why information campaigns fail. *Public Opinion Quarterly, 11,* 412–423.

IYENGAR, S., & SIMON, A. F. (2000). New perspectives and evidence on political communication and campaign effects. *Annual Review of Psychology, 51,* 149–169.

KAID, L. L., & BYSTROM, D. G. (Eds.), *The electronic election: Perspectives on the 1996 campaign communication.* Mahwah, NJ: Erlbaum.

KERR, J., & MCKENNA, J. (2000). A randomized control trial of new tailored walking campaigns in an employee sample. *Journal of Health Communication, 5,* 265–279.

LAPINSKI, M. K., & WITTE, K. (1998). Health communication campaigns. In L. D. Jackson & B. K. Duffy (Eds.), *Health communication research: A guide to developments and directions* (pp. 139–161). Westport, CT.: Greenwood.

MCALISTER, A., RAMIREZ, A., GALAVOTTI, C., & GALLION, K. (1989). Antismoking campaigns: Progress in the application of social learning theory. In R. E. Rice & C. K. Atkin (Eds.), *Public communication campaigns* (2nd ed., pp. 291–308). Newbury Park, CA: Sage.

MCGUIRE, W. (1989). Theoretical foundations of campaigns. In R. E. Rice & C. K. Atkin (Eds.), *Public communication campaigns* (2nd ed., pp. 43–66). Newbury Park, CA: Sage.

MCGUIRE, W. (2001). Input and output variables currently promising for constructing persuasive communications. In R. E. Rice & C. K. Atkin (Eds.), *Public communication campaigns* (3rd ed., pp. 22–48). Thousand Oaks, CA: Sage.

MI-KIM, Y., & MARANGWANDA, C. (1997). Stimulating men's support for long-term contraception: A campaign in Zimbabwe. *Journal of Health Communication, 2,* 271–297.

PAISLEY, W. (1989). Public communication campaigns: The American experience. In R. E. Rice & C. K. Atkin (Eds.), *Public communication campaigns* (2nd ed., pp. 15–38). Newbury Park, CA: Sage.

PAISLEY, W. (2001). Public communication campaigns: The American experience. In R. E. Rice & C. K. Atkin (Eds.), *Public communication campaigns* (3rd ed., pp. 3–21). Thousand Oaks, CA: Sage.

PETTY, R., & CACIOPPO, J. (1986). Communication and persuasion: Central and peripheral routes to attitude change. New York: Springer-Verlag.

PIOTROW, P., & KINCAID, L. (2001). Strategic communication for international health programs. In R. E. Rice & C. K. Atkin (Eds.), *Public communication campaigns* (3rd ed., pp. 249–266). Thousand Oaks, CA: Sage.

REARDON, K. (1989). The potential role of persuasion in adolescent AIDS prevention. In R. E. Rice & C. K. Atkins (Eds.), *Public communication campaigns* (2nd ed., pp. 273–290). Newbury Park, CA: Sage.

RESSLER, W. H., & TOLEDO, E. (1997). A functional perspective on social marketing: Insights from Israel's bicycle helmet campaign. *Journal of Health Communication, 2,* 145–156.

RESSLER, W. H., & TOLEDO, E. (1998). Kasdah B'Rosh Tov: A description and evaluation of the Israeli bicycle helmet campaign. *Health Education and Behavior, 25,* 354–370.

RICE, R. E. (1989). Campaign sampler: Smokey Bear. In R. E. Rice & C. K. Atkin (Eds.), *Public communication campaigns* (2nd ed., pp. 215–218). Newbury Park, CA: Sage.

RICE, R. E. (1992). Interview. In T. E. Backer, E. M. Rogers, & P. Sopory. *Designing health communication campaigns: What works?* (pp. 145–149). Newbury Park, CA: Sage.

RICE, R. E., & ATKIN, C. K. (1989). Public communication campaigns (2nd ed.). Newbury Park, CA: Sage.

RICE, R. E., & ATKIN, C. K. (1994). Principles of successful public communication campaigns. In J. Bryant & D. Zillmann (Eds.), *Media effects: Advances in theory and research* (pp. 365–387). Hillsdale, NJ: Erlbaum.

RICE, R. E., & ATKIN, C. K. (Eds.) (2001). *Public communication campaigns* (3rd ed.). Thousand Oaks, CA: Sage.

RICE, R. E., & ATKIN, C. K. (in press). Communication campaigns: Theory, design, implementation, and evaluation. In J. Bryant & D. Zillmann (Eds.), *Media effects: Advances in theory and research* (2nd ed.). Mahwah, NJ: Erlbaum.

RICE, R. E., & FOOTE, D. (1989). A systems-based evaluation planning model for health communication campaigns in developing countries. In R. E. Rice & C. K. Atkin (Eds.), *Public communication campaigns* (2nd ed., pp. 151–174). Newbury Park, CA: Sage.

RICE, R. E., & FOOTE, D. (2001). A systems-based evaluation planning model for health communication campaigns in developing countries. In R. E. Rice & C. K. Atkin (Eds.), *Public communication campaigns* (3rd ed., pp. 146–167). Thousand Oaks, CA: Sage.

RIMAL, R. N., FLORA, J. A., & SCHOOLER, C. (1999). Achieving improvements in overall health orientation: Effects of campaign exposure, information seeking and health media use. *Communication Research, 26,* 322–348.

ROGERS, E. M. (1992). Interview. In T. E. Backer, E. M. Rogers, & P. Sopory. *Designing health communication campaigns: What works?* (pp. 149–153). Newbury Park, CA: Sage.

ROGERS, E. M., & STOREY, D. (1987). Communication campaigns. In C. Berger & S. Chaffee (Eds.), *Handbook of communication science* (pp. 817–846). Newbury Park, CA: Sage.

SLATER, M. D. (1999). Integrating application of media effects, persuasion, and behavior change theories to communication campaigns: A stages-of-change framework. *Health Communication, 11,* 335–354.

SOLOMON, D. S. (1984). Social marketing and community health promotion: The Stanford heart disease prevention program. In L. Frederiksen, L. Solomon, & K. Brehony (Eds.), *Marketing health behavior* (pp. 115–135). New York: Plenum.

SOLOMON, D. S. (1989). A social marketing perspective on communication campaigns. In R. E. Rice & C. K. Atkins (Eds.), *Public communication campaigns* (2nd ed., pp. 87–104). Newbury Park, CA: Sage.

STEPHENSON, M. T., PALMGREEN, P., HOYLE, R. H., DONOHEW, L., LORCH, E. P., & COLON, S. E. (1999). Short-term effects of an anti-marijuana media campaign targeting high sensation seeking adolescents. *Journal of Applied Communication Research, 27*, 175–195.

STEPHENSON, M., & WITTE, K. (2001). Creating fear in a risky world: Generating effective health risk messages. In R. E. Rice & C. K. Atkin (Eds.), *Public communication campaigns* (3rd ed., pp. 88–102). Thousand Oaks, CA: Sage.

VALENTE, T. (2001). Evaluating communication campaigns. In R. E. Rice & C. K. Atkin (Eds.), *Public communication campaigns* (3rd ed., pp. 105–124). Thousand Oaks, CA: Sage.

VRIJ, A., & SMITH, B. J. (1999). Reducing ethnic prejudice by public campaigns: An evaluation of a present and a new campaign. *Journal of Community and Applied Social Psychology, 9*, 195–215.

WALLACK, L. (1989). Mass media and health promotion: A critical perspective. In R. E. Rice & C. K. Atkin (Eds.), *Public communication campaigns* (2nd ed., pp. 353–368). Newbury Park, CA: Sage.

ENDNOTES

1. (CPM is the *cost per thousand* audience members for one presentation of a message in a single medium.)

Media Effects
on Health

- A health communication campaign for AIDS awareness results in an increase in the use of condoms.
- The Mothers Against Drunk Driving (MADD) campaign achieved the passage of legislation with stricter penalties for drunk drivers and greater restrictions on alcohol advertisements.
- After seeing a news report about doctors detecting breast cancer in Nancy Reagan during a routine examination, women throughout the country phone their gynecologists to make an appointment for an exam.
- In the grocery store, a child begs his mother for a box of sweetened cereal that he has seen advertised during cartoon programming.
- After watching a movie that featured Julia Roberts smoking cigarettes, teenage girls decide to take up the habit.

Mass media messages often have considerable impact on personal and public health. As the first two examples reveal, mass media have served as essential components in a number of important health communication campaigns in recent years (Backer, Rogers, & Sopory, 1992). As you learned in the last chapter, communication campaigns attempt (often with successful results) to change or initiate attitudes and behaviors. The goal of the media health communication campaign is to present specific messages, designed by health and communication experts, which have intentional, positive, health-related effects on audiences.

The other examples, however, show that media campaigns are but one type of health communication by way of mass media. Every day audiences are inundated with health-related messages from other sources—news reports, prime-time entertainment programs, daytime soaps, countless advertisements—and the effects from such messages are not always positive in nature. Studies have shown that Americans obtain much of their health-related information from mass media (Sandman, 1976), and this creates a problem when one considers that much of that health information, and many of the health behaviors presented to audiences, result in negative (albeit many times unintended) effects on their health.

267

If we step back and look at the general picture of health provided in these most pervasive of media, we find a world in which people eat, drink, and have sex with abandonment but seldom suffer the consequences. Research shows that the audience does learn from these images and that, in general, what they learn is not good for their health. (Brown & Walsh-Childers, 1994, p. 409)

As with other types of media content, research has shown that effects from health-related messages may be positive versus negative and intended versus unintended in nature. This chapter will examine some of the research findings for effects from cigarette, alcohol, and food advertisements, and also explore the effects of entertainment portrayals and the nature of health news coverage. We will also discuss the use of health campaigns and other educational strategies designed to affect individual health improvements or cause positive changes at the policy level.

It should be remembered that the study of effects of health communications is a relatively young domain; many of the most important studies have been conducted since the 1970s (Brown & Walsh-Childers, 1994). Much has been learned from research so far, but much remains to be discovered.

RESEARCH FINDINGS

Many of the studies that have examined the effects of media messages on health have concentrated on advertisements, entertainment portrayals, and news reports. These messages have had either unintentional positive impacts (e.g., in the case of Nancy Reagan) or negative impacts (e.g., Julia Roberts film) on viewers, or they have been intentionally designed to promote healthier lifestyles.

Effects of Advertisements on Health

Research on the effects of commercial product advertising has focused primarily upon the health of individuals who use the products. Brown and Walsh-Childers (1994) reviewed the literature on the health effects from three types of advertisements: cigarettes, alcoholic beverages, and foods.

Cigarettes

The percentage of Americans who smoke cigarettes has declined steadily since the 1970s, but a substantial number continue to smoke. Cigarette advertisements have been banned from broadcast media in the United States since 1971, but the ban has not stopped tobacco companies from using other means to advertise their products. Print media, billboards, sponsorship of sporting events—such forums have kept cigarette ads in clear view of the public despite the broadcast ban.

Numerous studies have examined the effects of various cigarette advertising or promotional appeals. With the decline in smoking among white, middle-class males, tobacco companies have targeted cigarette ads to entice other segments of the population, such as women, minorities, and, arguably, children (Davis, 1987;

Basil & Schooler, 1990). Even though tobacco company executives say they do not direct their ads to children or adolescents, research has shown that youngsters recognize the symbols and slogans of various cigarettes (Aitken, Leathar, & O'Hagan, 1985; Aitken, Leathar, & Squair, 1986). The more likely the ad recognition, the more likely one is to smoke (Goldstein, Fischer, Richards, & Creten, 1987). Bloom and his colleagues (1997) found an association between cigarette use among adolescents and watching stock car racing (where tobacco products are heavily advertised).

Studies in Australia revealed that adolescents are particularly attracted to brands of cigarettes that use "lifestyle" appeals in advertising. More than 75 percent of the adolescent smokers used brands that advertised in this way (Chapman & Egger, 1980; Chapman & Fitzgerald, 1982). Another study of Australian children revealed that approval of cigarette ads was second only to the smoking behavior of peers as a predictor of a child's smoking behavior (O'Connell et al., 1981).

Other studies have explored various issues related to the warning labels on tobacco product advertisements. One study tracked the eye movements of adolescents who were shown tobacco ads in magazines, and it found that almost half the children did not read the warning at all. Those who did look at the warning did so only briefly (Fischer, Richards, Berman, & Krugman, 1989). In another study, Davis and Kendrick (1989) found that the warning notices for tobacco ads on billboards and on taxis were very hard to read—yet the brand name of the cigarette could be clearly seen.

Alcohol

Research on the effects of alcohol advertising on personal and public health has generally focused on (1) whether such ads entice adolescents to start drinking, or (2) whether such ads cause increased alcohol consumption and, perhaps, drunk driving among established drinkers. With regard to the first of these issues, Atkin and his associates (1984) surveyed a group of adolescents and found that their likelihood to drink either beer or liquor was directly related to their exposure to TV alcohol ads. Moreover, other factors such as age, sex, social status, or parental influence were not as strong predictors of drinking behavior as exposure to the TV ads. Rather than rely on evidence from this one survey, Atkin (1990) reviewed the body of research related to this issue and determined that alcohol ads on television *do seem to encourage* drinking among adolescents. More recently, another study showed that the exposure of adolescents to football and basketball events where alcohol was promoted was linked to subsequent use of beer (Bloom et al., 1997).

Researchers have found mixed evidence for the second research question related to the effects of alcohol ads. One study found a correlation between exposure to alcohol ads, increased consumption of alcohol, and drunk driving (Atkin, Neuendorf, & McDermott, 1983), but other studies suggested that such findings are inconclusive (Kohn & Smart, 1984). In a study of young schoolchildren, Austin and Nach-Ferguson (1995) found that knowledge of specific brands of alcoholic beverages and a liking for alcohol commercials predicted whether or not the children had ever tasted an alcoholic beverage.

Food

A large amount of research on the effects of food advertisements on consumer health has focused on children. Studies have shown that food commercials may have positive or negative effects, depending upon the nutritional value of the food advertised. Goldberg, Gorn, & Gibson (1978) found that TV food ads did affect the short-term and long-term food preferences of children, yet parental eating habits were much more influential than the commercials in determining a child's diet. When one considers the vast numbers of ads for food items that have low nutritional value, such a finding suggests negative health consequences. On the positive side, Kellogg's campaign for All-Bran cereal during the 1980s used information from the National Cancer Institute to stress the healthy (anticancer) benefits of a diet high in fiber and low in fat. Studies found that as a result of this campaign, more people started eating high-fiber, low-fat foods (such as All-Bran) and more people became aware of the importance of nutrition in preventing particular types of cancer (Freimuth, Hammond, & Stein, 1988; Levy & Stokes, 1987).

Effects of Entertainment Portrayals on Health

After a British medical television drama called *Casualty* featured a suicide by overdose of a drug called paracetamol, the number of patients admitted to emergency rooms for self-poisoning increased by 17 percent during the first week after the broadcast and by 9 percent during the second week. Of the patients who had viewed the episode, 20 percent indicated that what they had seen had influenced their decision to overdose, and 17 percent said they had selected the drug paracetamol because they had seen the program. The researchers concluded that it might not be advisable for mass media to portray suicidal behavior (Hawton et al., 1999).

As the study of the effects of *Casualty* revealed, entertainment portrayals sometimes have rather powerful (sometimes even dire) effects upon the health of audience members. Most studies of health effects related to entertainment portrayals have concentrated on television programs, films, music videos, and musical lyrics.

Television

One important aspect of research on the effects of entertainment portrayals on health has required the careful study of media content to assess the "world" being portrayed through the mass media, especially television. Signorielli (1993) and other researchers have found the world portrayed on television is very different from the real world, especially in matters related to health. For every doctor portrayed on television, the viewer sees only two people with some type of physical illness (Signorielli, 1990).

Another important way in which the world of television differs from the real world is in its numbers of overweight characters. In 1980 Kaufman determined that about 12 percent of TV characters had a weight problem, but in the real world about 25 percent of the adult population was obese. This creates

Most popular television characters are thin. The slim
standard contributes to health problems such as eating disorders among some audience members.
Source: © The Everett Collection

something of a paradoxical situation for viewers in that most of the characters
on TV are slim, yet they eat and drink what they please. Even though solid evidence has not yet been presented, one researcher has argued that the problem
of bulimia may be in response to this paradox, "because only bulimics can eat
everything they wish and remain thin" (Dietz, 1990, p. 76).

In recent years, the slim standard in America and its resulting health problems have spread to remote corners of the globe, by means of satellite television broadcasts. An article in *Newsweek* (May 31, 1999) noted that teenage girls
in the South Pacific island of Fiji (traditionally a culture with a full-figure ideal
body type) began showing signs of serious eating disorders after Western programs with their pencil-thin actresses arrived in 1995. Researchers are reluctant
to attribute all the blame to television alone, but it seems to be a central factor
in the mix. In a study reported to the American Psychiatric Association in 1998,
Fiji girls who watched the most television were precisely the ones who considered themselves too fat, and of those, two of three had resorted to dieting to
lose the unwanted pounds. Moreover, 15 percent of those studied said they had
used vomiting as a way of controlling their weight.

Other studies of the link between television viewing and nutrition have found that time spent watching television is a good predictor of weight problems in adolescents (Dietz, 1990; Dietz & Gortmaker, 1985). A study in the 1970s had already established that children who are heavy TV watchers also eat more snacks between meals than do light viewers (Clancy-Hepburn, Hickey, & Nevill, 1974).

As for cigarettes, alcohol, and illegal drugs, studies in the 1980s revealed that smoking had almost disappeared from television programs (Breed & DeFoe, 1984; Gerbner, Gross, Morgan, & Signorielli, 1981), and illegal drug use was rarely shown (Greenberg, 1981), but consumption of alcohol was a different story. DeFoe, Breed, and Breed (1983) found that characters drank alcohol more than any other beverage, and 7 out of 10 prime-time network dramas featured alcohol. The findings also indicated that even though many of the major characters drank alcohol, only 1–2 percent portrayed alcoholics.

References to sex and depictions of sexual activity on television rose more than 100 percent from 1980 to 1985 (Greenberg, Brown, & Buerkel-Rothfuss, 1991). But during that period, discussion about or mention of the negative consequences of sexual activities (e.g., unwanted pregnancy or sexually transmitted disease) were not common on TV programs, especially daytime soaps (Lowry & Towles, 1989) and prime-time programs (Louis Harris and Associates, 1987).

In recent years, studies from the Henry Kaiser Family Foundation have continued to find ever-increasing numbers of sexual messages on television. A recent Kaiser Foundation report found that 68 percent of the programs on television (excluding news, sports, and children's programming) during the 1999–2000 season contained some form of sexual content, a substantial increase over the previous season's 56 percent. The number of programs depicting or implying sexual intercourse increased from 7 percent in the 1997–1998 season to 10 percent in the 1999–2000 season (Kunkel, Cope-Farrar, Biely, Farinola, & Donnerstein, 2001).

Despite the increasing abundance of sexual activity on television, few sexual scenes show the use of contraceptions or the practice of safe sex. The problem has persisted in recent years. The 1998 study, conducted for the Henry Kaiser Family Foundation, examined more than 1,300 shows selected at random from the 1997–1998 television season (Kunkel, 1999). The 2000 study sampled more than 900 shows. As the 2000 study pointed out:

> Programs that emphasize sexual risk or responsibility issues are a rarity on television, in stark contrast to the widespread treatment of sexual topics across the television landscape. (Kaiser Family Foundation, 2001, p. 50)

Films

The images of sexual activities on film have been demonstrated to have various potential ill effects on the health of audience members. Studies in the 1980s on the effects of sexually explicit films revealed that male college students tended to trivialize rape as a crime and showed more sexually callous attitudes toward women after viewing such films (Zillmann & Bryant, 1982). Others found similar effects, but only in sexually explicit films that also contained violence (Linz,

Donnerstein, & Penrod, 1988). Zillmann and Bryant (1988) later determined that viewers (college students and nonstudent adults) of nonviolent but sexually explicit films were more likely than nonviewers to accept sexual infidelity or promiscuous behavior.

One interesting recent study by Goldstein (Sobel & Newman, 1999) found that two-thirds of children's animated feature films for the past 60 years in the United States have included at least one character who used tobacco or alcohol. Good characters were as likely as bad characters to consume drugs; moreover, presentations did not indicate that the use of the drugs was unhealthy in any way. According to Goldstein:

> Of 50 films reviewed, 34—or 68 percent—displayed at least one episode of tobacco or alcohol use. And 28 (56 percent) portrayed one or more incidences of tobacco use, including all seven films released in 1996 and 1997. . . Children are clearly seeing positive images of addictive substances that their parents, teachers and society all discourage. (McLean, 1999, p. 8)

Music Lyrics and Music Videos

Since the 1980s, many contemporary rock music lyrics and music video depictions have emphasized physical (rather than romantic) sex, violence, and sometimes, violent sexual encounters (Fedler, Hall, & Tanzi, 1982; Sherman & Etling, 1991). The preponderance of such lyrics and depictions in rock and rap music today has led some researchers to suspect a negative effect on teen health concerns, including teenage pregnancy, suicide, substance abuse, and sexual assault (Brown & Hendee, 1989; Gore, 1987). One study found that adolescents who watched a large number of rock music videos were more likely than other children to feel that premarital sex was OK (Greeson & Williams, 1986). Other studies revealed similar negative effects from heavy viewing of music videos and frequent listening to music with negative lyrics (Klein et al., 1993).

One criticism of such studies concerns the direction of causality, or even the potential absence of causality (i.e., a spurious correlation). For example, are music videos causing delinquent behavior or are delinquency-prone adolescents watching the videos? Also, studies have shown that different adolescents interpret videos differently, depending upon age, race, gender, and previous experiences and attitudes (Brown & Schulze, 1990; Walsh-Childers, 1990).

> In summary, large bodies of research point to the conclusion that the largely unintended health consequences of advertising for tobacco, alcohol, and food products are negative. Similar conclusions, although somewhat more tentative, can be drawn regarding entertainment media. (Brown & Walsh-Childers, 1994, p. 409)

Effects of Health News

Research on the effects of health-related news on personal and public health has generally been confined to two types of studies: those that measure the impact of news media as sources of health information, and those that compare public opinion regarding a health topic to news media coverage of that topic.

So far, we know very little about the health benefits or negative consequences of exposure to health-related coverage by the news media (Brown & Walsh-Childers, 1994). One exception to this statement is a study from the United Kingdom that examined the effects of exposure to positive and negative messages about alcohol in brief news items from popular magazines. Teens who read the positive messages became significantly more positive in their attitudes about alcohol, drinking, and health, and those who read the negative messages became significantly more negative in their attitudes (Guild & Lowe, 1998). This study represents one of the few attempts to examine consequences of exposure to health-related news items. Certainly more research along these lines is needed.

What we do know is that people obtain much of their health-related information from news media (Freimuth, Greenberg, DeWitt, & Romano, 1984; Simpkins & Brenner, 1984; Wallack, 1990), and this includes policy makers (Weiss, 1974). In this respect, news coverage of health matters takes on considerable significance, in that it has the potential to shape the impressions of average citizens and powerful policy makers alike.

We also know much about the *nature* of news media coverage of health issues. According to Milio (1985), broadcast and print media offer a similar, overall message when it comes to health: The way to deal with disease or medical problems is to take advantage of medical expertise or to make lifestyle changes.

Studies have shown that health news in national news media usually contains information about biomedical research, medical hardware, and drug treatments (Levin, 1979; Fisher et al., 1981). Such coverage "tends to ascribe the power to control individuals' health to medical experts using high-technology equipment" (Brown & Walsh-Childers, 1994, p. 402).

In the 1960s, 1970s, and 1980s, coverage of specific diseases such as coronary heart disease and AIDS revealed that the media often adopt a *"victim-blaming"* attitude (Fisher et al., 1981; Albert, 1986; Baker, 1986). This model places most of the responsibility for the health problem on the shoulders of the victim or patient. For example, the news media depicted AIDS patients as people who engaged in unsafe, promiscuous sexual practices, or those who shared needles with other junkies.

Another characteristic of media coverage of health issues seems to be an emphasis on reporting health concerns that affect mainstream America, or the greatest number of people in their audience (Klaidman, 1990). Stories about AIDS, for example, increased when public health practitioners began noting the increasing number of cases among nongay, monogamous individuals and other mainstream Americans (Baker, 1986; Kinsella, 1990).

The media were also found to offer little valuable information about practical matters such as symptoms for diseases, risk-reducing factors, and treatment facilities. These studies, conducted in the 1980s, examined health news in leading newspapers in the United States and Great Britain (Freimuth et al., 1984; Kristiansen & Harding, 1984).

Some evidence suggests that news coverage of health issues has a marked effect on policy makers. Positive governmental actions during the AIDS crisis of the 1980s occurred after protests by gays and nongays received coverage

(Baker, 1986), and the $1.7 billion congressional antidrug legislation passed only after much news attention to the drug problem during the summer of 1986 (Shoemaker, Wanta, & Leggett, 1989).

HEALTH COMMUNICATION CAMPAIGN EFFECTS

Health campaigns involve the purposive use of mass media for health education and behavioral change. Such campaigns have been used throughout the world with varying levels of success (Brown & Walsh-Childers, 1994).

For whatever reason, some media health campaigns have not produced long-term behavioral changes while others have; some have produced positive, intended effects whereas others have produced negative, unintended effects; and some have produced a variety of effects. For an example of the latter, a North Dakota media campaign to promote mammography screening found that although the campaign seemed to encourage women who had already been screened to have another screening, it seemed to adversely affect women who had never had a mammogram (McCaul, Jacobson, & Martinson, 1998).

You will recall from the previous chapter that adherence to the 10 principles of successful campaigns increases a campaign's chances for success. In many cases, it is likely that a failed campaign failed to meet one or more of the principles. For example, one of the principles of successful campaigns is to analyze and understand the audiences. The public health campaigns in the 1980s to raise AIDS awareness and change at-risk behaviors succeeded in raising the awareness of the general public, but they also increased *anxieties* about the disease. Moreover, these campaigns, both in Great Britain and the United States, failed to reach high-risk audiences such as drug users (Department of Health and Social Security and the Welsh Office, 1987; Snyder, Anderson, & Young, 1989). Subsequent research revealed that sometimes media interventions *are* consumed by at-risk audiences and *do* result in the desired effects—in this case more positive behavioral change (Elwood & Ataabadi, 1996; Guenther-Grey, Schnell, & Fishbein, 1995). The box offers two models aimed at persuading people to engage in healthy and risk-free behaviors.

The use of different communication channels has also produced inconsistent findings in different studies. Some studies have indicated that a campaign featuring a combination of mass media messages and interpersonal communications may be the most effective in producing desired attitudinal or behavioral changes (Flynn, 1994; Guenther-Grey, Schnell, & Fishbein, 1995; Svenkerud, Rao, & Rogers, 1999). Others, however, have shown that exposure to mass media messages alone was responsible for the changes in behaviors or attitudes (McDivitt, Zimicki, & Hornick, 1997). The differences in results may be attributable to fundamental differences in the campaigns themselves or to their adherence to the key principles for campaign success.

Different antitobacco campaigns also serve as good examples for campaigns that produced different results. A five-year antitobacco campaign in Minnesota resulted in teens reporting increased exposure to antismoking messages from the mass media, but these exposures had little effect on their beliefs

Risk Learning and Stereotype Priming Models

Pechmann (2001) offered descriptions of two different types of complementary models aimed at persuading people to engage in more healthy behaviors and avoid health risks. Risk-learning models operate with the goal of relating "new information about health risks and the behaviors that will minimize those risks," while stereotype priming models attempt to use "salient preexisting social stereotypes about people who do or do not behave as advocated" (p. 189) for the purpose of persuading people to avoid behaviors that cause health risks. Risk-learning models are based on protection motivation theory, which means they work to motivate behaviors that promote and protect good health. Four types of messages have been shown to increase a person's likelihood to engage in protective behavior. These include messages that (1) show the severe disease consequences of engaging in risky behavior (risk severity), (2) show how easy it is to contract the disease (risk vulnerability), (3) show how protective behaviors reduce chances for or prevent or cure the disease (response efficacy), and (4) show effectiveness when engaging in protective behavior (self-efficacy). The stereotype priming model depends upon a priming stimulus and preexisting links between a particular social group and particular behavior traits. For example, in a campaign that discourages smoking, cigarette smokers might be presented using negative stereotypical traits (e.g., having yellow teeth or smelling like tobacco), while nonsmokers would be shown with positive stereotypical traits (e.g., enjoying good health). According to Pechmann:

Risk-learning models do not require message recipients to have any prior knowledge of the substantive message content. The main goal is, in fact, to impart knowledge where it is lacking. By comparison, the stereotype priming model requires the use of messages that reflect people's prior stereotypes. In other words, the prime must mirror or correspond to a belief that already resides in long-term memory. Priming merely serves to bring a preexisting stereotype to the forefront of memory. (p. 195)

Source: Pechmann, C. (2001). A comparison of health communication models: Risk learning versus stereotype priming, *Media Psychology, 3,* 189–210.

---

about the health dangers of tobacco or on their smoking behaviors (Murray, Prokhorov, & Harty, 1994). On the other hand, a study by Flynn and his colleagues (1994), also conducted over several years, revealed that media interventions *in addition to* school smoking prevention programs resulted in rather positive behavioral effects. Students from two communities participated in smoking prevention programs at their schools. One group received mass media interventions in addition to the school program, and over time, the behavior of this group showed more positive results (Flynn et al., 1994).

Another study revealed that a different type of combination approach—in this case, a media antismoking campaign together with a cigarette sales tax—proved most effective in reducing cigarette consumption. The researchers examined cigarette sales from 1980 to 1992 and found that both tactics resulted in several million packs fewer being sold. The level of the effects varied, depending on the amount of the tax and the amount spent on the media campaign (Hu, Sung, & Keeler, 1995).

One health campaign approach that has regained attention in recent years is the scare tactic or fear appeal. Such campaigns targeted against smokers in Massachusetts and in Australia have resulted in much public attention (measured by phone calls to antismoking counseling services and phone interviews with those who saw the ads), but overall effects from these campaigns are not yet known. In Massachusetts, a campaign featured commercials showing a 29-year-old mother battling emphysema and awaiting a second lung transplant (Worden & Flynn, 1999).

Other findings suggest that the use of fear appeals in health communication campaigns has been rather successful (Hale & Dillard, 1995). Quantitative reviews of fear-appeal research have shown that such appeals are persuasive (Boster & Mongeau, 1984; Mongeau, 1998; Sutton, 1982). According to Hale and Dillard (1995):

> The most recent of the meta-analyses, and by virtue of including several newer studies perhaps the best of the lot, concluded that perceived fear and the attitude of the target were positively correlated, as were perceived fear and behavior. It is clear from these findings that fear-arousing message content is persuasive and that abandoning the use of fear would be to abandon an effective persuasive strategy . . . [T]he quantitative reviews also demonstrate that the relationship between fear and persuasion is a complex one. (p. 70)

Media health campaigns have sometimes been criticized for their "victim blaming" approaches (similar to victim blaming in news media coverage of health issues). These campaigns offer individuals information that will allow them to take responsibility for their health by changing their lifestyles or going for health screenings. Critics argue that victims cannot take full blame for their actions when they have been bombarded since childhood with advertisements or media portrayals that feature the use of unhealthy products such as cigarettes or alcoholic beverages (Wallack, 1989).

Finally, certain media channels used in a campaign have characteristic benefits over other media channels. Health communication planners must assess the advantages and disadvantages of different media when selecting channels for the delivery of their messages. We know a great deal about the various characteristics of different media choices (see Table 16.1). What we know *empirically* about the effectiveness of various media channels in health campaigns remains rather sketchy, but research continues to provide more illumination. Schooler, Chaffee, Flora, and Roser (1998) looked at five channels in a risk-reduction campaign: booklets, tip sheets, television programs, newspaper messages, and TV public service announcements (PSAs). They found that newspaper messages had the most impact upon audiences, followed by booklets, television PSAs, tip sheets, and then television programs.

OTHER TYPES OF MEDIATED HEALTH EDUCATION

Brown and Walsh-Childers (1994, 2001) identified two new educational strategies that have arisen in recent years as alternatives to traditional health campaigns. These strategies include *edutainment,* the implanting of health messages in entertainment content, and *media advocacy,* activities by public health agents that focus mass media attention on health issues at the social or public policy level, rather than at the individual level.

Table 16.1   Characteristics of Mass Media Channels

Television

- Potentially largest/widest range of audiences, but not always at times when public service announcements (PSAs) are most likely to be broadcast.
- Deregulation ended government oversight of stations' broadcast of PSAs, public affairs programming.
- Opportunity to include health messages by means of news broadcasts, public affairs/interview shows, dramatic programming.
- Visual as well as audio make emotional appeals possible; easier to demonstrate a behavior.
- Can reach low-income and other audiences not as likely to turn to health sources for help.
- Passive consumption by viewer; viewers must be present when message is aired; less than full attention likely. Message may be obscured by commercial "clutter."
- PSAs can be expensive to produce and distribute. Feature placement requires contacts and may be time consuming.

Radio

- Various formats offer potential for more audience targeting than television (e.g., teenagers by way of rock stations). May reach fewer people than TV.
- Deregulation ended government oversight of stations' broadcast of PSAs, public affairs programming.
- Opportunity for direct audience involvement through call-in shows.
- Audio alone may make messages less intrusive.
- Can reach audiences who do not use the health care system.
- Generally passive consumption; exchange with audience possible but target audience must be there when aired.
- Live copy is very flexible and inexpensive; PSAs must fit station format.
- Feature placement requires contacts and may be time consuming.

Magazines

- Can target segments of public more specifically (e.g., young women, people with an interest in health).
- No requirement for PSA use; PSAs more difficult to place.
- Can explain more complex health issues, behaviors.
- Print may lend itself to more factual, detailed, rational message delivery.
- Audience has chance to clip, reread, contemplate material.
- Permits active consultation; may pass on; read at reader's convenience.
- Public service ads are inexpensive to produce; ad or article placement may be time consuming.

Newspapers

- Can reach broad audiences rapidly.
- PSAs virtually nonexistent.
- Can convey health news/breakthroughs more thoroughly than TV or radio and faster than magazines; feature placement possible.
- Easy audience access to in-depth issue coverage is possible.
- Short life of newspaper limits rereading, sharing with others.
- Small papers may take public service ads; coverage demands a newsworthy item.

Source: Making Health Communication Programs Work: A Planner's Guide, NIH Publication #92-1493, U.S. Department of Health and Human Services, Public Health Service, National Institutes of Health, Office of Cancer Communications, National Cancer Institute, Copyright © April 1992. Cited in S. N. Di Lima (Manager) and C. S. Schust (Ed.) (1997). *Community health education and promotion: A guide to program design and evaluation* (p. 288). Gaithersburg, MD: Aspen.

Edutainment

Many of the daytime soap operas occasionally contain embedded health messages. Steamy love scenes sometimes end with the man reaching for a condom. Some soap characters contract AIDS and, as they learn about the disease, so does the audience. However, such instances of edutainment and their effects on audiences have not been studied extensively.

Media Advocacy

Media advocacy is an innovative use of mass media to promote public health by focusing attention on public policies related to health matters. Media advocacy campaigns differ in several ways from other types of media communication campaigns:

> First, as primarily an advocacy strategy it relies on coalition building and community organization for its base of support. Traditional strategies tend to focus on putting the health message out from a centralized point. Media advocacy, on the other hand, seeks to provide community groups with skills to communicate their own story in their own words.
>
> Second, agenda setting and framing are the key theoretical perspectives that media advocates use.
>
> Third, traditional strategies tend to see individuals and groups as parts of the audience to be addressed in one-way communication . . . Media advocacy treats the individual or group members as potential advocates who can use their energy, skills, and other resources to promote social change.
>
> Fourth, media advocacy develops healthy public policies rather than health messages.
>
> Fifth, media advocacy shifts the focus from changing the individual to changing the environment in which the individual acts.
>
> Finally, media advocacy moves the focus for media access from the public affairs desk to the news desk. (Wallack, Dorfman, Jernigan, & Themba, 1993, pp. 74–75)

A good example of a successful media advocacy campaign was the effort of the African-American community in Philadelphia to stop RJ Reynolds Nabisco (RJR) from test-marketing a new cigarette in an African-American section of Philadelphia. In the early 1990s RJR planned to launch the menthol cigarette "Uptown" to African Americans in Philadelphia, home of the famous Uptown Theater. After members of the community learned of the tobacco company's plans, the Coalition Against Uptown Cigarettes formed and used local mass media to mobilize their community and halt the test marketing. When the national media came calling, the coalition delayed responding to questions and completely turned down other invitations for exposure due to the local focus of the issue and the need to gain the support of local organizations (Wallack, Dorfman, Jernigan, & Themba, 1993).

Other Important Tools

In addition to media advocacy and edutainment, researchers have also identified other important tools for health education that either use mass media or focus on proper mass media use: journalism education; critical viewing skills or media literacy training; and interactive communication technologies. Print and broadcast journalism can be used to educate audiences about the prevention of particular health problems (Wilde, 1993). Also, teaching critical viewing skills to youngsters may lessen the negative health effects of particular media portrayals (Davies, 1993). A study of third-graders found that media literacy training had both immediate and delayed effects on the youngsters' decisions about alcohol (Austin & Johnson, 1997). Finally, new, interactive technologies may be used to achieve health-promotion goals for a variety of programs or interventions, such as disease management or maintenance of the highest possible quality of life (Street, Gold, & Manning, 1997).

RECENT RESEARCH AND FUTURE TRENDS

Recent research on the effects of mass mediated messages on individual and public health has continued to investigate unintended and intended messages from health-related communications and their negative and positive effects. In recent years, the Internet has become a source of health information to millions, and several studies have examined the effects on individual health and health policy. Research has shown that both the healthy and the chronically ill use the Internet to find health-related information (Cain, Mittman, Sarasohn-Kahn, & Wayne, 2000), and that many seek online sources to tell them about prescription drugs (Health on the Net, 1999). Research has also revealed that many teens find answers to sexual questions on the Internet because of its accessibility,

Mixed Effects of Access to Health Information Online

In mid-1999, if you typed "cancer treatment" into the Internet search engine Infoseek, almost 1.5 million entries popped up. These entries ranged from chemotherapy information and self-help guides to cancer support groups to directories of leading medical centers to herbal medicines and other alternative treatments not always condoned by the medical establishment.

Patients now have access to an enormous amount of health-related information with the simple press of a few buttons, but health care providers have mixed opinions about the effects of this new means of patient empowerment. They see the benefits of online support groups for those suffering from the same horrible diseases, but they also fear that online patients may be locating too much incorrect and even potentially harmful information.

A 1999 Harris poll revealed some 70 million Americans went online during the previous year to ferret out health-related information. About half of these people were searching for information about diseases such as cancer. Websites related to health matters are estimated to exceed 15,000.

Sources: Martin, J. P. (1999). A world of support; The Web is changing medicine for doctors and patients. But is this leading to better health care? *Washington Post*, 31 August, p. Z10; Miller, L. and Davis, R. (1999, 14 July). Net empowering patients: Millions scour the Web to find medical info, *USA Today*, p. 1A; Bly, L. (1999, 14 July). A network of support; Patients find emotional, practical advice—and each other, *USA Today*, p. 1D; Online health: number of users continues to grow (1999, 5 August), *Health Line*, NEXIS Online Library: NEWS, File: CURNWS.

affordability, and the anonymity it offers (Cooper, 1998; Wilson, 2000). Some seekers of health information on the Internet become involved in online support groups (Kassirer, 2000), and others make lifestyle changes or encourage others to seek medical attention as a result of the information they collect online (Cyber Dialogue, 2000).

The Internet promises to be a primary point of focus in the future for media effects researchers interested in health-related messages. For example, researchers will watch closely to see if the tobacco and alcohol industries turn to online marketing to reach young, potential smokers and drinkers. Other topics of interest will include the effects of advertising nonprescription and prescription drugs, the relationship between media messages and obesity, eating disorders, drug abuse, and mental health issues (Brown & Walsh-Childers, in press).

In their discussion of the effects of health-related media messages, Brown and Walsh-Childers pointed out the focus of future research.

> The media's impact on health beliefs and behaviors at both the personal and public level is becoming increasingly sophisticated and theoretically based, moving away from only content analyses to more complicated longitudinal designs that put media exposure into the context of individuals' lives.

Also, future research projects will probably examine the Internet as a source of health messages, and focus on the effectiveness of media literacy programs so that children and adults have the tools they need to understand and analyze media messages with a critical eye. Media literacy is especially useful in diminishing harmful effects from negative media messages, such as embedded health messages or subtle advertisements for harmful products within programs or motion pictures.

SUMMARY

Mass media messages often have considerable impact on personal and public health. As with other types of media content, effects from health-related messages may be positive, negative, intended, or unintended in nature.

The goal of the media health communication campaign is to present specific messages, designed by health and communication experts, which have intentional, positive, health-related effects on audiences. Other sources of health-related messages in mass media—news reports, entertainment programs, and advertisements—do not always produce positive results.

Research on the effects of commercial product advertising has focused primarily upon the health of individuals who use the products. Health effects from cigarette, liquor, and food ads have been the focus of numerous studies; most have found that such ads result in negative effects on individual and public health.

Entertainment portrayals sometimes have rather powerful effects upon the health of audience members. Most studies in this area have concentrated on television programs, films, music videos, and musical lyrics, establishing links between entertainment portrayals and nutrition, smoking, alcohol consumption, drug abuse, and sexual activity.

People, including policy makers, obtain much of their health-related information from news media. In this respect, news coverage of health matters takes on much significance, because it has the potential to shape the impressions of average citizens and powerful policy makers alike. Some news coverage adopts a "victim-blaming" attitude which places most responsibility for the health problem on the shoulders of the victim or patient. Most of the news reports on health issues focus on concerns that affect mainstream America.

Health campaigns involve the purposive use of mass media for health education and behavioral change. For whatever reason, some media health campaigns have not produced long-term behavioral changes while others have; some have produced positive, intended effects while others have produced negative, unintended effects; and some have produced a variety of effects. The appeal to fear has a persuasive power in communication campaigns. Some media campaigns have been criticized for using victim-blaming approaches. Certain media channels used in a campaign have characteristic benefits over other media channels. Health communication planners must assess the advantages and disadvantages of the different media when selecting channels for the delivery of their messages.

Other types of educational strategies that serve as alternatives to traditional health campaigns include edutainment, media advocacy campaigns, journalism education, critical viewing skills instruction, and use of interactive communication technologies.

REFERENCES

Aitken, P. P., Leathar, D. S., & O'Hagan, F. J. (1985). Children's perceptions of advertisements for cigarettes. *Social Science Medicine, 21*, 785–797.

Aitken, P. P., Leathar, D. S., & Squair, S. I. (1986). Children's awareness of cigarette brand sponsorship of sports and games in the UK. *Health Education Research, 1*, 203–211.

Albert, E. (1986). Illness and deviance: The response of the press to AIDS. In D. A. Feldman & T. M. Johnson (Eds.), *The social dimensions of AIDS: Method and theory* (pp. 163–178). New York: Praeger.

Atkin, C. (1990). Effects of televised alcohol messages on teenage drinking patterns. *Journal of Adolescent Health Care, 11*, 10–24.

Atkin, C., Hocking, J., & Block, M. (1984). Teenage drinking: Does advertising make a difference? *Journal of Communication, 34*(2), 157–167.

Austin, E. W., & Johnson, K. K. (1997). Immediate and delayed effects of media literacy training on third graders' decision making for alcohol. *Health Communication, 9*, 323–349.

Austin, E. W., & Nach-Ferguson, B. (1995). Sources and influences of young school-aged children's general and brand-specific knowledge about alcohol. *Health Communication, 7*, 1–20.

Backer, T. E., Rogers, E. M., & Sopory, P. (1992). *Designing health communication campaigns: What works?* Newbury Park, CA: Sage.

Baker, A. J. (1986). The portrayal of AIDS in the media: An analysis of articles in the *New York Times*. In D. G. Feldman & T. M. Johnson (Eds.), *The social dimensions of AIDS: Method and theory* (pp. 179–194). New York: Praeger.

BASIL, M. D,, SCHOOLER, C., ALTMAN, D. G., SLATER, M., ALBRIGHT, C. L., & MACCOBY, N. (1991). How cigarettes are advertised in magazines: Special messages for special markets. *Health Communication, 3*, 75–91.

BLOOM, P. N., HOGAN, J. E., AND BLAZING, J. (1997). Sports promotion and teen smoking and drinking: An exploratory study. *American Journal of Health Behavior, 21*, 100–109.

BOSTER, F. J., & MONGEAU, P. A. (1984). Fear-arousing persuasive messages. In R. Bostrom (Ed.), *Communication yearbook* (Vol. 8, pp. 330–375). Newbury Park, CA: Sage.

BREED, W., & DEFOE, J. R. (1984, June). Drinking and smoking on television, 1950–1982. *Journal of Public Health Policy*, 257–270.

BROWN, J. D., & HENDEE, W. R. (1989). Adolescents and their music: Insights into the health of adolescents. *Journal of the American Medical Association, 62*, 1659–1663.

BROWN, J. D., & NEWCOMER, S. (1991). Television viewing and adolescents' sexual behavior. *Journal of Homosexuality, 21*(1–2), 77–91.

BROWN, J. D., & SCHULZE, L. (1990). The effects of race, gender and fandom on interpretations of Madonna's music videos. *Journal of Communication, 40*(2), 88–102.

BROWN, J. D., & WALSH-CHILDERS, K. (1994). Effects of media on personal and public health. In J. Bryant & D. Zillmann (Eds.), *Media effects: Advances in theory and research.* Hillsdale, NJ: Erlbaum.

BROWN, J. D., & WALSH-CHILDERS, K. (in press). Effects of media on personal and public health. In J. Bryant & D. Zillmann (Eds.), *Media effects: Advances in theory and research* (2nd ed.). Mahwah, NJ: Erlbaum.

CAIN, M. M., MITTMAN, R., SARASOHN-KAHN, J., AND WAYNE, J. C. (2000, August). *Health e-People: The online consumer experience, 5-year forecast.* Oakland, CA: California HealthCare Foundation. [Online]. Available: http://admin.chcf.org/documents/ehealth/HealthEPeople.pdf.

CHAPMAN, S., & EGGER, G. (1980). Forging an identity for the non-smoker: The use of myth in promotion. *International Journal of Health Education, 23*, 2–16.

CHAPMAN, S., & FITZGERALD, B. (1982). Brand preference and advertising recall in adolescent smokers: Some implications for health promotion. *American Journal of Public Health, 72*, 491–494.

CLANCY-HEPBURN, K., HICKEY, A. A., & NEVILL, G. (1974). Children's behavior responses to TV food advertisements. *Journal of Nutrition Education, 7*, 93–96.

COOPER, A. (1998). Sexuality and the Internet: Surfing into the new millennium. *CyberPsychology & Behavior, 1*, 187–193.

CYBER DIALOGUE (2000). Cybercitizen Health 2000. Cited in Kassirer, J. P. (2000). Patients, physicians, and the Internet. *Health Affairs, 19*(6), 115–123.

DAVIES, J. (1993). The impact of the mass media upon the health of early adolescents. *Journal of Health Education, 24*, S28–S35.

DAVIS, R. M. (1987). Current trends in cigarette advertising and marketing. *New England Journal of Medicine, 316*, 725–732.

DAVIS, R. M., & KENDRICK, J. S. (1989). The Surgeon General's warnings in outdoor cigarette advertising. *Journal of the American Medical Association, 61*(1), 90–94.

DEFOE, J. R., BREED, W., & BREED, L. A. (1983). Drinking on television: A five-year study. *Journal of Drug Education, 13*(1), 25–38.

DEPARTMENT OF HEALTH AND SOCIAL SECURITY AND THE WELSH OFFICE. (1987). *AIDS: Monitoring response to the public education campaign, Feb. 1986–Feb. 1987.* London: H. M. Stationery Office.

DIETZ, W. H. (1990). You are what you eat—what you eat is what you are. *Journal of Adolescent Health Care, 11*, 76–81.

DIETZ, W. H., & GORTMAKER, S. L. (1985). Do we fatten our children at the TV set? Television viewing and obesity in children and adolescents. *Pediatrics, 75*(5), 807–812.

ELWOOD, W. N., & ATAABADI, A. N. (1996) Tuned in and turned off: Out-of-treatment injection drug and crack users' response to media intervention campaigns. *Communication Reports, 9,* 49–59.

FAT-PHOBIA IN THE FIJIS: TV-THIN IS IN. (1999, 31 May). *Newsweek, 70.* Article quotes Dr. Anne Becker, research director at the Harvard Eating Disorders Center, in her report to the American Psychiatric Association.

FEDLER, F., HALL, J., & TANZI, L. A. (1982, Spring–Fall). Popular songs emphasize sex, de-emphasize romance. *Mass Communication Research,* 10–15.

FISCHER, J., GANDY, O. H., JR., & JANUS, N. Z. (1981). The role of popular media in defining sickness and health. In E. G. McAnany, J. Schnitman, & N. Z. Janus (Eds.), *Communication and social structure: Critical studies in mass media research* (pp. 240–257). New York: Praeger.

FISCHER, P. M., RICHARDS, J. W., BERMAN, E. J., & KRUGMAN, D. M. (1989). Recall and eye tracking study of adolescents viewing tobacco advertisements. *Journal of the American Medical Association, 261*(1), 84–89.

FLYNN, B. S., WORDEN, J. K., SECKER-WALKER, R. H., PIRIE, P. L., & BADGER, G. J. (1994). Mass media and school interventions for cigarette smoking prevention: Effects 2 years after completion. *American Journal of Public Health, 84,* 1148–1150.

FREIMUTH, V. S., GREENBERG, R. H., DEWITT, J., & ROMANO, R. M. (1984). Covering cancer: Newspaper and the public interest. *Journal of Communication, 34*(1), 62–73.

FREIMUTH, V. S., HAMMOND, S. L. & STEIN, J. A. (1988). Health advertising: Prevention for profit. *American Journal of Public Health, 78*(5), 557–561.

GERBNER, G., GROSS, L., MORGAN, M., & SIGNORIELLI, N. (1981). Health and medicine on television. *New England Journal of Medicine, 305*(15), 901–904.

GOLDBERG, M. E., GORN, G. J., & GIBSON, W. (1978). TV messages for snack and breakfast foods: Do they influence children's preferences? *Journal of Consumer Research, 5,* 73–81.

GORE, T. (1987). *Raising PG kids in an X-rated society.* Nashville: Abingdon Press.

GOLDSTEIN, A. O., FISCHER, P. M., RICHARDS, J. W., & CRETEN, D. (1987). Relationship between high school student smoking and recognition of cigarette advertisements. *Journal of Pediatrics, 110,* 488–491.

GOLDSTEIN, A. O., SOBEL, R. A., & NEWMAN, G. R. (1999). Medicine in the media: Tobacco and alcohol use in g-rated children's animated films. *Journal of the American Medical Association, 281,* 1131–1136.

GREENBERG, B. S. (1981). Smoking, drugging and drinking in top rated TV series. *Journal of Drug Education, 11*(3), 227–233.

GREENBERG, B. S., BROWN, J. D., & BUERKEL-ROTHFUSS, N. (1991). *Media, sex and the adolescent.* Norwood, NJ: Ablex.

GREESON, L. E., & WILLIAMS, R. A. (1986). Social implications of music videos for youth. *Youth & Society, 18*(2), 177–189.

GUENTHER-GREY, C. A., SCHNELL, D., & FISHBEIN, M. (1995). Sources of HIV/AIDS information among female sex traders. *Health Education Research, 10,* 385–390.

GUILD, T., & LOWE, G. (1998). Media messages and alcohol education: A school-based study. *Psychological Reports, 82,* 124–126.

HALE, J. L., & DILLARD, J. P. (1995). Fear appeals in health promotion campaigns: Too much, too little, or just right? In E. Maibach & R. L. Parrott (Eds.), *Designing health messages: Approaches from communication theory and public health practice.* Thousand Oaks, CA: Sage.

HAWTON, K., SIMKIN, S., DEEKS, J. J., O'CONNOR, S., KEEN, A., ALTMAN, D. G., PHILO, G., BULSTRODE, C. (1999, 10 April). Effects of a drug overdose in a television drama on presentations to hospital for self-poisoning: Time series and questionnaire study. *British Medical Journal, 318,* 972.

HEALTH ON THE NET FOUNDATION. (1999, October–November). 5th HON survey on the evolution of Internet use for health purposes. [Online]. Available: http:222 .hon.ch/ Survey/ResultsSummary_oct_nov99.html

HU, T-W., SUNG, H-Y, & KEELER, T. E. (1995). Reducing cigarette consumption in California: Tobacco taxes vs. an anti-smoking media campaign. *American Journal of Public Health, 85,* 1218–1222.

KASSIRER, J. P. (2000). Patients, physicians, and the Internet. *Health Affairs, 19*(6), 115–123.

KAUFMAN, L. (1980). Prime-time nutrition. *Journal of Communication, 30*(3), 37–46.

KINSELLA, J. (1990). *Covering the plague: AIDS and the American media.* New Brunswick, NJ: Rutgers University Press.

KLAIDMAN, S. (1990). Roles and responsibilities of journalists. In C. Atkin & L. Wallack (Eds.), *Mass communication and public health: Complexities and conflicts* (pp. 60–70). Newbury Park, CA: Sage.

KLEIN, J. O., BROWN, J. D., WALSH-CHILDERS, K., OLIVERI, J., PORTER, C., & DYKERS, C. (1993, July). Adolescents' risky behavior and mass media use. *Pediatrics, 92,* 24–32.

KOHN, P. M., & SMART, R. G. (1984). The impact of television advertising on alcohol consumption: An experiment. *Journal of Studies on Alcohol, 45*(4), 295–301.

KRISTIANSEN, C. M., & HARDING, C. M. (1984). Mobilization of health behavior by the press in Britain. *Journalism Quarterly, 61*(2), 364–370, 398.

KUNKEL, D. (1999). Results of study for Henry Kaiser Family Foundation. Cited in too much TV sex, not enough education. *Television Digest,* February 15, 1999, [Online]. NEXIS: News Library, CURNWS File.

KUNKEL, D., COPE-FARRAR, K., BIELY, E., FARINOLA, W. J. M., & DONNERSTEIN, E. (2001*). Sex on TV2: A biennial report to the Kaiser Family Foundation.* Santa Barbara: University of California, Santa Barbara Press.

LEVIN, A. (Ed.). (1979). *Focus on health: Issues and events of 1978 from the New York Times Information Bank.* New York: Arno Press.

LEVY, A., & STOKES, R. (1987). Effects of a health promotion advertising campaign on sales of ready to eat cereals. *Public Health Reports, 102*(4), 398–403.

LINZ, D. G., DONNERSTEIN, E., & PENROD, S. (1988). The effects of long-term exposure to violent and sexually degrading depictions of women. *Journal of Personality and Social Psychology, 55*(5), 758–768.

LOUIS HARRIS AND ASSOCIATES. (1987). *Sexual material on American network television during the 1987–88 season.* New York: Planned Parenthood Federation of America.

LOWRY, D. T., & TOWLES, D. E. (1989). Soap opera portrayals of sex, contraception, and sexually transmitted diseases. *Journal of Communication, 39*(2), 76–83.

MCCAUL, K. D., JACOBSON, K., & MARTINSON, B. (1998). The effects of state-wide media campaign on mammography screening. *Journal of Applied Social Psychology, 28,* 504–515.

MCDIVITT, J. A., ZIMICKI, S., & HORNICK, R. C. (1997). Explaining the impact of a communication campaign to change vaccination knowledge and coverage in the Philippines. *Health Communication, 9,* 95–118.

MCLEAN, J. (1999, 31 March). Cartoon capers grow up in smoke; Tooned in: Are your children picking up bad habits from Cruella and Co? Daily Record, [Online]. NEXIS: News Library, CURNWS. Article quotes Dr. Adam Goldstein's findings, presented at an American Medical Association meeting in New York and reported in the *Journal of the American Medical Association.*

MILIO, N. (1985). Health education = health instruction + health news: Media experiences in the United States, Finland, Australia, and England. In J. D. Brown & E. Rubinstein (Eds*.), The media, social science, and social policy for children* (pp. 118–236). Norwood, NJ: Ablex.

MONGEAU, P. A. (1998). Fear-arousing persuasive messages: A meta-analysis revisited. In M. Allen & R. Preiss (Eds.), *Persuasion: Advances through meta-analysis*. Thousand Oaks, CA: Sage.

MURRAY, D. M., PROKHOROV, A. V., & HARTY, K. C. (1994). Effects of a statewide anti-smoking campaign on mass media messages and smoking beliefs. *Preventive Medicine, 23*, 54–60.

O'CONNELL, D. L., ALEXANDER, H. M., DOBSON, A. J., LLOYD, D. M., HARDES, G. R., SPRINGTHORPE, J. J., & LEEDER, S. R. (1981). Cigarette smoking and drug use in school-children: 11 factors associated with smoking. *International Journal of Epidemiology, 10*, 223–231.

SANDMAN, P. M. (1976). Medicine and mass communication: An agenda for physicians. *Annals of Internal Medicine, 85*, 378–383.

SCHOOLER, C., CHAFFEE, S. H., FLORA, J. A., & ROSER, C. (1998). Health campaign channels: Tradeoffs among reach, specificity, and impact. *Human Communication Research, 24*, 410–432.

SHERMAN, B. L., & ETLING, L. W. (1991). Perceiving and processing music television. In J. Bryant & D. Zillmann (Eds.), *Responding to the screen: Reception and reaction processes* (pp. 373–388). Hillsdale, NJ: Erlbaum.

SHOEMAKER, P. J., WANTA, W., & LEGGETT, D. (1989). Drug coverage and public opinion, 1972–1986. In P. Shoemaker (Ed.), *Communication campaigns about drugs: Government, media and the public* (pp. 67–80). Hillsdale, NJ: Erlbaum.

SIGNORIELLI, N. (1990). Television and health: Images and impact. In C. Atkin & L. Wallack (Eds.), *Mass communication and public health* (pp. 96–113). Newbury Park, CA: Sage.

SIGNORIELLI, N. (1993). *Mass media images and impact on health: A sourcebook.* Westport, CT.: Greenwood Press.

SIMPKINS, J. D., & BRENNER, D. J. (1984). Mass media communication and health. In B. Dervin & M. J. Voigt (Eds.), *Progress in communication sciences* (pp. 275–297). Norwood, NJ: Ablex.

SNYDER, L. B., ANDERSON, K., & YOUNG, D. (1989, May). *AIDS communication, risk, knowledge and behavior change: A preliminary investigation in Connecticut.* Paper presented to the International Communication Association, San Francisco.

STREET, JR., R. L., GOLD, W. R., & MANNING, T. R. (Eds.) (1997). *Health promotion and interactive technology: Theoretical applications and future directions.* Mahwah, NJ: Erlbaum.

SUTTON, S. R. (1982). Fear-arousing communication: A critical examination of theory and research. In J. R. Eiser (Ed.), *Social psychology and behavioral medicine* (pp. 303–337). London: John Wiley.

SVENKERUD, P. J., RAO, N., & ROGERS, E. M. (1999). Mass media effects through interpersonal communication: The role of "Twende na Wakati" on the adoption of HIV/AIDS prevention in Tanzania. In W. N. Elwood (Ed.), *Power in the blood: A handbook on AIDS, politics, and communication.* Mahwah, NJ: Erlbaum.

WALLACK, L. (1989). Mass communication and health promotion: A critical perspective. In R. E. Rice & C. K. Atkin (Eds.), *Public communication campaigns* (2nd ed., pp. 353–367). Newbury Park, CA: Sage.

WALLACK, L. (1990). Improving health promotion: Media advocacy and social marketing approaches. In C. Atkin & L. Wallack (Eds.), *Mass communication and public health: Complexities and conflicts* (pp. 147–163). Newbury Park, CA: Sage.

WALLACK, L., DORFMAN, L., JERNIGAN, D., THEMBA, M. (1993). *Media advocacy and public health: Power for prevention.* Newbury Park, CA: Sage.

WALSH-CHILDERS, K. (1990). *Adolescents' sexual schemas and interpretations of male-female relationships in a soap opera.* Unpublished doctoral dissertation, University of North Carolina, Chapel Hill.

WEISS, C. H. (1974). What America's leaders read. *Public Opinion Quarterly, 38*, 1–21.

WILDE, G. J. (1993). Effects of mass media communications on health and safety habits: An overview of issues and evidence. *Addiction, 88*, 983–996.

WILSON, S. N. (2000). Raising the voices of teens to change sex education. *SIECUS Report, 28*(6), 20–24.

WORDEN, J., & FLYNN, B. (1999, 2 January). Shock to stop? Massachusetts' antismoking campaign. *British Medical Journal, 318*. [Online]. NEXIS: News Library, CURNWS File.

ZILLMANN, D., & BRYANT, J. (1982). Pornography, sexual callousness and the trivialization of rape. *Journal of Communication, 32*(4), 10–21.

ZILLMANN, D., & BRYANT, J. (1988). Effects of prolonged consumption of pornography on family values. *Journal of Family Issues, 9*(4), 518–544.

Advertising Effects

We live in a country in which mass media receive most of their support from advertising revenue. As a result, we are bombarded with advertisements every day of our lives. Whether it is billboards, newspapers, magazines, radio, television, the Internet, the side of a bus, or some other conspicuous location, ads scream at us to try particular products or services.

When you consider the enormous sums of money spent on advertising each year in the United States, it probably comes as no surprise that a significant amount of research in various disciplines has been devoted to the effects of advertising messages. After all, advertisers want to make sure that they are getting their money's worth. In addition to advertising researchers, psychologists, marketing and consumer researchers, and others are interested in researching the effects of advertising on media users.

As with other research domains, some advertising research has been *theoretical* while other research has been *applied* in nature. Theoretical studies, conducted mostly by scholars in traditional disciplines, use a variety of research methods to test hypotheses and advance knowledge in the field. The primary purpose of theoretical research is to gain a richer understanding of a phenomenon, in this case, the role and effects of advertising for individuals and society. Applied research also employs a variety of research techniques to answer questions of practical value to advertising practitioners and media professionals.

Considering the connection between advertising and persuasion, researchers in mass communication have been very interested in studying the effects of advertising. The focus of these researchers has been either on the processes involved whenever advertising media effects occur or on the differences in effects produced by the media context in which the advertisement is embedded. Media context refers to program type, whether humorous, sad, serious, riveting, and so forth.

This chapter explores the various effects on individuals (rather than a group or culture) of reading, watching, or listening to advertising messages, and the individual's processing of those messages. We first examine advertising as part of the current media environment, then we review past research to discover what has been learned about the ways that individual audience members react to ads in various media. We look at particular characteristics of individuals, such as their moods, that cause them to use and react to media and advertising in different ways. We also explore the importance of media context to the success of the advertisement, and we examine other factors, such as repetition or the frequency of exposure, and comprehension and miscomprehension of advertising messages, as influences on effects. Finally, we take a look at recent research in the field and trends for future research.

ADVERTISING IN TODAY'S MEDIA ENVIRONMENT

A **medium** can be defined as "any transmission vehicle or device through which communication may occur" (Stewart & Ward, 1994, p. 317). Advertising media include the various types of mass media such as television, radio, and print sources. Advertising differs considerably from personal selling, which employs the medium of interpersonal communication.

Today's media environment offers an abundance of choices for advertisers. In recent years, the increased volume of advertisements in various types of mass media has caused some advertisers to select less conventional media. The segmentation of audiences and the personalized nature of today's media provide advertisers with new vehicles to reach specialized audiences. New media sources such as shopping networks on television and information services on the Internet have provided viable alternatives to the standard, 10-second commercial slot. Computer-assisted methodologies and specialized databases have caused a boom in telemarketing, which (although often annoying to recipients) allows advertisers to reach a more specific audience than would be available through traditional mass media sources. Direct mailings to targeted audiences also reach people with similar characteristics. The proliferation of television channels and increased knowledge about each channel's audiences also give advertisers access to large numbers of people with similar and desirable demographics. Additionally, some advertisers have opted to sponsor special events with wide reach, such as the immensely popular Super Bowl, the World Series, or the Olympic Games.

The matching of demographics with particular media has evolved considerably through the years. Early studies showed that the use of certain media was highly related to a person's level of educational attainment. Berelson and Steiner (1964) found that people with less education tended to read less, listen to radio more, and watch television more than their better-educated peers, whereas those with higher levels of education preferred print media to broadcast media. The increasing availability of computerized demographic information allows today's advertisers to know more than ever before about particular audience characteristics. The many activities and attributes of millions of consumers are recorded and matched to their likelihood for using particular media or engaging in certain purchasing behaviors.

Through the years, research has indicated that a person's attitudes with regard to a particular media product within a particular medium influence both media use and message effects. For example, an important study in 1962 measured differences in brand quality and preference ratings among readers of three different magazines, *McCall's, Look,* and *Life.* Readers perceived that products

Advertising messages bombard us daily.
Source: © *CORBIS*

appearing in *McCall's* were of much higher quality than the *same* products in *Look* and *Life* ads (Politz Research, 1962). Clearly, the individual's attitude about particular magazines made the difference.

New media choices continue to appear. In the future, as these choices increase, researchers will continue to examine individuals' attitudes regarding these media and the advertising messages they carry. Such information will be especially valuable to advertisers.

RESEARCH TRADITION

Throughout the history of media effects research, some people have believed that mass media messages have direct and powerful effects upon audiences, whereas others have held the view that direct mass media effects are rather limited. Research in the 1940s and after emphasized the importance of interpersonal communications among audience members in modifying media effects. The *transactional* model recognized that the presence of any number of factors—specific characteristics of the sender, the message, the transmitter or channel, the audience as a group, and the individual audience member—could mitigate the strength of media effects.

As you will recall from Chapter 10, "Persuasion," the elaboration likelihood model offers a modern take on the transactional model. The potential of a media message to persuade an audience member depends on myriad factors, such as an individual's mood and predispositions, other individual character- istics, or the likelihood that a message will be thought through carefully. The same holds true for the persuasive power of an advertising message. Effects from exposure to different characteristics of media content vary from person to person. Different people use media differently and react to it differently; there- fore, advertisements affect them differently.

Communication researchers have identified many different individual characteristics of consumers that influence media effects. Each person is moti- vated by different factors to use particular media. A person's emotional state at the time of media use also influences media effects, as does the person's prior experiences and knowledge (Thorson & Reeves, 1990).

One theoretical basis for such individualized effects is called **selective exposure** (Zillmann & Bryant, 1985). People tend to watch, listen to, and remember media messages that are consistent with their attitudes, interests, or predispositions. For example, someone with a beloved feline companion would be more likely to attend to commercials featuring products for cats than would someone who dislikes cats and dotes on a pet poodle.

A great amount of research has supported the idea of selective exposure (Broadbent, 1977; Greenwald & Leavitt, 1984; Krugman, 1988; Pechmann & Stewart, 1990). The related area of uses and gratifications research has also proven productive (Gunter, 1985; see Chapter 8). Research has shown that when people watch television, they tend to make their selections based upon what they *don't* want to see rather than what they *do* want to see. Stewart and Ward (1994) stated it in this way:

> Viewers appear to avoid programs they do not like rather than select programs that they do like. In contrast to the selection of a specific magazine or book, the critical decision for the television viewer appears to be whether or not to turn on the television. The choice of program is clearly secondary. What effect such processes have on advertising in the different media remains to be determined. (pp. 330–331)

One of the most important components of selective exposure, attitude for- mation, and attitude change is that of *involvement* on the part of the audience member. Involvement of the media user can be loosely defined as *personal con- nections with media content.* For example, a television viewer who watches a pro- gram and is reminded repeatedly of personal, real-life situations is said to be a highly involved viewer.

Much scholarly research has identified characteristics of audience members (or consumers) and links between *consumer and medium* that may cause an advertisement to be effective or ineffective. An audience member's attitude regarding the medium, uses of the medium, involvement while using the medium, and mood states that affect media usage have been found to be criti- cal factors in the mix (Stewart & Ward, 1994).

The emphasis on the role of involvement in advertising effects as a challenge to the traditional transactional model can be traced to the 1960s. Krugman (1965, 1966) applied "involvement" not only to the individual audience member, but also to characteristics of the medium and characteristics of the product. Based upon the amount of control exercised over a medium by a user and the level of cognitive processing required, Krugman described various media as either low involvement or high involvement. Print media were characterized as **high involvement,** considering the reader's level of control and necessity for information processing. For example, a reader has time to read a print advertisement carefully, ponder its ramifications, and possibly obtain new knowledge or change existing knowledge. Broadcast media such as television were labeled **low involvement** because of the viewer's lack of control over the rate at which the information is received and the low level of processing usually required.

Due to the low involvement nature of broadcast media, Krugman found the presence of only subtle advertising effects. Television advertising proved most advantageous for developing *product recognition* on the part of the consumer, and for *brand perception*. Attitude change as a result of exposure to TV advertising was not likely and, if present, difficult to measure.

Since Krugman's initial studies, others have investigated the issue of involvement and its connection to various advertising effects and responses. Two major studies in the 1980s offered evidence that high involvement print media provide advertisers with the best means for making product messages known to audiences (Lloyd & Clancy, 1989; Audits & Surveys, 1986). A few years later, Buchholz and Smith (1991) studied degrees of audience involvement among low involvement (broadcast) media. These researchers recognized that people do not always attend to commercial messages with the same level of involvement. Due to distractions, personal interest, or myriad other factors, some people at certain times or under some circumstances might pay more attention to a commercial than would someone else. The researchers set out to test these differences. They presented two groups with a commercial message embedded in other broadcast material (television and radio). The first group (high involvement) was told to pay close attention to the advertisement. They instructed the other group (low involvement) to focus on the broadcast material that surrounded the ad. The high involvement group processed the ads more thoroughly and thought about the personal relevance of the product much more than the low involvement group.

Five Important Consumer Characteristics

Stewart, Pavlou, and Ward (in press) provided a concise list of five different consumer characteristics that influence the effectiveness of ads. These five characteristics have been very important in empirical research and in the development of theory on advertising effects.

1. Attitudes toward the medium.
2. Uses of the medium.
3. Involvement while using the medium.
4. Mood states affecting media usage.
5. Interactivity of the medium.

Source: Stewart, D. W., Pavlou, P,. & Ward, S., (in press). Media influences on marketing communications, in J. Bryant & D. Zillmann (Eds.), *Media effects: Advances in theory and research* (2nd ed.). Mahwah, NJ: Erlbaum.

Certain types of television programs may cause people to experience certain types of moods. Comedy programs may produce lighthearted or cheerful moods. A serious drama might cause the viewer to experience a more contemplative mood. A highly suspenseful program may produce an intensely anxious mood on the part of the viewer.

Research has revealed the importance of media context on a person's mood, as well as the importance of a person's mood on a number of psychological processes, including memory, attention, the forming of attitudes, and so forth (Gardner, 1994). A person's mood affects involvement. It also affects a person's response to an advertisement and subsequent consumer behavior (Gardner, 1985).

Research has shown that the moods produced by watching particular kinds of television programs cause viewers to react differently to the commercial messages shown during the programs. Kennedy (1971) found that people who watched a comedy program had a less positive attitude toward the advertised product than those who watched a suspense program, but in this and another study (Soldow & Principe, 1981), viewers of comedy *recalled* ads far more readily than did suspense viewers.

Individual television programs or specific episodes within genres also affect viewers' responses to ads. In one study, viewers of situation comedies (sitcoms) and action programs offered similar ratings for the effectiveness of commercials embedded in each program type; however, significant differences emerged from episode to episode (Yuspeh, 1977). Specific episodes were more likely than others to affect both viewers' recollections of the brands advertised and their intentions to buy the advertised products.

Another study compared the differences in mood and advertising effects while viewing happy television programs as opposed to sad ones (Goldberg & Gorn, 1987). Overall, commercials shown during happy programs tended to be evaluated higher and to produce more positive thoughts. They also found that program-induced moods had more of an effect on viewers' responses to commercials with high emotional appeals than commercials with straight, informational appeals.

Subsequent research identified an important *interaction* effect between the mood invoked by the media context (program) and that of the embedded commercial. Specifically, commercials with emotional tones or moods consistent with the media context received higher ratings than commercials with tones different from those evoked by the media context. (Examples of inconsistencies would be a funny commercial that appears during a sad program, or a sad commercial shown during a comedy performance.) Researchers found that viewers not only rated context-consistent commercials as more likable, but said they would be more likely to purchase the products that were pitched (Kamins, Marks, & Skinner, 1991).

The theoretical explanation for this interaction effect can be found in **consistency theory.** This theory takes the position that viewers wish to maintain a particular mood for the duration of a program. Commercials with tones or moods that are consistent with those presented in the program are therefore more effective than commercials with tones that differ from the media context.

MEDIA CONTEXT STUDIES

Even though media context was an important part of many of the involvement studies discussed previously, those studies are usually not classified under the heading of "media context research." Involvement studies emphasize various consumer characteristics that result in media effects. Media context studies focus upon *media content or stimuli* rather than on *particular consumer characteristics*. These studies measure more immediate responses—cognitive, physiological, and even behavioral—to advertisements in different media.

Stewart and Ward (1994) identified several ways that researchers have explored the effectiveness of advertisements embedded in various kinds of media context. These different types of media context studies include cognitive response studies, observational studies, studies of psychological measures, and priming studies. In each branch, immediate responses to advertisements were measured in some way.

Cognitive Response Studies

People experience any number of different responses when exposed to advertisements. When the spokesperson for a brand of toothpaste claims that a survey showed that more dentists use Brand X than any other, one viewer may believe the spokesperson whereas another may have serious doubts about the claim. The viewer who does not know much about social scientific research methods might be inclined to take the spokesperson's word. This more knowledgeable viewer believes that the use of a survey provides enough evidence to support such a claim. Another viewer may question the claim due to the vagueness of the information regarding the survey. This viewer wonders: Was a random but representative sample of dentists surveyed? Were strict survey methods employed, or did the product advertisers search only for dentists who use Brand X? Would another survey produce similar results? If one of the viewers is a dentist who does not use Brand X nor know of any colleagues who use it, he or she might have serious doubts about the claim. If that same dentist had attended a recent medical conference in which survey findings revealed Brand X to be the preferred choice among dentists and their families, the claim would be much more trusted.

As shown from the previous example, the nature of a person's response to an advertising message depends on personal knowledge or personal experiences. In other words, advertising responses are affected by a person's level of knowledge about the product or service or claim. Someone with considerable knowledge about a particular product or subject would be more likely to listen carefully to related advertising claims and have a stronger opinion—pro or con—regarding those claims.

Wright (1973) studied several different cognitive responses to advertising messages, such as supporting arguments, counterarguments, and so forth. He examined users of different types of media under differing levels of involvement, then asked questions of the participants to measure certain factors. Media users were exposed to either print or audio versions of an advertisement for a new product. Prior to exposure, Wright created conditions of high involvement by telling a portion of the participants that they would be asked to make a decision about purchasing a new product that would be advertised during the session. Low involvement was created by not giving other participants such instructions. Wright found that people from both groups reacted differently to the print ads than to the audio ads. For the print version, members of the high and low involvement groups tended to think more about the ads, trust the source more, and think of more supporting arguments. More people who read the print version also expressed an intention to buy the product compared with respondents hearing the audio version of the ad.

Observational Studies

Rather than rely upon the self-reports of participants, some researchers prefer to gather information about advertising responses by *direct observation* of consumers as they view the ads. In one study of advertising on television, mothers were asked to observe as one of their children watched television and to record information about the child's behavior while viewing (Ward, Levinson, & Wackman, 1972). As might be expected, the research found that children were very active while watching television, and the levels of activity ranged from high (ignoring the television) to low (full attention to the programming). Whenever a commercial interrupted a program, it captured the attention of most of the children, but their attention waned steadily as more commercials were shown, then picked up toward the end of the commercial "pod" as they grew impatient for the return of the regular program.

Another TV advertising study attempted to determine what particular characteristics of television programs attracted the attention of children (Bryant & Anderson, 1983). Attention was measured as the portion of time a child's eyes were directed toward the television screen, or "eyes on screen" time. The study found that children tended to be attracted by changes in sound and in movement (depiction of much physical activity).

As for print ads, the eye movements of newspaper readers have been tracked using a unique device. A camera mounted on a helmet allows a video image of a person's field of vision to be transmitted to a computer. As the person focuses on different points, a light beam on the pupil is superimposed on the video image and allows researchers to track eye movements (Newspaper Advertising Bureau, 1987). Referring to this and other studies, Tolley and Bogart (1994) asserted that newspaper readers scan most pages. If they see something they are interested in, they read it, but they end up ignoring many other items. These findings confirmed earlier studies that showed many readers engage in an information-filtering process to decide if printed items are worth the effort of their full attention (Broadbent, 1977; Greenwald & Leavitt, 1984).

Studies Involving Psychological Measures

Another means of measuring responses to advertisements involves the use of equipment to determine if physiological changes occur. Electroencephalographic (EEG) responses measure changes in the brain waves of viewers. One study found considerable EEG activity during exposure to television commercials, and also a relationship between the EEG responses and the likelihood that a viewer would remember certain parts of the ads (Rothschild & Hyun, 1990).

Scientists have discovered that the left and right sides of the brain process information differently. Speaking very generally and in rather simple terms, the right side of the brain appears to specialize in processing pictures and music, while the left side of the brain performs the mental tasks involving words and numbers. This would lead one to hypothesize that print advertisements would tend to be processed more on the left side of the brain, while television ads would be oriented more toward the right hemisphere. Krugman (1977) made such a hypothesis, but research findings did not support the assertion (Weinstein, Appel, & Weinstein, 1980). Measurement of such a hypothesis proves difficult because most print ads contain pictures as well as words and television ads also typically contain spoken words (Rossiter, 1982).

Priming Studies

In these studies, researchers look for instances of priming in the media context. One approach to conducting such research is to examine the content of a program to determine if the viewer's attention might be drawn to certain aspects of an ad. For example, one of those fresh-face Cover Girl ads that feature gorgeous, pencil-thin supermodels might work better if embedded in a show that features hip, good-looking teens. Imagine the incongruity of seeing one of those ads in the middle of a heart-wrenching program about someone struggling to lead a normal life after surviving an accident or illness that left the person with a grossly disfigured face and body. The audience member has been primed to be especially sensitive about the importance of appearance and might react negatively to models who appear so fortunate and frivolous in contrast to the individual in the program.

Studies have revealed that media context "primes" viewers to pay more attention to particular ads or parts of ads (Herr, 1989; Higgins & King, 1981; Wyer & Srull, 1981; Yi, 1990a, 1990b). Readers or viewers can be primed *cognitively* or *affectively*. In other words, exposure to particular media content may cause audience members to *think* or *feel* more strongly about certain aspects of advertisements than they would have otherwise. If someone reads a positive-sounding editorial or news story, and then looks at an advertisement, that person usually feels more positively about the brand in the advertisement and usually reports a higher likelihood of purchasing the product (Yi, 1990a).

Advertising research on priming has focused on the power of media context to affect the reaction of audience members to ads. Studies to explore effects in the opposite direction (commercials priming responses to programs) have not been conducted but would prove interesting (Stewart & Ward, 1994). Using again the fresh-face Cover Girl ads as an example, such research would examine whether one of those "easy-breezy" ads shown at the beginning of a program would "prime" audiences or cause them to think or feel differently about the program than had they not viewed the commercial.

THE IMPORTANCE OF ADVERTISING FREQUENCY AND REPETITION

Media planners have attempted to measure many factors related to advertising exposure. One of these examines the effects of the cumulative number of exposures to an ad on a person's likelihood to buy the product.

Two different models of advertising response function have emerged. The first of these (depicted as an S-curve) posits that people must be exposed to an ad several times for that ad to have any effectiveness. After a number of exposures the ad achieves greatest impact, then begins slowly to decline in effectiveness (Burke & Srull, 1988). The other model does not have a threshold effect. Response to the advertisement begins with the first viewing and rapidly becomes more effective, then slows with subsequent exposures resulting in diminishing returns (see Figure 17.1).

Another factor related to exposure involves consumer attitudes toward long cycles of exposure to the same advertisements. A number of studies (see Pechmann & Stewart, 1988, for a review of the literature) have found that prolonged exposure to the same ad causes consumers to feel resentful and sometimes irritated, in a phenomenon called **advertising wearout** (Calder & Sternthal, 1980; Petty & Cacioppo, 1986). As a result, effectiveness of the ad declines. Most of us have experienced advertising wearout at some time in our lives—remember those Ronald McDonald TV commercials?

After reviewing studies concerning advertising wearout, Pechmann and Stewart (1988) determined that three "quality" exposures to a particular ad were needed for the ad to have an effect. A quality exposure is one in which the audience member pays attention to the ad and it evokes certain thoughts or feelings (i.e., it causes cognitive or affective processing). An audience member may have to be exposed to an ad any number of times for three "quality" exposures to occur.

FIGURE 17.1.
Source: From Bryant and Zillman, *Media Effects: Advances in Theory and Research,* p. 322. Copyright © 1994. Reprinted by permission of Lawrence Erlbaum Associates, Inc.

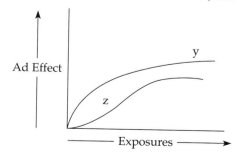

Sometimes too many exposures result in diminished returns. When a television advertisement has good persuasive power, repeated showings of that ad result in increased sales of the product. An ad that does not persuade does not result in increased sales, even if that ad is shown repeatedly. Moreover, once consumers have reached the point where they are either persuaded or not persuaded by a commercial, repeated exposure to that ad makes no difference (Blair, 1987, 1988). Finally, the consumer who already has a negative attitude about a product may become even more negative when exposed repeatedly to ads for that product (Stewart & Ward, 1994).

In terms of print advertising, frequency of ads has been found to produce a greater effect for low-awareness brands than high-awareness brands. The "effects" include consumer awareness of the brand, attitude toward the brand, and intention to buy the brand. Ads for brands that readers do not readily recognize need to be run more often for an effect to occur. The persuasive power of ads for more recognizable brands is not so dependent upon frequency (Time, Inc., 1981).

Frequent exposure to an advertisement results in a process of learning on the part of the consumer, but many factors may influence the learning process. Prior experiences and prior knowledge of the consumer or message variables within the advertisement may cause the learning process to be accelerated or slowed. Also, learning and memory research (Ebbinghaus, 1902) has shown that people tend to forget what they learn over time, that the first or last items in a series are more easily remembered than those in the middle, and that overlearning or overrepetition makes long-term memory possible—for overrepetition, consider how hard pressed one would be to find someone unfamiliar with the brand name associated with Snap, Crackle, Pop.

Several studies have tried to identify schedules of advertising frequency that result in greater learning and ad recognition among consumers. In the 1950s Zielske (1959) found that both short-term repetitions and long-term repetitions produced effective consumer recall of the messages in direct-mail ads;

Media Multiplier Effect

A recent study showed that advertising campaigns that use both print and television media are more effective than ad campaigns that use only one medium or the other. The proper mix of media in the ad campaign results in maximum brand awareness among consumers. Magazine Publishers of America (MPA) calls the phenomenon the "Media Multiplier Effect."

MPA commissioned two research companies, Millward Brown and A. C. Nielsen Corp., to study the effectiveness of ads in magazines and on television, separately and together. The studies found that 65 percent of consumers who see ads on television and in magazines are brand-aware, compared with only 19 percent who see magazine ads only and 16 percent who see television ads only.

Sources: Morris L. (1999, 2 August). Studies give "thumbs up" to mags for ad awareness—print ad scrutiny: Media multiplier effect urges combo buy over just one medium over another, Special Report, *Advertising Age,* p. S16; Chhaya (1999, 22 April), Print+TV=wow! *Business Today,* p. 89; Magazine world: Take a fresh look at print: New insights into the effectiveness of print in the media mix, (1999, 29 April), *Business Wire,* NEXIS, Online Library: NEWS, File: CURNWS; Proof that print advertising really works, (1998, 16 November), *Business Wire,* NEXIS, Online Library: NEWS, File: CURNWS.

however, those who received ads weekly tended to recall more about the ads than those who received the ads on a monthly basis. A later study of print advertising found that magazine ads with the greatest recognition effect also ran at weekly rather than monthly intervals (Strong, 1974, 1977). It is interesting to note that this same study also found that weekly ads had greater recognition effect than daily ads.

COMPREHENSION AND MISCOMPREHENSION

If an advertisement is to be persuasive, a consumer must fully comprehend the importance of its message. Miscomprehension may result in misunderstanding and severely limit the persuasive power of the ad. As with the reception of news (Robinson, Levy, & Davis, 1986; Gunter, 1987) persuasion research has long revealed that comprehension is an important mediator variable (Hovland, Janis, & Kelley, 1953; McGuire, 1972; Ratneshwar & Chaiken, 1991).

A number of studies have shown that miscomprehension is a problem with both print and broadcast advertisements (Jacoby & Hoyer, 1982; Jacoby, Hoyer, & Sheluga, 1980; Jacoby & Hoyer, 1989) but more of a concern with *broadcast* ads (Jacoby, Hoyer, & Zimmer, 1983; Morris, Brinberg, Klimberg, Rivera, & Millstein, 1986). In these studies, the advertisements were for the same products and otherwise equal, except for the medium in which they appeared. This suggests that comprehension or miscomprehension may be correlated with high and low involvement.

As for print ads, one study found that only 20 percent of the participants comprehended the magazine advertisements they were shown (Russo, Metcalf, & Stephens, 1981). Another study of print ads found that comprehension was related to a reader's age, educational level, and income (Jacoby & Hoyer, 1989). Other factors that have been identified as possible determinants of miscomprehension include the individual characteristics of a medium or a message or the individual expectations of a consumer.

RECENT RESEARCH

In recent years, the proliferation of interactive media—the Internet, mobile telephones, interactive television, and so forth—has created a completely new vista for researchers interested in the effects of marketing communications. New media present a new set of characteristics and concerns for today's advertisers and advertising researchers. According to Stewart, Pavlou, and Ward:

> This new form of communication is predominantly electronic, but it has many of the characteristics of other forms of communication: (1) it can be interactive, but without the human touch of personal selling, (2) it provides the opportunity for direct response from and to the consumer, (3) it allows mass communication among consumers without the marketer's intervention, and, (4) it shares some of the characteristics of print and broadcast advertising, at least with respect to the more traditional advertising that appears on it (banner ads, e-announcements). (in press)

Interactive media make the consumer an active part of the marketing process, forcing advertising researchers to reconceptualize the entire sales experience that involves marketing communications (Pavlou & Stewart, 2000), as well as consumer processing and perceptions (Rodgers & Thorson, 2000). The Internet is creating a new type of marketing communication that merges traditional advertising by way of mass media with the interpersonal advantages of personal selling (Stewart, Frazier, & Martin, 1996). Interactive media also have the advantage of facilitating word of mouth communications, long considered the most effective type of advertising (Rosen, 2000; Hoyer & Macinnis, 2001), through chat rooms, message boards, and the like. Researchers are increasingly addressing consumers' active participation in the marketing communication process.

Virtual showrooms and interactive consultations available by means of interactive advertising offer benefits to consumers and advertisers (Wikstrom, 1996). The use of interactive media often facilitates the creation of consumer profiling, either from information gathered directly from consumers or through tracking of online behavior. E-mail communications from sites such as *www.coolsavings.com* give targeted customers the advantage of information about specific products personalized to their interests.

Advertising and New Communication Technologies

Private research firms report that people who live in homes connected to the Internet are spending about 16 percent less time watching television. With such reports, advertisers are taking notice and investing more and more money in online activities. Advertising on the Internet exceeded $1 billion for the first time in 1998, and is projected to grow to at least $8 billion annually by 2005. According to the Internet Advertising Bureau, online ad revenues reached $491 million during the third quarter of 1998, more than double the amount posted for the same period during 1997.

Online advertising is considered superior to television advertising in that it offers the added advantage of accountability. Web advertising can be targeted to reach specific types of consumers. Results are readily measurable, unlike television advertising, which reaches vast numbers of people but cannot be easily measured for effectiveness.

Nielsen recently began researching Web audiences and found that Microsoft, Cataloglink, Amazon, and Yahoo were the top advertisers. Another digital media measurement firm, Media Metrix, listed AOL, Yahoo, and Microsoft sites as the three most popular websites. According to both firms, about 35 to 37 million homes in the United States were connected to the Internet early in 1999.

Advertising researchers have already begun to turn their attention to the Internet and other new communication technologies. Many of the same issues they have explored with advertisements and audiences on traditional media such as television, radio, magazines, and newspapers, are now being examined with regard to the Internet, interactive TV, online publications, and so forth.

Sources: Hall, L. (1998, 23 March). Web ads change online business: Net advertising could reach $8 billion a year, *Electronic Media*, p. 16; also, Harper, J. (1999, 24 March). Nielsen logs on to rate what's happening on line; Data for advertisers similar to TV tallies, *Washington Times*, p. A1; Elliott, S. (1999, 10 February). The media business: Advertising—addenda; on-line advertising doubles in quarter, *The New York Times*, p. C8; Internet advertising revenues exceed $1 billion for the first time, (1999, 9 February), Business Wire, NEXIS Library: News, File: Curnws. Internet advertising bureau—IAB—announces second quarter 1998 advertising revenue reporting program results (1998, 29 October), Business Wire, NEXIS Library: News, File: Curnws.

When a person sees a knockout sweater for sale on the Internet at a reasonable cost, one of the most important factors that determines whether the sweater is purchased is *trust*. Not only does the consumer trust the product, but does the consumer trust the website enough to enter a credit card number and buy the sweater? "Trust" on the part of a consumer toward an advertiser may be defined as:

> the subjective probability with which consumers believe that the marketer will perform a particular interaction in a manner consistent with their expectations. (Stewart, Pavlou, & Ward, in press)

The notion of trust on the part of the consumer toward the advertising source has received a good deal of attention in recent years, especially with the proliferation of electronic commerce. Trust on the part of the consumer has been found to make consumers more likely to do business with the same company (Doney & Cannon, 1997), and lack of trust has been found to be a stumbling block for many consumers when responding to Internet marketers who desire personal information (Hoffman, Novak, & Peralta, 1999).

Despite the drawbacks to e-commerce, some scholars are optimistic that interactive media will serve to enhance consumer trust (Forrest & Mizerski, 1996). Interactions between consumers and advertisers require the exchange of information, as in instances of technical assistance related to the product. Such interactions may serve to strengthen a bridge of trust over time.

SUMMARY

Advertising media include broadcast and electronic media and print sources. Advertising is distinguished from personal selling, which employs the medium of interpersonal communication.

Several models of media effects have been advanced through the years, including the bullet or hypodermic needle model, the limited effects model, and the transactional model. The last of these recognized that many factors—specific characteristics of the sender, the message, the transmitter or channel, the audience as a group, and the individual audience member—could mitigate media effects.

The power of an advertising message to persuade an audience member depends on many factors, such as an individual's mood and predispositions, other individual characteristics, or the likelihood that a message will be thought through carefully. Communication researchers have identified many different individual characteristics of consumers that influence media effects. One theoretical basis for individualized effects is called selective exposure. Each person is motivated by different factors to use particular media and seek different messages. People watch, listen to, and remember media messages that are consistent with their attitudes, interests, or predispositions. A person's motivation to use a particular medium, the person's emotional state at the time of consuming media, and the person's prior experiences and knowledge all influence effects.

Involvement on the part of the audience member is an important component of selective exposure, attitude formation, and attitude change. Involvement of the media user can be loosely defined as personal connections with media content.

Involvement refers to the amount of control exercised over a medium by a user and the level of cognitive processing required. Print media typically are *high involvement,* considering the reader's level of control and necessity for information processing. Broadcast media such as television typically are *low involvement,* owing to the viewer's lack of control over the rate at which the information is received and the low level of processing usually required.

Low-involvement television advertising proves most effective for developing product recognition on the part of the consumer, and for brand perception rather than attitude change. High involvement print media work best to make product messages known to audiences.

Different television programs evoke different moods. A person's mood affects involvement, a person's response to an advertisement, and subsequent consumer behavior. An *interaction* effect occurs between the mood invoked by the media context (program) and that of the embedded commercial. Commercials with emotional tones or moods consistent with the media context are more effective than commercials with tones different from those evoked by the media context. Consistency theory posits that viewers wish to maintain a particular mood for the duration of a program.

Involvement studies emphasize various consumer characteristics that result in media effects. Media context studies focus upon media content or stimuli rather than on particular consumer characteristics. Different types of media context studies include cognitive response studies, observational studies, studies of psychological measures, and priming studies.

Prolonged exposure to the same ad sometimes causes advertising wearout, when consumers feel resentful and sometimes irritated. As a result, effectiveness of the ad declines. Three "quality" exposures to a particular ad are needed for the ad to be effective. Print ads produce greater effects for low-awareness brands than high-awareness brands. Low-awareness brands need to be run more often, but high-awareness brands are not so dependent upon frequency for effectiveness.

If an advertisement is to be persuasive, a consumer must comprehend the message. Miscomprehension may result in misunderstanding and severely limit the persuasive power of the ad.

Recent research has focused on marketing communications in the interactive media environment. The dynamics of interactive media are causing researchers to enter uncharted territory with regard to marketing communications.

REFERENCES

AUDITS & SURVEYS. (1986). *A study of media involvement.* New York: Audits & Surveys.

BERELSON, B., & STEINER, G. A. (1964). *Human behavior: An inventory of findings.* New York: Harcourt, Brace, & World.

BLAIR, M. H. (1987/1988). An empirical investigation of advertising wearin and wearout. *Journal of Advertising Research, 27,* 45–50.

BROADBENT, D. (1977). The hidden pre-attentive processes. *American Psychologist, 32,* 109–118.

BRYANT, J., & ANDERSON, D. (1983). *Children's understanding of television: Research on attention and comprehension.* New York: Academic Press.

BUCHHOLZ, L. M., & SMITH, R. E. (1991). The role of consumer involvement in determining cognitive response to broadcast advertising. *Journal of Advertising, 20,* 4–17.

BURKE, R. R., & SRULL, T. K. (1988). Competitive interference and consumer memory for advertising. *Journal of Consumer Research, 15,* 55–68.

CALDER, B. J., & STERNTHAL, B. (1980). Television commercial wearout: An information processing view. *Journal of Marketing Research, 17,* 173–186.

DONEY, P. M., & CANNON, J. P. (1997). An examination of the nature of trust in buyer-seller relationships. *Journal of Marketing, 61*(2), 35–52.

EBBINGHAUS, H. (1902). *Grundzuge der psychologie* [Principles of psychology]. Leipzig: Viet.

FORREST, E., & MIZENSKI, R. (1996). Interactive marketing: The future present. Lincolnwood, IL: American Marketing Association, NTC Business Books.

GARDNER, M. P. (1985). Mood states and consumer behavior: A critical review. *Journal of Consumer Research, 12,* 281–300.

GARDNER, M. P. (1994). Responses to emotional and informational appeals: The moderating role of context-induced mood states. In E. M. Clark, T. C. Brock, & D. W. Stewart (Eds.), *Attention, attitude, and affect in response to advertising* (pp. 207–221). Hillsdale, NJ: Erlbaum.

GOLDBERG, M. E., & GORN, G. J. (1987). Happy and sad TV programs: How they affect reactions to commercials. *Journal of Consumer Research, 14,* 387–403.

GREENWALD, A. C., & LEAVITT, C. (1984). Audience involvement in advertising: Four levels. *Journal of Consumer Research, 11,* 581–592.

GUNTER, B. (1985). Determinants of television viewing preferences. In D. Zillmann & J. Bryant (Eds.), *Selective exposure to communication* (pp. 93–112). Hillsdale, NJ: Erlbaum.

GUNTER, B. (1987). *Poor reception: Misunderstanding and forgetting broadcast news.* Hillsdale, NJ: Erlbaum.

HERR, P. M. (1989). Priming price: Prior knowledge and context effects. *Journal of Consumer Research, 16,* 67–75.

HIGGINS, E. T., & KING, G. (1981). Accessibility of social constructs: Information processing consequences of individual and contextual variability. In N. Cantor & J. Kihlstrom (Eds.), *Personality, cognition, and social interaction* (pp. 69–122). Hillsdale, NJ: Erlbaum.

HOFFMAN, D. L., NOVAK, T. P., & PERALTA, M. (1999). Building consumer trust online. *Communications of the ACM, 42*(4), 80–85.

HOVLAND, C. I., JANIS, I. L., & KELLEY, H. H. (1953). *Communication and persuasion: Psychological studies of opinion change.* New Haven: Yale University Press.

HOYER, W. D., & MACINNIS, D. J. (2001). *Consumer behavior.* Boston: Houghton Mifflin.

JACOBY, J., & HOYER, W. D. (1982). Viewer miscomprehension of televised communication: Selected findings. *Journal of Marketing, 46,* 12–26.

JACOBY, J., & HOYER, W. D. (1989). The comprehension/miscomprehension of print communication: Selected findings. *Journal of Consumer Research, 15,* 434–443.

JACOBY, J., HOYER, W. D., & SHELUGA, D. A. (1980). *Miscomprehension of televised communications.* New York: American Association of Advertising Agencies.

JACOBY, J., HOYER, W. D., & ZIMMER, M. A. (1983). To read, view or listen? A cross-media comparison of comprehension. In J. H. Leigh & C. R. Martin (Eds.), *Current issues and research in advertising* (Vol. 6, pp. 201–218). Ann Arbor: University of Michigan.

KAMINS, M. A., MARKS, L. J., & SKINNER, D. (1991). Television commercial evaluation in the context of program induced mood: Congruency versus consistency effects. *Journal of Advertising, 20,* 1–14.

KENNEDY, J. R. (1971). How program environment affects TV commercials. *Journal of Advertising Research, 11,* 33–38.

KRUGMAN, H. E. (1965). The impact of television advertising: Learning without involvement. *Public Opinion Quarterly, 29,* 349–356.

KRUGMAN, H. E. (1966). The measurement of advertising involvement. *Public Opinion Quarterly, 30,* 583–596.

KRUGMAN, H. E. (1977). Memory without recall, exposure without perception. *Journal of Advertising Research, 17,* 7–12.

KRUGMAN, H. E. (1988). Point of view: Limits of attention to advertising. *Journal of Advertising Research, 28,* 47–50.

LLOYD, D. W., & CLANCY, K. J. (1989). The effects of television program involvement on advertising response: Implications for media planning. *Proceedings of the first annual Advertising Research Foundation Media Research Workshop.* New York: Advertising Research Foundation.

MCGUIRE, W. J. (1972). Attitude change: The information–processing paradigm. In C. G. McClintock (Ed.), *Experimental social psychology* (pp. 108–141). New York: Holt, Rinehart & Winston.

MORRIS, L. A., BRINBERG, D., KLIMBERG, R., RIVERA, C., & MILLSTEIN, L. G. (1986). Miscomprehension rates for prescription drug advertisements. In J. H. Leigh & C. R. Martin (Eds.), *Current issues and research in advertising* (Vol. 9, pp. 93–118). Ann Arbor: University of Michigan.

NEWSPAPER ADVERTISING BUREAU. (1987). *An eye camera study of ads.* New York: Newspaper Advertising Bureau.

PAVLOU, P. A., & STEWART, D. W. (2000). Measuring the effects and effectiveness of interactive advertising: A research agenda. Journal of Interactive Advertising, *1,* 1. [Online]. Available: http://jiad.org/vol1/no1/pavlou/index.html

PECHMANN, C., & STEWART, D. W. (1988). A critical review of wearin and wearout. *Current Issues and Research in Advertising, 11,* 28–330.

PECHMANN, C., & STEWART, D. W. (1990). The role of comparative advertising: Documenting its effects on attention, recall, and purchase intentions. *Journal of Consumer Research, 17*(2), 180–191.

PETTY, R. E., & CACIOPPO, J. T. (1986). *Communication and persuasion: Central and peripheral routes to attitude change.* New York: Springer-Verlag.

POLITZ RESEARCH. (1962, November). *A measurement of advertising effectiveness: The influence of audience selectivity and editorial environment.* New York: Politz Research.

RATNESHWAR, S., & CHAIKEN, S. (1991). Comprehension's role in persuasion: The case of its moderating effect on the persuasive impact of source cues. *Journal of Consumer Research, 18,* 52–62.

ROBINSON, J. P., LEVY, M. R., & DAVIS, D. K., IN ASSOCIATION WITH WOODALL, W. G., GUREVITCH, M., & SAHIN, H. (1986). *The main source: Learning from television news.* Beverly Hills, CA: Sage, 1986.

RODGERS, S., & THORSON, E. (2000). The interactive advertising model: How users perceive and process online ads. Journal of Interactive Advertising, *1,* 1. [Online]. Available: http://jiad.org/vol1/no1/pavlou/index.html

ROSSITER, J. R. (1982). Point of view: Brain hemisphere activity. *Journal of Advertising Research, 22,* 75–76.

ROTHSCHILD, M. L., & HYUN, Y. J. (1990). Predicting memory for components of TV commercials from EEG. *Journal of Consumer Research, 16,* 472–479.

RUSSO, J. E., METCALF, B. L., & STEPHENS, D. (1981). Identifying misleading advertising. *Journal of Consumer Research, 10,* 119–131.

SOLDOW, G. F., & PRINCIPE, V. (1981). Response to commercials as a function of program context. *Journal of Advertising Research, 21*, 59–65.

STEWART, D. W., FRAZIER, G., & MARTIN, I. (1996). Integrated channel management: Merging the communication and distribution functions of the firm. In E. Thorson & J. Moore (Eds.), *Integrated communication: Synergy of persuasive voices* (pp. 185–216). Mahwah, NJ: Erlbaum.

STEWART, D. W., PAVLOU, P., & WARD, S. (in press). Media influences on marketing communications. In J. Bryant & D. Zillmann (Eds.), *Media effects: Advances in theory and research*. Mahwah, NJ: Erlbaum.

STEWART, D. W., & WARD, S. (1994). Media effects on advertising. In J. Bryant & D. Zillmann (Eds.), *Media Effects: Advances in Theory and Research* (pp. 315–363). Hillsdale, NJ: Erlbaum.

STRONG, E. C. (1974). The use of field experimental observations in estimating recall. *Journal of Marketing Research, 11*, 369–378.

STRONG, E. C. (1977). The spacing and timing of advertising. *Journal of Advertising Research, 16*, 25–31.

THORSON, E., & REEVES, B. (1990). Consumer processing of advertising. In J. H. Leigh & C. Martin, Jr. (Eds.), *Current issues and research in advertising* (Vol. 12, pp. 197–230). Ann Arbor: University of Michigan.

TIME, INC. (1981). *A study of the effectiveness of advertising frequency in magazines, the relationship between magazine advertising frequency and brand awareness, advertising recall, favorable brand rating, willingness to buy, and product use and purchase.* New York: Research Department, Magazine Group, Time Inc.

TOLLEY, S., & BOGART, L. (1994). How readers process newspaper advertising. In E. M. Clark, T. C. Brock, & D. W. Stewart (Eds.), *Attention, attitude, and affect in response to advertising* (pp. 69–77). Hillsdale, NJ: Erlbaum.

WARD, S., LEVINSON, D., & WACKMAN, D. (1972). Children's attention to television advertising. In G. A. Comstock & J. P. Murray (Eds.), *Television and social behavior: Vol. IV. Television in day-to-day life.* HSM 70–9059. Washington, DC: Department of Health, Education and Welfare.

WEINSTEIN, S., APPEL, V., & WEINSTEIN, C. (1980). Brain activity responses to magazine and television advertising. *Journal of Advertising Research, 20*, 57–63.

WIKSTROM, S. (1996). An integrated model of buyer-seller relationships. *Journal of the Academy of Marketing Science, 23*, 335–345.

WRIGHT, P. L. (1973). The cognitive processes mediating acceptance of advertising. *Journal of Marketing Research, 10*, 53–62.

WYER, R. S., & SRULL, T. K. (1981). Category accessibility: Some theoretical and empirical issues concerning the processing of social stimulus information. In E. T. Higgins, C. P. Herman, & M. P. Zanna (Eds.), *Social cognition: The Ontario Symposium* (pp. 161–197). Hillsdale, NJ: Erlbaum.

YI, Y. (1990a). Cognitive and affective priming effects of the context for print advertisements. *Journal of Advertising, 19*, 40–48.

YI, Y. (1990b). The effects of contextual priming in print advertisements. *Journal of Consumer Research, 17*, 215–222.

YUSPEH, S. (1977, October). *On-air: Are we testing the message or the medium?* Paper delivered to J. Walter Thompson Research Conference, New York.

ZIELSKE, H. A. (1959). The remembering and forgetting of advertising. *Journal of Marketing, 23*, 239–243.

ZILLMANN, D., & BRYANT, J. (1985). *Selective exposure to communication.* Hillsdale, NJ: Erlbaum.

Mass-Mediated Political Communication Effects

You campaign in poetry. You govern in prose.
—**Mario Cuomo**, *New Republic*, **April 8, 1985**

The study of the effects on audiences from mass-mediated messages or symbols that are political in nature or have political consequences is but one division in the broad research domain of political communication effects. Within this particular area of inquiry, different levels of effects may occur—effects on individuals in society (called micro effects) or on the political system, institutions, or society as a whole (called macro effects). Effects may be periodic in nature, such as those produced by elections, or they may be continuous, such as the watchdog function the press performs in the United States, with the president and other elected officials under constant scrutiny. This chapter will discuss important findings in these various arenas.

Throughout the history of the study of media effects, researchers have been interested in the effects of political communication. As you have learned in earlier chapters, findings on the power of mass-mediated effects have varied through the years, and political communication effects are no exception. Studies of voting behavior in the 1940s and 1950s indicated that mass-mediated political communication effects were rather *limited* (Berelson, Lazarsfeld, & McPhee, 1954; Lazarsfeld, Berelson, & Gaudet, 1948). In these well-known studies, mass media were found to influence opinion leaders, who in turn influenced others through interpersonal communication. Later studies have put into question the integrity of the limited effects model by presenting findings of more direct and powerful media influence on voters from political campaign messages (Blumler & McLeod, 1974; Chaffee & Hochheimer, 1985; Gitlin, 1978; Iyengar & Simon, 2000; Noelle-Neumann, 1984). For example, Noelle-Neumann's Spiral of Silence theory suggests powerful effects result whenever people fear social alienation or isolation enough to keep quiet and not speak their views.

After the 1970s, an increasing number of researchers became interested in political communication, and the number of studies mushroomed. McLeod, Kosicki, and Rucinski (1988) identified four major reasons for this increased interest:

1. Voting behaviors became increasingly unpredictable due to various sociopolitical changes.
2. The societal concern for the negative effects of television increased.
3. Studies by European scholars (e.g., Spiral of Silence theory by Noelle-Neumann, and the Marxist and radical views of the Frankfurt and Birmingham critical schools) attracted attention and stimulated additional research.
4. An emphasis on cognitive dimensions expanded the focus of political communication research.

307

CHAPTER 18
Mass-Mediated
Political
Communication
Effects

In addition to their list, we might also add that researcher interest began to grow in the areas of negative political advertising (Johnson-Cartee & Copeland, 1991) and negative campaigning, and on the topic of decreasing voter turnout (Miron, 1999).

In recent years, several trends have emerged in political communication research (McLeod, Kosicki, & McLeod, 1994). Studies have begun to show connections between the various components of the communication process and effects on audiences (e.g., effects due to the news source or media organization) or effects from message content. Macro-level studies have become more popular and comparative studies have emerged that examine differences in media effects from political communications in various nations or communities or periods in history (Blumler, 1983; Blumler, McLeod, & Rosengren, 1992; Tichenor, Donohue, & Olien, 1980; Miron & Bryant, in press). Other trends include a growing interest in the language used in media content and its interpretation by audiences, and an increase in studies that use a combination of methodologies and different sources of data to answer research questions. As a result of these trends, scholars have developed increasingly sophisticated models to explain the processes of political communication.

In this chapter we will examine some of the research findings responsible for these several trends. We will also discuss aspects of mass media and society that affect the nature of political communications, the various goals of mass media in a democratic society, the content of mediated political messages, and factors responsible for media effects at micro and macro levels.

INFLUENCES ON POLITICAL COMMUNICATION

Several dynamic influences affect the nature of political communications in a society: the social scene, the political landscape, the media environment, and media content. We describe these influences as dynamic because they change, often considerably, over time with the introduction of new technologies, shifts in public opinion, fluctuations in the political climate, and other changes at the societal level.

Functions of Mass Media in a Democracy

Mass media attempt to provide a number of special functions for the body politic in democratic societies of the world. Gurevitch and Blumler (1990) identified eight such functions and McLeod, Kosicki, and McLeod (1994) paraphrased them in the following convenient way:

1. Surveillance of contemporary events that are likely to impinge, positively or negatively, upon the welfare of citizens.
2. Identification of key sociopolitical issues including their origins and possibilities for resolution.
3. Provision of platforms for advocacy by spokespersons for causes and interests.
4. Transmission of diverse content across the various dimensions and factions of political discourse, as well as bidirectionally between potential power holders and mass publics.
5. Scrutiny of government officials, their institutions and other agencies of power by holding them accountable for their actions and policies.
6. Incentives and information to allow citizens to become active informed participants rather than spectators in the political process.
7. Principled resistance to external forces attempting to subvert media autonomy.
8. Respectful consideration of the audience as potentially concerned, sense-making, and efficacious citizens. (p. 126)

According to Gurevitch and Blumler (1990), these special functions are actually *goals* or *standards* that mass media should try to attain in a democratic society. In reality, because of the fundamental nature of mass media as money-making, profits-dominated entities or to any number of constraints, news media sometimes fall measurably short of the standards. For example, news

The social scene, the political landscape, the media environment, and media content are dynamic influences on the nature of political communication.
Source: © Reuters/New Media Inc. CORBIS

media sometimes cover pseudo-events or other irrelevant but entertaining stories in their quest to attract the highest audience numbers. The tendency of the news media to cover *events* rather than *issues* represents another stumbling block in the path of the designated goals. When issues are addressed, they are often presented from the standpoint of the news network's institutional agenda (McLeod, Kosicki, & McLeod, 1994). Additionally, the media usually dramatize their coverage of political campaigns and present the event as they would a horse race, with candidates neck and neck in the polls, or a dark horse candidate gaining ground, or a front-runner pulling away.

309

CHAPTER 18
Mass-Mediated
Political
Communication
Effects

Media Content

Studies have focused primarily on two types of media content related to political communication: political advertising and news stories. The first of these, political advertising, constitutes the primary form of communication between political candidates and the voting public (Kaid, 1996). In major political campaigns, television advertising usually consumes much of the campaign budget.

Studies have shown that political ads on television have been effective in presenting particular candidate images to the voting public, providing information about key issues, and sometimes influencing voting decisions (Kaid, 1981). Content analyses have revealed that political ads often provide more information about campaign issues than candidate images (Joslyn, 1980; Kaid & Johnston, 1991).

In the area of news stories, several aspects of media content may influence political communication. Two common types of media content include framing and news flaws.

Frames are abstract notions that media professionals use to present news stories in a particular way. Gamson and Lasch (1983) defined a frame as a "central organizing idea for understanding events related to the issue in question" (p. 398). In terms of political communications, campaigns are often framed using metaphors or catchphrases. Campaigns are usually referred to as battles or contests like horse races, complete with "front-runners" and "dark horses." Such framing devices often influence audience perceptions and interpretations (McLeod & Detenber, 1999; Valkenburg, Semetko, & de Vreese, 1999; Nelson, Oxley, & Clawson, 1997).

Bennett (1988) identified four *news* **flaws** common in news coverage: personalization, fragmentation, dramatization, and normalization. *Personalization* refers to the tendency for news stories to concentrate on individuals when reporting on large-scale social concerns. *Fragmentation* involves the delivery of news in disconnected, brief capsule summaries. Hart (1996) referred to the fragmentary presentations as resulting in "cameo politics" (p. 109). *Dramatization* occurs whenever news is selected on the basis of its dramatic or entertaining value rather than its importance as an issue. *Normalization* takes place whenever news stories show how particular problems can be solved within the existing political system. Each of these flaws may affect the nature of a political communication.

RESEARCH ON POLITICAL COMMUNICATION EFFECTS

Most research on effects from political communication has concentrated on the individual rather than society at large; in other words, micro-level effects studies rather than macro-level studies dominate the literature. At the micro level are four major areas: formation and change of opinion; cognitive effects, including agenda-setting research, priming, knowledge gain, and framing; effects on individual perceptions of the political system; and effects on political behavior or participation. Macro-level studies seek to examine effects on systems, or effects on individuals that affect systems.

At either level, the nature and strength of effects from mediated political communication depend on a number of different factors. These factors have to do with certain characteristics or orientations of individual audience members and their processing of media messages.

Micro-Level Studies

Formation and Change of Opinion

A number of studies have explored the power of media messages to produce or change the political opinions of audience members. The voting studies of Lazarsfeld and his colleagues (1948) found only a limited amount of influence from mass media on the political opinions of audiences. Later studies indicated that political media messages produced much stronger effects than previously thought (Blumler & McLeod, 1974; Ranney, 1983; McLeod & McDonald, 1985; Iyengar & Simon, 2000).

Newer models of persuasion, such as Petty and Cacioppo's elaboration likelihood model (1986) and Fishbein and Ajzen's reasoned action model (1975) have been applied to the study of political communication effects. Several research studies have used these persuasion models as a basis for understanding campaign effects (Fazio & Williams, 1986; Granberg & Brown, 1989; Krosnick, 1988; O'Keefe, 1985; Rice & Atkin, 1989). Variables of interest in persuasion studies include message variables, channels, timing (as in campaign schedules), audience variables, and effects from polling information.

Effects of Cognitive Processes

In recent decades, four different types of research have examined cognitive effects from mediated political messages. These include agenda-setting research, priming research, knowledge gain, and framing (McLeod, Kosicki, & McLeod, 1994).

You will recall from Chapter 9 that the agenda-setting hypothesis states that the news media determine prominent issues through their expanded coverage of particular issues, and these issues are considered important by the public (McCombs & Shaw, 1972). Research supports the notion that the issues that receive the most coverage are the very issues that the public perceives as important (Funkhouser, 1973; MacKuen, 1981; McCombs, 1977; Tipton, Haney, & Basehart, 1975; McLeod, Becker, & Byrnes, 1974; Iyengar & Kinder, 1987). Studies have begun to identify whether the news media or some other source actually determine the agenda. Iyengar and Kinder (1987) found that news *sources* may be more influential in setting issues agendas than the news media. Other researchers have explored ways in which the news agenda is set (Ericson, Baranek, & Chan, 1989; Semetko et al., 1991), and especially the power plays between media and sources (Epstein, 1973; Sigal, 1973).

311

CHAPTER 18
Mass-Mediated
Political
Communication
Effects

Priming, you will recall, occurs when exposure to a mediated message activates related thoughts in the mind of the audience member. Priming has been shown to affect political opinions and voting decisions. Iyengar and Kinder (1987) found that issues that received prominent media coverage primed audiences in their evaluations of presidential performance. The way that presidents handled the high-coverage issues disproportionately influenced the overall performance rating for that president in the eyes of an audience member. In 1980, the daily coverage of the Iran Hostage Crisis has been blamed for priming voters to give more emphasis to foreign affairs, which may have resulted in a lower overall performance rating for Jimmy Carter and more votes for Ronald Reagan.

Other studies have found that while audiences may or may not be persuaded by mediated political communication, they often *learn* from such messages. News reports about campaign issues and candidates, political debates, and conventions have all been shown to be responsible for various amounts of knowledge gain among audiences (Conover & Feldman, 1989; Gunter, 1987; McLeod, Bybee, & Durall, 1979).

Several caveats must accompany these indications of political knowledge gain. First, other studies have revealed that Americans are not particularly knowledgeable about political affairs. Delli Carpini and Keeter (1991) found that the U.S. public's knowledge of politics increased only minimally in the decades following the 1960s, despite great increases in the number of Americans attending college. When the researchers controlled for education, they found that factual knowledge about politics had actually declined through the years. Also, studies have shown that very little factual information learned from news stories is retained (Neuman, 1976).

Some researchers have not focused on the mere retention of facts, but have tried to measure audiences' broader understanding of political information conveyed in news stories. Audience members are asked open-ended questions about news stories and they participate in group discussions. Using these techniques, researchers gain insights into the *cognitive complexity* of the audience members' understanding of the news stories (McLeod, Pan, & Rucinski, 1989).

Voter Perceptions

What influences a person's voting decision? Is a voter motivated to select a particular candidate based on self-interest or on broader perceptions about the system? In other words, does a voter select a particular candidate because promised tax cuts or other measures will provide personal economic advantages to the voter, or does the voter base the decision upon less selfish motives, such as perceived economic benefits to the country at large?

Some evidence suggests that voters are persuaded less by personal "pocketbook" matters than by their perceptions about the economic health of the country (Fiorina, 1981; Kinder & Kiewiet, 1983). Such findings are important when one considers that news media coverage usually shapes those perceptions. The press plays an essential role in providing the public with information about governmental operations, the economy, and other aspects of the system. Often, however, the press does not fulfill this role satisfactorily (Popkin, 1991).

Studies have shown that media coverage, especially television coverage, may cause voters to perceive that individuals, rather than society at large, are responsible for particular social problems such as poverty or crime. Many do not associate social problems with societal responsibility but prefer to blame individuals such as the poor, the homeless, or victims (Iyengar, 1989). Iyengar (1991) identified two types of frames for political news stories on television: *episodic*, using case study examples or reports of concrete events, and *thematic*, approaching an issue from a more abstract or general perspective. About 80 percent of the CBS news stories in his sample were episodic. A controlled experiment revealed that thematic framing caused audiences to associate social problems with societal and governmental responsibility rather than individuals. With episodic framing, however, the perceptions of system-level responsibility decreased. Results have been different in studies that involve political stories in newspapers, which tend to be more thematic than episodic (McLeod, Sun, Chi, & Pan, 1990).

Political Behavior

Political communication researchers have long been interested in media effects on voting behavior. Through the years, studies have revealed that media effects may be direct or indirect, and that interpersonal communication sometimes has a place in the mix. For the most part, studies have shown that voting is a complex behavior influenced by a number of factors, with media presentations being one of those factors.

Political advertisements have proven effective in influencing voting decisions (Kaid, 1981). For this reason, candidates spend millions of dollars on television ads alone. During the past four decades, the length of televised political ads has decreased considerably, from 30-minute biographical ads in the 1950s and 1960s to 4-minute spots in the 1970s to the 60-second, 30-second, and 15-second spots of the 1980s and 1990s (Devlin, 1995; Kern, 1989). The most popular time length for political ads today is 30 seconds, leading one scholar to call this the "age of the 30-second spot" (Perloff, 1998, p. 348).

Research shows that many people learn from political advertisements (Brians & Wattenberg, 1996; Just, Crigler, & Wallach, 1990), and evidence shows that people may be influenced by both positive and negative ads (Houston & Doan, 1999). Studies reveal that weak partisans—for example, those who are not staunch Democrats or Republicans—and those with little interest in politics are more affected by political ads than staunch partisans and high-interest voters (Ansolabehere & Iyengar, 1995). Yet, as Perloff (1998) pointed out, such findings must be qualified:

> It is difficult to parcel out the influence of commercials from all the other forces impinging on voters during the election campaign. Clearly, political spots can affect voters' evaluations of candidates and their interpretations of political

events. Ads also contribute to voters' storehouse of campaign knowledge, although even advertising consultants would agree that a campaign diet based exclusively on commercials would be an intellectually meager one. (p. 374)

313

CHAPTER 18
Mass-Mediated
Political
Communication
Effects

Negative political ads have proven effective in influencing voters when voters perceive them to be fair, and when they focus on issues that are important to voters (Perloff, 1998). Studies show that people tend to remember negative ads more and recognize them more than they do positive ads (Shapiro & Rieger, 1992; Newhagen & Reeves, 1991). Research has also shown that failure to answer negative ads can be disastrous for a candidate because such silence allows the opposition to define the persona of the candidate (Johnson-Cartee & Copeland, 1991). For example, George Bush's attacks on the social policies of Governor Michael Dukakis in the 1988 presidential election proved highly effective when Dukakis failed to answer the charges. One political consultant explained the situation in this way: "There's one thing the American people dislike more than someone who fights dirty. And that's someone who climbs into the ring and won't fight" (Johnson-Cartee & Copeland, 1991, p. 224).

In recent years, political advertising campaigns have become so conspicuous that print and broadcast media have begun to report on them. Such "adwatches" provide analyses, interpretations, and evaluations of the ads (Kaid, 1996, p. 451). These adwatches have become important dimensions in political advertising (West, 1993; Kaid, Gobetz, Garner, Leland, & Scott, 1993), and may influence voters reactions to the candidates and the ads themselves (Cappella & Jamieson, 1994; Pfau & Louden, 1994).

Traditionally, a number of personal factors not related to media influence have predicted voter turnout. These factors include educational level, age, marital status, church attendance, and so forth (Strate, Parrish, Elder, & Ford, 1989; Wolfinger & Rosenstone, 1980). Yet some studies have revealed instances of abstention from voting that can be attributed to mass media (Ranney, 1983; Blumler & McLeod, 1974). In a study of the 1970 election in Great Britain, panel participants revealed that they abstained from voting because they did not like the image presented by the candidates on television.

The strength of influence on voting behavior attributed to *interpersonal communication* rather than, or in addition to, *mass communication* has varied through the years. Lazarsfeld and his colleagues (1948) were the first to identify the influence of interpersonal communication on voters. They found that many people received information about the candidates or the election from other people rather than from news media reports. Later studies showed that conversations with others tend to work in conjunction with or complement news reports (Chaffee, 1982), and that media reports arouse interest in a campaign that leads to more interpersonal discussions (McLeod, Bybee, & Durall, 1979).

Macro-level Studies

Analytical macro-level effects studies that go beyond individual-level effects to explore consequences for society or the political system are few in number due to the difficulties encountered in measurement; however, purely *descriptive* macro-level studies abound. These studies provide much descriptive information about the American political system and its body of voters.

Descriptive Macro Studies

Descriptive macro studies suggest, for example, that only a small group of people in the United States is politically knowledgeable and active. The great numbers that constitute the remainder of the population are apathetic and politically uninformed (Neuman, 1986). People with high levels of education tend to vote more often, know more about politics, participate in politics, and know and discuss political news more than less-educated citizens (Burnham, 1982; Powell, 1986; Popkin, 1991).

Television has been blamed for many problems with the American political system. Ranney (1983) pointed out several of these problems. The expense of television commercials has made fund-raising an increasingly important aspect in political campaigns. Also, the brevity of the TV commercial spot encourages less focus on discussion of issues and more emphasis on superficial factors such as the candidate's appearance and image.

Effects on Policy Making

When the mass media influence politicians and policy makers, influences at the system level may also occur. One study (Protess et al., 1991) found that the use of investigative reporting contributed to civic reforms in a number of areas. Such reports did not arouse readers to contact their elected officials and insist on reforms; rather, effects occurred because of interactions between the journalists, special interest groups, and public policy makers.

The effects of mass media on policy making are apparent in other ways as well. Local media usually support civic or other local "improvement" projects, some of which may be rather costly (Kaniss, 1991; Logan & Molotch, 1987). Also, media publicity has been shown to help lawmakers achieve their goals and raise money toward reelection campaigns (Smith, 1988; Etzioni, 1988; Goldenberg & Traugott, 1984).

FACTORS INFLUENCING MEDIA EFFECTS

The impact from mass media political messages depends on a number of characteristics of the individual audience member and the way he or she processes the mediated information.

Individual Characteristics

Generally, the most politically active citizens are those with high educational levels. These politically sophisticated individuals are not only the most politically informed, but the most likely to learn new political information (Star & Hughes, 1950; Tichenor et al., 1970). Conversely, such informed people are less likely to exhibit agenda setting effects from either print or broadcast media, probably due to the strength of their personal issues agendas (McLeod et al., 1974; Weaver, Graber, McCombs, & Eyal, 1981; Iyengar & Kinder, 1987).

Other individual factors that influence the strength of political communication effects include political partisanship or party preference (Katz, 1987; Iyengar & Kinder, 1987; McLeod et al., 1974), personal images or evaluations of

The Internet as a Campaign Tool and Source for Political Information

As the 1990s progressed, the Internet became more important as a tool in political campaigning and a source for political information. In the 1996 and 2000 presidential election campaigns, all the candidates had websites up and running. In the weeks following the vote on November 7, 2000, millions of anxious Americans turned to Internet news sites for the latest information on the Florida vote fiasco.

During the vote-counting drama in Florida following the 2000 election, many news sites on the Internet reported record numbers of users. MSNBC .com reported that almost 7 million people accessed the site on election day, almost double the number of their previous single-day record. Boston.com (affiliated with the *Boston Globe* newspaper) saw new records for daily and monthly use following the election. A Gallup Poll in the aftermath of the election revealed that 18 percent of respondents considered the Internet as an "extremely important" source of information about the Florida vote. Another survey revealed that more than three times as many people cited the Internet as a chief source of news information in the 2000 election than in 1996.

Sources: Jurkowitz, M. (2000, 13 December). The media; Who's winning the election? The comedians. *Boston Globe*, p. E1; J. Omicinski (2000, 10 December). More believe news is biased; The poll was taken when the media were covering the Florida recount. *Des Moines Register*, p. 13; Reed, L. (1999). Online campaigning, In D. D. Perlmutter (Ed.), *The Manship School guide to political communication* (pp. 233–240). Baton Rouge: Louisiana State University Press.

the news media (Kosicki & McLeod, 1990; McLeod, Kosicki, Armor, Allen, & Philps, 1986), and personal motivations for particular gratifications (Blumler & McQuail, 1969; McLeod & Becker, 1974; McLeod, Becker, & Byrnes, 1974). Those with strong political partisanship are less likely to be influenced by political messages that are counter to their political predispositions. Also, a person's image toward the news media has a marked effect on how much that person learns from the news. Research has shown that people who give high ratings to news quality usually learn *less* from the media, as do people who are highly critical of or skeptical about the accuracy of news content. People who are moderately skeptical about news content tend to think about it more carefully and therefore learn more from it (McLeod et al., 1986). Finally, people with the strongest interest in political communications are usually those who attend to the messages most carefully and learn the most from them; in this way, personal gratifications sought from political communications mediate media effects.

Information Processing

The effects of political communication are also modified by factors related to the *processing* of the messages. The more attention a person gives to a broadcast or print news story, the more the person learns from the story (Chaffee & Choe, 1980; Chaffee & Schleuder, 1986). Studies have identified three levels of information processing among news audiences (Kosicki & McLeod, 1990; Kosicki, McLeod, & Armor, 1987). These range from skimming or scanning the story (level one) to reading through the story (level two) to reading and then thinking about the story and possibly discussing it with others (level three).

Lower measures of political learning, interest, and participation are associated with processing at level one; higher measures occur when processing occurs at the third level. When information processing occurs at level two, interest and participation are enhanced but learning is not.

SUMMARY

Findings on the power of mass-mediated political effects have varied through the years. Studies of voting behavior in the 1940s and 1950s indicated limited effects from mass media but later studies found more direct and powerful media influences on voters.

Since the 1970s the number of studies of political communication effects has increased considerably. These studies have examined micro-level (affecting individuals) and macro-level (affecting society or the system) effects from political communications.

Several dynamic influences affect the nature of political communications in a society: the social scene, the political landscape, the media environment, and media content. Media influence on political communications is considerable in the United States; therefore, the media have a responsibility to provide a number of special functions.

Political advertising constitutes the primary form of communication between political candidates and the voting public. Political ads on television have been effective in presenting particular candidate images to the voting public, providing information about key issues, and sometimes influencing voting decisions.

Political communication is also influenced by the content of news stories and, specifically, their frames and news flaws. Frames are abstract notions that media professionals use to present news stories in a particular way. Framing devices often influence audiences' perceptions and interpretations. The four common flaws in news coverage are personalization, fragmentation, dramatization, and normalization.

Media effects research at the micro level usually falls into four divisions: formation and change of opinion; cognitive effects (including agenda-setting research, priming, knowledge gain, and framing); effects on individual perceptions of the political system; and effects on political behavior or participation. Macro-level studies, though problematic, seek to examine effects on systems, or effects on individuals that affect systems.

At either level, the nature and strength of effects from mediated political communication depend on a number of different factors, which have to do with certain characteristics or orientations of individual audience members and their processing of media messages.

REFERENCES

ANSOLABEHERE, S., & IYENGAR, S. (1995). *Going negative: How political advertisements shrink and polarize the electorate.* New York: Free Press.

BENNETT, W. L. (1988). *News: The politics of illusion* (2nd ed.). New York: Longman.

317

CHAPTER 18
Mass-Mediated
Political
Communication
Effects

Berelson, B. R., Lazarsfeld, P. F., & McPhee, W. N. (1954). *Voting: A study of opinion formation in a presidential campaign.* Chicago: University of Chicago Press.

BLUMLER, J. G. (ED.). (1983). *Communicating to voters: Television in the first European parliamentary election.* Beverly Hills: Sage.

BLUMLER, J. G., & MCLEOD, J. M. (1974). Communication and voter turnout in Britain. In T. Legatt (Ed.), *Sociological theory and social research* (pp. 265–312). Beverly Hills, CA: Sage.

BLUMLER, J. G., MCLEOD, J. M., & ROSENGREN, K. E. (1992). An introduction to comparative communication research. In J. Blumler, J. McLeod, & K. Rosengren (Eds.), *Comparatively speaking: Communication and culture across space and time* (pp. 3–18). Newbury Park, CA: Sage.

BLUMLER, J. G., & MCQUAIL, D. (1969). *Television in politics: Its uses and influence.* Chicago: University of Chicago Press.

BRIANS, C. L., & WATTENBERG, M. P. (1996). Campaign issue knowledge and salience: Comparing reception from TV commercials, TV news, and newspapers. *American Journal of Political Science, 40,* 172–193.

BURNHAM, W. D. (1982). *The current crisis in American politics.* New York: Oxford University Press.

CAPPELLA, J. N., & JAMIESON, K. H. (1994). Broadcast adwatch effects: A field experiment. *Communication Research, 21,* 342–365.

CHAFFEE, S. H. (1982). Mass media and interpersonal channels: Competitive, convergent or complementary? In G. Gumpert & R. Cathcart (Eds.), *Inter/media: Interpersonal communication in a media world* (pp. 57–77). New York: Oxford University Press.

CHAFFEE, S. H., & CHOE, S. Y. (1980). Time of decision and media use during the Ford-Carter campaign. *Public Opinion Quarterly, 44,* 53–59.

CHAFFEE, S. H., & HOCHHEIMER, J. (1985). The beginnings of political communication research in the United States: Origins of the limited effects model. In M. Gurevitch & M. Levy (Eds.), *Mass communication review yearbook* (Vol. 5, pp. 75–104). Beverly Hills, CA: Sage.

CHAFFEE, S. H., & SCHLEUDER, J. (1986). Measurement and effects of attention to media news. *Human Communication Research, 13,* 76–107.

CONOVER, P. J., & FELDMAN, S. (1989). Candidate perception in an ambiguous world: Campaigns, cues and inference processes. *American Journal of Political Science, 33,* 912–939.

DELLI CARPINI, M. X., AND KEETER, S. (1991). U.S. public's knowledge of politics. *Public Opinion Quarterly, 55,* 583–612.

DEVLIN, L. P. (1995). Political commercials in American presidential elections. In L. L. Kaid & C. Holtz-Bacha (Eds.), *Political advertising in western democracies: Parties and candidates on television* (pp. 186–205). Thousand Oaks, CA: Sage.

EPSTEIN, E. J. (1973). *News from nowhere.* New York: Random House.

ERICSON, R. V., BARANEK, P. M., & CHAN, B. L. (1989). *Negotiating control: A study of news sources.* Toronto, Canada: University of Toronto Press.

ETZIONI, A. (1988). *Capital corruption: The new attack on American democracy.* New Brunswick: NJ: Transaction Books.

FAZIO, R. H., & WILLIAMS, C. J. (1986). Attitude accessibility as a moderator of the attitude-perception and attitude-behavior relations: An investigation of the 1984 presidential election. *Journal of Personality and Social Psychology, 51,* 505–514.

FIORINA, M. P. (1981). *Retrospective voting in American national elections.* New Haven: Yale University Press.

FISHBEIN, M., & AJZEN, I. (1975). *Belief, attitude, intention and behavior: An introduction to theory and research.* Reading, MA: Addison-Wesley.

FUNKHOUSER, G. R. (1973). The issues of the sixties: An exploratory study in the dynamics of public opinion. *Public Opinion Quarterly, 37,* 62–75.

GAMSON, W. A., & LASCH, K. E. (1983). The political culture of social welfare policy. In S. Spiro & E. Yuchtman-Yaar (Eds.), *Evaluating the welfare state: Social and political perspectives* (pp. 397–415). New York: Academic Press.

GANS, H. J. (1979). *Deciding what's news: A study of the CBS Evening News, NBC Nightly News, Newsweek and Time.* New York: Vintage Books.

GITLIN, T. (1978). Media sociology: The dominant paradigm. *Theory and Society, 6,* 205–253.

GITLIN, T. (1980). *The whole world is watching: Mass media and the making and unmaking of the New Left.* Berkeley: University of California Press.

GOLDENBERG, E., & TRAUGOTT, M. (1984). *Campaigning for congress.* Washington, DC: CQ Press.

GRANBERG, D., & BROWN, T. A. (1989). On affect and cognition in politics. *Social Psychology Quarterly, 52,* 171–182.

GUNTER, B. (1987). *Poor reception: Misunderstanding and forgetting broadcast news.* Hillsdale, NJ: Erlbaum.

GUREVITCH, M., & BLUMLER, J. G. (1990). Political communication systems and democratic values. In J. Lichtenberg (Ed.), *Democracy and the mass media* (pp. 269–289). Cambridge: Cambridge University Press.

HALL, S., CRITCHER, C., JEFFERSON, T., CLARKE, J., & ROBERTS, B. (1978). *Policing the crisis.* New York: Holmes & Meier.

HART, R. P. (1996). Easy citizenship: Television's curious legacy. *Annals of the American Academy of Political and Social Science, 546,* 109–119.

HERMAN, E. S., & CHOMSKY, N. (1988). *Manufacturing consent: The political economy of the mass media.* New York: Pantheon Books.

HOUSTON, D. A., & DOAN, K. (1999). Can you back that up? Evidence (or lack thereof) for the effects of negative and positive political communication. *Media Psychology, 1,* 191–206.

IYENGAR, S. (1989). How citizens think about national issues. *American Journal of Political Science, 33,* 878–897.

IYENGAR, S. (1991). *Is anyone responsible? How television frames political issues.* Chicago: University of Chicago Press.

IYENGAR, S., & KINDER, D. R. (1987). *News that matters.* Chicago: University of Chicago Press.

IYENGAR, S., & SIMON, A. F. (2000). New perspectives and evidence on political communication and campaign effects. *Annual Review of Psychology, 51,* 149–169.

JOHNSON-CARTEE, K. S., & COPELAND, G. A. (1991). *Negative political advertising: Coming of age.* Hillsdale, NJ: Erlbaum.

JOSLYN, R. A. (1980). The content of political spot ads. *Journalism Quarterly, 57,* 92–98.

JUST, M. R., CRIGLER, A. N., & WALLACH, L. (1990). Thirty seconds or thirty minutes: What viewers learn from spot advertisements and candidate debates. *Journal of Communication, 40*(3), 120–133.

KAID, L. L. (1981). Political advertising. In D. Nimmo & K. R. Sanders (Eds.), *Handbook of political communication* (pp. 249–271). Beverly Hills, CA: Sage.

KAID, L. L. (1996). Political communication. In M. B. Salwen & D. W. Stacks (Eds.), *An integrated approach to communication theory and research* (pp. 443–457). Mahwah, NJ: Erlbaum.

KAID, L. L., GOBETZ, R., GARNER, J., LELAND, C. M., & SCOTT, D. (1993). Television news and presidential campaigns: The legitimization of televised political advertising. *Social Science Quarterly, 74,* 274–285.

KAID, L. L., & JOHNSTON, A. (1991). Negative versus positive television advertising in U.S. presidential campaigns. *Journal of Communication, 41,* 53–64.

KANISS, P. (1991). *Making local news.* Chicago: University of Chicago Press.

319

CHAPTER 18
Mass-Mediated
Political
Communication
Effects

KATZ, E. (1987). On conceptualizing media effects: Another look. In S. Oskamp (Ed.), *Applied Social Psychology Annual* (Vol. 8, pp. 32–42). Beverly Hills, CA: Sage.

KERN, M. (1989). *30-second politics: Political advertising in the eighties.* New York: Praeger.

KINDER, D. R., & KIEWIET, D. R. (1983). Sociotropic politics: The American case. *British Journal of Political Science, 11,* 129–161.

KOSICKI, G. M., & McLEOD, J. M. (1990). Learning from political news: Effects of media images and information-processing strategies. In S. Kraus (Ed.), *Mass communication and political information processing* (pp. 69–83). Hillsdale, NJ: Erlbaum.

KOSICKI, G. M., McLEOD, J. M., & ARMOR, D. L. (1987, May). *Processing the news: Some individual strategies for selecting, sense-making and integrating.* Paper presented at the Annual meeting of the International Communication Association, Montreal, Quebec.

KROSNICK, J. A. (1988). The role of attitude importance in social evaluation: A study of policy preference, presidential candidate evaluations, and voting behavior. *Journal of Personality and Social Psychology, 55,* 196–210.

LAZARSFELD, P. F., BERELSON, B. R., & GAUDET, H. (1948). *The people's choice* (2nd ed.). New York: Columbia University Press.

LEE, M. A., & SOLOMON, N. (1990). *Unreliable sources: A guide to bias in news media.* New York: Lyle Stuart.

LEVY, M. R. (1981). Disdaining the news. *Journal of Communication, 31*(3), 24–31.

LOGAN, J. R., & MOLOTCH, H. L. (1987). *Urban fortunes: The political economy of place.* Berkeley: University of California Press.

MACKUEN, M. (1981). Social communication and the mass policy agenda. In M. MacKuen & S. Coombs (Eds.), *More than news: Media power in public affairs* (pp. 19–144). Beverly Hills, CA: Sage.

McCOMBS, M. E. (1977). Newspapers versus television: Mass communication effects across time. In D. Shaw & M. McCombs (Eds.), *The emergence of American political issues: The agenda-setting function of the press* (pp. 89–105). St. Paul, MN: West Publishing.

McCOMBS, M. E., & SHAW, D. L. (1972). The agenda-setting function of the mass media. *Public Opinion Quarterly, 36,* 176–187.

McLEOD, J. M., & BECKER, L. B. (1974). Testing the validity of gratification measures through political effects analysis. In J. G. Blumler & E. Katz (Eds.), *The uses of mass communication: Current perspectives on gratifications research* (pp. 137–164). Beverly Hills, CA: Sage.

McLEOD, J. M., BECKER, L. B., & BYRNES, J. E. (1974). Another look at the agenda-setting function of the press. *Communication Research, 1,* 131–165.

McLEOD, J. M., BYBEE, C. R., & DURALL, J. A. (1979). The 1976 presidential debates and the equivalence of informed political participation. *Communication Research, 6,* 463–487.

McLEOD, J. M., & DETENBER, B. H. (1999). Framing effects of television news coverage of social protest. *Journal of Communication, 49*(3), 3–23.

McLEOD, J. M., KOSICKI, G. M., ARMOR, D. L., ALLEN, S. G., & PHILPS, D. M. (1986, August). *Public images of mass media news: What are they and does it matter?* Paper presented at the annual meeting of the Association for Education in Journalism and Mass Communication, Norman, OK.

McLEOD, J. M., KOSICKI, G. M., & McLEOD, D. M. (1994). The expanding boundaries of political communication effects. In J. Bryant & D. Zillmann (Eds.), *Media effects: Advances in theory and research* (pp. 123–162). Hillsdale, NJ: Erlbaum.

McLEOD, J. M., KOSICKI, G. M., & RUCINSKI, D. M. (1988). Political communication research: An assessment of the field. *Mass Communication Review, 15*(1), 8–15, 30.

McLEOD, J. M., & McDONALD, D. G. (1985). Beyond simple exposure: Media orientations and their impact on political processes. *Communication Research, 12,* 3–33.

McLeod, J. M., Pan, Z., & Rucinski, D. (1989, May). *Framing a complex issue: A case of social construction of meaning.* Paper presented at the annual meeting of the International Communication Association, San Francisco.

McLeod, J. M., Sun, S., Chi, A., & Pan, Z. (1990, August). *Metaphor and the media: What shapes public understanding of the "war" on drugs?* Paper presented at the annual meeting of the Association for Education in Journalism and Mass Communication, Minneapolis, MN.

Miron, D. (1999). Grabbing the nonvoter. In B. I. Newman (Ed.), *Handbook of political marketing* (pp. 321–343). Thousand Oaks, CA: Sage.

Miron, D., & Bryant, J. (in press). Mass media and voter turnout. In R. A. Carveth & J. Bryant (Eds.), *Meta-analyses of media effects.* Mahwah, NJ: Erlbaum.

Nelson, T. E., Oxley, Z. M., & Clawson, R. A. (1997). Toward a psychology of framing effects. *Political Behavior, 19,* 221–246.

Neuman, W. R. (1986). *The paradox of mass politics: Knowledge and opinion in the American electorate.* Cambridge: Harvard University Press.

Neuman, W. R. (1976). Patterns of recall among television news viewers. *Public Opinion Quarterly, 40,* 115–123.

Newhagen, J. E., & Reeves, B. (1991). Emotion and memory responses for negative political advertising: A study of television commercials used in the 1988 presidential election. In F. Biocca (Ed.), *Television and political advertising, Volume 1: Psychological processes* (pp. 197–220). Hillsdale, NJ: Erlbaum.

Noelle-Neumann, E. (1984). *Spiral of Silence: Our Social Skin.* Chicago: University of Chicago Press.

O'Keefe, G. J. (1985). "Taking a bite out of crime": The impact of a public information campaign. *Communication Research, 12,* 147–178.

Perloff, R. M. (1998). *Political communication: Politics, press, and public in America.* Mahwah, NJ: Erlbaum.

Petty, R. E., & Cacioppo, J. T. (1986). *Communication and persuasion: Central and peripheral routes to attitude change.* New York: Springer-Verlag.

Pfau, M., & Louden, A. (1994). Effectiveness of adwatch formats in deflecting political attack ads. *Communication Research, 21,* 325–341.

Popkin, S. L. (1991). *The reasoning voter: Communication and persuasion in presidential campaigns.* Chicago: University of Chicago Press.

Powell, G. B., Jr. (1986). American voter turnout in comparative perspective. *American Political Science Review, 80*(1), 17–44.

Protess, D. L., Cook, F. L., Doppelt, J. C., Ettema, J. S., Gordon, M. T., Leff, D. R., & Miller, P. (1991). *The journalism of outrage: Investigative reporting and agenda building in America.* New York: Guilford Press.

Ranney, A. (1983). *Channels of power.* New York: Basic Books.

Rice, R. E., & Atkin, C. K. (Eds.). (1989). *Public communication campaigns* (2nd ed.). Beverly Hills: CA: Sage.

Semetko, H. A., Blumler, J. G., Gurevitch, M., & Weaver, D. H., with Barkin, S., & Wilhoit, G. C. (1991). *The formation of campaign agendas: A comparative analysis of party and media roles in recent American and British elections.* Hillsdale, NJ: Erlbaum.

Shapiro, M. A., & Rieger, R. H. (1992). Comparing positive and negative political advertising on radio. *Journalism Quarterly, 69,* 135–145.

Sigal, L. V. (1973). *Reporters and officials: The organization and politics of newsmaking.* Lexington, MA: D.C. Heath.

Smith, H. (1988). *The power game.* New York: Random House.

Star, S. A., & Hughes, H. M. (1950). Report on an education campaign: The Cincinnati plan for the UN. *American Journal of Sociology, 55,* 389–400.

321

CHAPTER 18
Mass-Mediated
Political
Communication
Effects

STRATE, J. M., PARRISH, C. J., ELDER, C. D., & FORD, C., III. (1989). Life span and civic development and voting participation. *American Political Science Review, 83*(2), 443–464.

TICHENOR, P. J., DONOHUE, G. A., & OLIEN, C. N. (1970). Mass media flow and differential growth of knowledge. *Public Opinion Quarterly, 34,* 159–170.

TICHENOR, P. J., DONOHUE, G. A., & OLIEN, C. N. (1980). *Community conflict and the press.* Beverly Hills, CA: Sage.

TIPTON, L. P., HANEY, R. D., & BASEHART, J. R. (1975). Media agenda-setting in city and state election campaigns. *Journalism Quarterly, 52,* 15–22.

VALKENBURG, P. M., SEMETKO, H. A., & DE VREESE, C. H. (1999). The effects of news frames on readers' thoughts and recall. *Communication Research, 26,* 550–569.

WEAVER, D. H., GRABER, D. A., MCCOMBS, M. E., & EYAL, C. H. (1981). *Media agenda-setting in a presidential election: Issues, images and interests.* New York: Praeger.

WEST, D. (1993) *Air wars.* Washington, DC: Congressional Quarterly Press.

WOLFINGER, R. E., & ROSENSTONE, S. J. (1980). *Who votes?* New Haven: Yale University Press.

CHAPTER 19

The Effects of Minority Portrayals

> *In this country American means white. Everybody else has to hyphenate.*
> —**Toni Morrison,** *The Guardian,* **January 29, 1992**

In 1999, when the new fall programs for the networks were unveiled, several minority rights activist groups were outraged because of the lack of new minority characters in the different programs. The National Council of La Raza (NCLR) encouraged Latino viewers to boycott the four networks during one week in September, in protest of the dearth of minority new character portrayals (Hanania, 1999).

During the turbulent 1960s, African Americans in the United States fought for and gained their civil rights. Since then, other minority groups have stepped forward and demanded not only equal rights, but also social acceptance and recognition. These other groups include those different from others due to race, religion, sexual orientation, physical challenges, or other factors.

In the past few decades, people of all colors and differences have begun to show more respect and tolerance for one another. But our society still has many miles to cover on the road to harmonious relations among the various races of diverse Americans. Many people still carry prejudices. Many are oblivious to the needs and feelings of others. Many wrongs remain to be righted.

Since the 1960s, portrayals of minority characters in mass media, particularly on television and in film, have reflected some of these societal changes. These changes in portrayals and, especially, their effects upon audiences' attitudes, values, and behaviors, are of particular interest to communication researchers. Most of the studies in this area were conducted in the 1970s and 1980s, and offer a large amount of informative data regarding those years.

Studies of the 1990s have shown that blacks have achieved very positive gains in both the number and the nature of their portrayals in entertainment programs, but other minorities have not fared so well. A recent study showed that African Americans are overrepresented in advertisements, far beyond their societal numbers (Taylor & Stern, 1997). Other minorities, however, such as Latinos, Asian Americans, and Native Americans continue to be grossly underrepresented in mass media, sometimes to the point of exclusion (Greenberg, Mastro, & Brand, 2001). When these groups are depicted, it is sometimes in stereotypical or demeaning ways.

Previous chapters have demonstrated the power of mass media to affect the cognitions or mental processes of media users. We learned that media messages are sometimes responsible for changing a person's attitudes and values. For better or worse, these changes may also alter a person's behavior.

This chapter explores the nature of minority portrayals in mass media and their effects upon audiences. You will recall from Chapter 6 on cultivation research that the real world is often very different from the world portrayed on television and in the movies. Research analyses of media content have examined whether or not minority characters are present, how they compare to other characters, the significance of the minority characters, and the interaction of minority characters with others. Other studies have explored the differences of minority and majority viewers in terms of their preferences for content and characters. First, we take a look at how the media convey social information to audiences through minority portrayals in entertainment programs, news reports, advertisements, and children's programming. We then examine the current content picture and conclude with results of studies on the effects of minority portrayals on audiences.

MEDIA AS CONVEYORS OF SOCIAL INFORMATION

Studies on minorities in mass media have generally fallen under two main categories: descriptions of minority portrayals or their effects on audiences (Greenberg & Brand, 1994). The first of these has been very important in determining what messages about minorities various media have been sending the public, or what social information has been conveyed. This research recognizes that television, film, videos, and other media—through entertainment, advertisements, news reports, and children's programming—are influential in providing information about minorities, especially for young people. We will first focus upon the descriptions of various media content that features minority characters before we turn to specific effects on minority audiences.

MINORITY PORTRAYALS IN ENTERTAINMENT

Researchers have used one of three different methods to describe minority characterizations (Greenberg & Brand, 1994). First, simply counting the number of different characters of various races (called "head counts") offers relevant information when the numbers are compared. Another method involves assessing the significance of each character in a program and, especially, comparing the roles played by minority characters to those played by majority characters. Finally, another method of study notes the similarities, differences, and interactions between characters played by people of different races.

For each of the three methods, studies have been much more numerous in years past than in recent years. This decline is a serious cause for concern. As Greenberg and Brand have noted, "new research efforts appear to be receding at a time when public consciousness about minority issues is rising" (1994, p. 273). Current and accurate numbers and findings are needed to ensure that the networks and moviemakers are attempting to reflect a more accurate picture of the world, and to ensure that any efforts on their part to correct inaccuracies in their portrayals of minorities are not going unnoticed. One of the few recent studies in this area revealed that the numbers and the nature of television characterizations in the early 1990s were different in many ways from those of the 1970s. Clearly, additional research is needed.

Counting Heads

Are minority characters underrepresented on television? Do their numbers on television match their numbers in society? These are the questions that **head count studies** attempt to answer.

Some of the first head count studies were conducted in the 1970s, when the number of minority characters on television fell far below their societal numbers. Two major head count studies examined the entire decade of the 1970s (Seggar, Hafen, & Hannonen-Gladden, 1981; Gerbner & Signorielli, 1979). The first of these found that white male characters increased from 81 to 88 percent during the decade and white female characters increased from 84 to 91 percent, while black male characters increased from 6 to 9 percent, and black females, from 5 to 6 percent. The number of nonblack minority characters (e.g., Latinos, Native Americans) as a whole fell in the 1970s from 13 to 3 percent. In summary, throughout the decade, the number of white characters increased even more beyond their actual numbers in society, the number of black characters increased slightly but remained below their societal percentages, and the number of nonblack minority characters were practically nonexistent. The programs assessed included comedies, dramas, and movies (Seggar, Hafen, & Hannonen-Gladden, 1981).

Another study during the decade of the 1970s also focused on television programs during the 1970s and reported similar findings. Communication scholars George Gerbner and Nancy Signorielli (1979) analyzed the minority representation in television programs as a part of their Cultural Indicators Project. They found that the number of nonwhite characters accounted for an average of 11 percent of all characters per year. The year of greatest representation was 1977, when 14 percent of characters in prime-time dramatic programs were nonwhite.

More recent studies have shown that network television is becoming more sensitive to the number of black character portrayals, but not other types of minorities. One head count study revealed that in the early 1990s, the number of black characters on network television came close to their percentage in society; however, Asian, Hispanic, and other minority characters remained underrepresented (Greenberg & Collette, 1997). The study examined the new season lineups of the major networks for 27 years, from 1966 to 1992. The researchers explained that "prior research identifying the various attributes of television's demography has never isolated new television characters for systematic analysis. The subsequent 'birth rate' that can be achieved by isolating new characters, and excluding ongoing characters, offers a more precise measure of the network efforts to alter yearly television populations" (p. 1). During the 27 years, almost 1,800 new characters were introduced. Of those, 88 percent were white and 10 percent were black. Asian, Native American, and Hispanic characters accounted for less than 1 percent each. (The 1990 U.S. Census indicated that Asian Americans made up 2.9 percent of the population and Hispanic Americans 9.0 percent.) Of all the new season characters, "only 12 Asians and 13 Hispanics could be identified as having major roles, with most of those occurring since 1980" (Greenberg & Collette, 1997, p. 8). Of the four networks, Fox featured the greatest percentage of black characters (13 percent), the least white characters (82 percent), and the most characters from other ethnic groups (6 percent). NBC and ABC posted the same numbers: 87 percent white, 11 percent black, and less than 1 percent Asian or Hispanic. The new programs for CBS contained the most white characters (90 percent) and Asian characters (1 percent), but the least number of blacks (8 percent) and Hispanics (.6 percent) (Greenberg & Collette, 1997, p. 8).

In the late 1990s, the networks responded to demands from minority activist groups by featuring more black characters on prime time, but not other minorities such as Asian Americans, Latino Americans or Native Americans (Greenberg, Mastro, & Brand, 2001). A recent study revealed that the number of black characters on prime-time television was in excess of their actual percentage in society at that time (12 percent), with blacks appearing in 16 percent of major and lesser prime time roles (Mastro & Greenberg, 2000). Still, television does not reflect America's colors accurately, as other minority groups remain as underrepresented in major network programming today as they were 20 years ago (Mastro & Greenberg, 2000; Greenberg, Mastro, & Brand, 2001). In the early 1990s, only 1.1 to 1.6 percent of characters on television were Latino, despite actual population numbers of 11.0 percent. A very recent study showed that Latinos made up 3 percent of the roles in prime-time fictional programming, Asian Americans only 1 percent, and Native Americans, less than 1 percent (Mastro & Greenberg, 2000; Greenberg et al., 2001).

Research Methods: Describing Minority Characterizations

For better or for worse, audiences learn from what they see on television. Children especially pick up a lot of social information by watching the interactions of characters on TV. Researchers have studied particular programs to find out what television is saying to audiences about minority characters— their status, their occupations, their similarities and differences from mainstream characters, and the nature of their interactions with others. They generally use three techniques to describe content:

Head Counts
Different characters of various races are counted.

Assessment of Significance
Significance of minority versus majority characters is assessed.

Similarities, Differences, & Interactions
Minority and majority characters are evaluated to determine similarities, differences, and the nature of their interactions.

Role Comparisons

The significance of roles for minority characters is another area of study that received a great amount of scrutiny in the 1970s and 1980s, but relatively few studies have been conducted in the 1990s (Greenberg & Brand, 1994). Researchers have examined the roles played by whites and nonwhites to discover how television is portraying them in terms of characterization, violence, occupations, age, and other factors. Most of these studies have focused on television programs, but a few have investigated print media and movies as well.

From 1975 to 1980, black men enjoyed more minor roles and bit parts on television, but they were featured in fewer leading and supporting roles. Blacks accounted for 9.0 percent of the men in major roles in 1975, while in 1980 their number dropped to 4.5 percent. In 1975, black males were featured in 12.0 percent of the supporting roles, and in 1980 only 4.5 percent. Black female appearances also declined, in major roles to 2.4 percent, and in supporting roles to 2.7 percent (Seggar et al., 1981).

Another study of minorities in major and supporting roles during the 1970s offered similar findings (Gerbner & Signorielli, 1979). Blacks appeared in 8.5 percent of the major roles in the programs examined, whereas Hispanics accounted for only 2.5 percent of the major roles. The numbers showed a decline toward the end of the decade.

Interactions between blacks and whites on television programs in the 1970s were found to be friendly in nature or to exhibit mutual respect only about 13 percent of the time. The black and white characters were rather equal in status in 7 of 10 episodes examined (Weigel, Loomis, & Soja, 1980).

Several studies have examined television characters in terms of their aggressiveness, heroism, and villainy. In 1970 Gerbner attempted to determine which television characters were committing acts of violence. He found that 66 percent of the nonwhites, 60 percent of the white foreigners, and 50 percent of the white Americans were responsible for acts of TV violence. Gerbner also found that nonwhite characters were usually victims. Ten years later, Gerson found that two groups of nonwhites, blacks and Native Americans, usually portrayed killers rather than victims, and that whites, Asians, and Hispanics usually played characters that were killed by others (1980). Nonwhites were not always depicted as the bad guys; they were about as likely as white characters to appear as either good guys or bad guys (Gerbner & Signorielli, 1979).

Characters of color usually appeared in blue-collar or service jobs rather than in prestigious positions during the 1970s and 1980s, yet the percentage of minority characters depicted in professional or white-collar jobs, although small, actually exceeded their numbers in society. In terms of age, three of five nonwhites were under 35. Two of three white males were over the age of 35 (Gerbner, Gross, & Signorielli, 1985).

During the 1970s and 1980s, disabled characters on TV rarely appeared in a positive light. They were usually portrayed as poor, out-of-work, or abused (Elliot & Byrd, 1982; Donaldson, 1981). Most were physically challenged (68 percent) rather than mentally challenged (22 percent), and only one in three of all disabled characters was portrayed as an independent, productive individual. Also, about one in five exhibited some type of abusive or socially deviant behavior (Gardner & Radel, 1978).

Movies in the 1980s were even more negative in their presentations of disabled characters. A 1989 study that examined 67 disabled characters in movies from 1986 to 1988 found that about three of four exhibited abnormal or deviant personality traits. One in two was victimized at some point in the film (Byrd, 1989).

In the 1990s role comparisons between blacks and whites found blacks overrepresented as police officers (Mastro & Robinson, 2000). Portrayals of criminal justice characters were similar to those of whites in terms of physical and verbal aggressiveness (Tamborini, Mastro, Chory, & Huang, 2000). Latino roles also occurred most frequently in the area of criminal justice, with Latinos depicted as either law enforcement officers or criminals (Greenberg et al., 2001).

Portrayals of Interracial Interactions

How does television portray whites, blacks, and those of other races in their interactions with one another? Do programs provide accurate portrayals or do they present people of color in stereotypical or demeaning ways?

One method of analysis used to answer such questions involves studying the characters of different races in the same program and examining how those characters compare with one another. In one study of the 1970s, black and white characters on sitcoms were examined for certain behavioral characteristics (Reid, 1979). Both black and white male characters exhibited similar behaviors, but the female black characters were found to behave in stereotypical ways. Black females were usually boastful and domineering, and they usually appeared on the black-dominated comedies. Reid also found that whites appearing on black-dominated comedies behaved differently from the whites on white-dominated comedies. Overall, whites on the black-dominated shows exhibited more aggressiveness and dependent behavior, and they were generally more negative toward others.

Most Asian characters appearing on television in the mid-1970s portrayed teenagers, criminals, or business owners. As a whole they were not representative of their true numbers in the population with regard to many factors, including age, jobs, and marital status (Shu, 1979).

Another study of shows with predominantly black casts and shows with mixed casts in the 1970s revealed that black characters who were part of the mixed casts exhibited more competence, more cooperation, and higher social standing. Their counterparts on predominantly black shows were generally less educated and troubled by more personal problems (Banks, 1977).

A 1980 study of black and white characters selected from the same shows during a week of programming found the black characters to be younger and funnier than the white characters, but more likely to be unemployed. One in two of the black characters and one in three of the whites appeared in comedies. White characters had eight times as many conversations with one another than with black characters, but the ratio of whites to blacks was five to one (Baptista-Fernandez & Greenberg, 1980).

Interracial relationships, romantic and otherwise, have become rather commonplace on many daytime soap operas and in films, but unfortunately no recent studies have examined the phenomenon or its possible influence on majority and minority audiences. In the 1970s interactions between people of color on television programs were rare. In a study that examined one week of prime-time programming in 1978, most whites interacted with other whites and most blacks interacted with other blacks (Weigel et al., 1980).

Two studies in the 1970s approached the study of TV race relations by focusing on the behaviors of black family members and white family members. One of these studies found that the black family was usually made up of a single parent (usually the mother) with children, whereas the white family normally consisted of two parents and children. The most notable difference between portrayals of the different families was in their propensity for conflicts. One in 6 interactions among black family members involved conflicts, compared to only 1 in 10 interactions among white family members (Greenberg & Neuendorf, 1980). Another study examined more than 90 episodes of 12 shows depicting the family unit—6 featuring whites and 6 featuring blacks. This was another decade-long (1970–1980) study. It found that black families were portrayed in negative and stereotypical ways. Females usually headed black households, and black family members were generally portrayed with lower levels of education and lower occupational standings than their white counterparts. Also, interactions among black family members featured more conflicts than interactions among the white family members (Sweeper, 1983).

The Current Picture

Some recent research along these lines is available, but its focus is rather limited. In 1994, for example, the Corporation for Public Broadcasting conducted a focus group study to find out, among other things, how Native Americans were responding to portrayals of American Indians on public television. The study found that Native Americans considered their portrayals on public television to be fair and ethical, but they wanted to see more programs of interest to them. The groups examined recognized public television for first-rate educational programming for preschoolers (Corporation for Public Broadcasting, 1994).

A recent study by Mastro and Greenberg (2000) that assessed the minority portrayals during the 1996–1997 television season found blacks overrepresented and other minorities underrepresented in terms of their percentage in the general population of the United States. Asian Americans made up only 1 percent of the television population; Latinos accounted for only 3 percent. The study found no represention of Native Americans.

As for current television and viewing habits, a study by a media group released in 1998 revealed that ratings for cable programs were much higher among blacks than among whites. As a result, several cable networks target black audiences with more programs that feature black casts. "Television Viewing among Blacks" by TN Media Inc., examined black viewers based on data from Nielsen Media Research in 1997. The study found that blacks watch more cable—both basic and pay—than whites. Black Entertainment Television (BET) was popular among black viewers, but the study found that the Cartoon Network, TBS Superstation, Turner Network Television (TNT), and others also pulled higher ratings among black audiences. A&E, The Nashville Network, MSNBC, and The Learning Channel (TLC) showed higher ratings among whites than blacks (Moss, 1998).

In recent years, many successful films have
featured blacks in starring roles.
Source: © The Everett Collection

The study also found that blacks watch 11 percent more prime-time television than whites. They also tune in more to networks such as WB and UPN. These networks feature a number of programs with all-black or almost-all-black casts (Moss, 1998).

In the absence of a great amount of hard data, industry insiders offer much insight into the minority situation on television and in movies. Many newspaper, magazine, and trade press articles are written on the subject of minorities. Also, a number of television programs that feature information on upcoming films and television programs usually note minority involvement.

For the most part, recent articles acknowledge the increases in minority numbers but note that problems still exist. Blacks and other minorities are usually cast in roles that specifically call for a minority character; however, this is starting to change. Film star Halle Berry felt that her supporting role in *The Flinstones* was a breakthrough because "it was a part that could've gone to anybody. It could've gone to a white actress. But it went to me" (Ivry, 1998). In another example, Will Smith's portrayal of James West in the action adventure movie *Wild Wild West* represented another instance when a leading role could have gone to anyone, but happened to go to a black actor.

Many films in the 1990s have broken new ground by featuring blacks in starring roles. Moreover, many of the more recent films do not portray the minority characters in stereotypical ways, that is, as criminals or inner-city residents. Stars such as Cuba Gooding, Jr., Will Smith, Denzell Washington, Samuel L. Jackson, Halle Berry, Vanessa Williams, Vivica A. Fox, and Whitney

Houston have landed roles that "could've gone to anybody," as Berry put it. These stars have also proven that they can attract audiences of different colors.

Daytime television portrayals of minorities and their interactions with majority characters have also changed considerably in recent years. Unfortunately, recent research has not examined these trends. On the ABC network alone, daytime soaps such as *Port Charles*, *One Life to Live,* and *General Hospital* have many minority characters, including blacks, Hispanics, and characters in wheelchairs. Interracial premarital and marital relationships are also depicted. The box summarizes the four stages of minority portrayals on television.

MINORITY PORTRAYALS IN NEWS REPORTS

Most of what we know about the presence and presentation of minorities in the news comes primarily from studies conducted during the 1970s and 1980s. Relatively few studies have been conducted in more recent years. Those that have been published reveal an increased presence of minorities in the news, although the nature of the portrayals is not always positive (Greenberg & Brand, 1992b) and far more negative than fictional portrayals have tended to be (Dixon & Linz, 2000).

Baran (1973) and Roberts (1975) each examined network television newscasts for the presence of blacks. They found that blacks appeared in 25 percent and 23 percent, respectively, of network newscasts. This was during the period when civil rights issues were at the forefront of public attention, and most of the stories had to do with busing and segregation.

One study compared newspaper coverage of black and white candidates in 19 cities during the 1970s. Chaundhary (1980) found that whites generally received more coverage than blacks on election day and two days prior to election day; however, stories on black candidates tended to be longer. Different newspapers covered black and white candidates differently, leading Chaundhary to conclude that individual newspaper policy played a major part in the coverage given to blacks and whites.

Several studies examined the content of newspapers in three decades, 1950–53, 1963–68, and 1972–80, to detect any changes that had occurred through the years in print coverage of blacks (Martindale, 1984, 1985, 1987). One of these studies found that the activities of blacks in the community became much more visible through the years with the appearance of many more photographs of African Americans; however, the newspaper ran few stories about minority life and the problems of blacks in the community. Another study focused on four major newspapers—The New York Times, Atlanta Constitution, Chicago Tribune, and the Boston Globe. From the 1950s to the 1970s, all but one newspaper increased the number of stories on the problems of blacks. From the 1960s to the 1970s, stories about black criminals remained relatively constant and stories about black entertainers and black politicians increased considerably. Far fewer stories about black protesters appeared in the 1970s than in the 1960s.

Several studies in the 1980s looked at local newspaper coverage in areas of the country with large numbers of Latinos. They found that local newspapers tended to include Hispanic news in proportion to the number of Hispanics in their communities; however, most of the "Hispanic news" stories were so labeled because they mentioned someone with a Spanish last name (Greenberg, Heeter, Burgoon, Burgoon, & Korzenny, 1983a). Also, news coverage tended to be negative and focused on Hispanics as "problem people" (Turk, Richard, Bryson, & Johnson, 1989). In one community, a study of Hispanic stories among various media found that television and newspapers offered coverage of Hispanics in proportion to their numbers in the community, but radio did not. Hispanic names on radio were mostly in crime stories, but less than half of the stories featuring Hispanics in newspapers and television were related to crime (Korzenny, Griffis, Greenberg, Burgoon, & Burgoon, 1983).

Asian Americans also received print coverage in relation to their numbers in the community. Mansfield-Richardson (1996) analyzed the content of 20 major newspapers from 1994 to 1995 to examine their coverage of Asian Americans. She found that newspapers that employed more Asian Americans were usually those in communities with the most Asian Americans. Those same newspapers were more likely to run stories on Asian Americans in the community.

One study of television news in Chicago during 1989 and 1990 found differences in the portrayals of black and white political leaders. Entman (1992) discovered that local TV news stories usually featured white leaders as representing the interests of all constituents. Stories portrayed black leaders as more concerned with the interests of the black community than the overall good.

In addition to individuals of color, researchers have also examined news reports concerning disabled people to determine the nature of such portrayals. A study of several daily newspapers with a national audience in the 1980s found that approximately eight articles concerning or mentioning disabled people were published daily. The majority of these stories focused on the person's disability. Approximately half the stories discussed the negative impact of the disability, but most of those also pointed out possibilities for positive improvements (Keller, Hallahan, McShane, Crowley, & Blandford, 1990).

One of the most interesting recent studies examined the prejudices in reporting on gays and lesbians in the United States from the 1940s until the present day (Bennett, 1998). The number of articles about gays and lesbians in *Time* and *Newsweek* have increased from 2 in the 1940s, to 25 in the 1960s, to 95 in the 1980s, to 151 in the 1990s. These increases reflect society's growing awareness of homosexuals and the issues that relate to them. The study found that the coverage of gays and lesbians through the years has been overwhelmingly negative and prejudicial. Writers have used derogatory terms such as "faggot," "fruit," "queer," "butch," and "pervert" to describe them. The study recommended that journalists take conscious steps to be aware of prejudicial and derogatory comments from sources, to avoid printing unfounded allegations against gays and lesbians, and to challenge "powerful" sources that disparage homosexuals.

MINORITY PORTRAYALS IN ADVERTISING

Like entertainment portrayals of minorities, advertising images historically have been mostly white until recently (Coltraine & Messineo, 2000; Wilson & Gutierrez, 1995). Recent studies have shown that blacks and Asian Americans have made significant gains in some media in the past few decades although other minorities remain underrepresented. The nature of the portrayals for blacks, however, has been a cause for concern in the past (Greenberg & Brand, 1994).

Studies from the 1970s forward offer a clear picture of the historical nature of minority portrayals in advertisements. They reveal an increased presence of certain minorities and a marked absence of others. More and more black and Asian faces have appeared in television ads through the decades, from virtual nonexistence to more representative numbers, to overrepresentation by more than double the numbers of African Americans and Asian Americans in society. By 1994 blacks appeared in more than 31 percent of all commercial advertisements featuring models (Taylor & Stern, 1997). Asian Americans appeared in more than 8 percent of all commercial ads featuring models. This compares rather favorably to their societal percentage of only 3.6 (Greenberg, Mastro, & Brand, 2001). The years have not been so kind to Native Americans and the disabled, who have been avoided almost completely (Wilson & Gutierrez, 1995; Greenberg et al., 2001).

From the 1940s to the 1960s, blacks appeared in only about 3 percent of the ads in national magazines. Those that appeared usually fell into one of three categories: well-known entertainers, famous athletes, or unknowns depicted as servants (Colfax & Steinberg, 1972; Kassarjian, 1969; Stempel, 1971).

Two studies in the late 1970s found that the situation for blacks in advertisements had not improved, and had actually deteriorated. One found a mere 2 percent presence of blacks in magazine ads (Bush, Resnick, & Stern, 1980). A second study reviewed 8,700 advertisements for new products or services in issues of *Time, Cosmopolitan, Reader's Digest,* and *Ladies' Home Journal* from 1968 to 1977. Of this total, less than 1 percent featured black models or characters (Reid & Vanden Bergh, 1980).

The situation did not change significantly in the 1980s. Jackson and Ervin (1991) examined almost a thousand ads from 1986 to 1988 that appeared in *Cosmopolitan, Glamour,* and *Vogue.* Only 2.4 percent of the ads featured black women models, and of those 83.0 percent portrayed the black woman from a distance. At that time, blacks accounted for more than 12 percent of the female population of the United States and a hefty 15 percent of the subscribers to the magazines examined.

Several studies in the 1970s and 1980s found that white magazine readers did not respond negatively to the use of black models in ads (Block, 1972; Schlinger & Plummer, 1972; Soley, 1983). One of these studies measured the actual readership of ads featuring black models. It found that the race of the model did not affect ad readership.

Broadcast commercials have tended to include more black models through the years, but studies have noted that blacks tend to appear in a crowd rather than alone (Atkin & Heald, 1977; Bush, Solomon, & Hair, 1977; Culley & Bennett, 1976; Dominick & Greenberg, 1970). As the 1960s progressed, black models on television increased from 5 to 11 percent. By the mid-1970s African Americans accounted for 10 to 13 percent of the models appearing on TV ads—numbers close to their actual societal percentages. A study of prime-time commercials in 1978 found that whites appeared in ads 97.0 percent of the commercial time, blacks 8.5 percent, and cross-racial appearances 5.0 percent (Weigel et al., 1980). Approximately 75 percent of the commercials were all-white, whereas all-black commercials accounted for only 2 percent. By comparison, animated commercials that lacked any human accounted for about 4 percent of commercials.

Other minority groups have not enjoyed such increases. In a study of television commercials in the late 1970s, Gerbner, Gross, Morgan, and Signorielli (1981) found that Hispanics appeared in fewer than 2 percent of the commercials shown during prime time, less than 1 percent of commercials during the day on weekends, and not at all in commercials shown during evening newscasts.

The Current Scene

The 1990s have seen a few breakthroughs. A number of black women have achieved the status of "supermodel" and now enjoy enormous visibility in the press. Tyra Banks broke the *Sports Illustrated* color barrier by being the first black woman to make the cover of the famed Swimsuit Edition. Black British supermodel Naomi Campbell teamed up with white superstars Elle McPherson and Claudia Schiffer to open trendy restaurants in major cities of the world. Their friendship and business partnership offered a highly visible example of positive relations between the races.

In terms of quantitative evidence, Bowen & Schmid (1997) found that the use of black models increased in major magazines in recent years; however, Hispanic and Asian models still rarely appear. Blacks were usually depicted as athletes or musicians. They appeared mostly in ads sponsored by the government and in public service messages.

Another recent study underscored the fact that Latinos, particularly, are highly underrepresented in the ads of general-audience magazines. Even though Latinos made up more than 10 percent of the population in the United States at the time of the study, they appeared in only 4.7 percent of the ads examined, and less than half of those pictured a Latino as a major character in the ad (Taylor & Bang, 1997).

MINORITY PORTRAYALS IN CHILDREN'S PROGRAMMING

As early as the 1970s, programs for children on public television began to focus on positive portrayals of minorities and harmonious racial interactivity. Award-winning programs such as *Sesame Street*, *Mr. Rogers*, and *Electric Company* were recognized as much for their sensitivity to minority issues as for their instructional and entertainment value. Even in the early 1970s, about 25 percent of the characters on these public television programs were minorities (Dohrmann, 1975).

Historically, a much different (i.e., a much less diverse) picture emerges when one changes to children's programs on the commercial networks. Greenberg and Brand (1993) conducted a qualitative analysis of 20 Saturday morning children's shows on commercial TV and concluded that "Saturday's commercial television program schedule is fairly empty as a carrier of multicultural information" (p. 142). The researchers summarized their findings in this way:

> (a) three programs featured regularly appearing racial minority characters; (b) all racial minority characters who appeared regularly were black; (c) in 10.5 hours, one Hispanic American was featured, zero Asian Americans and zero Native Americans; and (d) all racial minority characters featured were male— the adult minority woman was invisible, and younger minority females, when present, were background characters. (p. 295)

By and large, this study confirmed the results of previous landmark studies of the 1970s and 1980s that involved both head counts and examinations of roles. Barcus (1975) and Barcus and Wolkin (1977) studied advertisements and programs for children on the commercial networks during the 1970s. For weekend programs, they found that 7 percent of the characters on the programs were black, whereas other minorities were present in the range of 4 to 8 percent. Numbers on weekday/daytime programming were much lower (3 percent for blacks and 1 to 4 percent for other minorities), but at that time, weekday programs tended to be syndicated repeats of programs produced during earlier decades when minority issues had not come to the forefront. Seven percent of the characters in commercials, were black and only about 2 percent were some other minority. Other head count studies of the early to mid-1970s reported similar findings (Gerbner & Signorielli, 1979; Mendelson & Young, 1972).

Head count studies in the 1980s did not reveal dramatic changes in numbers, but studies that examined role portrayals in children's programming of the 1980s produced interesting findings. Barcus (1983) found that blacks had made significant inroads while other minorities had been left behind. Blacks on children's programs were almost as likely to be cast as heroes as whites, and much more likely to be the heroes as other characters of color. About 2 percent of the major characters on these programs were black. The study also found that blacks appeared in different types of jobs, and they were two times as likely as other minorities to appear in managerial and professional jobs. On the negative side for all minority portrayals, Barcus found that cartoon comedies usually portrayed ethnic minorities in stereotypical ways, and sometimes these stereotypes were cruel in nature. The box describes the influence of television on the perceptions of children ages 10 to 17.

In recent years, research studies that examine minority portrayals in children's programming have been sparse, but a number of innovative programs indicate that the networks are becoming more sensitive to issues of color in children's programs. Nickelodeon and its network for preschoolers, Nick Jr., have led the way for commercial television by offering interesting and highly successful programs that feature an abundance of minority characters portrayed in a positive light. One reason for Nickelodeon's success in producing programs sensitive to minority portrayals may have to do with an innovative intern program that recruits minority students to work on new and existing programs. Shows like *Gullah Gullah Island* and *Allegra's Window* have known commercial and critical success and have been lauded for their educational

A Different World: Media Images of Race and Class

This study from a children's advocacy group called Children Now polled 1,200 children from the ages of 10 to 17 throughout the United States in an attempt to understand television's influence on their perceptions. The study found that children (especially African Americans, Asians, and Hispanics) felt that it is important to see characters of their own race on television. White and black children say they frequently see people of their own race on TV, but Latino and Asian children say they do not see their race represented much. Almost half of the black children felt that their race was represented more accurately and fairly by entertainment media than news media.

White children usually selected white stars as their favorites, while minority children usually selected black stars. The exceptions were actor Will Smith and basketball great Michael Jordan, who were popular with children of all colors. Children of all races tended to associate positive characteristics with whites and negative characteristics with minorities on TV. When asked which race they would likely see playing particular roles on television, the children agreed that criminals or maids and janitors would be played by African Americans, while secretaries, bosses, police officers, and doctors would be played by whites.

One Asian girl in the study remarked: "You see African Americans getting along with other African Americans, and Caucasians getting along with other Caucasians, but you rarely see an African American and Caucasian together happy and as friends."

In light of the findings, communications scholar Joanne Cantor remarked: "There is evidence that as kids watch TV, what they see becomes their reality. This age group is very vulnerable to what they are watching."

Sources: Kato, D. (1998, 8 May), *San Jose Mercury News*, Study: Kids tuned in to ethnic stereotyping, In *The Arizona Republic*, May 8, 1998, p. A11; Lewis, D. (1998, 21 May), "When children see little of their own world on the screen," Gannett News Service, *Nashville Tennessean*, ARC; Burby, L. N. (1998, 11 July), Planned parenting/TV colors children's perceptions, *Newsday*, Part II, p. B02.

value and sensitivity to minority portrayals. The cartoon *Doug*, a nonviolent cartoon that originated on Nickelodeon but soon began appearing on the ABC network as well, features children of various exotic colors, including purple.

Additional content analyses that examine the numbers and, especially, the nature of minority portrayals are sorely needed to understand the current picture in children's programming. Media effects studies are needed even more desperately. The impact of minority portrayals in these new programs on minority and majority children's ideas and attitudes would be fascinating to learn.

THE EFFECTS OF MINORITY PORTRAYALS

The studies that describe television content provide interesting data and take a step toward answering the questions: "Are minority portrayals sending accurate and fair pictures to the American public? Are interactions among minority and majority characters promoting pictures of racial harmony or of racial conflict?" Such studies, however, do very little to answer other important questions. For example, "What effects do minority portrayals have on minority and majority audiences? What effects do such portrayals have on children of all colors?"

Media effects research attempts to provide answers to these difficult questions. You will recall that in Chapter 4 we discussed social learning theory and its underlying importance in understanding a large part of the research on media effects. Social learning theory lies at the heart of research that examines the effects of minority portrayals in mass media. This theory posits that individuals learn from what they see in the media. Children especially are likely to pick up attitudes and behaviors by simply viewing situations, actions, and interactions on television and in other media. For this reason, minority portrayals have the potential to educate children about race relations, for better or for worse.

The evidence for the effects of minority portrayals on majority and minority audiences will be discussed momentarily, but first we should note that several studies have provided insights into the perceptions of both majority and minority audiences. These studies reveal much about the differences in these audiences. Whites, blacks, and other people of color not only use the media differently and for different purposes, but they also vary in their disposition toward media portrayals of their own race and other races. They also perceive media messages differently.

Several studies have found that viewers enjoy seeing people of their own color in the media, particularly on television. They like these characters more, they trust them more, and they identify with them more. Black high school students have indicated a stronger liking than white students for shows featuring black characters (Dates, 1980). White high school students have rated white newscasters higher than black newscasters in terms of competency and the likelihood that those newscasters might some day be neighbors or relatives (Kaner, 1982). Grade school children tend to select their favorite characters on the basis of race. During a season when 85 percent of the characters on television were white, 96 percent of the white children selected a white character as their favorite, whereas only 75 percent of the black children and 80 percent of the Hispanic children chose a white character (Eastman & Liss, 1980). When programs featuring minority characters are available, minority audiences tend to prefer these shows to others that feature white characters (Liss, 1981; Eastman & Liss, 1980; Greenberg, Heeter, Burgoon, Burgoon, & Korzenny, 1983b).

Studies that compare the perceptions of young minority and majority audiences have produced interesting findings. One such study has indicated that black youngsters may be more prone to the effects of cultivation. Black children are more likely than white children to believe that television portrayals of blacks and nonblacks are realistic. Greenberg and Atkin (1982) found that approximately 40 percent of black children, compared to about 30 percent of white children, agreed that the portrayals they witnessed reflected the true state of affairs as they exist in the real world.

Young white and black viewers also differ in the ways they use information from television in their lives. White children use television as a primary source of information about black children (Greenberg, 1972). Black children use information from television much more extensively in their lives. They report that they learn about employment opportunities, problem-solving techniques, interactions between spouses and their children, and other areas to a much greater extent than white children (Greenberg & Atkin, 1982).

In a study of music videos among black and white adolescents, Brown and Schulze (1990) found significant differences in interpretation. Two Madonna videos, "Papa Don't Preach" and "Open Your Heart," were shown to the adolescents. Almost all the whites indicated that the theme of the first video was pregnancy, whereas almost half the blacks perceived the theme to be focused on the father-daughter relationship. For the second video, almost half the whites identified the theme to be pornography and sexual perversion, while more than 50 percent of the black males and 30 percent of the black females said that the video did not have a theme.

Effects on Majority Audiences

Media images of minorities have been shown to have a considerable impact on white audiences. The portrayal of a lazy, incompetent, rebellious, or violent person of color is an enduring mental image. Subsequent stereotypes on the part of the white viewer have been found to occur.

Most white children prefer to watch action-adventure programs on television, shows that contain a great deal of violence (Eastman & Liss, 1980). Children who spend the most time watching such violent programming are the most likely to have negative stereotypes of blacks. On the other hand, white children who watch less violent shows and more shows featuring black characters are less likely to have prejudicial attitudes or stereotypical beliefs toward blacks (Zuckerman, Singer, & Singer, 1980). The box illustrates an effort by the television producers of Sesame Street in Israel and Palestine to promote tolerance and understanding among children in those troubled countries.

The most recent study on stereotypes from the media found that whites tend to stereotype people of color on the basis of media messages and direct contacts with the people. For example, whites evaluated Native Americans based on their first contact with them. The tendency to stereotype depended upon whether or not the first contact was a pleasant one (Tan, Fujioka, & Lucht, 1997).

Combating Prejudice: Teaching Mutual Respect

In 1998 Israeli and Palestinian producers of *Sesame Street* decided to introduce a series of shows in each country that depicted Israeli and Palestinian characters living in peace and helping each other. The Hebrew *Rechov Sumsum* and the Arabic *Sharaa Simsim* were each produced without featuring mosques or synagogues in the story lines. The programs taught the usual *Sesame Street* fare, introducing children to their numbers, colors, letters, and words, except that Israeli characters lived on one street and Palestinian characters on another. In one episode, the Jewish child rode a bicycle into an Arab neighborhood and, after having a flat tire, Arab characters provided a new replacement wheel.

After watching the series of programs, children tested showed increased tolerance toward the other children. "The show is having an impact. Israeli and Palestinian kids are saying nicer things about each other," said the president of the company that produces America's *Sesame Street*, the Sesame Workshop. "After four month's exposure, kids were more likely to say positive things [about one another]," a researcher reported.

Unfortunately, the programs were not a hit with adults in the Middle East, especially those on the Palestinian side. One Israeli official said she heard Palestinian teachers complaining, "The Israelis have taken everything from us—our homes, our land—and now we're giving them a bicycle wheel?"

Sources: Jacobson, P. (2000, 9 January). International: Discord dogs Middle East muppets: Real-life rivalries are threatening to kill off a children's television show designed to heal communal rifts, *Sunday Telegraph* (London), p. 22; Viva Press (1999, 2 December). Peace prevails on Israeli version of Sesame Street, *Canadian Jewish News*, p. B3; Hockstader, L. (1999, 10 November). Middle East muppets at a crossroads; local "Sesame Street" hits more snags than the peace process, *International Herald Tribune*, p. 7.

White children who tune in to black TV programs on a regular basis report that they learn much about the behavior and appearance of black people from what they see on television. The white children who watched the most programs featuring black characters did so because they perceived the characters to be funny; in other words, they enjoyed the humor in the black situation comedies. Atkin, Greenberg, and McDermott (1983) also found that television tended to reinforce existing attitudes as well as to provide new information to the white children.

Effects on Minority Audiences

Much of what we know about the effects of television programming on minority audiences has come from studies performed in the 1970s and 1980s. Two reviews of research have summarized the findings from those important studies. The first review showed that as audience members, ethnic minority children:

1. Have distinct and different preferences in television programs.
2. Have particular orientations toward television and mass media.
3. Respond with similar behaviors to programs that include minority characters portrayals.
4. Learn from television and use the information as an important source of instruction or guidance (Comstock & Cobbey, 1979).

The second review indicated that:

1. As characters on television, blacks were becoming more visible after years of underrepresentation, but the portrayals were usually low in status or importance and sometimes negative and stereotypical.
2. As audience members, blacks relied heavily on television for information, including information about themselves.
3. Blacks could be counted among the heaviest consumers of television programs (with high preferences for shows with black characters and low preferences for news and public affairs programming).
4. Black children often could not distinguish between the fantasy and reality of television; they tended to learn behaviors by watching characters and to be influenced by the claims of commercials (Poindexter & Stroman, 1981).

Blacks tend to watch more television than whites, so for this reason they are especially at risk for effects of either a positive or negative nature. Nielsen data have shown that television viewing for black households exceeds viewing for other households by about 23 hours per week (Nielsen Media Research, 1988). Other studies have shown that black teenagers watch from five to six hours more television each week than white teens (Brown, Campbell, & Fischer, 1986), and that black youngsters (ages 12 to 14 years) watch about two more hours of television per day than their white counterparts (Brown, Bauman, Lentz, & Koch, 1987; Greenberg & Heeter, 1987; Greenberg & Linsangan, 1993).

Do heavy viewers and light viewers among blacks have the same perceptions of blacks in the real world? One study found that they did not. From a sample of blacks, Metabane (1988) identified heavy viewers as those who watched four or more hours of television each day, and light viewers as those who watched less than two hours each day. He found that the heavy viewers were more likely to overestimate the number of blacks that fell into the middle class, and to perceive blacks as sociable, acceptable, and similar to whites. In other words, television was responsible for *cultivating* a view of the world somewhat different from reality (see Chapter 6, "Cultivation"). The box, "Research Agenda for the Future," points to a number of suggestions concerning research on minority portrayals on television.

Television's impact on the self-esteem of black viewers has been another area of interest for researchers. McDermott and Greenberg (1984) examined black children to determine if peers, parents, and television programs featuring black characters affected the children's personal and racial self-esteem. They found that the children with higher measures of self-esteem tended to hear positive statements from their parents, and they tended to watch more black shows regularly. Racial self-esteem was related more to peers and parents than to black TV programs. When the researchers divided the children on the basis of their attitudes toward black TV characters, they found that the children with more positive attitudes toward the characters also watched the programs more frequently and measured higher for both personal and racial self-esteem. Another study of black children from the ages of 7 to 13 found that the girls who viewed the most television had the highest self-concept, while boys did not show such a relationship (Stroman, 1986).

Research Agenda for the Future

Dates and Stroman offered the following suggestions for future research in the area of minority portrayals on television. Future research, they said, should focus on:

1. The latent content of shows featuring people of color; for example, investigations that explore the more subtle messages about and meanings of relationships and interactions in families of color.
2. What people acquire from both fictional and nonfictional television content. Of particular relevance to African-American and other families is the role of television in the formation of ideas about how families should operate or interact . . . An equally important question is what effect the lack of people of color in dramas has on the formation of perceptions about people of color and their families.

3. The need to understand how people process family portrayals of people of color. Especially useful would be studies in which participants describe how they conceptualize and process television portrayals of African Americans.
4. Televised portrayals of people of color in advertising.

Have increased portrayals changed perceptions of African Americans? Has increased ownership by people of color changed their portrayals? We must continue to wrestle with question of how to use the media to "socially construct" a society in which portrayals of families of color will no longer be an issue. (pp. 221–222)

Sources: Dates, J. L. and Stroman, C. A. (2001). Portrayals of families of color on television. In J. Bryant & J. A. Bryant (Eds.), *Television and the American family* (pp. 207–228). Mahwah, NJ: Erlbaum.

The situation for other ethnic minorities remains in question. Minority groups, especially Latinos, but also Asian Americans, Native Americans, Arab Americans, and others apparently have not been the focus of similar types of studies, yet such studies would be highly interesting and informative. It is hoped that future studies will attract the attention of researchers and address such issues, especially as the Latino population in the United States continues to grow.

SUMMARY

Studies of minorities in mass media usually involve content analyses that describe minority portrayals or studies that examine the effects of those portrayals on audiences. Content analyses are useful in determining the social information conveyed by various media. Researchers use three methods to describe minority characterizations: head counts, assessments of the significance of characters, and evaluations of the similarities, differences, and interactions between characters of different races.

Head count studies have revealed that blacks have made significant gains in numbers as actors on network television, but Asian, Hispanic, and other minorities remain underrepresented. Of the four networks, Fox features the greatest percentage of black characters and those from other ethnic groups. Programs on CBS include the most white characters and Asian characters but the least number of African Americans and Hispanics.

Role comparison studies examine television portrayals of whites and people of color in terms of characterization, violence, occupation, age, and other factors. Most studies in this area were conducted in the 1970s and 1980s. Nonwhite characters were more likely to be victims, but they were about as likely as white characters to play good guys or bad guys. Most characters of color appeared in blue-collar or service jobs rather than prestigious positions. Disabled characters were usually portrayed negatively.

Studies of interracial interactions were also conducted in the 1970s and early 1980s. Portrayals of interracial relationships, romantic and otherwise, have become much more common on television and in film in recent years. Unfortunately, these have not received the attention of researchers.

Most of what we know about the presence and presentation of minorities in the news comes from studies conducted during the 1970s and 1980s. The few studies that have appeared in recent years reveal an increased presence of minorities in the news, but the nature of the portrayals is not always positive. Minorities are likely to appear in newspaper articles to the extent that they are present in the community and/or on the newspaper staff. Coverage of gays and lesbians has been overwhelmingly negative and prejudicial through the years.

As with entertainment portrayals of minorities, blacks have made significant gains in advertising portrayals in recent years, from virtual nonexistence to more representative numbers. The nature of some of the portrayals of blacks has been a cause for concern. Other minorities remain underrepresented. Supermodels such as Tyra Banks and Naomi Campbell have done much to break the color barriers at the top of the advertising scene.

Programs on public television have featured positive portrayals of minorities and harmonious racial interactivity since the 1970s. Even in the early 1970s, about 25 percent of the characters on preschool programs such as *Sesame Street,* *Mr. Rogers,* and *Electric Company* were minorities.

Historically, children's programming on commercial television has not been sensitive to issues of diversity. Blacks and other minorities have been underrepresented for many years. The most recent studies indicate that the number and nature of minority portrayals on children's programs of the late 1990s have changed both quantitatively and qualitatively. A 1997 study found that whites make up about 74 percent of the characters in children's programs, whereas people of color account for about 26 percent—numbers close to actual societal percentages. Such studies, as well as a number of innovative programs, indicate that the networks are becoming more sensitive to issues of color in children's programming. Additional research is needed.

Majority and minority audiences use the media differently and for different purposes. They also vary in their disposition toward media portrayals of their own race and other races. They perceive media messages differently.

Viewers enjoy seeing people of their own color in the media, particularly on television. They like these characters more, trust them more, and identify with them more. Blacks tend to watch more television than whites; for this reason they are especially at risk for either positive or negative effects.

Most studies have focused on black and white numbers and effects, even though the Latino population in the United States continues to grow. More research on different ethnic groups is sorely needed.

REFERENCES

ATKIN, C., GREENBERG, B., & McDERMOTT, S. (1983). Television and race role socialization. *Journalism Quarterly, 60*(3), 407–414.

ATKIN, C. & HEALD, G. (1977). The content of children's toy and food commercials. *Journal of Communication, 27*(1), 107–114.

BANKS, C. M. (1977). A content analysis of the treatment of black Americans on television. *Social Education, 41*(4), 336–339.

BAPTISTA-FERNANDEZ, P., & GREENBERG, B. (1980). The context, characteristics and communication behavior of blacks on television. In B. Greenberg (Ed.), *Life on television* (pp. 13–21). Norwood, NJ: Ablex.

BARAN, S. (1973). Dying black/dying white: Coverage of six newspapers. *Journalism Quarterly, 50*(4), 761–763.

BARCUS, E. F. (1975). *Weekend children's television.* Newtonville, MA: Action for Children's Television.

BARCUS, E. F. (1983). *Images of life on children's television.* New York: Praeger.

BARCUS, E. F., & WOLKIN, R. (1977). *Children's television: An analysis of programming and advertising.* New York: Praeger.

BENNETT, L. (1998, September). *The perpetuation of prejudice in reporting on gays and lesbians, Time and Newsweek: The first fifty years.* Research paper R-21. Cambridge: The Joan Shorenstein Center for Press, Politics, and Public Policy, Harvard University.

BLOCK, C. (1972). White backlash to Negro ads: Fact or fantasy. *Journalism Quarterly, 49*(2), 253–262.

BOWEN, L., & SCHMID, J. (1997). Minority presence and portrayal in mainstream magazine advertising: An update. *Journalism and Mass Communication Quarterly, 74*(1), 134–146.

BROWN, J. D., BAUMAN, K., LENTZ, G. M., & KOCH, G. (1987, May). *Young adolescents' use of radio and television in the 1980s.* Paper presented at the annual conference, International Communication Association, Montreal, Canada.

BROWN, J. D., CAMPBELL, K., & FISCHER, L. (1986). American adolescents and music videos—Why do they watch? *Gazette, 37*(1–2), 19–32.

BROWN, J. D., & SCHULZE, L. (1990). The effects of race, gender, and fandom on audience interpretations of Madonna's music videos. *Journal of Communication, 40*(2), 88–102.

BUSH, R., RESNICK, A., & STERN, B. (1980). A content analysis of the portrayal of black models in magazine advertising. In R. Bagozzi et al. (Eds.), *Marketing in the 80's: Changes and challenges* (pp. 484–487). Chicago: American Marketing Association.

BUSH, R. F., SOLOMON, P., & HAIR, J., JR. (1977). There are more blacks in TV commercials. *Journal of Advertising Research, 17*, 21–25.

BYRD, E. K. (1989). A study of depiction of specific characteristics of characters with disability in film. *Journal of Applied Rehabilitation Counseling, 20*(2), 43–45.

CHAUDHARY, A. (1980). Press portrayal of black officials. *Journalism Quarterly, 57*(4), 636–641.

COLFAX, D., & STEINBERG, S. (1972). The perpetuation of racial stereotypes: Blacks in mass circulation magazine advertisements. *Public Opinion Quarterly, 35*, 8–18.

COLTRAINE, S., & MESSINEO, M. (2000). The perpetuation of subtle prejudice: Race and gender imagery in 1990s television advertising. *Sex-Roles, 42*, 363–389.

COMSTOCK, G., & COBBEY, R. R. (1979). Television and the children of ethnic minorities. *Journal of Communication, 29*(1), 104–115.

CORPORATION FOR PUBLIC BROADCASTING. (1994). *Native Americans' perceptions of public broadcasting.* CPB Research Notes, No. 69. Washington, DC: Corporation for Public Broadcasting.

CULLY, J. D., & BENNETT, R. (1976). Selling women, selling blacks. *Journal of Communication, 26*(4), 160–174.

DATES, J. (1980). Race, racial attitudes and adolescent perceptions of black television characters. *Journal of Broadcasting, 24*(4), 549–560.

DIXON, T., & LINZ, D. (2000). Overrepresentation and underrepresentation of African Americans and Latinos as lawbreakers on television news. *Journal of Communication, 50*, 131–154.

DOHRMANN, R. (1975). A gender profile of children's educational TV. *Journal of Communication, 25*(4), 56–65.

DOMINICK, J. (1973). Crime and law enforcement on prime-time television. *Public Opinion Quarterly, 37*(2), 241–250.

DOMINICK, J., & GREENBERG, B. (1970). Three seasons of blacks on television. *Journal of Advertising Research, 10*(2), 21–27.

DONALDSON, J. (1981). The visibility and image of handicapped people on television. *Exceptional Children, 47*(6), 413–416.

EASTMAN, H., & LISS, M. (1980). Ethnicity and children's preferences. *Journalism Quarterly, 57*(2), 277–280.

ELLIOTT, T. R., & BYRD, E. K. (1982). Media and disability. *Rehabilitation Literature, 43*(11–12), 348–355.

ENTMAN, R. M. (1992). Blacks in the news: Television, modern racism and cultural change. *Journalism Quarterly, 69*(2), 341–361.

GARDNER, J., & RADEL, M. S. (1978). Portrait of the disabled in the media. *Journal of Community Psychology, 6*, 269–274.

GERBNER, G. (1970). Cultural indicators: The case of violence in television drama. *Annals of the American Academy of Political and Social Science, 388*, 69–81.

GERBNER, G., GROSS, L., MORGAN, M., & SIGNORIELLI, N. (1981). *Aging with television commercials: Images on television commercials and dramatic programming, 1977–1979.* Philadelphia: Annenberg School of Communication, University of Pennsylvania.

GERBNER, G., GROSS, L., & SIGNORIELLI, N. (1985). *The role of television entertainment in public education about science.* Philadelphia: Annenberg School of Communication, University of Pennsylvania.

GERBNER, G., & SIGNORIELLI, N. (1979). *Women and minorities in television drama 1969–1978.* Philadelphia: Annenberg School of Communication, University of Pennsylvania.

GERSON, M. (1980). Minority representation in network television drama, 1970–1976. *Mass Communication Review, 7*(3), 10–12.

GREENBERG, B. S. (1972). Children's reactions to TV blacks. *Journalism Quarterly, 49*(1), 5–14.

GREENBERG, B. S., & ATKIN, C. (1982). Learning about minorities from television: A research agenda. In G. Berry & C. Mitchell-Kernan (Eds.), *Television and the socialization of the minority child* (pp. 215–243). New York: Academic Press.

GREENBERG, B. S., & BRAND, J. E. (1992, April). *U.S. minorities and the news.* Paper presented at conference on Television News Coverage of Minorities: Models and Options for the Commission on Television Policy organized by the Communications and Society Program of the Aspen Institute and the Carter Center at Emory University at the Wye River House Conference Center, Maryland.

GREENBERG, B. S., & BRAND, J. E. (1993). Cultural diversity on Saturday morning television. In G. Berry & J. K. Asamen (Eds.), *Children and television in a changing socio-cultural world* (pp. 132–142). Newbury Park, CA: Sage.

GREENBERG, B. S., & BRAND, J. E. (1994). Minorities and the Mass Media: 1970s to 1990s. In D. Zillmann & J. Bryant (Eds.), *Media effects, advances in theory and research.* Hillsdale, NJ: Erlbaum.

GREENBERG, B. S., & COLLETTE, L. (1997). The changing faces on TV: A demographic analysis of network television's new seasons, 1966–1992. *Journal of Broadcasting & Electronic Media, 41*(1), 1–13.

GREENBERG, B. S., & HEETER, C. (1987). VCRs and young people: The picture at 39% penetration. *American Behavioral Scientist, 30*(5), 509–521.

GREENBERG, B. S., HEETER, C., BURGOON, J., BURGOON, M., & KORZENNY, F. (1983a). Local newspaper coverage of Mexican Americans. *Journalism Quarterly, 60*(4), 671–676.

GREENBERG, B. S., HEETER, C., BURGOON, J., BURGOON, M., & KORZENNY, F. (1983b). Mass media use, preferences and attitudes among young people. In B. Greenberg, M. Burgoon, J. Burgoon, & F. Korzenny (Eds.), *Mexican Americans and the mass media* (pp. 147–201). Norwood, NJ: Ablex.

GREENBERG, B. S., & LINSANGAN, R. (1993). Gender differences in adolescents' media use, exposure to sexual content, parental mediation and self-perceptions. In B. S. Greenberg, J. Brown, & N. Boerkel-Rothfoss (Eds.), *Media, sex and the adolescent* (pp. 134–144). Cresskill, NJ: Hamilton Press.

GREENBERG, B. S., MASTRO, D., & BRAND, J. E. (2001). Minorities and the mass media: Television into the 21st century. In J. Bryant & J. A. Bryant (Eds.), *Media effects: Advances in theory and research.* Mahwah, NJ: Erlbaum.

GREENBERG, B. S., & NEUENDORF, K. (1980). Black family interactions on television. In B. S. Greenberg (Ed.), *Life on television* (pp. 173–182). Norwood, NJ: Ablex.

HANANIA, J. (1999). White out: Latinos on TV. *TV Guide, 47*(34), 31–39.

IVRY, B. (1998, September 25). In movies, a question of race. *Buffalo News,* p. 3G.

JACKSON, L. A., & ERVIN, K. S. (1991). The frequency and portrayal of black families in fashion advertisements. *Journal of Black Psychology, 18*(1), 67–70.

KANER, G. (1982). *Adolescent reactions to race and sex of professional television newscasters.* Unpublished doctoral dissertation, New York University, New York.

KASSARJIAN, H. (1969). The Negro and American advertising: 1946–1965. *Journal of Marketing Research, 6,* 29–39.

KELLER, C. E., HALLAHAN, D. P., MCSHANE, E. A., CROWLEY, E. P., & BLANDFORD, B. J. (1990). The coverage of persons with disabilities in American newspapers. *Journal of Special Education, 24*(3), 271–282.

KORZENNY, F., GRIFFIS, B. A., GREENBERG, B., BURGOON, J., & BURGOON, M. (1983). How community leaders, newspaper executives and reporters perceive Mexican Americans and the mass media. In B. Greenberg, M. Burgoon, J. Burgoon, & F. Korzenny (Eds.), *Mexican Americans and the mass media* (pp. 55–75). Norwood, NJ: Ablex.

LICHTER, L. S., & LICHTER, S. R. (1983). Criminals and law enforcers in TV entertainment. In *Prime time crime.* Washington, DC: The Media Institute.

LISS, M. (1981). Children's television selections: A study of indicators of same-race preference. *Journal of Cross Cultural Psychology, 12*(1), 103–110.

MANSFIELD-RICHARDSON, V. D. (1996). *Asian-Americans and the mass media: A content analysis of twenty United States newspapers and a survey of Asian-American journalists.* Unpublished doctoral dissertation, Ohio State University, Columbus.

MARTINDALE, C. (1984, August). *Being black in America: The press portrayal.* Paper presented at the 67th annual meeting of the Association for Education in Journalism and Mass Communication, Gainesville, FL.

MARTINDALE, C. (1985). Coverage of black Americans in five newspapers since 1950. *Journalism Quarterly, 62*(2), 321–328, 436.

MARTINDALE, C. (1987, August). *Changes in newspaper images of black Americans.* Paper presented at the 70th annual meeting of the Association for Education in Journalism and Mass Communication, San Antonio, TX.

MASTRO, D., & GREENBERG, B. S. (2000). The portrayal of racial minorities on prime time television. *Journal of Broadcasting & Electronic Media, 44,* 690–703.

McDERMOTT, S., & GREENBERG, B. (1984). Parents, peers and television as determinants of black children' esteem. In R. Bostrom (Ed.), *Communication yearbook 8* (pp. 164–177). Beverly Hills, CA: Sage.

MENDELSON, G., & YOUNG, M. (1972). *A content analysis of black and minority treatment on children's television.* Boston: Action for Children's Television.

METABANE, P. W. (1988). Television and the black audience: Cultivating moderate perspectives on racial integration. *Journal of Communication, 38*(4), 21–30.

MOSS, L. (1998, February 23). Study shows races watch cable differently. *Multichannel News, 8*(19), 38.

NIELSEN MEDIA RESEARCH. (1988). *Television viewing among Blacks* (4th annual report). Northbrook, IL: Neilsen Research.

POINDEXTER, P. M., & STROMAN, C. (1981). Blacks and television: A review of the research literature. *Journal of Broadcasting, 25*(2), 103–122.

REID, L., & VANDEN BERGH, B. (1980). Blacks in introductory ads. *Journalism Quarterly, 57*(3), 485–489.

REID, P. T. (1979). Racial stereotyping on television: A comparison of the behavior of both black and white television characters. *Journal of Applied Psychology, 64*(5), 465–489.

ROBERTS, C. (1975). The presentation of blacks in television network newscasts. *Journalism Quarterly, 52*(1), 50–55.

SCHLINGER, M. J., & PLUMMER, J. (1972). Advertising in black and white. *Journal of Marketing Research, 9,* 149–153.

SEGGAR, J. F., HAFEN, J., & HANNONEN-GLADDEN, H. (1981). Television's portrayals of minorities and women in drama and comedy drama, 1971–1980. *Journal of Broadcasting, 25*(3), 277–288.

SHU, J. I. (1979). *The portrayal of Chinese on network television as observed by Chinese and white raters.* Unpublished doctoral dissertation, State University of New York at Stony Brook, NY.

SIGNORIELLI, N. (1985). *Role portrayal and stereotyping on television: An annotated bibliography of studies relating to women, minorities, aging, sexual behavior, health, and handicaps.* Westport, CT: Greenwood Press.

SOLEY, L. (1983). The effect of black models on magazine ad readership. *Journalism Quarterly, 60*(4), 686–690.

STEMPEL, G. (1971). Visibility of blacks in news and news-picture magazines. *Journalism Quarterly, 48*(2), 337–339.

STROMAN, C. A. (1986). Television viewing and self-concept among black children. *Journal of Broadcasting & Electronic Media, 30*(1), 87–93.

SWEEPER, G. W. (1983). *The image of the black family and the white family in American prime time television programming 1970 to 1980.* Unpublished doctoral dissertation, New York University, New York.

TAN, A., FUJIOKA, Y., & LUCHT, N. (1997). Native American stereotypes, TV portrayals, and personal contact. *Journalism and Mass Communication Quarterly, 74*(2), 265–284.

TAYLOR, C. R., & BANG, H. K. (1997). Portrayals of Latinos in magazine advertising. *Journalism and Mass Communication Quarterly, 74*(2), 285–303.

TAYLOR, C., & STERN, B. (1997). Asian-Americans: Television advertising and the "model minority" stereotype. *Journal of Advertising, 26,* 47–61.

TURK, J. V., RICHARD J., BRYSON, R. L., JR., & JOHNSON, S. M. (1989). Hispanic American's in the news in two southwestern cities. *Journalism Quarterly, 66*(1), 107–113.

UNITED STATES BUREAU OF CENSUS. (1990). *United States census of population.* Washington, DC: U.S. Government Printing Office.

UNITED STATES BUREAU OF CENSUS. (1993). *Statistical abstract of the United States* (113th ed). Washington, DC: U.S. Government Printing Office.

WEIGEL, R. H., LOOMIS, J., & SOJA, M. (1980). Race relations on prime time television. *Journal of Personality and Social Psychology, 39*(5), 884–893.

WILSON, C., & GUTIERREZ, F. (1995). *Race, multiculturalism, and the media: From mass to class communication.* Thousand Oaks, CA: Sage.

ZUCKERMAN, D., SINGER, D., & SINGER, J. (1980). Children's television viewing, racial and sex role attitudes. *Journal of Applied Social Psychology, 10*(4), 281–294.

CHAPTER 20

Media Entertainment Effects

We do not know what it is that gives us pleasure and what we laugh about.
—**Sigmund Freud, 1905**

Whether on television or in the movies, whether a comedy, drama, or suspense thriller, most messages from electronic media are meant to *entertain* their audiences. The term *entertainment* means different things to different people; however, most social scientists would agree that media entertainment as an overarching concept has to do with consuming media messages for sheer pleasure and without ulterior motives (Zillmann, 2000a). This definition reflects a rather modern view of entertainment and differs considerably from earlier conceptions of the term, as we shall see.

The study of mass media entertainment became a vital research domain only in the 20th century, after movies, radio, television, and other electronic devices became popular among mass audiences. Since the 1960s, especially, this particular area of research has been prolific. Studies that examined entertainment from mass media have told us much about people's reasons for selecting particular types of entertainment, their reasons for seeking entertainment in the first place, and the ultimate effects that various types of entertainment have upon them.

This chapter focuses upon the effects of entertainment, rather than upon the reasons why audience members select particular types of entertainment (e.g., suspense, drama, comedy). A discussion of the various reasons why individuals select particular media content was provided in Chapter 8, on "Uses and Gratifications." Entertaining media fare may produce either behavioral or affective (emotional) effects or both, and these are examined. Following a brief history of entertainment, we examine the methods of research used in studying entertainment effects, selective exposure to entertaining content, and enjoyment of different types of entertainment fare.

A BRIEF HISTORY OF ENTERTAINMENT

Entertainment from mass media is a relatively recent development, but entertainment itself is almost as old as mankind (Zillmann, 2000a). The phenomenon of entertainment is common among cultures throughout the world and throughout the ages. As people learned to cope with their environment and meet their needs for food and shelter, they found that they had spare time on their hands. Entertainment of some form was used to fill that time.

Throughout the centuries, entertainment has served a variety of purposes. In addition to providing relaxation, amusement, or merriment, rites of passage soon developed. These rites became well defined and helped to maintain social structures and social unity, and to provide comfort about an afterlife to the living who faced the inevitable—death (Malinowski, 1948).

The uses of entertainment were pondered by ancient philosophers such as Plato and Aristotle. In the ancient classic *Philebus* (1892), Plato acknowledged that witnessing the fortunes and misfortunes of others brought delight, but he believed such delight was morally wrong in some instances. Aristotle viewed entertainment with greater moral detachment, believing that dramatic performances should be free from the constraints of moral judgment.

In the Western world, after the invention of the printing press, books, newspapers, and pamphlets that did not conform to the views and morals of the ruling elite (and the church authorities) were condemned, censored, or restrained altogether. Writers were put in prison or fined for unorthodox or blasphemous views or fictional works that expressed such views.

Through the years, Western attitudes toward entertainment typically have been much more in line with Plato's views than Aristotle's. Merriment and fun were considered sinful by religious extremists. In the 17th century, Christian philosophers such as Blaise Pascal (1941) believed that people should seek salvation and engage in activities to improve the soul rather than seek entertainment.

The issue of entertainment's moral value continues to this day. Books, films, television programs, video games—you name it—with controversial themes or outrageous contents continue to draw critical moral scrutiny. In recent years, movies such as *Lolita, The Last Temptation of Christ,* or *Natural Born Killers* have met with condemnation, prior restraint, and even lawsuits.

The 16th century philosopher Michel de Montaigne (1927) and the 20th century philosopher Sigmund Freud (1930/1960a, 1915/1960b, 1919/1963a, 1908/1963b) were largely responsible for the modern view of entertainment as a recreational tool to relieve stress, boredom, or unhappiness. In contrast to Pascal, Montaigne viewed the merriment and joy of entertainment as very positive rather than sinful, with entertainment providing relief from the unhappiness of life. Freud believed that a person's impulses for pleasurable experiences were repressed and that entertainment allowed an indirect way to experience these pleasures and relieve a person's suffering.

Freud wrote much about entertainment and the mechanisms at work whenever people are entertained. While he did not propose any formal theory of drama, he did study and theorize about the topic of humor (1905/1960c).

METHODS OF RESEARCH

Much of what we know about entertainment has been accomplished mostly by communication researchers and psychologists using one of two research domains, either *uses and gratifications* or *behavioral research*. As you will recall from Chapter 8, the uses and gratifications approach assumes that audience members seek out different messages, use those messages differently and react to them differently because of individual differences derived from their psychological makeup and social background. Rather than examine direct effects from mass media, uses and gratifications research focuses on the motivations and behavior of viewers. This type of research usually involves interviewing audience members or having them fill out questionnaires that indicate the various reasons for their media choices.

Uses and gratifications research is helpful in providing researchers with indications about people's likes and dislikes and their perceptions and interpretations of their motives for selecting particular media fare. Such research does have its limits, however. When asked to report their feelings and reasons for selecting their entertainment choices, some audience members may not be able to properly articulate what they want to say. Others may not really know why they make certain choices. Moreover, some may exaggerate or distort their self-reports in order to present a better image of themselves.

The behavioral approach provides an alternative to the limits inherent in uses and gratification techniques. The motives of audience members are treated as hypotheses which are subsequently tested in controlled laboratory or field settings. This approach has been used for years by communication researchers and psychologists alike in studying the phenomenon of communication (Berscheid & Walster, 1969; Donnerstein, 1980; Geen, 1976; Knapp, 1978; Rosnow & Robinson, 1967; Rushton, 1979).

Only in recent years have researchers begun to employ behavioral approaches to the study of entertainment (Zillmann & Bryant, 1994; Zillmann & Vorderer, 2000). Such research is designed to explore the factors that determine enlightenment and enjoyment from entertaining media fare. Survey research is still employed to identify various motives behind people's entertainment choices, but those are the only self-reporting measures employed. The techniques of the behavioral approach are different from uses and gratifications in the sense that researchers exercise more control over variables or factors that could distort findings.

The major research in uses and gratifications has already been discussed (see Chapter 8). For this reason, the research discussed in the remainder of this chapter will focus on behavioral studies of the entertainment phenomenon. Behavioral research findings that report the various motives people have for selecting entertaining fare will be covered, along with research that explores the enjoyment of entertaining media content.

SELECTIVE EXPOSURE

Many different factors may affect a person's decision to select a particular entertaining program. Many faithful *X-Files* fans started making plans to go to a theater and see the movie as soon as they heard that a movie was in production. Green Bay Packers fans watch their team whenever they make appearances on TV during the football season. Figure skating enthusiasts regularly flip through the channels to see if any competitions or performances are being telecast.

The deliberate choices made by the people described are usually the exception to the rule in terms of program selection. Research has shown that most of the time people make impulsive or spur-of-the-moment decisions about their entertainment choices. These spontaneous choices depend upon many factors, such as the person's situation, mood, and underlying motives (of which the person may not even be aware).

The concept of **selective exposure** assumes that people make entertainment choices based on personal preferences and needs. For example, a person who has a very boring job day in and day out might enjoy becoming immersed in a thrilling suspense-adventure novel or movie each evening. In this case, entertainment provides some much needed excitement in an otherwise dull existence. A person with a highly stressful job may opt for evenings spent in an easy chair listening to a soothing symphony.

As the examples reveal, entertainment may be used by different people for different ends, especially in terms of mood management. For some, it is a means for excitement or arousal; for others, it provides a means for relaxation (Zillmann, 1982). Researchers have shown that a person's mood has much to do with his or her entertainment choices (Bryant & Zillmann, 1984; Zillmann & Bryant, 1985a). In a controlled experiment, the researchers put participants in one of two situations, either very stressful or very boring. Each participant was then given the opportunity to select whatever television program he or she wanted to watch from a choice of three exciting programs and three relaxing programs. Without their knowledge, the time participants spent viewing the various programs was recorded. The researchers found that the stressed individuals tended to select the relaxing programs and the bored individuals watched the more exciting programs. The researchers later wrote:

> Bored persons experience relief when watching exciting programs . . . stressed people experience relief when watching relaxing programs, and . . . the experience of relief constitutes negative reinforcement that shapes initially random choice patterns into mood-specific entertainment preferences. (Zillmann & Bryant, 1994, p. 442; 1985a)

Subsequent research has revealed that people make program selections based on their affective or emotional state of being. A person in a bad mood might choose an absorbing program to help forget about the bad mood. Those in good moods would not need to be distracted by such absorbing programs (1985b).

Additional research revealed that people in a highly agitated emotional state tended to avoid entertainment altogether (Christ & Medoff, 1984). For these people, the acute nature of their problem makes it very difficult or undesirable for them to become absorbed in a distracting program while they remain so upset.

Research has also shown that people often consume humor and comedy in order to put themselves in a better mood or to remain in a good mood. In an interesting study, Meadowcraft and Zillmann (1984) examined the viewing choices of women throughout various stages of the menstrual cycle. Due to hormonal changes immediately before and during a woman's period, she is more inclined to suffer from a bad mood or even depression during these times. The researchers hypothesized that during these times women would experience the greatest need and desire to watch programs that would lift their spirits, such as comedies, whereas midway through the cycle, when hormonal levels were normal, such program preferences should not be manifest. The experiment confirmed this. Midway through the cycle, the women were drawn to dramatic programs rather than comedy, while just before and during their periods, they were found to prefer the humorous relief of comedies. Other studies have produced similar findings (Helregel & Weaver, 1989).

Studies have also shown that people selectively expose themselves to comedy for reasons in addition to mood enhancement. Zillmann (1977) identified several components of television comedies, such as teasing, hostility, and put-downs. Subsequent research revealed that people who had experienced such conditions in their lives were not attracted to comedies that reminded them of the bad treatment they had personally experienced. Research participants who had been angered preferred to watch something other than comedy which included situations of hostility (Zillmann, Hezel, & Medoff, 1980).

This tendency to seek relief from an undesirable mood did have one exception. O'Neal and Taylor (1989) found that angry men who believed they would have the opportunity to get back at the person who had tormented them did not select calming programs. On the contrary, they made a point to select violent material. Those men who believed they would not have the chance to retaliate against their tormentor consistently selected more calming programs. In other words, when the angry men believed it was useful to *stay* angry, they selected programs that would sustain the emotion.

Studies of young boys and girls have revealed interesting differences regarding their uses of television programs to improve their moods. Masters, Ford, and Arend (1983) put four- and five-year-old girls and boys in social situations that were either neutral, hostile, or nurturing, then gave them the chance to watch either a neutral (nonemotional) or a nurturing (*Mr. Rogers' Neighborhood*) children's program. In the neutral social situation, a supervisor treated the child the same as his or her peer. In the hostile situation, the supervisor showered praise on the peer and ignored the other child, making the other child feel neglected and unimportant. In the nurturing situation, the supervisor heaped words of criticism and belittlement on the peer and said nothing to the other child, making the other child feel that everything must be fine because the supervisor was not being critical toward him or her.

Boys who were neglected watched the nurturing *Mr. Rogers' Neighborhood* more than twice as long as the boys in the nurturing situation. The boys who had been in the nurturing situation were the least likely to watch *Mr. Rogers*. Interestingly, girls tended to ignore the supervisor's discriminating behavior and the use of selective exposure to improve their mood could not be detected.

Other entertainment studies among adults have shown that, like the young boys in need of nurturing, people tend to select programs that will relieve their discomfort. Wakshlag, Vial, and Tamborini (1983) first made male and female participants feel apprehensive about crime and their chances of becoming victims. Then they allowed them to select from a group of dramatic films that depicted varying degrees of violence, victimization, and the capture and punishment of criminals. The most apprehensive participants tended to select the films that had fewer scenes of victims being violently attacked and more scenes of justice being restored. Watching these types of films tended to decrease their apprehensions about becoming victims themselves.

> The main message of television crime drama—namely, that criminals are being caught and put away, which should make the streets safer—apparently holds great appeal for those who worry about crime. (Zillmann & Bryant, 1994, p. 447; Zillmann, 1980)

As with the study of the children, gender differences also emerged among adults. Regardless of their initial levels of apprehension, men were found to prefer more violent fare, and women were more likely to favor programs that show criminals being captured and locked up.

ENJOYMENT OF ENTERTAINMENT

One definition of entertainment is that it is an effective and acceptable means of relief from discontent and the unavoidable stress of daily life. This definition presumes that entertainment may take a variety of forms. In most cases, it serves as an activity that delights or enlightens. It might involve witnessing others' happiness or sadness in a play, either a comedy or tragedy. Musical performances, dance performances, artistic showings, game shows, athletic competitions—all are considered forms of entertainment. Moreover, taking part in such activities can be as much a form of entertainment for the *participants* as for the audiences.

While there are many different kinds and forms of entertainment, not all satisfy us in the same manner; that is, some are more entertaining than others. Consider dramatic movies, for instance. Some keep us riveted to the screen. They move us and uplift us. Others leave us feeling unsatisfied and feeling that we have wasted our time and money.

Drama

To answer the question, "What makes mass media entertainment enjoyable?" we must look at the components of good entertainment. In particular, we will first examine some of the elements found in good drama. Drama is "a state, situation, or series of events involving . . . intense conflict of forces." Vorderer and Knobloch (2000) elaborated on the meaning of drama in this way:

> To put it in media-related terms, drama dwells on conflict and its resolution by depicting events that impact the welfare of persons, animals, and animated things. At the core of each drama are characters, the protagonists and antagonists, who are affected by these events and who are witnessed by readers, viewers, and other media users. (p. 59)

Researchers have identified a single element that is found in all good dramatic programs: *conflict* (Smiley, 1971). Even though conflict is found in good drama, conflict alone is not enough to ensure enjoyment of that drama. Other elements must be present. In particular, audience members must have "affective dispositions toward interacting parties" (Zillmann & Bryant, 1994, p. 447). This means that good, enjoyable drama has *interesting characters* whom viewers care about or despise. Last, and as important as the presence of conflict in enjoyable drama, is the *satisfying resolution* of that conflict.

As you would expect, character development is very important in the enjoyment of drama. Audience members either like or dislike characters, and they approve or disapprove of their behaviors. In other words, they pass moral judgment on those characters (Zillmann, 1991c). Based on the strength of their feelings toward the characters, audience members hope that good things will happen to beloved characters and that hated characters will get what's coming to them.

Examples abound for dramatic films, books, or programs that have all the criteria for being good and entertaining. One need only consider classic literature or film classics to see the elements at work. Consider the adored hero Dorothy and the evil Wicked Witch of the West in *The Wizard of Oz* or the beloved Luke Skywalker and the dreaded Darth Vader in *Star Wars*.

Based on previous research by Zillmann (1980) and Zillmann and Cantor (1976, 1996), Bryant and Zillmann (1994) outlined the following formal predictions about audience enjoyment of drama. Called the **disposition model,** these

Audiences pass moral judgment on characters. They hope that good things will happen to beloved characters and that evil characters will get what they deserve. *Source: © The Everett Collection*

predictions are based on the principles we have discussed; that is, interesting characterizations, affective dispositions (strong feelings) toward the characters, and satisfying resolutions to conflicts. Research findings have consistently supported this disposition model.

1. Enjoyment deriving from witnessing the debasement, failure, or defeat of a party, agent, or object increases with the intensity of negative sentiment and decreases with the intensity of positive sentiment toward these entities.
2. Enjoyment deriving from witnessing the enhancement, success, or victory of a party, agent, or object decreases with the intensity of negative sentiment and increases with the intensity of positive sentiment toward these entities.
3. Annoyance deriving from witnessing the debasement, failure, or defeat of a party, agent, or object decreases with the intensity of negative sentiment and increases with the intensity of positive sentiment toward these entities.
4. Annoyance deriving from witnessing the enhancement, success, or victory of a party, agent, or object increases with the intensity of negative sentiment and decreases with the intensity of positive sentiment toward these entities.
5. Propositions 1 through 4 apply jointly. Consequently, all contributions to enjoyment and/or annoyance combine in total enjoyment or annoyance. (pp. 449–450)

Humor

Researchers have found that the predictions of the disposition model also apply to the enjoyment of other forms of entertainment such as humor and sports (Zillmann, 2000b; Bryant & Raney, 2000; Zillmann & Bryant, 1991; Zillmann, Bryant, & Sapolsky, 1979; Zillmann & Cantor, 1976, 1996). Comedy itself is a form of drama. The only difference is in the many cues given to audience members that what they are watching or hearing should not be taken very seriously (McGhee, 1979).

Comparatively speaking, very little research has been done in the area of humor through the years. Most psychological studies examine negative or unpleasant emotional states rather than joyful emotions. For whatever reason, humor has not been taken very seriously within the social science community (Chapman & Foot, 1996). Today, a relatively small group of social scientists throughout the world continue to conduct studies to understand the workings of humor. These researchers have developed many models and advanced theories to explain what it is about certain jokes or actions that makes us laugh (Zillmann, 2000b; Nerhardt, 1996; Zillmann & Cantor, 1976, 1996; Rothbart, 1996).

Hostile-type jokes in which someone is victimized can be thought of as minidramas. In this sense, one can see how the tenets of enjoyable drama can also apply to humor. The listener enjoys the satisfactory resolution of conflict and feels that the victim deserved his or her fate.

The use of humor in mass communication, especially the use of humor to facilitate persuasion, has attracted the interest of some communication scholars (Gruner, 1996). One need think only of the scores of funny television commercials to know that many advertisers believe that humor helps to persuade

Researchers have examined several uses of humor in mass communication through the years, and further research is needed in these areas. The addition of humor to enhance the persuasive power of a message has been one topic of interest. Another has been the power of humor to facilitate the learning process.

Scholars have advanced several hypotheses to explain the persuasive power of humor in messages. Humor may make the message more interesting and more memorable for the listener. Audiences may attend to the message more closely. (Recall from Chapter 10 on persuasion the components of the elaboration likelihood model.) Humor may also enhance the image of the message source in the eyes of the audience. Audience members may be distracted from formulating counterarguments to messages, thus facilitating the possibility of persuasion (Gruner, 1996; Sternthal & Craig, 1973).

Some studies have shown that students learn more when humor is included in a lecture or speech; other studies do not find a relationship. Research findings do support the notion that speaker image is enhanced by the use of humor. (See Gruner, 1996, for a review of the studies in these areas.)

Sources: Gruner, C. R. (1996). Wit and humour in mass communciation, in A. J. Chapman & H. C. Foot (Eds.), *Humor and Laughter: Theory, Research, and Applications* (pp. 287–311). New Brunswick, NJ: Transaction; Sternthal, B. & Crai, C. S. (1973). Humor in advertising, *Journal of Marketing, 37*, 12–18.

us. Research has found that people enjoy humor—it lowers their guard and makes them have a more positive disposition toward the message source.

Research findings reveal that laughing is indeed contagious. When audience members hear others reacting with laughter, it also makes them laugh and evaluate the performance as more enjoyable (Chapman, 1973b; Chapman & Wright, 1976; Fuller & Sheehy-Skeffington, 1974; Smyth & Fuller, 1972). Canned or piped-in laughter also increases the likelihood that audiences will laugh at the contents and in many cases it has been shown to increase enjoyment of the program (Chapman, 1973a; Cupchik & Leventhal, 1974; Leventhal & Cupchik, 1975; Leventhal & Mace, 1970).

Sports

The dispositional model also helps explain enjoyment of watching sporting events (Bryant & Raney, 2000). Sports fans have been known to treat their favorite teams and players as beloved heroes, and rival teams as hated villains. Bryant and Raney wrote:

> Nirvana for these diehard fans is having one's favorite player or team not only defeat but humiliate and annihilate one's most hated player or team. Such is rooting; such are the manifestations of the disposition theory of sportsfanship circa the 21st century. (p. 162)

One study found that fans who saw their favorite team win had their personal self-esteem and personal confidence raised. When the home team lost, however, their self-esteem and levels of personal confidence were lowered. Dispositional factors were clearly at work (Hirt, Zillmann, Erickson, & Kennedy, 1992).

Other studies have supported disposition theory as a basis for explaining the enjoyment of sporting contests (Madrigal, 1995). See Bryant and Raney (2000) for a review of the findings.

Research has shown that several different factors influence the enjoyment of mediated sports entertainment. Suspense, or the fear of a negative outcome, has been shown to facilitate more enjoyment (Gan, Tuggle, Mitrook, Coussement, & Zillmann, 1997). Risky play is another factor that contributes to enjoyment (Sargent, Zillmann, & Weaver, 1998).

Gender differences also play a role in the enjoyment of mediated sporting events. Females prefer moderate suspense in sporting contests, while males enjoy highly suspenseful situations. Also, women rate enjoyment much higher than men for sporting events that include an artistic component, such as figure skating or gymnastics (Bryant & Raney, 2000).

Is the enjoyment of sporting events enhanced by the cheers and reactions of the crowd in much the same way as the sound of laughter from other audience members enhances the enjoyment of comedy? Research efforts have not been successful in determining the answer to such a question (Zillmann & Bryant, 1994; Hocking, 1982). We remain unsure of the effects of social interactions on the enjoyment of sporting events; that is, whether the social groups are large, such as a stadium, or small, as in front of a television.

Suspense

According to Vorderer and Knobloch (2000), suspense is an emotional response to a narrative or parts of a narrative in which audience members are unsure of a final outcome. The enjoyment of suspense has proven to be a little more difficult to explain than other forms of entertainment such as comedy, regular drama, or sporting events. During most suspenseful programs, the leading characters are in trouble or peril (Zillmann, 1980, 1991c). There are narrow escapes from evil forces and repeated dangers and disasters for the heroes with whom audiences empathize, yet audiences apparently enjoy subjecting themselves to such stress and distress. As with regular drama, the satisfying resolutions in suspense thrillers are thought to be one aspect that keeps audiences coming back for more.

The satisfaction achieved from the resolution of suspense thrillers is not enough to explain their popularity, however. Their appeal appears to be something of a paradox: There are far more scenes in suspense thrillers that should make audiences uncomfortable or distressed than scenes that provide audiences with satisfying resolutions. Why, then, are such programs enjoyed?

Some believe that the stimulation that suspense thrillers provide is the key to their popularity. Such programs are exciting to watch. Audience members who are attracted to them tend to be understimulated or bored and enjoy feeling the excitement (Tannenbaum, 1980; Zillmann, 1991b; Zuckerman, 1979).

Another viable explanation for the enjoyment of suspense thrillers is that great distress throughout brings greater enjoyment in the end. The more the audience suffers along with the leading character, the greater the satisfaction at the end of the program when all is resolved. Enjoyment of the final outcome is intensified. This explanation has been supported by research (Zillmann, 1980, 1991c).

Scholars in recent years have advanced several theories to explain the enjoyment of suspense among audiences (Carroll, 1996; Vorderer, 1996). One of the most compelling is empathy theory (Zillmann, 1991a). This theory explains why audiences of suspense become involved emotionally or psychologically with what they are watching, hearing, or reading. Audiences become involved because they are something akin to witnesses of narrative events that unfold before them. They empathize with heroes who are in trouble or danger or distress.

Zillmann's (1996) definition for empathy is rather lengthy because of certain stipulations it carries, but it stresses that empathy is first and foremost a *response* to particular stimuli. He defines empathy as any experience that is a response:

1. To information about circumstances presumed to cause acute emotions in another individual; and/or
2. To the bodily, facial, paralinguistic, and linguistic expression of emotional experiences by another individual; and/or
3. To another individual's actions that are presumed to be precipitated by acute emotional experiences; this response being
4. Associated with an appreciable increase in excitation; and
5. Construed by respondents as feeling with or feeling for another individual. (pp. 214–215)

Horror

Whenever people hear the laughter of others while watching a comedy performance, it makes them more likely to laugh and even more likely to enjoy the performance. Is the same true with fearful reactions to horror? Interestingly, the answer is no.

According to the audience-influences explanation, people should enjoy frightening movies even more if other audience members exhibit a great deal of fear. Studies have shown that this does not happen (Zillmann, Weaver, Mundorf, & Aust, 1984). Instead, gender differences and various social and cultural expectations come into play. In traditional cultures, young men are expected to master fearful situations and serve as protectors to young women.

Research has shown that men enjoy horror more when they are in the company of a terrified female. A man's mastery makes him feel good about himself because even though the movie is scary he displays strength and can comfort his terrified female companion. The experience is spoiled if the woman herself exhibits mastery (Zillmann et al., 1984).

Women are more likely to enjoy horror if they watch it with a male who exhibits mastery (i.e., denial of fright and ability to comfort others who are frightened). A man who is overcome with fright does not provide the security sought by the frightened female. Research findings confirm that women enjoyed horror more when viewing with a male companion who exhibited mastery rather than a male companion who was visibly distressed (Zillmann et al., 1984).

> The frightened maiden's desire to snuggle up on the macho companion is a cliché for horror movies. If there is any truth to it, we can see why boys want to master, why girls want to scream, and why both parties want to go to such movies in the first place. (Zillmann & Bryant, 1994, p. 456)

The technological wonders of the information age promise to bring more leisure time than ever before and more opportunities for entertainment from mediated sources. As Zillmann (2000a) announced enthusiastically:

> The Entertainment Age cometh! The never-ending talk of present times as the Information Age is not necessarily misleading. However, what is usually overlooked is that the monumental capacity to generate, manipulate, and transmit information is likely to serve leisure as much as labor, if not more so. (p. 17)

Entertainment research promises to be one of the premier areas of communication scholarship in the future. In recent years, researchers have begun to study the effects of entertainment through many different types of media, including the new interactive media (Vorderer, 2000; Chapter 21, "New Media Technologies") and interactive video games (Grodal, 2000), in addition to more traditional modes such as television, movies, and music videos (Hansen & Hansen, 2000).

SUMMARY

Most messages from mass media are meant to entertain their audiences. Entertainment can be defined as an effective and acceptable means of relief from discontent and the unavoidable stress of daily life. The study of mass media entertainment tells us why people seek entertainment, why they select particular types of entertainment, and the effects of entertainment on audiences.

Online Entertainment

One of the great challenges for designers of Internet applications has been to develop online entertainment. The major television networks now have websites that offer the latest news, but online entertainment has yet to materialize. Giants such as America Online and Microsoft have made attempts to develop entertainment applications on the Web, but so far their efforts have failed. The main problem has been creating new forms of entertainment that are especially suited for online audiences. It could take the form of a game, a type of video, or something else. The interactive nature of the medium makes it different from the standard media of entertainment such as television, motion pictures, and radio.

In the early years of television, executives faced similar problems. Newscasts appeared first while entertainment programs developed more slowly. Many early programs were spin-offs from radio shows. As time went on, program producers and directors discovered techniques to improve the quality of entertainment programming, and within a few decades the medium came into its own as a source of entertainment for millions.

One thing seems certain, however: Social scientists will continue to watch carefully as the Internet develops, especially its entertainment function. Already, uses and gratifications studies and behavioral studies to determine effects are being conducted on Internet users. In the future, effects of entertainment on the Web may prove to be a major research domain.

Through the ages, people have used entertainment for many reasons—relaxation, amusement, merriment, rites of passage, and so forth. Ancient philosophers debated the moral value of entertainment. Montaigne and Freud ushered in the modern view of entertainment as a recreational tool to relieve stress, boredom, or unhappiness.

Uses and gratifications and behavioral research studies are employed to understand entertainment. Uses and gratifications research focuses on the motivations and behavior of viewers. The behavioral approach allows researchers to test audience members' motives as hypotheses in controlled, laboratory settings.

Many different factors may affect a person's decision to select a particular entertainment program. The concept of selective exposure assumes that people make entertainment choices based upon personal preferences and needs. Research shows that most of the time, people make decisions impulsively or on the spur of the moment, depending upon the situation, mood, and underlying factors. Mood has much to do with entertainment choices. Bored people tend to watch exciting programs, while stressed people prefer calming programs.

Entertainment may take any number of forms. Comedies, tragedies, musical performances, dance performances, artistic showings, game shows, athletic competitions—all are considered forms of entertainment.

Conflict is found in all good drama, but other elements must be present for drama to be enjoyable. Interesting characters that viewers either care about or despise are essential to audience enjoyment. Also, a satisfying resolution to the conflict is needed. The disposition model has been developed to predict audience enjoyment of drama, humor, and sports.

Humor is often used in mass communication for the purpose of persuasion. People enjoy humor. It lowers their guard and makes them more positively disposed toward a message source. Laughter is contagious. When audience members hear others reacting with laughter (even canned laughter), it makes them laugh as well and evaluate the performance as more enjoyable.

The appeal of suspense is something of a paradox: There are far more scenes that should make audiences uncomfortable or distressed than scenes that provide audiences with satisfying resolutions. The stimulation provided by suspense thrillers is thought to contribute to their popularity. Also, greater distress throughout is thought to intensify enjoyment at the satisfying conclusion. Empathy theory proposes that audience members make psychological connections with heroes who emerge from trouble or danger to save the day.

Gender differences and various social and cultural expectations come into play in the enjoyment of horror. Men enjoy horror more when they are in the company of a terrified female. Women enjoy horror if they watch it with a male who does not seem to be frightened and who can provide security.

REFERENCES

Berscheid, E., & Walster, E. (1969). *Interpersonal attraction.* Reading, MA: Addison-Wesley.
Bryant, J., & Raney, A. A. (2000). Sports on the screen. In D. Zillmann & P. Vorderer (Eds.), *Media entertainment: The psychology of its appeal* (pp. 153–174). Mahwah, NJ: Erlbaum.

BRYANT, J., & ZILLMANN, D. (1984). Using television to alleviate boredom and stress: Selective exposure as a function of induced excitational states. *Journal of Broadcasting, 28*(1), 1–20.

CARROLL, N. (1996). The paradox of suspense. In P. Vorderer, H. J. Wulff, & M. Friedrichsen (Eds.), *Suspense: Conceptualizations, theoretical analyses, and empirical explorations* (pp. 71–92). Mahwah, NJ: Erlbaum.

CHAPMAN, A. J. (1973a). Funniness of jokes, canned laughter and recall performance. *Sociometry, 36*, 569–578.

CHAPMAN, A. J. (1973b). Social facilitation of laughter in children. *Journal of Experimental Social Psychology, 9*, 528–541.

CHAPMAN, A. J., & FOOT, H. C. (Eds.) (1996). *Humor and laughter: Theory, research, and applications.* New Brunswick, NJ: Transaction.

CHAPMAN, A. J., & WRIGHT, D. S. (1976). Social enhancement of laughter: An experimental analysis of some companion variables. *Journal of Experimental Child Psychology, 21*, 201–218.

CHRIST, W. G., & MEDOFF, N. J. (1984). Affective state and selective exposure to and use of television. *Journal of Broadcasting, 28*(1), 51–63.

CUPCHIK, G. C., & LEVENTHAL, H. (1974). Consistency between expressive behavior and the evaluation of humorous stimuli: The role of sex and self-observation. *Journal of Personality and Social Psychology, 30*, 429–442.

DONNERSTEIN, E. (1980). Pornography and violence against women: Experimental studies. *Annals of the New York Academy of Sciences, 347*, 277–288.

FREUD, S. (1930/1960a). Das Unbehagen in der Kultur. In *Das Unbewusste: Schriften zur Psychoanalyse* (pp. 339–415). Frankfurt, Germany: Fischer Verlag.

FREUD, S. (1915/1960b). Das Unbewusste. In *Das Unbewusste: Schriften zur Psychoanalyse* (pp. 1–40). Frankfurt, Germany: Fischer Verlag.

FREUD, S. (1905/1960c). *Jokes and their relation to the unconscious.* New York: Norton.

FREUD, S. (1919/1963a). Das Unheimliche. In *Das Unheimliche: Aufsatze zur Literatur* (pp. 45–84). Frankfurt, Germany: Fischer Doppelpunkt.

FREUD, S. (1908/1963b). Der Dichter und das Phantasieren. In *Das Unheimliche: Aufsatze zur Literature* (pp. 7–18). Frankfurt, Germany: Fischer Doppelpunkt.

FULLER, R. G. C., & SHEEHY-SKEFFINGTON, A. (1974). Effects of group laughter on response to humorous material: A replication and extension. *Psychological Reports, 35*, 531–534.

GAN, S., TUGGLE, C. A., MITROOK, M. A., COUSSEMENT, S. H., & ZILLMANN, D. (1997). The thrill of the close game: Who enjoys it and who doesn't? *Journal of Sport & Social Issues, 21*, 53–64.

GEEN, R. G. (1976). Observing violence in the mass media: Implications of basic research. In R. G. Geen & E. C. O'Neal (Eds.), *Perspectives on aggression* (pp. 193–234). New York: Academic Press.

GRODAL, T. (2000). Video games and the pleasures of control. In D. Zillmann & P. Vorderer (Eds.), *Media entertainment: The psychology of its appeal* (pp. 197–214). Mahwah, NJ: Erlbaum.

GRUNER, C. R. (1996). Wit and humour in mass communication. In A. J. Chapman & H. C. Foot (Eds.), *Humour and laughter: Theory, research, and applications* (pp. 287–312). New Brunswick, NJ: Transaction.

HANSEN, C. H., & HANSEN, R. D. (2000). Music and music videos. In D. Zillmann & P. Vorderer (Eds.), *Media entertainment: The psychology of its appeal* (pp. 175–196). Mahwah, NJ: Erlbaum.

HELREGEL, B. K., & WEAVER, J. B. (1989). Mood-management during pregnancy through selective exposure to television. *Journal of Broadcasting & Electronic Media, 33*, 15–33.

HIRT, E. R., ZILLMANN, D., ERICKSON, G. A., & KENNEDY, C. (1992). Costs and benefits of allegiance: Changes in fans' self-ascribed competencies after team victory versus defeat. *Journal of Personality and Social Psychology, 63*(5), 724–738.

HOCKING, J. E. (1982). Sports and spectators: Intra-audience effects. *Journal of Communication, 32*(1), 100–108.

KNAPP, M. (1978). *Nonverbal communication in human interaction.* New York: Holt, Rinehart & Winston.

LEVENTHAL, H., & CUPCHIK, G. C. (1975). The informational and facilitative effects of an audience upon expression and evaluation of humorous stimuli. *Journal of Experimental Social Psychology, 11,* 363–380.

LEVENTHAL, H., & MACE, W. (1970). The effect of laughter on evaluation of a slapstick movie. *Journal of Personality, 38,* 16–30.

MADRIGAL, R. (1995). Cognitive and affective determinants of fan satisfaction with sporting event attendance. *Journal of Leisure Research, 27,* 205–227.

MALINOWSKI, B. (1948). *Magic, science and religion, and other essays.* Garden City, NY: Doubleday Anchor Books.

MASTERS, J. C., FORD, M. E., & AREND, R. A. (1983). Children's strategies for controlling affective responses to aversive social experience. *Motivation and Emotion, 7,* 103–116.

McGHEE, P. E. (1979). *Humor: Its origin and development.* San Francisco: Freeman.

MEADOWCRAFT, J., & ZILLMANN, D. (1984, August). *The influence of hormonal fluctuations on women's selection and enjoyment of television programs.* Paper presented at the meeting of the Association for Education in Journalism and Mass Communication, Gainesville, FL.

MONTAIGNE, M. E. DE. (1927). *The essays of Montaigne* (Vols. 1–2), (E. J. Trechmann, Trans.). London: Oxford University Press.

NERHARDT, G. (1996). Incongruity and funniness: Towards a new descriptive model. In A. J. Chapman & H. C. Foot (Eds.), *Humor and laughter: Theory, research, and applications* (pp. 55–62). New Brunswick, N.J.: Transaction.

O'NEAL, E. C., & TAYLOR, S. L. (1989). Status of the provoker, opportunity to retaliate, and interest in video violence. *Aggressive Behavior, 15,* 171–180.

PASCAL, B. (1941). *Pensées* (W. F. Trotter, Trans.). New York: Modern Library.

PLATO (1892). *Philebus.* In B. Jowett (Ed. and Trans.), *The dialogues of Plato* (3rd ed., Vol. 4, pp. 519–645). New York: Macmillan.

ROSNOW, R. L., & ROBINSON, E. J. (Eds.). (1967). *Experiments in persuasion.* New York: Academic Press.

ROTHBART, M. K. (1996). Incongruity, problem-solving and laughter. In A. J. Chapman & H. C. Foot (Eds.), *Humor and laughter: Theory, research, and applications* (pp. 37–54). New Brunswick, NJ: Transaction.

RUSHTON, J. P. (1979). Effects of prosocial television and film material on the behavior of viewers. In L. Berkowitz (Ed.), *Advances in experimental social psychology* (Vol. 12, pp. 321–351). New York: Academic Press.

SARGENT, S. L., ZILLMANN, D., & WEAVER, J. B. (1998). The gender gap in the enjoyment of televised sports. *Journal of Sport & Social Issues, 22,* 46–64.

SMILEY, S. (1971). *Playwriting: The structure of action.* Englewood Cliffs, NJ: Prentice Hall.

SMYTH, M. M., & FULLER, R. G. C. (1972). Effects of group laughter on responses to humorous material. *Psychological Reports, 30,* 132–134.

TANNENBAUM, P. H. (1980). An unstructured introduction to an amorphous area. In P. H. Tannenbaum (Ed.), *The entertainment functions of television* (pp. 1–12). Hillsdale, NJ: Erlbaum.

VORDERER, P. (1996). Toward a psychological theory of suspense. In P. Vorderer, H. J. Wulff, & M. Friedrichsen (Eds.), *Suspense: Conceptualizations, theoretical analyses, and empirical explorations* (pp. 233–254). Mahwah, NJ: Erlbaum.

VORDERER, P. (2000). Interactive entertainment and beyond. In D. Zillmann & P. Vorderer (Eds.), *Media entertainment: The psychology of its appeal* (pp. 21–36). Mahwah, NJ: Erlbaum.

VORDERER, P., & KNOBLOCH, S. (2000). Conflict and suspense in drama. In D. Zillmann & P. Vorderer (Eds.), *Media entertainment: The psychology of its appeal* (pp. 59–72). Mahwah, NJ: Erlbaum.

WAKSHLAG, J., VIAL, V., & TAMBORINI, R. (1983). Selecting crime drama and apprehension about crime. *Human Communication Research, 10,* 227–242.

ZILLMANN, D. (1977). Humor and communication. In A. J. Chapman & H. C. Foot (Eds.), *It's a funny thing, humor* (pp. 291–301). Oxford, England: Pergamon.

ZILLMANN, D. (1980). Anatomy of suspense. In P. H. Tannenbaum (Ed.), *The entertainment functions of television* (pp. 133–163). Hillsdale, NJ: Erlbaum.

ZILLMANN, D. (1982). Television viewing and arousal. In D. Pearl, L. Bouthilet, & J. Lazar (Eds.), *Television and behavior: Ten years of scientific progress and implications for the eighties: Vol. 2. Technical reviews* (pp. 53–67). Washington, DC: U.S. Government Printing Office.

ZILLMANN, D. (1991a). Empathy; Affect from bearing witness to the emotions of others. In J. Bryant & D. Zillmann (Eds.), *Responding to the screen: Reception and reaction processes* (pp. 135–167). Hillsdale, NJ: Erlbaum.

ZILLMANN, D. (1991b). Television viewing and physiological arousal. In J. Bryant & D. Zillmann (Eds.), *Responding to the screen: Reception and reaction processes* (pp. 103–133). Hillsdale, NJ: Erlbaum.

ZILLMANN, D. (1991c). The logic of suspense and mystery. In J. Bryant & D. Zillmann (Eds.), *Responding to the screen: Reception and reaction processes* (pp. 281–303). Hillsdale, NJ: Erlbaum.

ZILLMANN, D. (1996). The psychology of suspense in dramatic exposition. In P. Vorderer, H. J. Wulff, & M. Friedrichsen (Eds.), *Suspense: Conceptualizations, theoretical analyses, and empirical explorations* (pp. 199–232). Mahwah, NJ: Erlbaum.

ZILLMANN, D. (2000a). The coming of media entertainment. In D. Zillmann & P. Vorderer (Eds.) *Media entertainment: The psychology of its appeal* (pp. 1–20). Mahwah, NJ: Erlbaum.

ZILLMANN, D. (2000b). Humor and comedy. In D. Zillmann & P. Vorderer (Eds.), *Media entertainment: The psychology of its appeal* (pp. 37–58). Mahwah, NJ: Erlbaum.

ZILLMANN, D., & BRYANT, J. (1985a). Affect, mood, and emotion as determinants of selective exposure. In D. Zillmann & J. Bryant (Eds.), *Selective exposure to communication* (pp. 157–190). Hillsdale, NJ: Erlbaum.

ZILLMANN, D., & BRYANT, J. (Eds.). (1985b). *Selective exposure to communication.* Hillsdale, NJ: Erlbaum.

ZILLMANN, D., & BRYANT, J. (1991). Responding to comedy: The sense and nonsense of humor. In J. Bryant & D. Zillmann (Eds.), *Responding to the screen: Reception and reaction processes* (pp. 261–279). Hillsdale, NJ: Erlbaum.

ZILLMANN, D., & BRYANT, J. (1994). Entertainment as media effect. In J. Bryant & D. Zillmann (Eds.), *Media effects: Advances in theory and research* (pp. 437–461). Hillsdale, NJ: Erlbaum.

ZILLMANN, D., BRYANT, J., & SAPOLSKY, B. S. (1979). The enjoyment of watching sport contests. In J. H. Goldstein (Ed.), *Sports, games, and play: Social and psychological viewpoints* (pp. 297–335). Hillsdale, NJ: Erlbaum.

ZILLMANN, D., & CANTOR, J. R. (1976/1996). A disposition theory of humor and mirth. In A. J. Chapman & H. C. Foot (Eds.), *Humor and laughter: Theory, research, and applications* (pp. 93–116). New Brunswick, NJ: Transaction.

ZILLMANN, D., HEZEL, R. T., & MEDOFF, N. J. (1980). The effect of affective states on selective exposure to televised entertainment fare. *Journal of Applied Social Psychology, 10,* 323–339.

ZILLMANN, D., & VORDERER, P. (Eds.) (2000). *Media entertainment: The psychology of its appeal.* Mahwah, NJ: Erlbaum.

ZILLMANN, D., WEAVER, J., MUNDORF, N., & AUST, C. F. (1984). *Companion effects on the enjoyment of horror.* Unpublished manuscript, Indiana University, Bloomington.

ZUCKERMAN, M. (1979). *Sensation seeking: Beyond the optimal level of arousal.* Hillsdale, NJ: Erlbaum.

CHAPTER 21

New Communication Technologies

> *Cyberspace is where a long distance phone call takes place. Cyberspace is where the bank keeps your money. Where your medical records are stored. All of this stuff is out there somewhere. There is really no point in thinking about its geographical location. Information is extra-geographical.*
> —**William Gibson, interview in** *Rapid Eye 3*, **1995**

In the past few decades, new communication technologies have caused numerous changes in our lives. Only since the 1980s have electronic mail (e-mail), video conferencing, voice messaging, voice mail, and other advanced communication technologies become part of our daily activities (Daft, 1989). In the 1990s the Internet began to impact day-to-day affairs and created new means for individuals to connect and communicate with one another and with databases worldwide and, in the process, revolutionized our lives.

New technologies have caused us to make changes in the ways that we conceptualize mass communication processes. In recent decades, traditional forms of mediated communication with large, heterogeneous, and anonymous audiences (e.g., television and radio broadcasts) have gradually been joined and often overshadowed by other forms of mediated communication in which audience members have far more potential for feedback and much more "user power." Looked at another way, one-way *mass* communication has been slowly evolving into a more *interactive* or *transactive* process. Many of the new communication technologies allow interpersonal communication as well as mass communication among users. Moreover, the interactive components of certain new communication technologies make it difficult to distinguish between the classic "sender" and "receiver" that for so long were regarded as the basic components of the mass communication model.

The characteristics of the new technologies force us to take a step beyond the realm of traditional mass communication. This new domain may be thought of as **transactional mediated communication.** *Transactional* implies a give-and-take situation—an interpersonal communication relationship in which parties alternate in their roles as sender, receiver, and information processor, and thereby exchange information or share symbols and thereby meaning. *Mediated* signifies that the media are still involved. In most media systems that support transactional communication, mass communication is also possible; in other words, communication transactions may still occur between many users. Any one individual or institutional entity has the opportunity to address numerous other users.

In today's information age, change has become the constant. As we shall see in the next section, the marriage of the computer to contemporary media is causing these sweeping changes to occur before our eyes. After a brief discussion of the new media environments, we will take a look at the characteristics of the new media audiences, as new media technologies are forcing us to change our traditional views of media audiences. We are also having to confront ethical issues and concerns that have not troubled us in the past. Such change ultimately forces revisions of existing communication theories and models and the development of new ones. Additional sections will examine these issues, along with research findings on the social and psychological effects that new technologies have on individuals.

THE DIGITAL FRONTIER

> Among the marvellous accomplishments of human study and genius, nothing, all facts considered, can well be regarded as more important than man's triumph over space and time in the matter of the intercommunication of widely separated individuals and nations.

This quotation only sounds like something from the 21st century. Believe it or not, it is actually a product of the 1870s! The quotation opens a chapter titled "The American Magnetic Telegraph" in *The Great Industries of the United States: Being an Historical Summary of the Origin, Growth, and Perfection of the Chief Industrial Arts of this Country* by Horace Greely and others (1872, p. 1111). The quote reminds us that "new" communication technologies have been around for some time.

When we say "new communication technologies" or "new media technologies" at the cusp of the 21st century, what exactly do we mean? Basically, we are referring to communications technologies on the cutting edge; therefore, our definition of new technologies continues to change, or perhaps evolve, as time goes on and new technologies emerge. This makes a discussion of new media difficult at best, when you consider that by the time this book is published the new media discussed in it will more than likely be well worn or in some cases even obsolete.

If we were pressed to list some of the new communication technologies of today, we might start with a list compiled by Rogers "way back when" in the 1980s—which included microcomputers, teletext, videotext, interactive cable television, communication satellites, and teleconferencing[1] (Rogers, 1986). We might add to his list the technologies listed in the first paragraph of this chapter, as well as high-definition television (HDTV) and interactive television. HDTV provides 1,920 vertical lines of detail and 1,080 horizontal scan lines and offers pictures and sound as sharp and crisp as a movie theater experience. Interactive TV, the result of the convergence of television and the computer, allows viewers to click on icons during television shows to get more information—for example, sports statistics on certain players or biographical information on stars. About 1 million homes in the United States have interactive TV capabilities; by 2005, the number of interactive TV subscribers is expected to skyrocket to 24.5 million (Haring, 1999).

In a bibliographical essay, Marien (1996) surveyed the literature and offered a comprehensive list of new technologies already in place or projected for the future. His list included voice-access computers, language translators, and 500-channel cable television, among many others.

One of the ways that communication scholars have attempted to define the new technologies is to describe their essential nature. Dizard (1994) has argued that new communication technologies cannot be accurately termed "mass media" by the conventional definition of that phrase. The specialized nature, decentralized products, and interactive format of these new media make them very different from traditional mass media.

> Mass media historically has meant centrally produced standardized information and entertainment products, distributed to large audiences through separate channels. The new electronic challengers modify all of these conditions. Their products often do not come from a central source. Moreover, the new media usually provide specialized services for large numbers of relatively small audiences. Their most significant innovation, however, is the distribution of voice, video, and print products on a common electronic channel, often in two-way interactive formats that give consumers more control over what services they want, when they get them, and in what form. (p. 2)

Rogers (1986) made many of the same points, and some additional ones, using a different vocabulary. He listed several ways that human communication had changed since the advent of new technologies:

1. All of the new communication systems have at least a certain degree of *interactivity*, something like a two-person, face-to-face conversation . . .
2. The new media are also *de-massified*, to the degree that a special message can be exchanged with each individual in a large audience . . .
3. The new communication technologies are also *asynchronous*, meaning they have the capability for sending or receiving a message at a time convenient for an individual . . . (pp. 4–8)

Perhaps the best way to come to grips with all the new technologies and facilitate a broad-based understanding of them is to identify the common bond that they all seem to share: their need for broader bandwidths to support digital technology rather than the old analog variety. Writers have described the conversion from analog to digital as significant as the fundamental change that occurred when transistors replaced vacuum tubes (Grant, 1997). Another commentator referred to the changes in broadcast production and transmission as "revolutionary," even though the conversion has been taking place for decades and continues to this day.

> The conversion to digital transmission represents the first fundamental change in television broadcasting since color was added to the NTSC standard more than 40 years ago. It is a transition with multibillion dollar consequences for

broadcasters who are the first adopters of these technologies, and consumers who will eventually need to replace their analog radio/TV receivers, VCRs, camcorders, and other related peripherals. (Seel, 1997, p. 8)

The key to understanding the nature of digital technology can be found in three *c* words: compression, conversion, and convergence. More information—*much* more information—can be transmitted and stored using digital technology than the old analog form. In addition, digitalization makes possible the integration or conversion of this compressed information into computer systems and applications. As a result of digitalization, broadcast communications, wireless communications, and telecommunications are *converging* because of their sudden ability to share information with one another.

The new digital formats require larger bandwidths or network pathways. Construction of these new networks is already under way throughout the world. Once fully developed, telecommunications will be very different from that to which we are now accustomed. Hodge (1995) described this transformation and its consequences:

> Highly evolved telecommunications networks, interconnected and delivering telecommunications and data services around the country and the world, will enable the delivery of virtually unlimited numbers of channels of video, telephony, switched data, wide area networking, business data links . . . These networks will carry services (sometimes called video dial tone) including broadcast video, time-shifted TV, Pay-per-view TV, multimedia services, premium channels, video on demand, home shopping, tele-education, interactive games . . . This interconnected high-performance network is often referred to as the Information Superhighway, or the National Information Infrastructure (NII). (p. xv)

The technological, operational, and functional shifts in the communications infrastructure of modern society can soon be felt by virtually everyone. Already more than half a million homes in the United States are wired for broadband services; by 2002 that number is expected to increase anywhere from 7 million to 16 million, depending on the research firm doing the forecasting (Berman & Bunzel, 1999; Bowles, 1998). In the transition period, the conversion box business is booming. About 10 million digital set-top boxes were sold throughout the world in 1998 for digital direct broadcast systems, and about 14 million satellite, cable, and digital television product sales with revenues of $4.7 billion were forecasted for 1999 (Brown, 1999). Digital set-top boxes allow people to use existing wiring in their homes to pick up digital signals.

In the future we will have an intelligent network, an advanced information system supported by a spinal column comprised of a fiber optic–based, broadband or wideband digital network. Fiber optic cable will comprise the backbone, but the veinlike extensions of the network often referred to as the Information Superhighway will also include coaxial cable, telephone lines, wireless, microwave, and satellite communications. This broadband network will have the potential to deliver diverse, customized functions and incredibly specialized media messages. When media messages are encoded into a digital format, video, audio, and textual messages can be combined in an almost unlimited way. As Brand (1988) wrote poetically in *The Media Lab: Inventing the Future at MIT*:

With digitalization all of the media become translatable into each other—computer bits migrate merrily—and escape from their traditional means of transmission. A movie, phone call, letter, or magazine article may be sent digitally via phone line, coaxial cable, fiber optic cable, microwave, satellite, the broadcast air, or a physical storage medium such as tape or disk. If that's not revolution enough, with digitalization the content becomes totally plastic—any message, sound, or image may be edited from anything into anything else. (p. 19)

This network of networks currently under expansion extends around the globe. Countries in Europe and Asia are rushing to construct fiber optic lines so that they can maintain parity with if not supremacy over the United States. A report to the European Union in 1994 emphasized the importance to its member nations of being among the first to construct information infrastructures (Commission of the European Communities, 1994). One corporation in Japan recently announced plans to wire all schools, homes, and offices in the country with fiber optic cable by the year 2010. This initiative will cost from $150 to $230 billion, according to the country's Ministry of Posts and Telecommunications. In Singapore a similar project undertaken by the island government is well under way. Ironically, that same government holds very tight controls on information access for its citizens (Hudson, 1998).

As some countries hurry to lay cable lines, others experiment with radio-wave technology that avoids the use of wires altogether for broadband network access. In recent years a number of wireless products and services have appeared on the market. Some believe that wireless may lead the way in broadband networking in the future. One electronics expert wrote, "There's every indication that wireless will begin to take a leading role in the broadband multimedia future" (Mathias, 1999, p. 6).

NEW INTERACTIVE ENVIRONMENTS

The move to digital communication has resulted in new media environments that are often interactive in nature and allow multiple functions and tasks to be performed on a single piece of equipment such as a home computer or a television. Mundorf and Laird (in press) pointed out that the convergence of technologies has "led to an increasing overlap between the telecommunications, television, and consumer electronics industries. For the user it means that the same appliance can be used for work-at-home, chat, children's entertainment, and online shopping or banking" (in press).

Interactive applications now allow some cable television and movie viewers various options that were unheard of several decades ago. For example, television viewers can now go online to participate in game shows. Another interactive technology allows movie viewers to choose between plot lines and endings. Interactive cable systems allow sports fans to select different camera angles at televised sporting events.

Stipp (1998) argued that interactive features may not be attractive for certain types of television content or for some people who prefer the old-fashioned, nondemanding way of viewing television. Interaction requires activity on the part of the viewer, and some people simply prefer to be passive viewers of their favorite dramas or sitcoms. Other content, such as sports programming or news, may invite interactivity more readily.

Mundorf and Laird (2001) pointed out that interactivity is a multidimensional concept. They cited researchers such as Fortin, Bryant and Love, and Goertz who have identified various aspects that define interactivity. According to Fortin (1997), interactivity involves interchangeability in the roles of senders and receivers. Users may be human or machine. Bryant and Love (1996) identified dimensions that distinguish interactive media such as selectivity by way of cable or satellite television, and an increased viewing diet due to expansion in viewing choices. Goertz (1995) also pointed out that the new, interactive media not only provide a greater amount of selectivity, but also added some other features. For example, the new media differ from traditional media in the amount of content that can be manipulated and changed by the viewer, and in the increased number of senses that may be activated during media use.

NEW CONCEPTIONS OF AUDIENCES

As a result of interactivity and user empowerment, the new media technologies are forcing us to reexamine our traditional concept of the media audience. The new media enable users to become more active in the communication process and to be more selective with regard to the messages they receive. They are active agents rather than passive receivers of information.

The decade of the 1990s has yielded a generation of *addressable users of micromultimedia*. By *addressable* we mean that media messages are no longer being sent "to whom it may concern." Indeed, media messages may be selected and "downloaded" by parties whose names, addresses, identification numbers, and demographic and marketing profiles are a part of the message distributor's database. The degree of efficiency and profitability such communication systems will provide surely will make them commonplace early in the new century, despite the increased expenses of initial installation and start-up.

What we formerly referred to as an "audience" must now be termed "users." How can we call an "audience" an active aggregate of media users who can and will, by programming their own gatekeeping technologies, actively select from thousands of informational, educational, and entertainment options? We cannot. Some have called this aggregate of users "the sovereign consumer of the information age." We prefer the less pretentious label of "media user."

Finally, what do we mean by *micromultimedia*? The changes that support this seemingly innocent term are revolutionary. They are also multidimensional. At the core are essential alterations to the communications skeleton of our nation—and, indeed, our world—a backbone of which many of us are not even aware. This plastic translation of message form by means of computers is what we refer to as a multimedia format. That the form can readily be shaped to suit the desires of an individual user is signaled by the term *micromedia*. Certainly the prototypical scenario for typical media use under the micromultimedia environment is miles removed from what our intellectual ancestors meant by mass communication.

Traditionally, communication scholars have debated the notions of an active versus a passive audience; that is, audience members as a passive mass of people exposed to a mass medium and influenced in some way by its messages compared with audience members as active individuals who make purposive selections based on individual choices. As a result of new media technologies, new theoretical models of the audience are moving away from this traditional passive-active dichotomy. They recognize the different nature of different media audiences.

Webster (1998) made a compelling argument against viewing media audiences as either all passive or all active in orientation and, at the same time, provided an interesting framework for conceiving the audience in today's world of interactive media and transactive mediated communications. He offered three models to describe media audiences, which he termed *audience-as-mass, audience-as-outcome,* and *audience-as-agent.* The audience-as-mass model defines audience members as those who have common exposure to a mass medium. With this model, the mass or "the body of the audience" assumes utmost importance (Webster, 1998, p. 192). Attempts to measure audience numbers fall under this category. The audience-as-outcome model focuses more broadly on media effects. Propaganda studies, media violence and pornography studies, attitude change studies, and other studies of media effects fall within this category. The audience-as-agent model differs considerably from the other two models. It recognizes the power that new media technologies offer today's audience members. It shows an audience member as an individual who enjoys more personal options and choices whenever consuming media fare. This audience member is more active and more involved in the communication process than ever before.

The beauty of Webster's conception of audience models is its capacity to classify combinations of the various perspectives of media audiences. He ingeniously uses a Venn diagram to denote the different areas of communication research that conceive of the audience as either mass, outcome, agent, or some combination of the three (see Figure 21.1). The areas of intersection on the diagram may be used to describe the various conceptions of the audience from all areas of communication research and theoretical approaches, including critical studies, cultivation, symbolic interactionism, and even postmodernism, in addition to the more conventional areas of effects research, propaganda studies, uses and gratifications, and cultural studies.

ETHICAL AND POLICY CONSIDERATIONS

In today's world, hungry for new technology, new communication technologies present us with a number of public policy and ethical considerations as they are developed and adopted. Some of these issues have been around for some time, whereas others are new concerns created by the advent of brand-new media technologies.

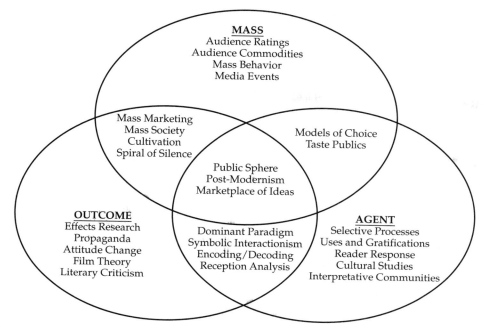

FIGURE 21.1. Various traditions of audience studies.
Source: From J.G. Webster, "The Audience." *Journal of Broadcasting and Electronic Media,*
42, p. 192. Copyright © 1998. Used by permission.

Cooper (1998) provided a useful and thoughtful inventory of 40 leading ethical concerns that are the result of the use of new communication technologies.

> Understanding effects and ethical issues accompanying new technologies includes studying a myriad of overt and submerged social, cultural, and institutional factors within corporations and countries. To have dominion over such new technologies and to predict at least some of their effects, it is important to recognize, systematize, analyze, and tentatively evaluate not only technologies but their relations to corporations, individuals, and societies. (pp. 86–87)

Included in his list were the diverse ethical issues associated with fairness or equality, an information underclass, obscenity and pornography, plagiarism, and bootlegging, or the copying of other people's data for resale purposes. On the issue of fairness or equality, Cooper wrote:

> One of the most ancient ethical issues is magnified when discussing resources (technology-rich and technology-poor countries, regions, and peoples), access, and even air space. Questions about how the air spectrum should be allocated, about whether foreign-owned satellites may orbit over domestic military sites, about who should be charged and how much for transmission and transponder time magnify questions of global equality, inequality, and fairness. Similarly, questions of intellectual property, ownership, royalties, and so forth raise questions of distributive justice. Who, if anyone, should profit from the distribution of information? (1998, p. 76)

A good example of the bootlegging issue is the recent controversy associated with MP3, a compression technology that results in computer files with sound quality that rivals compact disks. A senior vice president for a major recording label has called the MP3 music available on the World Wide Web "the biggest thing to happen in the business in about 40 years" (Jensen, 1999, p. 34). Music fans can "call up" tunes on their computer and download or copy them for future play or for resale. The difference between this type of bootlegging and the old variety (i.e., simply taping a song from an album or from the radio) is in the quality of the sound.

The MP3 bootlegging issue attracted the notice of the recording industry when a new device called the Diamond Rio came onto the market. The recording industry objected to its introduction because owners or users of PC peripherals such as the Diamond Rio are not required by law to pay royalties, even though the device allows digital audio recording and permits online music to become portable. The industry responded by filing suit against Diamond Rio. The Recording Industry Association of America and five major recording labels created a task force called the Secure Digital Music Initiative. The initiative studied the MP3 problem and came up with new standards to protect music distributed in digital formats.

In addition to ethical concerns, the new technologies are also associated with a number of public policy considerations. In 1998, the FCC complied with the Telecommunications Act of 1996 by forming an Advanced Networks Inquiry and Rulemaking initiative. This initiative is attempting to define a new regulatory framework to provide guidance as the country's public switched voice-based telecommunications network is transformed into a high-speed and broadband network. Another goal is to stimulate the growth of alternative networks such as hybrid wireless, wireline, CATV, and satellite networks (Pearce, 1998).

The policy associated with high definition television (HDTV) serves as another good example. The FCC has set several requirements that will facilitate the transition from analog to digital television in the near future. An April 1997 order required (1) that network affiliate stations in the top 10 television markets construct digital television facilities by May 1, 1999, (2) that network affiliates in the top 30 markets construct their facilities by November 1, 1999, (3) that all other commercial stations construct their facilities by May 1, 2002, (4) that all noncommercial stations construct such facilities by May 1, 2003, and (5) that all analog services cease by 2006 (Federal Communications Commission [FCC], 1997; Dupagne, 1998).

Since that order, however, former FCC Chairman Bill Kennard came under fire for not offering enough regulatory guidance to broadcasters during this period of conversion from analog to digital. In a newsletter of the Communication and Technology Policy division of the Association for Education in Journalism and Mass Communication, Dupagne criticized Kennard's apparent decision to curtail FCC involvement in HDTV policy.

> Such a call for disengagement is both premature and inconsistent with prior FCC policymaking. It is unreasonable to expect broadcasters to meet aggressive build-out deadlines without contributing appropriate policies enabling

them to achieve these objectives. As HDTV enters American homes, it is imperative that the commission continue to provide a nurturing, albeit flexible, regulatory environment, to ensure an orderly and expeditious transition to HDTV broadcasting. (p. 3)

Whether the government offers too many regulations or not enough is a matter of opinion, but it serves to illustrate the one constant in today's telecommunications policy: *controversy*. With so many players vying for a piece of the broadband network pie—broadcasters, cable companies, telephone companies, computer companies, satellite companies—finding a common regulatory ground that will satisfy all seems next to impossible. Additionally, policy makers are still searching for the balance between regulation and deregulation of the major players and assurance that various publics—including the disadvantaged—will be served.

One key issue is the question of digital must-carry on the part of cable companies. The National Association of Broadcasters has urged the FCC to adopt a ruling that will force cable companies to carry digital signals in the future, so that cable customers will have access to digital television. Cable operators, on the other hand, are resisting being forced to carry digital signals of broadcast stations in a particular market. They prefer to offer more cable channels on the extra channel capacity.

Perhaps the key to solving policy dilemmas lies in the conceptualization of the new technologies themselves, their uses, their users, and the stakeholders. In her award-winning dissertation, Holman (1998) offered a regulatory framework for emerging communication media based on First Amendment principles. This framework, which she called **Information Commons,** takes into consideration the interactive and convergent nature of new communication technologies and provides policy makers with an appropriate metaphor to describe new digital-based communication environments.

> Commons can be conceptualized as any set of social acts characterized by voluntary participation, common purpose, shared resources, mutuality, and fairness. This concept of the commons, or *koinonia*, which dates back to the ancient Greeks, has five principles: (1) participation must be free and uncoerced; (2) participants must share a common purpose; (3) participants must have something in common that they share, such as jointly held resources, a collection of precious objects, or a repertory of shared actions; (4) participation involves a sense of mutuality or friendship; and (5) social relations must be characterized by fairness and justice. A commons describes any self-defining collective of individuals who voluntarily associate to create communities and to reproduce social worlds—a setting very akin to the groups and communities that comprise the new information environment. (pp. 248–249)

Another framework for understanding current telecommunications policy involves a communication theory perspective, which also emphasizes an integration or common ground approach. Lenert (1998) used the concepts of liberalization and democratization to characterize two recurring themes in telecommunications policy discourse. He associated those concepts with two models of communication advanced by Carey (1989): the transmission model and the community-cultural-ritual (CCR) model. According to Lenert, *liberalization* (also known as deregulation) can be associated with the transmission model of communication, which emphasizes the transporting of messages, or "the movement of messages in space." Lenert defined *democratization* as "a focus on a political system characterized by popular participation in decision making in the context of liberal guarantees of equality and individual rights." He associated democratization with the CCR model, which views communication as "the representation of shared beliefs, rather than the imparting of information . . . directed toward the maintenance of society in time as well as the extension of messages in space." In his essay, Lenert called for an integration of the transmission and CCR models "to provide the basis for a more fully democratized telecommunications policy in the context of a liberalized global economy" (1998, pp. 4–7).

RESEARCH ON NEW MEDIA AND THEIR EFFECTS

"As new information technologies become available, a whole new program of research is required to learn techniques for their effective utilization." This was the farsighted opinion of Parker (1973, p. 596), one of the few communication scholars of the 1970s who believed that technology variables should be given greater attention in communication research.

Since the 1970s, the study of new communication technologies has followed a trend set by precedents. As each new communication technology has appeared, researchers have studied it using research methods that were employed to examine technologies immediately previous to the new one. For example, early television studies used methods of research on the effects of message content similar to those used in earlier film and radio studies (Williams, Rice, & Rogers, 1988).

Most recent research has followed tradition by making use of existing communication theories as a guide in exploring the uses and consequences of new media technologies. Williams, Strover, and Grant (1994) reviewed the literature and found a number of studies related to new media technologies, from the areas of uses and gratifications and diffusion of innovations research. Mundorf and Laird (2001) provided an expanded list of more recent research.

Researchers have studied the motives of cable television subscribers to learn what gratifications they obtained from cable (Becker, Dunwoody, & Rafaell, 1983; Ducey, Krugman, & Eckrich, 1983; Jeffres, 1978; McDermott & Medhurst, 1984; Metzger, 1983). Others have investigated the relationship between viewer motives and actual program choices to find that different people watch certain programs for different reasons at different times. Zillmann and Bryant (1985) found that people experiencing emotional distress preferred to watch soothing programs. Rubin (1984) distinguished two different styles of watching television: (1) instrumental, in which viewers selected a program carefully and with a definite purpose in mind, and (2) ritualized, in which viewers watched television habitually in an effort to pass time or to forget their loneliness. Heeter and Baldwin (1988) studied cable viewers and found that the variety of programming offered by cable provided opportunities for both instrumental and ritualized viewing.

Research has revealed that most people use the Internet at home for interpersonal communication such as e-mail, chat rooms, and participation in electronic communities (McKenna & Bargh, 1999). Papacharissi and Rubin (2000) investigated reasons for Internet use and found information seeking and entertainment to be the highest in rank, followed by convenience. Motives for computer-mediated communication included interpersonal communication (number one) as well as information seeking, a means to pass time, and entertainment.

Other researchers have studied new media technologies in relation to the rapidity of their diffusion among users. Some have examined the phenomenon of the *critical mass,* or that explosive point when the greatest number of people suddenly adopt the new technology. Markus (1987) pointed out that the success of certain technologies, such as e-mail or the telephone, was entirely dependent upon achieving the critical mass because of the reciprocal nature of these technologies. For example, if only a few people had adopted the telephone, those

New communication technologies such as virtual reality are making diverse content choices available to children
Source: © Raoul Minsart/CORBIS

users would have had very few people to call. Without achieving the critical mass, telephone usage would have declined and probably vanished entirely. E-mail and the fax machine are other technologies for which mass adoption was critical to their success.

Several studies have found that new technologies may have important effects on the social interactions of users. Internet use in the home has been cited as a reason for family conflicts (Oravec, 2000), and heavy Internet use is also associated with high levels of loneliness and anxiety (Kraut et al., 1998), depression and introversion (Petrie & Gunn, 1998), and decreased social interactions (Nie & Ebring, 2000). Other studies, however, have found beneficial effects from Internet use (Cole, 2000), especially for people who are shy or lonely (McKenna & Bargh, 1999), and for the elderly (White, McConnell, Clipp, & Bynum, 1999; Mundorf, Bryant, & Brownell, 1997).

Another arm of research into new technologies involves their effects upon children and adolescents. Van Evra (1990) provided a survey of research on children and their use of new communication technologies such as the VCR, video games, virtual reality, and the Internet. New technologies are causing changes in program content for children and making much more diverse content choices accessible to them. Sometimes this programming is educational and positive in nature; sometimes it is not.

The availability of additional channels through cable and VCRs has meant that children may be exposed to inappropriate content such as violence, graphic sex, or programs with adult themes. This, along with the interactive component built into many of the new technologies, has had important developmental and behavioral implications for today's children. Oftentimes children do not have the developmental maturity and experience to understand completely the adult information they are exposed to. The borders that separate reality from fantasy may become confusing for them.

> Children who are watching material intended for adults may still be having considerable difficulty sorting out real information from fantasy material; they may not be cognizant of some of the formal features of television and hence they may find flashbacks, dream sequences, and other dramatic techniques confusing and incomprehensible. They may still be unable to grasp subtle messages or "morals to the story" and hence they may overreact to salient, but irrelevant or inappropriate, aspects of a program. (Van Evra, 1990, p. 199)

With regard to children's programming, interactivity has been shown to make programs more enjoyable and enhance entertainment (Rockwell & Bryant, 1999). Children given the opportunity to interact also reported a higher level of liking for the program's characters.

As for the educational advantages of new media technologies, students may have the opportunity to become more involved in the learning process through the use of new media. Calvert (1999) surveyed the landscape and listed several characteristics of the new information technologies that should benefit children.

> As with television, children will be able to travel around the world without leaving their homes. But in the future, the images will be interactive and personalized.

The symbol systems will be visual, verbal, musical, and interactive. They will be three-dimensional, and children will be able to enter virtual realities they create. Mobile computers will allow children to take and to access information everywhere they go. (p. 247)

PRACTICAL ADVANTAGES OF NEW TECHNOLOGIES

New media technologies are already proving to be exceptionally valuable tools, especially for educational purposes, in many different areas. The computer has become a central part of modern day schooling (Papert, 1993; Marien, 1996). The ease and availability of electronic communication has made it possible for students in remote corners of the globe to gain access to information that was previously available to only a select few.

The use of new communication media in college instruction rose throughout the 1990s (Deloughrey, 1996; Panici, 1998). An increasing number of college instructors are making use of e-mail, the World Wide Web, and multimedia materials in their courses.

The introduction of new technologies has brought many changes in traditional modes of education for communication professors and students. In mass communication, especially, mastery of new technologies has become an essential part of undergraduate and graduate education. Instructors teaching skills courses in journalism, public relations, advertising, and broadcasting must keep abreast of new technologies in order to prepare their students for modern work environments. In communication and other fields, distance education has become more and more prevalent in recent years and has allowed and sometimes forced faculty members to embrace new technologies. Interactive distance learning has become accessible to many (Levy, 1999) and offers practical advantages such as reduction in travel costs and larger numbers than traditional classroom audiences (Mottl, 2000). Table 21.1 shows adoption patterns for the Internet, cable television, and broadcast television, 1995–2000.

Journalism and mass communication are not the only subject areas undergoing profound changes due to new media technologies. In the area of personal and public health, for instance, new media are viewed as tools for health care systems and individuals concerned about their health (Harris, 1995). These new media are allowing more public access to health information, and they are "making expertise portable" (p. 14). Interactivity and simulation are combining to make medical knowledge available to audiences who would not normally have access to such information (McGinnis, Deering, & Patrick, 1995). Multimedia programs are now being used in medical schools, allowing doctors in training to encounter simulated experiences that they might face in actual medical practice (Henderson, 1995). New media technologies are also viewed as a means for reducing health care costs. These new technologies allow patients to have more health information and take more responsibility for their own health and needs. Armed with such information, people may recognize when unnecessary services are about to be rendered (Vickery, 1995).

Table 21.1 Media Adoption Patterns in the United States, 1995–2000

INTERNET

	1995	1996	1997	1998	1999	2000
U.S. homes (in millions)	9	15	27	38	45	52
% of homes	10	15	27	39	44	50

CABLE TV

	1970	1980	1990	2000		
U.S. homes (in millions)	4	15	52	69		
% of homes	6	20	55	67		

BROADCAST TV

	1950	1960	1970	1980	1990	2000
U.S. homes (in millions)	4	46	59	76	92	101
% of homes	9	87	95	98	98	98

Sources: The history of U.S. media adoption (2000, 8 May). *Industry Standard,* p. 209; Mundorf, N. & Laird, K. R. (in press). Social and psychological effects of information technologies and other interactive media, in J. Bryant & D. Zillmann (Eds.), *Media effects: Advances in theory and research* (in press). Mahwah, NJ: Erlbaum.

NEW THEORY AND NEW MODELS

Attempts to build comprehensive communication theory that would account for transactional mediated communication and explain both the interpersonal and multimedia aspects of new technologies have occurred at two different levels. Macro-analytical models have been offered to guide our understanding of the relationships between communications infrastructure, technologies, communication policies, and society. Micro-analytical models (rare at this time) provide us with a clearer picture of the specific components of transactional communication among users by way of the new technologies.

Williams, Strover, and Grant (1994) suggested that two recent theories, media system dependency theory and social information processing theory, may prove useful in explaining in macro-analytical terms the complex nature of communication processes through new media technologies. *Media system dependency theory* (Ball-Rokeach, 1985, 1988) provides a framework for understanding relationships of dependency between mass media, various audiences, and societal groups or systems. For example, individual audience members may develop a dependency on a medium such as television to satisfy certain needs such as entertainment or instruction. The media system itself is dependent on advertisers for financial support, and this relationship is dependent on the individual viewers to provide audiences for the advertised products. *Social information processing theory* (Fulk, Steinfield, Schmitz, & Power, 1987) holds that when evaluating new media and making selections for use, media users are as much or more influenced by the information and evaluations they hear from others than by personal appraisals of media performance. The theory has been used to predict adoption and use of an electronic mail system (Rice, Grant, Schmitz, & Torobin, 1990) and electronic message evaluation (Schmitz & Fulk, 1991).

You will recall from Chapter 1 that one of the best examples of the macro-analytical model is the "Interactive Model of Communication and Society," provided by the U.S. Congress, Office of Technology Assessment (1990, p. 35). This model, contained in an extremely comprehensive report called *Critical Connections: Communication for the Future*, is useful if it accurately describes the overarching "players" and essential relationships in the realm of communication and society, and if it guides research that explains and predicts how technology changes society and vice versa. If such models are to be accurate representations of the new media environment and the communication processes of the users of new media, they must depart radically from orthodoxy. As Rogers (1986) indicated:

> The new media are having a powerful influence on the nature of communication research, unfreezing this field from many of its past assumptions, prior paradigms and methods. As we have stated previously, the predominant linear models of one-way communication effects must give way to convergence models of communication as a two-way process of information exchange, due to the interactivity of new media. (p. 213)

The Office of Technology Assessment report offered a slightly different slant but reflected similar concerns:

> The sender/receiver model is also much too orderly to describe many of today's mediated communication processes. It assumes that communication takes place as a consistent, linear sequence of events—an assumption that is not supportable in today's technology-mediated information environment. With a computerized bulletin board, for example, how does one identify and distinguish between who is the sender and who is the receiver? And, similarly, who is considered the sender when the receiver can now access information on demand? (1990, pp. 31–32)

The dearth of theoretical models to illustrate the transactional nature of modern mediated communications underscores the rapid development and deployment of the new communication technologies. Simply put, theory has not been able to keep up with technology. New communication theories that explain the uses of new technologies are sorely needed. As the new century progresses, the continual challenge for communication theorists will be to catch up and keep up.

SUMMARY

New communication technologies are forcing us to reconceptualize mass communication processes. One-way mass communication is giving way to transactional mediated communication.

Our list of new technologies continues to change as new technologies emerge. Scholars define new technologies by describing their essential nature. New media are characterized by specialized nature, decentralized products, and interactive formats. The key to understanding the nature of digital technology can be found in three "c" words: compression, conversion, and convergence.

The move to digital communication has resulted in new media environments. These are often interactive and allow multiple functions and tasks to be performed on a single piece of equipment such as a home computer or a television. Interactivity is a multi-dimensional concept.

New media enable users to become more active in the communication process and to be more selective with regard to the messages they receive. They are active agents rather than passive receivers of information. They may be called addressable users of micromultimedia.

New communication technologies present us with a number of public policy and ethical considerations. New policies must address broadband networking, high definition television, and other technologies. Conceptualizing the new media environment as an information commons may help in the development of regulatory policies. Fairness or equality, an information underclass, obscenity and pornography, plagiarism, and bootlegging, or the copying of other people's data for resale purposes are some of the diverse ethical issues associated with new technologies.

As each new communication technology has appeared, researchers have studied it using research methods that were used to examine technologies immediately previous to the new one. Most recent research has followed tradition by making use of existing communication theories as a guide in exploring the uses and consequences of new media technologies.

New media technologies are already proving to be exceptionally valuable for educational purposes. More and more college instructors are making use of e-mail, the World Wide Web, and multimedia materials in their courses. The introduction of new technologies has brought many changes in traditional modes of education for communication professors and students.

Theory building to account for transactional mediated communication and explain both the interpersonal and multimedia aspects of new technologies has occurred at two different levels—macro-analytical models and micro-analytical models. Theory has not been able to keep up with technology, however, and new theories to explain the uses of new technologies are needed.

REFERENCES

BALL-ROKEACH, S. J. (1985). The origins of individual media-system dependency: A sociological framework. *Communication Research, 12:* 485–510.

BALL-ROKEACH, S. J. (1988). Media system dependency theory. In M. L. DeFleur & S. J. Ball-Rokeach (Eds.), *Theories of mass communication* (pp. 297–327). New York: Longman.

BECKER, L., DUNWOODY, S., & RAFAELL, S. (1983). Cable's impact on use of other news media. *Journal of Broadcasting, 27,* 127–142.

BERMAN, S. J., & BUNZEL, M. (1999, 1 March). The rapid bandwidth explosion. *Electronic Media, 20.* The article quotes projections from The Yankee Group, a technology research firm.

BOWLES, J. (1998, 16 November). The future Internet: Faster, smarter, mobile, scarier. *Newsweek*, p. 12.

BRAND, S. (1988). *The media lab: Inventing the future at MIT*. New York: Penguin.

BROWN, P. (1999). Set-top box market frenzy: Industry trend or event. *Electronic News, 45,* 50.

BRYANT, J., & LOVE, C. (1996). Entertainment as the driver of new information technology. In R. R. Dholakia, N. Mundorf, & N. Dholakia (Eds.), *New infotainment technologies in the home: Demand-side perspectives* (pp. 35–58). Mahwah, NJ: Erlbaum.

CALVERT, S. (1999). *Children's journeys through the information age*. New York: McGraw-Hill.

CAREY, J. W. (1989). *Communication as culture*. Boston: Unwin Hyman.

COLE, J. (2000). *Surveying the digital future*. Los Angeles: UCLA Center for Communication Policy.

COMMISSION OF THE EUROPEAN COMMUNITIES. (1994). *Europe and the Global Information Society*, Brussels: European Commission.

COOPER, T. W. (1998). New technology effects inventory: Forty leading ethical issues. *Journal of Mass Media Ethics, 13,* 71–92.

DAFT, R. (1989). *Organization theory and design* (3rd ed.) St. Paul, MN: West Publishing.

DELOUGHREY, T. J. (1996, November 22). Campus computer use is increasing but not as fast as in previous years. *Chronicle of Higher Education, 43,* (13), A21–A22.

DIZARD, WILSON, JR. (1994). *Old media new media, mass communications in the information age*. New York: Longman.

DUCEY, R., KRUGMAN, D., & ECKRICH, D. (1983). Predicting market segments in the cable industry: The basic and pay subscribers. *Journal of Broadcasting, 27,* 155–161.

DUPAGNE, M. (1998, Winter). The two faces of HDTV policymaking: United States enters new era of TV broadcasting. *Communication & Technology Policy Newsletter,* p. 3.

FEDERAL COMMUNICATIONS COMMISSION (FCC). (1997). *Advanced television systems and their impact upon the existing television broadcast service (Fifth Report and Order)*, [12 FCC Rcd. 12809].

FORTIN, D. (1997). *The impact of interactivity on advertising effectiveness*. Unpublished doctoral dissertation, University of Rhode Island, Kinston.

FULK, J., STEINFIELD, C. W., SCHMITZ, J., & POWER, J. G. (1987). A social information processing model of media use in organizations. *Communication Research, 14,* 529–552.

GOERTZ (1995). Wie interaktiv sind die neuen Medien? Auf dem Weg zu einer Definition von Interaktivität. [How interactive are the new media? On the way towards a definition of interactivity]. *Rundfunk und Fernsehen, 43,* 477–493.

GRANT, A. E. (1997). Introduction. In P. B. Seel & A. E. Grant (Eds.), *Broadcast technology update, production and transmission*. Boston: Focal Press.

GREELEY, H., CASE, L., HOWLAND, E., GOUGH, J. B., RIPLEY, P., PERKINS, F. B., LYMAN, J. B., BRISBANE, A., HALL, REV. E. E., ET AL. (1872). *The great industries of the United States: Being an historical summary of the origin, growth, and perfection of the chief industrial arts of this country*. Hartford, CT: J. B. Burr & Hyde.

HARING, B. (1999, 20 January). Linking the clicker and the cursor: Interactive TV is finally real, but services are jumbled. *USA Today,* p. 4D.

HARRIS, L. M. (1995). Differences that make a difference. In L. M. Harris (Ed.), *Health and the new media: Technologies transforming personal and public health*. Mahwah, NJ: Erlbaum.

HEETER, C., & BALDWIN, T. (1988). Channel types and viewing styles. In C. Heeter & B. Greenberg (Eds.), *Cableviewing* (pp. 167–176). Norwood, NJ: Ablex.

HENDERSON, J. V. (1995). Meditation on the news media and professional education. In L. M. Harris (Ed.), *Health and the new media: Technologies transforming personal and public health* (pp. 185–205). Mahwah, NJ: Erlbaum.

HODGE, W. W. (1995). *Interactive television, A comprehensive guide for multimedia technologists*. New York: McGraw-Hill.

HOLMAN, J. M. (1998). *An information commons: Protection for free expression in the new information environment.* Unpublished Ph.D. dissertation. Indiana University, Bloomington.

HUDSON, H. E. (1998, April). Global information infrastructure: Eliminating the distance barrier. *Business Economics, 33,* 25.

JEFFRES, L. (1978). Cable TV and viewer selectivity. *Journal of Broadcasting, 22,* 176–177.

JENSEN, J. (1999, 12 March). Everything you wanted to know about MP3 but were afraid to ask. *Entertainment Weekly,* pp. 33–37. Quote is attributed to Paul Vidich, senior vice president of strategic planning for Warner Music Group.

KRAUT, R., PATTERSON, M., LUNDMARK, V., KIESLER, S., MUKOPADHYAY, T., & SCHERLIS, W. (1998). Internet paradox: A social technology that reduces social involvement and psychological well-being? *American Psychologist, 53,* 1017–1031.

LENERT, E. M. (1998). A communication theory perspective on telecommunications policy. *Journal of Communication, 48,* 3–23.

LEVY, S. (1999, 31 May). The new digital galaxy. *Newsweek,* pp. 57–63.

MARIEN, M. (1996). New communications technology, a survey of impacts and issues. *Telecommunications Policy, 20,* 375–387.

MARKUS, M. L. (1987). Toward a "critical mass" theory of interactive media: Universal access, interdependence and diffusion. *Communication Research, 14,* 491–511.

MATHIAS, C. J. (1999). An expert opinion: Wireless—still chasing wire, but catching up. *Electronic Design, 47,* 6.

MCDERMOTT, S., & MEDHURST, M. (1984, May). *Reasons for subscribing to cable television.* Paper presented at the conference of the International Communication Association, San Francisco.

MCGINNIS, J. M., DEERING, M. J., & PATRICK, K. (1995). Public health information and the new media: A view from the public health service. In L. M. Harris (Ed.), *Health and the new media: Technologies transforming personal and public health* (pp. 127–141). Mahwah, NJ: Erlbaum.

MCKENNA, K. Y. A., & BARGH, J. A. (1999). Causes and consequences of social interaction on the Internet: A conceptual framework. *Media Psychology, 1,* 249–269.

METZGER, G. D. (1983). Cable television audiences: Learning from the past and the present. *Journal of Advertising Research, 23,* 41–47.

MOTTL, J. (2000). Learn at a distance. *Information Week, 767,* 75–78.

MUNDORF, N., BRYANT, J., & BROWNELL, W. (1997). Information technology and the elderly. In N. Al-Deen, *Cross-cultural communication and aging in the United States* (pp. 43–62). Mahwah, NJ: Erlbaum.

MUNDORF, N., & LAIRD, K. R. (in press). Social and psychological effects of information technologies and other interactive media. In J. Bryant & D. Zillmann, *Media effects: Advances in theory and research* (2nd ed.). Mahwah, NJ: Erlbaum.

NIE, N. H., & EBRING, L. (2000). *Internet and society: A preliminary report.* Stanford, CA: Institute for the Quantitative Study of Society.

ORAVEC, J. A. (2000). Internet and computer technology hazards: Perspectives for family councelling. *British Journal of Guidance and Counselling,* 309–324.

PANICI, D. A. (1998, Spring). New media and the introductory mass communication course. *Journalism & Mass Communication Educator, 53,* 52–63.

PAPACHARISSI, Z., & RUBIN, A. (2000). Predictors of Internet use. *Journal of Broadcasting and Electronic Media,* 175–196.

PAPERT, S. (1993). *The children's machine: Rethinking school in the age of the computer.* New York: Basic Books.

PARKER, E. B. (1973). Implications of new information technology. *Public Opinion Quarterly 37,* 590–600.

Pearce, A. (1998). Exciting times in Washington: FCC rulemakings gives us respite from sex, lies and videotape. *America's Network, 102,* 74.

Petrie, H., & Gunn, D. (1998, December). *Internet "addiction": The effects of sex, age, depression, and introversion.* Paper presented at the British Psychology Society, London.

Rice, R. E., Grant, A. E., Schmitz, J., & Torobin, J. (1990). Individual and network influences on the adoption and perceived outcomes of electronic messaging. *Social Networks, 12,* 27–55.

Rockwell, S. C., & Bryant, J. (1999). Enjoyment of interactivity in an entertainment program for children. *Medien-Psychologie,* 244–259.

Rogers, E. M. (1986). *Communication technology: The new media in society.* New York: Free Press.

Rubin, A. (1984). Ritualized and instrumental uses of television. *Journal of Communication, 34,* 67–77.

Schmitz, J., & Fulk, J. (1991). The role of organizational colleagues in media selection. *Communication Research, 18,* 487–523.

Seel, P. B. (1997). The transition from analog to digital broadcasting. In P. B. Seel & A. E. Grant, (Eds.), *Broadcast technology update, production and transmission.* Boston: Focal Press.

Stipp, H. (1998, July). Should TV marry PC? *American Demographics,* pp. 16–21.

U.S. Congress, Office of Technology Assessment. (1990, January). *Critical connections: Communication for the future,* (OTA-CIT-407) Washington, DC: U.S. Government Printing Office, pp. 31.

Van Evra, J. (1990). *Television and child development.* Hillsdale, NJ: Erlbaum.

Vickery, D. M. (1995). Demand management, self-care, and the new media. In L. M. Harris (Ed.), *Health and the new media: Technologies transforming personal and public health* (pp. 45–63). Mahwah, NJ: Erlbaum.

Webster, J. G. (1989). Assessing exposure to the new media. In J. L. Salvaggio & J. Bryant (Eds.), *Media use in the information age: Emerging patterns of adoption and consumer use* (pp. 3–19). Hillsdale, NJ: Erlbaum.

Webster, J. G. (1998). The audience. *Journal of Broadcasting & Electronic Media, 42,* 190–207.

White, H., McConnell, E., Clipp, E., & Bynum, L. (1999). Surfing the net in later life: A review of the literature and pilot study of computer use and quality of life. *Journal of Applied Gerontology,* 358–378.

Williams, F., Rice, R., & Rogers, E. M. (1988). *Research methods and the new media.* New York: Free Press.

Williams, F., Strover, S., & Grant, A. E. (1994). Social aspects of new media technologies. In J. Bryant and D. Zillmann (Eds.), *Media effects: Advances in theory and research* (pp. 463–482). Hillsdale, NJ: Erlbaum.

Zillmann, D., & Bryant, J. (1985). Pornography, sexual callousness and the trivialization of rape. *Journal of Communication, 34*(4), 10–21.

ENDNOTES

1. Teleconferencing is considered by some to be an application of new media technology rather than a new media technology in itself.

Index